A MORAL HISTORY OF

WESTERN

SOCIETY

An Historical Review of the
West's Great Political, Social,
Cultural, and Intellectual Legacy

Volume One

From Ancient Times to the Mid-1800s

Miles Huntley Hodges

ISBN 979-8-9900799-0-8 (Hardback)
ISBN 979-8-9900799-1-5 (Paperback)
ISBN 979-8-9900799-2-2 (Laminate)
ISBN 979-8-9900799-3-9 (eBook)

Library of Congress Control Number: 2023924528

spiritualpilgrim.net

CONTENTS

A MORAL HISTORY OF WESTERN SOCIETY:

AN INTRODUCTION

* * *

THE KEY COMPONENTS OF ANY SUCCESSFUL SOCIETY

The necessity of strong moral foundations for any successful society. I find it very easy to identify with the ancient Aristotle, who in the 300s BC was forced to watch his beloved Athens, even all of Greece, fall into highly self-destructive social folly. Being the inquisitive individual that he was, Aristotle decided to take a close look at numerous societies of his day – and those even of previous ages – to see what he could discover about the cause of the rise and fall of societies. He wanted to know what made them work most successfully. And he wanted to know what made them fail. He wanted to know what made them be birthed, grow, even become strong … and then, almost as a matter of inevitability, go into decline and even collapse. Sometimes they made comebacks from low points in their existence … and were able to put the age of folly behind them and rise again to some kind of social strength – although deeply changed by the experience.

In fact, in his own days, he was able to watch the young Alexander, a Macedonian that had taken up the Greek social cause (largely against Greece's constant enemy, Persia) … and bring Greek culture not only to grand restoration, but in fact to what seemed like at the time even global dominance. This meant a lot to Aristotle, not only because he loved his Greek or Hellenistic society and culture deeply … but because Alexander had himself once been a student of Aristotle's.

What mattered most importantly in all of this was what it was that Aristotle finally concluded from all his studies … and his own personal investment in the whole Greek dynamic. Most amazingly (to modern Americans at least) he concluded that what made for a truly "good" society, was not the social form or shape by which it went at life, whether a society governed by a single person, or a society governed by a privileged few, or one even governed widely by the citizens themselves. What mattered most were a society's moral foundations – and ability of those foundations to hold a society on a healthy course of life.

In other words, a government of one could be a society governed singly by a king (good) or a tyrant (bad). It could be a society governed by an aristocracy (good) or an oligarchy (bad). Or it could be a society governed by a constitutionally guided citizenry (good) or an emotionally manipulated citizenry (bad – like the Athenian democracy had become).

So social morality found in the hearts of its people, but especially on the part of those most responsible for making a society's vital decisions – not some carefully-designed governmental structure – was understood by Aristotle to be the most important factor in building a strong society.

And in this matter, I have long been very, very inclined to agree. Indeed, this is why I composed this very work before you: *A Moral History of Western Society*. It's about the moral dynamic that shaped the various periods of Western history … the good times – and the not so good times.

Wise leadership. But also, and very clearly – to Aristotle as well as to me – whether or not a society would find itself going down a good road or a bad road depended not only on the moral foundations by which the members of that society directed their lives. It depended also on the leadership it was able to enjoy in the process … or have to suffer under. Like Alexandrian Greece, the leadership of one single individual can make all the difference in the success or failure of a society … for such leaders possess enormous power to inspire people to remain true (or not) to the moral imperatives that have long shaped and motivated their societies.

A grander sense of social purpose. But societies do not just exist. They exist to serve some larger social purpose … from families all the way up to great empires. Without that sense of larger purpose any society would soon find itself wandering through life wondering whether this or that was more important to pursue, which road it should take in the face of a rising challenge, or even whether it was important or not to do anything at all … and simply fall into a deadening sense of routine. Most tragically, a society does not long survive the loss of that larger sense of social purpose.

A guiding sense of divine appointment or "covenant" with God. My personal and quite detailed knowledge of America's own history – published as an earlier three-volume study, *America the Covenant Nation*[*] – also

____

[*]*America, The Covenant Nation – A Christian Perspective*, Bloomington, Indiana: Westbow Press, 2020 … in three volumes: (1) *Securing America's Covenant with God: From America's Foundations in the Early 1600s – To America's Post-Civil War Recovery in the late 1800s*; (2) *America's Rise to Greatness under God's*

has made it very clear to me how vitally important it was that America had founded itself in the early 1600s on the idea that it was designed to serve the larger world as a "Light to the Nations," a "City on a Hill." Thus whatever "good purpose" America might feel justified its existence, it was acutely aware from its very founding in the early 1600s that this had better be focused very carefully on the sense of what God – and not mere human ambition – demanded of it.

Thus it was that (until fairly recently) America went forward in its growth over the decades and even centuries very, very prayerfully in facing the many challenges that continually rose before it … from the days of America's first Founding Father John Winthrop (early 1600s), through its Constitutional Founders George Washington and Ben Franklin (late 1700s), and its Saving Father Abraham Lincoln (mid-1800s) … all men of prayer – keenly aware of how much their work as American leaders was sustained and directed by God's own hand – as they took on the nation's huge challenges.

Sadly, as America has reached the grandness of great wealth and power (since the mid-20th century), it has increasingly lost the sense of that need for such a divine relationship … supposing that it now possesses all the "natural" human knowledge needed to keep the country – and the West that it leads – moving forward down that road of great wealth and power. It no longer needs the "superstitions" of the leaders of those earlier generations.

Thus "modern" man is self-supposed to be much more "realistic" and much more "progressive." As far as morality goes, he is now "free" to live by any inner directives that he chooses. All is well because social harmony is supposedly a natural instinct of everyone … provided that the social institutions that a person lives in and under are well-designed. For this, society needs only the brilliance of educated leaders ("Sophists" they were termed in Aristotle's days) to do that very designing.

As anyone who has studied history closely knows quite well, this kind of "Idealistic" thinking is itself worse than "superstition." It is pure folly … self-destructive folly. And Western history since the arrival of the 20th century is full of examples of such folly – much like Aristotle's 3rd century BC. Most sadly, such folly continues today* because modern Sophists

---

Covenant: From the Late 1880s to the end of the 1950s; and (3) *The Dismissing of America's Covenant with God: From the Early 1960s to the Present*. See thecovenantnation.com for details.

*Bush Junior in the early days of the 21st century convinced America that planting democracy (by military intervention) in Afghanistan and Iraq would do the people of these countries a great deal of good … as did Obama with his similar efforts in Syria and Libya. The results of such "democratic idealism" proved to be murderous for countless civilians in each of these societies … which never asked for such enlightened American intervention in the first place.

continue to demand the implementation of their Idealistic dreams ... at the cost of the horrible death of thousands of innocent people.

Consequently, I have undertaken this written work to put the recently abandoned social perspective of our forefathers back in place ... by examining the Western "narrative" describing the rise and fall of generations past – focusing on these four elements: social morality, social leadership, social purpose, and divine appointment as the four key elements in a society's success or failure.

✻ ✻ ✻

THE PARABLE OF THE FOUR GENERATIONS

In my days as a university professor, and in the subsequent writings I have authored about America's own social dynamics, I have told a parable about a society as it developed across four generations – a parable I now want to put before you, the reader of this particular work. This narrative has long seemed to me to summarize all of this political, social, cultural and spiritual dynamic that goes into the rise and decline of any society.

It is the story of four generations of a leading, guiding, governing family – and of the society they are supposed to be directing ... and that society's rise and fall across those four generations. It is a tale well worth retelling here as we dig into the question of Western society's own social dynamics.

The First Generation. In this story, a small society forms around the mastery or leadership of a very strong-willed individual, a young man who climbs out of very tough – actually brutal – circumstances. And in overcoming those circumstances he achieves a self-discipline in the face of dangerous challenges, one which so strongly impresses a gathering circle of young warriors that he is able to turn this group into a similarly disciplined band of conquerors. The warrior-leader is very generous to those who would follow his lead bravely, against even the most dangerous of challenges. But he could also be equally unforgiving of those who would fail to live up to his very precise warrior code or his high expectations of a very brave performance in carrying out the warrior duties of those who would dare join him.

But what drives this leader is not just some hunger to force others under his direction for the sheer joy of it. That can come to certain people as a big ego-high. But usually that same urge will blind and ultimately destroy such wannabe leaders. No, what drives this First-Generation leader is vision, a higher vision or sense of call that comes from some source other than the approval of the immediate world around him. It comes typically from a sense, even at a very early age, that Heaven itself has a special commission for this young man to build a society that will serve the greater will of Heaven, God, Providence, Allah, Zeus, Tian – or whatever name is given to this Higher Power. It is the ability of our young warrior to keep his eyes on this higher call that allows him not to fall victim to the flattery of those who would try to use him for their own personal gain. He is immune to such human willfulness. Thus such vision – with its call to bold action as well as an unshakable resolve to keep himself and others under the inflexible moral discipline required to see that vision come to reality together – makes him the powerful leader that he is.

He also occupies a special place in history because his arrival on the social scene is timed with developments well beyond his own political-social designs. In fact, he himself is no such political-social designer.   Instead, he is an individual fully capable of taking on fearsome challenges immediately in front of him as they arise to confront him on an almost daily basis. He does not design life, like some lofty intellectual working at a desk and living in a bubble of beautiful ideals and wonderfully rational plans designed to achieve utopia. His world is tough, messy, and unpredictable. But he is fearsomely brave as he pursues this political-social call placed on him by the very power of Heaven. He resolves simply to keep moving forward, even in the face of the most discouraging circumstances.

And thus it is that this man of valor is able to inspire others to join him on this path of overcoming – and ultimately this path of social conquest. He is thus able through sheer doggedness to produce social greatness.

And in our parable, that conquest would include even the great civilization just over the next mountain range, a civilization that is in deep trouble because it is no longer led by such powerful leaders as our First-Generation founder. This once-great civilization has fallen into deep moral decay, one that inevitably comes along with the rise to power of the Fourth and final Generation. This civilization finds itself caught at this point in time in the throes of social collapse. It is ripe for conquest by some kind of rising power outside itself. And that is where the First-Generation leader finds himself and his men headed in history.

Timing is, of course, also key to success in history.

The Second Generation. The son (the Second Generation) of the original founder-warrior will also have grown up in tough circumstances, though only because of the disciplined social environment established by his father, not because of a threatening political world immediately around him. By the time he is a rising young man, much of that has already been cleared away by his father's early successes. However, the father's grand vision, in which he understood rather clearly the ultimate destiny of his small but growing society, has had the father over the years preparing his son to take up the responsibilities that one day will be passed on to him. The First-Generation father therefore has had his Second-Generation son train and join him in battle, learning the responsibilities of leadership. There is, after all, a world to be conquered by both of them, father and son.

And that conquered world one day will need to be administered by a competent ruler. But it will fall to the son, not the father, to be just that individual. Anticipating this, the father perhaps will have, early along the way, sent his son off to live and study for a number of years within that larger civilization, one that is destined to be ruled by his own rising dynasty. This certainly occurred in the case of Philip II of Macedon, when he sent his son Alexander off to Greece to study under Aristotle. As a result, the son will know and understand the ways of the larger world that one day will be his responsibility to rule.

The son will also know of the Heavenly Commission upon which his society was originally founded by his father, though perhaps only secondarily, through what his father has told him about it. The son will respect that Higher Power and will take its ruling principles into account in his governance. But he will also be shaped by his knowledge of the political codes and moral rules of the society he is about to inherit, its wise counselors, its civilized ways. All of this will come as a blend of the son's own vision and self-discipline. He is more the person of Reason, like the civilized world he has come to know, than of dangerous risk-taking, something required by the social conditions his father grew up in.

Typically, the era of the Second Generation will be understood by historians as constituting the political height of that society or civilization, the one created or restored through the conquering efforts of the First Generation, and the considerable administrative talents of the Second Generation.

The Third Generation. The grandson/son of the two preceding generations will be personally familiar only with life as lived within the palace that he was raised in. He will know well the stories of the great valor of his grandfather, although such knowledge will have more the nature of folklore than reality to him. He will see and experience directly the blessings of his father's well-administered social-legal order. It certainly will have already benefited the son greatly. And thus he will be entirely devoted to the idea of completing and securing the full development of that perfect social order. He will spend his time in his royal chambers working on that perfect design, working closely with his highly-educated advisors on the specifics of a proposed legal order he wants them to put into place by royal decree.

Along with the proposed legal order, his own vision typically will include the perfecting or beautifying of the visible features of the civilization he has inherited: the beautification of the palace dwellings; the building of magnificent homes for his huge administrative staff; the upgrading of the public places such as the all-important central market and the houses of worship; the development of public parks and places of leisure (mostly for the privileged urban classes).

Of course all of this will come at a great cost, especially to those least able to fend off the tax collectors, who fleece the poorer classes to pay for these extravagant projects, projects which will bring little or no benefit to the lower social orders. Restlessness and even occasional revolt will from time to time upset this utopian social order that Generation Three is attempting to put into place. And our ruler will be uncomprehending as to why such turmoil is accompanying his efforts to perfect his people's world. But that is because he lives largely in a social-intellectual-moral bubble of his own making. He is far removed from the hard realities of the larger world around him. Most importantly, he has lost touch with those he is expected to govern. He no longer relates to his people as a moral compass or spiritual guide for them. Trouble brews.

The Fourth Generation. Having grown up in a world of total privilege – and being surrounded by flattering supporters looking to be brought into that world of privilege – our Fourth-Generation leader will have lost touch completely with the hard realities facing his society, the challenges that as society's governing authority he is expected to address and resolve. But he lives in a world of massive disinformation (who would dare to contradict the presuppositions of the Great Ruler). He is clueless as to his responsibilities.

Not only is there a total loss of dedicated discipline to his governance, there is not even any particular direction to it. He is a person of no particular vision, except to hang on to all the entitlements coming his way as Great Ruler. He is bored, listless, and dangerous, not only to those immediately around him but also to himself. Thus he is also a great danger to the society he is expected to lead. He indulges in every known diversion possible, being able (he believes) to afford them all: gambling, drugs and alcohol, sex (in various ways), wild spending sprees (for nothing in particular), cruel games (including the torture of individuals he does not particularly care for), and so on.

And as for the general moral order of the society he is supposed to be leading, it now finds itself in a state of collapse. Hungry gangs wander the streets, violating persons and property as they see the urge to do so. It is dangerous for women and children to go to market for the day's needs, or even to enter the streets at all. Extortionists come around to exact the price of protection on the defenseless people. The social order is simply collapsing. And as for the people's affection for their government, its Great Ruler in particular, there is none. They wish him dead, and would support anyone inclined to cause that to happen.

And that brings us back to the First Generation, for that is where such help is to come from. And thus the cycle begins all over again.

✳ ✳ ✳

THE WESTERN LEGACY – IN SHORT OR SUMMARY FORM

The West's narrative or historical record or story of this kind of rise and fall of its many great societies is long ... and reaches way back thousands of years. But most thankfully, Western history is a well-recorded narrative concerning this process of social rise and fall. So it is that in this study we propose to make a fairly complete picture of how the "Western Narrative" actually developed through good times – and times not so good – politically, socially ... but especially morally.

The Greek legacy

At a time period I like to call the "Axial Age" (the 500s BC) – because of the deep changes that hit a number of world cultures at that time – a group of Greek philosophers were beginning to look past their own older vision of the universe – a world directed by gods and heroes – to consider a basic material or natural order that seemed to underpin all things. As life settled down and prosperity increased, this natural "order" of things became more and more obvious – at least to some of the thinkers or "philosophers" of Greek Ionia. But as these philosophers contemplated this natural order, they arrived at two distinctly differing conclusions as to how this order worked. And this division of opinion on the matter helped produce in part a philosophical dualism that still exists within the West today.

One group – Thales, Anaxagoras and Democritus, and others – claimed that this order was basically just material and naturally inherent in all life itself. Creation was a complex system of various materials (such as earth, wind, fire and water ... or even atoms!) which interacted with each other in rather fixed or mechanical ways to produce the world that we find around us. These "materialist-mechanists" were the ones who laid the foundations for the secular viewpoint within Western civilization.

But another group – founded principally by Pythagoras (but promoted principally by Plato 150 years later) – asserted that the source of this order was to be found beyond the rather disorderly visible or material world itself.

Instead, the source of this order was to be found in some eternal, perfect, or transcendent/heavenly realm which inspires or directs the more unstable or imperfect visible world that we see around us. This higher world is the mainspring of the oneness, of the order, of all things. Ultimately this kind of thinking helped pave the way for the spread of mystical theism (belief in a supreme deity or God) through Western civilization.

However, despite all this grand intellectual speculation, the Greeks ultimately went down a tragic path intellectually and temperamentally ... a path always designed to lead any society into a spiritual sickness – a sickness that afflicts societies jaded by too much wealth and power and too little moral restraint to use that wealth and power humanely.

Decline. The Greeks too (at least some of them) had a sense of failed righteousness – though they had no particular remedy to the situation ... except over time to become existentially cynical. At best, this produced a movement called Stoicism – which belied Western optimism and took on qualities of Eastern quietism (such as Buddhism).

The problem was material success itself. In fending off quite handily the aggression of the neighboring Persian Empire, a period of peace came to Greece – with Athens the leading city in this new Greek world. But political and economic greed crept into the Athenian social dynamic ... against some of its own better citizens (political jealousy) and against its allied Greek city-states (moneys sent to Athens by its allies for the purpose of mutual defense against Persia being used instead to beautify Athens itself). Ultimately Athens' allies rose up in revolt (with help from the city-state Sparta) and several wars resulted (the Peloponnesian Wars) ... which worked out disastrously for Athens – but for the rest of the Greeks as well.

The Alexandrian legacy. Then the grand military-political success of Alexander the Great (300s BC) revived Greek spirits. A young Alexander was able to reunify the Greeks in order to go on the offensive against the persistent Persian threat ... succeeding masterfully in the process in crushing the Persian Empire – and bringing the much-expanded Greek world back to unity. However he would soon die – and his vast empire would be divided up among various Greek generals (founders of major dynasties).

But the Greek world would remain rather united anyway. Indeed, the Alexandrian enterprise made the Greek language and culture the dominant feature throughout much of the Eastern Mediterranean and Middle Eastern world. But it was a world whose moral foundations were now based on the power of its military-based dynasties ... not on the moral fiber of the Greek citizenry itself.

Ultimately, the Alexandrian world would soon be overridden politically by the Romans (100s BC). Yet despite Roman rule, much of the Alexandrian cultural legacy would continue (for a very long time) to underlie all of Eastern society.

The Roman legacy

The Romans, who took over the Western political-military program from the Greeks a century or two before Christ, were an odd combination of traditional polytheists and skilled materialists. Their minds did not fuss much with higher thought such as the Jews and Greeks engaged in. For the longest time they were content to stay with their older gods ... and do their most inventive thinking in the material world around them. Here they proved themselves to be geniuses.

Political greatness as a Republic. But they would do so also politically ... building not a democracy like the Greeks, run on the whims of the citizenry, (led by manipulative politicians) but instead on a very fixed set of laws (the Roman Constitution) which forced political dynamics to stay within precise boundaries. And wisely, in expanding the Roman realm, instead of simply conquering their neighbors, they invited them into the Roman realm as fellow citizens.

Rome eventually becomes an Empire. But the Republic faced the huge problems of a vastly expanding population ... without an equal growth in the economic resources to support that population (no more easy conquests). Conquests continued ... more for political than social-economic reasons – undermining the morale of the Roman citizen-soldier whose ever-longer terms of military service brought no apparent rewards. Eventually mercenary troops were brought in to serve the various generals (imperators or emperors) ... increasingly made up of mercenary troops drawn from the various Germanic tribes pushed up to Rome's northeastern borders.

And although Rome would continue to call itself a Republic, by the year 1, it was in fact a society run largely by the military generals – the emperors. Thus the Roman "empire" drifted into existence ... and the emperors became ever-greater in social stature – even godlike. Some of these emperors were very capable political leaders. Others were not – especially those that seem to come along in the 200s AD.

Rome thus found itself in decline, morally and thus socially as well. It was finding that Eastern worldviews were making great inroads into Roman culture – despite the efforts of emperors to block and destroy these invading viewpoints on life.

The Jewish legacy

Divine faith versus human works. One of these worldviews was coming from Judaism (and subsequently its stepchild Christianity) which saw a basic dualism in life ... between a "rational" or materialistic approach to existence – and a mystical approach (keeping covenant with God).* Indeed, in the Jewish Bible this dualism forms the very central theme of the whole ... starting from the very beginning of its historical narrative, reaching back in time before time itself was even counted with any accuracy. This dualism indeed constitutes the key dynamic in the very opening episode of those Scriptures, with the story of the primal couple, Adam and Eve, and the matter of having to choose between two options in moving their life forward.

Were they going to continue to build their lives on a vital faith in the mystical powers of God himself? Or would they choose to "eat of the fruit of the Tree of the Knowledge of Good and Evil," which the Satanic tempter, in the form of the Serpent, assured them that by doing so they would take on such knowledge that they themselves would become like God, possessing importantly the power to design their own lives, according to their own personal plans? They chose the latter option. And most tragically, the story did not end well.

So, this matter of where we are to place our greatest faith has been at the heart of Western society's own story, from its very beginning. Is it to be on ourselves and our ability to control the surrounding world, or is it to be on a God who goes before us so that in faith we can move forward into an unfolding world? In fact, this is a story of a moral-spiritual debate that reaches back countless centuries (thousands of years most probably) even before the coming of Christ.   Indeed, this debate within the West seems to have reached a point of clarity five to six centuries earlier – during the 500s BC† "Axial Age" – on a number of fronts.

Previous to that Axial Age of the 500s BC, life was understood In

---

*The Hebrew word for "God," *El*, is similar to the Arabic *Allah* (the God). We recognize El in the term *El Shaddai* (God Almighty). It is also found in *Elohim* ... which is actually the dual form of El, thus literally "gods" ... though clearly it is used in the Hebrew to signify one God – the one and only God.

†On our Western or Christian calendar, BC stands for "Before Christ," indicating *the years prior* to the approximate year of Jesus Christ's appearance on earth as a baby born in Bethlehem – occurring a little over two thousand years ago. Likewise, *the years since* that event are designated as happening AD, or *anno domini*, or "the year of our Lord." More "modern" minds have changed the BC and AD designations to BCE and CE, that is, "Before the Common Era" and the "Common Era" ... trying to cover over the fact that our shaping of events, however you want to designate them, was deeply centered on the all-important event of the birth of Jesus Christ. What is tragic is that the "modern" church has even fallen into the use of these "non-Christian" designations ... in order to appear to be more "progressive." This is another very sad example of moral abandonment by the very institution created to keep the Western moral foundations intact in the face of human folly.

polytheistic terms: life was primarily the result of a number of contending gods who laid claim to particular powers or particular areas of jurisdiction. These gods tended to be whimsical, violently passionate, and at times even lined up against each other in fierce competition.   But life was also filled with heroes, men and women who faced the gods, faced overwhelming struggles – and yet survived, even rising victorious in the struggle. Life therefore was viewed as some kind of dynamic between the gods of heaven and the mortal heroes of the earth – a dynamic that ultimately did produce some kind of sense of order to life.

The Ancient Jews, who strongly favored the mystical side of the great cosmological debate, saw life in terms of personal and collective righteousness which their own God YHWH* (we will translate this as "Yahweh") demanded of them. But they also had their earlier heroes (Abraham, Jacob, Joseph, Moses, Joshua, Gideon, David, etc.) and the stories or epics surrounding them as examples they should follow. And they also had their God-given system of law. And together – God, heroes, and the Law – these produced a strong sense of order in Jewish life.

Judaism actually founded in Babylonian captivity (500s BC). When the Jews of the tribe of Judah, as the last surviving tribe of the original 12 Hebrew or Israelite tribes, were led off to captivity in Babylon in the early 500s BC, they had a serious question facing them. Who or what had failed them? Had their tribal protector Yahweh failed them in competition with the Babylonian god Marduk? Was Marduk greater than Yahweh? Or had Yahweh simply abandoned them because they had failed miserably in maintaining the covenant of faith and the standards of righteousness required of them by Yahweh? It had been, after all, centuries since they had produced any heroes of significant stature to lead them in the paths of righteousness;

---

*Concerning the personal name for God – in biblical scripture written as the tetragram YHWH – there is much uncertainty. So holy was the personal name of God – never ever to be "taken in vain" (or simply used carelessly or wrongly) – that it was never pronounced. In the Jewish writings only the four consonants YHWH were recorded, and thus the vowels are unknown to us today. Was the name to be pronounced something like "Yehovah" or "Jehovah," or was it "Yahveh" or "Yahweh"? What exactly was the name to sound like? In any case, when the Jews read the name aloud, they typically substituted another name in the place of YHWH ... usually *Adonai* ("My Lord") but also *Elohim* or *El Shaddai*.

There is also much uncertainty about the original meaning of the tetragram itself. YHWH could possibly mean "I am what I am" or "I am the creator" or "I am the one who is above all that is" ... in the sense that God himself has no beginning or end, though creation itself, which his God's own handiwork, does have finite qualities. In other words, YHWH is the one who stands far above that which merely "is" ... that is, above the very universe that materialists are so caught up with in believing that "things" themselves are the ultimate reality – falling far short of the Judeo-Christian understanding of ultimate reality.

prophets, such Isaiah and Jeremiah, had also warned them that their lack of keeping covenant with God was going to draw Yahweh' s wrath?

Or was it that Yahweh was the God of all nations, that even the Babylonians were part of his ruling hand – and that God had sent the Babylonians to discipline the Jewish remnant of God's own covenant people Israel, as Isaiah had previously stated and as Jeremiah reiterated – much to the discomfort of the Jews?

Jewish monotheism. In the end, the Jews came to see the situation posed in the last- mentioned terms: Yahweh was the only God, the Creator of the universe, the Judge of all. There was no Marduk. But there was plenty of Divine judgment to be faced. Yahweh had used the Babylonians to punish the Jews for their failure to maintain his righteous covenant. And with that, the Jews turned urgently to keeping covenant with God by studying and practicing God's Law revealed to their people through previous heroes and prophets (most importantly Moses). This is when the ancient stories of their former "greats" handed down verbally by generation after generation were most earnestly collected and put in written or Scriptural form, the foundation of the Judeo-Christian Bible.

Messianic Judaism. But also, as a key part of this covenant, they also came to find themselves waiting for a new hero, a Messiah or "Anointed One," to come to them, one who as the heroes of old (particularly David, who had lived centuries earlier, in and around the year 1000 BC) would lead them personally to a greatness under Yahweh – a greatness that would bring the world to worship God at Zion (Jerusalem). They would then be reconstituted as an entirely priestly people, serving the world as God' s holy priesthood.

That was certainly to happen ... but just not in the way they expected.

The legacy of early or "Scriptural" Christianity

Undoubtedly, the most important – and totally life-changing – of these various worldviews was Christianity. As the Romans headed off strongly in the secularist direction, the Christians – as inheritors of the Jewish vision of life – headed off strongly in the theistic or mystical direction. Their view was that their leader or "savior," Jesus of Nazareth, was indeed the long-awaited Jewish Messiah – though more along the lines of a prophet like Moses or Isaiah than of a soldier like David. Jesus had come to open the way to a new world ... one that lived in total love with the God of Heaven – and thus also with each other.

In his own life and death, Jesus opened the way for those who chose by deep faith to rely on this very personal God – whom Jesus termed as Abba (Father) – as opposed to relying on their own human reason and in the workings of the materialist-mechanist or secular social systems that human reason always sought (and still seeks) to build.

This put the early Christians at distinct odds with everything that the Roman Empire stood for, especially at odds with the notion that the Empire – and its semi-divine emperors at its head – ought to be the object of veneration by every member of the Empire. Christians refused to offer sacrifices to the emperors, claiming that such a privilege belonged to God alone ... and suffered harsh persecution for their stand.

This also put them at odds with their own Jewish community, not merely because Jesus was not the kind of Messiah that most of the Jews had been led to expect, but because Jesus taught a Godly righteousness drawn not from the faithful observance of the Jewish Law but instead a righteousness drawn from the heart, from personal compassion towards others, and from a total devotion to God as Abba (a term of great blasphemy to "proper" Jews, because it was actually a term of familiarity more on the order of "Daddy"!)

The synthesis: Imperial Christianity or "Christendom"

During almost three centuries of persecuted existence, Christian "martyrs" (or "witnesses") revealed themselves to fellow Romans as possessors of an amazingly high moral character and personal bravery long missing in Roman life. So impressive was their Christian faith that eventually (early 300s AD) the Christian faith was taken up personally by the Roman rulers themselves. Thus it was that it then became the official religion of the Roman Empire.

However, both the faith and the Empire were significantly changed in the process of Christianity becoming thus officially "Romanized." Christianity joined Roman law to become the moral-ethical underpinning of the Empire. Jesus Christ was moved up alongside the emperors in status to become *Christus Rex* (Christ the King), friend and supporter of the emperors – and at this point a lofty figure quite removed from the common Christian. The latter now looked to the Virgin Mary and the saints for more intimate or personal spiritual support.

In turn, the Empire saw itself as defender of the Christian faith through a variety of formal offices – including the military. Out of this new amalgam arose the firmly-established Roman Catholic Church in the western half of the empire and the equally firmly-established Orthodox Church in the eastern or Byzantine half of the empire.

In short, while the Roman Empire took on certain theistic dimensions, the Christian faith gave up some of its pure theism in favor of a politically stronger, more secular religious position.*

The "Middle Ages"

But the synthesis of Roman Empire and Christian faith did not shore up the sagging Roman system, which finally crumbled – at least in the West – under the pressure of Germanic tribes who were pressing for resettlement within the Roman lands (400s). Though the Germanic tribes only wanted to possess the Roman order, not destroy it, their tribal touch only collapsed what little was left of the old imperial system.

However, two developments within Christianity helped keep the Christian faith intact in the West, even as the empire collapsed there. One of these was the belated conversion of the Irish to Christianity – thanks to the work of Patrick and his disciples (early 400s). These Irish converts in turn infused the faith with new vigor and sent missionaries from the outer island of Ireland into the midst of the Germanic settlements, both in England and on the Western European continent. Their brand of faith was of the very theistic variety: personal and Christ centered.

The other development as Rome was collapsing was the influx into the ranks of the church of good Roman patrician blood, which gave the Catholic church sufficient political expertise to thus be able to stave off the Roman collapse, at least with respect to the Roman church itself. Notable were the Roman popes Leo (mid-400s) and Gregory (late 500s) – who rebuilt the powers of the religious hierarchy centered on Rome. From Rome then went forth Catholic missionaries, drawing the Germanic tribes into the last standing institution of the old Roman imperium: the Roman Catholic Church. The Franks (in the future France), under Clovis (c.† 500), adopted in whole the Roman version of the faith. England, facing two versions of Christianity, finally decided to follow the Roman rather than the Irish variety. Thus a tendency of Christianity toward political or secular order rather than a personally theistic spirit won out in the end (mid-600s). But even then, it was a feeble version – invested with huge doses of pagan superstition and subject to the political whims of its Germanic rulers.

---

*More secular religious position" may sound like a contradiction in terms, because in today's world, secularism is treated as simply "scientific fact" – not "religion." Actually, secularism is no less a religion than any other "worldview" or system of belief that instructs people about why life exists as it does ... and what the people are to do to make the most of such a life. And the attack by modern Secularists on Christian "superstition" – or anciently, "mysticism" – is hardly a new thing ... going all the way back to the times of the ancient Greeks. Such secularism is no more "progressive" today than it has ever been.

†c. means circa – or around or about.

The Muslim intervention (600s/700s).   In its weakened political condition, Western Europe in the 700s found itself vulnerable to new intruders: the Muslims who had also just overrun most of the Roman Empire in the East (630s-640s) ... although in a way the Muslims revitalized – even as they transformed – the Eastern or "Byzantine" Empire into a quite prosperous Muslim order, rather than collapse those lands into poverty as the Germanic tribes had done in the West.

And these Muslims had achieved this grand success by simply building on the simpler Christian faith of many of the Byzantine commoners ... especially among the Semitics (Syrians, Palestinians and Arabs) most of whom had difficulties understanding the mystical character of the Trinitarian faith (God in three co-equal persons: Father, Son and Holy Spirit) that Greek minds so readily grasped. The Semitics tended to be Unitarians (only one God – the Heavenly Father ... with Jesus attaining divine status only in completing his work on earth). Islam's founder, Muhammad, in fact was really only something of a Christian Unitarian ... adding some key works of his own as the last of the Judeo-Christian prophets – thus "completing" the line of prophets. And Islam could be even more tolerant of dissenting religious groups – such as the Eastern Christians – as long as they accepted Islamic political ascendancy – and paid the required tax (the *jizya*).

The brief Carolingian revival in the West.   But very significantly, the Franks under Charles Martel not only turned back this Muslim tide when it tried to enter deeply into Western Christian territory, but his grandson, Charlemagne, even began the consolidation of Christian Western Europe under his personal rule through what is today France, Germany and Italy (most of Spain, however, was lost to Muslim domination for centuries).

Charlemagne was crowned Emperor in Rome in 800, and one might have believed that somehow the ancient Roman Christian Empire had come back to life in the West. But it was Germanic and not Roman ways that directed Charlemagne's Empire – and in accordance with Germanic custom ("Salic Law"), Charlemagne's lands were divided equally among his grandsons – and the impetus toward the reorganization and unification of the West was lost.

Viking domination (800s-1000s). Soon the Vikings or "Northmen" were taking up from the Germanic tribes in assaulting Western and Northern Europe – except that their hand was even more violent. This spun these regions of Europe back into two more centuries of "Dark Ages." But eventually, here and there, these Northmen (or Normans) settled into conquered Europe and were eventually drawn into the Christian order, giving it new blood – of the military variety.

The crusades (1100s/1200s). By 1100 their military talents were being put to use in a counter assault against Islam, carrying Christian "crusaders" all the way to Syria, Palestine and Egypt. This marks the beginning of the period of revival of Western culture, one which has continued down to the present day.

Growing East-West contacts. Though in the end the crusades proved to be a military failure (the Muslims pushed the Crusaders back out of the East during the 1200s), the Muslims indicated a willingness to replace Western efforts at conquest of the Muslim East with Western efforts at trade instead – and pilgrimage – as long as the Western Christians were willing to behave themselves! So a new relationship was established between the Christian West and the Muslim East, one which proved to be a major benefit to the West.

Also, and very importantly, the Muslim East (or actually to the West's great benefit, the Muslim South in Spain) had carefully preserved the ancient writings of the Greeks – writings that the Western Christians had previously destroyed because they were pre-Christian and thus "pagan." Aristotle and Plato had been known to the West; but now also other ancient Greek philosophers, mathematicians, and scientists came to light – as well as the Muslims' own contribution to learning (such as their Arabic numerals and their advanced methods of mathematical calculation known as al–jabr or algebra.)

The High Middle Ages (1200s-1300s). A period of peace began to settle in within the West itself during this time – which allowed the West to come into its own revival in Christian learning. Actually, this had begun even as early as the late 1000s but reached a highly sophisticated level during the 1200s. This new learning produced on the one hand a rich spirituality or "mysticism" (led in part by the Franciscans) and on the other hand a deep revival of intellectual order known as "scholasticism" (led in part by the Dominicans). The first of these emphasized a deep personal relationship with a loving God (theism) and the other tended to emphasize the benefits of a close examination of God's created order (the secularist instinct). An old dualism thus showed its ongoing hold on the Western mind even after centuries of dormancy.

By the 1300s this stirring intellectual curiosity had begun to shift its focus away from God and was casting it more and more on human life – even just ordinary human life. Also stirring was a deepening interest in the cultural offerings of the pre-Christian pagan Roman past. Things Roman (and not just Roman-Christian) and Greek were beginning to fascinate the West – particularly the Roman and Greek achievements in art, architecture and literature (both poetry and prose). Secular-humanism was stirring.

The Renaissance and Reformation (1400s/1500s)

The Renaissance. In the West, attitudes of the Christian church toward these new secularist developments were actually favorable, with the church even being a major patron of this revived spirit of secular-humanism (even elements of paganism).

Also, the Western church had never been averse to holding political power – and soon it began to demonstrate that it was not averse to holding big portions of economic power or wealth either. By the 1400s popes and bishops vied with newly rising industrialists, merchants, bankers – plus a new breed of national princes and kings – in gathering up the fruits of a fast unfolding secular order of power, wealth, art – and moral abandon.

Part of this came from the vastly expanded trade running across the Mediterranean to the Muslim East ... particularly by way of a number of powerful Italian city-states (Venice, Genoa, Florence ... even Papal Rome as well) ... which thus made Italy something of a base camp for this Renaissance.

But by the beginning of the 1500s, the scene shifted away from the Mediterranean to the Atlantic and the key monarchies located along its shores: Portugal, Spain, France, the Netherlands, England principally. And their wealth came from discovering the path south around Africa to the wealth of the Far East ... but also the path across the Atlantic to the New World or America ... where the vast plunder in Indian gold made Spain the wealthiest power of the 1500s – by far.

Luther's Protestant "Reformation." By the early 1500s this secular spirit growing in the Roman Catholic Church – and the Spanish Holy Roman Emperor as powerful protector of the Church – was about to find itself in opposition to two major social groups. One was the piety of the traditional rural order which was growing increasingly offended at the secularism or materialism of their holy church. The strongly theistic reformer Martin Luther demanded that reforms be undertaken within the secular church to restore it to the theistic purity of the early church, as founded by Jesus and the Apostles – clearly outlined in Holy Scripture ... the Bible now widely available thanks to the discovery of the printing press ... and the quickness by which the Vulgate Latin version was translated into the languages of the European commoners – a highly illegal act on the part of these "Protestants" in the eyes of the Roman Catholic Church.

The Calvinists. Another Protestant group, which found its voice in John Calvin, was the fast-rising urban society which had no place in the old rural feudal order – and which saw itself as better able than the rural feudal order to realize the ideal community life of early Christianity. This urban group, though pious in its theistic affections for God, happened also to command considerable intellectual and material or secular resources which could not be easily co-opted back into the feudal Catholic Church – nor easily subdued by the power of the fast-rising national princes of Spain, France and England.

By the 1600s Europe was plunged into bitter war on a number of fronts – as all of these old and new forces vied for mastery of the Western culture and soul.

The stirrings of "modern" culture

The path to the European Enlightenment. By the late 1600s two things were happening which would shift European culture away from the religious agenda of the Reformation: the first was the sheer exhaustion of Westerners from all the warring over the theological differences between Catholics and Protestants … over the issue of which religious group held the Truth. The feeling began to grow up among Westerners that the Truth would never be found through bloodshed. Toleration of differing religious opinions seemed to be more high-minded than all this sectarian squabbling.

The second thing was the rapid expansion of science (termed at the time "natural philosophy") and its seeming ability to explain all manner of natural events, whether in physics, chemistry or human anatomy. Science had already in the 1500s started to challenge traditional theism in the West over the issue of whether the earth was or was not the center of the universe. All theological tradition said that it had to be – for Scripture clearly places the earth as the center point of God's creation. But astronomers such as Copernicus, Galileo and Kepler offered powerful mathematical theories that undermined the church's traditional position.

As the 1600s progressed, social and natural philosophers such as Descartes, Spinoza, Newton and Locke began to speculate and design theories about a physical and social reality which seemed to function quite apart from the issue of God. This new science began to put the pieces together of a great mathematical puzzle which needed no particular involvement of God to make it all work. At best, God could be congratulated for having set the whole mechanism in motion – long, long ago. But now that it was up and running, it no longer gave evidence of further involvement of God in the process. The universe seemed to run simply under its own fixed or eternal physical or "natural" laws. Thus it was that modern science was born.

The colonization of the Americas. During the 1500s there had been some effort by the Portuguese and Spanish to bring their American territories under greater control by encouraging the settlement of their people in these lands of the New World ... thereby extending Europe's feudal social system to America. And the Portuguese and Spanish Catholic Church supported this endeavor by sending accompanying priests and missionaries – and building churches where they could. And economically speaking – as well as morally or spiritually – it all seemed to work out fairly well (for the Europeans at least) ... especially in the face of an expanding population back at home in Europe.

Not wanting to be left of out this enterprise – as the lands to the north of the Spanish holdings looked as if they might offer the same opportunity – the French, Dutch, English and even Swedish sent off various individuals to lay claim to North American territory ... in the hopes of establishing similar settlements of their own there.

The French sent priests and a small number of settlers to the habitable regions furthest north in "Canada" ... and then down along the Mississippi River valley. But it proved not to be a grand success.

The English sent settlers in the late 1500s to an Atlantic middle-region of North America ... which turned disastrous, and slowed the English enthusiasm for a while. But in the early 1600s the hope of discovering Indian gold – thus securing for themselves a higher position in the English feudal order – sent a new group of men off to "Virginia" ... they too having a very hard time of it – and dying in vast numbers in wave after wave of new arrivals.

The New England experiment as a "covenant" society. But curiously to the north of Virginia – in a region that came to be termed "New England" – a very different type of English society was established. It was not intended to be based on anyone's dream of "striking it rich in America" ... but rather on the intent of breaking from England to plant a new Protestant society (Calvinist style) in America – free from the persecutions these "Puritan" Protestants were experiencing in England under their king.

And the experiment was vastly successful ... avoiding the ongoing dying times that had afflicted Virginia. Some 20,000 English flocked to New England in the 1630s and early 1640s to become part of this new society – covenanted to live with God the way the Israelites had themselves once covenanted to live with God. And this covenant would become the key moral foundation of what was to become a very outstanding and quite powerful "Christian America."

Theism and secularism turn on each other. By the early 1700s, secularism seemed to be elbowing theism aside in the West. Those who continued to hold theistic views of the universe were looked upon by the newly "enlightened" thinkers of the day as being either deeply self-deluded or just simple-minded. Universities once given heavily to preparing ministers for their pastoral calls were now shifting the focus of their studies to the exploration of the secular world and the truths of "natural philosophy" which undergirded a growing sense of a natural or secular order standing behind everything.

The ultimate victory for secularism over theism finally began to register itself in terms of a shift in the sense of the nature and purpose of Western societies and governments. Whereas the old Catholic feudal order and the newer Protestant commonwealths had justified their existence in terms of God's own will and pleasure, by the late 1700s political communities were being refashioned around purely secular principles in which man – not God – was the justifier of the enterprise. Political reformers (Rousseau, Condorcet, Hume, Smith, Kant and others) were calling for reform of the political, economic and social systems of their days ... reform according to "rational" principles of governance – principles designed to enhance human stature, not the stature of God.

The Protestant "Great Awakening." But theism was by no means dead. Protestant pietism on the European continent and a spirit of Protestant revivalism in England and America (known in America as the "Great Awakening") stirred the theistic passions of many Westerners just prior to the mid-1700s. And although within a generation this passion had once again subsided, it left in its wake nonetheless a strengthened church and a resolve among Christians not to let the fires of their faith flicker out.

Unitarianism/Deism. Not all Protestant Christians had approved of these emotional outpourings – especially those of a more "reasoned" Christian faith. Unitarianism and deism stood halfway between pure secularism and theism – acknowledging God as the source of the blessings of creation and Jesus as the master moral teacher of mankind. But this viewpoint also tended to see Christianity as a moral responsibility rather than as a personal spiritual passion. It dismissed much of the fervency of those swept up by revivalism and looked with disbelief and disdain on all the tales of miraculous events as key to the Christian faith – either at that particular time or even previously, in Biblical times. Unitarianism and deism ultimately believed in a practical reality facing the Christian which was best approached through reason and science. Such Christianity was well on its way toward pure secularism.

English America breaks from its British monarchy. The fact that English Americans had made themselves politically self-governing virtually from the founding of their colonies many generations earlier decided the English king George III to break that spirit of independence ... lest it infect his subjects back in England as well. But the endeavor proved to be disastrous for George's oppressive armies (1775-1782) – and George had to face up to the humiliation of a people successfully rising against their monarch ... something unheard of in history. But the Americans themselves understood that the God they had covenanted with was highly responsible for this grand change in the course of history. Then with this success, American leaders gathered in 1787 to draft the ground rules (their Constitution) establishing a new Republic.

The French Revolution. This American success in turn was soon to serve to inspire the "enlightened ones" in France to attempt the same popular uprising against their Bourbon King. And there were also some deep cultural spiritual ingredients also involved in this French decision. But these went in a moral-spiritual direction quite opposite the one that had guided "revolutionary" America.

In Catholic France – and then elsewhere on the European Continent – the French Revolution which broke out in 1789 took a more militant attitude toward theistic Christianity, blaming such "superstition" for having undergirded centuries of political tyranny in Europe. French militants spread the accusation that Christian piety had dulled the spirits of the people in the face of feudal tyranny, by keeping them willingly submitted before traditional political authority because of the belief that this Old Regime had been ordained by God. Christianity was also accused of weakening the people's resolve to improve their lot in this life through political revolution and the rule of human reason ... by deflecting their hope instead toward an afterlife – something Enlightenment philosophers viewed as dangerously superstitious escapism.

Reaction. Ultimately such French secularism destroyed its own moral credentials through the blood-bath produced by the Paris guillotine – as French intellectuals, after having slaughtered the former ruling class, turned on each other in their quest to "rebuild" France around a more "rational" order, an order they seemed to be unable to agree on. Indeed, their use of "reason" merely deepened their mutual opposition. Soon they took to slaughtering each other. This was a very ugly display of intellectual arrogance, and social blindness.

Then, the cultural imperialism undertaken by Napoleon in the early 1800s – in order to refocus French militancy away from France itself and outward, toward France's neighbors – ultimately stirred up anti-French nationalism around Europe. This reaction to French haughtiness in fact also induced much of Europe to cling even more closely to its traditional Christian Order. Thus, after the defeat of the French in 1815, Europe returned to the safety of older theistic views on life. This coincided in America with wave after wave of yet another round of religious revivals (including the birthing of Mormonism) that swept across the country in the early 1800s.

The industrial revolution. But secularism was soon rescued by the ongoing industrial revolution – which produced unprecedented wealth, even eventually for the humbler classes, without the apparent aid of God. Human reason and effort alone seemed to be the necessary force behind this wondrous material development in the West. But unlike the French Revolution, it needed to find no cause against Christianity. The newly emerging industrial culture paid lip service to theistic Christianity – while in fact putting its greatest energies behind secular development.

Karl Marx. Not all voices of the industrial revolution, however, were so respectful of Christianity. In the mid-1800s, Marx, in explaining the servile condition of the European worker under the new industrial leaders, blamed Christian hypocrisy – in much the same language that the French Revolution had used. Marx called Christianity – and its belief in a better afterlife for the weak and downtrodden – as the "opium of the masses," dished out to them to keep them dumbed down and submissive. He called not only for the overthrow of these new industrial leaders in a grand workers' revolution, but also for the elimination of this Christian superstition.

In counter to any theistic understanding of the human social order, Marx counter-proposed a purely secular or materialist interpretation of society and its historical development. He claimed that forces inherent in the material means by which societies historically had produced their own wealth (land holding, slave labor, capitalism) produced dialectical or opposing class interests whose historical conflicts actually progressed societies to an ever-higher social state or condition. Thus it was (to Marx anyway) that materialist forces, not a divine hand, moved history ever-progressively forward.

Ultimately, he boasted that his theory was "scientific socialism" ... not theistic superstition.

Charles Darwin. This was coupled in the mid-1800s with an even more devastating indictment of the traditional theistic interpretation of life's dynamics. Darwin tackled the entire question of the origins of all biological life – including human life. He came up with a theory that claimed that life had progressed over the long run of the earth's history from simple life forms to very complex life forms. This progression had occurred, Darwin claimed, through genetic accidents in reproduction – accidents which would give a non-normal creature a slight advantage over its cousins in its adaptability to newly arising changes in the environment. This better adapted creature would eventually establish itself as a new species. And thus, over the long run of history, one species produced another more complex species – which would eventually produce yet an even more complex species – until through a process of biological evolution the whole biological panorama of the present world eventually came into being. Even human life emerged through this process – emerging from less complex biological life, indeed emerging recently in this long biological history as a better-adapted ape.

The impact of Darwin's theory was that it in no way necessitated the hand of a Creator God. It ran on its own as a completely self-sustaining process, simply through the accidents of history. God was a meaningless concept in Darwin's theory of biological evolution through natural selection.

This was a devastating challenge to theism – for which, to many Westerners, theism seemed to have no adequate response.

Progressivism, nationalism, and imperialism

Progressivism. This Marxist-Darwinist "evolutionary" or "progressivist" view of life, of human history, had a tremendous impact on the intellectual moral character of Western society in the latter half of the 1800s. Darwinism, in its social form, undercut deeply Roman Christendom's long-standing political-social doctrine of noblesse oblige, whereby the wealthy and powerful had a moral responsibility to care for the humbler or poorer classes. Darwinist "Progressivism" claimed that it was the very heart of nature – and crucial to all historical progress – that the strong not be burdened in any way by the plight of the poor. It was the destiny of the strong to rule – to take history forward – and the destiny of the weak to be cast out in the struggle for survival.

This "ethic" helped justify the huge wealth that was being amassed in the hands of the new industrial-commercial-financial elite – at the cost of the working poor, who were forced to work long hours for the rich with only the barest of compensation for their contributions to the industrial age. But this is also what gave Marx the inspiration for his theory that history would advance to its next and final stage when the industrial worker realized his true strength and revolted against the ever-smaller industrial capitalist class (the capitalists highly competitive urge towards monopoly driving each other to ruin and thus ironically reducing their own ranks in number) – producing a revolution of the newly strong (the rising working class) over the weakening former dominators (the dwindling capitalist class).

Nationalism. But this competitive or Darwinist ethic not only set the European "working class" against the European "propertied class," it also set European nation against European nation. Darwinism produced an ever-growing instinct or spirit of each European nation, aggressively moving to prove itself historically superior to its neighbors. For France and England, this nationalist competition already had a long history. But it served in the 1800s to soften the class lines within the French and English nations as the lines of one nation against the other hardened. Thus it was allowed – even encouraged – to develop, through the creation of "Romantic" national history, poetry, operas, anthems, etc. ("jingoism"), as a means of preserving social harmony within Europe's increasingly self-aware national units.

This urge also drove the Germans and Italians – who had long been divided internally into a number of fiercely competitive smaller states – to create the new nation-states of Italy (1860) and Germany (1870). It also stirred ethnic minorities within the remaining European multi-ethnic empires to demand the same national independence.

The nation and its quest for glory came to command the full, overriding loyalty of its members – even to the extent of a call to die gallantly in war for the nation's rightful place in the sun. Complements of Romanticism's ability to stir the hearts of still rather theistic European commoners, the nation became celebrated as the supreme instrument of God's will on earth – as well (to the more noble intellectuals of society) as the ultimate source of all material well-being, justice and right-mindedness here on earth. Indeed, Westerners were creating a new god of sorts: their beloved nation – whether England, France, Germany, Italy, Russia, Bulgaria, America or elsewhere.

Imperialism. This hotly competitive national spirit flung itself outward into the larger world – uniting imperial armies, industrialists and traders, and Christian missionaries in the effort to extend the influence of their sending nations among the "pagans and heathens" of the world. The West was on the move, impelled by zealous forces which seemed to have no limit to their ambitions for mastery or dominance in the world. The British pushed for global commercialism, headquartered in London; the French pushed for a global French language and culture, headquartered in Paris. The Americans pushed for constitutional democracy and commercialism, mostly focused on its neighbors to the south ... and quite beneficial to the American business world! And the Germans and Italians, coming lately to the game, struggled to find imperial colonies for themselves to rule, in a demonstration of Germanic or Italian greatness. And the Russians and Austro-Hungarians looked to grab pieces of their Muslim neighbor, the Turkish Ottoman Empire, in their own program of imperial expansion.

But by the end of the century they had run out of "overseas" territories to grab in this Darwinian contest. It was inevitable that these different sending forces would ultimately clash with each other – right at home in Europe itself – in a most ferocious sort of way.

The 20th and 21st centuries

Violent war. The first half of the 20th century saw the inevitable clash of these nationalist forces – in two world wars and in the startup of a "cold war" which drew most of the world into a vortex of unprecedented violence. These nationalist urges which had their origins in the West not only dragged the rest of the world into the violence as victims, but eventually infused the same nationalist zeal among non-Westerners. Everyone, it seems, wanted a place in the sun for their beloved national or cultural communities – as if the forces that directed the universe itself depended on the ultimate victory of one or another of these communities.

Standing behind the outrageous level of violence of 20th century wars was the power of modern materialist science. Man had learned to control, even unleash, enormous powers – both to create and to destroy. Long range artillery could reduce towns and cities to rubble; air power could do the same. With the discovery of the nuclear bomb – and the missile that could send these bombs from one side of the earth to the other – cities could potentially even be disappeared in a single flash. Gone were the days of the heroic warrior. In the warrior's place stood the anonymous engineer who from the safety of his or her headquarters could conduct terrible war without the enemy having any idea of who or what was coming their way.

Thus it was that clearly any kind of actual shooting war must now be avoided ... at all costs.

Western Europe goes "international." Consequently, most Europeans now tended to be very suspicious of nationalist appeals ... and quite decided to build as much as possible a post-war Europe on the basis of multinational executive authorities. Thus they were glad to join America in the creation of the multinational defense force NATO. But they also put their strategic industries, coal and steel, also under multi-national authority. And soon they simply moved to join their economies ... and even their workforces into a single economic zone – the European Community. And Europe prospered ... at least in the Western half of the continent.

The Soviet Empire. But Eastern Europe found itself (since 1945) under occupation by Stalin's Russian or Soviet troops ... giving the dictator Stalin the opportunity to put into place his own ideas as to how the Eastern half of Europe was to move ahead. He was careful to place Eastern European countries under the authority of Communist leaders he himself picked and directed ... leaders that seemed to have little ability to inspire the societies they controlled. Supposedly Eastern Europe now lived according to the Marxist vision (secular and very anti-Christian). But in fact, it was merely whatever Stalin deemed it should be politically, economically, and socially.

When Stalin eventually died, his legacy was passed on to Soviet leaders Khrushchev and then Brezhnev ... who continued the dictatorship.

Cold War America. America understood that it was called on to protect what it could of Western Europe (and the rest of the world, for that matter) from Stalin's expansionist instincts. This was the basis of the Marshall Plan of economic assistance to Europe (1947 and after) and NATO (1949). Beyond that, America simply encouraged Western Europe to move ahead with its multinational impulse, America seeing in this the advance of the grand cause of "democracy" ... the political philosophy which had been driving America forward (its own form of nationalism) since the beginning of the 20th century.

No shooting war with its arch-rival Soviet Russia was ever involved. But something like a chess game was going on between these two superpowers ... a move of either America or Russia to put itself in a position of influence in some new part of the world quickly answered with a countermove by its opponent. Thus a "Cold War." And of course, each move was justified morally by the idea that the action undertaken by the superpower was either in advance of "Free World Democracy" (America) or "The People's Democratic Republic" (Russia). But such moves in fact seldom resulted in progressing "democracy" ... of whatever variety. These were actions taken in accordance with the political and economic interests of the superpowers themselves!

The Soviet Empire collapses. Finally (1980s), Soviet premier Gorbachev felt called on to reform Soviet society along more truly democratic lines, freeing speech, economic opportunity ... and whatever the people themselves might want from society. The only problem was this set a bad example to the East European Communist dictatorships ... which found themselves unable to fend off revolts of their citizens when the latter also demanded such reforms. One by one these East European dictatorships fell ... and with it, the Soviet Empire in East Europe.

But Russia itself did not fare well under the reforms, confusing a Russian citizenry not all acquainted with the responsibilities of self-rule. Gorbachev was followed by Yeltsin, who tried to hold things together ... though even huge sections of the Soviet Union itself simply declared independence from the Russian center. Putin would then take over ... and attempt to rebuilt a Russia along more familiar lines. But the days of Russia as a superpower were definitely over.

America stumbles. Meanwhile in America, there was much celebration over the fall of the Soviet system. But America was actually having its own troubles ... its Cold War unity being replaced by an ever-stronger contention between its political "Left" (Democrats) and "Right" (Republicans) ... a battle shaping up among the generations and also among the different regions of the country over which worldview America is supposed to be living by. Republicans tried hard to hang onto older American moral-cultural traditions ... whereas Democrats saw those traditions as horribly evil on so many fronts (race and ethnicity, sex, religion, urban vs. small-town mentalities) and did what they could to progress or "change" America.

The latter group, the Democrats, had to their advantage, younger generations who sought personal freedom and status rather than conformity to any larger social responsibilities (marriages, family, jobs) ... and were quite content to see the older American worldview cut away.

In this they had the Supreme Court as their best political ally, needing only 5 of the Supreme Court's 9 members to completely rewrite the legal foundations of the country – power which even Congress itself could not command. Indeed, the Supreme Court had somehow managed to make itself America's chief law-making body.

Not surprisingly, the very disciplines of Congressional politics itself underwent decay ... as national politics became a matter solely of one side defeating the other side ... and the all-critical political "center" cut out of the dynamic completely.

And with Trump playing president as some kind of celebrity rather than experienced statesman (and his Mussolini-like call for his "troops" to march on the Capitol to block the Congressional presidential vote) and Biden seeming to be nothing more than a mouthpiece for the Democratic Party and its particular political agenda – and with no one else seeming to be able to come to prominence against these two political figures – it is hard to see how America is going to get up from its huge political stumble ... and continue its superpower responsibilities as an international referee in the world's political games.

China on the move. At the same time Gorbachev's Russia was moving to make democratic reforms (the 1980s) so too was a post-Mao China under Deng Xiaoping doing the same ... although with much better success. There was still enough of an entrepreneurial mentality among key components of

Chinese society that in fact the Chinese economy was able to boom at a huge 10% annual rate of economic expansion, year after year. Thus China moved quickly from being merely another Third World country … to something of a superpower itself. In fact, under the premiership (another dictatorship?) of Xi Jinping, China has been moving rapidly to make itself not only a true superpower … but the sole superpower on earth – presuming that a deep decline politically, economically (and in every other respect) awaits America now that it is on the path it has chosen for itself (an unpayable national debt, no sense of any unifying purpose, a lack of strong moral leadership). The Chinese recognize a Fourth-Generation society when they see it!

Looking to the future. Where that leaves the Western world at this point remains a huge question. Western Europe seems quite content simply to enjoy the fruits of a truly multinational economic system. Politically, it seems to feel no particular need to have some grand purpose beyond the simple enjoyment of these economic achievements. But where that would put Europe in relationship with a weakening America and an ever-stronger China is not exactly clear.

For America, it seems that the only serious possibility for a comeback is to find itself once again on the same road that, over the centuries, led to its 20th century greatness. There was truly a moral reason behind what America was ultimately able to shape itself into. It didn't just happen by accident or by some natural or inevitable process. It came down a very strongly Christian path, under the leadership of Christian men who understood very clearly the call placed by God on the nation they were called to preside over.

But getting America to understand this challenge in this manner will never be achieved by human reason. It is human reason that got America in this fix in the first place. Truly, like Israel of old – and like America itself at various points in its history – it is time for the nation to call on God to guide it out of the moral morass it has fallen into.

Thankfully, it takes only a few good souls to ignite the fires of religious revival – as America's own history demonstrates. So … let us look beyond Washington for some kind of deliverance (that's just not going to happen) and instead to Christian leaders … truly "born-again" individuals committed to restoring the great Western – and American – legacy, the legacy that once led the Christian West to greatness.

Indeed, let our call be "Maranatha" … may the Lord come!

✱ ✱ ✱

A GRAPHIC PORTRAYAL OF THE WEST'S
MORAL-SPIRITUAL LEGACY

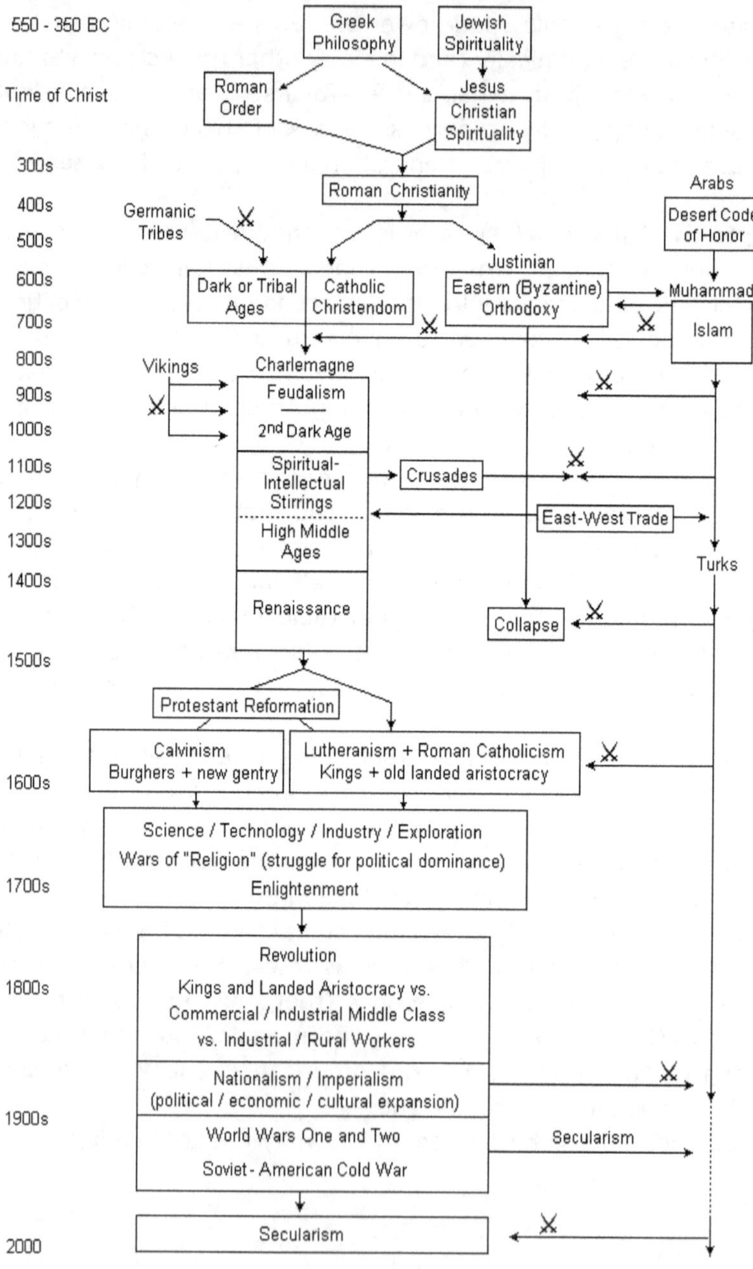

CHAPTER ONE

THE ANCIENT GREEK LEGACY

* * *

THE ANCIENT GREEK POLITICAL-INTELLECTUAL LEGACY

It is of vital importance to note that America's "Founding Fathers" who gathered in Philadelphia during a very hot summer in 1787 to draft a new Constitution uniting their thirteen* newly-independent states were college educated – or at least self-taught in the intellectual areas that a college education would have included – and were therefore well-informed about the ancient Greeks ... and the political and intellectual lessons to be drawn from Greek history. And it was a huge legacy ... highly instructive of both the good – and the bad – in any society's political and intellectual development. Thus this Greek legacy would factor hugely in how those that were called to put together a new American Constitution would finally design or "frame" this most fundamental American political foundation. They knew to build on the positive part of the Greek – especially the Athenian – legacy ... and avoid the horribly negative parts of that same legacy.

At the heart of that legacy was the immense intellectual energy that a large number of Greek individuals were able to generate. Greek scholarship brought Greece forward out of its original neolithic (farming and animal herding) world ... and into a highly civilized world – urbanized on the basis of the very independent Greek city-states. Such development sparked deep inquiry into a newly awakening world ... and what that meant to the Greeks in terms of the social "progress" they were seeking to achieve.

But unfortunately, that same highly intellectual spirit would also come to lead the Greeks, notably the leading Greek city-state Athens, into very self-destructive political rationalizing. Tragically, the Athenian "Sophists" (wise ones!) of the 400s and 300s BC used their intellectual gifts to lead

---

*Actually, only twelve of these new states sent representatives to Philadelphia that summer ... because tiny Rhode Island was afraid to join the new Union, fearing it would lose all sovereignty to a new governing authority. Rhode Island would, however, soon join ... when it was clear that the new Constitution protected the states' authority – rather than removed it.

a very gullible Athenian citizenry to take up very self-destructive political causes ... ones that led to a series of totally ruinous wars.

Thus the cleverly rational Greek Sophists demonstrated to the American Framers the dangers of human "reason," always clever – but hardly the kind of Truth that elevates life. After all, half of these Framers were lawyers, and already knew that a very convincing rational argument laid before a jury on behalf of a client of theirs was simply the business they offered their clients. For the jury, deciding the actual "Truth" of a dispute involving a "rational" defense put before them by opposing – but equally clever – lawyers was a very delicate, often very uncertain, matter.

Thus the Framers knew very well that Reason itself never equaled Truth. Reason merely advantaged one side of a dispute over its opponents. The actual truth of things thus always stood above – and often well beyond – human reason. The Greeks proved that quite clearly.

"Democracy" as Greece's great legacy. Undoubtedly when Greece is remembered today as a major contributor to Western civilization it is in the area of "democracy" that Greece – but especially Athens – is mostly noted. But actually, for almost two thousand years, the Greek concept of "democracy" dropped from view or discussion ... and for good reasons.

Democracy or rule by the people (the Greek *demos*) is an almost sacred concept today ... but one not well understood by those very ones today loudest in their promotion of the glories of democracy. The way they go at this matter comes from their instincts favoring a purely rational Humanism or Idealism ... not from actual experience across the ages.

Greek government by the demos at one point served the Greeks well ... and then proceeded to dishonor that record – especially in the leading Greek city-state of Athens – by engaging in very stupid politics, "democratic" politics that ultimately brought Athens down from its power and greatness. The Athenian demos, as it turned out, was easily led by unscrupulous politicians, who manipulated the masses into making horrible political decisions ... such as ordering the death of Athens' premier philosopher Socrates, because he annoyed these unscrupulous politicians with his constant criticism of their behavior. That same stupidity was found also in the decision of the Athenian demos to turn a deaf ear to their fellow Greeks who complained that the money being sent to Athens, as Greece's leading city-state, to equip a Greek army designed to protect Greece from the Persians, was being used instead to dress up Athens with fancy new buildings and other public works. The other Greek city-states would have been happy to have kept this money, if it was not going to the intended purpose of Greek defense, to undertake the same architectural upgrade to their own communities. Ultimately, Athens' selfishness led to a horrible series of Peloponnesian Wars among Greece's various city-states, (431-378 BC), wars that finally destroyed not only Athens politically, but much of the rest of Greece as well.

Consequently "democracy" was not well remembered in the West. As we have already noted, the philosopher Aristotle himself (who was widely read by educated Westerners ... up until recently), made it clear that it is not the form of government – whether government by one, a few, or the many – that produces better government ... but instead the moral intentions of those who do govern. Dictators are not the only problem affecting mankind. Democracies (Hitler's Germany was actually a "democracy") can be horrible, if horribly led.

Thus it is that the men (who had read their Aristotle!) who gathered in Philadelphia in 1787 to put together a new American Constitution in order to perfect the Union of their thirteen states were definitely not intending to create a democracy. They instituted instead a "republic" built on a regime of foundational law ... which itself called for a "mixed" system, one of political checks and balances. The Republic's Constitution was carefully designed to permit, yet restrict, popular participation in the nation's politics – out of a fear of democratic instincts getting out of control. Their new Federal Union would include government by one (the President), the aristocratic few (the Senate) and the democratic many (the House of Representatives) ... understanding that this system would work only when all three forms of rule worked together. This was to prevent any one of the three forms of government to take over the other two and establish a monopoly on power ... which unchecked always leads to great social evil.

It would be until only the beginning of the 20th century – notably with the arrival on the scene of the highly Idealistic American President Woodrow Wilson, who saw "democracy" as the cure-all for the world's ills – that "democracy" would come to have the glamor and intense devotion that it does today. Thus it is only recently that Western political philosophers have rejected the wisdom of the ancients and moved to the call for pure "democracy" both at home and abroad.

This is so much so the case that it is now almost religious heresy to voice any hesitations about bringing (especially imposing) democracy as some kind of wonderful benefit to the world's societies ... without having also laid the accompanying moral groundwork that democracy would need in order not to lead to horrible social chaos and even cruel tyranny. Democracy is not a basic human right. It is a major social responsibility.

GREEK ORIGINS

The Mycenaeans or Achaeans. At some very distant point in time, dating anywhere between 1900 BC and 1500 BC, a number of different Aryan-speaking peoples moved westward from southwestern Russia and invaded and settled in wave after wave into the land we know as Greece.

These invaders, sometimes identified as "Mycenaeans" or sometimes as "Achaeans," spoke an early form of Greek and would become known to later Greeks as the military heroes in Homer's epic war story or poem, the *Iliad*. There on that southernmost Peloponnese Peninsula they established fortified towns in the valleys between the many mountainous ridges that reach down to the sea and divide Greece into a number of distinct geographic units.   Each town was headed by a chieftain or warlord (or "king" as we later termed them).

Eventually a number of important Greek cities, such as Athens and Thebes that developed later, could easily trace their origins back to Mycenaean times.

The Dorians ... and a Greek "Dark Age." But this Mycenaean/Achaean strength eventually began to decline, and after approximately 1150 BC Greek culture fell into a 400 year-long Dark Age. This was either caused by, or led to, yet another wave of Greek invaders from the Northeast, the "Dorians."   All archeological evidence seems to indicate that probably (though not certainly: debate lingers on) the Dorians disrupted life in Greece in a very major way.

Certainly the Doric invasion set off a reactive wave of Greek migrations in around 1000 BC – principally to the shores of western Asia Minor (the western shores of today's Turkey). Ionians from Attica (around Athens) retreated across the Aegean to those central western shores of Asia Minor to Miletus – and gave their name "Ionia" to this particular region along the Asia Minor coastline. Aeolians (perhaps a later group of Greeks to appear on the scene) settled the northwestern shores of Asia Minor. Dorians themselves eventually continued their own migration across the Aegean to the shores of southwestern Asia Minor and then onward to Crete.

In any case, the warlike Dorians eventually settled themselves into the Peloponnesian peninsula – where they ruled over the helots, the enslaved or enserfed Greeks who had originally lived in the area. Eventually Sparta grew up as the leading city-state at the heart of Doric culture – famous for the intense military discipline all its citizens (women as well as men) were put under. But interestingly, Athens (and its hinterland of Attica) managed to fend off the Dorians – and retain its older Achaean culture.

Greece's "Archaic Period" (700s BC to the late 500s BC). In the 700s BC Greece began to experience a commercial revival, growth of its population, and emergence of political powers in reviving Greek towns in the form of local aristocracies (rule by the heads of prominent families). But prosperity also strengthened the power of the more numerous commoner class, who found champions in the form of tyrants ("champions of the poor") – who would use their political power to support the political cause of the Greek lower classes. Political revolutions of sorts thus shook the Greek world as new prosperity put power in the hands of all sorts of people. As a result, democracy (rule by the common people or demos) – or something like it – resulted in a number of cities.

This rise of the common classes however inspired a strong political reaction in Sparta, where a small elite of Spartan military citizens, who ruled over the vast numbers of subject peoples (helots) in surrounding towns and villages, took an ever-tougher stance of rulers-over-ruled – creating Sparta's famed military aristocracy.

More Greek colonization around the Mediterranean. With this economic revival of Greece there was also a large increase in the population – causing a serious strain on Greece's available farmland to feed that population. However, the surrounding seas, which the Greeks viewed not as a barrier but as a source of life (in fact a superhighway for them to move across), offered them an escape from their problems. Thus, excess population was sent out to create new settlements or colonies – extensions of sorts of the sending cities. A new wave of Greek migration thus developed.

During the 700s and 600s BC Greeks sailed east and west and discovered lands that they could colonize with their excess population (much as other cultures were doing at the time, notably the Phoenicians – located along the Syrian coast – with whom the Greeks had active commercial relations).

From the city of Corinth colonies were established to the West on the island of Sicily and on the southern Italian peninsula (this would eventually come to be called *Magna Graecia* or "Greater Greece"). One of those colonies, Syracuse (founded in 733 BC), soon became a major city by its own right. Some of the Euboean towns (just north of Attica) sent settlers to the Syrian coast. From Miletus and other coastal towns in Ionian Asia Minor settlers were sent north through the Dardanelles straits into the Black Sea where they then established numerous Greek towns around the coast. Settlers also headed south to the Egyptian and Libyan coasts of Africa. Others sailed west beyond Sicily and established towns along the coast of what is modern day France. By the 500s BC, they were even reaching Spain.

Thus in the course of the 600s BC "Greece" came to describe an area much larger than the land we today call Greece. In those ancient days "Greece" encompassed a whole huge area along the northern half of the Eastern and central Mediterranean Sea. And if we include the various Greek cities planted along the coast of the Western Mediterranean (such as Marseilles in southern France) we are describing a culture that was very extensive.

Soon Greek towns along the Western coast of Ionia and Magna Graecia would achieve tremendous cultural growth of their own – often surpassing in quality the level of culture of the sending-cities back home.

✱ ✱ ✱

EARLY PHILOSOPHICAL DEVELOPMENT

The Greek cosmic vision: Materialism versus Mysticism

It is easy to look to the ancient Greeks for the startup of what we have come to know as "Western culture." The Greeks were great thinkers. Although they had started out as much of the rest of the world with rather neolithic ideas about how events on earth were regulated by gods and goddesses in the heavenlies above (and in the depths of the earth below), some of them began to notice a high degree of order around them, one not so easily explained by the doings of rather human-like and human-acting gods and goddesses. Greek thinkers began to explore the possibilities of other things being the source of this order. Thus Greek philosophy was born. And thus the Greeks put Western culture on the road to intellectual and spiritual enquiry – one still very much a part of Western culture to this day. And it all began so very long ago.

This Greek legacy was so strong that it even influenced deeply the Roman world that eventually took over the Mediterranean heartland from the Greeks, and indeed also the Christian society that emerged from the decline of Rome, and even the modern secular world that would one day in turn challenge the thousand-year tenure of Christendom. This legacy would be strongly philosophical and ideological in its early shaping of the West's fundamental cosmology or world view – but in the process would take on not one but two distinct forms: on the one hand an earthy *philosophical materialism* ... and on the other a lofty *mysticism*.

From Chaos to Order. Greek culture had grown up in a cosmos of rather fickle and often cruel gods who, from Mount Olympus, called the shots on earth. It was often a wild and crazy affair – as witnessed in the sagas of Homer in his works, the *Iliad* and the *Odyssey*. But by the 700s BC, the poet Hesiod was describing in his well-received work, *Theogony*, an Olympic realm in which the gods themselves lived under some kind of a divine order – with Zeus as the presiding figure over this order.

Philosophical Materialism. By the 500s BC a number of Greek thinkers were already dismissing the idea of human-like gods living atop Mount Olympus directing life on earth, especially concerning the affairs of the Greeks themselves. From the Easternmost reaches of the Greek world in Western Asia (Ionia in modern-day Turkey) to the Westernmost reaches of the same world in Southern Italy and Sicily, a number of Greek thinkers or philosophers were reflecting deeply on this matter of a basic order underlying all creation ... an order that seemed to work quite "naturally" (as in its very nature to do so) rather than as a result of some kind of Olympian or divine manipulation.

The "Miletus Triad"

It is perhaps surprising to note that it was not in Athens or the Greek mainland, but in the eastern Greek realm of Ionia across the Aegean Sea, that this program of "natural science" really got underway. In the Ionian town of Miletus, the well-traveled teacher Thales (c. 624-546 BC) showed his students the power of mathematics and engineering in the construction of everything from pyramids to ships. But he was also the first Western philosopher on record (and thus acknowledged as the "Father" of Western philosophy) to seek to find the substance that was the source – material in nature ... not spiritual or divine – that was the foundation of all reality. And he was certain that it was simply the primary physical reality: water.

His legacy was then picked up by Anaximánder (most probably a student of Thales) and then carried forward by Anaximander's student Anaximénes. Anaximander (c. 610-547 BC) claimed that it was the balance of forces inherent in all matter (cold v. hot; wet v. dry) that formed the underlying dynamic moving all of life forward. Then Anaximenes (mid-500s BC) went back to Thales' single-substance theory ... except that he claimed that it was *pneuma* (breath or spirit) that was the primal material and the source of all life. But according to Anaximander, pneuma could take on mass, even take form as fire, as well as form the foundation for all material substance.

And thus the "Miletus Triad" opened up the materialist pathway for Greek philosophy to take. Thus these materialistic philosophers were early forerunners of our modern scientists – with this same tendency to look to the material order for answers to the "natural" structure and dynamics of the universe.

According to these early philosophers, Greek gods had no role to play in the dynamics of life.

Pythagoras (c. 570-480 BC)

But the materialism of the Miletus school was answered by another individual located on the opposite side of the Greek world – in Southern Italy at Croton. Today he is remembered for his skill in the field of mathematics ... for instance, the discovery of the "Pythagorean Theory" of the dimensions of a right triangle, his discovery of the mathematical rules for the musical harmonies or scales; his assurance that the sun, moon and earth - as well as the universe itself – are all perfect spheres.

But unlike the Miletus School of Materialist philosophy,[*] Pythagoras was noted for being a mystic ... even of the Orphic school – rather than a materialist. Unfortunately, it is hard to say what his cosmological beliefs actually happened to be ... because he worked with his students in mystic secrecy ... although elements of his thinking slipped out publicly so that we can see that he was an exceptional philosopher in the mystic category as well.

We know that his philosophy was closely related to Orphism[†] ... although we can't tell whether Orphism impacted him greatly – or he impacted the

---

[*]With Pythagoras actually growing up on the island of Samos just opposite Miletus, it is even probable that he was once a student of Anaximander's.

[†]Orphism shared many features in common with another worship form found further to the East: Hinduism. Orphism developed a theology of reincarnation and transmigration of the souls through endless cycles of birth, growth, decay and death – in which escape from the grip of this eternal dance was the desired goal of the Orphic devotee (as with Hinduism's offshoot, Buddhism).

Orphic school greatly. But certainly, the Orphic mysteries became much more sophisticated in his days … a Greek philosophical development for which Pythagoras is probably greatly responsible.

As a mystic he looked beyond the mathematical precision of the world that so fascinated the Materialists … in the search for the higher causes of such precision. Certainly this mathematical precision underlying all physical reality was not achieved by accident … but had a much higher cause – some divine force behind it all. It was to this higher realm that Pythagoras was certain that we needed to direct our search … in order to better understand reality.[*]

The challenge to unite the Materialist and Mystical cosmologies

Heráclitus (c. 500 BC) was another Ionian … who certainly had his foundations in the Ionian Materialist camp but who was also interested in exploring the higher dynamic behind all reality. As a Materialist, he concluded that fire was the primordial element of life … even though it is not a "thing" but merely a life process we are presently observing. But as something of a Mystic, he also believed that life is actually a dynamic in which divided forces governing physical reality are always seeking to recover full unity with the higher order or *Logos* from which they were once separated. Unity with the Logos is thus that higher order or full reality to which we should ourselves seek to be rejoined.

Interestingly, Christians would later identify that same Logos [†] as the dynamic "Word" of God from which all things in creation were originally derived … but also a Logos which came to earth in the form of man (Jesus) to live among us in order to show us the way back to that unity with the Creator himself, our heavenly Father.

Ultimately however, the Materialists came to some kind of agreement, thanks to Empédocles (mid-400s BC), that reality was made up of four elements – earth, air, fire and water – which combine in different ways to shape the physical world.

Of course the Materialists would still find the one most important question in life to be also the most difficult question to answer: where did all of this material order come from? Parménides (early 400s BC) answered the question by affirming that the question itself was an absurd one … because something could not just come out of nothing. Reality always is …

---

[*] Einstein's discovery of the shockingly simple mathematical relationship between all matter and all energy, E=mc2, would have greatly excited Pythagoras. In fact, to call Einstein a mystic would not be inaccurate at all! He and his scientific friends often engaged in discussions about the precise nature of the Lord God!

[†] John 1:1 and John 1:14 … some of the opening verses of the Gospel of John.

and has always been. That thus supposedly answered the question.

But another Ionian philosopher, Anaxagóras (mid-400s BC) would not stop with that conclusion. Being from Ionia, he was quite naturally a Materialist. For instance, he saw the sun as an enormous red-hot stone ... and the moon as merely reflecting the sun's light. But he had some Mystical instincts as well ...holding the view that the Eternal Mind (the *Nous*) gave life its beginning ... and continued to shape and activate all life.

And very importantly for Athens, he left Ionia and moved to that city to do his study and teaching ... helping to start up Athens as a major intellectual as well as political center.

Democritus

Another Greek Materialist, Demócritus (c. 450-370 BC), would take Greek philosophy its furthest down the Materialist path. He was widely recognized even in his own days as a brilliant thinker ... who brought to the ancient Greek world the atomic theory of the cosmos. Basically, his view was that all life is merely the composite structure of invisibly minute particles of hard matter: atoms (from the Greek *atomos* meaning "not divisible"). These atoms – eternal in their being – are structured into the more visible material entities we observe in our world – through the laws of motion – also eternal in their existence.

Democritus was also a profound materialist in his view of human life. To him life is simply patterns of motion of these soul-less atoms – operating in accordance with equally soul-less laws. The human soul itself is simply a brief pattern in the working of the atoms – a pattern which forms in the human womb, developing, and then breaking down over a human lifetime ... until it simply ceases to exist when we draw our last breath.

To Democritus there was no such thing as eternal life. Likewise, God or Divinity was to him simply a construct of human thought – and had no real existence in the cosmos.

Thus in so many ways Democritus anticipated – by thousands of years – the direction modern secular science would take in its development with the modern rise of post-Christian Western culture and society!

✳ ✳ ✳

THE "GOLDEN AGE" OF GREECE
Greek democracy

The Greeks were also a people given to much thought about the best way to shape, run, and occasionally reform Greek society.

All Greeks originated as proud tribal peoples, complete with their tribal assemblies that all men were expected to attend ... for their services would be frequently called on and it was best that they personally had "bought into" the social decision, especially on the matter of war, in order to assure their commitment to the cause. And out of this experience grew the idea of the people governing themselves. Each tribe, even when it grew in number and became "civilized" (meaning the people now lived in cities with temples, commercial buildings, apartments, town walls, etc.), saw itself as practicing "democracy" – government (*kratos*) by the citizens (*demos*) of the towns or cities themselves.

However, the definition of demos or citizen was not as broad as it is today. As already pointed out, the category "citizen" by no means included all inhabitants of the city-states, but only those males of a recognized tribal pedigree ... meaning full members by birth of one or another of the old tribes originally making up the community. Foreigners or *xenoi* living in the cities – which often included a huge number of the industrial or commercial workers (and certainly also the many slaves) – were actually quite numerous in Greek culture. These individuals did not qualify for democratic privileges ... even if they were descendants of several generations of xenoi living and working in these "democratic" city-states.

Athenians and Spartans

Leading the way in this democratic development was the city-state of Athens. But the path by which Athenian democracy would develop was very, very stormy ... just as was the rise to political prominence of Athens itself.

During most of Greece's Archaic Period the Spartans had been considered the dominant political power or *hegemon* in Greece. But during the 500s BC Athens, which was well-positioned at the center of this huge Greek world, and possessing a number of natural advantages (a very strong citadel, a wide fertile region surrounding it, and closeness to the sea), soon rose to its own prominence. Also, having the strongest navy of all the Greek city states (thanks to its political leader Thucydides), Athens was early looked to in order to provide leadership in organizing the city states into a great Greek navy, one designed to keep the Persians away from Greek shores. But the Athenians proved themselves as well on land as foot soldiers.

Thus Greek leadership was divided between – and often competed for – by both Sparta and Athens (Corinth and Thebes were also powerful, though only at a secondary level).

Athens' struggle to secure democracy

But Athens was wracked by internal problems. Athens' rich and powerful aristocracy, long used to dominating Athens' political and economic life from its political council, the Areopagus, found itself increasingly challenged by the Athenian commoners (not really all that common, since they still occupied a much higher status than the more numerous "foreigners" in Athens and the even more numerous slave portion of the Athenian population).

The aristocrats first attempted to control Athens' affairs with a very tough legal code or constitution (in which the penalty for a wide range of offenses was death) laid down by Draco (c. 620 BC) – and thus very "Draconian" – which, though an improvement over the older oral laws and traditions, still did not satisfy the political desires of the commoners. However, his constitution did provide for the creation of a Council of Four Hundred, its members drawn from the commoners by lot.

A generation later, in the early 500s BC, another aristocrat, Solon, serving as *archon* (one of several leaders governing Athens), was commissioned to reform this constitution. He attempted to find a compromise between the contending social classes by ranking the citizens into four classes and giving each of them a certain number of economic and political duties and rights. But soon after his departure from power, class rivalries gradually returned. Peisistratus, a nephew of Solon, seized power on behalf of the poorer citizens, thus becoming tyrant. However, his political base was never secure and he was in power – and exiled – frequently from 546 to 527 BC as political confusion continued to grip Athens.

Eventually a compromise was achieved (509 BC) – in no small part due to the need to secure unity in the face of the political threat posed by both Sparta and Persia. A popular politician named Cleisthenes was elevated to power to reform the constitution. He reorganized the tribal basis of Athenian citizenship from four to ten tribes – membership based no longer on class but on residence in the city. From these tribes were drawn (by lot) members of the all-important legislative and judicial councils. He saw this not so much as "democracy" as *isonomia*: full legal equality of all (male) citizens.

The challenge of the Persian Wars

In the latter part of the 500s BC, just as a number of Greek towns were beginning to grow in power as "city-states," the Persians surprised the world by conquering Mesopotamia, Syria, Egypt, and Greek Ionia. Thus was the mighty Persian Empire born. This was the first time ever that nearly the whole of the Near East had been brought under a single rule.

Some of the Greeks living in Ionia did not particularly take well to this Persian domination (though others did, even serving in the Persian military) and rose up in revolt against Persian rule in the 490s BC. The citizens of Athens were quick to back the Ionian rebels – who, however, were eventually forced back under Persian rule.

This action of Athens and other Greek city-states in supporting the Greek Ionian rebellion drew the wrath of Persia, and led to the intense desire of Persian king Darius to crush any further Athenian or other Greek "meddling" in Persian affairs. In fact, he wanted Athens completely destroyed. Thus the Persian-Greek wars began.

This Persian response to Greek "meddling" in turn forced the two leading Greek city-states, Sparta and Athens, into cooperation (in fact forcing a general Greek unity among all the Greek cities that had previously been lacking).

The Battle of Marathon (490 BC). Quite surprisingly (to the Persians, anyway!), in a number of major encounters, the Greeks succeeded in defeating the Persian armies and navy sent to Greece, thus not only helping to secure Greek freedom, but elevating Greece – and in particular Athens – to a new status politically.

In the first encounter, Athenian hoplites (troops) were able to surround, attack directly, and completely rout the Persian troops that had just arrived by sea at the Greek coast at Marathon (the Spartans were no help in this engagement, claiming to be deeply involved in a religious ceremony at the time). The Persian survivors (they lost over 6,000 troops, in contrast to Athens' loss of 190 troops) retreated to Asia, where they prepared themselves for a second attempt. However, a revolt in Egypt against Persian domination delayed that second attempt.

The Persian king Xerxes, who took over when his father died in 486 BC, was as dedicated to the reduction of Greece, and the total destruction of Athens. After having crushed the Egyptian revolt, and after three-years of military preparation, Xerxes was finally ready to undertake just such a mission. However, Sparta now joined Athens in the effort to fend off the Persians. But most of the other Greek city-states still chose to stay out of the action.

Setbacks at Thermopylae and Artemisium (480 BC). The Persians now approached Greece both by land and by sea, with the first encounter taking place at a narrow pass at Thermopylae, along the eastern coastal road in Thessaly (northern Greece). A small group of Spartan-led troops were able for three days to hold off the invading Persians, before a Greek traitor showed the Persians a path around the pass, and the Greek troops were ultimately surrounded and slaughtered there

At the same time the Athenian-led Greek fleet managed to fight off the Persian fleet at Artemisium, until news of the Greek defeat broke the Greek spirit and the Greek fleet withdrew to Salamis. The Persians then continued their advance through Greece, destroying city-state after city-state as they went, including the city of Athens as well.

The sea battles at Salamis (480 BC) and Plataea (479 BC). But the Persians were blocked at the narrow isthmus that opens the huge Peloponnesian peninsula to the rest of Greece, and thus Xerxes decided that a victory at sea would be required to finish off the Greek resistance. But under the brilliant leadership of the Athenian general Themistocles, the Greek navy was able to gain a very decisive victory at Salamis over the Persian navy.

The next year, Xerxes was ready to try again to conquer Greece, and sent his troops to Greece, where they assembled at Plataea. A battle which then took place there did not go well for the Persians, who lost their commanding general and then found their camp surrounded, and ultimately destroyed by the Greek hoplites. At the same time, another sea battle – at Mycale – did not go well for the Persian fleet, making the Persian defeat even more obvious.

These were horrible setbacks for the Persians, ones they would never recover from – at least in their dealings with the Greeks.

Yet for the Greeks it proved to be a major turning point in the history not only of Greece but even of Western civilization itself. From this point on, Greece, led most importantly by Athens, would leave a deep political, social, intellectual and moral impact on Western civilization ... one that would shape that civilization not only in the many centuries of Greek political and cultural greatness, but even down to today, where that same legacy is built deeply into the ways of the West.

The "Golden Age" of Athens (and Greece)

The Delian League. By the mid-400s BC Athens was the dominant sea power in Greece, Sparta the dominant land power. But the sea was the more important element in Greek life at that time – and thus Athens naturally tended to dominate Greek affairs. In fact, although the Persians had been twice defeated by the Greeks, their shadow continued to loom over Greek thinking – and thus Greek defenses stood always at the ready, headed up primarily by Athens which had organized a number of Greek cities into a defense organization known as the Delian League.

"Periclean Athens." The fact that the Greeks had escaped Persian rule was to become important in the future development of Greece. Spurred on by the continuing threat of Persia, Greece developed its own strength, especially under the leadership (even dominance) of Athens. Athens, after the two grand defeats of the Persians at Salamis and Plataea, soon became the center of a newly rising Greek civilization, with Athens itself reaching the height of its power and glory about 450 BC, roughly the time of the political leader Pericles (490-429 BC).

Pericles was born to a highly-placed noble Athenian family ... and followed in his father's footsteps to command the Athenian military in some of its most important engagements – most notably those conducted during the First Peloponnesian Wars of Athens versus Sparta in the period 460-445 BC. Pericles was also a very close friend of the philosopher Anaxagoras. And Pericles became very active in the world of politics, becoming the primary prosecutor against the politician Cimon, who had succeeded in having the great general Themistocles (a warrior that Pericles greatly admired) expelled or "ostracized" from Athens. Pericles eventually was indeed able to have Cimon himself ostracized.

Pericles was a practitioner of "democratic" politics ... doing what he could to use state resources to support the poor – winning obvious favor from that huge sector of the population. Indeed, he identified himself as a champion of the little people (tyrant). And he also limited voting rights to only those Athenians with both parents being Athenian citizens ... so as to keep the voting privileges enjoyed by even the poorest Athenians from being diluted by the massive entrance of the foreigners or xenoi into the ranks of Athenian citizenship.

This all seemed to support the idea that indeed, Athens was a very grand city ... everyone (at least its citizens) able to afford the pleasures of a highly successful society.

Athens' great cultural achievements. And yes, indeed, the mid-400s marks the grand age of Athens. Athens' democracy and the leadership of the very capable general/statesman Pericles combined to offer Athens' citizens a very rich life. A lavish building program turned the city into an architectural marvel. And the tendency of Greece's finest minds to gravitate to Athens made it "the school of Greece."

THE "GOLDEN AGE" COMES TO AN END

Athenian democracy under challenge

Actually, Athenian democracy was more an attitude than a political institution or policy. The commoners were jealous of their political rights and quick to defend them against any appearance of usurpation from any source. Tragically, this "democratic" attitude was easily molded by the shapers of "popular opinion" – by the political satire of the popular theaters of Athens ... and by the political maneuvering of clever speakers in the Athenian Assembly, in particular by the Sophists and their wealthy disciples – sort of the ancient version of modern day trial lawyers, who specialized in playing on the prejudices and fears of the people in order to whip up this or that popular mood ... which they skillfully directed according to their own personal ambitions.

The Sophists. As the Athenians' public life in the middle and second half of the 400s BC developed in its richness and importance, wealthy families hired tutors for their sons in order to prepare them for leadership roles in the public assemblies. This was where the laws guiding Athens would be shaped. This was where economic, diplomatic and military decisions that were key to the well-being of the community would be made. They wanted their sons to become persuasive in their rhetoric, quick in public debate and noble in their public bearing – so that they would find themselves at the heart of the doings of these public assemblies.

A particular class of wise ones or "Sophists" (Greek *sophia* = "wisdom") gladly offered their teaching services for a fee to these families. They built their learning or wisdom around the need to produce practical results in the form of skilled or adept students. These Sophists were sort of the ancient version of modern-day trial lawyers, who specialized in using very clever and highly persuasive "rational" arguments in order to win their cases. As demagogues, they proved highly skillful in cultivating the prejudices and fears of the people, to whip up this or that popular mood

As for the higher issues of life such as truth, goodness, justice, etc., in general the Sophists tended to be agnostic – that is, they professed to have no knowledge about (or even concern for) such ultimate or transcendent things. Indeed, they functioned as if such things did not really matter in the course of actual existence. Success was measured not in possessing the knowledge of ultimate truth, but in knowing how to use truths (or "truthiness" as it is sometimes termed today) for personal political and economic gain.

Democratic cruelty

Ostracism. At the same time that wealthy Athenian families were very busy in creating something of a newly-rising ruling class of "more enlightened" individuals, at the level of the lower social orders tendencies were also developing that would serve to weaken further the moral foundations of Greek democracy.

One of these tendencies was the long-standing practice of "ostracism" or the exiling of Athenians by their fellow citizens, because for one reason or another they had fallen out of popular favor. At a special general assembly, citizens were invited (usually by these Sophist-trained demagogues) to record the name of a person they might want exiled on a broken piece of pottery and deposit it in urns. These pottery shards or *ostraka* were then tallied by a public official. The person receiving the most votes (although at least a minimum of 6,000 votes) was "ostracized" and thus automatically exiled for ten years.

Themistocles is ostracized. In 472 or 471 BC the Athenian general Themistocles, who had been one of the Athenian commanders at the Battle of Marathon, who then led the Athenians to develop massive sea power and subsequently devised the scheme to trap and destroy the Persian navy at Salamis, and who was the leading political figure over the next ten years, was brought before the ever-suspicious Athenian Assembly – fed by rumors coming from the Spartans of a role in a political conspiracy (entirely false in fact, designed cleverly by the Spartans to destroy their rival Themistocles) – and adjudged by the Athenian commoners to be guilty of the crime of arrogance. He thus was ostracized. He fled to Macedonia – then moved on to Ionia, where the Persian Emperor Artaxerxes offered to bring him into Persian service as a regional governor!

Tragically for Athens itself, it would take some time and distance from this sad episode before the Athenians would recognize the cruelty that they had delivered to the one man who not only had saved Athens from Persian destruction, but had put the Greeks on the path to greatness.

Athenian arrogance / Athenian imperialism

Another (and similar) major problem facing the Athenian democracy would be the arrogant attitude it came to assume with respect to its fellow Greek city states – and the resentment this would breed among these other Greeks. At this point Athens no longer was led by wise men with a deep sense of high-minded virtue, but by cynical, manipulative, self-serving politicians, setting a similar moral tone for the entire Athenian community.

With the passing of time, as the Persian threat seemed to dwindle – but Athenian collection of dues from its allies for "defense" purposes continued nonetheless – resentment by members of the Delian League against Athens grew, especially when it became obvious that this money the other cities were sending to Athens had little to do with Greek defenses and more to do with a lavish Athenian building program going on during Athens' "glory days." Consequently, Athens' Greek allies in the Delian League felt as if they had been seduced into surrendering their independence to a growing Athenian Empire. Certainly also, the money they were sending Athens could have been used to improve their own cities. Anger against Athens began to grow among the other Greek city-states.

Sparta, the major rival to Athenian power, with its well-disciplined land army, was quick to take advantage of this discontent and organized a rebellion against Athens in 431 BC. Also Thebes, seeing the growing mood of Greek rebellion against Athens, decided to make a bid for dominance in Greek affairs.

The Peloponnesian Wars, and the decline of Athens. Thus wars (the "Peloponnesian Wars") broke out in Greece (431-421 BC; 421-404 BC; 395-378 BC), wars that tended to ravage Greece – yet seemed to resolve nothing. The worst of these were the engagements between 431 and 404 BC. Truces would be declared only to have one party or another decide that it was advantageous to break those treaties and start up a new round of wars. Also political leaders played treacherous games of shifting their loyalties according to their personal advantage.

Pericles' efforts to keep Athenian spirits high. For a while the great general and Athenian political leader Pericles was able to keep Athenian spirits high as it struggled with the hostility of the surrounding Greek world. But Athens had taken on a war that would drain it economically and spiritually ... and offer no gain whatsoever in return. Consequently, Athens found itself bleeding to death economically and spiritually.

Decline. Thus things went quickly downhill for Athens. A long-lasting siege of Athens by Sparta created devastating conditions within Athens, taking the lives of many Athenians, including Pericles (429 BC). Athens' new leader Alcibiades (Pericles' nephew) proved to be largely a disaster for Athens, as he led Athens on ruinous expeditions and switched loyalties constantly ... including even siding with Athens' enemies, first Sparta (415-412 BC) and then Persia (412-411 BC) during his cynical political career!

Ruin. The war gradually led not only Athens but also much of the rest of Greece to ruin. Finally, in 405 BC, the Spartans (now allied with the Persians) defeated Athens even at sea – and Athens was forced into a humiliating surrender, forced to tear down her town walls, surrender her fleet and give up all her overseas possessions. Only Sparta's compassion prevented Corinth and Thebes from getting their wish to level all of Athens and also enslave the entire Athenian population.

Socrates is condemned to death. Even more tragically, the West's most famous philosopher, Socrates – who was loudly critical of the amoral antics of the Sophists – would eventually (late 400s BC) become the object of the satire of the playwrights (notably Aristophanes) and the demagoguery of the Assembly speakers. Both groups turned the public against him.

In 399 BC the Assembly voted for Socrates' death ... given somewhat honorably in that he was to inflict this punishment on himself (poison, usually). Actually, they expected Socrates to do what most Athenians did when the Assembly turned against them: flee Athens. This was certainly the counsel of Socrates's devoted disciples. But Socrates reasoned that to flee would be to discredit the very truths and moral principles to which he had dedicated his life in his teachings. Thus he took the poisonous hemlock and died, surrounded by his disciples.

Socrates's death by the decision of Athens' democratic Assembly consequently caused democracy to be intensely distrusted by some (Socrates' famous student Plato, for instance) or at least not highly regarded (Plato's equally famous student Aristotle, for instance).

✳ ✳ ✳

SOCRATES, PLATO, AND ARISTOTLE

Socrates (469-399 BC)

Socrates is known largely through Plato's heroized representation of him. We know that subjects such as social ethics or public morality were of great interest to him – though he was also interested in such subjects as justice, beauty, goodness, and even physics and metaphysics. Above all, he was interested in conveying to his students the understanding of how to live a life of honor and truth ... particularly in service to the larger social order.

He was keenly aware that objective reality and what our minds understand of reality are separated by a great mental divide (the general consensus of Greek philosophy by that time). But to the optimistic Socrates, rational inquiry, meticulously but humbly pursued (his dialectical method), could close this divide. In using rational methods of inquiry, human mind and soul could be brought to discover transcendent (thus absolute) truth and goodness – and personal happiness.

Socrates felt optimistically that knowing the truly good would necessarily direct a person to act in line with this knowledge. Also, the quest for such knowledge was the very heart of life itself – its highest form (almost a divine enterprise).

Unfortunately, the Athenians proved not to be so enlightened by the truth as he had hoped, and ordered him to poison himself ... for "teaching the youth not to reverence the gods" (something actually not the case at all).

Plato (427-347 BC)

His pupil Plato took up Socrates' cause and carried the matter further – much further. Reflecting on life in a way not dissimilar to Pythagoras, Plato felt that though the visible world itself might at times appear chaotic and threatening, behind this visible world was a world of perfection. Our visible world was only a dim reflection of this perfect world. This perfect world on the other hand was composed of perfect formulations: mathematical and geometric – like Pythagoras' world. But to Plato such abstract perfections also included things such as goodness, virtue, beauty.

The realm of the Ideon. These perfections were idealized Forms or Ideas (*Ideon* or *Eidei* – terms he used interchangeably) like geometric forms that describe life *ideally*. But though these Forms existed only as ideas, they were more real than the visible world around us. But how could Plato be so sure that these Forms we had never ever seen were so real?

His thinking went something like this. We know, for instance, that there are no perfect circles to be found anywhere in nature. Some things in nature only *tend* toward a perfect circular form and thus may be called circular. But how is it that we know that they are not perfectly circular? Only because for some strange reason our minds can indeed hold clearly a distinct understanding of a perfect circle – though we have never seen such anywhere in the world around us.

We can thus make such assertions about circularity – not because we have seen perfect circles, but because we certainly hold the idea of a circle clearly in our mind. If we could not conceive of such perfect ideas in our minds, then we would not be able to think clearly or rationally. The fact that we can think about circles, to Plato proved their existence. This existence, of course, was not in the immediate world around us, but in some mysterious realm of higher being or thinking.

Plato was interested in uncovering this perfect world of the Ideon or Forms – in bringing it to light to human understanding. Indeed, this was to Plato (and by many "Platonists" who came after him) a religious enterprise – not just a matter of detached scholarship.

Plato and the realm of politics. With regard to the world of politics, most understandably, after what the Athenian Assembly did to his teacher Socrates, Plato was no lover of democracy. But Plato did believe that there existed part of the realm of the Ideon ... able to guide our shaping of an ideal state. In his *Republic*, Plato described that ideal state as one that was divided by classes or castes into three levels of society: workers, guardians (soldiers) and governors ("philosopher kings").

Tragically, when later in life Plato was called to Syracuse (Greek Sicily) by Dion (a former student of Plato's) to help Dion's young but dissolute nephew Dionysius II become just that "philosopher king" and put such an Ideal State into effect, the whole thing ended up most disastrously. Dionysius's older brother-in-law Dionysius the Elder, who was actually ruling Syracuse at the time, was deeply irritated by Plato's disdain of his attempts at being a popular tyrant ... and had Plato arrested. Plato was spared death only by being sold into slavery ... from which a friend of Plato's went on to purchase his freedom. Oddly enough, when Dionysius the Elder died, Plato was invited back by Dion to Syracuse to try again with the young Dionysius. But Dionysius fought with his uncle Dion, and had him expelled ... but forced Plato to stay on. Plato was finally able to get out of Syracuse. Ultimately the "philosopher king" Dionysius found himself facing a popular uprising ... in which he was ultimately driven from power.

What Plato actually learned from all this very non-Idealist experience in the realm of politics is not known to us today. Nothing in Plato's writings points to any kind of development of his political thinking because of this sad experience.

Aristotle (384-322 BC)

Aristotle went in a direction opposite that of his teacher, Plato. While Plato focused his attention on the mysterious world of the perfect Forms, Aristotle focused his attention on the messier visible world immediately around him. Aristotle was greatly fascinated by this empirical or physical world. He was looking for Plato's Forms actually contained within this visible world.

But Aristotle eventually surmised that these Forms were merely abstractions in our mind which we use to categorize the immense information that comes to us about the surrounding world. These Forms, though useful to human logic, were themselves only mental constructs or *kategoriai* (categories) ... useful to the human mind in developing an organized understanding of how to understand and work with the surrounding world. "Dog," or "barn", or "hot", or the color "red" were just such categories. They had no separate existence like gods or defining spirits (as Plato had asserted).

But Aristotle was deeply interested in exploring this world of categories, trying to discover as many different categories as possible ... in all fields of life, from biology to geology, but also in the realm of logic, ethics, and politics.

As already mentioned, in the field of politics, he was not particularly interested in one or another particular category of social organization, whether a society governed by a single person, or a few, or even the many. What he understood as the "good society" was one which – whatever the specific form – was carefully ordered by a set of very strong moral foundations ... ones that human cleverness would not be able to manipulate – but which would offer clear guidance to that society as it took on life's various challenges.   He made this very clear in his famous publication, *Politics*.

Most interestingly however, when it came to discussion of things beyond this earthly realm – the heavenly realm of the sun, moon and stars – Aristotle evidenced a religious awe. Though the earth might be marked with physical imperfections, these heavenly bodies were the essence of the divine, for they were perfect – perfect in their circular shape and circular movement. Thus for Aristotle the perfect-imperfect dualism in life occurred not between things seen and unseen (as it had for Plato), but between the imperfect things seen on earth and the perfect things seen in the heavens.

Thus even in his religion, Aristotle remained focused on the visible universe around him. "Heaven" was not a place found beyond the visible world ... but instead was located quite visibly in the skies above. Beyond that, Aristotle had no particular opinion about the "heavenly realm" of the gods or whatever.

✻ ✻ ✻

THE ALEXANDRIAN EMPIRE

Philip II of Macedon (r.* 359-336 BC). While the city-states of Classical Greece seemed to be enjoying tremendous prominence (when not fighting each other), a new power was growing to the North of Greece: the semi-Greek kingdom, Macedonia, under its ruler Philip II (382-336 BC). Many of the Greeks, including some influential Athenians, looked to Philip to rescue Greece from its military and political follies.

But others, most notably the Athenian statesman and orator Demosthenes, saw in the ascendancy of Philip the end to Greek political values and liberties. Demosthenes spoke fervently and often (his *Philippics*) about the dangers to Athens posed by Philip. But all to no avail.

Philip was able to throw Macedonian control over the surrounding

---

*"r." means reigned or ruled.

states in northern Greece, securing valuable gold fields in the region, bringing him frequently in conflict with Athens. He spread Macedonian dominance to the south in Thessaly (356-352 BC), turned again to focus on consolidating his power at home in growing Macedonia, then in 349 BC resumed his movement against Athens, Thebes and the other leading city states in southern Greece. Only Sparta, which more or less allied with Philip in this enterprise, was spared the threat of Macedonian domination. Finally in 338, he defeated the armies of both Athens and Thebes at the Battle of Chaeronea, opening for him the opportunity to create the League of Corinth, with himself as its hegemon or leader. By this diplomatic action he finally brought peace to Greece, under Macedonian supervision, of course – despite ongoing political opposition urged by Demosthenes.

Then in 336 BC, he was murdered by one of his bodyguards on the way to the wedding of one of his daughters. At this point the Macedonian challenge seemed to have suddenly disappeared as quickly as it had arisen. Or so many hoped.

Alexander the Great (r. 336-323 BC)

No one was giving much thought to Philip's son, a young man of only 20. But Alexander surprised everyone by quickly revealing himself to be every bit the man (even more so) than his father. Under his father's sponsorship, he had been carefully raised in Greek ways, studied under Aristotle (when not off somewhere fighting battles!) – thus combining personally the scholarly interests of his Athenian teacher with the political talents of his Macedonian father.

Coming to power in 336 BC, he quickly put down challenges to his kingship in Macedonia ... and in Greece. He crushed and destroyed the city-state of Thebes, sending a clear message to Athens to behave (Demosthenes had turned his invective on Alexander since Philip's death). Thus very quickly, Alexander demonstrated to the surrounding Greek, Thracian and Illyrian peoples* that, though young, he was very much made of the same stuff as his father.

He then, in 334 BC, moved to further galvanize his rule by turning the combined Macedonian-Greek state he now ruled toward the idea of ending the Persian threat to Greece forever. He intended to invade Persia – and not just wait as they had in the past for the Persians to take the initiative in their strained relations.

He divided his Macedonian army (leaving some behind to keep his

---

*Illyria is north of Macedonia (roughly equivalent to the 20th century Yugoslavia) and Thrace is to the East of Macedonia (today's Western Greece, southern Bulgaria and Northwestern Turkey).

power secure in Greece) and added a large number of Greek soldiers to his ranks and then crossed into Asia Minor to raise the flag of anti-Persian rebellion by the various subject peoples living there under Persian tutelage.

When he and his army set off toward Asia Minor in 334 BC no one had any idea of how far Alexander's ambitions in Asia were going to take them.

The Battle of the Granicus (334 BC). Persian royal power had been in decline for a while, corruption within the bureaucracy was growing rapidly, and the subject peoples were quite restless. Alexander saw his incredible opportunity as liberator or deliverer of these subject peoples.

To meet this challenge from Alexander, a Persian army was quickly organized by the satraps of Asia Minor ... and proceeded to come out to meet him at the Granicus River. The Persian forces expected to demolish Alexander and his Macedonian-Greek forces in short order.

But instead, Alexander and his army proceeded to crush the Persian forces ... much to the Persian dismay. However, Alexander was wounded in battle ... but continued to fight until the Persians fled before him.

At this point the Persian regional capital at Sardis capitulated to Alexander ... and Alexander moved his troops onwards along the Ionian coast (today's western coast of Turkey), with city after city going over to his side (depriving the Persians of naval bases along the Aegean Sea).

Then Alexander used the next months to consolidate his position as the new master of Asia Minor.

The Battle of Issus (333 BC). He then headed east towards Syria where, in late 333 BC, he met near the town of Issus a huge Persian army ... led by the Persian king Darius himself. But the area of the battlefield was narrow in scope, not allowing Darius to bring the full force of his 400,000-man army against Alexander's mere 40,000 troops. Alexander himself led a cavalry charge straight into the Persian ranks ... startling Darius and causing him to flee ... thus breaking the morale of his Persian army and turning the battle into a slaughter of retreating Persians (and again, also Greek mercenaries serving in the Persian ranks).

Onwards, towards Egypt. This victory then opened up the eastern end of the Mediterranean to Greek expansion. Indeed, Alexander easily entered Syria and Palestine as liberator/conqueror, facing serious resistance only from Tyre and Gaza, both of which he destroyed. Most other cities opened their gates to the conqueror without resistance – and were met with fair treatment.

Then at this point he strangely turned away from chasing the humiliated Persian Emperor ... and headed instead to Egypt. Here too he was received without resistance ... in fact being received even as a liberator rather than as an enemy.

Was Alexander the son of a God? What might seem to be a mere side incident in the story is actually a very major piece in Alexander's life. No doubt out of a desire to get to the bottom of a story (and perhaps in part also out of a desire to impress his troops) that Philip was not his true father – that Alexander was actually descended on his father's side from one of the gods – Alexander journeyed to the Siwa Oasis in the Libyan desert to inquire of the famed priests of Ammon there as to the truth to the story. They confirmed that indeed the story was true. Indeed, Egyptian priests greeted him as a divine instrument of their god Ammon and crowned him Pharaoh.

The establishment of Egypt's greatest city, Alexandria. While in Egypt he planted a Greek colony at the edge of the Nile delta – a fabulous Greek-Egyptian city bearing (as did so many of the towns or cities he founded) his name, Alexandria. It would soon grow to outclass all other cities around the Mediterranean ... and hold that position for centuries. Even with the rise of Rome, Greek Alexandria retained the reputation for being the most sophisticated city in the Western world. It would be the center of fabulous Greek scholarship for at least another thousand years.

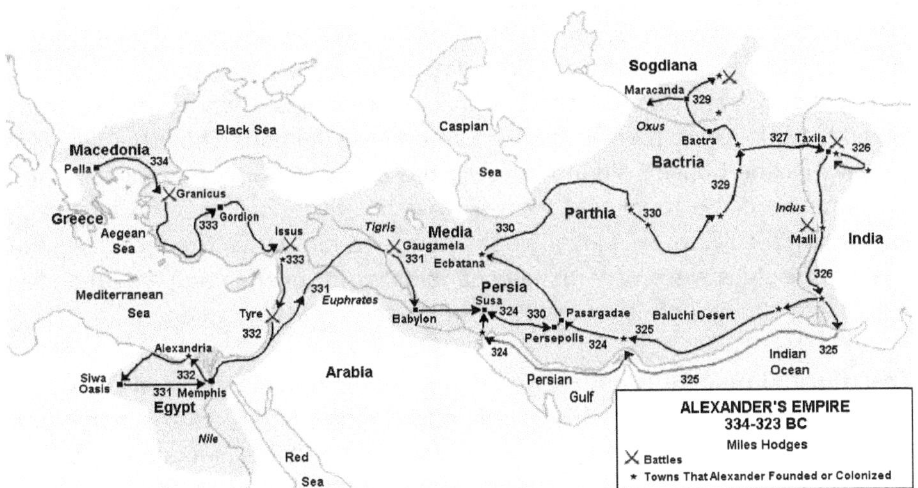

The Battle of Gaugamela (331 BC) and the defeat of Persia. But soon it was time for Alexander to turn his attention back to the Persians. The Persians had been assembling the largest multi-ethnic army ever seen before in western Asia. But Alexander's army was more disciplined, more maneuverable and more personally loyal to its leader than the Persian army. The two prior defeats of the Persians also contributed to the high morale of the Greeks and the nervousness of the Persians. Thus when the two armies met at Gaugamela, the Persians were once again routed, the new Persian king Darius was forced to flee - with Darius soon killed by his own men as Alexander continued to advance against the Persians.

Victorious in battle, Alexander now focused his attention on consolidating his rule over his newly acquired territories. Interesting, and convenient for Alexander, even in the very heart of the Persian empire Alexander was greeted as a liberator/conqueror. Babylon and even Susa, the old Persian capital, greeted him as a liberator, and indeed Alexander did what he could in service as "protector" of these grand cities. He wanted to rule over a land of wealth, not ruin.

The sack of Persepolis. However the new Persian capital of Persepolis proved to be a different matter. The city tried to take a military stand in its own defense – and chose the unwise tactics of parading before Alexander's army 800 badly mutilated Greeks who had been captured earlier, presumably as a ploy to demoralize the Greeks. Instead it merely infuriated them (and Alexander) – and the Greek troops went wild, slaughtering its inhabitants and burning Persepolis to the ground.

Creating an East-West synthesis. Though Alexander's power was clearly based on the support of his very practical-minded Macedonian-Greek army, Alexander soon began to envision himself as a great Oriental god-king sent to rebuild civilization in what he supposed was the entire reach of the world. He planted cities with Greek colonists wherever he went, urged his soldiers to take wives from among the Persians and other Oriental peoples (as he himself did in marrying the Bactrian princess, Roxana), and did what he could to rebuild Western Asian civilization on a mix of Greek and Oriental culture. His loyal troops humored him in his thoughts, though they themselves were very unlikely candidates for ever seeing Alexander as a god – as the Orientals so easily came to see their new ruler.

The final days. Alexander would not let up on his conquering ways, particularly as he began to learn of other lands that lay to the north and east beyond the Persian empire. He pressed on with his Macedonian-Greek army, first into central Asia (328 BC), where he faced bitter conditions and bitter resistance and where there was very little of value (Roxana excepted!) to add to his already vast dominions. He then turned eastward (327 BC), again passing through bitter situations in Afghanistan in an attempt to reach India with its rumored wealth and splendor. Crossing the high Hindu Kush Mountains he descended into the Indus River Valley (326 BC) where at the Jamnia River he defeated King Porus and his Indian army – though turning them into allies after all.

But at this point, he found himself faced with firm resistance from his troops. They would go no further East. In fact, after nine years of conquest, they were ready to return home to Greece and Macedonia. For the first time ever, Alexander and his ambitions faced defeat. Against the resistance of his own troops he could do nothing.

He thus turned South along the Indus River, ran into trouble at Malli, where he led a charge and was nearly killed – but rescued by his own troops – putting him in convalescence for several months, before continuing his journey back towards the West. He divided up his troops, able to send only half of them back to Babylon by ship, the other half having to take the desert route (today's Balochistan) – which through heat and thirst left ten thousand of his soldiers dead along the way and Alexander himself physically and mentally exhausted in his arrival back in Persia.

On arriving at Babylon, he cleaned out much of the corruption that had set in on his administration during his absence. He then returned to the program of integrating his Greek and Persian supporters – including organizing (in 324 BC) a massive marriage ceremony between his Greek soldiers and Persian women, taking two Persian princesses as additional wives of his own (a very non-Greek concept). He then had rebellions to face down, including one among his own Greek troops (also 324 BC). His last enterprise (323 BC) was to have been a massive exploration of the water link between Babylon and Egypt by 1000 ships he had built for the occasion. But his body was spending itself out – not only because of his constant exertions, but because of his deep drinking and carousing that went on for hours. Just prior to his departure on this grand sailing expedition he caught a fever which his tired body could not shake – and as he lay dying ten days later his army passed silently before him to bid their hero farewell. He died the next day, June 13, 323 BC.

Most interestingly, Alexander is remembered greatly not only in the West but also in the East ... where he is known as Iskandar ... and his exploits celebrated there as much as they have come to be celebrated in the West. He was truly an outstanding individual ... empowered by the forces of heaven, which every religion (except secular materialism) knows well as being the ultimate source of all human greatness. Alexander himself knew this to be so in his own case.

✳ ✳ ✳

THE DIVISION OF ALEXANDER'S EMPIRE

With Alexander's sudden death, a crisis arose over the matter of who was to succeed him in overseeing his empire. Alexander's Bactrian wife Roxana was pregnant, and if she were to deliver a son it was assumed that he should rule, under the regency of Antipater of Macedonia. But this set the generals themselves to fighting among themselves for power (the "Wars of the Diadochi").

At first Alexander's cavalry general Perdiccas took control by killing Meleager, the commander of Alexander's foot soldiers – leaving himself in unquestioned command. But when Perdiccas attempted to make his own assignments with regard to the governance of the various regions of the empire, he found himself strongly resisted by Ptolemy of Egypt and Antipater of Macedonia - individuals previously assigned their regional commands by Alexander.

When Perdiccas was then assassinated by his own officers (321 or 320 BC), the foundations of the Alexandrian Empire began to break up. And then when in 310 BC Cassander – once an early friend of Alexander and fellow student of Aristotle - had Alexander's wife Roxana and their 13-year old son Alexander poisoned, any likelihood of a continuing single Alexandrian domain ended. What at that point was taking place was the rise of a number of independent kingdoms, usually founded by one or another of Alexander's generals.

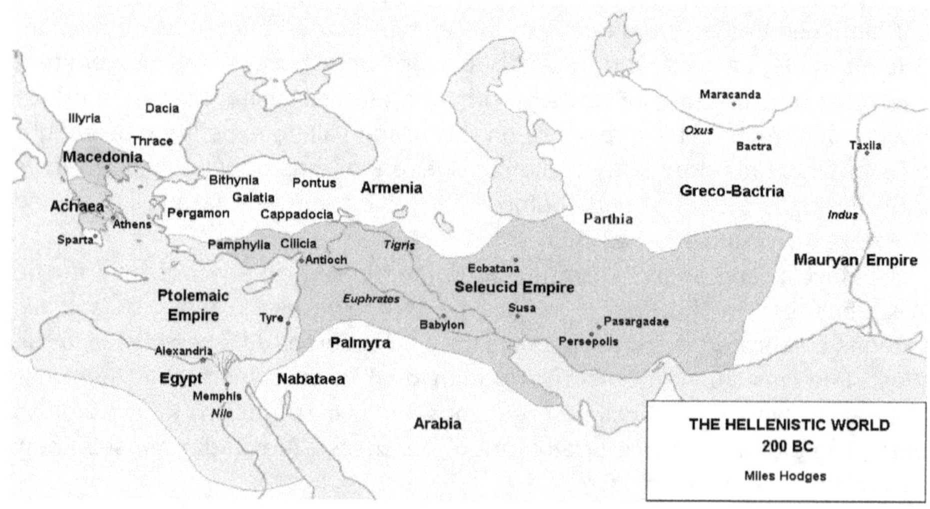

Antigonid Macedonia

Antigonus, governing the region of Syria and Asia Minor (today's central Turkey), first stayed out of the in-fighting among the Alexandrian generals. However, the migrating Celtic-speaking Gauls began to invade a weakened

Macedonia and Asia Minor at this point. This is what brought Antigonus II to action, and in defeating the Gauls in 277 BC, brought him to kingship in Macedonia, and then in Greece itself. But then he had to face another challenge, from the Greek general Pyrrhus, who had been off fighting and defeating the Romans in Italy, but at a great cost to himself financially and in the loss of many of his troops (thus the term "Pyrrhic" victory). At first Antigonus was brought to defeat by Pyrrhus. But then Pyrrhus was killed in another battle deeper into Greece, effectively returning Antigonus to power in Macedonia and Greece.

But the Greeks themselves were attempting to regain their independence from Macedonian rule ... resulting in a string of Greek rebellions – even on into the reign of the next Antigonid, Demetrious, and after him, Antigonus III. But the latter was able not only to hold off a new group of invaders from the north, the Dardanians, but also put down a Spartan rebellion – largely by working diplomatically with the Achaean League (cities of the Peloponnese Peninsula – excepting the hostile Sparta).

In 221 BC, the 17-year-old Philip (221-179 BC) was finally able to take the Antigonid throne ... and soon proved his worth in forming a new Hellenic League, which brought to an end the "Social War" (220-217 BC) between the Achaean League and the Aetolian League (Corinth and cities on the northern mainland), giving Philip full respect in both Macedonia and Greece.

Rome now enters the picture. But mounting problems with Rome would occupy Philip greatly. At one point he entered into a treaty with Carthaginian General Hannibal (then ransacking the Italian countryside) ... only to have the Romans enter into an alliance with the Aetolian League – which tended to remain hostile to Macedonian rule. But with the Romans deeply occupied with their 2nd Punic War with Carthage, Philip was able to finally crush the Aetolian League in 205 BC. But in 200 BC, the Romans took up the cause of some of the still-rebellious Greek cities and attacked Philip's Macedon, bringing Philip and his army to defeat.[*]

The Romans allowed Philip to keep his throne, but put him under Roman dependency ... and forced him to pay an indemnity of a thousand talents annually. But Philip proved to be cooperative with the Romans in their war with the Seleucid King Antiochus III and eventually the indemnity was lifted and Philip was allowed to rebuild his weakened rule.

Perseus (179-166 BC), who followed upon the death of his father Philip, would be the last Antigonid king. At first Perseus conducted fairly friendly relations with the domineering Romans. But the Romans finally decided that he was a bit too independent and went to war with him (Third Macedonian

---

*The Roman legion proved itself to be a military formation superior to the traditional Greek phalanx (even more easily maneuvered in battle).

War, 171-168 BC) ... in which Perseus was defeated and captured at the Battle of Pydna, was paraded in Rome in chains and was imprisoned by the Romans. Additionally, some 300,000 Greeks were deported and enslaved by the Romans ... and their land given to Roman settlers. This would finally bring an end to the rule of the Antigonid dynasty in Macedonia-Greece.

Finally in 146 BC, Rome simply declared Macedonia to be a Roman province. This then prompted the Greeks – spurred on by foolish demagogues of the Greek cities of the Achaean League – to rise up in revolt ... which turned out to be suicidal for the Greeks. As a result, the city of Corinth was laid waste (similar to what happened to Carthage that same year).

Following this, there were no further thoughts among the Macedonians or Greeks about the possibilities of independence from Rome. They were now permanently part of the Roman Empire.

The Seleucid Empire in the East

In the division of Alexander's Empire, infantry General Seleucus Nicator would receive the largest section of the empire, approximately the equivalent of the former Persian Empire, and all the problems that went with it. Locating his own capital at Babylon in 305 BC, Seleucus ruled Anatolia, Syria and Palestine, Mesopotamia, Persia, Kuwait, Bactria (Afghanistan and Turkmenistan), and parts of what is today Pakistan. However when Seleucus ran into serious opposition in the eastern reaches of his empire from the Indian general Chandragupta Maurya,* he entered into an alliance with Chandragupta, handing over to him not only much of the far eastern portions of the Empire (Afghanistan and Pakistan) but also his daughter in marriage, receiving 500 elephants in return – which Seleucus subsequently used to great advantage in his battles elsewhere.

But much territory still remained to the new Seleucid dynasty that he established. And into this land the Greeks migrated in large numbers, bringing their language and culture ... leaving a permanent mark on Central and West Asia that would only be replaced very slowly by a return of the pre-Greek cultures (but much changed through Greek influence).

Seleucus' son and grandson, Antiochus I and Antiochus II, faced constant challenges in the West as well, from the Egyptian Ptolemies and the Celts (Gauls or Galatians) who were migrating into Asia Minor. This ended up distracting Antiochus II so much that he lost control of the satrapies of Bactria and Sogdiana (Afghanistan and Turkmenistan) which moved to independence as Greek Bactrian States (c. 250 BC), Greek power centers by their own rights (Greek Bactrian King Demetrius would invade India in

---

*It is said that in a battle in 305 BC between the Greek and the Indian generals, Chandragupta was able to field 600,000 troops and 9,000 elephants.

180 BC to set up a Greek Indian kingdom that lasted over a century and a half).

Parthian independence (247 BC). And Parthia (northeastern Iran) also moved to independence under the Greek satrap Andragoras (also around 250 BC), but was not able to maintain its independence. An Asian (of Scythian origin?) named Arsaces soon overthrew him and laid the foundations in Parthia for the Arsacid Dynasty, which would eventually come to dominate all of Persia for five centuries (and offer constant problems for the West) as the powerful "Parthian Empire" (247 BC – AD 224).

Antiochus III and the Romans. Antiochus (r. 223-187 BC) then made the fateful political decision to cooperate with the Carthaginian General Hannibal – whose army at the time was thrashing the Romans in their own homeland – in Antiochus's effort to liberate mainland Greece from Roman influence. That was a huge mistake. The Romans slowly ground down his troops, requiring him in 188 BC to accept humiliating terms for peace (enormous loss of territory and huge indemnity in gold required to be paid). The next year Antiochus was killed while raiding Persia in an attempt to gain the gold the Romans required of him … in the process merely helping the Arsacid dynasty plant even deeper roots in the Persian world.

Rome now pretty much dictated matters … at least within the Western reaches of the Seleucid Empire (while the Eastern portions became increasingly rebellious and independent). Seleucid kings came and went in rapid succession … and containing (or causing) civil strife occupied most of their time in power.

By the beginning of the 1st century BC, little more than Damascus and the area of Syria immediately around it was all that the Seleucids truly governed. Far greater in power and importance by that time was the Greco-Persian (semi-Seleucid) kingdom of Pontus, to the north of Seleucid Syria, and encompassing all of Asia Minor and Anatolia (modern Turkey). For a while Pontus's leader Mithridates VI was able to hold off Roman power, defeating a Roman army in 89 BC. But Rome was not going to let matters stand at that, and in 66 BC Roman General Pompey took on Mithridates and set him and his army in flight. Three years later. With Pompey closing in on him … and not wanting him and his family to be subjected to a triumphal parade in Rome – Mithridates chose suicide. At this point Seleucid Syria was simply converted into a Roman province under the rule of a Roman governor.

Ptolemaic Egypt

With Perdiccas's death, wide support existed for Ptolemy (r. 323-283 BC) to head up the Alexandrian Empire. Ptolemy wisely refused the honor, understanding the many problems such an position would create for him. Instead, he further consolidated his well-established position in Egypt ... as well as outlying areas along and across the Mediterranean Sea.

Then in 305 BC, he took the title of Pharaoh, helping to legitimize his position among the Egyptians themselves. He hereby established the beginning of a dynasty that would rule Egypt for the next three centuries.

He also began the process of turning the Ptolemaic capital city Alexandria into not only an economic and political power center ... but also the most noble of all Hellenistic cities in terms of its intellectual achievement (founding the great Royal Library of Alexandria) ... one that even the eventual conquest of Egypt by the Romans would not diminish.

His son and successor, Ptolemy II Philadelphia (283-246 BC) proved to be an equally capable ruler, his navy succeeding in fending off a Seleucid attempt to grab southern Syria (Palestine/Judah). And he also held off an attempt by invading Celts or Gauls to try to establish themselves in Egypt (they did take control of part of Asia Minor ... known subsequently as Galatia

He also continued the policy of his father to support the intellectual development of the capital Alexandria ... expanding the Library and supporting scientific research. It was during his rule that Greek culture would establish itself as the dominant culture of Egypt.

The Septuagint Bible. And most importantly for Western Civilization, he was instrumental in having the Hebrew Bible translated into Greek as the *Septuagint Bible.** This brought this key piece of Jewish law and literature out of its narrower Hebrew cultural world into the much broader Hellenistic world, offering that almost "universal" Greek speaking world of the day easy access to what would eventually become the start-up section of Western civilization's most foundational writing.

More Ptolemies, and Cleopatras! Following Ptolemy II's death, there were a succession of Ptolemies (for a total of thirteen!). They increasingly took on Egyptian ways ... especially in marrying their sisters (frequently of the name Cleopatra) such as the ancient Egyptian pharaohs had done. Indeed, one of these Cleopatras (II) would rule from c. 175 BC to her death in 116 BC ... through a series of husband-brothers (Ptolemy VI: 180-145 BC; Ptolemy VIII: 144-132 BC) and then by herself (132-127 BC) and again

---

*"Septuagint" from the idea of "Seventy" ... the number of Jewish scholars commissioned by Ptolemy II to come up with a Greek translation of the Hebrew Scripture or Bible. These 70 scholars worked independently of each other. In the 70-day period in which they did their work, they presumably came up with exactly the same Greek translation – word for word – something considered miraculous then ... and today!

with Ptolemy VIII and her daughter Cleopatra III (131-127 BC). It was all very incestuous ... and all very Egyptian.

And as a general rule among the Alexandrians, these Ptolemies found themselves usually at war with the Seleucids of Syria as well as the Macedonians of old Greece. And of course these dynastic quarrels and the political confusion they generated began to weaken seriously the Ptolemaic dynasty ... so much so that the Romans simply moved themselves gradually into the position of protectors of Ptolemaic Egypt (just as they had done initially with Macedonia), after 80 BC when an Alexandrian mob lynched Ptolemy XI (who ruled only a few weeks) after he murdered his stepmother – who was also his cousin and probably half-sister.

The next Ptolemy (Ptolemy XII, popularly known as "Auletes" or "Flute player"), was actually more of a Roman client than a true Egyptian ruler. At one point he was driven from power (58 BC) and exiled to Rome by his daughter Bernice IV ... but restored to his throne in 55 BC by the Romans (after Ptolemy made a payment of 10,000 talents to one of Roman Consul Pompey's Generals). But at this point Auletes enjoyed his power only through the support of Rome.

Cleopatra VII and Mark Anthony. When he died of illness in 51 BC, he was followed on the throne by another daughter, the 18-year-old Cleopatra VII – who had served with him as co-regent during the last year of his life – as well as her brother and husband Ptolemy XIII ... but the latter only briefly. After a failed attempt to win Julius Caesar's support by murdering Pompey, who had fled to Egypt to escape Caesar, Ptolemy XIII was defeated (with the help of Caesar, who was her lover!) and died in 47 BC in a civil war he waged against her. Cleopatra then chose another younger brother (and husband) Ptolemy XIV to rule with her.

When Caesar was assassinated in 44 BC, she attempted to have her son, Caesarion (born from the affair with Caesar) to take his place in Rome. But Caesar's grandnephew Octavian took that position instead. Nonetheless, she had her brother Ptolemy XIV murdered (also 44 BC) and then elevated her son Caesarion to co-rulership with her in Egypt.

Following the assassination of Caesar, Rome itself fell into a series of civil wars among a number of Roman contenders for power. During this period the Eastern half of the Roman Empire (including Egypt) came under the command of the Roman politician and general Mark Antony (c. 42 BC) ... with the Western half under his ally Octavian Caesar.

This eventually brought Mark Antony into a relationship where he and Cleopatra openly became lovers (including the birthing of three children) ... despite the fact that Mark Antony was married to Octavian's sister, Octavia. This would become part of the reason for a growing split between the former allies Octavian and Mark Antony. By 33 BC the two Roman leaders were in full conflict with each other and in 31 BC, in a major battle at Actium, Octavian's forces decisively defeated the forces of Mark Antony and Cleopatra.

Both Mark Antony and Cleopatra presumably chose suicide rather than face the humiliation at the hands of Octavian. Cleopatra's 17-year-old son Caesarion was executed soon after. The Ptolemaic line of pharaohs had come to end. Egypt was now formally a Roman province under the rule of a Roman governor (30 BC).

✳ ✳ ✳

THE ALEXANDRIAN OR "HELLENISTIC" CULTURAL LEGACY

The dominating role of the Greek language. With Alexander's success, the civilized "Western" world was united by a new sense of Greek cultural hegemony. Although local peoples might cling to their more ancient tribal or regional ways, the Greek language and culture quickly established themselves throughout the whole of the Eastern Mediterranean (and the hinterland) as the medium of literature, philosophy and science.

Thus Alexander did more than any actual Greek in establishing the Greek language as the dominant international tongue used by scholars, scientists, tradesmen, governing officials, not only in Alexander's day but for centuries to come. Even when Rome expanded its military power into the Eastern Mediterranean it did not supplant Greek with its own Latin. Indeed, the Roman government itself took up the use of Greek in administering its Eastern holdings.

The original works of Christian Scripture were not in Hebrew (which anyway had passed out of daily use in Jesus's times) or even Aramaic (a local Semitic language used in Syria/Palestine) ... but in Greek, considered the only language adequate to cross the lines separating the various cultural groups making up the Middle East. Even Paul's letter to Rome was written in Greek, not Latin. Eventually a translation had to be made from the Greek into Latin (the Latin "Vulgate" translated by the monk Jerome in the late 300s, long after Christianity had been formally accepted as the official religion of the Roman Empire) – which the Western Church then went on to adopt as its official translation of the original Greek.

A shift to a new sense of order in life. But this great Greek achievement came at a time of continuing confusion among the Greeks as to what the ideals of life ought to be. Certainly Alexander's imperial political legacy made trivial any residual Greek affections for the city-state – though certainly such sentiments were slow to die. The domain of politics now rested in the hands of lofty rulers – ones who even took on the Eastern affectation of being "gods." The noble Greek citizen directing the course of his cherished city was now an anomaly, even a dangerous one at that.

But even beyond these changes in political style and vision lay other major changes in Greek life. Just as politics seemed to slip out of the hands of the Greek commoner and move to the loftier realm of royal, almost god-like authority, so even the sense of the source of life seemed to move away in the same direction. Life now seemed shaped by forces that greatly transcended direct human management. To achieve any sort of sense of connectedness with such transcendent sources, a person now had to look well beyond the realm of the surrounding physical or material reality – to the mystical realm of the Divine. True, the Greeks held on to their gods, personal protectors whom they hoped would protect them and intercede on their behalf with the higher forces of the universe. But ultimately, they knew that it was from these higher forces that all things in the end drew their power, their direction, their life.

Such a realm was not necessarily hostile. It was not necessarily chaotic. Indeed, a new Order seemed to be the rule of the day. But it was distant, beyond the easy understanding of the common man, mysterious in its nature and action. To reach such a realm required enormous amounts of concentration of human thought and understanding. Perhaps only those who had the luxury of free time could ever achieve such a connection, such a relationship with the ultimate.

Thus in general, common folk turned increasingly to the mystery cults and religions brought forward out of older times ... such as the Eleusinian Mysteries involving the secret cults of Demeter and Persephone – cults that reached all the way back to the Mycenaean age. They also looked to religions brought in from outside the Hellenistic world ... such as Mithraism, a part of the Persian or Iranian Zoroastrian tradition.

But while this tended to satisfy the general population, it seemed to have less impact on the more educated of Hellenistic society ... who attempted to keep alive the rich Hellenic philosophical tradition of intellectual inquiry into the kosmos and its ways.

However, Hellenistic philosophy began to take on a more complex character. It could no longer be found just in simple dialogues between a teacher and a citizen-student as in Socrates' days. It now required profound devotion to study, a deep focusing of oneself on the task, meditation, prayer even, to reach the goal of understanding. Philosophy was now itself a mystical, spiritual enterprise – engaged in by specialists.

A big part of that mysticism came from the deep reverence for the starry heavens, which Greek philosophers (such as Aristotle) had been certain presided over life on earth. Thus ongoing "scientific" study of the heavens was supposed to bring new insights into related events on earth … even the power to predict the course of future events, both social and personal. Thus there was a huge development of astrology.

However, this derived not only from the research that the Greeks had undertaken in their study of the heavens, but also from the quite sophisticated astrological mysteries brought in from the East – thanks to Alexander's conquest and subsequent uniting of the Asian East with the Greek West.

In short, the mysticism of the East inserted itself deeply into the pragmatism of the West, producing an amalgam, Greek in language but Asian in spirit … which we call "Hellenism."

Cynicism and Skepticism

Cynicism and Skepticism involve two different degrees of questioning life's underlying or fundamental order … the two philosophies being in ancient Greek times almost the reversal of what they have come to represent today. Today, skepticism implies that someone is holding some doubts about how things seem to appear to be. To the skeptic, they may not be what they seem to be. Cynicism today means having no doubts at all about such matters … for to the cynic, nothing is ever to be trusted! To the ancient Greek, these ideas were quite the opposite of what we hold them to be today.

Cynicism actually started even before the Alexandrian era … most notably under the Greek philosopher Diogenes of Synope (c. 412-323 BC). Diogenes, a contemporary of Plato and Aristotle, simply chose to escape the world of wealth and power and try to live the simplest life possible, such as does an animal. To Diogenes, the life of a dog (Greek: *kuon* or *kyon*, from which the word "cynic" is derived) has greater integrity than the life of the wealth-and-power-grasping human. But like his contemporaries, Plato and Aristotle, Diogenes still believed that it was possible, by deciding to go down the right road in life, to come to excellence as a person. In short, he was not at all cynical about human possibilities … though skeptical at times! He truly believed that there was hope that humankind could pull out of the mess he was observing around him in his pre-Alexandrian Greece.

But in the post-Alexandrian world, that optimism seemed to fade away. Pyrrho of Elis (c. 360-270 BC) took on something similar to a Buddhist or Hindu attitude in concluding "skeptically" that true knowledge, true goodness, true anything, was humanly unattainable. He felt that life would be simpler and happier if people simply gave up trying to find perfection … and accepted the fact that life has its times of grand disappointment as well as moments of glory – and that there is little that we can do to determine those results. Also to Pyrrho, simply following tradition – rather than trying to come up with new, more progressive ideas intellectually – worked better for everyone in the long run.

But exactly what those more useful traditions actually happened to be Pyrrho never clarified ... leaving the matter for the individual to decide. Ultimately, there was nothing to keep a skeptic from disavowing all intellectual standards and simply following a life of wantonness.

Epicureanism

Epicurus (342-270 BC) was not actually the "eat, drink, and be merry" individual that we associate with being an "Epicurean" today. He did however certainly support the idea of the pursuit of pleasure. But to him, such pleasure was found in a life free of pains and hurts, because a person has chosen to live a life of virtue. But what that life of virtue actually consisted of Epicurus was not of Socrates's variety ... that is, of finding the higher realm of truth and goodness and then staying focused on living according to those standards. Rather, to Epicurus, the definition of the virtuous life that brings real pleasure was a rather subjective one ... not really anchored on standards lying above an individual's own preferences on the matter. In short, because to Epicurus pleasure was purely subjective, a person was easily led to the understanding that whatever a person craves is the ultimate good for that person.

Epicurus also believed that we were wasting our time speculating on the nature of some kind of higher realm, especially one that perhaps follows death, that we would do well simply to explore the material-mechanical world around us ... and make the most of that practical or physical world.

Stoicism

Stoicism actually had its origins in Cynicism ... although Zeno of Citium (336-264 BC) took the matter well beyond a simple retreat from the material world in to a life of simplicity. Zeno, who came to Athens to teach his ideas to students gathered under him at the Stoa (Porch) located in the Athenian marketplace (thus "Stoicism"!) believed that there was great purpose in bringing to anyone's life the practice of deep contemplation about the mysteries of the world ... bringing human life under such mystical discipline in order to truly free up that life.

Following something of a Socratic or Platonic tradition, Zeno was confident that there existed some kind of Divine Reason (the Logos), an ultimate reality beyond mere physical appearances. Thus he taught that the human mind could – and most certainly should – attach itself to this Logos in pure devotion.

He also taught (in strong distinction to Epicurus) that we should bring our personal cravings under the mastery of a mind-over-matter life. In the face of life's many difficulties, this was particularly important ... that is, important to stay focused on the Logos – and not the worries or hurts of the moment. This "quietism" ultimately became the hallmark of the Stoic.

Most interestingly – perhaps because it offered such hope to a world that seemed to find little logic in the way political and social affairs seem to be moving at the time – Stoicism soon became a widespread philosophy across the Greek world. It would even make its way into the Roman realm.

The development of the physical sciences

But at the same time, the larger Alexandrian world seemed to offer a new sense of order ... or at least point to the possibility of one being achieved – in the same way that Alexander had so quickly achieved so much.

Thus Aristarchus of Samos (c. 310-230 BC) came to have a very lofty view of the universe, even as a young man publishing a work (lost to us today) declaring that the sun was 19 times the size and distance of the moon (actually the figure is about 400 times the size and distance) – something that seemed to defy the common sense of his times that the sun and moon differed only in the intensity of their light, not their size and distance. He even stated that the sun was much larger than the earth ... and therefore it was most likely that the smaller earth circled the larger sun (the heliocentric theory), rather than the reverse (the geocentric theory) – as it was viewed at the time.   Of course all of this was ridiculed in Aristarchus's day ... though defended and promoted (a century later) by Seleucus. But sadly, it ultimately got dropped in Western thinking for the longest time.

Then there was Eratosthenes (c. 276-192 BC), the head librarian at the huge museum and library of Alexandria Egypt, who conducted an unheard-of experiment in calculating the curvature of the earth by measure the length of shadows at the exact same moment in two different locations in Egypt ... and came up with a figure that gave the earth the estimate of being (by today's measurements) 24,660 miles in circumference ... only 200 miles less than the actual measure! He also made the bold claim that a person could theoretically sail around the world and arrive back at the same staring point, provided that he never changed course along the way. And additionally, he cataloged nearly 700 stars ... as well as a system of calculating prime numbers.

Tragically these amazing discoveries did not fit well with the preconceptions of the times ... and were dismissed by other intellectuals.

For instance, Hipparchus (fl.* 145-130 BC) argued strongly against Aristarchus'sheliocentric theory ... pointing out that there were serious problems mathematically with the theory. Of course, neither he nor Aristarchus had taken into account the gravitational effect of the sun's surrounding planets or the elliptical way that things seemed to move in the heavens. That would come only many, many centuries later. Thus it was that he would help the mathematician Ptolemy (fl. early 100s AD) use very complicated mathematical formula to put the earth back at the center of things ... the geocentric theory that would last all the way to the time of the West's Renaissance in the 1500s (Copernicus) and the early 1600s (Brahe, Galileo, and Kepler).

   Mathematics was another field of great accomplishment, Euclid (fl. c. 300 BC) putting together in his *Elements*, a clear and precise explanation of the laws of geometry ... used all the way down to modern times as the model for that mathematical field. And there was Archimedes of Samos (c. 310-230 BC) who in his *Sand Reckoner* (212 BC) not only laid out the major laws of engineering and physics ... but was able to put those to use in helping his native city of Syracuse defend itself using his clever inventions against besieging Romans (although tragically the Romans won anyway). Interestingly also, he came very close to inventing the calculus, something not finally attained until 1,900 years later (Newton and Leibniz).

____

*"fl" – "flourished" ... as an approximate dating.

SUMMING THINGS UP

Materialists	**Mystics**

Homer - mid 700s BC?
There is some great force (Fate) more
powerful than the Olympian gods.

Hesiod - 700 BC
There is an underlying Order to life both in
the Olympain heights and here on earth.

Thales - Miletus (Ionia) - early 500s BC
All matter in the universe comes from
a single substance: water (not the gods)
and acts in a purely natural or mechanical way.

Anaximander - Miletus (Ionia) - early 500s BC
Life comes from some invisible, formless substance.
The matter we see around us is a corruption of this
substance — forming separate substances which strive
to return to harmony with/in this primal substance.
This striving has evolved all things over time into
their present forms (humans most recently).

Anaximenes - Miletus (Ionia) - mid 500s BC
Life comes from air (pneuma) in varying
thicknesses.

Pythagoras - from Ionia to S. Italy - late 500s BC
Visible life is an imperfect reflection of some higher
divine Order — perfectly mathematical in character.
This Order or *Logos* can be apprehended by the
human mind through disciplined reflection or study.

Heraclitus - Ephesus (Ionia) - 500 BC
Fire is the primal substance of life — though it (as with all life)
is not a thing, but rather a process in which all separate things
are striving to return to a oneness, a unity with the great *Logos*.

Parmenides - Elea (S. Italy) - early 400s BC
Visible life is an imperfect reflection of some higher
divine Order: the *Logos*.
All things strive for a return to oneness with the *Logos*.
"Time" is a meaningless concept; all that truly exists
is the present.

Empedocles - Sicily - mid 400s BC
There are four substances that make up
all matter: earth, air, fire, and water.

But all substances strive for unity with
the *Logos*.

Anaxagoras - Ionia to Athens - mid 400s BC
The eternal *Nous* created all things from
an undifferentiated mass of tiny elements
- by spinning things out into groups of like
elements - till they took form as "things.
The sun is a red-hot stone (as are the distant stars).
The moon merely reflects the sun's light.
Things operate rather mechanically ("naturally"
or scientifically).

But the eternal *Nous* is what activates all
life.

Materialists

Protagoras (Sophist) - Athens - mid 400s BC

Truth is a concept relative to the needs of society.
Knowledge is valued as a path to social success.

Democritus - Thrace
late 400s to early 300s BC

All that truly exists is mere matter composed of
the union of atomic particles in various forms.
Even man himself, including his mind, comes
from such material substance.
The is no God or ultimately heavenly goal behind
life; death is simply the breakdown of matter.
The life forms we see about us are simply the
result of a long period of biological evolution.

Aristotle - Athens - mid to late 300s BC

The only reality the human mind can comprehend
practically is the flawed but visible life on earth.
Plato's *Ideon* are merely mental *Categories* our
minds devise in order to understand reality.
The human mind can bring reality to a scientific
understanding by categorizing and analyzing
our world in accordance with strict rules of
logic.
While life on earth is broken and imperfect, life in
the heavens (sun, moon, stars) is perfect and
complete.

Mystics

Socrates - Athens - late 400s BC

In our broken world, the noble mind seeks
oneness with the great, divinely transcending
(or Absolute) concepts of Ideas (*Ideon*) of
Truth, Justice, Beauty, etc. through the
straightforward process of logical study.

Plato - Athens - 400 to mid 300s BC

Visible life is an imperfect reflection of some
higher Order composed of various Forms or
Ideas (*Ideon*).
The Order of Forms or Ideas can be apprehended
by the human mind through disciplined study.
The quest for such intellectual union with the
realm of Forms or Ideas is truly the most noble
of all human enterprises.

Diogenes (Cynic) - Athens - early to late 300s BC

The Athenian quest for material wealth and
power has corrupted life in Athens.
Life lived simply in nature (such as a dog's
life) is more noble.

Crates of Thebes (Cynic) - Athens - late 300s BC

Crates gave away a fortune and dedicated
himself to teaching others how to live happily
with a simpler life.

Philosophers of The Alexandrian or Hellentist Era that followed (after 330 BC)

Pyrrho of Elis (Skeptic) - Athens
late 300s to early 200s BC

The quest for Absolute Truth is a fruitless,
frustrating act which should be avoided.
We should discipline ourselves to live simply
in accordance with useful social traditions.

Zeno of Citium (Stoic) - Athens
late 300s to mid 200s BC

Through simple, unadorned living, and the
stilling of the cravings of the human body,
the mind can focus itself on achieving
oneness with the *Logos*

Epicurus - Athens - late 300s to early 200s BC

The virtuous life is focused on the pursuit
of pleasure and the avoidance of pain by
living simply in accordance with basic
human desires

CHAPTER TWO

ANCIENT ROME

* * *

AN OVERVIEW OF EARLY ROMAN SOCIETY AND CULTURE

The Romans, coming along behind the Greeks (after defeating the Greeks militarily in 146 BC and turning Greece into a Roman province), put into effect a wonderfully ordered material civilization. This civilization indeed gave witness to the power of human reason or human engineering to work with the natural world in producing a place that people often thought was perfection itself. Roman civilization bore out the hope of the Greeks – by giving the West a practical example of the orderly life.

The Romans were not intellectual innovators – as the Greeks were with their powerful philosophies.   Rather, the Romans were powerful administrators – such as the Greeks themselves were never able to be. The Romans, with their sense of legal or administrative order, put the Greek ideas to work in life. Probably had not the Romans done so, the Greek contribution might itself have been put aside with its own growing cynicism and skepticism. Thus the Romans contributed immensely to (materialistic) Western civilization by demonstrating clearly that orderly cooperation with nature could produce amazing results.

The ongoing influence of Hellenistic thought

Yet even under the practical-minded Romans, Western philosophy continued to develop. But Roman philosophy tended to follow the lines laid down by Hellenistic Greece in the two previous centuries. Indeed, as once Eastern thought captured its Greek conquerors centuries before, now Greek thought began to capture its Roman conquerors. Thus did Greek Platonism and Stoicism continue to draw Western philosophy forward, though now under Roman patronage. Indeed, despite Roman political ascendancy, the Greek-speaking eastern provinces of the Roman Empire continued by their own right to be vibrant and at times even dominant cultural-intellectual centers within the Roman Imperium.

Actually, once the Romans conquered the Greeks and turned Greece into a Roman province, actually things Greek rapidly became the standard for "higher" or "more civilized" ways of thinking and behaving just in general.* A Roman's ability to read, write and speak Greek fluently was considered a necessary sign of higher social standing. Thus schooling for Roman youth included lessons in Greek at a very early age – and almost always instruction in Greek by Greek professors at the higher levels of Roman education.

Thus it was that Roman art, literature, drama, philosophy, and even religion were strongly shaped by Greek tastes and interpretations. There were unique Roman contributions to each of these intellectual forms of course. But at the foundations, the Greek character of Roman culture was unmistakable. Indeed, despite Roman political ascendancy, the Greek-speaking eastern provinces of the Roman Empire continued by their own right to be vibrant and at times even dominant cultural-intellectual centers within the Roman Imperium.

The Roman concept of the "legal order"

Where things Roman differed from things Greek was mostly in the area of politics and social organization. The Greeks (in particular the all-dominant Athenians) seemed to see politics more in terms of the general will of society – wherever that might take things, greatly directed of course by clever manipulators of public opinion, such as the Sophist-trained orators who specialized in the art of "demagoguery" or manipulation of the public will. The Romans thought of politics more in terms of what the legal order permitted or required of those who would practice politics. In this area the Romans strangely enough proved to be more abstract than their Greek counterparts.

The Romans were greatly enamored with the idea of "order" in almost everything they designed or developed. The Romans had a very well organized law code which allowed them to rise above the tribal mentality (all members of society related by blood and members of a single genealogical line) and instead create a monumental society built on a mutual respect for a politically neutral Code of Law ... one that made all who came under its authority coequal partners in the Roman social experiment. Thus Roman Law, though abstract in its design, was highly effective in bringing a wide variety of peoples into a vibrant state of political unity.

In Roman eyes the Law – not the public will – dictated what was

---

*This however was also due in part to the earlier Etruscan influence, for the Etruscans themselves had modeled much of their cultural ways after the Greeks.

supposed to be done ... and how it was to be done. Thus lawyers rather than orators tended to dominate the Roman political scene – at least during the Republican era. And thus also it was the Romans who came up with the concept of the "state," a powerful but impersonal institution that granted authority to various assemblies and officers acting on behalf of this state – termed a "Republic"* – in fulfilling the duties of their "office" as defined by the Roman legal system.

Indeed, in this realm of social development, Rome left a legacy in the West that exists to this day: the understanding that society ought to be a community of laws, not of personalities or special social groups.

Of course that is a very high standard to which to aspire ... or to maintain if achieved. Ultimately Rome itself could not maintain such a lofty concept ... and declined as it left that standard behind it. But the legacy remained and still serves to this day as a major political ideal among Western societies ... whether actually achieved or not.

Thus it is that we tend to idealize the Republic – probably a bit caught up too much in the idealized vision of the Republic put forth (and still read today) by Cicero, who wrote even as he saw his beloved Republic coming to an end. Actually, for most of its days, the Republic was run by a privileged elite, drawn from the very old aristocratic patricians and from upstart plebeians who were able to attain incredible wealth (usually at the expense of the other commoners) and status through intermarriage with the patricians and through acquiring a place in the Senate, which they guarded jealously. There were Tribunes, selected for short terms (one year) to watch out for the interests of the commoners, plus the Assembly, which was supposed to give voice to commoners' interests. But by and large during the Republic, the Senate did what it could to keep a tight hold on the political life of the Republic.

Rome's cultural-religious pluralism

Another reason for its grand success was that Rome proved to be quite tolerant of the social and cultural "pluralism" within its borders – as long as everyone showed due respect to Roman authorities and their gods. When the authorities themselves posed as gods, this all became quite curious. But for the most part everyone was willing to play along with the Roman thing. Morally and ethically, Rome didn't reach deeply into the private hearts of its

---

*The word *republic* is derived from Rome's Latin language, much as the word democracy is drawn from the Greek language. In the Latin, republic is written as *res publica*, meaning "thing of the people," that is, a government created by Roman law belonging to no particular social group, no dynasty, but to all the people.

subjects. That belonged to their local gods and religious traditions.

The Roman economic order

The Romans also organized the world around them physically and materially as they conquered it, building roads (still standing today in many places) to provide rapid communication, troop movement and ultimately commerce connecting the Roman center to its outlying territories. Wherever they conquered, they planted military camps on a perfectly uniform grid pattern ... which became the heart of new commercial towns which quickly grew up around these garrisons. They cleared the seas of pirates and kept marauding tribal raiders from central and east Europe closed out beyond a well-defended line running from the Rhine River in Germany to the Danube in the Balkan Peninsula. Consequently, under Roman rule, Europe, North Africa, and the Eastern Mediterranean area experienced an unprecedented peace and prosperity that made "Rome" the very model of civilization itself to millions of people.

However, ancient Rome went through a number of deaths – and a number of reincarnations, springing back to life as Roman society reinvented itself into some new form, always "Rome" but never the Rome it once was. Maybe such change was a good thing. Maybe it was not. But in any case, those who loved the Rome they were born to would suffer tremendously from the loss or death of the Rome familiar to them.

The Roman military

In the very early days of the Republic the army was basically a citizen militia whose soldiers, like the Greek hoplite army, supplied their own armor and weapons and who trained and fought in tightly packed formations (similar to the Greek phalanx) hurled at similar enemy formations. With time this heavy but cumbersome structure was broken up into a more flexible system of forming smaller and more mobile units called *centuria* of approximately 100 (later 80) men or legionaries each ... led by a centurion. Six of these centuria formed a cohort, and ten cohorts constituted a legion ... a huge military unit also made up of cavalry and more lightly armed but very maneuverable light infantry.

Overall, such formation gave the Roman military tremendous advantages in the conduct of battle, a major reason for Rome's incredible political expansion across the Mediterranean world.

In those earlier years of Rome, its soldiers originally were simply farmer-soldiers, propertied and thus with a personal vested interest in the outcome of battle. But as time went on, with the increased use of soldiers for political as well as frontier service, the ranks thinned out from the huge number of casualties – and *proletarii* (landless, usually urban, citizens) were recruited and salaried for their service. Also foreign troops (often tribal cavalry units) were recruited – for pay. By the end of the Republic, Roman soldiers were more or less paid professional soldiers – motivated less by a sense of civic duty than an affection for their commander who rewarded or supported them with pay and whose own political fortunes were what seemed most to motivate his legions. This shift in the nature and purpose of the Roman legions was probably the single most important factor in the death of the Republic and its replacement by the Empire.

✳ ✳ ✳

ROMAN ORIGINS

The first Italians. Three groups of Italian-speaking tribes – the Latins, the Umbrians and the Samnites – migrated down into Italy from the north just about the same time that the Dorians were overrunning Greece (around 1000 BC). They too conquered with iron weapons, thus introducing the iron age to Italy. They eventually settled into the mountainous center of the Italian peninsula and in the west-central lowlands facing the Mediterranean Sea. Basically, these peoples were farmers, cattle raisers and sheep herders.

The Etruscans. This wave of conquest and settlement was followed in around 900 BC by another – that of the Etruscans, who invaded central Italy from the east.* The Etruscans established ascendancy over the Italians, and reached the peak of their power during the mid-500s BC. They established cities and a high order of a material civilization – quite like the Greeks, who seemed to have influenced deeply Etruscan culture over the centuries.

Greek Italy. We have already seen that the southern part of Italy, including Sicily, was settled heavily by the Greeks as Magna Graecia. Here Greek civilization attained great heights of achievement. It certainly, along with the Etruscan culture, left a strong material legacy among the Italians – though the latter held tenaciously to their distinct Italian language.

The founding of Rome. The actual origins of Rome itself are submerged beneath a heavy overlay of patriotic myth – and thus it is hard to get at the "facts." The town was created through the joining of a number of settlements found among the "seven hills" located along the middle Tiber River. These eventually came to comprise early Rome.

Myth says that two Latin brothers, Romulus and Remus, were responsible for laying out the foundations of Rome on the Palatine Hill in 753 BC. But an Etruscan royal line (the Tarquins) seems to have established itself in Rome by the 500s BC. The Tarquin monarchy ruled the town and environs – though it was by and large a positive rule, building up Rome with an extensive city wall, public buildings and public water and drainage works and bringing commercial prosperity to Rome. It also developed a very effective military force.

The Etruscans also gave Rome its first experience in representative government, laying out Rome's basic governmental framework of several councils (*comitia* and their leaders or consuls) to oversee Rome's various civil and military functions. It was at this time that a body of local "first citizens" or Roman patricians grew in prestige and influence within Rome itself.

Rome's early rise among the Latins. In the late 500s BC, Rome began its expansion by entering into alliance with other Latin cities against Etruscan dominance. In 509 BC they expelled the Etruscan King Tarquin ... and established their own Republic.

But gradually over the next century and a half, Roman leadership within the alliance turned to dominance within the alliance (much as Athens

---

*The origins or ethnic background of the Etruscans remains a grand mystery to historians. They apparently spoke a non-Indo-European language unrelated to the Greek, Roman, Celtic languages of the region ... perhaps having roots in the region even prior to the arrival of these Indo-Europeans.

was doing at about the same time).

Against the Etruscans.   With this growing power, Rome put increasing pressure on the Etruscans. In 396 BC, during an ongoing conflict with the nearby (and quite wealthy and powerful) Etruscan city of Veii, the Romans awarded the temporary position of dictator to Furius Camillus, who led the Romans finally to success in the conflict ... slaughtering the entire male population of Veii and enslaving its women. Henceforth the Etruscans would remain troublesome – but no longer a major threat – to Roman designs in Italy.

The Celts.   But just as the Romans were beginning to enjoy the fruits of victory, Celts or Gauls invaded from the north and not only crushed the Etruscans, they sacked Rome itself (but failed to capture its citadel) in 390 BC. Once again the Romans called on Camillus (who had been banished by jealous rivals) ... and at the head of a 12,000-man army he and his army slaughtered the Gauls – who had fallen into a drunken stupor after pillaging Rome.   Then – largely to restore unity within a socially divided Rome (plebeians or commoners against the patrician class) – Camillus turned his troops on neighboring cities in the region.

   After that, as quickly as they had come, the Celts also retreated from Rome. Soon the Celts settled back into northern Italy, leaving Rome to recover quickly.

Etruscan collapse.   But the Etruscans were quite thoroughly devastated by the Celts. The Etruscans soon lost power as a vibrant society – and mysteriously their culture disappeared. They left us with no knowledge of their language and very little of their history.

Roman expansion.   This began the process of the extensive development of Rome's citizen army ... and the aggressive policy by which Rome approached the rest of Italy. This in turn sparked bloody wars with Rome's neighbors – which Rome crushed one by one.

Absorption of the fellow Latins and the Samnites.   In 338 BC a number of Latin cities rose up in revolt against Roman dominance. But the Romans responded swiftly both militarily in crushing the Latin uprising and diplomatically in extending Roman citizenship to the conquered Latins.

   Also, the fellow Italian Samnites in the mountain valleys of central Italy tried to block Roman expansion through a series of wars or uprisings beginning in 343 BC – though they too (along with some Umbrian, Etruscan and Celtic/Gallic allies) finally fell to Roman power at Sentinum in 295 BC.

Relations with the Greeks in Southern Italy. For a while, the Greeks and the Romans were cooperative, with the Romans in fact adopting many Greek cultural features – many of them transmitted earlier to the Romans by the Etruscans during the monarchy. Notably there was the Roman adoption (with many modifications) of the Greek alphabet. Indeed, by 300 BC the process of Hellenizing Roman culture was moving rapidly forward – especially through the romanticizing of Alexander and his exploits, which led the Romans to idealize Greek power, Greek culture, Greek philosophy, Greek religion.

But Roman political expansion and the question of which of the two powers was to dominate southern Italy was destined to produce friction with the Greeks in Italy. A Greek reaction – joined by some Latin allies also resenting Roman dominance – finally took form around the ambitions of King Pyrrhus of Epirus, who (equipped with some awesome elephants) managed at first to defeat the Romans in several battles. But these victories were so costly to Pyrrhus that it depleted Greek power and discouraged their Latin allies – to a point where the Romans were finally able to defeat Pyrrhus in 275 BC at Beneventum. Quickly thereafter Roman mastery of southern Italy became complete. But there was still a mighty Greek presence in eastern Sicily in the form of prosperous Syracuse.

Against Carthage. Carthage was a great sea power located on the North African coast just across from Sicily, as well as in western portions of Sicily itself. At first competition with the Carthaginians came from the Greeks (during a century-long war from 367 BC; the Romans were fairly friendly to the Carthaginians). But after the defeat of the Greeks by the Romans, the Romans and Carthaginians were left facing each other for ultimate dominion over the seas around southern Italy and the lands around the western Mediterranean ... which began to interest the Romans.

The clashes came in the form of a series of wars – the Punic Wars – fought between Rome and Carthage over the next 120 years (264-146 BC). Carthage was a formidable opponent, with a powerful navy and a huge, prosperous urban population able to put muscle to their war effort. But Rome had an experienced, battle-tested land army.

The First Punic War (264-241 BC) linked Hieron II of Syracuse with the Romans in expelling the Carthaginians from Sicily.

The Second Punic War (220-201 BC) started when the Carthaginian leader Hannibal Barca attacked Roman Saguntum in Spain, then crossed the Alps with a mighty army and for 15 years held off Roman efforts to dislodge him from northern Italy – until Rome decided to take the war to Carthage itself, where at Zama (202 BC) Hannibal lost his only battle (but also the war) to the Roman general Scipio "Africanus" (considered still today as one of the best generals in history). Carthage was stripped of its war-making powers as a result of the war. Tragically, the Roman patricians (upper-class) were jealous of the popular Scipio and brought him to trial for unfounded charges of bribery and treason, resulting in his retreat in disgust from Roman public life.

The Third Punic War (153-146 BC) occurred when the leading families in the Roman Senate decided that they wanted no further competition from a fast-reviving Carthage, found an incident that permitted them to return to war, eventually marched on the city, and after a 3-year siege, burned it to the ground. Carthage was destroyed and Africa (the region around Carthage) became a Roman province.

Against the Greeks. Philip V of Macedonia unfortunately had chosen to ally himself with Hannibal during the Second Punic War. Once Hannibal had been defeated, the Romans turned their attention to Philip and led a rebellion of Greek states against the Macedonian monarchy in 214 BC. This drew Rome deeply into Greek affairs and a number of wars involving Rome in Greece – and also in Macedonian Asia Minor and Syria under Antiochus. Rome "liberated" these Greek cities and placed them under Roman protection – as Macedonian power was chipped away.

But eventually, Roman dominance bred its own opposition in the Greek East. Perseus of Macedonia tried to rally these Greek sentiments – but the Romans quickly marched out to defeat him at Pydna (168 BC). The Romans did not follow up their victory in such a way to discourage further thoughts of rebellion ... until 148 BC, when a final war with the Greeks and Macedonians (148-146 BC) brought Macedonia under full Roman dominion as a Roman province and the rest of Greece under the full "protection" of the Roman governor in Macedonia.

In Asia Minor and Syria the Romans continued the pretense of a mere "protection" placed over local Greek power – but made and unmade kings and rulers at will. Roman rule was in fact complete in these regions.

THE ROMAN REPUBLIC

The monarchy and the comitia. The Tarquinian monarchy in Rome shared its power with several assemblies or comitia whose power increased/ decreased over the centuries: the Comitia Curiata or popular assembly of all freemen, the Comitia Centuriata or military assembly, and the Comitia Tributa or tribal assembly – presided over by 10 Tribunes. There was also the Senate, a council of elders serving for life as advisors to the king – a council which grew in power over the years.

The patricians and the plebeians. There were among some of these early Romans a number of families of "worthier" nature – the patrician families – marriage into which offered a preferential placement in the Roman scheme of things. The powerful Senate of course was dominated by these patrician families.

Yet simple membership in any of the families of the permanently settled Romans – the common citizens or "plebeians" – accorded itself some important rights in the life of the Roman community. Indeed, there was a most unusual openness about Roman life, its readiness to adopt others into its communal life – even freed slaves. In fact a freed slave living in Rome automatically became a Roman citizen.

The Republic. According to tradition, the Tarquinian monarchy was overthrown in 509 BC. The patricians were behind this action and it represented the victory of the traditional Latin agrarian gentry over the newer commercial groups closely connected to the Etruscans and Greeks through trade. It marks a time of decline of Etruscan power – and the growth of Roman military expansion.

With the new Republic, two patrician Consuls (serving one-year terms) replaced the king as the head of the Senate and the military Centuriata. But eventually (through plebeian pressures) a number of Tribunes, representing the interests of the plebeianss, were accorded both the power to protect the poorer Romans and certain veto powers over the acts of the aristocratic Republic.

There were a number of other Roman officials, the Quaestors (judges), the Censors (tax officials), Aediles (public works supervisors) and others whose powers, along with the whole governmental structure, were carefully defined in the bronze *Twelve Tables* of the Roman constitution (c. 450 BC) – posted in the Forum for all to see. All Romans knew these laws well.

The dominance of the Roman Senate. This rise from an expansive agrarian power in west-central Italy to the point where Rome now commanded the fabulous civilizations that ranged around the Mediterranean (Ptolemaic Egypt, however, had not yet fallen to Roman rule) – all this change was bound to have a profound effect on the internal disposition of Rome.

Over time, but particularly during the wars with the Carthaginians, the Roman Senate had become the center of all Roman power. It was a club of old patrician families and new plebeian wealth (new landowners) which closed its ranks and became a ruling oligarchy. Meanwhile rising taxes and competition from slave labor were bringing the Roman commoners to ruin. Roman power, especially the power of the Roman military, was built on the services of these commoners. Something drastic needed to be done to save Rome from collapse or revolution.

The efforts to "reform" the Roman Constitution

For three centuries the unchanging character of the Roman Constitution, fixed on those *Twelve Tables*, had served Rome well in keeping political ambitions under fair control. But political ambition is very difficult to manage, and for Rome the difficulty merely increased with the increase in power of Rome itself.

Much of the social-political trouble was between the patricians or the "equestrian" class dominating the Senate and controlling the wealth of the countryside and the *populare* or common citizens demanding greater influence in the life of the Republic. This conflict was greatly complicated by the demands of the Italian allies for full Roman citizenship (entry to which had been tightened up since it had become so much more profitable since the Punic Wars).

Tragically for Rome, well-intended reformers finally stepped forward with proposals to bring economic and political reform to Rome. But what they did not realize was that such reform would merely open the door wider to political contests, as "reforms" in favor of one political group soon led to "counter-reforms" of an opposing political group. Thus the rigidity of the 12-tabled Constitution now became more "flexible," that is, subject to political intrigue. As a consequence, Rome's firm foundation on Law rather than Human Will began to shatter, and the Constitution became no longer "constitutional."

Roman Law would now read according to the interests of one group or another that had managed to take control of Rome's political dynamic. And tragically Rome's legal standards now became simply the matter of the political interest of this group or that. Rome's Republic was in trouble, deep trouble ... and sadly had no idea of what could be done about mounting political animosities that only worsened once the process of "reform" got underway.*

---

*The great American sage, Ben Franklin, was well aware, thanks to Rome's own historical witness, of this problem facing any constitution. Franklin had personally observed the severity of the political splits hindering the creation of America's Constitution of 1787, and the difficulties involved in getting these groups to rise above self-interest in order to finally develop a Constitution for all Americans. Thus when questioned at the end of the long Constitutional

The Gracchi brothers (133-121 BC). Two brothers, Tiberius and Gaius Gracchi, elected successively as Tribune, tried to act on behalf of the plebeians to bring economic and political reform to Rome. Essentially, they proposed the increase of common lands for the use by the small farmers, the allotment of newly acquired lands to retired soldiers, and the broadening of the powers of and the electorate for the Assembly. But the brothers' reforms were blocked by the Senate. When riots resulted, martial law was declared by the Senate and Tiberius was murdered in the confusion. Gaius, who took his brother's place at the head of the plebeian party, had Senate partisans sent after him and he committed suicide rather than face arrest. Nothing serious came of the reform efforts.

Marius (108-100 BC). A mix of events then brought to the fore a capable military leader, Gaius Marius, who through his important military victories became so influential that he was repeatedly elected consul (seven times!). On numerous occasions he moved to clean out political corruption or incompetency in the army and public administration, save Rome itself from invading barbarians, and institute reforms in the army to make it more democratic and higher in morale. But the power to enact such reforms came not from the people through the workings of the constitution ... but instead through the use of the intimidating power of the Roman armies that Marius led – plus his own dangerous and bloody obsession with removing anything or anyone who got in his way. Having succeeded in his reforms, he then retired.

The "Social War"

This title describes various events that accompanied a shifting of power within Roman society as Rome moved through the last century BC. Reformers now fought back and forth in support of this political interest or that political ideal – violently. Marcus Livius Drusus was assassinated in 91 BC after alienating the Senate with his efforts to move things in favor of the Roman commoners – and Italian allies desiring full citizenship as members of the Empire.

After revolts by Rome's Italian neighbors, and after Marius was returned to military service – along with a new figure, Lucius Cornelius Sulla – order in Italy was restored ... although the Senate decided in 88 BC to go ahead and extend citizenship to its neighbors anyway. But this merely promoted a further spirit of reform under the Tribune, Publius, bringing the

---

Convention (May-September 1787) and asked what kind of government the delegates had finally come up with, he answered: "A Republic ... if you can keep it."

Senate again to reaction.

Thus Sulla decided to march his army into Rome and end the reform momentum ... in the process decreeing a number of political changes which reduced the powers of the people's Tribune and made the aristocratic Senate more absolutely the ruler of Rome. He also had numerous individuals arrested and executed ... and even turned on Marius – declaring him to now be an outlaw. He then headed off to Asia Minor to put down a rebellion there.

This prompted Marius to make his own military move on Rome, killing a number of opponents, and in 86 BC having himself elected as Consul (his 8th time) ... to once again put in place a number of popular reforms. But he died a few weeks later and chaos thus simply spread throughout Italy.

Then in 82 BC, with his campaign in the East completed, Sulla returned to Rome – again in full accompaniment by his army – and confirmed his, not Marius's, reforms as the model for Rome. Sulla then retired.

The slave rebellion led by Spartacus. However, a reign of terror now rested over the land – producing the semblance of peace only through fear. Whole regions lay desolate. And in 73-71 BC the slaves (joined by the Roman paupers) even went into revolt led by the gladiator Spartacus, conditions having become so bad.

Finally, the Senate called on the very wealthy patrician, Marcus Licinius Crassus, to suppress the rebellion. Crassus's legions chased down Spartacus's rebel army, crushed the rebellion, and lined the Appian Way with 6,000 crucified bodies (hung on wooden crosses) – from Rome all the way south to Capua (120 miles).

The end of the Republic

Ultimately Rome was finding itself being captured by its captive cultures ... and by those most responsible for such capture, the Roman army. Ultimately the Empire, built on military rather than Roman family power, both noble and common, would replace Republican Rome – for better or worse

The Triumvirate: Caesar, Crassus and Pompey. Three key figures would soon come together in an effort to bring Rome back to some kind of order. All three, of course, were military leaders. One of these was Julius Caesar, nephew of Marius and of the reform party. Caesar was not only a capable military commander, he was a skilled politician – who understood how important it was to sell his greatness ... by making the Roman world aware of his successes in war – specifically in the publication of his account of his actions in the Gallic Wars (58-51 BC). Previously, in 62 BC, Caesar skillfully aligned himself politically with the well-respected Crassus, and with the Senate, getting an agreement – with the equally well-respected Pompey – to form a three-way joint rule or triumvirate for Rome. Each of the three would be given areas to govern (on the basis of the military power under each of them): Crassus was given Syria and the Roman East to govern; Caesar was given Gaul and the regions across the Alps (thus his *Gallic Wars*); and Pompey was given Spain.

Pompey was understood to be the key figure in the triumvirate – and took the lead in putting down rebellions in Syria (bringing it in as a Roman province) and even marching his armies all the way East to the Euphrates River (modern central Iraq) and the Caspian Sea.

But Caesar was just as energetic, not only in bringing Celtic Gaul under Roman rule, but in undertaking popular public works projects ranging from public games to new roads. He also pushed for the extension of Roman citizenship to the Italians of north Italy.

Marcus Tullius Cicero. Cicero was a self-appointed spokesman for conservative middle-class interests – neither in favor of the patrician Senate nor the urban mobs that threatened the old Republic. Cicero's election as Consul in 63 BC was in testimony of his appeal to this middle class, plus the willingness of the patrician Senators to back him in fear of a worse fate from the populist radicals.

He was opposed by the fellow Senator Catiline, a very corrupt former governor of Africa,* who conspired to engineer widespread discontent among a whole spectrum of people within the Republic (from the supporters of Sulla, to the slaves, to even the people recently brought by conquest into the Roman order), in order to make himself dictator. Cicero, informed by Crassus of Catiline's plans, exposed Cataline's plot – forcing Cataline to leave Rome ... and take on a Roman army sent after him, which resulted in Catiline's defeat and death in battle.

Cicero was very alarmed at what was the clear deterioration of the constitutional foundations of the Roman Republic – and thus of the Republic itself ... which he made in his many speeches (recorded in *Orations*) and his writings (for instance, his very popular *De Officiis*). Sadly, his efforts availed little in keeping the Republic on its original foundations ... although those same efforts would serve very well in getting much later generations to understand what constitutes excellent, and what constitutes destructive, social dynamics.

---

*Africa was simply a Roman province roughly equivalent – not to the continent we know today as Africa - but to today's Tunisia, the Eastern portions of coastal Algeria, and the Western portions of coastal Libya.

Caesar takes full power. When in 53 BC Crassus was killed in battle against the Parthians (Persians), a two-way power division now existed between Caesar and Pompey. Also, despite the putdown of Cataline, riots and general disorder were increasing in the capital – and in 52 BC even Cicero admitted to the need to confer extraordinary powers on Pompey, now sole Consul. Pompey became flattered by his title, and by all the attention of the Senate … and was soon drawn into a Senate-inspired conspiracy against Caesar.

The plan was not to renew Caesar's appointment as Consul – and indeed to have him step down from his military command immediately. This would then require Caesar to return to Rome to stand for re-election without the military support that had by this time become all-essential for success in Roman politics. Caesar refused. The Senate then expelled his supporters – and Caesar at that point knew that he had to take drastic steps to save himself. In March of 49 BC he crossed with his troops into Italy, entered Rome at the head of his army (Pompey and the majority of the Senate fled to Greece) and became the sole ruler of Rome.

✳ ✳ ✳

THE INTELLECTUAL CULTURE OF THE ROMAN REPUBLIC

Rome never achieved the intellectual uniqueness of the Greek world … nor did it attempt to do so. It was impressed enough with its ability to simply draw on that Greek intellectual legacy for its own cultural purposes. But nonetheless, there were numerous Romans who did indeed add important items to that now Greco-Roman legacy.

Polybius (c. 200-118 BC). Polybius was not a Roman, but instead a Greek scholar and politician, who wrote a history about the rise to power of Rome. When Macedonia was defeated by Rome in 168 BC. he was brought as a political prisoner to Rome. But he was able to use this misfortune to intervene on behalf of his Greek compatriots to secure fairly gentle treatment by the Romans of the Greeks (the Romans tended to be quite impressed with Greek civilization anyway.)

Living there another 18 years, and becoming part of the political circle of the powerful Scipio family, he became familiar with a number of Roman notables. Thus when he eventually wrote the story of Rome's rise to power (40 volumes covering the period up to the final conquest of Greece in 164 BC – with only the first 5 volumes having survived to today), he did so with particular insight.

Lucretius (96-55 BC). The Roman poet and philosopher, Lucretius (Titus Lucretius Carus), was a strong contributor to the Roman sense of material order. He was a naturalist in the tradition of Democritus and Epicurus – holding a very low view of the religion of his times. In his work *De rerum natura* (*On the Nature of Things*) he claimed that popular religion was the source of the worst superstitions and sources of human evil.

Cicero (06-43 BC). Although Cicero considered his political work to be his most important activity, his writings left a huge mark on the intellectual culture of Western society. His writings set the standard for Latin scholarship all the way up to modern times. He was a devoted translator and commentator on Greek philosophy ... in particular Plato ... and wrote extensively on Greek philosophy in order to introduce it easily to the Roman citizen. His essay *De Officiis* (*On Duties*), written to his son, set out the principles of honorable or noble public service ... and had such an impact on Western scholarship that it was the second book after the Bible printed by Gutenberg. He also developed the art of oratory to professional standards ... being only second to the Greek Demosthenes in rank as the greatest orators in Western history.

Cicero's prose and oratory changed Latin from a rather ordinary or just useful language into a powerful verbal tool able to give intricate expression to the most complex ideas ... building Latin into the foundational language of Western civilization ... which was then carried forward in the West by the Christian Church ... and through the ages the primary reading of young scholars developing their Latin abilities.

Virgil (Publius Vergilius Maro) (70-19 BC). Virgil was a Roman poet who dignified the Roman nationalist aspiration with his vivid writings. His biggest project, one that had not yet been completed to his satisfaction at his death, was the *Aeneid*. This was the story of Aeneas, a Trojan survivor of the deadly war with the Greeks, who set out on his own across the Mediterranean, lived for a while in North Africa with the beautiful Dido, but in the end tragically left her in order to journey to Italy and there establish a settlement at Rome (a version very different from the older story of the founding of Rome by the brothers Romulus and Remus). This was, in short, the Roman answer to the Greek works of Homer, the *Iliad* and the *Odyssey* – designed to put Roman culture on a par with Greek culture, at least in terms of its supposed antiquity and heroic origins.

But it also struck a deep moral-ethical cord (something lacking in Homer's works) in the way it portrayed Aeneas as a man who understood the bitter-sweet of his destiny and was willing to face that destiny as a matter of honor and duty (*pietas*) – even against odds that were greater than life.

Horace (Quintus Hortius Flaccus) (65-8 BC). Horace was a military officer turned poet during the time of Rome's transition from Republic to Empire ... actually rather closely associated with Octavian's new regime. Well-born and well-educated, he found himself on the losing side of tough Roman politics, but was pardoned and eventually became a civil servant in the new regime.

Poetry was a sideline of sorts for Horace ... but where he truly left his mark on his times. He never lost his interest in Roman politics, and his writings offered some important insights into the dynamics of his times. His poetry was often satirical, even caustic at times, such as his *Epodes* and *Satires* ... uncovering faults in the world around him – and in his own life (he was very autobiographical in his writings). He himself was also deeply influenced philosophically by the rising Epicureanism and – to a lesser extent – the Stoicism of the times ... evidenced strongly in his *Satires, Epistles* and *Odes*. But ultimately, his real talent was in putting before Roman society a higher standard of Latin literary form ... studied carefully by succeeding generations.

Ovid (Publius Ovidius Naso) (43 BC to AD 17 or 18). Ovid was a poet ... who actually wrote a huge history of the world (from the "beginning" or "Creation" up to the time of the death of Julius Caesar) in the form of some 250 myths – in the 15 books comprising the *Metamorphoses*. He was very popular in his time because of the very artful way that he presented these historical sketches ... and would be a person of great interest again in the late Middle Ages / Early Renaissance (1300s/1400s). These "histories" gave him the opportunity to present matters of virtue and morality ... especially as these touch on man's relations with the gods.

Livy (Titus Livius) (59 BC to AD 17). Livy created an invaluable *History of Rome* covering the period from the rise of Rome up to his own time ... just as the empire was beginning to replace the republic under Augustus Caesar. Understandably, Livy was very well appreciated in his own time. Unfortunately, only portions of his work have survived down to today, probably lost sometime during the Middle Ages. But we have today Books 1-10 and 20-45 ... the rest (books 11-20 and 46-142) being lost to us. Nonetheless, what we do have gives us an excellent glimpse, from a very practical standpoint, of Rome's development ... beginning as far back as the period of Etruscan domination and Rome's spread across Italy.

*** * ***

THE ROMAN EMPIRE

The Birth of Imperial Rome

Julius Caesar (r. 49-44 BC). Caesar's rule proved to be surprisingly generous in its response to his opposition – and in his bringing his own followers in Rome to order.* In his land allotment to his soldiers he opened new lands – colonies in Carthage (Africa) and Corinth (Greece) – rather than confiscate land from his opponents. He tightened up on the administration of the wheat dole and the number of public events that had made him once so popular with the Roman masses. Towns in decline in Italy were rebuilt and resettled and labor was opened up to the many unemployed commoners. He established the new Julian calendar,[†] regularized the public administration, straightened out the treasury, and removed a great deal of corruption among public officials. And for himself, he acknowledged only his title as *imperator*[‡] – head of the Roman military. But the old constitution still remained in force – even as it accepted this new approach to governance (but not unprecedented – as in Sulla's dictatorship). Thus although Rome continued to present itself as a constitutional Republic, Caesar ran the government personally and totally.

But he mistakenly believed that he had finally won the hearts of the Senators. And thus, just as Caesar was about to depart for the East to fight the troublesome Parthians (March 44 BC) – and despite warnings not to do so – he presented himself before the Senate … only to be assassinated by those he thought were his friends. Supposedly this plot was undertaken to save the Republic. But in fact, all that these senators achieved was chaos

---

*So important did the family name "Caesar" become, that it came to be used simply as a title of authority by Roman rulers … all the way down to the 20th century, when Russian rulers were called Czars or Tsars – simply a Russian rendering of the name Caesar – in the same way the German emperor was called the Kaiser.

†This replaced the previous Roman calendar based on 12+ annual lunar cycles, reallocating days of the lunar calendar, plus adding an additional day in February ("leap year") to compensate for solar drift. This would remain as the West's calendar up until 1582, when Pope Gregory XIII put the new Gregorian calendar into effect – simply accounting for the slight drift over the centuries … thus, for instance, the 13 days difference between the Julian and Gregorian calendars as of today – with the Julian calendar still being used by the Eastern Orthodox Church!

‡The words "emperor" and "empire" are simply modern English's translation of the ancient Latin *imperator* and *imperium*. In short, an "empire" (imperium) is a society built on the power of its military and its military commanders (imperators) – as so many societies even today find themselves. They may not be huge "empires," but they are definitely run by the military … … as was the First French Empire under its Emperor Napoleon Bonaparte (1804-1815)!

in Rome ... and the need for another strong figure to take control – so as to bring Rome back to good order.

The Republic was now dead ... even though Rome would continue to call itself a "Republic."

Civil war. Again Cicero tried to organize the pro-Republican sentiments among the people. But Rome was deeply divided in sentiment over the restoration of the old Republic. In the meantime, Marc Antony took up the cause of avenging Caesar. Also Octavian Augustus Caesar (63 BC - AD 14), the 20-year-old great nephew (adoptive heir) of Caesar, recently elected consul, soon joined forces with Antony – after a period of bitter rivalry – in 43 BC). The following year they gathered a huge army (17 legions) and took on the "Liberators" responsible for Caesar's death (defended by 19 legions) ... with Octavian and Antony ultimately victorious at the Battle of Philippi (in Macedonian Thrace).

Antony and Octavian thus divided the empire between them, the East going to Antony and Italy and the West going to Octavian. Upon that agreement, Antony (who had married Octavia, Octavian's sister in 40 BC as part of their alliance) proceeded to settle into Eastern cultural ways – in company with Egyptian queen Cleopatra – by whom Julius Caesar supposedly had previously fathered her young co-ruler Caesarion ... and by whom March Antony fathered three more children! Thus it was that Marc Antony took up Alexander's old dream of instituting a "divine" imperial rule over the East.

Octavian meanwhile consolidated his political position in Rome. Then when Sextus Pompey, son of Caesar's old rival – who had tried and failed to challenge Octavian in the West – died in 35 BC, this finally left Octavian unchallenged in the West.

Soon Octavian turned to matters in the East. Mark Antony divorced Octavia in order to marry Cleopatra (33 BC) – more a political than a sexual matter actually – effectively ending his alliance with Octavian. Seeing how this was designed to increase the power of both Marc Antony and Cleopatra, Octavian decided that it was time to fight. The two met in a huge naval battle at Actium in 31 BC ... with Octavian the winner. Then with Octavian advancing on Egypt, Marc Antony and Cleopatra ultimately (30 BC) chose suicide rather than public humiliation. This ended Ptolemaic rule in Egypt ... as Egypt now came under Octavian's direct rule (29 BC).

Octavian "Augustus" Caesar builds all Roman power around himself as "Emperor." Two years later (27 BC) Octavian presented a plan for a restored Republic with powers supposedly returned to the Senate and the people of Rome. But his reforms of the Roman constitution did quite the opposite ... by turning over to Octavian all major public offices. He took for himself the title of princeps, an old title not unknown to the Republic, and also the designation as *augustus*.[*] In that same year the Senate accorded him for a 10-year period (renewed several times) oversight of the Imperium as commander-in-chief of the Roman Army. He also took for himself the civil title of Tribune (*tribunicia potestas*) – to broaden the look of his power base so that it appeared as if it had a traditional Republican foundation as well as just a military foundation.

Then in 23 BC he let the older, formerly more important title of consul lapse ... but retained the military title of imperator for himself – a clear indication that the military foundation of his power was much more important than the old leadership position of consul. Thus it came to be that it was not the constitution, nor the Senate that mattered most in the new regime, but it was solely the military and its role in Roman public life that now stood behind all Roman public power.

And thus Rome as an "Empire" was born.

Also in 12 BC, when an old political ally died, his priestly position as *pontifex maximus* was taken up by Augustus. He was careful to avoid trying to appear in Rome as a mystical ruler, a representative of the gods. But he easily took up that role in the East where that was exactly what was expected of their rulers. Eventually this mindset would enter Rome itself — especially through the slaves brought in in huge numbers from the East.

The deeper social impact of these changes. Unfortunately, Octavian based himself on the power of the military at a time (just about the time of Christ) when the military was depending less and less on recruits from the Roman middle class and more and more on fortune hunters drawn from conquered peoples. Their loyalties were less to Rome than to their generals. Thus also – and most sadly – under the new Imperial dynamic, it was often in rapid succession that rising generals (emperors) would take command – as the military (or at least military fortunes) made and unmade emperors at will. The Roman public played no role in these developments.

Also, the military needs and military expenses of the Roman Empire were limitless. After a while there were no more rich neighbors for Rome to plunder and the Empire had to rely on the resources of its own people to pay for its ongoing and extravagant military ventures. Mercenaries hired from Rome's former (or even continuing) enemies replaced the patriotic free citizen-soldiers of Rome, the latter, impoverished from too great a demand for their increasingly lengthy term of military service, now falling into terrible poverty. Soon the city's slums were filled with the once free

------

[*]A term derived from the Latin, augere (to increase) and thus meaning approximately "one who increases," or "majestic" or "venerable."

citizen-soldiers and their families. And thus the Empire lost touch with what it once was.

True ... military governance acted to unify the Empire. But actually it was the economic prosperity which Rome clearly brought its world that kept human hearts loyal to the whole program.

At first the new imperial system seemed to work well enough. Octavian Augustus' long rule provided the sprawling empire with the kind of stability needed for prosperity to become widespread everywhere. By and large, revolts disappeared and the scene of Roman legions gathering against each other to secure a change in political leadership was no longer to be seen ... for quite a long while.

The Julio-Claudians (AD 14-68)

Tiberius (AD 14-37). Tragically, those that followed Octavian did not have the same strength of character. And Rome would suffer as a result. Tiberius started out well. But with time, Tiberius descended into a highly paranoid condition, executing many around him that he suspected of personal disloyalty (including many of his personal relatives). His grandnephew Caligula (37-41 AD) was probably insane ... and was soon assassinated.

Claudius (AD 41-54). Caligula's uncle (and Tiberius's nephew) Claudius replaced him – just as the Senate was giving thought to restoring the Republic. But the army's Praetorian Guard (personal body guard of the Emperor) stepped in and declared Claudius emperor – putting an end to the matter. This would tragically mark the beginning of the role of the Praetorian Guard as emperor-makers – as well as emperor "unmakers" or assassins, according to their own political preferences. Claudius too developed violent suspicions of those around him, in particular a number of Senators. In AD 54 he was probably poisoned – possibly by his wife (who was certainly afraid that he was going to pass over her son Nero in favor of another imperial candidate).

Nero (AD 54-68). And then there was Nero who, with the help of his conniving mother (whom he would anyway execute in 59!), became emperor at age 16. He started off his reign fairly popular with the people – whom he was always trying to please. He did what he could to beautify Rome, building theaters and sponsoring gladiatorial contests to amuse the people. However, his projects grew increasingly extravagant and became a serious burden on the finances of the Empire. Also, arrogant and by nature suspicious, Nero became increasingly paranoid and ruthless (even murderous) to a large circle of individuals immediately around him, including his old tutor, Seneca.

In 64, much of Rome burned (actually not an entirely uncommon occurrence). Rumors were that he himself had done this in an effort to clear the Roman slums to make way for his expensive, ever-expanding urban beautification projects. According to the historian Tacitus, Nero attempted to deflect the blame for the fire onto the Christians … who were growing rapidly in number in Rome – and also gaining a bad reputation for their un-Roman "secret" ways. He attempted to validate his own accusations against the Christians by offering the Roman public the entertaining spectacle of horrible deaths inflicted on members of this "vile sect."

On the more positive side of the picture, during his reign he encountered – and largely overcame – rebellions in various parts of the Empire, most notably in Britain (Queen Boudica's Revolt of 60-61). Also, Nero actually demonstrated diplomatic talent in the way he resolved a dispute with Parthia (the former Persia) over the kingdom of Armenia (63) and in securing a peace between these two empires that would last 50 years.

But eventually revolt also touched the heart of Rome itself: Nero found himself facing down rebellion and conspiracy – from many different directions. Even the army was growing unreliable in its support of him. Finally hearing of a major rebellion brewing, and finding that no one supported him any longer, he took his own life (68). He was only 30 years old at his death. And with his death the Julio-Claudian line came to an end.

The early development of the Roman Empire

With no direct heir to the imperial title, and with Roman armies now more personally loyal to their generals than to imperial authority, chaos reigned throughout the empire. Four different emperors, commanding four different armies, rose and fell in rapid succession in the year and a half after Nero's death (68-69).

Vespasian (69-79). Finally Vespasian – one of the Roman generals to have helped bring Britain into the Roman Empire (43) during Claudius's reign … and the leader of the Roman effort to crush a huge Jewish revolt which broke out in 67 – was declared emperor by his troops in mid-69 and then by the Senate in late 69. He proved to be as excellent an administrator as he had been a general. He brought Roman public finances that Nero had squandered back into order – even into surplus – by raising taxes and by a closer oversight of how public funds were spent. He broadened the sense of Roman politics and culture by extending to Spain and Gaul rights and responsibilities that had previously belonged to Italy alone. He expanded the membership of the Senate (depleted by the murderous policy of his predecessors) from 200 to 1000, giving representation to new families and the new regions of the Empire he recently "Romanized."

Titus (79-81).   Vespasian's eldest son Titus succeeded his father as emperor. He had distinguished himself under his father's rule as the commander of the eastern legions that forced Judea back into submission. As emperor his rule was short – and troubled. Pompeii was destroyed by the eruption of Mount Vesuvius in 79 and in 80 much of Rome was destroyed by fire. Otherwise he too was proving to be an excellent administrator. But Titus died in 81 – seemingly of natural causes.

Domitian (81-96).   His place was immediately taken by Titus's brother Domitian … thanks to the support of the Praetorian Guard.   Domitian assumed tremendous powers as the society's "divinely-ordained and highly-enlightened" despot in his effort to rebuild the imperial character of Rome … including the physical rebuilding of the city itself, which had suffered tremendous damage from the recent fires and civil war.

No effort was made to continue the pretense of the Republic's existence. He ignored the Senate (which grew to hate him) and surprisingly gave no special favors to his family, very unusual in imperial politics. He presided over a tightly organized and surprisingly uncorrupt bureaucracy. He spent most of his time away from the capital city, leading battles or conducting inspection tours … and thus the seat of his government tended to be wherever he himself was located. It was during his emperorship that Celtic Britain was finally defeated (by General Agricola) and brought into the Roman Empire … except for the northern portions (Scotland) whose troops managed to escape the grip of the Roman legions.

He cultivated the support of the crowds – with lavish gladiatorial games in the new Coliseum and through distributions of monies to the residents of Rome. Surprisingly, his regime ended with money still in the state treasury, probably because of all the wealth he accumulated by seizing the property of people he had begun to fear.   In 96 he was assassinated in a plot directed by his own court officials.   But in any case, this brought the Flavian line to an end.

The height of the Roman Empire: The "Five Good Emperors"*

The next century or so proved to be a time of relative peace and prosperity. Five emperors peacefully succeeded each other – by the previous emperor's

---

*A term assigned to this next group of Emperors in the early 1500s by Niccolò Machiavelli in his *Discourses on Livy* … seeing in them the qualities that he longed to see in Italy's ruling class of his day.

adoption during his lifetime, as none but the last of these five had a natural heir of his own. Thus the transfer of power was based purely on a sense of true merit and not just family interest. Rome benefited greatly from this principle.

Nerva (96-98). The first of the five was Nerva … who however ruled only two years.

Trajan (98-117). He was followed by Trajan, who proved to be a capable administrator as well as a promoter of further military successes for Rome. He built in Rome both a new forum and market and some important ceremonial landmarks (Trajan's column). But it is in the area of military and diplomatic policy that he is best remembered. Under his rule the Empire reached its furthest extent. He marched into Armenia and placed his own man on the Armenian throne. Then in 116 Trajan continued his conquest into Parthia itself, seizing Babylon, Ctesiphon, and Susa, deposing Osroes, and placing his own ruler on the Parthian throne. But the venture overtaxed his energies – and he faced rebellion in many places in the newly expanded Empire. Mesopotamia was restless, and once again the Jews rose up in rebellion against Rome. Very ill, he managed to return to Rome before he died there in 117. The Romans knew that they had lost a great Emperor – one of their very best.

Hadrian (117-138) was named as successor as Trajan lay dying. The Senate quickly endorsed the choice. Hadrian had served with Trajan as something of a military administrator during Trajan's military campaigns – and was in fact appointed by Trajan as Governor of Syria in order to pacify the rebellious Jews. He took the view that trying to hold Mesopotamia against Parthia's claim to the region cost Rome more than it was worth … and let the area return to Parthian rule. He did however act strongly to protect Roman Britain from the fearsome Picts – by building a 80-mile-long wall (thus "Hadrian's Wall") across the northern border of Roman Britain.

He saw himself as something of an intellectual as well. He greatly admired Greek philosophy and literature (he even started the fashion of wearing a beard, Greek-style) and considered himself a poet and a Stoic and Epicurean philosopher.

The end of his rule was marked by a major crisis in Judea – where he faced a massive and destructive revolt by the Jews, led by Bar Kokhba. The problem began when Hadrian had Jerusalem rebuilt (destroyed in the earlier 67-70 Jewish rebellion) – but as a Roman city, Aelia Capitolina. He also erected a temple to Jupiter on the foundations of the leveled Jewish Temple. And he decreed an end to the "barbaric" Jewish practice of circumcision. This proved to be too much to the Jews and in 132 they rose up again in rebellion. The Jews proved to be very difficult to tame: Hadrian lost possibly an entire legion to the Jews, and had to call in legions from all around the Empire to finally bring the Jews to submission (135). The loss of Jewish life and social position was enormous. Furthermore, from that point on, a vindictive Hadrian dedicated himself to rooting out Judaism from the Empire.

But his health at this point was failing ... and he died in 138.

Antoninus Pius (138-161). Antoninus was a devoted follower of Hadrian, even pressuring the Senate to deify Hadrian – thus himself receiving the title "Pius" for his devotion to Hadrian. Interestingly, Antoninus did not come to prominence as a military man – nor did he ever develop any relationship with any of the legions, as had those before and after him. His rule was the most peaceful of any in the long run of the Empire – though he had to deal with relatively small military disturbances from time to time. He never left Italy to personally face disturbances, but always worked through Rome's governors – drawing praise from many for his relatively peaceful handling of Roman politics. However, this seemed to have produced the impression of Roman weakness in the estimation of many of Rome's enemies (such as the ever-troublesome Parthians) – which his successors would have to deal with.

Marcus Aurelius (161-180). However, the next "Good Emperor," Marcus Aurelius, was very much the military man ... as well as an excellent Stoic philosopher!

But during his first years in power, he shared the position as emperor with his adoptive brother, Lucius Verus, whom he raised to power in order to help him run the huge Empire. Verus proved to be a huge help in getting the Parthian threat reduced. But Verus would fall ill and die in 169, leaving Marcus Aurelius to continue his rule alone.

Marcus Aurelius had the very best education of the time and demonstrated a keen intellect very early in life. He had a natural affinity for philosophy – which would reveal itself later when he became Emperor.

Marcus Aurelius was very much the military man – called upon to deal with not only the ongoing Parthian problem to the East ... but to the increasingly serious problem of the movement of Germanic tribes up to Rome's northern borders – the Germanic tribes themselves pushed into that position by other tribes behind them, trying to escape the pressures of population growth, climate problems, and hunger.

As ruler of a mighty empire, there was something Solomon-like about Marcus Aurelius. From 170 until his death in 180, he recorded his thoughts (in Greek) on life, death, virtue, human purpose, etc. – that had all the qualities of Solomon's philosophical reflections found in Ecclesiastes in the Hebrew Bible ... or even of Buddha's teachings about the folly of human desire. His writings were later collected into a single work, *Meditations*. It is a classic in Stoic thought.

In 178, he was forced to turn his attention back to the Germans along the Danube. He again defeated the Germans soundly. But Marcus's health was failing him and he died in 180 at Vindobona (Vienna) along the German border.

✳ ✳ ✳

THE INTELLECTUAL CULTURE OF THE ROMAN EMPIRE

Lucius Annaeus Seneca (the Younger) (4 BC – AD 65). Seneca was a Spanish-born Stoic philosopher/statesman who stressed – and practiced – a gentle virtue in his living. He was of a distinct intellectual background, his father (Seneca the Elder) having been a notable rhetorician (polished public advocate before the law) and author in his time. The younger Seneca was educated in Rome under the Stoic Attalus, studying rhetoric and philosophy in preparation to become an advocate (lawyer) like his father.

As Seneca grew in stature and respect at Rome, he also drew suspicious political scrutiny from the imperial party. And in AD 41, he was banished to Corsica by the emperor Claudius. Eight years later he was brought out of exile to become the tutor of the young Nero – who for a while was brought up under the positive influence of Seneca.

In AD 57, Nero (now emperor) appointed Seneca Roman consul. From this important position Seneca hoped (for a few years) to augment a regime of enlightenment in Roman political life. But imperial pride once again worked against the virtuous (and increasingly popular) Seneca. Nero, now emperor and coming under the influence of an ambitious and flattering court circle – and presuming himself to be a great luminary of his age and thus resenting the greater light cast by Seneca – began to undermine his old tutor's position. Sensing the danger, Seneca quietly retired from public life.

But in AD 65, the elderly Seneca was accused (along with his rhetorician-statesman nephew Lucanus) of being part of the failed plot (led by Gaius Calpurnius Piso) to assassinate Nero. Nero thus ordered Seneca to take his own life.

With Stoic reserve and resolve, Seneca did as ordered – ending his life in keeping with his Stoic understanding of life: not to place too much thought on one's physical existence, but instead find such inner peace that neither life nor death might distract someone from his deeper sense of inner being.

Plutarch (c. 45 to 125). Plutarch was a Greek historian and biographer of a large number of famous Greek and Roman individuals (*Lives of the Noble Greeks and Romans* – also known as *Parallel Lives* – being his best-known work) – and the source of much of our in-depth knowledge of many historical figures. He came from a noble Greek family, was well educated, and became a Roman citizen … soon finding himself moving in a circle of prominent Romans. He ultimately served as a magistrate of his hometown of Chaeronea – and a representative of his town on various missions abroad. Thus it was that he wrote his biographies on the foundation of his own personal knowledge of Greek and Roman politics from a very practical standpoint. It was even claimed that in Plutarch's later life Hadrian made him procurator of Achaea. But interesting also was that in the mid-90s, Plutarch also became a priest at the Temple of Apollo at Delphi … thus a mystic – as well as a political secularist!

Claudius Ptolemy (85-165). Following (three centuries later!) the line of thought of Hipparchus, the Alexandrian-Greek mathematician, astronomer, and geographer Ptolemy, in his work – known primarily as *Almagest** – rejected the opinion of Aristarchus that the sun was the center of our cosmos (the heliocentric theory). Ptolemy "demonstrated" mathematically what appeared to be the much more "reasonable" and ancient view that the earth is the center of the cosmos (the geocentric theory) and that all heavenly bodies rotate around the earth as the epicenter of the universe.

In order to get his theory to work, he (and others after him) had to add a large number of secondary mathematical explanations (following Hipparchus' use of eccentrics and epicycles) of the peculiar movement of heavenly bodies around the earth in order to get them to fit his theory.

His theory was widely adopted by Western thinkers – down until the approach of modern times when it became dislodged – with much resistance, not least of all from the Christian church.

Plotinus (205-270). Plotinus was a developer of Neoplatonism. He headed Plato's Academy in Athens and there wrote *The Six Enneads* (250).

Like Plato, Plotinus accepted that our material world was a mere shadow of the World Soul (*Psychè Kósmou*) from which human souls derive

---

*Actually an Arab rendering of the title of this work *The Great Treatise* ('H Μεγάλη Σύνταξις – *Hē Megalē Syntaxis*) … because Ptolemy was highly regarded in the Muslim world … and it was by way of an Arab translation that Ptolemy was reintroduced to the Western world in the 1100s.

their power), which in turn was a shadow of an even higher world, that of the Nous (or Mind, where the Ideon are located), which was itself a shadow of the unknowable One (*ἕν – Hen*) or God. In other words, the world has four levels of reality: the "Divine Triad" of the One at the highest level, then the derivative world of the divine Nous, then the level of the World Soul (the bridge between the material world and the Divine Nous, which actually activates the material world). Finally, derivative of this Divine Triad, is the visible or "sensible" material world – with its tragic potential for evil.

According to Plotinus, the wise man would try, by means of very rigorous self-discipline, to free his soul from the material world or "matter," and seek contemplative unity as high up as possible within the Divine Triad, even possibly attaining a degree of unity with the One. Very much like an Eastern mystic, Plotinus claimed to have achieved this unity several times.

His pupil Porphyry (c. 234-305) edited and published the treatises of Plotinus (the *Enneads*) and also wrote a biography of his master.

The Neoplatonic philosophy was subsequently adopted by the fathers of the church, Ambrose (c. 339-397) and Augustine (354-430), and was to remain the philosophical school par excellence ... until Aristotle was rediscovered in the twelfth century.

Diogenes Laërtius (fl. 200s AD). Through Diogenes's important 10-volume work, *Lives and Opinions of Eminent Philosophers*, we possess a vastly richer knowledge about many of the ancient Greek philosophers ... although we know very little about Laërtius himself.

✳ ✳ ✳

THE DECLINE OF THE ROMAN EMPIRE

Following the rather grand period of the "Five Great Emperors," Rome then headed into a decline ... one that Rome did not really know how to break free from. It was all very tragic.

Commodus (180-192). Commodus, Marcus Aurelius' son, brings the period of the "Five Good Emperors" to an end. His rule marks the transition to very troubled times for the Roman Empire. Although his rule began well, a conspiracy in 182 (promoted primarily by members of his own family) to assassinate him turned him paranoid. And from paranoia he slipped into insanity. He loved to project himself as Hercules, a god of great physical strength. He renamed Rome after himself, termed all Romans as "Commodians," redrafted the months of the calendar in using his own twelve names for the months of the year. He did this less out of guile than out of a case of increasing simple-mindedness. But it was his behavior in the public arena that finally braced the Senate sufficiently to organize his death (he would entertain Roman crowds with his slaughter of hundreds of animals and hundreds of disabled Romans – and hold hundreds of bloodless gladiatorial combats, which he always "won," of course). Finally in 192 he was strangled in his bath by a wrestler that the Senate had paid to do the job.

Needless to say, Commodus had made no arrangements for a smooth succession upon his death. Roman politics fell into further chaos. Over the next year there were five different generals who laid claim to the title of Emperor. Assassinations and bribes followed in rapid succession as claimants attempted to line up soldiers and Senators behind their claim to the throne.

Septimius Severus (193-211). The Roman general Septimus Severus fought his way to power by having his army defeat the armies of other Roman generals contending for the position as Roman emperor. He then took on the Parthians, sacked the Parthian capital Ctesiphon and retook Mesopotamia for Rome. He was naturally suspicious of the Praetorian Guard … and replaced individuals with his own supporters to cover for him while he was away fighting Rome's enemies. However he let his cousin Plautianus take on too much authority in the Guard – and had him put to death (205).

Severus ended his days personally directing military operations against Rome's tribal enemies who were constantly threatening Rome's borderlands. In 208 he traveled to Britain in order to extend Roman rule even to northern Scotland. In the process his troops slaughtered countless Scottish Celts …. but he also lost 50,000 of his own men. In late 210 he became ill while still in Britain … and died early the following year.

Caracalla (211-217). Severus's sons Caracalla and Geta succeeded him, though Caracalla immediately murdered his brother. Then when a satire about his murder of his brother was produced in Alexandria, Caracalla took revenge by sending troops to Alexandria to loot and slaughter (over 20,000 Alexandrians killed) … earning Caracalla the reputation as one of Rome's cruelest emperors.

He treated his army lavishly – understanding the importance of keeping happy this institution which he both admired and feared deeply. He also created the last of the great architectural wonders of Rome: a giant bath that could accommodate over 2,000 at a time (named, appropriately, the Baths of Caracalla). He was busy during much of his reign defending Rome's borders against the Germanic Alamanni at the Rhine frontier. He was, in fact, on his way to renew the war with Parthia in 217 when he was assassinated by a member of the Praetorian Guard.

Macrinus (217-281) and Elagabalus (218-222). The two emperors that followed Caracalla were put in place by the Praetorian Guard (Macrinus was actually its Prefect) and also brought down by the same organization. Elagabalus turned out to be a disappointment (but only 14 when put in his position as emperor) because of his crude sexual adventures ... which led to his assassination.

Alexander Severus (222-235). Elagabalus's cousin Alexander too was only 14 when he ascended the throne. In fact it was his mother, Julia Mamaea, who was the real power behind the throne. In general, his reign was a stable one for Rome. He did what he could to put Rome back on something of a moral-legal basis, he attempted to place Rome's governmental structures on a more rational footing, and he strengthened the economy by cutting back on governmental extravagance, lowering taxes, improving the quality of Roman coinage, placing controls on interest rates, etc.

His problems on the Roman frontier would however make his rule deeply troubled. A new Parthian dynasty, the Sassanids, had extended Persian control deep into Roman territory in the eastern reaches of the Roman empire. When Alexander marched his army out to meet the Sassanids in 232, the results were something of a standoff for both sides.

Two years later, Alexander led his armies out to expel the German armies that had crossed the Rhine and had overrun eastern Gaul. He crossed into Germany – and then offered to pay tribute to the Germans rather than fight them to resolve the issue. The soldiers were incensed – and plotted his removal and replacement by a soldier popular among the troops. Thus in 235, Alexander and his mother were both murdered in a mutiny of his troops.

Fifty years of imperial turmoil (235-285)

The rapid turnover of Emperors. The assassination of Alexander marked the beginning of a long period of political, economic and social chaos in which emperors rose and fell in rapid succession – frequently because they were murdered by the Praetorian Guard as these "emperor-makers" shifted their loyalties from one imperial candidate to another (as many as 25 emperors during this period, depending on how one counts the numerous pretenders to power). Unfortunately for Rome, generals were more interested in fighting each other for the title of emperor than in offering battle to the many tribal peoples who began to cross the Rhine and Danube in raids into

Roman territory. Meanwhile the Sassanids, taking advantage of this chaos within the higher reaches of Roman power, extended Persian control into Mesopotamia.

Economic decline.   Direct barter in goods and services (a terribly cumbersome way to do business) became the accepted means of economic exchange as Roman coinage became increasingly debased by emperors, who used cheap metals to pay their soldiers the tribute or financial reward that the soldiers expected when they threw their support behind a new imperial candidate. With the military no longer doing its job in protecting the empire, roads became unsafe – and thus shipping and trading declined dramatically. Thus also Roman farms ceased being commercial enterprises – and instead became local enterprises (manorial estates) producing only for their own immediate needs. Towns were forced to erect walls and look to themselves for their own protection. And as farms and towns developed this local, self-sufficient status, they were less inclined to give significant tax support to a Roman authority that was increasingly removed from the world that concerned them.

Distress in the countryside. Life for the Roman commoners became so difficult during this period that they were forced to abandon the cities and head to the countryside in order to find enough to feed themselves and their families ... offering owners of these countryside estates, in exchange for their personal survival, a rather permanent servant status – a status that was transferred to their descendants as well (the beginning of serfdom). Also many small farmers were just as unable to provide for themselves and thus, in order to survive, fell into legal bondage to the more successful large-scale farmers.

Buying popular support. The Roman government itself attempted to buy the support of the people for this decaying system through what was termed by the Roman poet Juvenal: "bread and circuses" (or bread and games). In a piece of sharp satire about the state or condition of Rome, Juvenal commented that the Romans no longer had any interest in defending the integrity of Rome itself. They had abandoned the older generations of Romans' noble interest in their public duties, in their civil and military service to Rome. Instead the people now anxiously set their hope on just two things: bread and circuses (wheat distributions and chariot races, gladiatorial contests and an occasional feeding of Christians to the lions). These were very expensive entitlements – and huge drain on the public treasury – that the Roman authorities had accorded the people in order to keep them subdued.

For a vast empire, undergoing obvious moral decay after about 200 AD, such crass payoffs were not enough. Rome and the Romans were suffering from a deep moral emptiness that could not be filled with bread and circuses.

Moral confusion. Rome was relatively tolerant of the social and cultural "pluralism" within its borders – as long as everyone showed due respect to Roman authorities and their gods. When the Roman emperors themselves posed as gods this all became quite curious. But for the most part everyone was willing to play along with the Roman thing. That was because morally and ethically, Rome was no longer reaching deeply into the private hearts of its citizens. Such affections now belonged principally to their local gods and religious traditions.

Given Rome's obvious lack of moral-spiritual focus at this point, a number of exotic (foreign) religions began to enter vigorously the Empire from the East – with loftier ideals than the old Roman pantheon of humanlike gods and goddesses. Mithraism from Persia, with its severe good/evil dualism, offered its services for a while as the moral underpinning of an Empire seeing evil swallow up good everywhere. It was especially very popular within the Roman legions, where life was either do or die. Also mystery cults from Syria, Babylon and Egypt were becoming quite popular – though they had no well-organized advocacy group. Then too the practitioners of Judaism were numerous in the Empire ... and Judaism was opening up its ranks to newcomers – though it never really developed a full zeal for bringing the whole of Rome into its ranks.

The heroic Christian witness. Christianity had no such hesitations, being quite evangelical. At first it appealed mostly to the poor and helpless who had flocked to the Roman cities in the desperate hope of finding some remedy to their plight. In Christianity these Romans found not only comfort, but an incredible degree of heroic dignity – especially in the face of the numerous rounds of persecutions that the emperors inflicted on the members of this strange (very un-Roman) Eastern sect when its members refused to acknowledge the emperors as gods.

But this persecution seemed only to present Christianity in an ever more-heroic or glorious light to the other Romans watching this murderous persecution. The bravery of the Christians in the face of certain death began to move sympathetically the crowds that gathered to watch these horrifying events. Eventually Christianity's obvious moral and spiritual strengths were beginning to attract the interest of even nobler Romans ... which drew even greater wrath from emperors who saw the old Roman pagan order now coming under serious challenge from Christianity.

Political fragmentation. This loss of Roman civic spirit was so pronounced that at one point (258-274) the Roman empire broke into three separate empires: the Gallic Empire in the West (Britain, Gaul and Spain), the Palmyrene Empire in the East (Egypt, Palestine, Syria) – with what was left as "the Roman Empire" somewhere in between.

Attempts at reform

There were however some emperors during this period, who attempted to bring Rome back to order.

Decius (249-251), though his reign was short, left a major mark on Rome in his efforts to purge Rome of all but its original state religion (the Christians suffering greatly as a result) and in his efforts to expel the recently arrived Germanic Goths (which resulted unfortunately in his army's destruction and his own death in battle).

Valerian (253-260), though he ruled longer, faced one disaster after another: the Goths who were pillaging Asia Minor, a plague which broke out within his troops, and finally his defeat and (presumably) execution by the Sassanids in his struggle to drive them from Rome's eastern provinces. Also his reign marked another period of intense persecution of Christians – many of whom were well-placed socially and politically.

Aurelian (270-275) was able in 274 to defeat the Empress Zenobia and restore to Rome the eastern territory she had ruled as the Palmyrene Empire – and in the same year to bring the Gallic Empire in the west back under Roman authority. Thus the Roman Empire was once again a united domain. But he too was assassinated by the Praetorian Guard.

Diocletian and the Tetrarchy (285-305)

We conclude our survey of imperial Rome with Diocletian, a reformer who attempted to bring this sorry period of Rome to an end. But the irony is that in his dedicated efforts to restore Rome to some kind of original purity, he succeeded very unintendedly in closing out the age of Classical Rome and setting up instead Rome's transition into Christendom (our next section).

The division of the Empire into eastern and western halves and the "Tetrarchy" ("rule of four"). Diocletian was another non-Senatorial figure (born of Dalmatian commoners) who simply worked his way up the ranks of the Roman legions to his position of dominance. Aware of the difficulty of one man giving effective governance to the whole of the Empire, soon after his acclaim as emperor by Rome's troops in 285 Diocletian recognized fellow soldier Maximian as co-emperor. Diocletian would then serve as emperor or "Augustus" over the eastern half of the Empire and Maximian would serve as Augustus over the western half. Then in 293 Galerius and Constantius Chlorus were called into service as assistants – termed "Caesars" – and also as future successors to the co-emperors, with Galerius serving as Caesar under Diocletian and Constantius Chlorus serving as Caesar under Maximian.

The Empire at that point had four rulers, each given different portions of the Empire to rule. Unfortunately, when it came to fill vacant positions, this formula proved to be as confusing as Roman politics ever had been.

The old city of Rome's loss of status. Not surprisingly, during Diocletian's tenure as Augustus or emperor, the city of Rome itself (and the Senate) suffered politically ... and socially. Diocletian tended to avoid Rome, preferring to use Milan or Ravenna as a base of operations when in Italy. Furthermore, Diocletian's taking for himself the assignment of the eastern half of the Empire was a clear sign that the political center of the Empire was also shifting eastward from Italy to the Eastern Mediterranean.

Religious persecution. Foreign-born himself, Diocletian compensated by being "super-Roman" ... detesting any foreign intrusions, whether military or cultural, into Roman life. He also hoped that religious uniformity within the Empire might further buttress its political unity. Thus both Diocletian and his assistant or Caesar Galerius took increasingly hostile attitudes toward a number of popular eastern religions which were spreading rapidly in the Empire. This became particularly the case when the traditional temple priests claimed that they were losing their powers due to the growing influence of these alien religions, at first most notably Manichaeism.

This was a religion originated by the prophet Mani in the second half of the 200s, who claimed to be a prophetic successor to Jesus ... and the prophets before him. Manichaeism blended gnostic Christianity with elements of Persian or Zoroastrian light-dark, good-evil dualism.[*]

Diocletian detested Manichaeism intensely because of its Sassanid or Persian connections – because Persia was Rome's main enemy at the time. Consequently, he began persecutions of the Manichaean faith in the Eastern Roman Empire in 302, seizing Manichaean property and executing or enslaving the members of this religion.

----

*The Manichaeans professed the old Persian idea of a dualistic divinity: 1) the creator/god of this physical world is Evil; 2) the god of Good is master over the spiritual world. The two are in struggle with each other for supremacy over life.

Intense Christian persecution. But he then turned on the Christians. His persecutions would turn out to be the worst by far that the Christians were ever to experience. In early 303 he ordered the destruction of all churches and the end to Christian worship anywhere in the Empire. At the initiative of his assistant Galerius, Christians were ordered to be dismissed from the Roman legions. The similar principle was applied to the Roman bureaucracy. And Christian freedmen (former slaves) were reduced back into slavery.

This was followed by ever harsher measures: execution by sword or fiery stake – left mostly to the discretion of local officials, some who were rigorous in their attempt to eradicate the faith by whatever means necessary … others less rigorous. For instance, Maximian's assistant or Caesar Constantius ignored Diocletian's orders in his western territory of Britain and Gaul.

In 304 Diocletian issued another edict which commanded all Christians to be brought to a public place and offered the option of sacrificing to the Roman gods – or facing execution.

This was a very serious problem for Rome itself because at this point approximately one in every ten Romans was some kind of a Christian.

Pacifying the Empire. Meanwhile German tribal hostilities in the North, rebellion in the East (Egypt) and a renewed war with Sassanid Persia kept the four rulers very busy. With respect to the German tribal hostilities, Diocletian was able to strengthen Roman fortifications along the Danube River – bringing both peace along that front, but also a heavy increase in the tax burden on Rome. With respect to rebellion in Egypt, Diocletian was successful in 298 not only in restoring control there but also in placing a tighter Roman grip over the region. With respect to the Sassanids, Diocletian was successful in 299 in forcing Persian recognition of the restoration to Rome of most of Mesopotamia and Armenia.

Problems of succession. Then, probably much to everyone's surprise, in 305 both Diocletian and Maximian stepped down from power, allowing their assistants, Galerius and Constantius to step up from their positions as Caesars to the full positions as Augustuses or Emperors. But this now merely opened the question as to who now was to take the positions as supporting Caesars. The rivalry became intense

Thus with so many would-be Caesars contesting each other, in 308 Augustus Galerius and the retired Diocletian and Maximian called a conference to try to work out a settlement so as to bring things back to balance. But the effort merely produced even more imperial claimants (seven) when new appointments were challenged by those left out of the deal. Thus military chaos would continue to reign over the Empire.

The Christian persecutions continue.   Meanwhile, the persecutions continued under Galerius, and supporting Caesar, Maximinus (actually his nephew) – the latter being particularly a strong enforcer of Christian persecution. Such persecution continued until 311 when Galerius, now on his deathbed, issued a decree officially ending the persecutions. However Maximinus – self-elevated to full status as Eastern Augustus in 310 – soon ignored the decree and continued the persecutions in his eastern realm … at least until shortly before his own death in 313.

Constantine versus Maxentius.   At the same time, with the death of Galerius, former (uneasy) allies Constantine and Maxentius now found themselves facing each other in the matter of assuming supreme imperial powers in the West as its Augustus … a position already held by Licinius (resulting from the 308 agreement).

How this conflict would play out would have tremendous implications for the way Western civilization would develop from this point forward.

CHAPTER THREE

THE ANCIENT JEWISH LEGACY

✳ ✳ ✳

ISRAEL AS THE "LIGHT TO THE NATIONS"

How Ancient Israel inspired the development of young America

The Framers of the American Constitution (1787). Undoubtedly in their look back in history to find guidance in shaping their new American government, the Founding Fathers of the young and rising American nation – one that had come to view itself as being specially covenanted by God to be a "City on a Hill" or a "Light to the Nations" – were also quite knowledgeable about ancient Israel. It was, after all, the forerunner and major part of the spiritual foundation on which their own Christian faiths stood.

They had just gone through a grueling struggle to preserve their political independence from Britain and its king and armies, who materially speaking were far better equipped to win this engagement than were the simple American colonists. But these Americans were mystics, and knew full well that it was God ("Providence") that had given them the win in this struggle – just as it was God who had been their protector and guide in founding and building this covenant nation a century and a half previously. Now (the summer of 1787) they were called to put this venture into writing – a fundamental or constitutional law that would carefully define how a newly independent America was at that point to be governed.

But getting the 55 delegates to be "reasonable" in developing a relatively short document defining their ongoing union as the United States of America proved to be a very difficult task. They all had their own good ideas of how this should be done. And with half of them being experienced lawyers, all the careful legal reasoning they employed to get their own views accepted was getting them nowhere … except into ever-deeper contention.

Thus at a point that the convention seemed doomed to failure, the American sage, Ben Franklin, called on the delegates to stop their contentious self-serving political reasoning and instead go to God in prayer

– in fact begin each day in prayer in order to get God's counsel in this enterprise of theirs. He quoted the Biblical passage, "Except the Lord build the House, they labor in vain that build it" (Psalm 127:1). He warned them that not to look to God in this matter was clearly going to result in failure in their efforts, and possibly the discouraging of any other society from ever attempting to establish a government on human wisdom, and instead leave it to chance, war and conquest. And that admonition seemed to have sobered them enough to back off from their high reasoning … and find ways to work together – through much compromise of course. ("enlightened" idealists hate the very idea of compromise).

Fortunately, besides their own long experience (a century-and-a-half) of self-rule, they also had in front of them (as Franklin clearly demonstrated) the clear example of Israel itself as the very model of what a society that had been covenanted to God was to look like, how under the rule of God's Laws it was to operate … and not operate. So it was that Biblical Judaism was very instructive on just such matters that these Framers of a new American Constitution themselves were facing.

The Puritan-American legacy. That very moral-spiritual foundation that the Constitutional Framers themselves enjoyed was well laid out in America because of a large number of English Puritans who came to America a century and a half earlier (the early 1600s). These Puritans were very much into the laws of God … ones they knew well on the basis of personal experience to be the most reliable instruction set to live by in both their personal and their social affairs. And these Puritans lived by means of a huge faith that gave them the necessary confidence to move boldly into a previously unexplored world. Thus it was that by all instinct they were great explorers … even adventurers

Indeed, the Puritans were well-known in their days for how they were the most active in studying carefully the world that seemed to be opening around them … looking for the patterns in all of life, in all of Creation, that God himself had put in place. Thus not only were the Puritans major experimenters in their days in the fields of math, physics and chemistry (for instance, England's Royal Society, founded in the 1600s, was filled with numerous Puritan "natural philosophers" or scientists),* they were also social visionaries, attempting to develop social improvements based on God's very Word itself.

---

*No … Christianity and science are not enemies! It is just that Christians oppose very much the idea that the laws of science just "happened" into existence and had nothing to do with a Creator or God who willed these into existence. Christian scientists, such as the Puritans, have long believed that every discovery made in the field of science simply proclaims all the more the marvelous glories of a very complex Creator/Sustainer God.

They were thus excited to put into place in the new American setting the life patterns that they knew that God himself had set up at the very foundations of the world, of the universe itself – patterns or "natural laws" not only to be discovered in their scientific research, but also, and most importantly, already well-founded on God's very Word – laid out quite clearly in their Bibles..

Ancient Israel and the laws of God. Thus it was that ancient Israel was well understood in America to be God's "Light to the Nations," revealing to all the peoples, all the nations, how God's social laws worked – have always worked and will always work accordingly – because social experiments, unlike physics and chemistry experiments, do not fit the strict requirements of laboratory experimentation. You can't conduct social experiments with whole societies the way you can conduct laboratory experiments with objects of a more physical nature!

Understanding this, and due to the enormous complexity of the laws directing all social dynamics – especially those concerning the rise and fall of societies – God simply demonstrated through the "Israelite experiment" the all-important laws of society as he himself made them. God made them very explicit not only through social example, bad and good, but also through words given directly to Israel by way of the prophets.

God intended for all of this social dynamic to be studied ... and learned from. And indeed, that was a set of lessons that the Founding Fathers would have known in great detail. And as they themselves affirmed, that was what enabled them to get all the human politics that arise when deep social challenges face a people. Putting themselves under God's guidance rather than their own self-serving political instincts, they were able finally to make the right decisions in founding America's new Constitutional Republic.

✳ ✳ ✳

THE EARLY FOUNDATION OF THE COVENANT PEOPLE

It is very hard to know where to start the Jewish narrative. Judaism as a mature religion really came into being only with the captivity of the Jewish ruling classes in Babylon during the 500s BC ... when, with no Temple to worship at where they could perform the anciently required sacrifices, and thus with their priests unemployed during their Babylonian captivity, the Jews found that to survive they had to reinvent themselves ... in the process becoming something of a "People of the Book" (as Muslims would later term them) ... that is a people whose religious life now turned around their own well-recorded narrative as a "chosen people" of God ... now disciplined and led not by priests but by teacher-preachers or Biblical scholars knows as rabbis – well familiar with that narrative, and on that basis able to give skillful moral-spiritual guidance to the various – and often quite scattered – Jewish communities under their leadership. Thus the 500s BC certainly would be a good place to start the narrative.

But the Jews did not just happen into existence at that point. Rather, they were one of the tribal components (over the long run however, the most important tribal component) of the multi-tribal Israelite people or kingdom. And that kingdom got its start some 500 years earlier (c. 1000 BC) under Saul, his competitor David, and David's famous son, Solomon. So, starting up the narrative with the all-important founding of the Davidic monarchy around 1000 BC would be a good starting point.

But here too, the Kingdom of Israel had its origins centuries earlier ... as a Hebrew people who were led out of Egyptian captivity by the prophet Moses ... to establish for themselves in the "Promised Land" a society where they were to live, worship, and prosper under their god YHWH / Yahweh (and have no other gods before him) ... against the neighboring tribes that they constantly found themselves up against, and thus having to call on Yahweh constantly to come to their rescue. That took a lot of faith in Yahweh – a faith which constantly strengthened and then waivered – as a critical lesson in the dynamics of faith put before the Israelite/Jewish generations to follow. Thus starting with Moses and the early Israelites would be a good place to start.

But Moses was himself of a line of Hebrews descending from much earlier patriarchs, Abraham and his offspring – four generations of earlier Hebrews well-known to Abraham's descendants, a family which originated the idea that they were to live in accordance with a very precise "covenant" that Abraham had taken up with Yahweh centuries earlier. So we could start our narrative there.

But the Biblical narrative that served as the Jewish national narrative actually started even before Abraham ... going all the way back to a primal couple, Adam and Eve, and their sons Cain and Abel. Thus we could go all the way back to the "beginning" – the "Genesis" or opening chapters of Jewish scripture!

So ... just to keep things simple, we will go chronologically, starting with the Genesis account ... then bringing us up step by step even to Roman times. It's a very long story. So this will have to be presented in very summary form!

The Genesis account

The Jewish Bible begins with God's creation of the universe, and then the bringing to life of Adam or "Earthman" (from the Jewish *Adamah*, or "earth") and his wife Eve (from the Jewish *Chava* or "life"). They lived in full trust in God's providence ... until they were lured by the serpent (representing Satan or the Adversary) into eating of the forbidden fruit of the knowledge of good and evil. The misleading promise was this would put God's powers in their own hands ... so that God would no longer be needed. They could live by their own godly powers. Of course, this was a disastrous deception (one that lives on even today!).

This kind of self-serving intellectual-moral power then carries on into their rather "neolithic" offspring, Cain and Abel ... in which the farmer Cain jealously puts to death his herdsman brother Abel ... and then plays "lawyer" before God, trying to justify this horrible deed. He suffers the natural consequences of his action ... but oddly enough still enjoys God's loving protection nonetheless.

But wickedness merely spreads across the human landscape, especially with the rise of urban Babel (Babylon?) ... until God gets fed up with the whole thing and decides to destroy his human creation – with the exception of the faithful Noah and his family ... and progenitors of a new animal kingdom ... who, by Noah building a massive boat (in the desert no less) survives when God sends a massive flood lasting "40 days" (meaning a very long time) to finish the job!

Then there is Job (not part of the Book of Genesis but part of the very ancient narrative), whose full faith in God is put to the test by Satan ... and in the face of crushing tragedy after tragedy (even his wife urges him to give up on God) Job holds on to his faith in God ... and in the end is rewarded for keeping faith in midst of the turmoil and terror.

Abraham and the Covenant with God

The narrative focusing on the people of "Israel" themselves actually begins many generations later. It takes up with the ever-faithful Abram, a man of faith who follows God's command to migrate to a new land – one that God promises him and his descendants. No one is exactly sure of the time, but a fair guess is anywhere from 1900 BC to 1500 BC. Abram was a nomadic Hebrew tribal elder or chief who, in following God's instructions, moved his family and herds around the Middle East ... migrating from the lower reaches of the Tigris-Euphrates River (in modern-day Iraq) upriver along probably the Euphrates River and arriving at Syria. Here he then had a call from God to take his people further south along the highlands ... into the "Promised Land" (modern Palestine).

Abram is a man who exemplified all the virtues of a "Man of God" ... yet experienced all the personal weaknesses that humans have to contend with. In many ways he is a typical herdsman facing problems of plenty and scarcity … which at one point has him turning to Egypt for relief … where there, to advance his position, he presents his wife Sarai as his sister to Egypt's Pharaoh … having then to return to the Promised Land when the deception becomes known by the Pharaoh.

But mostly he was a "great man" because of his total submission to the will of God. As a 99-year-old man, he covenanted with God Almighty to be his faithful servant … just as *Elohim/El Shaddai/Yahweh* was to be his faithful God.* From this point on Abram was finally to be known as Abraham (father of many people) … a strange irony since at this point, Abraham and his wife were very, very old. But this new dispensation also led Sarai to becoming Sarah (from a "striving" or "contentious" woman … to now a "princess"). To make Abraham's faith stand out even more starkly, they then most miraculously had a son … named Isaac (*Yitzhak* – "he will laugh") – because they both "laughed" when they were told that Sarah, at her old age (90), would have a son.

But then Abraham's faith is tested deeply when he comes under divine call to perform the sacrifice of his son Isaac. Seeing that Abraham is willing to do even this in service to God, God calls off the event. Abraham has passed the test.

The "many" offspring promised by God develops slowly over the generations, Isaac having only two sons, the twins Esau and Jacob – the latter having to live the life of a trickster since he was by mere minutes second-born. But clearly God's favor falls to Jacob … and through numerous trials and errors Jacob is brought to success in the Promised Land. In the trip back from his stay in Mesopotamia, he encounters an angel of the Lord – and the two wrestle all night, with Jacob finally able to win the match … and gain the label "Israel" – "he who struggles with God." Ultimately, Jacob – or "Israel" – is able to father a dozen male offspring (and a daughter) by way of his four wives.

But it is the young Joseph who shines among his older brothers – to their great jealousy. Joseph is spared his life by his angry brothers who instead sell him to a slaver heading to Egypt. But in Egypt Joseph shows himself to be a man of integrity, wisdom and mystical insight … saving himself and ultimately all of Egypt from disaster with his prophetic power, which brings him from prison to Egyptian chancellorship … but also brings him into reunion with his brothers who have had to come to Egypt to the find the food that is lacking across a hungry Middle East. But the reunion is graceful … and brings Joseph's brothers and his father Jacob and family to

---

*All three names in reference to God – *Elohim, El Shaddai*, and *Yahweh* – appear in the first few verses of Genesis 17, describing the making of this covenant between God and Abraham.

Egypt to live – where they will do so over the many generations to follow.

Moses and the return to the Promised Land

Centuries would go by, and the descendants of Jacob and Joseph would lose their special status in Egypt, even becoming bondsmen or slaves under the Egyptian system. But these "Hebrews"* have become a nuisance in the eyes of Pharaoh, and he orders the slaughter of all Hebrew babies in Egypt. But the baby Moses is hidden in the bulrushes by his sister, is discovered by the Egyptian princess, and is brought to the Egyptian court, and raised as a nobleman ... though his Hebrew origins come to haunt him. One day he finds himself acting on this understanding when he kills an Egyptian overseer beating a Hebrew worker. He now flees Egyptian justice ... into the Sinai wilderness or desert ... where he believes that his role in life is to live it out as a lowly shepherd.

It is at this point (as Moses finally reached his 80th year) that God appears to Moses in a burning bush, and orders the reluctant Moses to return to Egypt and demand of the Pharaoh to "let his people go." This he does ... which runs into a most resistant Pharaoh ... and Pharaoh's priests who engage Moses in a dual to prove which of the two, Moses's or the priests' gods are the more powerful. Even though YHWH proves himself as the most powerful god of all, the tests continue ... until finally God simply calls on Moses to have his Hebrews paint their doorposts with blood so that an angel of death that God is sending to Egypt will pass over (thus the most important Jewish holiday, the Passover) their homes – and strike dead the firstborn males of the rest of the Egyptian population ... including the son of Pharaoh.

This finally breaks Pharaoh's resolve and he orders the Hebrews to be released to return to their lands in the East ... then foolishly changes him mind and has his army chase after them, only to have that army destroyed when the waters of the Red Sea, that God has held back so that the Hebrews can exit Egypt, are released upon the Egyptians, and they are all drowned.

But the question of Moses's faith touching deeply the hearts of the Hebrews he is leading now becomes of paramount importance. Food and water are scarce and the trek is long. And, at one point, God calls Moses to the heights of Mount Sinai – there to outline the laws that he expects his newly freed Hebrews to live by. But on his return down the mountain after

---

**Hebrew*: A term indicating "those who came from beyond the river" implying nomadic origins ... and, in any case in Egypt, alien status because of not being originally from Egypt. But it also has in the Biblical narrative the idea of those who have passed through baptismal waters from an old world, old life, to a new one ... a covenanted one. This would have very strong symbolic value in Judeo-Christian spirituality.

an absence of "40 days,"* Moses discovers that the people have set up their own "Golden Calf" to worship ... and in his fury smashes the stone tablets containing the all-important Ten Commandments. But Moses convinces God to give his people a second change ... which he does – despite all their moaning and complaining about their situation – claiming that slavery back in Egypt was not this bad.

When upon finally reaching the border leading into the Promised Land (or Canaan), God calls for a single person from each of the twelve tribes to be sent as scouts into the land, take careful note of what they discovered, and then report back to the people. This they did ...with ten of the twelve going on about how impossible the idea of entering Canaan happened to be, the Hebrews merely tiny creatures in comparison to these Canaanite giants. Once again, this set up wailing and bitter complaining by the Hebrews about the dangers of entering the Promised Land. But Joshua[†] and Caleb, two of the scouts, affirmed that the reports of the nature of the Canaanites were correct. But given that God himself had promised that land to the Hebrews, they were standing with the idea of entering the Promised Land ... and taking on whatever challenges they faced, because God would be with them. But those two could not convince the rest of the Hebrews. As a result, God gave up on them, promising that only Joshua and Caleb would finally enter the promised land. Thus the complaining Hebrews found themselves stuck there ... for another "forty years" ... until the youngest of the Hebrews had grown into maturity and the older, faithless generation had died off.

Joshua and the Judges

At this point, with Moses also dead, under the leadership of Joshua, the Hebrews or Israelites finally made their entry into the Promised Land. This was the time (several centuries in duration) that the Israelites found themselves fighting the surrounding tribes, Canaanites, Hittites, Jebusites, Amorites, Philistines, etc. – when they weren't coming up against each other. And in all of this, there was always the test as to whose will they would follow, that of their God Yahweh ... or would they most humanly and most foolishly "walk in their own counsel" – the former bringing dazzling success, the latter bringing shameful defeat.

---

*Clearly 40 days or 40 years – the number or figure 40 used very frequently (157 times?) in the Bible – simply means enough time for God to do what he needed to do in a particular matter. Thus it rained 40 days and 40 nights during Noah's flood. Jesus was in the wilderness for 40 days. Moses's life was broken into three 40-year periods ... etc.

†"Joshua" (actually in Hebrew: *Yehoshua*, but also in Greek, *Jesus*) probably meaning "YHWH saves," or "YHWH is Lord/Savior."

Thus Joshua brought down the walls of enemy Jericho by following God's strict orders, Gideon and his small band of warriors produced the destruction of the entire Midianite army, Sampson, though badly wounded and blinded by his Philistine enemies, was able to break from his capture, destroy the Philistine temple to their god Dagon, and bring down 1000 Philistine warriors in his own ultimate battle.

And these events would strengthen greatly the faith in Yahweh and consequent strength of Israel ... only to be followed a few generations later by the foolishness of Israelite successors who knew little of such powerful faith. And the results for Israel would always be tragic ... until God appointed yet another judge (such as also Ehud, Deborah, Jephthah) to once again deliver Israel from its self-inflicted catastrophe!

* * *

THE DAVIDIC KINGDOM

But by the year 1000 BC, the Israelites were becoming very envious of the surrounding kingdoms ... and began to demand of their spiritual leader, the prophet (and Israel's last "judge") Samuel, to appoint them a king. Samuel warned them that to do so would cause them to lose their liberties and merely produce a very heavy political load to carry. But they insisted ... and so Samuel bowed to their wishes and had the very popular Saul anointed Israel's first king ... although earlier he had followed God's instructions and prophesied that one day the young shepherd David, would lead God's people, the Israelites. And very soon, still the youth that he was, he astonished Israel (and his older brothers) by coming out to take up the challenge by the Philistine monster Goliath to meet in personal combat ... and bring down the mighty Goliath – strictly on the basis of David's faith that God was fully with him in this most dangerous enterprise.

This brought David both political appointment and public adoration – that he had to carefully navigate in the presence of an increasingly jealous Saul ... until it was time for David to flee Saul's wrath. In his exile, he twice rejected the opportunity to kill Saul when the latter was off guard ... understanding that his destiny was to come at the moment of God's choosing, not his own. And that would finally come when Saul, overstepped his authority, took on Samuel's priestly powers for himself in preparation for a huge battle, and suffered the consequences of his own death and his son Jonathan's in the battle as a result. David now stepped into the kingship.

But even David got caught up in the pride of power when he took for his own sexual pleasure the wife of a very faithful military officer of his, Bathsheba ... and made her pregnant. The betrayal was discovered by the prophet Nathan, who brought David to repentance ... but still could not rescue David from the consequences of his action.* The baby did not survive, though David went on to have a second son by Bathsheba, Solomon ... who would actually go on to become a great king. But he would have horrible troubles from his other sons, Amnon and Absalom ... and die a brokenhearted king.

But Solomon would bring Israel and its Judaic capital Jerusalem to political greatness ... expanding considerably the realm of the kingdom, and through diplomatic alliances, the political reach of Israel to the nations around them. But in doing so, he would dilute greatly the position of Yahweh in the scheme of things ... building a fabulous temple to Yahweh ... but also other temples dedicated to the gods of his various foreigner wives (hundreds of them!). Thus David's political simplicity and directness was replaced by Solomon's highly sophisticated but also highly complex political programming ... which in his later years a fairly wise Solomon realized was just thin appearances and not deep reality. Indeed, his reflections on these matters became the foundations for what was to become the expanded "wisdom literature" of later Judaism (Proverbs, Ecclesiastes, Song of Solomon, etc.).

The North-South split between Israel and Judah

After Solomon, the Davidic kingdom split between Solomon's son, Rehoboam, and the Israeli General Jeroboam. The larger and much wealthier northern portion, which Jeroboam set up as an independent kingdom, would continue to enjoy the use of the name Israel, and construct smaller temples at Bethel (the original Israelite worship center) and at Dan ... and locate its capital at Samaria.

The Southern portion would be known from that point on as Judah (from the southern tribal region it was largely built on) with its Davidic Capital and Temple still at Jerusalem.

The two Hebrew states often fought – or sometimes allied with each other – usually in response to what was going on around them in Egypt, Syria and Mesopotamia (Iraq). They continued to act as if they were the major power that they had been under Solomon ... though Judah tended to be a bit more realistic about this than Israel and thus a bit more cautious in its diplomatic and military diplomacy.

Perhaps because of the location of the Temple in Judah in the South at

---

*Muslims, however, claim that this story of David and Bathsheba is told falsely. David was one of the true prophets and thus characterized by the principle of *ismah* (infallibility). He could not have done this. Thus Jews and Christians who tell the story as they do are guilty of *qazf* (falsely accusing a person of adultery) and defaming a prophet, two huge crimes in the eyes of Islam.

Jerusalem – and the strong influence of the Zadokite (Greek: "Sadducee") priesthood there – Judah stayed more closely in line with its religious focus on YHWH ... whereas the Israelite kings of the North tended to be more "inclusive" – (much like Solomon had been) in erecting temples to even the Canaanite gods.

Ahab, Jezebel, Elijah and Elisha. This became especially the case when King Ahab (r. 871-852 BC), in his bid to widen the power of Israel, married the Phoenician princess Jezebel. But she in turn brought her priests of Baal and Asherah with her to Israel – and set about killing whatever YHWHist priests she could get her hands on.

Finally, she and her prophets of Baal were challenged by the bold Yahwist prophet Elijah – resulting in the humiliation and subsequent slaughter of the priests of Baal ... and also Asherah.*

King Ahab subsequently died in battle and was succeeded by his sons Ahaziah and then Jehoram.

But Jehoram was challenged by the Israelite General Jehu (r. 841-814 BC), whom the prophet Elisha (Elijah's successor) had anointed as the new king. Then Jehu (under Elisha's instructions) set about purging Israel of the family line of Ahab-Jezebel – including Jezebel herself, who was thrown from her palace window to dogs below.

Meanwhile Athaliah, daughter of Ahab and Jezebel, had married King Jehoram of Judah (so many Jehorams!) and also introduced her mother's Baal worship to Judah. Jehoram's rule in Judah (c. 849-842 BC) was generally catastrophic ... and he and most of his family died at the hands of Philistine, Arabian and Ethiopian raiders.

Athaliah meanwhile survived as queen mother ... who when Jehu killed off her family in Israel then responded by turning on the descendants of David in Judah, nearly wiping out the entire Davidic line.

Only the baby Jehoash survived when he was hidden from the vengeful Athaliah. But finally, Athaliah was overthrown and executed ... and Jehoash (although only seven at the time) was then crowned as King of Judah. Jehoash – according to his YHWHist chroniclers – subsequently gave Judah 40 years of righteous government (c. 836-796 BC).

The rise of Assyria ...
and the destruction of the northern kingdom of Israel

----

*Sadly, the enormous courage of the prophet Elijah would give way to deep fear – and Elijah's flight into the desert – in the face of Jezebel's death threats aimed at Elijah for what he had done to her priests, a Biblical lesson in spiritual dynamics, demonstrating that true spiritual courage comes directly as a gift from God – and not from well-designed human intentions.

In the meantime, a northern Mesopotamian people, the Assyrians had challenged much of the Middle East with their ruthless military domination, begun in earnest in the early 800s BC by Ashurnasirpal II ... who conquered cities everywhere, executing or enslaving his defeated enemies and leveling their cities to the ground. But eventually the Assyrian danger seemed to subside ... as Assyria subsequently came under a number of weak rulers.

Then. in 745 BC, Assyrian general Tiglath-Pileser III seized power and put Assyria back on the path of dominance through destruction ... again striking terror in the hearts of the people throughout the region.

The kings of Israel and Syria appealed to King Ahaz of Judah to help them fight the Assyrians ... but Ahaz refused (Judah's relations with both countries had not been good, especially with the Syrians), and Israel and Syria foolishly attacked Judah upon Ahaz's refusal. But equally foolishly, King Ahaz put himself at the mercy of Tiglath-Pileser and appealed to him to come to his aid against Syria and Israel ... which Assyria immediately did, in 732 BC crushing both Syria and Israel – and placing them also under Assyrian control.

Then King Hoshea of Israel stopped paying tribute to Assyria (and its next King Shalmaneser) and instead appealed to Egypt for help ... which naturally infuriated the Assyrians, who laid siege to the Israelite capital-city Samaria for three years. The Assyrians finally (724/723 BC?) captured the city ... and carried off to captivity the inhabitants of all ten northern tribes of Israel.

The Israelites would be scattered widely across the Assyrian Empire, soon lose their identity as YHWH's people (not that they had been that loyal to him in the first place) and neither they nor any of their descendants would ever return again to the land of Israel. In their place the Assyrians brought in various other subject peoples from around their vast empire and settled them in the vacated Israelite territory ... thus creating the "Samaritans" – who took up some of the religious ways of the Israelites who had once lived there, but were themselves not descendants of Abraham nor possessing any part of the all-important Israelite tribal lineage.

Judah as the sole surviving part of ancient Israel. At this point (about 600 BC) of the original twelve tribes of Israel now only Judah, the Southern Kingdom (and small parts of some of the other tribes) were still standing in the Promised Land. This poorer, more humble, Judaic – or "Jewish" – people tended to stay closer to God ... though hardly perfectly. But in any case, with Judah being the only Israelite tribe to avoid the Assyrian devastation, "Judah" and "Israel" were now one and the same thing.

Now it's Judah's turn

Hezekiah and Isaiah.   Nonetheless, Judah itself was not free of the Assyrian threat ... which under a new Assyrian King Sennacherib (ruled 705-681 BC), overran Judah. Sennacherib then sent an emissary to King Hezekiah at Jerusalem, demanding massive tribute in silver and gold ... and warned Hezekiah in front of his own people of what the Assyrians would do to him (and his people) if he were to continue to rely on Egypt for help. He even scorned them with the claim that their God YHWH was not in a position to protect them.

But the prophet Isaiah informed Hezekiah (who had always been amazingly faithful to YHWH – and him alone) that indeed YHWH would actually make short work of Assyria because of its arrogance ... and as a sign, Judah would revive immediately from the devastation caused by Assyria. And indeed, this happened when Sennacherib's own sons assassinated their father ... seriously weakening Assyria in the face of a rising regional power centered on the ancient city of Babylon ... thus a rising "Babylonian" power.* In 626 BC under Nabopolassar, these "Babylonians" had secured their independence from the greatly weakened Assyrian power to the North. This then also became the opportunity for Egypt, Syria and others to try to secure their own independence – in various alliances with each other.

Judah defeated by the Babylonians.   But eventually Judah too got caught up in the politics of the bigger players – especially as the regional power structure seemed so undetermined. But most tragically for Judah, step by step, things went from bad to worse – as Judah got caught up in the middle of an Egyptian-versus-Babylonian contest. Ultimately, in 597 BC, an angry Babylonian king Nebuchadnezzar assaulted and conquered the Jews at Jerusalem ... consequently carting off the Judaic royal court, high priests and upper classes to Babylon as hostages.

But not long thereafter (ten years) – against the warnings of the prophet Jeremiah not to do so – Judah's king Zedekiah joined with the Egyptians in a revolt against Babylon. But this merely led Nebuchadnezzar to again attack Jerusalem (587 BC) ... this time destroying the Temple, tearing down Jerusalem's walls, burning the city to the ground, and carting off another – but now quite huge – group of the citizens of Judah (possibly as many as 20,000) to captivity in Babylon.

✳ ✳ ✳

THE "BABYLONIAN CAPTIVITY" ... AND ITS LEGACY

---

*These Babylonians were actually "neo-Babylonians," for they had no connection with the Babylonian Empire built up by the great Hammurabi about twelve-hundred years earlier – other than both having the city of Babylon serve as their capital-cities.

Judaism is born in Babylon. Thankfully, the Jews were not scattered around the Babylonian kingdom as the Assyrians had done to the Israelites. The Jews were allowed to live in Babylon in their own communities … where they actually would come to prosper. But therein was a huge danger – that of losing their offspring to Babylonian culture. But what were they to do as Jews? There was now no Temple where they could bring their sacrifices to the priests in accordance with Jewish tradition. In fact, the priestly class, the Levites, were rather unemployed in Babylon.

But what they did have was their strong religious traditions … and most importantly, their own Jewish narrative, the *Mishnah*, as a chosen people to inspire them. Thus they gathered on a regular basis, the Shabbat, to "worship" … prayers, songs, even dances, being offered in Jewish worship at these gathering centers or synagogues. But most importantly, as something like sermons, they were told and retold the stories of the Mishnah by their elders or teachers (eventually "rabbis") … narratives about their ancestors which they began to gather carefully … thus beginning the assembly of their Jewish Bible, the *Torah*.

Thus it was that they grew as a religious unit, dependent – unlike the world around them – not on priests and temple sacrifices … but on a sense that as a people they possessed a very special "Word" from God about how, as his chosen people, and by the example of their ancestors before them, they were to live … amidst a "Gentile" (non-Jewish) world. Thus as a Jewish people they not only survived. They prospered.

They still had some theological questions that needed to be answered in all of this. How was it that, as a people of God, they found themselves captives in Babylon? Was the god of the Babylonians, Marduk, greater than their god Yahweh? The answer came in the form of a new understanding that in fact there was only one God responsible for the creation of the universe … in fact, of all that there was in life. There was only one god, Yahweh. But he had to bring the Jews to their present circumstances (as he had done so many times previously with their ancestors) to get them to see what exactly he had in mind for his "chosen people" to be doing in this larger human realm. In a sense, they were brought to Babylon to be "awakened" from their human political-social obsessions and consequently be brought into God's higher spiritual realm. Thus as his "chosen people," they were to serve Yahweh as a priestly people. As Isaiah put it (Isaiah 49:6), they were to be a "light unto the nations." They were thus called to bring all humankind to worship God in Zion … to demonstrate to the larger world how to "walk in His ways" (Psalm 128:1).

The return of the Jews

Rebuilding life in the Promised Land. When in 521 BC, the Persians –

under the rule of King Cyrus – overran the Babylonians, Cyrus allowed the captive nations, including the Jews, to return to their homelands ... if they chose to return. In fact only a portion of the Jewish community in Babylon found their way back to their Jewish homeland ... although even then, the group that returned was reported to number over 40,000 – although it is believed today that this did not occur as a single event, but involved a continuing movement of such returnees over the years. Indeed, a second great migration occurred almost a century later under the direction of the prophets Ezra and Nehemiah.

Yet at the same time, most Jews chose to remain in the city of Babylon – where life there was fairly comfortable and where their community structure and its unity was generally under no deep danger (some exceptional occasions however).

In any case, on their return to the Promised Land, these returnee Jews encountered a much-changed Judah – even though only the oldest of this group were able to remember what life in Judah was like before they were carted off to Babylon.   The local population that had been left behind in Judah had, over the leaderless years, wandered from their Jewish religious-political ways – and did not recognize any special relationship with the returning Jews.   Coupled with the fact that the Assyrian program of resettling foreigners in the lands they had conquered had also filled the land with "Samaritans" – there was actually considerable local hostility aimed at these returnees.

Thus the first order of the day of the returned Jews was to rebuild, under the direction of Zerubbabel, the protective walls of Jerusalem as a matter of great emergency.   With that accomplished, the Jews then looked to the second order of the day, the rebuilding of the Jewish Temple in Jerusalem.   It would take some 20 years – with a couple of serious disruptions in the process – to complete the build. And sadly for those able to remember the original Temple before its destruction by the Babylonians, this reconstructed Second Temple fell way short of the grandeur of the First or Solomon's Temple.

Yet even with the Temple rebuilt in Jerusalem and the sacrifices commenced again under the direction of the restored temple priesthood, he rabbis or teachers continued to operate much as they had in Babylon. Not only in Jerusalem but also in the various towns of the rest of restored Judah/Israel, the rabbis continued to preserve their Biblical scholarship as a major undergirding of the Jewish nation. Jews would visit Jerusalem on very special religious occasions. But their Jewish faith and social-spiritual life was actually built on their involvement with the local synagogue, where they gathered on a regular weekly basis, the Shabbat or Sabbath, to follow closely their rabbi's teachings or sermons – giving powerful social structure to their lives.

The Jewish "diaspora." But as already notey, the majority of the Jews however opted to remain in Babylon, where life was good, and their Jewish religious life was in no danger of being extinguished in doing so. And thus began the Jewish "diaspora" ... the reality that Jews required no particular homeland to identify themselves by ... though certainly Judea and its capital Jerusalem still held special interest to them as a people. But what ultimately identified them was their lives built around the Sabbath practice of regular worship, instruction, fellowship ... and a set of social-moral rules to live by – and be identified by as a distinct people. And this would take place not only in Babylon ... but among the huge number of Jews living in Egypt.

Earlier, many Jews had accompanied the prophet Jeremiah to Egypt rather than face the Babylonian captivity – and then when the Alexandrians took over Egypt and made Alexandria a spectacular city, many more Jews found good reason to choose to live there. It was a great place to live out Jewish life. It was after all the Greek Ptolemies of Egypt that had offered them the invaluable gift of translating their Torah into Greek ... allowing them to fit easily into Egyptian society – and retain their strong Jewish identities.

✳ ✳ ✳

FURTHER DEVELOPMENTS IN JUDEA

With the coming of the Greeks by way of Alexander's conquests of the lands of the Eastern Mediterranean, Judah or Israel as it tended to call itself, found Greek culture becoming deeply invasive of its traditional Jewish culture ... especially among the rising generations. Indeed, Greek views on sex were deeply shocking to Jewish sensitivities.

Nonetheless, Greek culture was making deep inroads into Jewish culture ... even becoming the preferred language of scholarship - although ancient Hebrew remained central to Jewish worship. But the two worlds of scholarship and worship were becoming rather separate.

Then with the arrival of the Romans to the region in the 100s BC, Jewish culture feared an even deeper absorption into "Gentile" (non-Jewish) ways. Thus a spirit of rebellion found itself growing among many (though by no means all) of the Jewish people. They needed an Anointed One, a Messiah, to deliver them from this Gentile bondage.

The Maccabean resistance to Hellenism

Antiochus IV "Epiphanes" (r. 175-164 BC). Within the larger Greek Seleucid realm – which included the Jewish lands of Judea and Galilee – when Seleucid King Antiochus III died in 187 BC, he was eventually (175

BC) succeeded by his son Antiochus IV ... a truly insane individual who called himself "Epiphanes" ("God in appearance"). Nonetheless, being very ambitious, Antiochus was able to take control of the neighboring – and much-weakened – Ptolemaic Egypt in 170 BC ... but found the Romans blocking his attempt two years later to firm up his control there.

This political failure of Antiochus's in Egypt delivered by the Romans was interpreted in Judea as a sign of serious Seleucid weakness ... which in turn inspired in Judea a political reaction ... one wh ich expelled the Seleucid appointed (and very Hellenistic or pro-Greek) high priest, Menelaus. This act then angered Antiochus in his return from Egypt (168 BC) to the point of attacking, pillaging and slaughtering Jerusalem and its inhabitants (carrying off 10,000 survivors as prisoners) ... and supporting the party of the Hellenized Jews (who had adopted Greek culture and its very un-Jewish ways) by suppressing the religious culture and practices of orthodox Judaism.

The Maccabean Revolt. Then Antiochus rededicated the Temple to himself and forced the Jews to perform sacrifices to him personally, burning or crucifying those that refused.

In 167 BC, Jewish priest Mattathias refused, in fact killed a Jew who was about to offer just such a sacrifice ... and then did the same to the Seleucid general supervising the event. He and his sons then fled to the mountains ... and there began to gather a following of Jews ready to face martyrdom in defending Judaism from the intrusion of Greek pagan culture into their homeland.

The rebels under the leadership of Mattathias's son Judah "Maccabee" (the "Hammer")* were finally able in 164 BC to take Jerusalem ... and cleanse the Jewish temple of the Greek statues and adornments (the event celebrated as Hanukkah) – the first step towards a growing independence from Seleucid authority. This revolt then spread quickly around much of the region of old Judea – aimed as much against Hellenized Jews as against Seleucid authority itself.

But Seleucid General Nicanor was able to retake Jerusalem ... and then lose it again to Judah Maccabee – who executed Nicanor. But once more, the Seleucids made a comeback and Judah and a small group of followers who had not deserted the cause were defeated (Judah actually killed) in 160 BC.

Jonathan and Simon. However, the ongoing dynastic rivalry within the Seleucid dynasty once again offered opportunity to the Maccabees (now

---

*The Hasmonean family or dynasty would be known popularly as the "Maccabees" after Judah took the lead in the family.

under brother Jonathan) to overwhelm the Jewish Hellenized party ... and take and rebuild Jerusalem, cleanse its Temple – and restore conservative Judaism. But at the same time, clever political maneuvering by Jonathan resulted eventually actually in his Seleucid appointment as Jewish High Priest (153 BC) ... the Seleucids, most strangely, even promising him protection against the Hellenized Jews. Then in 150 BC Jonathan was in effect made governor of Judea.

But the civil strife between the Hellenized and Orthodox Jewish parties continued ... with Jonathan gaining ground for the Orthodox Jews. In 145 BC Jonathan saw the opportunity to press forward politically even more – because of a dispute involving both the Ptolemies and the Seleucids. But in 143 BC Jonathan was drawn into a Seleucid diplomatic trap, imprisoned (soon executed), and his army destroyed.

At this point, Jonathan's brother Simon took over the Orthodox cause ... and in 141 BC the Hasmonean family was officially recognized by a Jewish assembly as the rightful rulers of Judea. Two years later the Roman Senate confirmed that decision. Judea was now officially an independent kingdom.

This official status however did not exempt Judea from involvement in the dynastic struggles of the Ptolemies and Seleucids ... or the interests of the expanding Roman Empire ... or their own dynastic conflicts. The Hasmoneans themselves got caught up in much of the military and diplomatic maneuvering that would go on for another century.

John Hyrcanus (r. 134-104 BC). In 134 BC Simon was assassinated by a son-in-law at a banquet ... and nearly all his family executed. Only Simon's son John (Yohanan) escaped the slaughter ... and would eventually make a comeback as a conqueror (and High Priest) ... and also a clever diplomat playing on the difficulties of the Greeks caught up in their continuing dynastic rivalries, plus both the rising power of Parthians (Persians) to the East and Romans to the West. By allying with the Egyptian Ptolemies and the Romans, John was able to extend his Jewish kingdom's boundaries considerably (earning him the title "Hyrcanus"*) ... at the same time rebuilding the defenses of Jerusalem. Also, as High Priest, he relaxed some of the strict rules of Judaism ... in opposition to the Pharisees – and in support of the more "pragmatic" (or secularist) Sadducees.

The last days of the Maccabees (or Hasmoneans)

When John Hyrcanus died in 104 BC, the behavior of his sons revealed clearly how much Greek culture had made its way into Jewish culture. Aristobulus, after imprisoning his mother and three brothers, declared

---

*It is not clear today what exactly that title meant!

himself Jewish king (unacceptable to the Pharisees because he was not of Davidic lineage). His wife Salome Alexandra then convinced him that the one brother he favored, Antigonus, was conspiring against him and he had him murdered ... and then he himself immediately fell ill and died ... only one year into his reign.

Salome then (103 BC) released the remaining brothers from prison and placed her brother Alexander Jannaeus on the Jewish throne ... soon becoming even his wife.

However, although Salome was a supporter of the Pharisee party, her brother/husband Alexander hated them. The Pharisees were very critical of his sadistic and cowardly behavior and his use of Greek mercenaries, which in 93 BC he turned on his people, slaughtering thousands. But this served only to undercut his own rule – even forcing him to flee to the Judean hills. But he regained his throne ... and once again turned on his people, killing some 50,000 of them over a devastating six-year civil war. At one point he was even able to enjoy observing his crucified enemies being forced to watch their wives and children being slaughtered prior to their own deaths.

His ferocious personality however did bring considerable expansion to the kingdom of Judea ... before he himself died of alcoholism in 76 BC. At this point, Salome again took charge ... and in the nine remaining years of her life finally brought both peace and economic development to the kingdom ... as well as the advancement of the Pharisee party.

The Hasmonean Civil War ... and the arrival of the Romans. With her death in 67 BC, the intense rivalry between the "modernizing" Sadducees and the conservative Pharisees took the form of a bitter war between Salome's two sons, the older brother Hyrcanus II, who stepped up as King and High Priest – and supporter of the Pharisee party – and his younger brother Aristobulus II, supporting the Sadducees ... and far more popular among the people.

The feuding Jews appealed to the Roman general and political leader Pompey to help them sort out their civil war. Pompey eventually moved strongly against Aristobulus and his Sadducee supporters when the latter foolishly turned against Pompey. Pompey's forces attacked Jerusalem, destroying its walls and massacring much of the population inside. Pompey then formally ended the Hasmonean monarchy, but at least confirmed Hyrcanus as Jewish Chief Priest ... and Hyrcanus's Idumaean ally, Antipater, as governor of the recently Judaized Edomites or Idumaeans.   And then Pompey returned to Rome.

The rise of the Herodians

The Edomite governor Antipater proved to be a skilled political maneuverer and eventually chose to support Julius Caesar in his war with Pompey. Consequently, in 47 BC, Antipater was given the position of Roman procurator of Judea by Caesar. And Antipater in turn named his sons Herod governor of Galilee (the Judean north) and Phasael governor of Jerusalem (the Judean south).

But when Caesar was assassinated in 44 BC, the new Roman ruler in the East, Cassius, forced the payment of tribute to Rome so heavy that it plunged the Jews into poverty. Antipater's official collector of the tribute, Malichus, was so enraged by his duties (but also personally ambitious) that the following year he had Antipater poisoned.

But in agreement with Caesar's successor, Octavian Caesar, Octavian's friend Marc Antony was assigned the Eastern half of the Roman Empire ... and Antony in turn in 41 BC awarded Antipater's sons Herod and Phasael the rank of tetrarch in their two jurisdictions (Galilee and Jerusalem).

Herod. When in 40 BC Parthians from the east of the Seleucid Empire raided west all the way to the Mediterranean Sea, the Herodians were deposed and the Hasmonean Antigonus was appointed by the Parthians as Judean king.

But now the Hasmonean Antigonus (grandson of Salome) made an attempt to gain the throne against Herod and Phasael, calling on Parthian support in the endeavor ... the Parthians bringing a huge army to Jerusalem in 40 BC. Tragically, Phaseal was lured into negotiations with the Parthians over the matter, but was seized ... and then killed himself.

But Herod escaped to Rome and convinced the Senate to support him in his effort to overthrow the pro-Parthian Hasmoneans. With considerable Roman help, it took him until 37 BC (or 36 BC) to take full command of Judea ... before beginning 34 years of rule as Judean King (under Roman sponsorship).

In those years he would rebuild Jerusalem extensively ... including its walls (that Pompey had destroyed). But most importantly, he would construct a new and much grander Jewish Temple and Temple Mount. This would please the people ... though his taxes needed to pay for these projects did not. In the end, the people's view of Herod weighed strongly to the negative side ... despite his efforts to show himself to be a strong supporter of Judaism. His dependency on Roman power did not help his standing with the people ... nor did his reputation for cruelty (to even his immediate family).

Herod would die in 4 BC (or 3 BC?) ... soon after a calendar-changing event occurred: the birth of Jesus in Bethlehem.

CHAPTER FOUR

THE FORMATION OF CHRISTENDOM

* * *

THE LIFE AND MINISTRY OF JESUS

A word of caution: Original Christianity and today's Christianity are not exactly the same thing. It is important to note up front that the Christianity that Jesus founded and what has come down to us two thousand years later as Christianity are not necessarily the same thing. Over the centuries, the simple Christian faith that Jesus founded evolved into a formal religion, complete with doctrine, offices, rituals, etc. ... which have very much changed the character of Christianity since its early days. Also, different cultural and political influences have profoundly impacted the Christian faith – giving it not only a very much more complex character than it had at its founding but also a huge variation in how that faith has taken on different shapes and behaviors across the world.

Jesus's birth. When was Jesus born? A medieval monk five centuries after Christ sat down and counted the years back from his time to the time he felt that Jesus had to have been born – and that then became to him and to the Christian world since then, "Year One." But more recent scholarship has shown that he miscalculated a bit, for Herod died several years before this Year One – and if Jesus had been born before Herod died (as Matthew tells us) then Jesus might have been born 4 or 5 years prior to Year One. Close enough!

In the four Christian gospels – Matthew, Mark, Luke, and John – that open the Christian "New Testament" of the Bible, we have a very comprehensive reporting on Jesus and his ministry. However, two of those gospels, Mark and John - the earliest, Mark, and then the latest, John, of the four in terms of when they were written – jump straight to the beginning of Jesus' ministry as an approximately 30-year-old, skipping the part relating to his birth and early development. For that, we have to rely on Matthew and Luke. Their narratives on this matter vary somewhat ... due to the purpose behind their composition in the first place.

128

Matthew, focused on answering the Jewish question about the Christian claim that Jesus was indeed the Jewish long-awaited Messiah, starts with a long genealogy, tracing Jesus's roots back to the Davidic Kingship … then brings the narrative up to the times of Herod, Jesus's birth in Bethlehem, the visit to the baby Jesus of the Wise Men from the East (Zoroastrians, most likely), the jealousy of Herod in hearing of this visit to the newly born future Jewish "king" … and the angelic-inspired escape of Jesus's parents, Mary and Joseph, to Egypt to avoid the slaughter Herod enacted upon the male babies of Bethlehem in his effort to kill off any such potential "king." Eventually Mary, Joseph and Jesus return to Judea … but to Galilean Nazareth, where Jesus grows up as presumably a carpenter alongside his father.

Luke seems to be addressing more of a Greco-Roman audience … and starts the story off with the miraculous conception by the unmarried and thus virgin Mary of a child, fathered not by man but by the Spirit of God. Graciously, her fiancé Joseph accepts Mary's strange pregnancy and marries her. But while still pregnant, a decree by Caesar Augustus goes out to have all citizens of the Empire report to their ancestral birthplaces to be counted (a tax-focused census). This brings Joseph and the pregnant Mary to Bethlehem, where Jesus is born … and visited by shepherds made aware of the birth by a heavenly host of angels (the eventual visit of the Wise Men is not mentioned in Luke). When the baby Jesus was then brought to Jerusalem for dedication, Jesus is confirmed by the "righteous and devout" Simeon and the prophetess Anna to be the long-awaited Messiah or Christ (Anointed One). Luke then adds the story of a later visit to Jerusalem by Joseph and Mary and their 12-year-old son, Jesus … who departs company from his parents to find himself in amazing discourse with Jerusalem's rabbis… or as Jesus put things, to be in his "Father's (God's) house."

Jesus's early ministry

From Matthew, Mark and Luke – writers of the "Synoptic" Gospels … meaning, seen through the same eyes or perspective – we get a picture of Jesus's ministry that seems to follow a fairly closely scripted scenario: Jesus's ministry lasted only a single year, in and around Galilee – and his journey to Jerusalem was the closing of that ministry.

However from John, we get the idea that Jesus's ministry lasted over two and possibly as many as three years – on the basis of his many trips to Jerusalem to be present at the important Jewish festivals.

All four gospels point to the start of Jesus's ministry at a time when the appearance of the Messiah was strongly expected. John the Baptist was preaching a baptism-based repentance at the time ... with many wondering if John might be the Messiah. But John affirmed that he was not – but announced that the Messiah was coming. Then when Jesus came to be baptized by John, John found the opportunity to testify that it was indeed Jesus who filled that Messianic role ... as the Lamb of God who takes away the sins of the world. This was confirmed by John then seeing the Holy Spirit descend upon Jesus "like a dove." Thus God the Father, Jesus the Son, and the Holy Spirit completed the "Trinitarian" power in that all-important baptismal moment.

Matthew, Mark and Luke mention – as the follow-up to Jesus's baptism – Satan's wilderness testing of Jesus ... to see if Jesus could be seduced into following the agenda of the quite unspiritual world around him. Despite his "forty days" of fasting, Jesus stood firm in his commitment to follow only the instructions of scripture: to worship and serve God alone, not human ambition.

In his follow up to this episode, Luke tells of Jesus's early ministry to an amazed public ... but also a conflict in Nazareth over serving God versus serving the religious expectations of his own hometown folks – just to drive this point home.

Jesus then began to assemble a special group of followers, the twelve disciples ... men of quite ordinary social status – a number of them simply fishermen. None of these were Biblical scholars or persons of high religious standing ... because Jesus's ministry was not about high theology, but was about the spiritual salvation of the people – the rich and the poor alike.

Jesus's miracles. At this point begin the numerous miraculous healings and other miraculous events ... such as the changing of vats of water into wine, the stilling of the storm, the feeding of the 5,000, even the raising of the dead. These were designed not only to demonstrate that Jesus indeed had the power of God with him ... but also to make even clearer and stronger the messages or teachings that Jesus understood himself called to deliver. Indeed, the gospel of Mark is a running account of a huge number of miracles ... and the gospel of John uses a select number of miracles to illustrate the various aspects of Jesus's teachings.

Jesus's teachings. Actually, Jesus taught as much by example as he did by words or speeches ... especially since the heart of his message, his Good News or gospel, was that it was faith in God, not the works of our hands – no matter how "good" those might be – that God wanted to see coming from us. And faith is more than just excellent ideas brought forward in great oral discourses. It is instilled or inspired by personal example in the face of life's many challenges. Thus Jesus's miracles as the demonstration of the power of authentic faith were key elements of his teachings.

And these miracles were truly amazing ... giving cripples the power to walk again, healing lepers, giving sight to the blind ... and even bringing the well-dead back to life. His disciples were also amazed to see him walk on water to come to their boat ... and he could stop storms with a simple command. Jesus was not a show off. He was only illustrating what could be achieved simply by full faith in the Heavenly Father.

And that faith was directed to a loving God, a Father in heaven – whom Jesus called "Abba" ... a child's name for its "Daddy." Of course such personal familiarity with the mighty Yahweh of Heaven was considered highly scandalous by proper, or orthodox Jews.

In fact, pretty much everything Jesus did was scandalous to the Pharisees and their orthodox followers ... for it was clear to Jesus that the Law that the Pharisees tried religiously to live by was simply summed up for Jesus as the Law of Love ... love of God and the love we have for each other. Religious ritual seemed to be of little importance to Jesus.

And that Law of Love even carried to the point of forgiving the unforgivable ... because if unforgiveness was the law of life, then God himself would find good cause to destroy all of us. None of us are perfect. Thus, when the religious Jews tried to set a moral trap for Jesus ... by bringing before him a woman caught in adultery – to test Jesus to see if his "forgiveness" would lead him to break the Law of Moses on such a taboo matter – Jesus turned the tables against them by inviting the person who was without sin to cast the first stone in their punishment of the woman. The wise ones dropped their stones and quietly retreated ... soon followed by the others. They all knew that they too, at some point were sinners.

Jesus's atonement for all human sin on the Roman cross.   But this ultimately was the reason for Jesus's appearance among us ... to indeed be what John the Baptist called Jesus, the Lamb of God who takes away the sins of the earth. Jesus would be a guilt-offering by God himself for human sin ... all human sin – provided that by faith we took up that freely offered gift. Sadly, as with all Jewish sacrifices of "atonement" designed to wash away our sins, a blood-offering was required. But no birds, no lambs, no oxen would be offered in sacrifice. What would be offered at the altar would be the blood of God's own Son, Jesus. That was more – much, much more – atonement than that secured by the Jews at their altar's offerings of animal blood. Those animal offerings supposedly cleansed a person only for the sins of the previous year. Jesus's blood offering would atone for all sins, for all people, for all times ... so deeply desirous was God to bring us back in full union with him, one that would last for all eternity.

But the sacrifice was not to be made at a Temple altar ... but on the most humiliating of means of torture and death – the Roman cross. Jesus himself was aware that this was where his ministry was ultimately headed ... finding his disciples, especially the straightforward Peter, in no mood to see this happen. But at the time, this act of atonement by Jesus was way beyond their understanding.

And thus it happened ... during the Jewish celebration of the Passover. Jesus was arrested and brought before the Roman governor, Pilate ... who actually did not understand why the Jewish authorities were so fully committed to ending Jesus's life. Most ironically, these Jews were themselves not understanding that, unknowingly acting as agents of Satan in bringing down this Son of God, they were indeed conducting the most important atoning sacrifice ever! Finally, bowing to Jewish pressure, Pilate went ahead with Jesus's crucifixion (death on a cross).

The resurrected Lord. But imagine the shock when some women came to the tomb a couple of days later – only to find the tomb empty. Then when the disciples heard the news, they too came to inspect things. When they returned to their upper room (trying to stay away from the authorities that most likely would be looking for them as followers of Jesus), first one of his women followers, then the majority of his disciples found themselves encountered by a "risen Lord." This crazy encounter hit them deeply. Then over the following days, there were more appearances (Paul said as many as 500 individuals encountered the risen Lord ... as well as later Paul himself did). This was such a testimony of the power of heaven to shape life.

But there was more to come. After a 40-day period of such encounters, Jesus gathered his disciples, and told them to stay alert. God's own Holy Spirit was about to come to them – and lead them forward by divine design... no longer as disciples but as apostles ... ones "sent" out to spread the gospel. And when that happened on Pentecost, Peter and the others were indeed transformed into powerful evangelists. Christianity was about to explode out onto the Roman world!

✷ ✷ ✷

THE GOSPEL IS BROUGHT TO THE GRECO-ROMAN WORLD

Early carriers of the Gospel to that larger world

Certainly at first that world that the apostles supposed they were to evangelize (spread the "good news") was their Jewish world. Jesus was the Messiah the Jews had long been waiting for. But now it was no longer Jesus that orthodox Judaism was opposed to, it was this spreading "Way" of Jesus as the Christ, the Messiah, the Jewish savior – being spread by his followers. Thus the orthodox community hit back (although the number of Jewish converts was significant.

Paul (mid-first century AD). A major opponent and persecutor of this new movement was Saul of Tarsus, a highly educated Pharisee ... who dedicated himself to eradicating this heretical Jewish movement. But he was on the road to Damascus when he encountered – and was blinded in the encounter – by the appearance of the risen Lord. Finally recovering from his infirmity, he found his heart deeply changed (including the name he would now go by, "Paul") ... and now became one of the most active of the evangelists ... starting up Christian fellowships (or churches) here and there. And he did so across the Greco-Roman Gentile world as readily as he did among his fellow Jews. In fact, Paul played a major role in this cultural expansion of this new faith.

In fact, his letters to the various Christian churches – especially to the churches in Corinth and Rome – would play a huge role in explaining the basic theology behind the Jesus event described in the four Gospels. Indeed, his explanations would basically become the doctrines on which subsequent Christianity would rest.

His own experience made it clear to him that receiving the favor of God's salvation was hardly an earned entitlement. When God in Christ encountered – and thus "saved" – Paul, Paul was doing anything but trying to secure for himself such Christian favor. The choice for Paul to become a Christian was clearly God's ... not Paul's – although Paul certainly accepted – even ultimately celebrated greatly – the life-altering intervention by God. Thus Paul saw that God himself "elected" or chose those "predestined" to divine salvation. Salvation was God's choice ... not man's.

Thus he also lamented deeply the fact that not all of his Jewish compatriots were destined to receive what he received. But to Paul, such matters were God's, not his, to determine ... although certainly he would do his best to at least spread the good news as widely as he could. But how that evangelism would be received – whether it would be accepted or rejected – was a matter of the spiritual realm, both the hearer's spirit and God's Spirit ... and the way those two realms came to relate to each other.

The Gospel of John also justifies a bit of a closer inspection. Its high level of Greek thought seems strange for someone once just an Aramaic-speaking fisherman. But the gospel was written late in John's life ... a prisoner on the Isle of Patmos (the rest of Jesus's disciples presumably had been executed). John probably at that point at least enjoyed the company of a younger Greek scholar or two ... who, in their dialogues, helped John

    A Moral History of Western Society (Volume One)

develop in both his gospels and personal letters this high level of Greek thought. At the same time, the details by which John narrated the various miracles performed by Jesus, make it clear that John was intimately familiar with Jesus and his doings.

In a very Platonic and Stoic sense, John opens his gospel by identifying Jesus with the Divine Logos ... the source of all creation – in other words, with God himself. In Jesus, God is brought to earth to illustrate his concern for human life ... especially those bypassed in life's status competition (the poor, the crippled, and the outsider).

But the Jewish authorities were not buying what Jesus was selling ... seeing Jesus as just another one of the many that had followers claiming Messianic status for their leaders – whose movements all seemed inevitably to come to nothing. Nicodemus, a member of the Sanhedrin or Jewish Council was curious, but John tells us that he came at night to inquire of Jesus if he was the One – at night because he did not want to be seen visiting Jesus. And it is John that narrates at length Roman Governor Pilate's detailed interrogation of Jesus ... to determine exactly what it was that Jesus was guilty of – by Roman law, of course. Although finding nothing in the process, he simply decided to let a whipped up Jewish mob decide the matter for him. And thus by "the will of the people" Jesus was sentenced to death. These key details (and others) are not found in the synoptic Gospels – Matthew, Mark, and Luke.

The actual process by which these writings were "canonized." Actually, the amount of material and the follow-up commentary on Jesus's ministry was quite large. Very popular early on were Tatian's Diatessaron (a Gospel "harmony"), and the widely-read Shepherd of Hermas. But over time they would lose importance ... because they did not claim to be written by one of the apostles – an increasingly important criterion in deciding the authoritative nature of these many Christian writings. Mark and Luke however were considered authoritative, not because they had been apostles – like Matthew and John – but because they certainly were close disciples of such apostles, Mark serving under Peter in Rome, and Luke serving with Paul in his long ministry.

But some groups, in particular the Gnostics,* developed their own

---

*Gnostics (from "ones who know") viewed the cosmos as a supposedly dark, fallen second order of life created by a mere secondary order god: Yahweh. True God (not Yahweh) could not have made such a flawed creation. Further, they believed that there were two orders of Christians: the spiritual and the worldly. The spiritual or the saved (or "elect") were privileged spiritual beings who were raised above this flawed world and accorded special entrance into the secret world of original light, where God was found in truth. Moreover, such Gnostic "spirituals" were freed from the moral requirements of this darkened world of flesh (and many acted accordingly).

literary tradition – deeply shaped by Greek or Eastern mysticism ... writings clearly rejected by the more conservative or orthodox Christian groups. Eventually bitter controversy would result. It would not be until three centuries after Christ – when Christianity actually became endorsed by Roman authorities, that these disputes as to what should actually constitute the "canon"* of Scripture would finally be resolved – somewhat.

Christianity and Judaism go their separate ways

Besides the record of numerous claimants to Messiahship who proved to be grand disappointments to the Jewish community ... Jesus didn't even pretend to be what any supposed Messianic candidate should measure up to by way of character and deeds. This did not help his cause with the more rigorous of the Jewish militants ... who, for instance, found Barabbas – the Jewish rebel leader – more to their liking than Jesus.

Judaism had numerous sub-groups, with varying religious tendencies. But Jewish Christianity – as it was understood to be in its early days – just wandered too far off course as a Jewish sect. They ignored the rigors of the halakhic midrash ... strict in the matters of the washing of hands, about when and what to eat, the necessity of observing required fasts, burial restrictions, etc.

And the idea of Jesus dying and then coming back to life all seemed to be derived from a Greek or pagan world. Such an event made no sense to someone with a Jewish or Semitic mindset. True, Judaism understood the power of a blood sacrifice as part of the way their sins were atoned for with God. But human sacrifice ... by one even claiming to have god-qualities? That seemed more Orphic or Dionysian than Jewish in nature.

And the Christian talk of God in Three Persons also sounded more Greek than Jewish. A Greek mind would have no trouble coming to such a complex understanding. But to a Jew, this was just more paganism ... pure heresy or blasphemy on part of those "Jews" making such claims about Jesus.

Then there was the crisis of AD 66, when the Jews – tired of Rome's economic and social oppression – rose up in rebellion ... and a very bloody Judeo-Roman war resulted. But the Christians did not join the action – finding sanctuary in Pella (in today's Jordan) when Roman troops were sent

---

*The word "canon" is of Greek origins, meaning a rule or measuring stick. Thus for a particular writing to be considered part of the canon (being "canonical"), it had to measure up to a certain standard of authenticity. Deciding what material was canonical and what was not was a matter of great importance to the Christian community ... for Christians felt it vitally important that Scripture be entirely "God breathed" ... and not be just a human by-product – no matter how philosophical or even "useful" it might appear to be.

to crush the Jewish rebellion. In the eyes of the patriotic Jews, the passivity of the Christians in the face of this Roman assault – especially with the total destruction of the Jerusalem Temple in AD 70 – definitely qualified the Christians in the eyes of their fellow Jews as traitors. Christians were thus considered to be people who should be despised by any good Jew.

Indeed, in around AD 90, Jewish authorities made it clear to the Roman authorities, that Christianity was not to be considered a recognized Jewish sect … and to receive none of the protections that Judaism enjoyed under the Roman law

Yet many Jews did receive the gospel of Jesus Christ as their new faith, their new understanding of their own personal relationship with God. But these tended to be Hellenized Jews … especially among those joining more recently the Jewish community – which was doing its own form of evangelism at the time.

Indeed, with time, Christianity was finding an easier fit in the Greco-Roman world (when not persecuted by suspicious Roman authorities) … becoming more and more Greco-Roman in character and less and less Jewish in the process.

Early Greco-Roman church organization

As Christian communities began to develop across the Greco-Roman world, each local Christian community established its own structure for fellowship –all of them having one or more (usually several) overseers (*episkopos*) or elders (*presbuteros*)* to lead them. As defined in 1st Timothy (Chapter 3), an episkopos was one of the congregation, a person of excellent repute whom the congregation could rely on as a trustworthy overseer.

Some of the churches were recognized as apostolic churches – that is, founded by one or another of the original apostles – and thus their governing structure commanded regional respect (Jerusalem until 70, Rome, Antioch, Smyrna, Ephesus and others).

The early definers and defenders ("apologists") of the faith

Quite ironically, the intense persecution of Christianity served the faith by tending to exemplify those who, at the cost of their own lives, remained true

---

*"Bishop" is a shortening of the Greek word *episkopos*, meaning "overseer" or "one who watches over" … rendered into Latin as *episcopus*. And the word "Episcopalian" means simply a religious community directed by a bishop. "Priest" is a shortening of the Greek word *presbuteros* or "presbyter," originally meaning simply "elder" – an older person of some degree of wisdom that reputedly comes with age. "Presbyterian" means simply a religious community directed by just such elders.

to the faith. This actually served to attract to the faith people hungry to find a life of true integrity. This gave the church some outstanding defenders and definers (termed "apologists") of the faith – presented before a Roman world taking greater and greater note of this new faith … by both those supportive of – and those extremely hostile to – the new Christian faith.

Thus there was Clement, Bishop or Presbyter of Rome (late first century), offering counsel in his *Letter to the Corinthians* (AD 95?) about leadership, and avoiding certain doctrines such as Docetism.* Then there was Ignatius, Bishop of Antioch, who on his way to Rome to be executed (early 100s) wrote a number of letters advising also on the matter of selecting leaders and avoiding false doctrines. There was Polycarp, a disciple of the apostle John and Bishop of Smyrna, whose martyrdom as an old man in around 160 became a narrative told widely around the Christian world. And there was Papias, Bishop of Hierapolis, a friend of Polycarp, who wrote five books (only excerpts survive) explaining the authenticity of such gospels as Mark and Matthew … and explaining further facts about Jesus and his disciples.

With time, the work of the apologists became quite sophisticated as philosophical treatises about Christian doctrine … especially as ideas about what constituted the best version of Christianity became quite numerous.

Justin "Martyr" (beheaded in 165 rather than sacrifice to the Roman gods) came to Christianity by way of Stoicism, Aristotelianism, Pythagoreanism, then Platonism. The latter, Platonism, proved to be a strong bridge for him into the Christian faith … Justin agreeing with John the importance of understanding Jesus as the *Logos*. Indeed, he felt that Christianity ultimately was the summation of all that Greek philosophy was striving to discover.

There was Irenaeus, Bishop of Lyons (c. 130-202), a disciple of Polycarp – also later influenced deeply by Justin's philosophy. Irenaeus was particularly focused on Gnosticism's claims to have exclusive insights into the nature and meaning of Christ … which Irenaeus refuted with the counterclaim that the apostles were quite clear and quite united in their reporting about such matters. And there was nothing very secretive about Christianity … as the faith was presented quite clearly in the four Gospels and the other apostolic writings well-recognized across the Christian realm. By the same token, he was very critical of Montanism.†

----

*According to the Docetists, Jesus could not have been truly human – for that which is of God could never have taken the flawed form of a creature of this world. To have actually been flesh would have made him captive to evil. Thus Jesus only appeared to have been such a worldly creature.

†Montanism was Gnostic in character. This movement began as a "New Prophecy": as part of the continuing role of the *Paraclete* (Holy Spirit) in further developing the life of the church. It was guided heavily by the ecstatic utterances

Two individuals, contemporaries – but of different cultural settings – were the Greek apologist Clement of Alexandria (c. 150-215) and the Latin apologist Tertullian (c. 160-225). The separate directions that Greek and Latin thinking were taking at this point was quite apparent in the writings of these two apologists.

Clement basically agreed with Justin about Christianity being the fulfillment of Greek philosophy. And he disagreed strongly with the Gnostics, who were becoming quite influential in Egypt ... especially with their quite mystical view on things ... especially the "secret knowledge" ("gnosis") behind life's dynamics. To Clement, true Christian knowledge came in the form of ethical living and the disciplined contemplation of God. But Clement himself actually shared some of Gnosticism's negative views about natural life ... about its inherent darkness ... views similar to Gnostic Docetism. Clement believed that Jesus, being of God, was himself above such things. Thus Jesus surely did not need to eat, drink and sleep like mere mortals – but did so only so that his disciples might more easily follow him and his teachings.

Tertullian, being both trained in the law and a Latin Carthaginian, evidenced strongly the Roman love of order. As a religious legalist – and a teacher (apparently never an officer of the church ... but a very active writer) he felt it very important to give definition to Christianity along some very strict doctrinal or orthodox lines – lest it wander off into one of the many heresies impacting the faith. Monarchianism was particularly troublesome to Tertullian ... because of its "Unitarian" views of the Godhead.* Tertullian was very clear in his writings about the Trinitarian nature of God ... impacting strongly subsequent Latin theology of the Western world. But he was also something of a Christian "Montanist," very admiring of its Stoic moral rigor. And later, when the question of returning to office repentant Christians who had once bowed to Caesar in order to save themselves from execution, Tertullian could be quite unforgiving ... seeing no way back into the faith of "back sliders."

Then there was Origen (c. 185-254), a teacher at the catechetical school (instructed those about to enter the church) of Alexandria – until a disagreement with the Alexandrian bishop caused Origen to move to

---

of Montanus (from whom it got its name), and the female "prophets" Priscilla and Maximilla. It was also apocalyptic: viewing Phrygia (a Roman province in Asia Minor) as being the New Jerusalem of the End Times – which we were soon approaching. It too held a very rigoristic view of the Christian life: fasting, celibacy, martyrdom – and looked down on those Christians who were less rigoristic than they.

*Monarchianism opposed the view of God as *Logos*, seeing God simply and only in the form of the Father in Heaven ... rejecting the idea of Jesus as God or the idea of a Holy Spirit ... thus strictly "Unitarian" in theology.

Palestine and continue his work there. As an ascetic, Origen lived a simple life. But as a teacher he was also a very prolific expositor of the Bible – carefully studying Scripture verse by verse. But being a Greek, he tended to see such matters less as "fact" (as Tertullian did) and more as allegory ... taking the reader deeper into Scripture as a spiritual task to go to the deeper meaning of things.* Thus he also understood the death of Jesus on the cross as a way of bringing commoners to salvation. But for the more enlightened soul, Origen took the rather Socratic/Platonic view that proper intellectual or spiritual contemplation could lift the human soul more directly to God. Such views would later get him and his writings in trouble with later Christian Orthodoxy.

An individual who would have to address this question of the return to the faith of those who, out of fear, had bent a knee to Rome, was Cyprian, Bishop of Carthage (martyred in 258). Cyprian was of a well-born patrician family who came to the faith because of its well-demonstrated high moral qualities. As Bishop of Carthage (actually, soon after his conversion to Christianity in 245), he would have to answer Christians bitter over the restoration of fellow Christians – most notably bishops and presbyters – who had "apostatized" or folded in the face of the horrible Decian persecutions of 249-251. Cyprian himself escaped death only by being able to go into hiding ... giving opponents who resented his fast rise to office something to hold against him. But Cyprian recognized quite well that, at this point, the Church needed not religious rigorousness, but unity and forgiveness. Furthermore, Cyprian was very clear that it was not moral rigor that made the Christian bishop a leader worthy of devout support ... but simply the office itself – filled by sinners forgiven by God. And likewise, it was the bishops, not the most rigoristic individuals ("confessors"), that had the right to restore the apostates. His views on these very matters would serve greatly to strengthen the move of the church into a more "apostolic" or hierarchical order.

Then there was Anthony of Egypt (251-356) who moved from a life of asceticism (age 20) to a life fully isolated as a hermit living in the Egyptian desert (age 35) – in order to struggle against a hard-pressing Satan ... and to look to the perfecting of his own spiritual life. So exemplary was his rigorous life that others – including Athanasius who would later write about it in his *Life of Anthony* – took great note of his actions ... inspiring a large number of ascetics to gather around him in the desert in order to live a similar highly-disciplined spiritual life. Later Anthony would leave the desert ... to instruct others in the monastic life, even organizing a monastery

---

*This was a principle well established in Greek learning and used widely in the study of the ancient Greek legends. Thus Philo used this in his commentaries on the Jewish Scriptures. However, this put Origen in strong distinction to the attitudes of the more literalist Tertullian on the matter!

(Dayr Mari Antonios) on a mountain near the Nile (still standing today).

✳ ✳ ✳

CONSTANTINE AND THE "ROMANIZATION" OF CHRISTIANITY

Constantine's rise to power

We return to the point where we left off in the earlier account of the Roman emperors. Things were very confusing for the Romans as there were claims and counterclaims going back and forth as to who was emperor … and in what capacity.

Maxentius. PPart of the dynamic was set by Maxentius, son of the Eastern Augustus Maximinus. Angry that he had been left out of the 308 deal – Maxentius accordingly had made a move (not very popular ultimately) to take control of Italy … giving him what he thought entitled him to designate himself as Western "Augustus." Meanwhile, over in the East, and feeling left out in all this, Maximinus decided to enter into an alliance with his son Maxentius to press forward Maxentius's claim to some form of imperial title. Soon wars – one after another – broke out across all of the heartland of the Roman empire.

Christian persecution. In all of this confusion, the Christian community was beginning to play an increasingly important role in Roman affairs. The horrible persecution under Diocletian – and possibly even worse under Galerius – had simply sifted out the weak-of-heart among the Christians, and left the remainder strengthened in character – and enhanced in stature among increasingly admiring Romans. As already noted, just before his death in 311 Galerius had decreed an end to the persecution of the Christians – although Maximinus ignored the decree and continued the intense Christian persecution in the East. On the other hand, in Italy Maximinus's son Maxentius attempted to woo the Christians to his side by allowing the Christians to elect a new Bishop of Rome.

Constantine. But Constantine was not unsympathetic to the Christian cause himself. His father had been tolerant of them as emperor in the West and his mother Helena was a fully-practicing Christian. Constantine himself seemed to have some interest in the faith – though at what point and how much early on is difficult today to determine.

The Battle of Milvian Bridge. In 312, Italy became the scene of the worst of the encounters ... as Constantine crossed the Alps to attack Maxentius in northern Italy. Step by step, Maxentius was pushed back. Along the Tiber in October of that year, just outside of Rome at the Milvian Bridge, the two forces took their final stand.

According to the account of the contemporary Christian historian Eusebius (the story varies slightly from one ancient source to another), Constantine went into battle with a distinct Christian symbol painted on the shield of each of his soldiers, presumably the *labarum*, made up of the superimposed Greek letters *X* (*Chi*) and *P* (*Rho*), representing the first two letters of Χρίστος, that is, the name *Christos* or Christ. Constantine told his troops that Christ (or a heavenly voice), in a dream the night before the battle, had instructed him to go into battle with that painted on their shields ... under the command *en touto nika* – "in this conquer."[*]

And conquer they did. The result the next day was a rout of Maxentius's army – despite the fact that his army was twice the size of Constantine's army. Maxentius was drowned in the Tiber amidst the panic. And Constantine was now able to enter Rome, an Augustus in fact as well as in name.

And very importantly, this event would ultimately be interpreted as a battle waged by the Christian God as well as by the Roman legions themselves.

The Edict of Milan (313) and the final path to sole rulership. The next year Constantine and Licinius (Licinius, although actually the Western Augustus, found himself in charge of huge regions of the Eastern Empire as well) met in Milan and formed an alliance, sealed with the marriage of Constantine's half-sister to Licinius (March 313). At the same time, they jointly published the Edict of Milan, announcing the end to all religious persecution in the Empire and restoring all the property seized during the Diocletian/Galerian persecutions.

But Licinius had to leave abruptly for the East as news reached him that the Eastern Emperor Maximinus was organizing a revolt against him. Maximinus was defeated (April 313), leaving Licinius finally unchallenged in the East. With Maximinus out of the way, Licinius was able to take full command of the East ... and agreed to let Constantine have command of the West.

But politics being politics, it was inevitable that these two political giants would fall into conflict. Thus over the next ten years they fought, then found a way to peace, then returned to battle, etc. On and on it went,

---

[*]ἐν τούτῳ vika ... later translated into Latin as *in hoc signo vinces* (by this sign shall you conquer).

one thing after another stirring a new round in their contention. Meanwhile, Licinius also found himself deeply caught up in battle with the Sassanid Persian Empire to the East of the Roman Empire ... and Constantine the same with the troublesome Sarmatians and Goths to the North and East ... Constantine going after them into territory that Licinius considered to be his realm. This then provoked an all-out war between the two emperors (324) ... fought at the very walls of Byzantium and then at Chrysopolis ... where Licinius was defeated and imprisoned – and executed the following year. Constantine was thus the sole ruler of the Roman Empire.

The first Christian emperor –
and the foundation of "Christendom"

But Constantine's interest in Christianity now became a much greater matter than mere toleration of the faith. Clearly, Constantine saw in this faith the foundations of a revitalized moral order that had been lacking in Rome for centuries ... and that Diocletian's recent efforts to put a stronger order under Rome through political reform at the top had brought no particular improvement – perhaps even a worsening of the very divisive political situation Rome had been experiencing for decades ... even centuries. No ... Constantine was deeply determined to bring Rome back to good order through the virtues of the Christian faith. And basically he succeeded.

That meant having to decide what parts of the widely diverse doctrines associated with Christianity were to be upheld as critical to this new Roman-Christian order ... and what parts were to be dismissed – even suppressed. After all ... the central issue for Constantine was about social order.

But other influences that came from outside of the original founding of the faith in Jewish Palestine should possibly be accommodated – especially in the way they spoke clearly to the hearts of the commoner Christians. While these stood outside of the canon of Scripture, they certainly could be accommodated by some degree of religious "expansion" of the original faith.

Constantine as *Pontifex Maximus*. Constantine made it very clear early on in his rule that he was to be seen as more than just a political ruler. He took for himself the title *Pontifex Maximus* ("High Priest") – not however as someone intending to lead in some form of traditional temple sacrifices ... but simply and clearly as the ultimate "Protector of the Faith." If Rome was to be a religious empire as well as a political empire, it would have to be made clear that he was as much the head of the religious portion as he was of the political portion of the Empire. That was very Roman of him. But what that had to do with Jesus was not entirely clear.

The Donatist controversy: works versus grace. Within six months of his victory at Milvian Bridge Constantine was asked by the Donatists in North Africa to intervene in their dispute with "apostate" bishops (ones who under the pressure of the Diocletian persecutions had denied their faith). The Donatists refused to recognize the authority of these bishops to administer the sacraments (ordination, baptism, the eucharist or Lord's Supper, last-rites, etc.). In a way the question was one of works versus grace, or successful self-discipline versus forgiveness for failure. The vast majority of the *catholic* ("universal") or *orthodox* ("correct-thinking")* bishops were opposed to the stance of the Donatists. The Catholic/Orthodox view favored the forgiveness of the fallen bishops. Forgiveness was, after all, one of the key principles of the faith.

Constantine finally did intervene in 314 – but took the Catholic/ Orthodox position and found in favor of the compromised but restored bishops against the Donatists, and ordered the Donatists to submit to the authority of these bishops.

But the Donatists would have none of it. The Donatists had, after all, stood the test of persecution and could see no reason to bow to the authority of those they saw as having conveniently (albeit briefly) denied their faith in order to save themselves from the wrath of Diocletian.   Moreover, the Donatists had faced the hostility of emperors before without yielding – and they felt no need to start doing so at this point.

The results of defying the emperor – even a Christian emperor – had predictable results. In 317 Constantine sent troops to North Africa to force the Donatists into submission to his decision, thus setting off the first instance of Christians persecuting other Christians because of differences in the way they interpreted their faith. A large number of Donatists were banished – though ultimately even this did not bring the Donatists into compliance, so tough was their stance. Indeed, it was not until the Muslim conquest of North Africa in the 600s that the Donatist movement finally died out!

The "Nicene" decision: Trinitarianism rather than Unitarianism.
Then there was the matter – one that would never really go away over Christianity's long history – of Trinitarianism versus Unitarianism.

A works-versus-faith dispute had developed between Alexander, Bishop of Alexandria, and a presbyter (priest) of his, Arius. Arius was a strong advocate of the Monarchian or "Unitarian" position ... which saw Jesus as attaining divine or godly status only upon his arrival in heaven –

---

*Both terms, "catholic" and "orthodox," were originally more or less interchangeable – until gradually the term the word "catholic" tended to refer to the Latin-speaking Roman church in the West and the term "orthodox" tended to refer to the Greek-speaking Roman church in the East.

as something of a reward for his Messianic work while on earth. In other words, while on earth Jesus was not part of the godhead, not really the Logos of John – but simply a Messiah or Christ called by God to exemplify the perfect Christian life. Jesus was therefore not a God fully able to pay for the sins of all humankind on a Roman cross – but simply an outstanding moral example. True, he now could be considered something of a god … although of derivative or lesser standing than the sole eternal God of heaven. And as for the Holy Spirit … Arius as a Unitarian had little thought on the matter – since it was by man's own decision, rather than by some kind of intervention of a Holy Spirit, that the test of faith was to be lived out. Righteous works of a holy man or woman – following the high moral example set by Jesus as the Christ – was, to the Unitarian such as Arian, what Christianity was ultimately all about.

In response to Arius, Alexander requested a hearing on the matter before Constantine, resulting in the Council of Nicaea of 325 … Constantine presiding.   Alexander and the "Trinitarians" saw "God" in three different manifestations or "persons": God the Father, God the Son, and God the Holy Spirit – "Three in One" … all of a single God-nature, but relating to humankind in three different ways or roles.

Thus the Jesus that died on the cross was not merely a morally perfect individual but indeed God himself. The sins of a good man – even a perfect man – could possibly atone or pay for the sins of others … at least a few others. But only a God dying on that cross could pay for the sins of all humankind.

And as all humans are guilty of "original sin" – inherited from their ancient ancestors – sin would be a problem they would struggle with all their lives on earth. No one was perfect … as Christ made clear when he rescued the woman purposely caught in the act of adultery (John 8:1-11) by challenging those without sin to throw the first stone in her death sentence. But recognizing their own sinfulness, the accusers, starting with the oldest and wisest of the gathered "enforcers" quietly exited from the scene. Thus to the Trinitarians – we are all sinners … despite our efforts to atone for our sins or redeem ourselves through our good works. Only God can offer such atonement.

Furthermore, faith itself is not earned or achieved through human effort … but solely as a gift of God given to us … a wonderful mystery of God's pure grace (Romans 8). Claiming that such faith is a human achievement is a sad attempt to substitute human works for God's grace.

In any case, there was no way that Arius was going to win that contest … for the vast majority of the Christian bishops and presbyters or priests were strongly supportive of the Trinitarian view. And for good reason. Holy Scripture (the Bible) clearly supported the Trinitarian understanding of the

Divine Dynamic!

Thus resulted the Nicene decision ... and its Nicene Doctrine – and what is often described as "Nicene Christianity" ... another term for Trinitarianism.

But the problem was that while the better-instructed of the Christian community (the priests or clergy) would be able to come to such a complex Trinitarian understanding of things, many of the commoner Christians could not – or even would not. To them, religion was a social duty ... necessary for the good order in their lives. Anything beyond that was too "intellectual," too lofty, for serious usefulness in a person's daily life.

And being either of Greek, Roman, or even Semitic cultural background would also play a role in this Trinitarian-versus-Unitarian contest. The Greeks, already of something of a mystic mindset, had less difficulty following Trinitarian logic. The Romans perhaps had some difficulties in understanding such matters ... but since their ruling authorities supported the Trinitarian doctrine, being good Romans, they did so as well. But the Semitics of Syria, Palestine and Arabia would find themselves highly resistant to the complexities of Trinitarianism (also too "Greek" for their tastes). And later, when the German tribes would be absorbed into the Roman order, at first they readily accepted Christianity – but in the simpler Unitarian form. It would take some time before their tribal leaders converted to Trinitarianism – with their tribes then being brought into Trinitarianism along with them.

The Christian "add-ons"

Although these next items did not obtain official recognition as "Christian" during Constantine's days, their roots were there ... in fact actually even before Constantine. And two of these innovative items would soon come to play a huge role in the understanding of the Christians as to the dynamics of their own faith: the adoration of the saints (all the apostles, plus a number of outstanding early Christian martyrs and leaders) ... and the special reverence directed to Jesus's mother Mary.

No doubt these items would develop at the heart of the Christian faith ... because of the way in the 300s, step by step, pagan worship was outlawed – particularly under subsequent emperors. In earlier times, the Roman citizens could look to one or another pagan deity for help in this or that matter ... from business, to travel, to love life, to family support, etc. Also, very important in the religious thinking of the Romans, Greeks, Egyptians and others was one or another version of the "Earth Mother," out of whose womb all life – whether plant, animal or human – came forth (Isis, Demeter, Astarte, Aphrodite, etc.). Earth Mother, in whatever form, was an object of deep affection by a people hungry for a warmer relationship with the world around them.

But the banning of these pagan religious items by the new Christian order left hearts among the commoners hungry for the personal support that these deities once offered.

Jesus himself once offered that satisfaction. But now it seemed that Jesus existed mostly to appoint and confirm (like the old Senate and the Pretorian Guard) the appointment and authority of the emperors ... Jesus now something of a *Christus Rex* (Christ the King). This made him more distant ... less accessible than he was in the first days of the church.

Mary - the Blessed Virgin. Thus "the Virgin Mary" – Jesus's mother – came to fill that emotional gap between the realm of heaven and the believer on earth ... something like the former Earth Mothers. Actually, something of this tendency had started even before Constantine's establishment of Christianity as Rome's new moral-religious foundations. For instance, in the late second century (late 100s), Irenaeus commented about how Mary played a key role in the act of salvation.

But there was nothing scriptural about this – in that, except for Luke's beautiful narration of Mary's pregnancy and Jesus's birth in Bethlehem, Holy Scripture itself makes little mention of Mary beyond the birthing of Jesus. In the course of Jesus's ministry, other Marys – Mary the Sister of Martha and Mary Magdalene – get most of the Mary attention. Indeed, at one point when Jesus's mother and brothers were at the door, ready to take Jesus into their own care because, following the opinion of others, they believed that Jesus was acting most peculiarly in his actions and teachings (Mark 3:21) ... Jesus responded to their arrival by announcing that those that followed him were actually his mother and brothers.* That does not exactly put his mother on the plateau where she would later be placed.

Indeed, over time not only was Mary the one more likely to be prayed to, but her virtue was considered to be so great that she came even to be seen as "co-redeemer" with Jesus ... able to bring salvation to the sinners as readily as Jesus. And eventually she would become even not only *Christotokos* – mother of Christ – but even *Theotokos* - Mother of God.

Churches would eventually be dedicated to Mary ... and in those churches, pictures of her holding the harmless baby Jesus in her protective arms hung at their altars – as well as in the homes of the faithful. Thus it was that she seemed to loom even larger than Jesus in the way she offered counsel, protection, and even salvation to the faithful. Prayers to Mary (the "Hail Mary") were the focus of the act of redemption to be offered by the sinner – in the constant need for the cleansing of their sins.

The adoration of the saints. Likewise, Christians found themselves

---

*Matthew 12:46-50; Mark 3:31-35; Luke 8:19-21.

quietly praying to former "saints" that were reputed to possess miraculous powers in this matter or that – in the same way that the pagan deities had been prayed to. There was nothing illegal about this – though it too had no Scriptural warrant. But indeed, since it seemed to serve the emotional needs of the people so readily, it became a regular feature of Christian life over the centuries. And here too, churches would be dedicated to, and thus be named after, this saint or that saint.

The crucifix versus the empty cross and tomb. As far as the Christian cross went – as the central logo of the Christian faith – the image of Jesus nailed there in torturous pain served as a ready reminder of the cruel results of human sin. Jesus had to suffer extreme agony because of human sinfulness. Thus images of Jesus on the cross (the crucifix) were there more to remind or convict us of our sins and sinful natures ... than to present the good news or Gospel of God's grace in offering divine atonement or payment for exactly those same sins. Later reformers would empty the cross – as a rather different symbolic reminder (like the empty tomb) of Jesus's victory over sin and death – and the resultant liberation of the truly faithful from the clutches of sin.

The "Romanization" of the Church. In accordance with the typical Roman love of excellent social order, the Church itself underwent constitutional reform ... not only of its doctrines but also in the development of its organizational structure. Not surprisingly, a hierarchy of priests developed, ranging from the lower order of lay priests and deacons, upward through the district bishops, and above them the regional archbishops, and finally, at the head of it all, the emperor. Eventually, of the group of archbishops, five would emerge to dominate the array of bishops and archbishops: the patriarchs* of Rome, Constantinople, Alexandria, Antioch and Jerusalem. Every effort of the five was made to keep their responsibilities cooperative ... although different political priorities in different parts of the Empire would eventually cause these five religious bureaucracies to move along more independent lines.

Quite naturally, the assignment of various powers to the Church's clergy became central to the whole Christian religious process. Faith of the believer in Jesus Christ was increasingly replaced by the atoning gifts offered to the faithful by the officers of the Church. Priests and bishops came to be able to grant tremendous salvation powers through their worship rituals

---

*Also known as Fathers of the faith ... although the Father or Papa or "Pope" of Rome was considered the "first among equals" – because he was supposedly the inheritor of the legacy or "keys" of the first bishop of Rome, Saint Peter – Jesus's preeminent disciple.

and in their administration of the "sacraments" to their communicants: formalized prayer and worship, required confession, the celebration of the Holy Eucharist (Holy Communion of Christ's bread and wine ... although the wine part would later be open only to the clergy themselves), the rite of marriage, baptism, the last rites before death, etc.   Thus it was that the Church – not Christ – offered the faithful the salvation that would open for them at their death the doors to heaven. This too would become a critical matter of contention that the later reformers would demand that the Church address.

And worship itself took on the ritualistic character of Rome's former temple worship ... complete with the dramatic entrance of lavishly dressed church officers, chanting and burning incense as they moved towards the elevated altar at the front of the church ... where they then would seat themselves in front of an attentive congregation, leading that congregation through the various rituals they were required to perform.

And so things went – as Christianity opened these new religious paths to go down ... ultimately inspiring (many centuries later) protesters or "Protestants" to call for reform of just such church doctrines and practices ... to bring them back into alignment with the more informal and collegial – yet carefully defined – Scriptural standards of the early Church. But the growing movement for such reforms (the Protestant Reformation) would be deeply resisted by the established Church ... and ugly war would result. But details of that huge moral struggle are reserved for a later chapter.

Constantine's impact on Christianity. Maybe the matter is put better as Christianity's impact on Constantine. We know that he and his mother Helena were responsible for the building of many churches ... though in naming them after various departed saints, he was following a common pagan Roman practice of naming their temples after various gods. In fact, certain pagan influences seemed to remain with Constantine ... the way he set up a statue of himself in the Forum - honoring the Son God Helios or the *Sol Invictus* (the "Unconquered Sun") in the process ... even establishing "Sunday" as the day of rest or worship – honoring the Sol Invictus.

Sadly also, his Christian soul seemed not to be moved deeply by Christ's ethics – when (for reasons not clear to us today) he had his wife Fausta and oldest son Crispus murdered.

In any case, making Christianity now "politically correct," this led those seeking political favor to take up "membership" in the Church as new "Christians" ... undermining considerably the moral character of the faith that once was refined by the fiery tests under previous Roman persecution. Was this what Christ died for?

Shifting the political center of Rome to the East.   Soon after Constantine's defeat of his former ally, Licinius – receiving emperorship of the East in the process – he began the work of redeveloping the town of Byzantium, located at a very strategic point along the narrows where the Black Sea begins to connect with the Mediterranean, into a new imperial capital. This capital was not intended to rival the old city of Rome (which was suffering terribly from "inner-city" decay) – but to greatly exceed it. In a way this brought the Roman command center closer to its border problems with the Germans to the north (across the Danube) and the Persians or Sassanids to the East. Strategically this made a lot of sense.

But this move to the East also worsened greatly the status of the old city of Rome. About the only thing of note that still gave some importance to old Rome was that its bishop located there typically commanded the voice of all of Western Christianity ... something that would come to have increasing importance to "Western Civilization" in the centuries to follow.

✳ ✳ ✳

"POST-NICENE" CHRISTENDOM

Constantius II moves to suppress paganism. Constantius, who after his father Constantine's death in 337 (by sickness – not assassination!) finally – in a process taking over fifteen years – rose above his brothers and other imperial contenders to take over the Empire ... and continue the work of bringing the Empire around to full Christianity. But he was a fervently Arian Christian ... and intimidated the bishops into an anti-Nicene position. At the same time, pursuing religious conformity within his empire, he pushed the Christian cause against paganism more forcefully than his father had – closing the temples in 356 and removing the altar of Victory from the Roman Senate in 357.

Julian the Apostate (361-363). Julian was a nephew of Constantine who had miraculously escaped the murderous intrigues that took the life of most of the rest of his family after Constantine died in 337.

Upon becoming emperor in 361 (Constantius II had conveniently died in 361 just as a civil war was beginning to brew between the two cousins), he disclosed his pagan loyalties and began to try to undo the work of his Christian uncle Constantine and cousin Constantius. He tried to substitute a new religion based on Platonism in which the Supreme Being was identified with the Sun God Helios (akin to the popular Mithras). He tried also to establish the same moral rigor for his faith that made Christianity so respectable – and even copied the ecclesiastical organization of the Christian church.

He did not directly persecute Christianity but did remove Christianity's privileged position within the government and forbade Christians from teaching in the public schools (in an effort to bring the empire back to its pre-Christian traditions through the children). But there was no real zeal among the populace for his reforms – which was already apparent soon after he took over. When he died in 363 his efforts effectively closed the book for traditional paganism.

More Christian "greats" to further advance the Christian faith. During the later 300s and early 400s, Christianity was blessed by the writing and works of a number of "saints" ... who further refined the features of the faith – in the face of ongoing disputes ... and external threats to Rome itself (particularly the Germanic tribes).

There was Athanasius (c. 296-373), Bishop of Alexandria ... caught in the middle of the Unitarian-Trinitarian controversy – and exiled five times as a result because of his strong Trinitarian views. But his *The Incarnation of the Word of God* was a powerful work explaining in layman's terms the importance of the Trinity.

There were the "Cappadocian Fathers," Basil of Caesarea (c. 330-379), his younger brother Gregory of Nyssa (c. 335 -394), and their close friend Gregory of Nazianzus (c. 330-390) also strong Trinitarians – pointing out that only God – not human works of any kind – could forgive the sins of man. It was thus a God, not a man, that died on that Roman cross.

And there was Ambrose (c. 340-397), a Roman governor based in the city of rising importance in the West, Milan ... who was subsequently called to be the Bishop of Milan. He exemplified the highest virtues of the Christian, giving up his wealth to the poor and devoting himself to the call to be a teacher to those around him. But he also understood the world of politics – particularly critical at a time when the Unitarian-Trinitarian contest was so fierce – and although a strongly committed Trinitarian, he could be flexible on secondary issues ... such as how worship was to be conducted. This kept him from being caught in the deadly ideological trap set by the Trinitarian-Unitarian contest.

Augustine (354-430)

But without a doubt, the greatest of these theologians – one who would impact Christianity greatly – was Augustine. He would serve the Western world as very a strong light in a growing Roman darkness – helping it stay focused on higher spiritual realities when the surrounding world was rapidly losing its cultural, moral, spiritual appeal. Things were dark in Augustine's days because the Germanic Visigoths (West Goths) had, at the beginning of the 400s, crushed the city of old Rome ... and were pretty much in a dominant position around much of the rest of the Western Roman territory. And since such a "Dark Age" would persist through the following centuries (approximately a thousand years), Augustine's light would remain invaluable to a Western world trying to stay grounded – culturally, morally and spiritually – on its Christian faith. And it would even eventually serve to help the church reform itself in the 1500s.

Augustine was born in Thegaste (in the Roman province of Africa) to a pagan father but a Christian mother ... and raised in the Christian faith. But his philosophical mind eventually went well beyond the Christian doctrines he had been trained in during his youth – and he found himself exploring other realms of social ideas. Cicero inspired him to look to the higher world of social and political reality, and Plato directed his thoughts to the world (the realm of Logos and the Ideon) that loomed above even the social-political realm.

Eventually Augustine became a professor of rhetoric in Milan – and soon found himself intrigued by the sermons of Ambrose. And to Augustine, Ambrose finally made sense ... at least in the way he explained the Jewish Old Testament as allegory – rather than as material fact – something that had troubled Augustine's Materialist instincts in his earlier years. But he still was not sold on Christianity – in part because it seemed that the strong Christian was expected to remain celibate (unmarried) ... when he had no intention of dismissing his mistress, with whom he already had a baby boy. Nonetheless, he continued to remain curious about the Christian faith.

It was finally in 386, while in his garden, that he heard a voice commanding him to "take up and read" – obviously referring to the Bible. And there he immediately came across Romans 13:13-14, which called for the abandonment of the urges of the flesh. And thus began his journey ever deeper into the Christian faith.

He finally came to the understanding that faith, not reason, was the powerful means given to man to find ultimate truth ... faith that came from God – not from some kind of human skill or work. So impressed was he with this discovery, that he called his Platonist friends to explore with him this higher realm of Christian theology ... strengthening a strong personal foundation as a theologian and teacher in the process.

He returned to his home in Africa ... but tried to stay out of the limelight – having no interest in getting called into Christian ministry. But in 391 he was recognized and pressured to take up the priestly call. He relented. Then in 396, when the bishop of Hippo died, Augustine was directed to take that position ... thus serving as the Bishop of Hippo until his death in 430.

Hippo was located at the very center of the African controversy over Donatism – and it was inevitable that Augustine would have to address that painful controversy. Augustine's view on the matter was that it was the office of the man (such as bishop), not the man himself or his personal virtues, that weighed most importantly in the life of the Christian community or Church. And although the Donatists would never accept that explanation ... Augustine found his views on the matter to impact rather widely the rest of the Church – which readily accepted his explanation of the powers of the church office itself.

Furthermore, Augustine would stress that in other areas of life the same held true: it was the work of the Spirit, the blessings of God, the power of the cross – not the will of man – that made for goodness, for holiness. In this he was merely restating what the apostle Paul had made quite clear in his letter to the Romans some centuries earlier.*

This then brought Augustine into the debate that was beginning to stir around this same time (around 400) – over the teachings of a popular Christian teacher in Rome, Pelagius. Pelagius seemingly took a position not that different from the Donatists – stressing the vital importance of strict moral self-discipline as central to the Christian life. In this, Pelagius seemed to deny the central role of God's atoning self-sacrifice on the cross. And he seemed to ignore the problem of "original sin" in his optimism that human works were going to be quite sufficient to bring a person to true purity – and thus access to a heavenly reward at death.

Interestingly, when Alaric and his Visigoths attacked Rome again in 410, Pelagius – and his "Pelagians" – fled to Africa ... although Pelagius himself would then move on to Palestine. Those that remained in Africa – under the leadership of Coelestius – would generate the same challenges as posed by the Donatists ... and thus Augustine was now required to address the problem of Pelagianism.† He would do so, largely using the same arguments he had presented against Donatism.

But Pelagianism did succeed in stirring great controversy across the Roman Empire ... bringing it to be condemned as heresy by the Bishop of Rome in 418 and by a general council at Ephesus in 431 (the year after Augustine's death). However, despite this action, Pelagianism – or "Semi

-----

*But Augustine also believed that only through baptism are people, even babies, saved from eternal damnation – an idea later downplayed by the Protestants of the 1500s.

†Also most interesting, when Pelagius headed on to Palestine, Augustine wrote to the authorities there warning about the doctrines and controversies which would accompany Pelagius. But then Pelagius himself testified that he held no such strict "Pelagian" views ... for most of those had been developed by Coelestius!

Pelagianism"* (through John Cassian) – continued to be very influential within Christendom.

Augustine went further in his explanation of the Christian faith and its role in life. For one thing, he made clear that there was a huge difference between the "Visible Church" – that is, the Church that all good Roman citizens belonged to ... and the "Invisible Church" – actually made up only of the "true believers." But Augustine also affirmed that only God alone – who searches all human hearts – knew exactly who it was that constituted that true Church.†

And ultimately, with the collapse of Rome and the clear arrival of a Dark Age, Augustine's strong contrast between the glories of heaven and the tough and deeply challenging dynamics of earthly life would make great sense ... and help keep alive Christian hope amidst a despairing world.

The hermits – and the monastic movement

Understandably, a great number of Christians would find retreat from the world to be a good choice ... given the turmoil hitting the Roman world. The Syrian and Egyptian deserts seemed particularly attractive as places to retreat to in order to purify or mortify the flesh – in total surrender to God.

At first, the official church was hostile to all this ... until Jerome (347-420), working in the Syrian desert, gave this monastic development a great deal of legitimacy. He did so by devoting his seclusion to the translation of the Greek New Testament into Latin – the foundation of the Vulgate Bible. He then moved to Bethlehem to take up the study of Hebrew ... and there – in a cave reputed to be the same one Jesus was born in – he undertook the translation of the Old Testament into Latin. Also, he wrote a number of scholarly commentaries on Scripture – as well as critiques of Pelagianism.

Consequently, not only did he bring to his monastic efforts a deep respect from the fellow Christian community – including Augustine, who praised his work – he gave the monastic movement itself the respect it would need to place it in a very honored position within Christendom. And monasticism would retain that high respect not only during the long Dark Ages ... but even down to today.

---

*Semi Pelagianism: God extends by His grace salvation to those who are well disposed or of good will toward Him. Thus people possess through free will the potential to choose salvation. But only God's grace, in response to this good will, can actually confer such salvation. However this still leaves man – not God – as the initiator of the act of salvation.

†This idea was quite novel at the time – but came to be widely accepted after Augustine. The Protestant reformer John Calvin, in the mid-1500s, pushed this concept strongly in his own doctrine of the church.

CHAPTER FIVE

INTO THE "DARK AGES"

* * *

THE EARLY MIDDLE AGES: AN OVERVIEW

This next time period begins with the final stage of the decline of civilization in the Western half of the Roman Empire sometime during the 400s. This period lasts about 900 to 1000 years – until the beginning of the Renaissance in about 1400.

Thus it was that eventually (the 1800s) in looking at that thousand years or so since the decline of the grandeur that was once Rome's – and the rebirth of a similar material culture in the 1400s, Western scholars came to the point in the where they simply described everything in between as being the of the "Middle Ages."* That was when they were being kind. When many spoke of how they really thought about that time they referred to it as the "Dark Ages."†

Why the decline

Moral-Spiritual crisis: The loss of affection for the very idea of Rome itself. The co-opting of Christianity as the moral-ethical underpinning of the Roman Empire did not hold off the disintegration of the Empire. In fact the very theological ardor of imperial Christianity probably hastened its demise.

Christianity had made great advances among urbanized Romans ... at first among the poorer Romans who had flocked to the cities, or who had simply been part of the rapidly expanding landless class of Romans

---

*Latin: *medium aevum* for "middle ages" – from which we get the word "medieval" – appears as early as the beginning of the 1600s ... although the term "medieval" really comes into full use only in the 1800s.

†The term "Dark Age" actually goes back at least as far as the early 1300s, when the Italian scholar Petrarch used this term to describe the time-period that followed the collapse of the Roman Empire.

born and raised in the extensive urban slums of Rome. But over time, Christianity had also reached into the hearts of many of the upper classes of Romans ... even into the Senatorial class. But the rural and small-town parts of the Empire (which Rome had depended heavily on to support its extensive military presence everywhere) were still more closely attached to their former pagan ways ... and found urban Rome less and less easy to identify with – or have any continuing affection for.

Military loyalties. From the earliest times, the strength of Rome had been its independent, prosperous, pious and fiercely patriotic farmers and urban middle classes who had filled the ranks of the Roman armies – making for a fierce fighting machine, one that succeeded in conquering the Western world. But over time, the ranks of the military had become filled with foreigners, mostly Germanic tribesmen, whose loyalties rested not with the abstract idea of Rome but instead with their personal commanders ... who fought with each other constantly in the effort to command the Empire. These ongoing civil wars did nothing to create a unified sense of "Romanness" ... but did quite the opposite, draining Rome not only of its material assets but also its social and spiritual assets as well.

The crushing economic burden placed on Rome's citizens. Added to this loss of popular support of the Roman "idea" was the immense and wasteful cost of maintaining the huge Roman administrative, military and now also religious bureaucracy. The imperial bureaucracy (as all bureaucracies) grew in size and cost to the Empire, requiring the raising of taxes from those who created the Empire's source of wealth – the humbler social orders. Slowly, wealth gravitated to the bureaucracy (especially the Emperor and his friends) and drained away from the middle classes.

With the establishment of Christianity as the official religion of the Empire in the early 300s – and the confiscation of the wealth of the pagan temples and treasuries – the flow of wealth to the imperial rulers and their bureaucracy (which now included the Church) created an inflation which destroyed the real wealth of the middle classes. Taxes were now ruinous and lands were confiscated – or abandoned. Finally things got so bad that it seemed wiser for these humbler classes simply to abandon their farms and shops and go into service to the ever richer nobility.

Eventually laws had to be passed to keep them from doing this, for the countryside was depopulating and the empire needed their services. Thus they were forbidden to leave their work and homes except with imperial permission. But these laws served only to remove the last of their political rights.   Basically, they were now serfs – unwilling captives to the system.

Consequently, the commoners who once built the Roman empire

now were alienated from this same empire. Indeed, they saw themselves increasingly as living within an alien world.

Resentment increased – and revolts broke out – and were cruelly repressed. In the East, revolt tended often to take the form of rallying behind one or another Christian "heresy" which served to galvanize the frustration and anger of the humbler social orders.

Thus by the early 400s – the Empire was ripe for treason. In the West this came to fruition during the time of the German invasions. The people of the land simply refused to offer resistance to these alien intruders (who actually came in relatively small numbers) – having little love for the old imperial system.

The place of the Church in the breakdown of the old Roman Order. It was a Dark Age not because of the Church and its teachings – as so many during the Enlightenment would imply. The Church did not cause these developments, but like the Germanic tribesmen, moved into the moral vacuum that these developments created. And the Church survived this catastrophe, when little else of the Roman legacy did, because it was able to touch the hearts of the people the way the Imperium no longer could.

Indeed, about the only thing of old "Rome" that survived during this collapse of the social order in the Western half of the Empire was the Christian church. The Church gave what little bit of cultural unity to the West that it could. Even that was relatively little, at least during the first half of the Middle Ages.

Yes, there was a pope based in the city of Rome – and little else by way of authority in this once proud center of the great Roman Empire (the Roman imperial political center, such as there still was one in the West, had been moved to the city of Ravenna in the north of Italy). Actually, beyond Rome the pope originally had little real influence or authority. The power of the Church rested – as with all things in those days – with whatever powers it possessed at the local level.

Monks and priests managed to preserve what portion of the Church there was that was still intact. In this they acquitted themselves fairly honorably, especially once the monastic movement had been reshaped by Benedict (early 500s), whose rule was widely honored throughout the West. Indeed, missionaries sent out by the Irish monasteries* helped to bring to the Germanic tribesmen to the East of them in Britain and the European mainland aspects of the Roman Latin Christian legacy that otherwise would have been lost entirely to Western Europe.

––––––––––––––––

*Ireland, until the Vikings came along in the late 700s, had escaped the worst of the northern migratory disruptions.

The infighting within Rome's leadership. What really brought down Roman power – at least the increasingly unprotected Western half of the Empire once leadership had moved to the Byzantine East – was the constant infighting among those who sought Roman leadership. Of course this had been going on for some time. But it reached particularly catastrophic proportions after the reign of Theodosius at the end of the 300s. And it was at this point not just unhappy troops making and unmaking Rome's leadership … but also conspiracy and murder occurring within the families that did succeed to put themselves in power that crippled Roman leadership so badly.

The invading Germanic tribes. Taking advantage of the collapse of Western Rome's social-political morale were the various Germanic tribes at the Rhine-Danube borders – anxious to get themselves across these borders not merely to take advantage of the greater glory of Roman civilization … but also to get away from the invading Asian tribes pressing down on them from the East.

Compared to the size of the huge Roman population, the Germanic tribes were quite small. But they possessed the political determination that Rome now lacked … making a huge difference in the balance of power. And in particular, they were led by some of the most determined warriors of the day.

Even Rome understood this and opened the door for those of semi-Germanic – even full Germanic – origin to fill political and military positions that the Roman citizens themselves were failing to fill. Thus when during the 400s the Roman Empire fell apart in Western Europe – when Germanic tribes ranged widely across the Western Empire – there was almost nothing of the Old Roman Order stopping them. The Pax Romana or Roman peace simply ceased to function in the West. There were no more Roman magistrates backed up by the Roman legions to stand behind the Roman social order. Whatever social order existed did so at the mercy of local tribal lords acting in accordance with Germanic tribal customs.

Beyond or among these local, mostly tribal, principalities, there was no authority to enforce order. Consequently cross-European or even regional commerce and shipping came to a halt … as the highways and the sea routes became infested with brigands and pirates. In turn, cities, whose life blood existed around either commerce or public order, lost their function – and their population. But even the countryside became depopulated.

The Germanic "barbarians" did not produce this cultural vacuum. They merely moved into it once they understood that it was there … that there was no longer any real Roman counter-pressure to hold them back as they scrambled for grazing and farming lands for their own growing populations.

When they did move into the Roman domains, they attempted to capture the glory of the Rome that they once envied. But it was no longer there to be grasped. In consequence their own traditional tribal ways took over where they settled.

However ... "Rome" survives in the East as the Byzantine Empire

In the Eastern or Byzantine Roman Empire – which except in small parts of Italy and Sicily was no longer in touch with the West and its troubles – Roman life (now fully Greek rather than Latin in culture) seemingly continued as usual.

Indeed, eventually under Justinian (Emperor 527-565), Roman power was considerably revitalized in the East ... at least temporarily. Justinian was even able to retake large portions of the Western Empire, particularly in the areas immediately surrounding the Mediterranean Sea. But such success came at great expense to the Byzantines – an expense they really could not afford. The ancient and ongoing wars with the Sassanid Persians to the East had reached new levels of violence and were draining the energies (and tax sources) of the Byzantine Empire. [These wars were also draining the energies of Sassanid Persia.] Subject peoples within the Byzantine Empire were getting very restless under this heavy tax burden.

This situation was made only worse by the tendency of the imperial capital Constantinople to want to stamp out various Christian "heresies" widespread around the further reaches of the Empire – especially among the non-Greek peoples of the Eastern and Southeastern Mediterranean borderlands. A large number of Christians in these regions held philosophies or theologies not quite "Trinitarian" or Orthodox enough to suit the tastes of the imperial authorities in Constantinople. But the effort to stamp out these heresies resulted only in alienating the people of these regions all the more. As a result, by the beginning of the 600s much of the Eastern Roman Empire was exhausted and restless – physically, morally and spiritually.

This, in turn, would open the door for a rapidly rising Islam to finish off the largest portion of Byzantine Rome ... in quite short order.

✳ ✳ ✳

THE DISINTEGRATION OF THE WESTERN ROMAN EMPIRE

The Valentinian dynasty (364-392)

Valentinian and Valens (364-378). With Julian the "Apostate" dying childless, the military took the initiative once again to choose their emperor, a Pannonian officer named Valentinian. But they also demanded a co-regent so as to assure a more secure political succession. Consequently, Valentinian was elected to be western Augustus – and named his younger brother Valens as Eastern Augustus.

But these would be very troubled times for Rome. By the early 370s, the Germanic tribes were starting to act very nervous along the Roman borders. A group of fierce central Asian nomads – called "Huns"* by the Romans – had pushed westward into Germanic lands, driving the Germanic tribes up against Rome's Rhineland border ... which the tribes then attempted to cross. So angry was Valentinian during a meeting with a delegation of Germanic tribesmen that he suffered a stroke and died (375).

Meanwhile in the East, Valens finally agreed to allow Germanic tribes to settle in Roman lands along the Danube as foederati – groups who by treaty or foedus agreed to serve as soldiers in exchange for land rights within the Roman Empire. But these soldiers and their families were actually treated rather contemptuously ... forced to pay high taxes and unable to afford the food they needed.

The Battle of Adrianople (378). Thus in 378, the Visigothic tribesmen under their leader Fritigern rose up in revolt. Then when Valens went out to put down their revolt, he and most of his troops were killed in the battle ... and the rest completely routed.

And this defeat would result in the loss of Rome of most of its capable officers and veteran soldiers – and would now find it impossible to rebuild the ranks with Romans. The Romans would instead have to resort to the use of Germanic mercenaries to man their legions – a difficult (and expensive) situation considering the fact that Germanic tribes were also their natural enemies. This would mark an important turning point in the relations between the Roman Empire and their Germanic neighbors.

Theodosius (379-395). With Valentinian's death in 375, the Western emperorship had gone to his cousin Gratian. And upon Valens' death in 378, Gratian then chose Theodosius (of a Roman family of former military leaders) as Augustus for the East. For a while this arrangement worked fairly well. But soon Gratian began to lose effectiveness as a Western Augustus. His friendship with the tribesmen and his allowing Bishop Ambrose of Milan and the Frankish (another Germanic tribal group) general Merobaudes to actually run the Empire in the West all acted to alienate his troops. Gratian was finally challenged by his own troops and defeated and killed in battle.

---

*The precise origins of the Central Asian Huns remain a mystery ... though the Huns certainly came to Europe by way of the steppes of Southern Russia – possibly fleeing an extensive drought that hit central Asia about this time.

Theodosius now co-ruled the Empire, first with one then another individual, until 392 when his young co-ruler Valentinian II was found hanged in his home (possibly a suicide; more probably as a result of a fight with Arbogast, the Germanic Frankish leader who was at this point the effective military governor in the West). Theodosius was now the sole ruler of all the Empire, both East and West … but only for three more years.

Rome is now officially "Trinitarian." One of the critical developments under Theodosius's rule was the establishment of Trinitarian Christianity as the official religion of Rome. Up to this point, Christianity had been strongly favored but not yet Rome's official religion. But now, under Theodosius's orders, Trinitarian or Catholic/Orthodox Christianity became the sole religion supported by the state. All pagan worship was to be shut down, the Temples closed, pagan holidays ended* … and the Vestal Virgins – the most ancient and most revered of the pagan religious icons – disbanded.

However … Theodosius's relationship with Ambrose, bishop of Milan, is indicative of the new dynamics emerging within Christendom at that time. In 390 Ambrose excommunicated (cut off from the privilege of receiving the Christian sacraments) Theodosius for his massacre of 7,000 inhabitants of Thessalonica after his military governor stationed there had been assassinated. As directed by Ambrose, Theodosius underwent several months of public penance for this deed. Theodosius was of course no wimp. But neither was Ambrose. The church was in fact coming to be led increasingly by such figures of power and authority.

Meanwhile in the East, the Germanic tribesmen continued to give Theodosius considerable trouble.

Religious troubles brewed, as there was an attempt by Eugenius, a military usurper who seized control in the West and then – though a Christian himself – sought to build popular support for himself there by restoring some of Rome's pagan practices. Theodosius and Eugenius met in battle at the Frigid River in 394, and with the help of a "divine wind" (which turned a near defeat of Theodosius into a grand victory) Eugenius was defeated and executed. Thus again, the entire Empire found itself under the sole rule of Theodosius … at least briefly. Early the next year Theodosius died of natural causes.

Honorius (nominal Western Emperor, 395-423) and Arcadius (Eastern Emperor, 395-408). The Empire now passed to Theodosius's two sons, Honorius ruling in the West – with his capital at Milan, and then

---

*The ones anyway that had not yet turned themselves into Christian holidays … such as the year's end celebration of Saturnalia – which turned itself into Christmas!

later Ravenna* – and Arcadius ruling in the East from Constantinople. The Roman Empire was again divided ... however, never to be united again. Actually, from this point on, the Western Empire fell increasingly under the control of the Bishops of Rome and various semi-Roman / semi-Germanic or even fully-Germanic military strongmen or "patricians" (such as Arbogast – and subsequently Stilicho). Thus the Western emperors would now rule in name only.

Stilicho the "Patrician" versus Alaric the Visigoth

Stilicho.   As the 11-year-old Honorius became officially emperor of the Western Empire, Flavius Stilicho became de facto governor of the West.

Stilicho was born a Roman mother, but a Germanic Vandal father. In his upbringing he was treated entirely as "Roman." He rose quickly within Theodosius's army and ultimately was given the task by the emperor of defending the Empire against the Visigoths.   In the battle between Theodosius and Eugenius in 394, Stilicho was one of the generals who – along with a major storm (the "divine wind") – helped turn the battle in favor of Theodosius. Theodosius was so impressed by Stilicho's performance that he appointed him guardian of his son Honorius just prior to his death in 395.

Ultimately, Stilicho's main task at this point would be to stop the rise of his former colleague, the Visigothic foederati commander Alaric, who had replaced Fritigern as leader of the Goths. With Alaric threatening the Eastern Empire in Thrace in 395, and the Eastern Roman army fully occupied further east in battle against the Huns, this left Stilicho the full responsibility of stopping Alaric.

Alaric.   Alaric was a Visigoth chieftain principally interested in becoming recognized within the Roman Empire as a military "protector" over the imperial household. He was rebuffed in his effort to do this through a normal rise up the ranks of the military – and thus Alaric took to conquering. Recognition, not plunder, seemed consistently to remain his aim in life.

As a young man, Alaric served in the army of the Gothic foederati – becoming a general in 394 and serving under the Emperor Theodosius. At this point he began to take note of the weakness of the Roman hold over northeastern Italy.

Having been bypassed by Theodosius's sons in the distribution of imperial offices, Alaric decided to make his own move on Rome. As newly

---

*Honorius had ultimately moved the Western capital to the well protected town of Ravenna – well-protected because of the surrounding swamps which made siege by any enemy almost impossible. Ravenna – not the declining city of Rome – would then serve as the capital of the Western half of the Roman Empire for quite some time.

proclaimed Visigothic "king," he moved his disgruntled foederati (service pay had slacked off) against Constantinople. But finding the city well-defended by its walls – and by Stilicho's leadership – he then turned his soldiers West towards Greece. Then Alaric found himself trapped in Greece by Stilicho. But just as Stilicho was in a position to destroy Alaric and his army, Arcadius (the eastern emperor) strangely ordered Stilicho back to the West. This allowed Alaric to pillage the lands of Thrace and Greece for almost two years (395-396) – although he spared Athens.

In 397 Stilicho again moved against Alaric – crushing his army. But Alaric managed to escape to the mountains in the north along the eastern Adriatic Sea (Illyricum), where he was welcomed as a liberator, even as king of the lands that reached all the way up to the middle Danube River.

Then Stilicho was sent that same year to put down a rebellion in Africa. His reputation now was so great that in 400 the Senate named him "consul."

Stilicho took on Alaric two more times (401 and 403) ... and fell short of total success – with Alaric finding a way to escape total misfortune. But all of this was wearing down Stilicho's armies ... so much so that by 406 Germanic tribes were crossing the frozen Rhine and pillaging Gaul. The situation became so bad for Stilicho, that at one point he even called on Alaric for help – a development that Stilicho's enemies would soon use to bring him down.

Also Alaric, who had moved his armies into Greece, seeing mounting weakness in Rome's (Stilicho's) defensive forces, became so bold as to demand a huge tribute payment as the price of peace. Stilicho recommended payment ... and the Senators refused to go along with the idea ... although they had no alternative plan to deal with the mounting German problem.

Stilicho's fall (408). Instead, Stilicho's political opponents (which now included Honorius), who had become very jealous of Stilicho's popularity and fearful of his support among the Roman troops, began to spread wild rumors about his complicity with Alaric. This clever deception successfully alienated sections of Stilicho's army ... which rose up in revolt against Stilicho. Stilicho's enemies now felt that they had good grounds to have Stilicho arrested ... and executed (408). Stilicho's son was soon executed after him.

Confusion now reigned as Roman troops went on a rampage ... with Roman soldiers turning on the Germanic foederati soldiers and their families in Roman cities. The slaughter was extensive, and the Germanic survivors fled the Empire ... adding enormously to the ranks of Alaric's army.

Alaric's assaults on Rome (408, 409 and 410). Alaric then (408) turned on the defenseless city of Rome, cutting off all relief, including food – to the point of starvation for the city's citizens.   Alaric was finally bought off by the citizens of Rome themselves with an impossibly high ransom, which stripped the city of most of its wealth ... and certainly its honor. But still not getting the imperial recognition he felt he deserved he assaulted Rome a second time (409) – and gained the position from the Senate as unofficial overlord of an imperial usurper, Attalus. But it was not long before Alaric simply drove Attalus from power ... and then tried to negotiate a deal with Honorius – but was out-played diplomatically with the intervention of a Gothic rival, Sarus. Thus it was that Alaric turned on Rome a third time (310) ... this time his troops breaching the city's wall and then going on to plunder, slaughter and enslave much of the city and its population. But then heading south to take the grain fields of (North) Africa – now to make him a "benefactor" to a hungry Empire, storms at sea destroyed his navy ... and a feverish Alaric himself died in the effort (also 310).

Alaric's larger impact. Overall – despite his ultimate failure at establishing some kind of Gothic regime of his own, Alaric left a huge mark on his age. Principally, he had exhausted the Roman resistance in the West, and opened the way for the various Germanic tribes to invade Gaul and Spain. It was his marauding of Rome that also caused the withdrawal of the Roman legions from Britain in 410 (to protect the Italian homeland from Alaric) – leaving Britain vulnerable to the invading Picts and Scots to the North and the Saxons to the East.

Passing around the blame. Paganism had by no means been eradicated in Rome with Rome's embrace of Christianity ... and immediately the two religious groups laid blame for the city's humiliation at the feet of their opponents, each claiming that it was the failure of the other's God or gods that had brought this curse on Rome ... with the stronger argument seeming to lie with the pagans (though Augustine would offer a very effective answer of his own with his work, *The City of God*, written at this time.)

Whatever was the "divine cause," the net effect was a sense of curse that had fallen on Rome. Its centuries-old image as the power center of Western Civilization was shattered ... and in its place Rome now appeared to be a poor, broken city, a mere shadow of its former greatness.

And such an image of weakness would become simply an invitation for other rising powers beyond the Empire to see the Roman Empire – at least in the West – as an easy target. For the Germanic tribes of north central Europe (Goths, Franks, Alemanni, Burgundians, Angles, Saxons, Frisians, Thuringians, Vandals, etc.), the rush to move into the western half of the Roman Empire now began in earnest.

The Empire exhausts itself in foolish in-house power struggles. These were times of tremendous turmoil for the Empire. Various claimants to imperial power (Constantine III, Sebastianus, another Maximus, – and, again, Attalus) drained away Roman power as they fought each other – at a time when Rome needed all the resources it could muster just to control the influx of Germans. Honorius kept himself in power in the chaotic West actually hardly outside the surroundings of Ravenna) with the help of some able generals – and a lot of negotiating. Finally he died in 423, leaving no heir. The eastern emperor Theodosius III named his six-year-old cousin Valentinian III as Western emperor.

Aetius: the last great Roman leader in the West (433-454). In its continuing struggle for survival, the Western Empire was well served for twenty years by the Roman general Aetius, born of an aristocratic Italian mother and a Roman general of Germanic ancestry. Aetius began his career as a general commanding Hun troops and supporting an unsuccessful contender to the imperial throne. But his arrival before Rome with his Hun army was so impressive that Valentinian's mother, Galla Placidia, the effective ruler of Western Rome (or whatever was left of it) agreed to name him head of the Roman army in Gaul if he sent his Huns back outside Rome's borders. This he did.

He then turned his attention to the Visigoths, forcing them to retreat to southwestern Gaul, and the Franks ... Aetius retaking some of the land along the Rhine which they had seized. One by one he faced other Germanic tribes – forcing them also into submission.

Meanwhile he had battles of his own within the Roman political circles – principally against Boniface, his primary military commander. He eventually defeated Boniface, and was declared supreme military commander (patrician) in the West. Then he turned his attention again to the Germanic tribes: the Burgundians (whom he decimated), the Suebi, the Visigoths, the Alans – settling each of them in more or less stable situations around the Western Empire under some form of treaty arrangement.

Attila and the Huns. Meanwhile another problem presented itself ... this time in the form of the Huns, and their leader Attila.

Attila was born near Budapest in Central Europe to the royal family of Huns. In 433 he became king of the Huns and began the process of turning his tribesmen into a powerful fighting instrument. With his new army he brought the Germanic Ostrogoths (East Goths), located around the Huns, under Hunnic sway.

Then in 448-452, Attila – having reorganized his Huns into a new fighting machine – marched into the very heart of the Roman Empire.

Claiming to defend the honor of Honoria, granddaughter of the Eastern Emperor Theodosius II, he pressed her cause all the way up to the gates of Constantinople. He attacked Constantinople in 448 ... and was bought off with ransom money.

Then he turned westward in 451 with his huge Hunnic-Germanic army against the Emperor of the West, Valentinian III – again claiming to defend Honoria's honor. He ravaged Gaul (France) and was about to lay waste to Orleans along the Loire River when a huge coalition of Romans, Visigoths, Franks and Alemanni led by Aetius gathered to fend off Attila at the Battle of Châlons. The devastation was vast on all sides of the conflict. Theodoric, king of the Visigoths, was killed. But Attila was also forced to retreat back behind the Rhine.

But the next year (452), Attila slipped past Aetius in the Alps and descended down upon northern Italy – to burn and pillage city after city. Aetius, with a greatly depleted army, did what he could to slow up Attila's advance. Attila stopped at the Po River and received a Roman delegation (including Pope Leo I) – which convinced him to return north of the Alps (hunger among his troops and an attack on his homebase in the north by other Roman legions also contributing factors). Then before the waiting world could see what he would do next, he died suddenly at the feast celebrating his marriage to Ildico.

Valentinian III brings the Roman Empire to its death in the West (454-455). Meanwhile, Valentinian was growing paranoid about Aetius's popularity and power and was easily convinced by ambitious conspirators (Maximus and Heraclius) of the need to assassinate Aetius, which in 454 Valentinian did by his own sword – thus eliminating the one source of strength Rome possessed during his emperorship. But then when Maximus found that Valentinian did not name him as Aetius's replacement, he turned against Valentinian and his co-conspirator Heraclius and had them both murdered, while soldiers who had come to love Aetius, though standing close at hand, did nothing to stop the murders.

Valentinian would be followed by a rapid succession of Roman emperors, each reigning for only a few years, some only for months or even days. Finally, only two decades later, the fiction of a Roman ruling as Western Emperor was brought to an end. The Western Empire was gone.

✻ ✻ ✻

A CLOSER LOOK AT THE GERMANIC TRIBES (c. 375-568)

The Early days of the Germanic intrusion into the Roman Empire.

The Germanicm the Asian Huns coming in from further East) had found the eastern half of the Roman Empire a solid barrier to expansion. But as they slid west, they found a very different dynamic: only a very weak Rome trying to hold its own ... an easy pickoff.

Within the Roman Empire there was very little stopping them. Whole regions seemed largely deserted, either because the inhabitants had fled before the approaching tribal groups, or because the owners had abandoned their farms even earlier due to economic failure. Other groups such as the Celts of Britain (and Gaelic Brittany) tried to hold out from mountainous regions they had escaped to. Others just simply allowed themselves to be integrated into the social-political complex of the invading tribe. In any case, by 500 it was accurate to say that there was no longer a Roman Empire in the West. Rather the region seemed to be a loose patchwork of various tribes – themselves often in contention for dominion in the land.

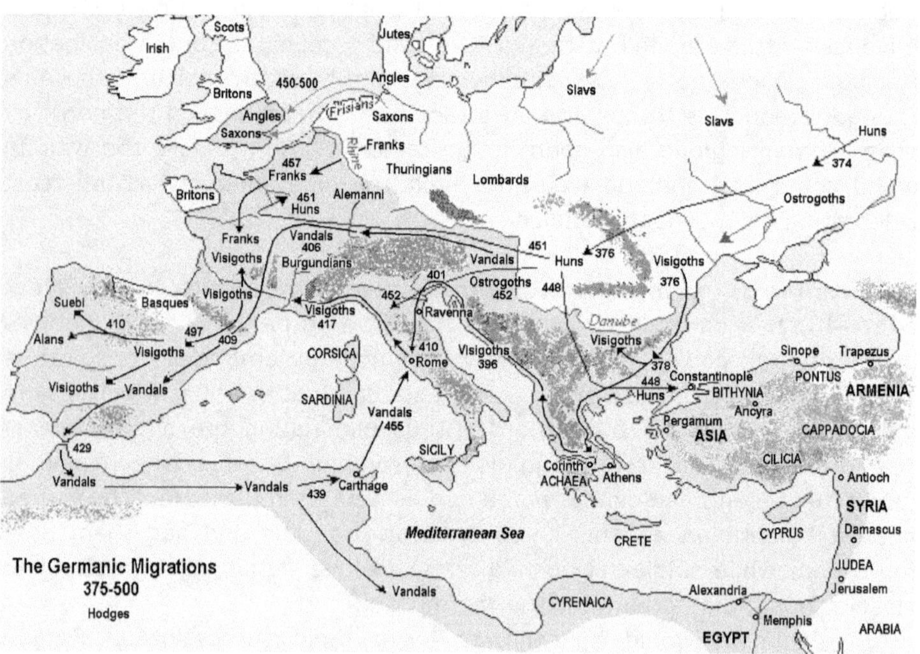

The Goths. In the East – along the Danube River near the Black Sea – it was the Goths (originating in Southern Scandinavia and Northern Poland?) who first troubled Rome, crossing the Danube in 267 to sack Byzantium (well before it became Constantine's capital city). They were eventually driven back across the Danube – but allowed by Aurelian to settle in the old Roman province of Dacia (north of the Danube) which the Romans had abandoned – establishing a Gothic kingdom there. At this point some of the Goths were entered into the ranks of the Roman armies.

In 332, Constantine attacked and crippled the Gothic kingdom and then settled Sarmatians just north of the Danube in order to act as a buffer to the Goths. But then two years later he expelled the Sarmatians after they revolted against Roman authority.*

Gradually the Goths were Romanized – and brought into Christianity as Arians. And the ranks of the Roman armies were composed heavily of Germanic tribesmen.

With the appearance of the Huns into the area (376), the Goths were given permission to settle on the south side of the Danube. But (as we saw above) they were treated shabbily (no famine relief) and, led by Fritigern, rose up in revolt – leading eventually to the Battle of Adrianople in 378, in which the Emperor Valens was killed and the Roman legions decimated.

The Franks. Actually, the first group to enter Roman territory – and take a permanent position within the Empire – were the Franks (in particular the Salian Franks). This name probably included a number of separate tribes located just east and north of the lower Rhine River as it enters the North Sea. During the 200s they raided deep within Roman territory on several occasions (even reaching Spain during a raid in 250) before being expelled by Roman forces. They settled the lower reaches of the Rhine (today's Netherlands) where they raided shipping to Britain. Finally they were settled down by the legions – though not removed from the territory.

In 258, Salian Franks were permitted to settle in northern Gaul as "foederati," offering military service to Rome in exchange for the privilege of settling just within the Empire's northern borders (on the Roman side of the Rhine River). Not much is recorded about them as they seemed to have caused the Romans no particular concern, mostly serving to protect the northern borders of the Empire from other Germanic tribes – including other Frankish sub-tribes ... although more importantly the more violent Saxons.

Mostly, the resettlement program of the Salian Franks worked ... for, like most of the German tribes, their desire was ultimately to move in and take for themselves the benefits of higher Roman civilization – not to destroy it.

They really come into history only with the dazzling conquests of Childeric and his son Clovis ... who finally succeeded later in bringing all of Gaul under Frankish rule (late 400s/early 500s) ... forcing the Visigoths to have to abandon to the Franks that portion of their once-extensive kingdom north of the Pyrenees Mountains.

———————————————

*The Sarmatians were a people of northern Iranian descent that had earlier migrated westward as far as an area reaching from Southern Poland to Eastern Romania.

The Vandals, Alans, and Suebi. With huge pressure coming their way from the Huns – and with the obvious deep decline of Roman military power in the West – Germanic Vandals, allied with Iranian Alans (part of the Sarmatians), were able to defeat the Franks, rendering the Franks unable at this point to be able to hold back the Germanic pressure on the Roman borders. Thus the Vandals and Alans were able to cross the frozen Rhine at the beginning of 406 and head westward, plundering as they went.

They soon established themselves in what is today Southern France ... but then in 409 continued even further South into the Iberian Peninsula (modern Spain and Portugal). Then pressure from the ever-expanding Visigoths forced the Vandals to move again, this time across the Straits of Gibraltar (429), where they then spread themselves eastward across the north African coast, taking Carthage ten years later.

Besides the Iranian Alans, another group – the Germanic Suebi – accompanied the Vandals in this sweep across Western Europe, the Suebi finally settling themselves in the northwest corner of the Iberian Peninsula.

Visigoths. Following Alaric's sack of Rome in 410 the Visigoths settled themselves in southern Gaul, first as Roman foederati and then as an independent Germanic kingdom (418) with their capital at the city of Toulouse (in today's southern France). From this base they would later extend their domain south across the Pyrenees Mountains into Hispania (Spain) where they secured their position against the Germanic Suebi and Vandals who had just moved there, forcing the Suebi to come under Visigothic rule and – as we have just seen – the Vandals (those anyway that did not submit themselves to Visigothic rule) to move out of Hispania and into coastal North Africa.

Ostrogoths. Ostrogoths went their own way under the very capable Theodoric ("the Great"), who in 488 defeated Odoacer – who himself had just overthrown the last Western Roman Emperor Romulus Augustulus in 476. Theodoric thus took control of all of Italy and the area across and north of the Adriatic Sea. Under his rule (until 526), the Ostrogoths assumed Roman character as much as possible and brought a degree of political strength back to the lands they controlled. But in the mid-500s they fell before the expansionist program of the Eastern Roman (Byzantine) Emperor Justinian I.

The long war with Justinian (535-554) not only badly destroyed social life in Italy, it also exhausted the Byzantine Empire ... leaving the Byzantines susceptible to conquest, first by the Persians and then by the Arabs. And the Ostrogoths themselves were also thus unable to ward off a new Germanic tribe anxious to take control of their lands: the Lombards.

The Alemanni. Just to the north of the Alps, in the upper reaches of the Rhine River (today's Alsace and northern Switzerland) was another Germanic tribal confederation, that of the Alemanni, a people who suffered terribly from the cruelty of the Emperor Caracalla who turned them into dedicated enemies of the Romans. In the mid-200s they made raids into Roman Gaul and into Italy north of the Po River. Finally they were defeated in battle in 268 and driven back across the Rhine.

But they would continue to trouble Rome, fighting – but defeated – at Argentoratum (Strasbourg) in 357 and then again in 366, after having crossed the frozen Rhine. They remained intact as a people ... and finally in the confusion caused by Alaric at the beginning of the 400s they were able to move successfully across the Rhine to settle the area of Alsace. In 451 the Alemanni would be part of Attila's alliance that was defeated by Aetius. But they again would still hold their position around the upper Rhineland region.

The Burgundians. The Burgundians (who might have been a sub-group of the Vandals) moved west – possibly from the Baltic coast of today's Poland – towards the Rhine Valley, initially locating themselves between the Franks to the north and the Alemanni to the South. They would serve as foederati in the Roman legions ... although Roman General Aetius had to call on his Hun allies to break their growing power ... killing the majority of the Burgundian tribe in the process. But Aetius then resettled the remnant group ... who then became Roman allies again (against Attila).

Then with the total collapse of Roman authority in Gaul, the Burgundians expanded their reach south to the area that today constitutes Southeastern France. But eventually they would be absorbed into the Frankish kingdom (when not upon occasion also quite independent in operation!).

The Saxons. There is some uncertainty about the name "Saxon" as to whether it refers to a particular ethnic or tribal subgroup of the Germanic peoples ... or whether it was simply a term applied to a group of tribesmen that as fishermen and sailors (ultimately "pirates") raided ships operating in the North Sea.

At some point "Saxons" (coming from the Baltic shores of southern Denmark?) drove the Franks south of the Rhine basin and took control of the coastal region along the North Sea coast of the European continent. They are closely associated with other Germanic peoples of the region, the Frisians, the Angles and the Jutes. It is indeed from this broader association that they produced the label "Anglo-Saxon."

The beginning of the Anglo-Saxon migration to Britain. Eventually this group crossed the North Sea to settle in the Roman province of Britain. Tradition* states that Saxons led by Hengest and Horsa were invited in the mid-400s by British (Celtic) King Vortigern to help ward off the attacks of the Picts and Gaels ... attacks that had begun after the withdrawal of the Roman Legions in 410 (to help fight Alaric).

However – according to some accounts – following their victory over the Picts, a dispute arose with Vortigern about payment. They thus felt free to take land for themselves – and thus established the kingdom of Kent. Others hold the opinion that the Saxons, simply seeing how defenseless the Britons were, sent word back to their kinsmen on the continent to come and help them take possession of the land. In any case, a mass migration of Saxons now got underway, filling the ranks of a growing Saxon presence in Britain.

Establishing Saxon England.   The advance of the Germanic Saxons against the Celtic British was steady ... until the Battle of Mons Badonicus (c. 500) when the British[†] halted the Saxon progress ... at least for a while. By the end of the 500s, starting from their base in Kent, the Saxon expansion resumed – aided by in-fighting among Celts. The Saxons – particularly those under King Aethelberht, King of Kent – drove the Celtic population further West into Wales and Cornwall ... as well as across the water to Brittany in France. Meanwhile, other Saxon kings also were establishing their rule in the regions of Sussex, Wessex, Essex, East Anglia, Mercia and Northumberland.

But the Saxons would end up fighting each other as often as they would be taking on the Celtic kings and their people.

The Lombards.   North-German Lombards – joined by a variety of other Germanic tribes – migrated south at the beginning of the 500s and settled along the upper Danube. Then in 568 under a very capable king, Alboin, they migrated west down into a very exhausted northern Italy, greatly weakened by the Ostrogoth-Byzantine war (the "Gothic War"). Sadly, the Roman army found itself totally unable to offer any kind of effective defense against such a large Germanic enemy (568-569) ... there being perhaps as many as half a million tribesmen on the move. Consequently, city after city quickly fell to them. By 580, they occupied nearly all of northern and most of central and southern Italy. The great Roman cities of Rome and Ravenna held out – but little else of strategic value in Italy was able to do so.

---

*Derived from *Ecclesiastical History of the English People*, composed by the English monk Bede around the year 730.

†This resistance was most likely the basis for the medieval development of the legends concerning Celtic King Arthur and his Knights of the Round Table.

A Lombard Kingdom was immediately established ... on the basis of a number of Lombard duchies located here and there around the Italian peninsula ... shared with the Byzantines, with Byzantine Italian holdings also scattered here and there – which included the city of Rome itself.

But it was a very loose arrangement, as the Lombard dukes were careful to protect their relative independence ... and thus Lombard kingship was normally a very unstable political office. Also the independence of the Popes at Rome weakened the position of the Lombard king. And the division among the Lombards between those trying to hold onto their traditional Germanic gods and culture and those who had become Christian and Latinized constantly roiled Lombard politics.

The Lombards would remain in control of Italy for the next two centuries – although, divided into 36 duchies, the Lombards lacked the political unity that Italy sorely needed. But this division served to keep the city of Rome independent – and still dominant in religious matters and influential in political affairs throughout the West.

* * *

KEY LEADERS RESPONSIBLE FOR THIS GERMANIC EXPANSION

Leadership problems. The Romans had always been fairly accommodating to non-Romans whom they had come to have some degree of ascendancy over. It was natural for the Romans during the 200s and 300s to suppose that they could continue this policy with the Germanic tribesmen. Indeed, they found the tribesmen to be excellent fighters willing to serve the interests of the Roman imperial armies.

But what began to change this relationship was not so much a change in the tribesmen themselves as it was a change in the talents of the Roman leaders. The personal character of Roman emperors had been variable, bad mixed in with the good. But it seems that Rome was increasingly experiencing a long run of incompetent emperors. Everyone sensed this.

And this in turn brought forward a number of bold Germanic eaders willing to challenge Roman authority. We have already met Alaric and Attila as excellent examples. But there were others.

Gaiseric (or Genseric) and the Vandal Kingdom (r. 428-477). The Wendels or Vandals were a small tribe allied with the Alans – who in the early years of the 400s crossed into Gaul. But the resistance of the Franks was so intense that they moved on through Gaul and crossed the Pyrenees into northwestern Spain. Conflicts with the Suebi (who had also recently migrated to the area) forced the Vandals into southern Spain. Here also troubles with the Visigoths – an even stronger German tribe which had moved to the area – brought the death in battle in 428 of their king Gunderic. At this point his half-brother Gaiseric (born c. 390) was named king by the Vandals and Alans.

Gaiseric had already made the decision that the Vandals had to leave Spain – even preparing a fleet prior to the events which made him king. Thus in around 428 or 429, Gaiseric led approximately 80,000 Vandals (or Wendels) from Spain to Carthage in North Africa where he ravaged Roman power there. Most tragically, Augustine died during the long Vandal siege of Hippo Regius (430-431), which subsequently became Gaiseric's capital. Eight years later Gaiseric forced the city of Carthage to submit – and made it his new capital. In the process, he had captured Carthage's large fleet – and added it to his own, giving himself a very large navy.

His intentions then were to challenge Rome for control of the Western Mediterranean. He forced Sicily, Sardinia and Corsica into submission – and then for the next several decades raided Roman shipping at will. Finally in 442 Gaiseric secured from Western Roman Emperor Valentinian III recognition of his kingdom as independent (not under Roman authority) – and some semblance of peace resulted.

When in 455 Valentinian III was murdered, Gaiseric took the position that the peace treaty he had made with Valentinian was no longer valid. He sent his fleet off to Rome – which was totally unprepared to deal with the Vandal attackers. It was only three years since Attila had ravaged Italy and nearly assaulted Rome (Pope Leo I had persuaded Attila to leave Rome alone). Rome was defenseless – and for two weeks the Vandals "vandalized" Rome – although with Pope Leo's intervention (again), Rome was spared from arson and slaughter of the population.

In 468, the Romans sent a huge fleet to attempt to crush the Vandals and end their control (or piracy) in the Mediterranean. But instead the Roman fleet was destroyed by Gaiseric's navy. This merely emboldened Gaiseric – who subsequently invaded Greece. But this time his victorious streak failed him and he had to retreat back to Carthage (but taking 500 hostages whom he hacked to pieces and threw overboard on the trip home). Finally in 474, he made peace with the Byzantine Empire. Three years later he died at Carthage.

Euric and the Visigothic Kingdom (r. 466-484). The Visigoths had offered critical support of Aetius in his battle at Châlons with Attila in 451. But the battle had cost the Visigoths the loss of their king, Theodoric. His son Theodoric II took the throne in 453 by killing his older brother, Thorismund. In 458, Theodoric lost to the Roman Emperor Majorian much of the Visigothic territory in Spain and in Septimania (today's French Mediterranean coastal region) but was able to regain the territory with Majorian's assassination in 461. But then in 466 Theodoric himself was assassinated ... by his own younger brother Euric.

As king, Euric was successful in forcing other Visigothic chieftains under his direct rule ... and establishing the Visigothic Kingdom as fully independent of Roman authority. To the south from his capital at Toulouse, he drove the Suevi (or Suebians) into the northwest corner of the Spanish peninsula thus taking over most of Hispania. And he extended Visigothic control north into Gaul ... all the way up to the borders of the Frankish kingdom in the north of Gaul. This marked the height of the Visigothic kingdom ... for, by the time of his death in 484, he and Roman general/ duke/king Odoacer had come to hold much of Roman Western Europe between the two of them.   But his death would also mark the beginning of Visigothic decline ... at the hands of the expansive Franks.

Childeric and the Frankish Kingdom (r. 458-481). In the continuing chaos which followed the sack of Rome by the Visigoth leader Alaric in 410 and then the sacking again of Rome in 455 by the Vandals, the Franks under their king Childeric I – in cooperation with the Gallo-Roman forces of Aegidius – were able in 463 first to fight off the Visigoths under Odoacer and then some Saxons along the Loire River valley. But then Childeric allied with Odoacer in fighting off invading Alamanni attempting to invade Italy. Consequently, Childeric succeeded in stretching Salian Frank rule from the Lower Rhine in the North to the Somme River in the South (a region eventually to be known as Austrasia).

Odoacer ... the last Roman patrician (r. 476-493). Odoacer was born (434) along the Danube River among the Germanic Scirii tribesmen who had just invaded the area a few years earlier. He entered service in the Roman army in around his thirtieth year and rose quickly within its ranks as a leader of a band of foederati.

In 475, the Western Emperor Nepos was driven from his throne by the military commander Orestes, who had built his support among thousands of foederati with promises of good land in Italy. Orestes's son, Romulus, was placed on the Western imperial throne. But Orestes did not deliver on his promise of land.

The following year, Odoacer led a group of disgruntled foederati in revolt. They captured the imperial capital at Ravenna and forced the youth Romulus to abdicate. However, Odoacer refused the imperial title, declaring himself simply "patrician" in the West ... although at this point little more than Italy was still under Roman control in the West.

Nepos appealed to the Eastern Emperor Zeno to restore him to the imperial throne. But there was initially no enthusiasm from Zeno in this matter – or from the Roman Senate which, pleased by the stability brought to Italy by Odoacer, asked Zeno to recognize Odoacer as a patrician entrusted with care of the "diocese" of Italy. Odoacer created a strong Italian-Germanic army and, upon Nepos's death, brought Dalmatia (opposite Italy) under his control. He then drove the Vandals from Sicily – and formed an alliance with the Goths and Franks to hold back the expansionist Germanic Burgundians, Alemanni and Saxons in the north.

But eventually Odoacer's power grew to the point that it embarrassed Zeno, who then decided to deflect the growing power of the Ostrogothic king, Theodoric, by directing him into action against Odoacer – promising him the rule of Italy should he defeat Odoacer (a policy designed by Zeno to move the Ostrogoths away from the Eastern Empire and get rid of the growing power of Odoacer at the same time). In 488, Theodoric and his Ostrogoths invaded Italy and defeated Odoacer in a series of battles. Odoacer took refuge in Ravenna where he remained impregnable – but also hungry. Then when disease broke out among the besieging Goths, a peace (493) was declared between Odoacer and Theodoric. But Theodoric personally murdered Odoacer at a supposedly friendly banquet the following month.

The net historical effect of Odoacer was to end for all times the fading tradition of Roman rule in Italy and the West (no more emperors ... until Charlemagne in 800). The West was no longer Roman – but instead, Germanic (Visigoth, Frank, Alemanni, Burgundian, Saxon, Vandal, etc.).

The Ostrogothic King Theodoric "the Great" (r. 475-526). Odoacer's rival Theodoric was born (454) in Pannonia (today's Western Hungary), son of Theudemir, one of the kings of the Ostrogoths. He was sent as a Gothic "guarantee" (hostage) of peace to the Byzantine court in Constantinople where he lived for ten years. Upon his return to Pannonia, he began the conquest of neighboring kings and their territories, including Macedonia. This gained him recognition as a *foederati*, titled holder of Roman territory in the Balkans to which his Ostrogothic kinsmen were entitled to settle.

This Roman privilege was intended to pacify the barbaric tribesmen ... even make them allies of the Roman imperium. But Theodoric preferred instead to use his power to consolidate his people's hold over his Germanic neighbors. He also attacked Roman lands at will – though not with any definitive success.

Theodoric's murder of Odoacer meant Ostrogothic dominion over Italy. But this proved to be a quite lasting time of peace and stability for Italy – the first in a long time. Bureaucratic corruption, brigandage and other social diseases were brought under control. The Italian economy began to revive and urban life underwent restoration. Indeed, Italy became a food exporter under the stimulus of such peace.

But toward the end of his reign some unwise political or diplomatic decisions began to undermine his legacy. As an Arian Christian he had generally been tolerant, even supportive, of the Catholic Christianity of the Italians. Yet when the Eastern Emperor Justinian began to take action to suppress Arian Christianity in Byzantine lands, Theodoric began to be cruelly reactive to the Catholic Church in his own Italian lands. Unfortunately, he is also remembered for his execution in his last years of the philosopher Boethius.[*]

The Frankish King Clovis (Chlodwig) (r. 481-511). Childeric's son Clovis I stretched Salian Frank rule even further than had his father, eliminating the power (and lives) of other Frankish kings in Gaul (including his own brothers). In 486 he defeated a Roman army under Syagrius at Soissons, thus establishing unquestioned Frankish ascendancy over northern Gaul. He then allied with the Ostrogoth King Theodoric and went on to defeat the Alamanni in 496. He then secured Paris as his own capital.

The Catholic archbishop of Reims, Remigius, was quick to recognize Clovis as a possible solution to the anarchy that ruled over the Gallo-Roman world.   Also, his Burgundian princess wife, Clotilda, had been working to bring him from paganism to Catholic or Trinitarian Christianity (perhaps he himself had been considering Unitarian Christianity). In any case, he finally decided to cooperate with the Roman church by converting and being baptized into Catholic Christianity in 496 (or was it 507? ... accounts vary). This made him the first of the major Germanic leaders to move to the Catholic or Trinitarian Christian confession.   His people then followed him into a similar baptism. This gave the Salian Franks special standing with the Catholic Church.

Meanwhile, in 500 he tried – but failed – to acquire the Burgundian kingdom ... although he did acquire all of Swabia two years later.   He then directed his attention South to Aquitaine, in 507 taking this huge region from the Arian Visigoths under the weak Alaric II.

In that same year the Byzantine or Eastern Roman Emperor Anastasius I decided to assign Clovis the old Roman title of Consul ... and then in 511 the Byzantine Emperor appointed Clovis to preside over the Christian Council of Orleans – adding further legitimacy to his rule.

With this, the Merovingian dynasty of Frankish kings was established

---

[*]Boethius (c. 480-524) was a Roman senator and scholar who spent much of his time translating the Greek classics into Latin ... as well as demonstrate the connection between Christianity and the works of Plato and Aristotle. In fact, it was Boethius who was most responsible for having the works of Aristotle preserved for later (Renaissance) study.

– to rule Frankish northern Europe* ("Francia," the land of the Franks) until the dynasty was put aside by the Carolingians in 751.

The Merovingian follow-up. However, in accordance with Salian tradition, at his death in that same year (511) Clovis's lands were divided among his sons into four smaller kingdoms: Paris (Childebert), Orleans (Chlodomer), Soissons (Chlotar) and Metz (Theuderic). Not surprisingly, much energy was spent by Clovis's sons fighting each other. But they also expanded the reach of their realms elsewhere, especially Childebert, fighting Visigoths in Spain and Burgundians (in today's southeastern France). But Childebert had no sons, and ultimately the youngest of Clovis's sons, Chlothar was able to reunite Francia briefly simply by surviving his brothers. But once again, Francia was split into separate kingdoms among Chlotar's sons when he died in 561.

Chlotar's son Chilperic received the Frankish heartland of Neustria (today's northwestern France) and attempted to conquer the rest of Francia, in particular to the East against his brother Sigebert, King of Austrasia (Eastern France and Western Germany). Family feuds grew bitter, involving also the wives, Fredegund (Chilperic) and Brunhilda (Sigebert). Fredegund eventually killed Sigebert (575) and an assassin killed Chilperic (584).

Eventually feuding among the Merovingian kings simply strengthened the powers of the local barons ... and the church. In 614 Neustrian King Chlothar II – who as King of the Franks (son of Chilperic and Fredegund) presumably ruled over the entire Merovingian domain – was forced to recognize (*Edict of Paris*) the increased powers of the local nobility.   Then in 617, hoping to rebuild royal power, Chlothar created the position of "Mayor of the Palace" – something of a prime minister or chancellor – given wide powers to administer the realm.

Finally, having Austrasian Queen Brunhilda executed in 613 and thus laying claim to Austrasia, Chlothar was able to unite most of Francia. But then in 623 he handed off Austrasia to his young son, Dagobert!

And so it went!

Merovingian government ... and the foundations of feudalism. Germanic or tribal Europe was not equipped to govern its lands and people in the manner that the Romans had ... through a huge bureaucratic network supported by a fairly efficient tax system. Neither administrative expertise nor money were available to administer the lands ruled by the Merovingian kings. So instead, key personal supporters of the kings – family members or trusted individuals – were assigned portions of the king's domain as

---

*The dynastic name is derived from a semi-mythical Salian Frank king Merovech ... who in the mid-400s ruled what is today's Belgium and northern France.

"counts" and "dukes" (from the Roman *comites* and *duces*). They were obligated to administer the law and protect the land ... in the name of the kings that appointed them.

But even these territories were quite large, so feudal lords (the counts or dukes) could sign out portions of their own feudal assignments to lesser gentry as vassals ... a process we today call sub-infeudation.

The whole thing was held together not by some strong realm of law ... but simply by interpersonal relations between lord or sovereign and vassal.

But over time, feudal lords would work hard to keep these feudal assignments in their family ... and thus the flexibility of a sovereign being able to appoint those he wished was lost. Politics – not legal norms – thus drove this system ... most often in a very bloody manner – as even brothers fought among themselves (or even rose against their fathers) over these inheritances.

The all-powerful mayors of the palace. The kings, however, would keep some section of the larger domain as their own personal property, the royal *demesne* (domain), for their own material support. To help oversee the daily administration of the royal domain, the kings would appoint personal assistants, "mayors of the palace." Over time, the position of mayor of the palace grew increasingly important, especially as Merovingian kings came to the throne quite young and died after fairly short reigns ... thus leaving the oversight of not only the royal domains but the entire kingdoms to the mayors of the palace. In time, dynasties would form themselves around this key office – more powerful in fact than the kings themselves. This became especially the case as the Merovingian kings increasingly slipped into the position of being mere ceremonial figures – even *rois fainéantes* (weak kings).

The early rise of the Carolingians: Pepin of Herstal. In 687, Pepin II of Herstal, "mayor of the palace" in Austrasia since 680, conquered the other Frankish kingdoms of Neustria and Burgundy ... and then awarded himself the new title "Duke and Prince of the Franks" (*dux et princeps Francorum*) ... declaring his own sovereign powers as Frankish leader. To prove his point, he then went on to conquer the neighboring kingdoms of Alemannia (today's Southwestern Germany), Frisia (Northern Netherlands) and Franconia (Southcentral Germany).

But his conquest was intended to be as much cultural as political ... for also as "defender of the faith" he sponsored evangelism among the Germans to bring them to Catholic (Trinitarian) Christianity.

Then he secured the right to have his own family succeed him in office ... thereby laying the foundations for the Carolingian dynasty. But (as was typical of the Germanic tribesmen at that time) he had more than one wife ... and his first wife Plectrude (whose sons died before the elderly Pepin finally died in 714) got Pepin to designate his grandson Theudoald as his heir ... in opposition to his second wife Alpaida, who had two surviving sons by him, but one in particular, Charles. Thus when Pepin died, a rather well-expected civil war broke out among Pepin's offspring.

Out of this, Charles "Martel" (the "Hammer") would emerge victorious ... and open France to a new greatness (more about this in the next chapter).

The Anglo-Saxon World

Æthelberht of Kent (r. c. 565-616*). Not much is known about how the Anglo-Saxon world developed – until Æthelberht took the Saxon crown upon his father's death (in 560 or 580?). The Christian monk Bede in his *Ecclesiastical History of the English People* (c. 731) mentions Æthelberht as the third of the Saxon kings to rule over several Anglo-Saxon kingdoms – from his base in Southeastern England (Kent). Bede also mentions his conversion to (Trinitarian) Christianity – thanks to the mission of the monk Augustine, sent in 597 to England by Pope Gregory to bring the area to Christ.[†] Æthelberht and Augustine would together establish a church at Canterbury ... which eventually would become the seat of the English Archbishops – and the starting point of bringing the Saxons to Christianity.

Edwin of Northumbria (r. c. 616-632). Way to the North were the kingdoms of Deira and Bernicia[‡] – ruled by Edwin, son of a Deira king ... with his base at the town of York. Edwin managed – with the help of East Anglia's king Rædwald – to come back from early exile and take command of the region – and be its first Christian king.[§] He would go on to conquer many of the surrounding Saxon kingdoms (Mercia, Wessex, Anglesey, for

---

*These dates are highly debated as Bede's *Ecclesiastical History* and the *Anglo-Saxon Chronicles* (late 800s) give at least a 20-year variance in dating Æthelberht's birth, marriage, and reign.

†But he may have already been something of a Christian ... thanks to his Frankish wife, princess Bertha – who apparently had a bishop accompany her to England upon her marriage to Æthelberht.

‡Probably originally British (Celtic) kingdoms, conquered by the Saxons. They would later (mid-600s) be joined as the kingdom of Northumbria ... that is, England north of the Humber River.

§This seemingly occurred when Edwin married Æthelburh, the sister of Eadbald of Kent ... under the provision that just as Eadbald's father Æthelberht had become Christian upon marring Bertha, so also Edwin should do the same in marrying Æthelburh.

instance) ... but ultimately would die in one of his many battles. After that, older Saxon paganism seemed to reassert itself in the north.

✻ ✻ ✻

CHRISTIANITY MOVES FORWARD AMIDST THE DARKNESS

In the West it was a very hard time. There was no reliable order in the land, and road and sea travel became very dangerous. Trade and industry ground to a halt. Urban life withered away to nothing. Even the population dwindled rapidly in size. People became dependent on a local tribal leader for protection – whose fortified domain offered some small amount of protection against wandering bands of trouble makers.

Politically, the city of Rome was now irrelevant, as what was left of the Roman imperial order in the West was supervised now out of Ravenna, in the north of Italy.

However, although Roman politics and economics collapsed under the German conquests in the Western portions of the Empire, the Roman religion, Catholic Christianity, did not. Indeed, Christianity became the all-important carrier in the West of what was left of Roman civilization: in the social organization of the church, its bishops and popes, and in its use of Latin in worship and study.

A number of Bishops of Rome (later termed "Popes") – most notably Leo I (pope: 440-461) and Gregory I (pope: 590-604) – managed to preserve and strengthen what little remained of Roman or Latin moral-cultural order in the West. Indeed, the church of Rome not only survived the Germanic impact but converted some of the most important Arian tribes to Roman Christianity and restored the city of Rome to a position of some degree of religious-cultural importance – at least within the West itself. Admittedly this was not very glamorous by comparison to what Rome once was.

Closely connected with this survival of the Christian church was also the monastic movement which at the time of the fall of Rome in the early 400s was widespread. Numerous monks and priests at the local level preserved something of the old Roman order, working under the monastic rules set out by Benedict in the early 500s. Then too, thanks to Patrick – who brought Christianity to Druid Ireland in the early to mid-400s – Ireland would send out many missionaries to help bring to the German (and Celtic) tribesmen in Great Britain and on the European mainland vital elements of the now-Christianized Roman social-moral legacy.

Patrick – Missionary to the Irish. Patrick served as a missionary to the

Irish for some thirty years. It is claimed that in that time he brought the nation to Trinitarian or Catholic Christianity, establishing over 300 churches and baptizing over 120 thousand Irishmen.*

He was not himself Irish but British – developing an extensive familiarity with this isolated Celtic island when he was taken there as a 16-year-old slave. He miraculously escaped after about 6 years of hard and dangerous service and made his way back to his home in Britain, rejoining his family, but was shocked to find the land itself devastated by the Germanic pillaging during his absence in Ireland. It took him quite a while to locate his refugee family ... who hoped that he would join them in their new life. But he could not refuse a sense of divine call ... and journeyed to southern France to become a priest. He was serving there when God called him to return to Ireland to bring that fierce Druid nation to Christ. So he put this sense of call before Celestine, Bishop of Rome – acknowledged as the person with the sole authority to authorize such a Christian mission. Sadly, Celestine appointed another priestly team to undertake the mission. But that mission was ultimately very unsuccessful. Thus Celestine finally commissioned Patrick and a small team for the task.

This was a wise choice since Patrick was one who knew the Irish well, and had an incredibly fearless heart. He knew the power of the Druid priests – and the importance of winning the respect of the Irish chiefs. He also was aware of an ancient Irish prophecy well known to all in Ireland that heralded the arrival of a small group of foreigners attired and adorned almost exactly as he and his small group of missionaries were. He was ready to challenge the Druid priests (the exact details have become so "expanded" in the retelling that it is impossible to know what really happened). In any case he succeeded in impressing the Irish chiefs – and was allowed to establish himself in Armagh as the nation's first bishop.

From this key spiritual center he began to involve himself in the political affairs of the nation – even intervening to protect Christian Irish from raids by British Christians. But he was no less involved in the social life of the country, establishing schools and monasteries throughout the country to raise the level of learning of the nation. Under his direction Irish monks began translating works from the Greek and Hebrew and developing libraries of considerable importance. But most of all he looked after the spiritual needs of Ireland – leading the nation into a wholesale embrace of Christianity.

The irony is that just as Roman Europe was undergoing a terrible

---

*What we know of Patrick comes from parts of his personal testimony, *Confessio* and also from his *Letter to the soldiers of Coroticus*. We do not know exactly the dates of his birth or death however ... although certainly he flourished in the mid-400s. His name "Patrick" came from the Latin, Patricius ... perhaps derived from the fact of his own British-Roman ancestry.

cultural eclipse caused by a general Germanic darkness – Ireland was undergoing quite the opposite in the form of a true cultural awakening. As the lights began to go out in the continental West, in Ireland they began to burn – burn brightly.

Eventually it would be the Irish who would go forth as missionaries to Germanic Europe – in an effort to restore Roman Catholic culture where they could.

Noble Roman churchmen
lay strong church foundations in the West

Leo I "the Great" (pope: 440-461). Leo I, the bishop of Rome, played the most important hand in tightening church organization in the West at a time that the Roman political order was disintegrating there. During his tenure as Bishop of Rome he became the unquestioned head of the Western church – that is, "pope." The other bishops, especially the North African bishops, simply declined in importance or even disappeared from view as the German tribal leaders undercut the bishops' power bases.

Early on, Leo lined up the other bishops of Italy and North Africa behind his lead in driving out of the church a number of heresies that were drifting into the faith. Later, with the help of the Western Emperor Valentinian III, he was able to draw a resistant church of Gaul (France) under his authority. And when Attila and his Huns threatened Rome, it was Leo who met him and got him to withdraw his troops, making him the primary political figure in Italy.

He was unabashed in his view that the Bishop of Rome was the head of the church – not only in the West but in the church universal. He based his claim on the logic of being of the apostolic line of succession descending directly from Peter, the first Bishop of Rome. His claim was not accepted in the East – though he certainly was respected there. But his claim went unchallenged in the West. From Leo's time on, the Bishop of Rome was acknowledged in the West as the "pope," the head of the Roman Catholic Church.

Benedict of Nursia (480-547). In the early 500s an Italian aristocrat-turned-monk, Benedict, founded some fourteen monasteries (the first and most important at Monte Casino in Southern Italy) and then laid out for the good order of these monastic communities his "Benedictine Rule." This proved so successful that it was widely copied among abbeys or monasteries throughout the West. His Rule served to give form and strength to the monastic movement. Indeed, over time, resulting from such order and discipline, these monasteries themselves grew very rich.

Gregory of Tours (538-594). This well-born (of the Roman Senatorial class) Bishop of Tours was not only an excellent Roman cleric, he became for the West something of the father of French history, carefully recording the story of the Franks, their Merovingian rulers, and some of the notable clerics of his days ... in ten volumes, the *Decem Libri Historiarum* (*Ten Books of Histories*). His writings present a very clear picture of the time of deep transition from Rome's traditional culture ... to the fast-rising, and quite rough, Germanic culture around him.

Gregory I "the Great" (pope: 590-604). This Gregory was chiefly responsible for reorganizing the structure of the Western Church – giving it the broad features that it would have for the rest of the Middle Ages – and indeed, through the ongoing Roman Catholic Church, even down to the present. Gregory was born of a noble or patrician Roman family – a family possessing not only great wealth but also a distinguished placement in the Christian community as a family of deep Christian devotion. As a youth Gregory received the typical patrician schooling at which he proved to be highly accomplished. He eventually stepped into a public career (as would have been expected of one with his family background) and by his early 30s he had become the prefect of the city of Rome.

But soon thereafter he abandoned his public life and took up the vow of poverty in becoming a monk. Eventually he turned his family inheritance of considerable landholding to use as the sites of a number of monasteries. But Pope Pelagius II pressured him to come out of seclusion and first had him appointed as a deacon of Rome and then as papal ambassador to the Eastern Roman or Byzantine court in Constantinople.

Here he revealed his highly organized mind in a controversy he had with the Eastern Patriarch – a controversy in which the Emperor eventually placed himself squarely on Gregory's side of the argument. Eventually he was returned to Rome and soon became abbot of St. Andrew's monastery – where he also became a widely respected teacher of the Scriptures. But he became fascinated with the idea of becoming a missionary to the Anglo Saxons of Britain – but at the insistence of a very upset Roman populace was recalled to Rome shortly after his departure. Under a promise never to leave Rome, he soon became a special assistant to Pelagius II. But he never lost his fascination for the idea of a mission to the Anglo-Saxons of Britain.

In 590, during the middle of a horrible plague which had followed upon equally devastating floods, Pelagius II died – and the unanimous Roman choice for pope went to Gregory – who nonetheless did what he could to duck the responsibility. Nonetheless, the Eastern Emperor confirmed the appointment and Gregory was forced to take up the position as bishop of

Rome (pope).

Soon after his accession to the papacy, he began to demonstrate his brilliance as a church administrator (including the management of the vast land holdings of the church, which he used generously to support the poor) – and as a dominating authority throughout the whole Christian world. With respect to church organization, the personal behavior of priests and bishops, and the handling of church monies, he was deeply demanding of papal discipline throughout the ranks of the church. He even claimed authority over the Patriarch of Constantinople, insisting that the church at Rome was the true Apostolic See.

He also drew the church into active politics – particularly when it became evident that the Byzantine Emperor was not going to do anything to stop the advance of the Germanic Lombards across Italy. Gregory not only appointed a new tribune to Naples to organize that city's defenses against the Lombards but eventually entered directly into negotiations with the Lombards for peace in Italy.

He finally had a chance to fulfill an old dream of sending a mission to the Angles in Britain – sending Augustine to begin the conversion of the Angles and Saxons in Britain. He also worked closely with the monastic movement reformed by Benedict – by drawing monasteries more closely into the ecclesiastical system that he presided over and disciplining it according to his strict standards ... and at the same time acting as a protector of the monasteries against the efforts of bishops to bring these monasteries under their own control.

The Christian (mostly Irish) missions to the Germanic nations

The monasteries (found significantly in unconquered Celtic Christian lands in Ireland and Britain) became very important pockets of learning in this dark Germanic world – sending out missionaries to the German tribes, converting them to Catholic Christianity, planting new monasteries in their midst, and keeping the hope of a better world alive.

These monasteries were not under papal control – nor was there any real "order" to them – but they provided a refuge for people who wanted to devote themselves to God and serve their fellow man in charity (something utterly lacking in the Roman Empire).

The most influential of these monastic havens within this darkened Germanic world – perhaps because they were furthest removed from the impact of the Germanic invasions – were the Irish monasteries started up by Patrick. They not only kept the flame alive, but sent out missionaries in the 500s and 600s to establish monasteries in England, Scotland, the Netherlands, France, Burgundy, Saxony, and Italy.

Columba (521-597) was a monk and missionary, known also by his Irish nickname, Columcille ("Dove of the church"). After his banishment from Ireland for opposing the King, he and twelve of his disciples founded in Scotland the missionary settlement at Iona (563) – which became the launch site for bringing Scotland into the Christian faith.

He had also been very active in shaping the Irish church in his earlier years, founding several hundred churches and monasteries in Ireland as well. And even after establishing himself in Iona he remained active in Irish affairs, helping to shape the governmental structure of Ireland at the council of Druim Cetta in 575.

Columban (c. 540-615) was another Irish monk who in 591 (at age 50+) traveled with twelve of his disciples to the European continent, to the Burgundian kingdom (in Southeastern Gaul or present-day France) to establish monasteries among the Celtic Gauls. But his strong disapproval of the lax moral and spiritual conditions within the Burgundian government and Roman church in that region brought him under attack. In 610 (at age 70!) he was forced out of Burgundy. He eventually settled in Switzerland to preach the faith to the pagan Alamanni – though he was soon chased from this region as well because of his having chopped down sacred pagan trees and because of a continuing conspiracy against him in the courts of Theodoric II. Thus he moved south into Italy (c. 612-614) and established a monastery at Bobbio, where he died a short time later.

In his sermons, teachings, writings and personal example, he left a legacy of spiritual integrity and vitality which gave inspiration to Christians generations after him.

Augustine of Canterbury (?-ca. 605). As already noted, Augustine was sent by Pope Gregory from Rome (where he had been prior of a Benedictine abbey) to England to convert the Anglo-Saxons to Catholic Christianity. Augustine arrived in Kent in 597 accompanied by forty monks. Kentish King Æthelberht was supportive of Augustine's mission and gave him a place at Canterbury to base his mission.

Augustine's mission proved to be highly successful. Ethelbert and thousands of English were brought to the faith in the first year alone. Within a few years a number of other missionaries were sent to England to assist Augustine, including twelve bishops – over which Augustine presided as archbishop. His church (Christ Church) was recognized as the cathedral for England.

Aidan (?-651). Aidan was a humble Irish monk at Iona, when he was consecrated in 635 as bishop and sent to evangelize the English under King

Oswald (and King Oswin who succeeded Oswald in 642) in Northumbria. Just off the Northumbrian coast, Aidan established the mission center of Lindisfarne for the training of more missionaries to the English, including the brothers Chad and Cedd (missionaries to the Mercians and East Saxons respectively) and Hilda (founder and abbess of a number of monasteries, including the notable monastery of Whitby in Northumbria, England).

The Synod of Whitby (663/664). One of the growing questions of the day was whether these missions ought to remain independent, or at least connected solely to the sending authorities back in Ireland – or whether they ought to affiliate themselves with the Bishop of Rome (the Pope). This was both a cultural and political issue. Would they follow Celtic or Roman patterns of church organization and life? Would they preserve their autonomy or submit themselves to the Roman religious order? Thus English Christians convened at Hilda's Whitby to come to some kind of a decision. Ultimately the decision was made in favor of the Roman formula.

Cuthbert (634-687). Cuthbert was a profoundly spiritual and humble Celtic monk who entered Melrose Abbey (Scotland) as a youth, became very close to its prior, Boisil, and succeeded him in 661 after a plague killed Boisil. Cuthbert quickly gained a reputation as a miracle worker after he went about the countryside praying for and treating plague victims.

When, after the decision of the Synod of Whitby to adopt Roman and drop Celtic church traditions (a decision which Cuthbert supported), Colman, who had been a leader of the Celtic position, resigned his post as prior of Lindisfarne. Cuthbert was invited to take his place. As prior of Lindisfarne, Cuthbert supervised the changeover from the more informal Celtic to the much more highly structured Roman church style.

But Cuthbert had more of a heart for quiet piety than for administrative duties. In 676, searching for solitude, he ventured to the Farne Islands and established himself in a hermit's cell there. However, his fame would not go away. He was recalled briefly as prior of Lindisfarne and then once again retreated to the Farne Islands where he lived out his days in prayer.

So well-loved was Cuthbert that the beautiful *Lindisfarne Gospel* (a treasure today of the British Library!) was published by Bishop Eadfrith of Lindisfarne in Cuthbert's honor shortly after his death.

✳ ✳ ✳

BYZANTINE (ORTHODOX) CHRISTIANITY HANGS ON IN THE EAST

By the mid-400s, the Eastern Roman Empire was distancing itself rapidly from the Western portion of the Roman Empire (except in the Byzantine parts of Italy and Sicily). The West's problems seemed far away from life in the East (the Balkans, Asia Minor, Syria and Egypt). Eastern Roman culture (fully Greek rather than Latin in character) seemingly continued as usual. Meanwhile within the Eastern or Byzantine Church itself, the patriarchs in Constantinople, Antioch and Alexandria vied with each other for a dominating role in this Eastern Christian or Byzantine world.

Struggles with heresy. For reasons that could be clear to only a Greek mind, the church in the early to mid-400s fell into deep dispute over the question of the nature of Christ. Was he of one or two "natures"? Was he in fact one or two "persons"?

Nestorius, the patriarch of Constantinople and his followers (strong in Syria and Asia Minor) took a view that Jesus was really two "persons" in the form of the Son of Man and the Son of God. This view was strongly opposed by Cyril, the patriarch of Alexandria, who took the view that Jesus was not only a single person but also of a single nature.

The debate grew so heated over this matter that a council was called in Ephesus in 431 to decide the matter. Cyril's supporters arrived first and quickly decided in favor of their own view that Jesus was a single person – and declared "Nestorianism" a heresy. But shortly after Cyril's death another council was called at Ephesus in 449.*   It went further with the position that Jesus was "Monophysite," that is, of a single nature. But the Monophysite position in turn was condemned as a heresy at yet another council held two years later in 451 at Chalcedon, where the "Chalcedonian formula" was adopted (Christ: of two natures [truly God / truly man] coming together in one person).

Thus the Byzantine church, in so tightly defining the theological details of the faith, and so rigorously rejecting all groups not able to agree in all details with the quite complicated orthodox position, succeeded in alienating both the Nestorians (popular in much of Asia Minor and the Syrian East) and their opponents, the Monophysites (popular in Egypt). This would later come to haunt the church when Islam came roaring out of Arabia ... and – helped by the widespread alienation of many Christian groups in the East by the actions of the official church – found it relatively easy to drive the domain of Eastern or Byzantine Christendom into humiliating retreat.

Eastern Roman or Byzantine Emperor Theodosius II, 408-450. During the middle years of Theodosius II's rule, the East was spared much of the turmoil consuming the West. Constantinople, already situated in a

––––––––––––––––––

*The meeting was so violent that Flavian, at that time the patriarch of Constantinople, was attacked and died shortly thereafter of his wounds!

strongly defensive position, had its walls so strengthened by Theodosius[*] that no army would be able to breach the walls (until fellow Christian crusaders did so in 1204). However, peace was kept with the bothersome Huns only through the payment of large amounts of gold in annual tribute (growing from 350 to 700 pounds annually over a 15-year period).

But then in 440 the Vandals began their attacks on the Eastern Empire. Soon thereafter the Huns and Persians, noting the weakness of Rome, began their attacks. Two Roman armies were destroyed by the Huns – and the amount of tribute now required of Rome to keep the Huns happy was increased to 2100 pounds annually.

Yet, one of Theodosius's greater achievements was the creation of a Roman law code updated since the time of Constantine. He also created the University of Constantinople.

Emperor Marcian (450-457). Marcian was a Thracian who came to power by rising up through the ranks of the Roman army. Marcian altered the policy of his predecessor, Theodosius, by ending the annual gold payments to the Huns. Attila, realizing that he could not conquer Constantinople, turned his wrath on Italy and the West instead. Marcian did nothing to help the West. Instead he turned his attention solely to cleaning up the Eastern Roman government finances and bureaucracy. He was also the Byzantine Emperor who called the Council of Chalcedon to settle the church's dispute over the nature of Jesus.

Leo I (457-474). Leo I was another Thracian, placed on the throne by the supreme commander of the Eastern Army, an Alan named Aspar (as an Arian Christian he himself was forbidden to take the throne). Aspar thought that Leo would be a mere puppet that he could control. But Leo allied with the Isaurians (the Isaurians were a people of long-standing residence in southern Asia Minor) and was able to thwart Aspar's plans. Aspar then attempted to assassinate Leo in 469 and failed. Consequently, he and his son were killed in 471.

Leo I reversed Marcian's policy of seeming indifference to the West. He in fact organized a very expensive major assault in the West against the Vandals in 468 – which failed miserably, reducing greatly the resources of the Roman Empire in the East.

Zeno (474-491). Originally a semi-barbaric Isaurian chieftain named "Tarasicodissa," Zeno married the imperial princess, Ariadne, daughter of

------

[*]They were actually reworked by the praetorian prefect Anthemius, who was the power behind the throne in the first years of Theodosius's reign ... for Theodosius was only seven years old when he was proclaimed Byzantine Augustus!

Byzantine Emperor Leo I. Through this marriage he eventually became elevated to the position of Eastern Roman Emperor.

It was he that in 488 convinced the Ostrogothic leader Theodoric not to invade the Eastern Roman Empire – but to invade Italy and "liberate" it from its German chieftain Odoacer, who had deposed the last Western Roman Emperor, Romulus, and who had taken over as direct ruler of Italy.

This effectively spared the Eastern Roman Empire from the German overlordship that was collapsing Roman society and culture in the West. But it looked as if it were confirming the shift of imperial power to the Isaurian tribes – in parallel with the power shift to the barbarians in the West.

Anastasius I (491-518).   Anastasius was a Roman civil servant who was elevated to emperorship in 491. Not only was imperial rule returned to Roman hands – unlike the developments in the West where various Germanic tribes had taken over Roman rule completely – but the Isaurians (an Indo-European ethnic group probably descendents of the Hittites), the primary challenge to Roman rule in the East, were defeated by Anastasius in 498. Indeed, so complete was the Roman victory over the Isaurians, that the Romans had many of the Isaurians resettled in Thrace as a security measure.

However Anastasius was not able to bring religious unity within his Eastern Roman domains. The split between the Orthodox and Monophysite positions on the human/divine nature of Jesus Christ deeply divided Eastern Christian society. Though Anastasius had pledged to support the Orthodox position in his accession to power, he eventually moved into the Monophysite religious camp.

Also, the Eastern Empire was constantly threatened from the East by the Zoroastrian Persians – who wanted to regain Armenia and other former Persian areas that had converted to Christianity and had thus come under the Roman imperium.

Nonetheless, the governance of Anastasius coincided with a period of economic growth – not only for the imperial government but for Eastern Roman society as a whole. These were relatively peaceful and prosperous times in the East – quite in contrast to the poverty and chaos that had settled over the former Roman West.

Justin I (518 to 527).   Justin was an illiterate peasant from Illyria who rose through the ranks of the Roman military because of his considerable ability as a soldier and leader. He was humble enough to recognize his limitations and gathered a circle of very capable advisors around himself. Nonetheless the latter years of his reign were marked with considerable troubles with Ostrogoths to the North and the Persians to the East.

Justinian I (527-565). Justinian was promoted to power by his uncle, the Byzantine emperor, Justin. After a very brief co-emperorship with his uncle, Justinian became sole Roman emperor in 527 (at this point there was no longer a Western Roman emperor).

The Nika riots (532). The first five years of his rule were uneasy. Constantinople was a rough place. Political factions confronted each other in increasingly violent fashion (something like modern urban gangs). The biggest outlet was the chariot races – which provided the opportunities for gangs (principally the Greens and the Blues – backed also by influential members of the Senate) to vent. Justinian had been trying to keep order – though he was not popular, having raised taxes in an attempt to straighten out the finances of the state. His wife Theodora was an object of ridicule – having been an actress and a well-known courtesan of humble birth (but as events would soon prove, was an exceptionally capable individual).

In early 532, just as he was negotiating a (very expensive: a one-time Roman tribute of 11,000 pounds in gold) "eternal" peace with Sassanid Persia, riots broke out in the city. This would prove to be the worst that the city was ever to see. It occurred over the arrest of two Blue and Green individuals recently involved in murderous chariot riots. The city was convulsed by even greater rioting – and the imperial palace was blocked off for five days. The crowds were taunting Justinian – who was turning to the idea of fleeing. But Theodora stiffened his resolve with her words: "those who have worn the crown should never survive its loss" and "Royalty is a fine burial shroud." She would rather be dead than flee. And so he faced down the crowd – and unleashed his general Belisarius (who would serve him loyally during his reign) on the rioters in the Hippodrome (race track). In the end, half of Constantinople was burned to the ground and 30 thousand people killed before the riots were finally suppressed (and many Senators plus a pretender to the throne executed). But his rule was now secure.

War against the Germans: First period (533-540). The next year (533) Justinian sent Belisarius to begin the reconquest of lost Roman territory in Africa held by the Vandals. This he did fairly easily. Two years later (535) Sicily was retaken – and Belisarius (eventually joined by Narses) then turned his attention to Italy and the Ostrogoths. This took longer, five years, and involved some reverses as well as advances. But in the end (roughly by 540) he had pried Italy loose from the Gothic grip – and even held the well-defended Ravenna, which became the Byzantine capital in the West.

The plague of 541-543. The empire was then hit violently by a plague, which left it greatly depleted of manpower. At its height, the plague was killing 10,000 people a day in Constantinople (so the contemporary chronicler Procopius reports). The depopulation of the empire not only cut back on the empire's tax sources at a time of huge need (and saddling the survivors with huge new taxes) the loss of manpower also made the empire an easier target for its enemies. The plague would return – in wave after wave – causing in Europe a population loss of probably more than 50% over the next century (but after 750 the plague would not reappear in Europe until it broke out again in the mid-1300s as the Black Death).

War against the Persians (540-562). Troubles with Sassanid Persia continued throughout this period. Seeing that the "eternal" peace was giving his Byzantine rival the opportunity to increase Byzantine power by retaking lost Roman territory in the West, Persian king Khosrau in 540 decided to end the truce with Rome. He invaded Syria – all the way up to the Mediterranean – and looted Antioch, and took its inhabitants back to Persia as prisoners.

Roman-Persian relations then continued with periods of war, truces and more war until 562, when Persia and Byzantium agreed to a 50-year peace (which cost Rome an annual subsidy of 5,000 pounds of gold).

War against the Germanic tribes: Second Period (544-554). Meanwhile, the Ostrogoths were experiencing something of a comeback in Italy. General Belisarius was sent again to Italy in 544 – with mixed results. Rome was attacked by the Ostrogoths several times, retaken by the Romans several times – and slowly reduced in population to a pathetic state.

In 552 the Ostrogoths were finally defeated by a major Roman force and two years later an invasion of Italy by the Franks was turned back. Italy was thus back in Roman (Byzantine) hands – but at a cost that the Empire was not really prepared to pay.

At the same time, Inter-tribal German war in Spain in 552 brought the Romans to that region, retaking for the Roman Empire a section of southeastern Spain.

Then it was also during this period that Slavic and Turkic invaders began raids into the Danubian provinces (across the Danube). Finally in 559, the aged general Belisarius was able to drive back a group of Turkic Avars who attempted to occupy the area.

Religious and civil activities. Both Zeno and Anastasius had been relatively tolerant of the Monophysites – a matter of great irritation to the bishops of Rome. Justinian thus ended the toleration in an attempt to force religious unity in his empire ... and peace with the bishops of Rome. His wife Theodora however was a Monophysite sympathizer and eventually, toward the end of his reign, Justinian became more tolerant of them.

This role of the emperor in religious affairs pointed to a widening difference between Eastern and Western Christianity. In the West, the bishops of Rome were clearly the leading authority of the church. Their influence, and at times even dominance, over the Germanic tribal kings was also great. But in the East, the authority of the emperor was paramount. The patriarchs of the Eastern Churches (particularly Constantinople, Antioch and Alexandria) were powerful – but not dominating. Domination belonged to the eastern emperor – in religious as well as civil policy. Thus it was that Justinian and Theodora were active supporters of the church, creating rules for the management of foundations, monasteries, episcopal (bishop) elections, etc. Justinian built and repaired churches ... such as the burned out Hagia Sophia in Constantinople which he actually had rebuilt at great cost to the imperial treasury.

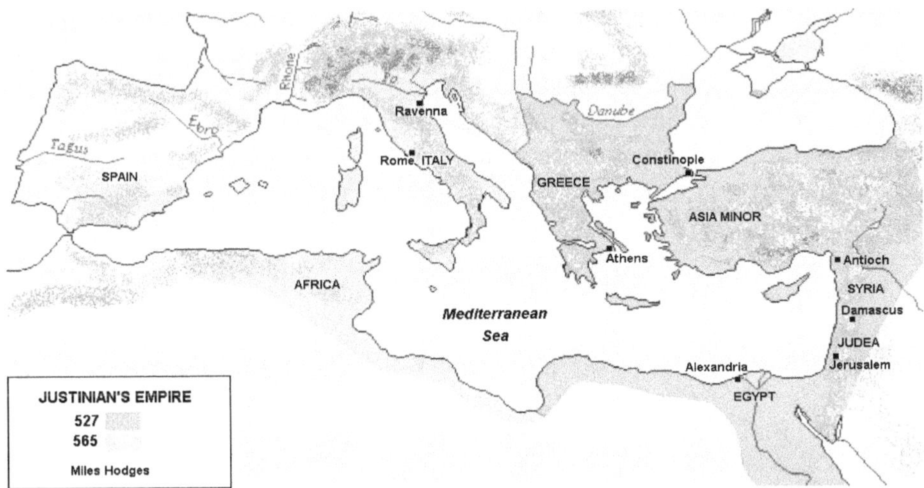

Mounting problems after Justinian. By the end of his reign in 565, Eastern Rome was at relative peace. But beneath the surface lurked serious problems. The ancient and ongoing wars with the Sassanid Persians to the East had reached new levels of violence and were draining the energies (and tax sources) of the Byzantine Empire. (These wars were also draining the energies of Sassanid Persia.) The state treasury was depleted, even though taxes were enormously high. The general population within the Byzantine Empire was getting very restless under this heavy tax burden.

Also, this situation was made worse by the tendency of the imperial capital Constantinople to want to stamp out various Christian "heresies" widespread around the further reaches of the Empire – especially among the non-Greek peoples (mostly Semitic) of the Eastern and Southeastern

Mediterranean borderlands. The concerted effort of the authorities in Constantinople to stamp out these heresies resulted only in alienating the people of these outlying regions all the more.

As a result, by the beginning of the 600s much of the Eastern Roman Empire was also exhausted and restless – physically, morally and spiritually. At the same time, Rome's enemies were simply waiting for an opportunity to find a point of weakness where they could start their assault again on the empire.

His immediate successors. Thus Justinian's successors had their hands full. Power changed hands fairly peacefully, to his nephew, Justin II (565-578), then to Justin's capable general Tiberius II Constantine (578-582), and his general Maurice (582-602). They attempted to restore the empire's finances, yet at the same time keep at bay the troublesome Germanics, Avars, Slavs and Persians.

Tiberius focused, with what was still available of Roman military might, on Eastern Rome's ongoing struggle with Persia. He tried to buy peace with the Avars with extensive subsidies – but the Avars, seeing the desperate situation of the Romans, continued their expansion into the southern Balkan peninsula (just northwest of Constantinople). Tiberius's successor, Maurice, had helped a Persian claimant, Khosrau II, to the Persian throne – and thus secured something of a peace with Persia, one which lasted until Maurice's death in 602. This freed up Rome so as to be able in 602 to push the Avars and Slavs back across the Danube.

Phocas (602-610), Heraclius (610-641), and the Persians. But Maurice's effort to restore state finances by cutting costs outraged his troops along the Danube ... troops who felt unsupported in their efforts to hold the Avars and Slavs – and who thus rose up in revolt (602). Under the leadership of a general Phocas, they marched on Constantinople in protest. The Greens of Constantinople declared Phocas emperor and Maurice fled, was soon captured, and then executed.

At first Phocas's rule was greeted with hope for an easing of the heavy financial and religious burdens felt by the ordinary citizen. But with the withdrawal of the Roman troops from the Danube area, the Avars and Slavs once again became a serious threat to Constantinople. Worse, Phocas's overthrow of Maurice offered Khosrau the pretext to renew the Persian war with the Byzantines, at a time when Byzantine power was at a very low point. Using a Persian-supported pretender to the throne, Theodosius, as his justification for Persian intervention, Khosrau invaded Roman territory in northern Mesopotamia – and then proceeded to conquer much of Asia Minor and Syria (608).

At this same time, Roman governor Heraclius started a revolt against Phocas in his civil diocese of Africa – which then spread to Egypt (609) and then up to Constantinople (610) – where Heraclius received little resistance ... and Phocas was quickly arrested and executed.

But Heraclius's accession* did not shake Khosrau from his cause to install Theodosius as emperor. The Persians pressed forward against a very exhausted Byzantine Rome, taking Damascus (613), Jerusalem (614) and Egypt (618). At one point they even raided all the way into Asia Minor almost just across from the city of Constantinople itself.

A stunned Heraclius finally gathered a Roman army and took to the field himself against Persia in 621. He also gathered allies among the Turks and took advantage of a political division within Persia itself to weaken Persian resistance. In 627 he was able to crush the Persian army at Nineveh.

Khosrau still refused to make peace and Heraclius marched onward to the Persian capital Ctesiphon (628). At this point Khosrau was deposed by his people ... and their newly appointed king, Kavadh II, made peace with the Romans, restoring to them the territory seized by Khosrau. But the war left the Persians exhausted. And it produced the same effect on the Romans. Peace – but also political exhaustion – reigned over both lands.

---

*Heraclius was the first of a long series of Byzantine rulers to entitle himself Basileus – meaning monarch or king – rather than Augustus or emperor.

CHAPTER SIX

ISLAM AND THE WEST
DURING THOSE DARK DAYS

* * *

MUHAMMAD AND ISLAM

Explosion.   Seemingly without warning, out of the obscure Arabian Peninsula roared highly fired-up Arab troops (633), rolling back everything set before them in the name of some obscure Arab prophet named Muhammad. It happened so quickly and so forcefully that both Byzantine Rome and Sassanid Persia, exhausted from their own long-drawn out and mutually destructive wars, found themselves rapidly losing territory to these frenzied Arab troops. Indeed, the Persian Empire was completely overrun and forced under duress to convert to Islam – however choosing a deviant version, Shi'a Islam, that "orthodox" or Sunni Islam would soon come to consider heretical. Meanwhile huge sections of the Byzantine Empire (Southern Iraq, Syria, Palestine and Egypt) were also lost to Islam. All of this occurred in less than a 10-year time frame. What ju`st happened?

While Rome and Persia were blasting each other with all the might they could muster, neither was paying much attention to what was going on to the south of their lands in Arabia. A movement that was both religious and political was gathering there like a dark storm and was about to be unleashed on both extremely exhausted kingdoms to the north.

Muhammad (c. 570-632). This new movement, *Islam,** was founded by an at-first obscure, self-proclaimed prophet born and raised in Mecca, a city situated on the western Arabian trade route linking Yemen in southern Arabia with the Byzantine lands to the north. Muhammad was orphaned as a boy and raised by his uncle Abu Talib, leader of the Banu Hashim (or

---

*Islam: The Arabic *I* plus *Salaam* (similar to the Jewish *Shalom*) is the fundamental concept of Islam. *Salaam* refers to the blessing of true *peace* or success in life ... which comes only in *submitting* to the will of Allah. The two, peace and submission, are thus vitally interconnected.

Hashemite) clan of the Quraysh tribe. The Quraysh tribe dominated life in the city of Mecca – though the Banu Hashim were a rather unimportant clan within that tribe. Life was not easy for Muhammad, being both an orphan and member of a relatively impoverished clan. But his uncle did what he could to help raise Muhammad – taking him on trade journeys north to Syria, where Muhammad was first exposed to the Byzantine-Christian culture.

Islamic tradition states that in an early journey to Syria he encountered a Christian monk, Bahira, who detected in Mohammad a future prophet of God ... and who thus took the time to instruct him in Judeo-Christian thought ... most importantly, Judeo-Christian thought of the Unitarian variety popular among the Semitic (Aramaic or Arabic) speaking people – rather than of the Trinitarian variety popular among the Greek-speaking people of the East. Basically, through this process, Muhammad became something of a Unitarian Christian.

As a tradesman (the only career open to an Arab orphan) Muhammad proved to be a hard and reliable worker – and was eventually hired by Khadijah, a woman 15 years older than him, to be in charge of her caravans to the north. Eventually (595) Khadijah proposed marriage – which he accepted. This not only secured a comfortable life for Muhammad, it proved to be a happy marriage.

The beginning of the *Qur'an* (Muhammad's prophetic recitations). Muhammad was of a philosophical bent and strongly interested in learning the ways of the superior Roman-Christian civilization to the north of Arabia. At the same time, he was deeply embarrassed by the paganism and chaotic tribalism of his Arab world. When back home in Mecca, he would spend a lot of time to himself in a cave in one of the hills just outside the city – in deep meditation about these matters.

In the year 610 he reportedly received a vision or visit from the archangel Gabriel, God's former heavenly messenger to Daniel and the Jewish people of Persia and then later to Mary – announcing Jesus's coming birth to her. Now in his visit to Muhammad, the angel Gabriel commanded Muhammad to memorize and recite some verses which he dictated to Muhammad (Sura 96:1-5). This visit confused and upset Muhammad – though when he told Khadijah of the event, she told him to take the matter seriously. He continued his meditations in the cave – but received no further visit from the archangel. Three years later the visits of Gabriel resumed. He was instructed not only to learn new verses, but to begin preaching them to his fellow Arabs. Basically, these were pronouncements against the paganism of the Arabs and a warning of pending judgments against them if they did not give up these practices and come to Allah (Arabic for "the

God," similar to the Hebrew *El*) ... in submission to his will The verses also included instructions on the proper life of a *Muslim.**

Mounting troubles in Mecca. At first, he attracted only a handful of followers who took his pronouncements seriously: his wife, Khadijah; a slave he had freed, Zayd; his very young cousin, Ali; a close friend, Abu Bakr, and one or two others. Mostly, Mecca scorned him – especially when the numbers of his followers began to increase.

A serious problem facing Muhammad was that Mecca was not only a trade center, it was also a religious center. Once a year, for about a month, the tribes of Arabia would declare a truce and gather peacefully in Mecca to worship their tribal (pagan) deities in the city's center, ranged around the *Ka'bah*, a large cubic structure approximately 40+ feet in each direction, containing in one corner a black stone (possibly a meteorite) twelve inches in diameter. This was very important commercially for the city of Mecca. And to have Muhammad year after year shouting prophetic warnings against the tribes' pagan practices during this high holy month was more than the Quraysh town fathers could tolerate. They could not simply execute Muhammad, because he enjoyed tribal protection as a fellow Quraysh. But his followers, who had no such protection, they were not hesitant to remove by whatever means necessary.

Thus in 615, under Muhammad's direction, a number of his followers left Arabia and moved to Ethiopia (importantly Islam's first *Hijrah* or journey – one of "freedom from oppression"), coming under the protection of the Christian Ethiopian Emperor or *Negus*, Ashama. On their arrival (according to the Maryam or 19th Sura) it was pointed out that Muhammad's Muslims venerated Jesus and the Virgin Mary. However, apparently Ashama was a Trinitarian Christian and thus it was not pointed out that Islam viewed Jesus only as a prophet (though the greatest of all prophets prior to Muhammad) ... even though now in heaven Jesus was seated at the right hand of God and was the one who would one day return to earth to bring the world to its last days. And Mary, though among Muslims a highly venerated woman, certainly was not viewed by Islam as the *Theotokos* or "Mother of God" – as she was by the Trinitarian Christians of those times.

In any case, through a misunderstanding about some of Muhammad's recitations (the "Satanic Verses" in the 53rd Sura), the Quraysh forgave Muhammad and invited his followers to return to Mecca. Muhammad later recanted on these particular verses ... and the persecution of the Muslims in Mecca thus resumed. In 617 Quraysh leaders ostracized the Banu Hashim

---

*A Muslim (*Mu* plus *Salaam*) is simply one who has submitted thusly. The goal of Islam is to bring all the world to such submission ... by whatever means necessary.

for its protection of Muhammad, cutting off not only trade with but also food for the Banu Hashim. This situation persisted for two or three years – however ultimately producing no repentance on the part of Muhammad, although a very shameful treatment of fellow Quraysh. Eventually the ostracism was stopped.

The *Isra* and *Mi'raj* (620). Muhammad claimed that one night Gabriel took Muhammad on a journey. During the first part of the journey, the *Isra*, he was taken from atop the Ka'bah in Mecca by way of a winged horse to a distant mountain (what Muslims believe was the Temple Mount in Jerusalem) and proceeded to lead other prophets in prayer. During the second part of the journey, the *Mi'raj*, the horse takes him from this mountain to heaven, speaking to the ancient prophets and to God (Allah). Here he is instructed by God on prayer – which, thanks to the intervention of Moses – is reduced to only five in number per day.   He is then returned to earth. One of the effects of this journey was that it made the Jerusalem mount, or al-Aqsa, the third most holy site in Islam (after Mecca and Medina).*

The *Hijrah* (622). Muhammad's situation in Mecca remained dangerous – and Muhammad began to explore the possibilities of moving elsewhere. Negotiations with citizens of the city of Yathrib (which would later be termed simply *Medina*, meaning, "city") proved fruitful. His Islamic religion had reached north to Yathrib. A delegation from Yathrib met secretly with Muhammad to invite him and his followers to move to their town. They were having tribal conflicts in Yathrib – largely on-going blood-feuds between the pagan Arab and Jewish tribes of the town. Accompanying the offer was the hope of the delegation that Muhammad might come to the town as a "judge" and restore order and peace there. Muhammad agreed.

When word of the pending migration (the *Hijrah*) reached the Quraysh, they attempted to stop it (as they had with those who had moved to Ethiopia). But most of Muhammad's followers (who came to be termed the *Muhajirun* or "emigrants") were able to slip away to Yathrib. Then in the dark of night Muhammad himself (and his friend Abu Bakr) made their escape to Yathrib. This was the year 622 on the Christian calendar. For the Muslims, this event (the *Hijrah*) serves their calendar as the beginning of year one, and the official beginning of Islam.

In Yathrib (Medina) Muhammad immediately set about establishing a new legal order on which his "peace" (or *salaam*) might stand. The

____

*Jerusalem was initially very central to Muhammad's sense of religious orientation. Similar to the Jews of Arabia, the Muslims had been praying toward Jerusalem (the *Qiblah* or direction of prayer) – until Muhammad abruptly changed the Qiblah toward the Ka'bah in Mecca.

Medinans (people of Yathrib) began a massive conversion to Muhammad's Islamic faith – and closed forces with the Muhajirun as Ansar or "helpers" of the immigrants. The Jewish tribes of the area were included in the new arrangement.

Yet some of the Jews and some recalcitrant pagan tribesmen of Medina were bitter about this new order. When some pagans produced verses mocking Muhammad and his Muslims, they were assassinated. As Muhammad did not disapprove of the assassinations, no one dared to take revenge for the murders. This would be the end of overt pagan opposition to Muhammad in Medina.

The Islamic movement begins to grow. Thus it was that Muhammad was no Jesus II ... but rather one of the nature of an Old Testament Joshua or Gideon or Sampson, slayers of those who stood in their way. Thus to finance his program, Muhammad ordered the raiding on caravans passing Medina on their way from Mecca to the north (wealthy Syria mostly) ... in the process killing many of these tradesmen (and Mecca's soldiers attempting to protect them) and taking the rest for ransom.

Then he turned on the Jewish communities in Arabia when they spurned his religious advances – even made the deadly mistake of mocking him as a "prophet." At first, he simply wanted to kill all the Jews of Medina – but backed down at the urging of a leader of a major Medinan tribe. Instead he merely banished them ... and took their property and distributed it among his followers, with Muhammad himself receiving 20% of the value of the plunder. Muhammad was now a rich man.

But he was soon to become even richer. One Jewish settlement after another Muhammad's troops overran ... with the same results: expulsion of the Jews and the confiscation of their property.

When in 627 the Jews of Khaybar* finally allied with the angry Meccans, a huge army was sent against Muhammad's army – with disastrous results for both the Jews and the Meccans ... all according to God's will, as the Muslims tell the story. The Jews were allowed to continue to live in Arabia – but at the cost of fully one half of their production sent to the Muslims as *jizya* (tribute).

The Meccans now found trade to the north cut off by the Muslims at Medina ... and finally came to some kind of agreement with Muhammad and his Muslims. The Meccans would now allow the Muslims to come to their city for the annual *hajj* (pilgrimage) ... to make their offerings to Allah – not

---

*Khaybar was a large settlement of Jews, who had moved south to Arabia to avoid the ongoing Roman-Persian conflicts. In doing so, they had brought to the region agriculture – instead of just animal-herding, as was common throughout Arabia.

to the Arab pagan deities.

Then two years later (630), an Arab tribal feud led Mohammed to march his troops on Mecca ... ultimately putting Muhammed in full command of the city. And with that, the pagan deities were destroyed ... although the central monument, the Ka'bah, was preserved ... as now the center point of all Islamic worship.

Over the next two years Muhammad's Islam would spread across Arabia, tribe after tribe accepting the faith as part of a new political domain.

His death ... and Islam's deep political division. Soon after completing the great annual Hajj to Mecca in 632, Muhammad gathered the huge crowd of pilgrims (perhaps 120,000) and delivered a long sermon explaining some of the last details completing the full requirements of the Muslim. He concluded with an admonition to follow the Qur'an and ... ?

Here debate within Islam as to what followed in Muhammad's address is intense. The *Shi'ites* ("faction" or "party" of Ali) claim that he added the name of his nephew (and son-in-law) Ali. Sunnis claim, however, that he added the word *Sunna* (the proper "way" of the Muslim). Which of those two options was it that Muhammad wanted the faithful to then follow?

From the very beginning, Islam was thus destined to split into two deeply hostile factions: the Shi'ites and the Sunnis.

Muhammad then returned to Medina ... and a few months later became sick and died. He was buried in Medina (his tomb is now housed in Medina's Mosque of the Prophet).

The fundamentals of Islam

The *Qur'an* and *Hadith*. In so many ways Islam is an extension of the Judeo-Christian legacy ... but a spinoff much simpler in form than its Judeo-Christian parent. Islam has its own holy Scripture, the *Qur'an* (or Koran) ... a recording of what Muhammad claimed were the social-spiritual instructions given him by the archangel Gabriel* ... organized into some 114 *surahs* (chapters) – not chronologically but instead simply by size, the longest surahs presented first and the shortest last. Then there is the *Hadith* – a supplemental collection of sayings and doings of Muhammad ... compiled a couple of centuries later ... although the two competing Islamic subgroups, the Sunnis and the Shi'ites, each have their own versions of the Hadith.

Most interestingly, there is much in the Qur'an that relates closely to

---

*Thus translations of these verses into languages other than the original 7th century Arabic of Muhammad earns such translations the reputation of being merely commentaries on the Qur'an – and are not considered the Qur'an itself.

the Judeo-Christian Bible ... except that it is reshaped considerably under Muhammad's own interpretation of things. For instance, Adam is not the primal sinner that he is in the Judeo-Christian Genesis story ... but instead is the first prophet of the true faith – and thus incapable of sin. Abraham is presented as the father primarily of the Arabs through his son Ishmael and only secondarily through his second son Isaac. Moses and David are part of the account ... although too as sinless prophets. They are part of the prophetic lineup leading to its fulfillment in Mohammed – Muhammed considered as the last or the "seal" of the prophets. Jesus is there also ... as the second to the last and thus very important. But he is viewed in the Unitarian fashion – as a very good man, a moral example to us all sent by God to show us how to live according to the will of God. And Mary is also given considerable attention (a large surah devoted to her) ... as the greatest of women because she was the God-gifted mother of Jesus.

The *Shari'a*. Islam also has its own carefully recorded code of law as per the instructions of Muhammad ... although most unsurprisingly, it is completely in line with the harsh social-moral code of the Arab tribes, a code developed in the face of a very challenging desert environment. And there can be no amendment or updating of this code – because it was set out by Muhammad himself.

The "Five Pillars" of Islam. In comparison to Christianity – especially given the complex theological arguments that produced so much Christian controversy (and bloodshed) – Islamic theology is very simple. Becoming a Muslim is quite easy: simply recite the *Shahada* "There is but one God, God (Allah); and Muhammad is His prophet." This single line is not only the identifying label of the true Muslim – but also the opening line of the prayer or *Salah* that Muslims are required to recite five times a day. Being a social order as well as simply a religion, the Muslim is also required to pay – the *Zakat* or tax – a portion of their wealth to provide for the poor and support the faith in its various works. There is also the annual fast or *Sawm* – which requires them for a full month (Ramadan) to refrain from eating or drinking during daylight hours. They are supposed to use this time to meditate on their faith walk ... to see what they could do to improve that walk. Then there is the *Hajj* or purifying pilgrimage to one or another holy site ... although the lifetime goal of making such a hajj to Mecca itself is considered the highest of all honors.

And that is about all that is required in terms of his or her personal walk as a true Muslim.

Islam's "style." Muhammad himself comes across to Westerners not as a scholarly prophet but instead as a very powerful tribal chief capable of leading his warriors on very bloody engagements with the surrounding world. Muhammad was most capable of slaughter or forced slavery on the part of those who got in his way ... and a very wealthy man on the basis of this trade in human lives and property.

Therefore to a Westerner, Muhammad was hardly a second Jesus. But to a Muslim, he was the very personification of what they believed that Allah or God expected them to be: fierce warriors for the cause of Islam. Thus the *jihadist* or "one who struggles or fights" is considered to be the finest version of the Muslim man of faith. Indeed, dying in the course of jihad or battle is the ultimate guarantee of gaining heaven's greatest reward: the massive sensual pleasures of the afterlife.

On the other hand, since Muhammad had deep respect for the Judeo-Christian world – Judeo-Christians being "People of the Book" – there was an amazing degree of tolerance of Judeo-Christianity ... provided that Judeo-Christians submitted to the political sovereignty of the Islamic political-social order. Indeed, as *dhimmis* (protected peoples), Judeo-Christians were given a fair amount of respect ... provided of course they paid the *jizya* or tribute to their Muslim overlords.

However, this tolerance of other peoples or nations – ones not "People of the Book" (such as the Zoroastrian Persians) – did not exist. Such people brought under Muslim overlordship by conquering Muslim armies either converted to the Islamic faith ... or were killed on the spot.

The rapid spread of Islam

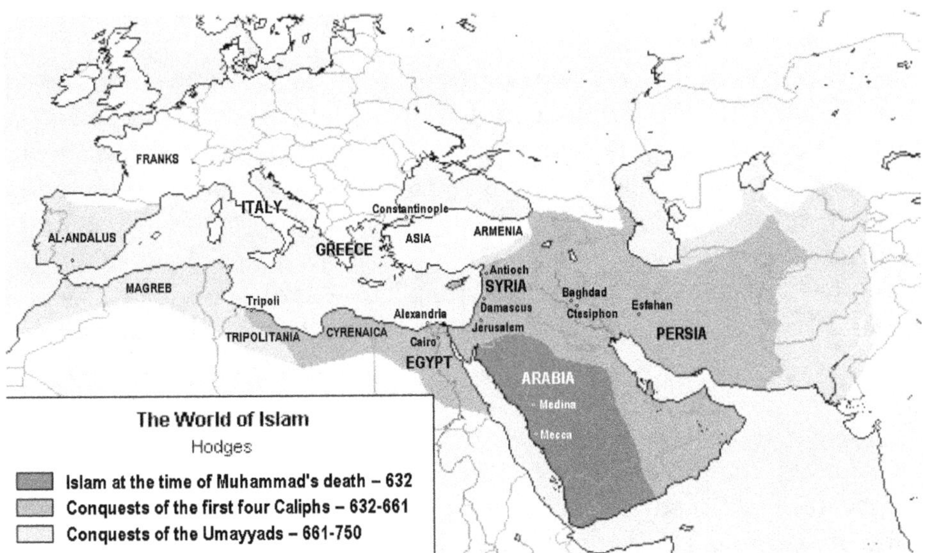

The first ten years. Muhammad's followers were quick to respond to the loss of their leader and called on Muhammad's long-time friend Abu Bakr to be his "successor" or caliph. At the same time, they sent their respected military commander Khalid to bring the rebellious Arab tribes back under Islamic control. Achieving this fairly quickly, Khalid then took his army north to face the Byzantine and Persian empires. But they came not as typical Arab raiders – plundering ... then returning to their bases in Arabia – but as raiders intent on planting themselves as successful invaders of these northern regions.

At first they met client Arab tribes of both empires ... easily convincing them to join them in this enterprise because as Monophysite Christians, they found themselves treated as religious heretics by both Orthodox Rome and Zoroastrian Persia. Then in 633 Khalid ventured even more deeply into the Euphrates River valley and defeated a much larger Byzantine-Persian coalition army ... and established a garrison at Firaz in order to lay strong claim to the region. From this point, Islam would then begin to spread itself westward against the Byzantines and eastward against the Persians.

Abu Bakr would serve only two years before dying ... his place as caliph then taken by another military commander, Umar ... even though there was a group that felt that this position should have gone to Muhammad's nephew and son-in-law Ali. They would subsequently form some kind of small political party, the Shi'a al-Ali, or simply the "Shi'ites." Islam was already beginning to split into two opposing units – the Shi'ites ... and the "Sunnis" – the latter being the "right-thinking" or orthodox portion of Islam. The Sunnis would always be by far the larger of the two groups. But the Shi'ites would never allow themselves to be brought back into union with the Sunnis ... even down to today!

Nonetheless, during Umar's ten-year caliphate (634-644) Islam would explode out onto the world of both Byzantium and Persia ... succeeding in that time period in fully defeating Persia (641) and doing nearly the same to Byzantium. Syria fell quickly to Islam in 634, Jerusalem in 637, Alexandria and Egypt in 641, and the western portions of Africa's Mediterranean coast (Cyrenaica) in 643-644.

The Byzantines would of course attempt to retake lost territory ... though things always worked out better for the Muslims than for the Byzantines. Thus the Byzantine loss extended to the islands of Cyprus and Crete (649) thanks to the military and diplomatic skills of the Islamic governor of Syria, Mu'awiya. Mu'awiya was even able to defeat a huge Byzantine navy along the southern coast of Asia Minor ... the Byzantine emperor Constans able to escape back to Constantinople only by disguising himself. It was all very humiliating for Constans ... and glorifying for Mu'awiya.

The deepening Sunni-Shi'ite split. Meanwhile, political troubles back in Mecca deepened over this ongoing problem of choosing a new caliph … especially with the death of Umar and his replacement by Uthman (r. 644-656) … more of a businessman than a soldier. There to challenge Uthman was A'isha … the highly ambitious daughter of one of Muhammad's 13 wives or concubines. She brought to the ruling council claims of corruption on the part of Uthman and his ruling group. But not getting the satisfaction she wanted, she encouraged a spirit of rebellion – in which one result was for a group of conspirators to break into Uthman's home in Medina and murder him while he was seated, studying the Qur'an.

The spirit of rebellion now spread … A'isha for some reason now opposing Ali's Shi'ite group that had been working with her. But finally (656) the hope of the ruling council was that in appointing Ali as caliph (who at first refused the offer), peace within Islam could be restored.

Ali finally accepted … although Uthman's Umayyad relatives refused to accept the decision and moved to Syria. Then the spirit of rebellion exploded … with Arab armies fighting Arab armies … and with the Umayyad Mu'awiya simply refusing to accept Ali as caliph.

Ali attempted to employ the ancient Arab diplomatic tool of compromise (very helpful under the harsh conditions of desert life) … which merely infuriated some of his more radical supporters, the Kharijites. And thus Ali too experienced the fate of Uthman when he was stabbed in 661 by a Kharijite while he was praying in the mosque of Kufa (Islam's new political capital to the north of Arabia).

Mu'awiya's Umayyad caliphate at Damascus. At this point Mu'awiya simply took the title of caliph for himself … and soon made his Syrian capital of Damascus also the political center of the Ummah or Islamic empire.

Mu'awiya made no pretense to be a very religious man … but understood his call in life to make his domain a most powerful one. He even engaged Christians as advisors … infuriating Muslim purists in the process. But there was little they could do, because his rule was proving to be a highly steadying experience for a deeply divided Islam.

Actually, he seemed fairly uninterested in converting anyone to Islam … as the revenues from the Christian and Jewish jizya proved to be much greater than the taxes or zakat imposed on the Muslim faithful. In fact, despite Mu'awiya's disinterest in the matter, there would be extensive conversion of the citizens of his empire from Christianity to Islam … simply because it meant for them a considerable lowering of their tax rates! So much for official religiosity!

In any case, the Umayyads would offer Islam 14 caliphs, governing from their capital in Damascus … as well as a century of steady growth and consolidation of the Ummah.

✳ ✳ ✳

ISLAM CHALLENGES WESTERN EUROPE

The Muslim conquest of Spain (Muslim "al-Andalus"*). By the early 700s, there seemed to be no stopping the spread of Islam. It headed West across the Mediterranean coastline of North Africa – under the conqueror Tariq – reaching the Atlantic and then turning north across the narrow Gibraltar straits[†] in 711 to head into Christian Spain. Tragically, Visigothic Spain at the time was deeply caught up in a civil war among the Visigoths. Thus the Muslims ended up rolling easily over the entire Visigothic kingdom after defeating the Visigothic army at the Guadalete River in 712.[‡]

Then soon joined by a larger Arab army led by Musa ibn Nusayr, Muslim governor of Ifriqiya, the two Muslim groups spread Umayyad rule even deeper into Spain over the next seven years ... even capturing Visigothic Septimania in coastal southern France.

However a small group of Christian Visigoths were able to hold off the Muslim onslaught by retreating into the Cantabrian mountainous in the north of the Iberian Peninsula ... where, restructured as the small Kingdom of Asturias, Christians would take refuge for the next few centuries.

And thus was the foundation of a huge Islamic Spain, then known as al-Andalus, with its capital at Cordoba.

Action north of the Pyrenees Mountains into Southern France

Duke Odo and the Battle of Toulouse (721). In 721 the Umayyad governor al Samh decided to complete the conquest of Southern France by heading west from Umayyad controlled Narbonne in coastal Septimania (where al Samh had established his capital) with an immense Muslim army. His goal was Toulouse, the capital of Christian Aquitaine. He had almost brought the city of Toulouse to defeat ... when he and his army were suddenly surrounded by an equally immense Christian army led by Odo, Duke of Aquitaine. Surprised Muslims fled or were cut down in such

---

*The Muslim Arabs first encountered the Germanic Vandals (or Wendels) coming from that direction, and thus identified the region as al-Andalus (dropping the V sound) ... even though it was Visigoths and not Vandals that they would encounter there.

†"Gibraltar" is the Spanish rendering of the Arabic *Jabal Tariq* or "Mountain of Tariq," named after the Arab general Tariq ibn Ziyad who led the advanced attack of the Umayyads into Spain.

‡Also (apparently) the ease of this Islamic victory occurred at least in part because the Latin population seemed not to be particularly fond of their Visigothic (German) rulers.

huge numbers that the battle amounted to a very bloody, very humiliating defeat for the Umayyad army (though at a cost almost as high among Odo's Christians). The Umayyad governor al Samh escaped, but died soon thereafter from his wounds.*

Frankish governor Charles Martel enters the picture. Despite Odo's huge victory over the Muslims at Toulouse, the Umayyads were able to regroup and continue their raiding of Odo's Aquitaine from their well-supplied coastal base at Narbonne. At one point Odo attempted an alliance with the frustrated Muslim Berbers (though Muslim, treated contemptuously by their Arab governors) – as much in defense against the expansive Franks to the North as the expansive Umayyads to the East. But this did not

---

*Muslim tradition stated that the Muslims lost over 350,000 soldiers ... and the Christians near that number at 300,000. The number seems to be probably a huge exaggeration ... but in any case, very indicative of the huge loss that both sides experienced at this battle. Also, the Muslim historians themselves placed greater significance on their strategic loss at the hands of Odo at Toulouse than they did on the disaster they experienced eleven years later at Tours at the hands of Charles Martel.

seem to suffice to fend off the Umayyad Arabs ... and the situation grew so desperate that Odo finally appealed to his Frankish rival to the north, Charles Martel, for help. Charles agreed, on the condition that Odo submit to Charles' authority.

The Austrasian Mayor of the Palace (located at Cologne), Pepin of Herstal, had been directed by one of his wives, Plectrude, to appoint their grandson Theudoald to replace him at his death ... ultimately 714. But at that point, Theudoald was a mere 8-year-old child. Then Charles, one of Pepin's sons by another wife, escaped the imprisonment imposed on him by Plectrude, and moved decisively to put down rebellions among the Neustrian nobles (the Frankish civil war of 715-718) ... restoring the unity of Francia – and making very clear who was exactly in charge in Francia. Graciously, Plectrude was sent to a convent and Theudoald lived out his life under his uncle Charles's protection.

Then – as the Austrasian Mayor of the Palace – Charles proclaimed Chlothar IV as King of Austrasia ... and replaced Rigobert as Archbishop of Reims with a political ally of his, Milo, Bishop of Trier. But when Chlothar died, Charles switched his support to Chlothar's rival, Chilperic ... on the condition of being named Mayor of the Palace for all of Francia. Then, in the name of King Chilperic, he went conquering to the East in Germany, bringing Alemannia and Bavaria under Frankish rule. Then when Chilperic died, Charles brought the young Theuderic IV to the throne – though keeping real power in his own hands. Meanwhile he continued the military task of bringing kingdoms both at home and abroad under his rule. By 730 he had a wide realm solidly under his control.

At the same time, Charles had been professionalizing his Frankish troops. In those days, volunteer troops, the basis of most tribal armies, would only serve the short period between the time when crops were established and growing and then when they had to be harvested. Charles instead paid his troops ... by confiscating the wealth of the churches and monasteries in his realm – bringing on him the danger of excommunication by Catholic authorities.

But having a professional – and well-tested – army available in 732 would be a surprise to the Muslims ... and the possible salvation of Western Christianity (the Church would recognize this soon enough!). At the same time the Muslims were not particularly observant of how well the Franks under formerly Pepin and now Charles were growing as a Christian military power. That would be a huge mistake.

The Battle of Tours/Poitiers (October 732). In 732 the Umayyads under Abd al-Rahman undertook a massive invasion of Odo's Aquitaine – this time delivering Odo a crushing blow ... and then heading north towards the Loire Valley, burning and plundering as they went, with the wealthy abbey of Saint Martin of Tours as their next objective. Suddenly, just north of Poitiers, they ran into Charles Martel's well-positioned and highly experienced army blocking the route to Tours. For seven days the Muslims attempted small skirmishes to draw out the Franks ... or at least dislodge them from their well-defended position. Finally on the seventh day, the Muslim cavalry charged Charles's infantry ... only to find Charles' troops surprisingly unyielding. Then a rumor spread among the Muslims that some Franks had raided their base camp to steal the plunder and free the slaves they had taken at Bordeaux ... and groups of Muslim troops broke off the battle to retreat to the base camp. But the retreat turned into an undisciplined rout ... with Abd al-Rahman himself killed in the retreat. At the dawn of the next day the Franks were surprised to discover the Muslim camp abandoned.

Continuing Muslim attacks. Umayyads under a new governor would attempt another large invasion of Francia in 735 ... and reach northeastward into Burgundy ... even as far north as Lyons. Charles Martel would counter with attacks into Septimania (736 and 739), taking various cities as he went ... but fail to dislodge the Muslims at Narbonne. The Muslims would, in fact, remain in Narbonne for another 20 years.

Berber rebellion. In the meantime, huge communities of Muslim Berbers (from Ifriqiya) and Arabs had been brought to settle al-Andalus, with the Berbers being assigned the areas of the north most susceptible to Christian counterattacks ... a matter of some bitterness infecting the relationship between the Muslim Arabs and Berbers. In fact, Berber rebellions were frequent, especially one that took place across Spain and North Africa in 740 ... which was put down only in 742 by an Arab Syrian army and then occupied by Syrian governors. The latter strengthened the Muslim hold over Spain ... but also formed the foundation for a number of rather autonomous feudal estates.

Alfonso I starts the Spanish *Reconquista*. Meanwhile, the Berber rebellion and the Berber evacuation of the frontline against Asturias – as well as the humiliating thrashings the Umayyads received at Toulouse and Tours – allowed Christian King Alfonso I (ruled Asturias 739-757) to take over the abandoned Berber forts in northern Spain and add the provinces of Galicia (740) and Leon (754) to his northern kingdom.

The *Reconquista* or "reconquering" of Spain by the Christians had thus begun. It would take another 650 years to finish the job.

The End of the Umayyad Caliphate in Syria (750)

Meanwhile, huge problems developed for the Umayyads when a member of the Hashemite group, Al-Saffah, put forward his own personal claim to dominion over the Islamic Ummah – on the basis of his direct descent from an uncle of Muhammad named Abbas (thus giving a name to him and his future dynasty as the "Abbasids"). He also cultivated an ever-widening power base among the Persians, who resented the pretensions of the Arab aristocracy, considering desert Arabs to be naturally inferior to those born to what was clearly the superior Persian civilization. Thus a bit of nationalism (Persian versus Arab) was rising within the world of Islam ... a nationalism that al-Saffah was glad to exploit in order to bring himself to power.*

In 747, the Abbasid military seized control from the Umayyad governor in Persia ... and under the command of the Persian general Abu Muslim moved their troops westward, driving back the Umayyad forces facing them. In 749, the Abbasids were so bold as to declare their leader al-Saffah as the new caliph (749-754). And the following year, Al-Saffah's Abbasid army defeated a huge Umayyad army in northern Iraq.

The Umayyad caliph was able to escape to Egypt, but was caught and beheaded ... thus bringing the Umayyad caliphate in Damascus fully to an end (750).

Now began the eradication of Umayyad power everywhere ... in a highly brutal fashion – including the slaughter of 80 members of the Umayyad clan leadership at a banquet supposedly called to work out an Arab-like compromise.

At this point the central seat of Islamic power was moved East from Damascus in Syria to Baghdad in Persia ... also bringing Islam under greater Persian cultural influence (art, music, literature).

However ... although the Abbasids used all the Persian Shi'ite support they could gather, they would remain staunchly Sunni in character.

The Umayyads continue to rule in isolation in Spain
for the next seven centuries

Abd al-Rahman I. Only one Umayyad, Abd al-Rahman (another individual with that same name!), escaped the slaughter of his kinsmen ... and made his way to al-Andalus. Here he took control of the Islamic government at

---

*This Persian spirit of hostility towards their Arab overlords was a major reason that the Persians identified themselves with the minority Shi'ites, in opposition to the majority (and largely Arab) Sunnis. Persia or modern Iran even today takes very seriously this same quite hostile – and quite nationalist – Shi'ite position.

Cordoba and declared himself Emir or Governor ... of a fully sovereign Emirate operating independently of the Abbasid Caliphate seated at Baghdad.

But his rule was not secure – neither along the north with the border with the Christian principalities nor to the south across the straits of Gibraltar in Africa.

The emirs after him had an even harder time holding onto their power ... for by 900 the power of the Umayyad Emir did not extend much beyond the capital of Cordoba itself.

Abd al-Rahman III. Then in 912, Abd al-Rahman III was able to bring all of al-Andalus and parts of Northwestern Africa back under Umayyad power ... restoring the region to a peace that it had not enjoyed for generations ... and taking for himself the title of Caliph.

This brought the Umayyad Caliphate to a level equaling even the Shi'ite Fatimid Caliphate based in Tunisia, the Umayyads' major competitor for control of North Africa.

For the next century the region grew greatly prosperous, expanding its trade ... and strengthening the character of its intellectual and artistic culture ... to a level unsurpassed in the rest of Islam ... and to the great admiration of even Christian Europe.

The gradual breakdown of Umayyad power in Spain. However a civil war among the Spanish Umayyads greatly weakened their power ... and little by little, during the 970s al-Mansur (known to the West as Almanzor) – the vizier or advisor to a very young Umayyad Caliph Hisham – took ever greater control over the affairs of state ... until by 980 he was in total control of the caliphate. With his incredible energy he took on the Christian states in Northern Spain ... winning a number of battles ... but thereby driving the Christians into a greater unity of effort against him.

Then when al Mansur died in 1002, his first son ruled a short six years before dying, and a very ambitious half-brother took over as vizier, even trying to take the title of caliph away from Hisham. This precipitated a huge civil war among the Muslims... which in turn by 1030 had broken the Muslim state into a number of now fiercely competing Muslim *taifa* or principalities – thus shattering Umayyad power and bringing the Umayyad caliphate to an end (1031).

The Spanish Reconquista gains momentum. This in turn now gave the Christian kingdoms (Asturias, Leon, Castile, Navarre and Aragon) the opportunity to advance the Reconquista against the various Islamic states ... a process which would continue until the last Muslim taifa or state of Granada was overthrown in 1492, closing out permanently the long Muslim presence in Spain (also the year of the Spanish-sponsored discovery of America by Columbus!).

El Cid.* A Christian Castilian knight of the second half of the 1000s would play a huge symbolic role in this process of the Christian reconquering of Spain, although for his personal traits as a warrior – rather than on the basis of any full loyalty to the Christian cause! In fact, Rodrigo Diaz de Vivar served both local Christian and Muslim lords, depending on the various shifts in his personal political status. Nonetheless, "El Cid" would not only come to be a major icon (even down to today) as an agent of the Reconquista, but would also exemplify the extreme complexity of the Muslim-Christian mix that dominated so much of Spain for seven centuries.

In many important ways, a Muslim-Christian Spain would leave an intellectual-cultural legacy that would run deep within a reviving post-Roman Christian world, in close conjunction with the Muslim impact on Western culture that would also come to Europe via the Christian crusades to the Muslim Middle East, crusades that were about to break forth also at the closing of the 1000s.

* * *

THE CAROLINGIAN DYNASTY

Charles Martel's legacy. In 737, Theuderic, King of the Franks, died ... and Charles Martel neither took the royal title for himself nor selected another member of the declining Merovingian family to take the position. The position of King remained vacant for the rest of Charles's days.

But of course Charles was totally in charge of the politics of this vast kingdom ... principally by forcing the rather self-governing dukes and counts to acknowledge his sovereign rule over them, or by personal appointments of new dukes and counts ... not infrequently achieved by brutal military action. However he continued to respect the relative autonomy of Odo in Aquitaine ... and Odo's son Hunald who took title as Duke of Aquitaine when Odo died in 735.

Charles was also a very active agent of the Catholic Church ... providing heavy support to (Saint) Boniface as archbishop of Charles's extensive holdings east of the Rhine River ... with Boniface offering in return strong church support for Charles's rule.

Pepin the Short (or "Lesser"). In 740, a year before his death, Charles

---

*From al-Sayyid: An Arabic political title meaning "the Lord" – received by Rodrigo in his military service to the Muslim King of the Taifa of Zaragoza.

designated his two sons as governors of his extensive kingdom: the older Carloman receiving Austrasia, Alemannia and Thuringia and the younger Pepin receiving Neustria, Burgundy, and Provence.   Though both sons were devout Christians, educated by the monks of St. Denis (Paris), the quite pious Carloman in 747 took up monastic life at Monte Casino (Italy), leaving all of Francia to Pepin.

Then an "understanding" developed between Pepin and Pope Zachary in 751, the latter who in exchange for Pepin's support against the hard-pressing Lombards in Italy declared the useless Merovingian kingship to have ended.   This then allowed an assembly of Frankish nobles to elect Pepin as King of the Franks ... and then have his friend Boniface officiate at Pepin's coronation that same year.   Thus was established the foundations of the new Carolingian dynasty as Frankish kings.

The following year, the new pope Stephen II traveled to St. Denis to officially anoint Pepin as Roman Patrician (and thus protector of the Roman papacy) ... and his sons, the 12-year-old Charles (Charlemagne) and 3-year-old Carloman as eventual inheritors of their father's positions and titles.   In return, Pepin forced the Lombard king to return Italian lands taken from the Church ... an action which came to be known as the "Donation of Pepin" ... certifying the Church as a major participant in what was beginning to take shape as the European feudal system.

Pepin was naturally busy forcing local rulers to either acknowledge his suzerainty ... or be replaced by Pepin's own appointments.   He also took the offensive against the Muslims of Septimania at Narbonne ... requiring seven years (752-759) to drive the Muslims – permanently – from this last bit of territory they held north of the Pyrenees.   He then turned his attention to the duchy of Aquitaine in order to force that region as well to submit to his sovereign rule.   It would take eight long years (760-768) of bloody warfare and brutal devastation to complete the task ... achieved just before he died in 768.

Charlemagne

In coming to power in 768, Charles (eventually "Charlemagne" or "Charles the Great") found himself facing a serious revolt in Aquitaine ... which he was able to put down fairly quickly ... even without the assistance of his brother Carloman, with whom relations became strained.   But Carloman would not factor long in the scheme of Carolingian politics, for he died in 771 – only 20 years old.

Against the Lombards.   Charles now turned his attention to the Lombards ... and their contention with Pope Adrian over the title of the lands of northern Italy. Charles sided with the pope, and attacked the Lombards at Pavia in 773 to force them to yield ... which, surrounded and now quite desperate, they surrendered the next summer (774). This then allowed Charles to take the crown as King of the Lombards ... not that this would not be contested by Italian dukes. Indeed, Charles in 776 had to put down a rebellion led by two of the Italian dukes. Eventually Charles was able to extend Frankish rule all the way south to Salerno (787), also pressuring the Duke of Benevento to recognize Charles's suzerainty in 788 ... influenced in part by a countering pressure coming from the Byzantine Empire based to the south at the base of the Italian peninsula.

In 781 he had designated his son Pepin (originally at birth "Carloman") – still yet a child – as King of Italy (and confirmed by Pope Adrian). Pepin would eventually take up heavy responsibilities of governance and military leadership quite well ... leading some of his father's regional armies in the constant warfare that took place during his father's rule.

Against the Umayyads of al-Andalus (Spain). On another front, an opportunity to extend Christianity back into Spain seemed to present itself when local Muslim rulers promised to acknowledge him as their king ... if he would break the power of the Umayyad Emir Abd al-Rahman. But despite gathering a huge army of Franks, Burgundians and Lombards at Saragossa in 778, they were not able to defeat the city ... and Charles finally gave up ... only to have hostile Basques* – bitter because of Charlemagne's destruction of the walls of their capital city, Pamplona – attack the rear of his army at Roncesvalles as he retreated north across the Pyrenees.† Charles reacted by taking direct control of Aquitaine and placing another son Louis (the Pious) over the province as its new king.

However, despite the humiliation at Saragossa, Charles continued to receive homage as nominal ruler in the Catalan region of Northeastern Spain ... because of the bitter feelings the local Muslim leaders felt towards the Muslim authorities at Cordoba. Thus Charles's troops received Barcelona without a fight in 797 ... lost it in 799 to the Umayyads and then regained it again in 801. From there the Franks extended their boundaries deeper

---

*The Basques – located primarily in Northern Spain – are a people whose language is unlike any of the Indo-European languages ... and for that matter any language spoken elsewhere in the world. The supposition is that they are the descendants of a people who once inhabited a larger portion of Europe prior to the migrations of the Indo-European tribes into Western Europe.

†This was the famous Battle of Roncevaux Pass in which Roland, leading the rearguard of the Frankish army, put up a brave resistance before being cut down by the Basque rebels. This event was to become legendary when it was retold as the earliest of the French epic poems, *La Chanson de Roland* (*The Song of Roland*).

into Spain along the Mediterranean coast, all the way to the Ebro River ... thereby founding the "Spanish March."

Against the Saxons. Meanwhile, Charles had been pressing his borders deeper across northern Germania, defeating one Saxon tribe after another (pretty much over the entire course of his years of rule) ... bringing the Saxons to convert to Catholic Christianity as a part of his effort to solidify the foundations of his growing domain. But revolts among the Saxons were not uncommon.

The Avars. Also, his son Pepin fought the nomadic Asian Avars when – from their huge Avar Empire or Khaganate located in Eastern Europe – they invaded Germanic Bavaria and the Germanic lands further South along the Danube River ... finally defeating them in 796 and bringing them into the Catholic faith.

The Slavs. To the East of Germania were the Slavs, against whom Charlemagne led his army ... only to have the Slavs offer little resistance – but instead submit rather willingly to his rule, accepting his Catholic faith in the process. Indeed, the Slavs would become important allies in some of Charlemagne's further efforts to put down Saxon rebellions. They also served as allies in Pepin's battles with the Avars.

Charlemagne crowned Emperor by Pope Leo III (800). In December of 800 Charlemagne was in Rome visiting his friend Pope Leo III – who had taken refuge at Charlemagne's court the previous year when the Pope found himself in danger from local Romans. On Christmas Day Pope Leo crowned Charlemagne as "Augustus" (Roman Emperor).

The exact meaning of this action was not clear ... even at the time. Some claimed that this made him Emperor of all the Roman Empire – taking up the inheritance of an unbroken line of Roman emperors that had continued via the Eastern or Byzantine Empire. At the time, the Byzantine Empire was headed by Irene, who held her position as Empress by having had her son Leo VI blinded (who soon died of his wounds) ... making her position appear highly illegitimate to many. Thus, to those same people, this coronation made Charles – not Irene – Rome's true Emperor. But Charles was not interested in involvement in Mediterranean politics ... having enough problems to deal with at the borders of – or even within – the territories where he had extended Frankish rule directly. Nonetheless, this matter of Emperorship would continue to vex East-West Roman Christian relations for many centuries to come ... as the imperial title granted to Charlemagne by the Pope would be passed on (with a brief break) by future popes to future Western leaders.

The development of the feudal system. European feudalism, though basic elements had been put in place by earlier Frankish kings, took a highly developed form under Charlemagne. In conquering these numerous German and Slavic tribes (Franks, Visigoths, Burgundians, Lombards, Alemanni, Avars, Croatians, etc.),* he had a far-flung and culturally highly diverse Empire to govern.

Charlemagne saw himself not just as a military dominator over numerous tribes – sort of a tribal super-chief. Instead, he understood himself to be something of a landlord, in full personal ownership of the lands and people he had conquered, to do with as he himself personally chose. Thus by receiving from the hands of the Pope the title of Emperor, Charlemagne had received the recognition and support – even blessing – of the powerful Church to this amazing political claim.

The relationship of Lord and Vassal. But Charlemagne had no extensive bureaucracy at hand to help him govern this massive estate, to organize the repair of roads and towns, to police the highways, to collect the taxes, etc. such as the earlier Roman emperors possessed. So Charlemagne had to improvise. Instead he placed sons where he could over portions of his territory – now legally an Empire – and leased portions of the rest of his empire to personal supporters termed "vassals," giving sons and vassals the right to govern in his place at the more local levels of society. This privilege – and responsibility – placed supporters of this system under the obligation not only to supervise the peace of Charlemagne's realm in their particular assigned districts (duchies, counties, principalities, etc.), but to provide taxes and military service when called on by the emperor to do so. Once assigned a place in Charlemagne's organization, these vassals could then turn around and, as lords (dukes, barons, counts) themselves of one of Charlemagne's regional realms, appoint vassals of their own to help govern smaller portions of their duchies or principalities.

Thus feudalism. And thus the system of sub-infeudation (sub-leasing) or "feudalism" was born ... a system by which the older, somewhat "democratic" Germanic idea of tribal territories presided over by elective tribal councils and tribal kings was replaced by a new "proprietary" system in which all-powerful "landowners" placed at various levels of this feudal system were put in total control of what was now considered almost "personal" (or family)

---

*However the Saxons of England would maintain their tribal independence until conquered by the French Normans ("Northmen" originally from Scandinavia) in 1066 – at which point England also came under the same system of feudalism.

territory.

This new "feudal" setup was given legitimacy by special rites of anointing extended to these landed rulers by officers of the Church (bishops, archbishops, and even, when the position was important enough, the Pope at Rome). Who then dared to contest what the Church (and thus supposedly God himself) had ordained?

The rightless masses (peasants). The masses of common people who worked the farmlands of these feudal proprietors were now relegated to the level of possessions, something like cattle. They were peasants with only the rights accorded them by the lords (and ladies) who ruled absolutely over them. The peasants and their lands could be bought, sold, exchanged, or gifted freely – without any consultation with the peasants themselves – to other lords belonging to the privileged circle of the feudal aristocracy that Charlemagne had created ... and that the Church authorized and certified.

This system would remain intact in Europe for the next thousand years – until the rise in the 1800s of nationalism and the accompanying doctrine of popular democracy.*

The roots of a significant cultural revival

The "Carolingian Renaissance." When the Pope crowned Charlemagne as Roman Emperor, it seemed that Europe was possibly on track to restore the lost grandeur of Roman society and culture. Charlemagne's new empire brought political stability ... and consequently economic development. And that in turn stirred to life a dramatic intellectual-cultural revival ... developed largely because Charlemagne himself was extremely interested in cultivating scholarship within his empire ... especially as he himself (typical of Germanic political leadership) could not read.

Consequently, his capital at Aachen became a gathering place for scholars, artists and builders. They came from all around this diverse empire – and even beyond. His chief minister Alcuin was an English clergyman, scholar, author, poet and teacher of logic from York (not part of his empire). Charlemagne's court included also the Spanish Visigoth poet and scholar Theodulf, the Lombard historian Paul the Deacon, Roman-Italian grammarian Peter of Pisa, and master theologian Paulinus of Aquileia. And certainly there were numerous Franks – the mathematician Einhard, the librarian Waldo, and the poet Angilbert, among them.

---

*Avoiding this feudal system were the city-states of Renaissance Italy and Flanders – at least for a few centuries (1300s to early 1500s). Also the English colonists of New England would come to their own "democratic" development a couple of centuries before the rest of Europe moved in that direction in the 1800s.

Huge number of Latin works were rewritten in a simplified Latin script (not just capitals but also "minuscules" or lower-case letters) ... to make learning easier ... especially among the priests, many of whom were illiterate. And the collection of valuable writings occurred ... producing key libraries.

Art and architecture also began a significant revival ... because of the German contact with the Mediterranean world where "Romanesque" architecture was still prevalent. Also, commercial relations with the Muslim world (built heavily on the sale of slaves) exposed the Carolingian world to more sophisticated art and architecture. Overall, the Carolingian building program was immense – with numerous new cathedrals, hundreds of monasteries and around a hundred royal residences constructed during the 80-year Carolingian period of Charlemagne and his immediate successors.

But perhaps most important – certainly at least to Charlemagne – was the moral and spiritual reform and strengthening of the Church ... Charlemagne becoming involved in refinements of the Church's theology and doctrines. Charlemagne understood that a strong empire depended on a strong moral culture at its base.

The breakup of the Carolingian Empire

Louis the Pious (814-840). In 813, Charlemagne had his only surviving son, Louis the Pious (king of Aquitaine), elevated to the position of co-emperor with himself ... shortly before Chalremagne died at the beginning of 814. Ordinarily, under the Salian Law of the Franks, Louis would have been required to have shared his rule with his two brothers.[*] But both died before Louis finally took the throne. Thus the Empire remained united.

But when Louis nearly died of an accident in 817, he decided to draw up his will ... arranging for the future division of the Empire among his three (eventually four) sons. His oldest son Lothair was to receive the imperial title and the greatest portion of the Empire. Pepin was assigned Aquitaine and Louis was assigned Bavaria. Furthermore, in accordance with Salian law, the children of his own sons were then to receive the right to various portions of their fathers' lands. Supposedly all this then provided for an orderly transfer of the realm in case of his own death.

----

[*]On the other hand, in England the Saxons practiced primogeniture, in which only the oldest son inherited all of the father's lands. That certainly was viewed as unfair by the other sons. But it kept the work and thus inheritance of the father intact from one generation to the next. The Salian law of the Franks was "fairer" to the sons, but left the father's legacy greatly weakened when it was divided fairly equally among his sons. However, the Franks eventually were forced to adopt primogeniture as the only serious solution to the problems caused by a constant subdividing of the family's feudal inheritance.

That was not to be. It became virtually the declaration of war among his sons – Lothair, Pepin, Louis and then, later, Charles – as they maneuvered to improve their inheritance ... mostly against Lothair and his privileged position in all this. Despite Louis's efforts to keep his sons in line, periods of bitter rivalry broke out (beginning in 829) among the brothers – and some of their sons as well – thoroughly disrupting life in the Carolingian Empire. Then when Vikings descended on the Empire to begin their raiding, plundering, and slaughter in 837, the situation grew horribly worse. Finally in 840, Louis was able to put a halt to the rebellion. But then an exhausted Louis died that same year.

The Treaty of Verdun (843) dividing the empire. With their father dead, the three surviving brothers – Lothair, Charles,* and Louis (Pepin had died in 838) – once again turned on each other. Lothair claimed the entire inheritance ... minus Aquitaine, which he assigned to his nephew Pepin II. But neither Charles nor Louis acknowledged Lothair's claim and war broke out again among the brothers. In 841 Charles and Louis defeated Lothair at the Battle of Fontenay ... and the following year (842) they were so bold as to declare Lothair unfit as emperor. At this point Lothair was willing to yield to negotiations held at Verdun.

The results of the negotiations were that Louis was awarded sections of the Empire East of the Rhine River, Charles the Western sections of the Empire, and Lothair a central strip of land – one reaching from the Netherlands in the North, then south along the Western bank of the Rhine ("Lotharingia" or "Lorraine"), then Burgundy and Italy in the South ... plus the right to keep his imperial title.

Whereas Lothair's territory lacked any centralizing tendency – plus having the grand impediment of the Swiss Alps positioned in the middle – Louis was able to take control of a land that would remain culturally largely "German" (thus his title, "Louis the German"). At the same time Charles's more Latin-based Western territory would become the foundation for the country of France.

This division would weaken greatly the peace, stability and prosperity of the Carolingian Empire – gradually driving Northern Europe back into something of another "Dark Age" ... especially with the Vikings taking advantage tremendously of the disunited and thus greatly-weakened Empire.

---

*He would eventually come to be known as Karolus Calvus, Charles the Bald ... although it had nothing to do with his hair ... of which he always had plenty! Speculation today is that instead it was in reference to the fact that at one time he was a son without any holding of land. But no one knows for sure why the title.

*** * ***

THE HOLY ROMAN EMPIRE ... AND THE PAPACY

The loss ... and then the restoration of the imperial title. The imperial title was passed through future generations of the Carolingian dynasty, then placed under challenge by Vikings from the north and then by a mass of dynastic contests – enfeebling the dynasty greatly. The imperial title got lost, was restored again, then just passed out of existence as the Carolingians lost their political positions in most places.

Then the Italian King Berengar came forward to claim the imperial title finally in 915 ... holding onto that claim until his death in 924. Then the title again fell into disuse.

Otto I the Great.   In 962 Saxon[*] King Otto I – who had succeeded in bringing a number of German duchies under his rule, who then in 955 decisively defeated invading Magyars (Hungarians) from the east, and who then in 961 absorbed the Kingdom of Italy – was crowned in Rome as Roman Emperor[†] by Pope John XII.

This Germanic central European (and northern Italian) imperial state – ultimately the "Holy Roman Empire" – would remain intact through many centuries – in fact all the way up to 1806, when the French Emperor Napoleon formally put an end to the title and position.

The elective nature of the imperial position. At first the title was hereditary, with a series of Ottos (II and III) and a cousin Henry inheriting the position and title after Otto I. But with Henry's death in 1024 the position became elective among a group of prominent dukes and other noblemen – constituting a College of Electors. Dynasties would subsequently come and go in the imperial position ... and, because of the ultimately elective nature of the office, the Emperor would seldom enjoy full power.

The Investiture Controversy. At the same time, the rise of emperors, kings and dukes under the new "imperial" (and feudal) system now posed a new problem for Western society. The working relationship between the secular rulers (dukes, kings and emperors) with their military power and the Church with its absolute religious authority left unanswered the question that would dog the Western political system for centuries: of the two, who had the greater authority, the secular or the religious leaders of Europe?

---

[*]The Saxony located in Germany ... not the Saxony established in Britain.

[†]The formal imperial title would become that of "Holy Roman Emperor" by the 1200s.

This question centered particularly on the question of naming local bishops (the process of investiture), where kings and dukes wanted to name members of their own families (upper-level church officials were almost always drawn from the aristocratic class) to the cathedrals located in their feudal districts. However, the Popes and archbishops felt that this was strictly the Church's prerogative. Compromise usually worked. But sometimes not. And the stress on medieval Christendom would become murderous when a deadlock over the matter occurred.

Emperor Henry IV and Pope Gregory VII. A particularly famous blowup occurred between the German King (and subsequently Holy Roman Emperor) Henry IV and the Roman Church and its officials, particularly Pope Gregory VII. In 1059, Church reformers moved swiftly during Henry's infancy to take the appointment of the Roman bishop (Pope) out of imperial hands and place that responsibility fully in the hands of a newly created College of Cardinals made up solely of church officials. Then in 1075, a new pope, Gregory VII, went even further to declare that the appointment of the Emperor could be done only by the Pope. But at this point Henry was an adult ... and fought back and proceeded to appoint his own bishops ... and even called for the election of a new pope (which Henry fully expected to control).

Henry's humiliation. Pope Gregory retaliated by excommunicating the emperor. Jealous German princes were more than happy to see Henry thus humiliated ... and defeated his army and seized the imperial lands for themselves. At this point (1077), Henry had no recourse but to make amends with Gregory ... and went before the pope at the castle of Canossa in the dead of winter, barefoot and wearing the penitent's hair-shirt. Gregory ultimately forgave Henry ... but the princes did not. They elected a rival, Rudolf, to Henry's place as emperor ... and Gregory then also moved his support to Rudolf and once again excommunicated Henry.

Henry then proclaimed Clement III to be the pope and moved on Rome with his army ... only to be faced by Normans* called out by Gregory to support him.

But the Normans instead sacked Rome ... causing the Roman citizens to rise up in revolt against Gregory and his Normans ... who were then forced to flee. Gregory, however, died soon after. But the controversy continued.

The Concordat of Worms. Then in 1106, Henry's son, Henry V, supporting

----

*"Norman" is simply an abbreviated form of "Northmen" ... a general term for the fierce raiders who came by sea out of the far North (Scandinavia) – known also as "Vikings."

the papal party, took over his father's throne. But then he too appointed his own candidate Gregory VIII as pope, starting the whole investiture controversy up again. However eventually (after much back and forth struggle between the emperor and various popes and anti-popes), with the signing of the Concordat of Worms in 1122, Henry V abandoned his papal candidate and agreed to end the emperor's right of investiture of church officers.

But this would not end the issue ... for it would spread elsewhere (England for example) and be a constantly troubling issue involving the relationship between church and state in Christian Europe.

THE VIKINGS (OR "NORTHMEN")

The sacking, burning (of its immense library) and slaughter in 793 of the wealthy and famous monastery and its monks at Lindisfarne (coastal Northeast Britain) was the announcement that a new, crude, and extremely violent set of players had emerged out onto the European political stage. The Vikings had finally made their appearance ... and would terrorize Europe for the next several centuries.

Behind this activity were factors similar to the Germanic incursions into the Roman Empire: land hunger. The population of Scandinavia had been expanding in a land that is mountainous and cold ... and thus not well suited to bringing new lands under cultivation to feed a growing population.

In their forays out of the North, they were determined and focused ... and learned quickly how defenseless the Christians to the South of them were to unexpected surprise attacks coming from these warriors in their longboats. These longboats were an amazing piece of naval technology, one that allowed them to go most anywhere on the high seas, yet move deeply upriver along any of the European tributaries to those high seas.

They ventured far and wide, settling Iceland and reaching North America in the West, in the East venturing deep into the Slavic lands of what would eventually (under their domination) become Russia, and in the South venturing into the Mediterranean and even establishing Viking or Northmen (simplified to "Norman") settlements on the strategic island of Sicily.

The Vikings in England. For the next 40 years following the sack of the abbey at Lindisfarne, little would be heard from these Nordic marauders ... until around 835 when Viking raids resumed ... and became a regular feature of English life.

By the 860s raids had become complete invasions by Danish Viking

armies accompanied by Danish settlers (the "Great Heathen Army"). One by one (865-875) the Saxon kingdoms fell before the Danish invaders ... until Wessex, the western portion of Mercia and the northern portion of Northumbria remained as the only Saxon kingdoms still intact. In the middle of what had once been the Saxon heartland, the Danish established a Viking state operating under Danish custom ... eventually known as the Danelaw.

Alfred the Great (871-899). Alfred was the fourth in a line of brothers to come to rule Wessex ("West Saxony") after their father, Aethelwulf died in 858. He fought alongside his older brother Aethelred against the Vikings in a series of battles that varied between Saxon victories and Viking victories. Then when his brother died in 871, Alfred found himself at age 23 as the new leader of Wessex.

But things got off to a bad start for Alfred ... even though he was able to get the Danes to leave Wessex ... probably at some great cost in tribute. For the next five years the situation stabilized around this arrangement.

Then in 876 the Danes came under an ambitious leader, Guthrum, who disregarded truces and agreements in the attempt to spread his personal rule deeper into Saxon England. Alfred fought back fiercely ... but in January of 878 he barely escaped with a small group of followers when Guthrum suddenly attacked and slaughtered the inhabitants of a town where Alfred had been staying for Christmas. At this point Alfred went into hiding.

In May of that year he emerged to rally again a Saxon army ... and then at the Battle of Edington was able to deliver the Danes such a blow that they retreated to a position that Alfred then encircled ... and slowly pushed the defending Danes to a point of starvation. Guthrum's Danes surrendered ... and as part of the terms of surrender had Guthrum and his court baptized.

Eventually (880?) a treaty was agreed on between Alfred and Guthrum, respecting Alfred's sovereignty over Wessex and the western part of Mercia with Guthrum acknowledged as ruler of East Anglia and the eastern portion of Mercia ... the foundation of the Danelaw.

This did not end the Viking threat ... for not all Vikings were in agreement with this arrangement – and a number of them crossed to the European continent to raid and sack towns there. Also independent Viking bands continued to descend from Denmark to raid the shores of England ... although they presented themselves more as a bloody nuisance than as a serious political threat – except for one Danish attack in Kent (885) which weakened but did not undo Alfred's position there.

But with Guthrum's death in 889 the Saxon-Dane truce began to disintegrate as local Danish warlords went to battle to claim ascendancy in Guthrum's place.

Then in 892 (or 893) a large fleet of Danes crossed from the European continent to invade Kent ... with the obvious intent of seizing and settling the land there. As Alfred was confronting this group of Danes, others arrived at other parts of England, requiring Alfred to keep his troops constantly on the move ... forcing the Danes back here and there (the Danes, being mostly raiders rather than settlers, and thus lacking their own food and supplies, were not prepared for long encounters).

And thus he busied himself protecting (rather successfully) his domain ... reclaiming even much of what the Vikings had taken from the Saxons – including the strategic city of the north, York. For this he was well-beloved by his people ... some who considered him to be virtually a saint!

Alfred was remembered not only for his fighting skills but also for building a small but effective navy, for his hard work at organizing his Saxon domain into effective political units, structured by a law code of his own making, and for his efforts to raise the level of learning within his kingdom (abysmally low given the damage the Vikings had done to the monasteries which had long served as England's educational centers). Of particular importance was his effort to promote such educational improvement in terms of the English language rather than the usual Latin.

He died in 899, having given Saxon England a relative degree of peace in the face of the constant Viking threat ... a threat that was still making life in coastal Europe miserable.

The Vikings in France. Charlemagne's feuding grandsons gave the Danes next door to the north the opportunity in the 830s and 840s to conduct raids of Frankish coastal cities (while they were doing the same across the channel in Saxon England). In 850 a huge Viking raiding party (5,000 men) under Ragnar sailed all the way up the Seine River to attack the strategic city of Paris ... sacking and slaughtering in the process. Only a major plague – and Carolingian King Charles the Bald's payment of 7000 livres (pounds) of silver and gold, and the promise of continuing payments after that (eventually termed the Danegeld) cause the Danes to leave.

Vikings would return again and again ... but encountering much more secure town walls guarding Paris.

Then in 885 the Danes returned with hundreds of ships and tens of thousands of warriors to attack Paris but even then found the Parisians, led by Count Odo, able to hold out against this massive onslaught. Months went by (Vikings venturing from there to sack and plunder in the region). Only the next summer did the Carolingian King Charles the Fat arrive ... not to fight the Vikings but to let them continue upriver to attack the rebellious Burgundians, and to offer a huge payment in silver. This was hardly a satisfactory solution to the Parisians ... and when in 888 Charles died, the stronger Odo was elected King of West Francia – the first non-Carolingian to take that title.

Also of note was the last Viking leader to undertake the siege of Paris was Rollo ... who would come to play a huge part in the rise of these Vikings or "Northmen" (or "Normans") in France.

Rollo ... and the dukedom of Normandy. Rollo in 876 had already taken control of the city of Rouen (downriver from Paris) – and the coastal city of Bayeux probably prior to even that ... where he captured, married and had a son, William, by the daughter of the local Frankish count. He also seems to have had some kind of working relationship with Guthrum, the Danish king of East Anglia across the channel. In short, Rollo was busy establishing himself as something of a local lord in northwestern coastal Francia.

In 911 French king Charles III of West Francia (France) finally came up with the brilliant idea of negotiating a deal with Viking leader Rollo after he and his Vikings had burned and sacked Paris (again). He gave formal recognition to Rollo and his Norman warriors and their families (after being baptized) ... assigning Rollo ducal rule (under the sovereignty of the king himself, of course) over the region at the mouth of the Seine River (eventually "Normandy"). He did so, understanding that with a vested interest in the peace of the region, Rollo's Viking military prowess would be the best way of keeping Paris from being regularly sacked and burned by future Viking predators. It worked. And eventually the Norman Vikings were assimilated into French culture.

Continuing Viking attacks on England. Viking raids on England never really ceased. But it was not until 947 that they were truly threatening to the Saxon kingdom – for in that year Erik Bloodaxe was able to take York and add it and the region of Northumbria to his Norwegian kingdom. But actually this was only part of the ongoing relationship (peaceful and warlike) that united the destinies of England and Scandinavia.

Sweyn Forkbeard. Another challenge to Saxon England began to brew in the mid-980s when Sweyn Forkbeard seized the Danish throne from his father Harald Bluetooth ... but was driven into exile for the next fourteen years by his father's allies (including the kings of Sweden and German Saxony). But by the year 1000 Sweyn rebuilt his power base ... and then led a series of attacks on England – off and on between the period 1003 and 1013 – in retaliation for Saxon king Aethelred the Unready's savage attacks on Danes living in the Danelaw. Sweyn was so successful that even the Saxons of England were ready to acknowledge him as the King of England in late 1013.

Cnut the Great takes the English throne. But Sweyn died only a few weeks later in early 1014. At this point his sons took over, Harald in Denmark and Cnut in England ... although it took a long struggle against Aethelred's son Edmund Ironside for Cnut to achieve this position (finally in 1016). In 1017 the Saxon Archbishop of Canterbury officially crowned Cnut as King of England. To further secure this throne, Cnut had most of the Saxon nobility and the sons of Aethelred executed – but married Aethelred's widow, Emma ... eventually elevating as royal heir his son by her, Harthacnut, above his sons by his first (Danish) wife. He extracted a huge indemnity from the English in order to pay off his troops – most of whom he then dismissed – but retained a large navy (presumably to protect his kingdom from other Viking invaders). He reorganized the lay of his kingdom into a group of four earldoms, appointing key supporters to each as "earl" – some of these earls eventually drawn from the ranks of noble Saxons.

When his brother Harald died soon thereafter (1018), Cnut then moved to take the position as King of Denmark (converting it into another of his earldoms). But his greatest work was in the way he united the English Saxons and Vikings of the Danelaw into a single society ... joined together in a military expedition into the Baltic and then to Norway, where he took position there as King of Norway (including part of southern Sweden).

By 1026, Cnut was the ruler of a vast kingdom. And so well established was he that he dared to take a trip (or pilgrimage) all the way to Rome in 1027, to attend the coronation of Conrad as Holy Roman Emperor ... indicating Cnut's own rank among the Christian "greats" of his day.

But aside from the successful challenge to his rule in Norway by Norwegian nobility, Cnut's rule was quite stable, all the way up to his death in 1035.

The Norman conquest of England (1066)

Edward the Confessor (r. 1042-1066). But that stability was not to last long. Upon his death his huge kingdom was divided up into a number of smaller kingdoms ... with his descendants fighting among themselves for supremacy. Ultimately in England, actually a Saxon nobleman of the House of Wessex, Edward "the Confessor" was able peacefully to take the position as England's new king. However, Edward seemed more interested in piety than in political power ... thus the name "the Confessor."* This tended to weaken greatly the 24-year rule of Edward ... to the advantage of local Saxon lords. This proved to be especially the case for the house of Godwin ... earls of the powerful Wessex domain.

Harold Godwinson – the last Anglo-Saxon king (1066). Then as death approached, Edward named the well-proven warrior Harold Godwinson, Earl of Wessex, to be his successor. But the Norman-French Duke William of Normandy then claimed that earlier, on a trip to the continent, Harold had sworn fealty to William – in support of William's claim to the English throne. Supposedly also, the childless Edward the Confessor had earlier named his cousin William to be his heir in England.

So then, who had actually the right to the English throne upon Edward's death? Ultimately, the contest between Harold and William for this position would prove to be deeply life-changing for English society.

The Battle of Hastings (October 1066). At the time, Harold was engaged in a fierce conflict with his brother Tostig ... while over in France, William was assembling a huge navy (700 ships), ready to convey a massive army across to England and seize control (and the throne) there.   Furthermore, Pope Alexander II took the side of William, claiming that he did so because Harold had broken his earlier oath to William. Hearing this, other English noblemen also took William's side. Things were not looking good for Harold. Then things got much worse in mid-September, when Norwegian king Harald Hardrada – joined by Harold's brother Tostig – invaded Northumbria and defeated the English earls there. This forced Harold to have to move his troops quickly to the north ... where the invading troops were defeated and Hardrada and Tostig were killed (late September).

But at the same time, William of Normandy's huge navy and army arrived at England's southern shores in East Sussex. Thus Harald had to quickly force-march his army 240 miles back to the south.   Then on 14 October the two sides went to battle. The Saxon lines held over the course of most of the day. And then a retreat by the Normans Harold interpreted as the path to victory ... only to find that his army had just marched into a

____

*He had once been called on by the Holy Roman Emperor to use his navy to help put down a revolt in Flanders. But it was his action against Welsh raiders in the West that drew the attention of other English noblemen ... that eventually brought his name forward as England's new king.

trap. Harold was then killed ... and the Saxon effort fell apart. It was a huge victory for the Normans.

The larger outcome.   This, of course, established a Norman-French feudal rule over the English-speaking Saxon commoners. By doing so, it established a strict class-based society, with French-speaking Norman families now ruling over the English-speaking Saxon commoners ... and with a class barrier erected between the two groups that was almost totally unbridgeable. And it would be lasting.

However also, with this event, Britain was now finally closely linked to continental European affairs.

CHAPTER SEVEN

THE HIGH MIDDLE AGES

* * *

NEW STIRRINGS IN THE WEST

After the mid-1000s, the West began to stir from its entrenchment. It got enough of a reprieve from invasions that it was able to see some order return to life. The West began to shake off its defensiveness … and begin to consider new possibilities. Energy was beginning to return to the European continent.

In part all this new energy resulted from the fact that Europe had absorbed so much of the energies of former invaders, such as the Normans. In part it was because their enemies, in particular Islam, were having organizational problems of their own that absorbed their energies. In any case, once Europe came out from under the threat of more invaders, it amazingly quickly began to show signs of life. By around 1050 AD the tide was turning in favor of Europe.

Economic and intellectual growth. Indeed, by the 1100s Europe was clearly undergoing a cultural revival of major proportions. Cities were growing up all around Western Europe, a sign of the revival of commerce and shipping. Learning centers were growing up – especially around the cathedrals of Europe's bishops. These were the early foundations of the universities that would be so vital to the redevelopment of the European intellect.

The Church powers up. At the same time the Church, which was still the main cultural underpinning for all of Western society, began to regain strength under powerful popes. Notable in this regard were Leo IX (pope: 1049-1054) and Gregory VII [Hildebrand] (pope: 1073-1085). They tightened the governing structure of the church and restored some degree of discipline within the priesthood.

Now Europe would move from the defensive to the offensive (one which would not cease until the twentieth century!).

Early intellectual stirrings

Anselm of Canterbury (1033-1109). An early sign of the changing times was the work of Anselm. Although a Christian monk, Anselm explored the nature and meaning of life on the basis of pure reason rather than on traditional theological intellectual foundations. He was highly critical of how logic and language were used traditionally ... and was eager to explore the realm of how we humans actually come to an understanding of things – both good and bad. Among his many works, *Proslogion* and *Cur Deus Homo?* became very influential in awakening Christian Europe to the world of deep intellectual enquiry. Eventually he was elevated to sainthood by both the Catholic and Anglican churches.

Unfortunately, much of Anselm's time as archbishop of Canterbury was spent in political conflict with English King William Rufus ... then Henry I after him.

Peter Abelard (1079-1142). An individual who stands out in stark contrast to the way scholars and intellectuals were expected to act ... Peter Abelard was dazzlingly brilliant in instruction and debate on this rising matter of the nature and use of pure logic. But Abelard was also very well aware of his own brilliance, and managed to both fascinate the masses ... and irritate deeply fellow scholars, such as Anselm (early on) and then Bernard of Clairvaux (later in life) ... among many others. Thus he was forced to move often to escape the wrath of this or that individual, someone that his arrogance had alienated.

Also his relationship with Héloise, with whom he birthed a son, and then got himself in deeper trouble when – as still a monk – he tried to fix matters.* But this sparked an angry uncle of Héloise to send agents to have Abelard castrated. This in turn ruined Abelard in the eyes of the Church ... though not in the heart of Héloise, for whom her love for Abelard ran deep ... as well as his love for her. In fact, their love itself became legend ... and would contribute greatly to a rising Western Humanism and its priorities.

Bernard of Clairvaux (1090-1153). Bernard was born of an aristocratic family from Burgundy ... and took up the challenge of founding a monastery at Clairvaux (with his brothers and even father joining him there). His work, both writings and monastic organization, became well-known ... and multitudes of young men flocked to his monastery to be joined in his enterprise of "Benedictine reform" (disciplining the life of a monk).

His incredible talents at political and social organization led him in

------

*The idea that monks should remain celibate or unmarried and childless was just getting underway at the time.

1128 at the Council of Troyes to write the Rules of the Knights Templar ... which became the code of honor not only for the crusaders heading to the Muslim East but also something subsequently of an honor code for Europe's ruling classes.

In the realm of politics, Bernard could become very unbending ... taking up causes that would bring victory to particular parties in a Christian world caught in deep social change ... and destruction and death to the Christian groups that took an opposing position on things. For instance, he became an ardent supporter of Innocent II in his battle for the papacy with Anacletus II, the latter being elected to the position by the majority of bishops gathered in Rome, but Bernard taking Innocent's case to the princes of Northern Europe to gain their political support. Bitter civil war would result ... and end not even with Anacletus's death in 1138, but continue as the two groups that the civil conflict had created would remain deeply divided. Bernard was also instrumental in having the Church go after the Cathars of southern France, driving them from their homes and even slaughtering them because of their "heresy."

He also became a very vocal opponent of Abelard's "logical" rather than "faith-based" approach to Christianity ... organizing opposition to Abelard when Abelard wanted to debate the matter before the Second Lateran Council in 1139 (Abelard had to flee).

For all of his extensive service to the Church, Bernard was canonized in 1174 as a saint by Pope Alexander III ... only 21 years after Bernard's death in 1153.

* * *

THE CRUSADES (1100s AND 1200s)
... AND THE WESTERN SOCIAL-CULTURAL REVIVAL

The call to crusade. But it was truly an event in the year 1095 that was to signal the beginning of a great material (especially military) rise of Western Europe that would bring it to roughly total world domination eight centuries later.

While new social-cultural stirrings were taking place in the European West, Islamic power was undergoing a period of decline in the East. This became an opportunity for Europeans to redirect some of these contentious instincts away from West Europe itself. It gave free-booting princes the promise of plunder – and the popes a way of getting a lot of these same princes out from under them so that they could continue in their restructuring of the church around Roman rule.

It was also a euphoric time. Christians in the West were very self-aware of their own growing power – and were desirous of putting it to good use. In particular they were easily stirred by the idea of retaking from the "infidel" Muslims the most holy sites of all Christendom: Jerusalem and Palestine.

The Council of Clermont (1095). There were a number of factors that came together in 1095 to cause Pope Urban to call for a great crusade to liberate Jerusalem and the surrounding Holy Land. Most directly was the appeal issued during the Council of Clermont held that year by the visiting Byzantine emperor (1081-1118) Alexius Comnenus. He asked the Pope and other nobles who were present at this Council to send aid to the East to deliver the Holy Land from the grip of the Seljuk Turks. Since the military defeat of the Byzantine army by these Turks at the Battle of Manzikert in 1071, these Muslim Seljuk Turks had seized Antioch, had pushed deeply into Asia Minor, and had cut off or badly disrupted the important paths of Christian pilgrimage to Jerusalem.

This came at a time when the population of Europe was expanding rapidly, not only among the common peasantry but also among the nobility, whose third and fourth sons were promised no inheritance or income – outside of what they personally could gain through battle or military service to another, wealthier noble. It was also a time of pilgrimage, enabled by more stable political conditions in Europe, and favored by the Christian as a means of receiving special grace or favor in reducing the penalty of one's sins. Also, Pope Urban made it very clear at the Council that if the French knights were to devote their energies to fighting the Turkish Muslim infidels rather than each other, God would be greatly pleased. In fact, God willed it (*Deus vult*). And thus the Pope declared a full indulgence (forgiveness of sins) for those who took up the call to this "crusade."

So it was that the idea of a pilgrimage to Jerusalem, especially to free Christ's lands from the infidel Muslim, seemed to be a highly rewarding proposition to many of Europe's young, devout adventurers. The result was an enthusiastic response which hugely exceeded the expectations of both the Roman Pope and the Byzantine Emperor.

The First Crusade (1096-1099). Planning and organizing such a major undertaking fell to a number of individuals, mostly European noblemen of fairly high rank (kings, however, did not participate in this first crusade).

An exception was Peter the Hermit, who organized a huge band of common soldiers and peasants, and marched them through southeastern Europe to Constantinople ... slaughtering Jews along the way. Rather than await the rest of the crusader force, Peter's soldiers insisted on pushing on ahead toward their goal of Jerusalem – so confident were they that God

was going to bless their rather unruly undertaking with glorious victory. But instead of victory, they walked into a Turkish ambush at Cibotus (August 1096) and were annihilated ... though Peter survived.
There were other rather spontaneous massings of commoner crusaders, but most of those failed even to reach Constantinople.

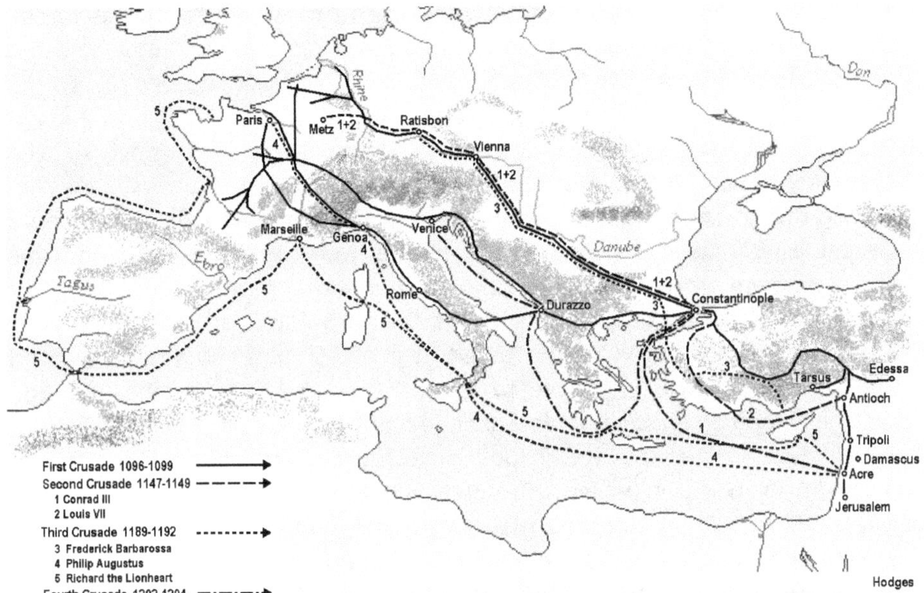

But a number of French-speaking noblemen would set an indelible mark on the crusading tradition, in that the crusaders' land-holdings in the Holy Lands would eventually become known as "Frankish" domains.

With about 4,000 knights and 25,000 foot-soldiers, they left Constantinople for the Holy Lands in May of 1097. With the assistance of Greek warriors, as they advanced through Asia Minor, they began to throw back the Turks that came out to meet them. By October they reached Antioch. At this point, Baldwin parted company with the crusaders to join the Armenians and take command of the all-important city of Edessa in eastern Syria. Not until next June did their siege of Antioch finally bring the collapse of the city, as Bohemond was finally able to breach the walls and lead his troops – to a massacre of the Muslim inhabitants of the city. But the Antioch citadel held out – though a relief force of Muslims was thrown back by the crusaders. At the end of the month the Muslim defenders surrendered the Antioch citadel under a promise of safe conduct if they left the city. So the city was delivered into the hands of Bohemond. But the victory was spoiled by an epidemic that broke out among the crusaders, taking the life of Bishop Adhemar.

Early the following year (1098) other crusader leaders and their armies set out for Jerusalem – accompanied by the fiery preacher, Peter the Hermit. Here they encountered not the Seljuk Turks (Sunni Muslims) but the Fatimids (Shi'ite Muslims) from Egypt, who had recently seized Jerusalem from the Turks. Despite the crusaders' greatly reduced numbers (about half of what they had left Constantinople with) they were able to breach the walls of Jerusalem in mid-July … and then proceeded to massacre the city's Muslim and Jewish inhabitants – despite Tancred's efforts to hold the crusaders to a promise of safe conduct he had given the city's leaders.*

Efforts to consolidate the victory.   Soon thereafter most of the crusaders, having completed their "pilgrimage," departed for home, including the crusade's leader, Raymond. Godfrey was then elected to serve as Jerusalem's new ruler. But Godfrey's death two years later brought his brother Baldwin from Edessa to take the position, now termed "king" of Jerusalem (he turned Edessa over to his cousin Baldwin of Le Bourg).

Within the next ten years, aided in part by more crusaders coming from Europe, Baldwin was able to extend the crusader holdings up and down the Eastern Mediterranean coast (except Ascalon and Tyre). Then in 1109 a fourth crusader state, Tripoli, was added to the crusader states of Edessa, Antioch and Jerusalem. Tripoli was led by a descendant of Raymond of St. Gilles (who had died in 1105). With the acquisition of Tyre in 1024, this would be the greatest extent of the crusader holdings in the Holy Land.†

Whereas the strong competition between the Sunni Turks to the North and the Shi'ite Fatimids to the South allowed the crusaders to use diplomacy to fend off Muslim threats from these two directions, a new challenge arose from the East in the 1130s from the Muslim governor of Mosul, Zangi. Improved diplomatic relations with the Muslims of Damascus allowed the next generation of crusaders (who were quickly adapting themselves to the political style of the surrounding Muslim world) to prevent Zangi from achieving a strategic advance against nearby Damascus. But the crusaders were unable to stop his assault on Edessa, which fell to Zangi in 1144. This was a huge loss for the crusaders – and a shock to the Christians of Western Europe when news of the loss reached them.

Meanwhile a similar crusade was undertaken in Spain and Portugal against the Umayyads, taking a number of key cities (importantly, Lisbon and Barcelona) also around the mid-1100s.

---

*The sheer barbarity of the crusaders shook the Muslim sense of religious toleration of the Christian communities in their midst … and eventually the word "crusader" would become for the Muslim a term of sheer ugliness and spite, representing in the mind of the Muslim the lurking danger of barbarity in the Christian heart.

†The promise of the crusaders to restore to the Byzantine emperor land taken from the Muslims was completely ignored.

Mixed Success. Of course the Crusaders in the East were not finished ... and fought back, recovering some of the lost territory. Needless to say, there would be little peace in the land between the Crusader Kingdoms and the Muslim principalities. Thus more crusades (a second and third crusade) were commissioned by future popes ... now involving German and French kings and even the Holy Roman (Western) Emperor.

The crusaders fared poorly in their efforts to expand their conquest to Fatimid Egypt, thanks largely to the military skill of Saladin, a Sunni Kurd serving as vizier to the Shi'ite caliph al-Adid. With al-Adid's death in 1171 Saladin took personal control of Egypt, submitted his territory to Sunni Abbasid authority (stirring Shi'ite Fatimid revolts, which he crushed) ... and then took on the crusader states, regaining control of Syria for Islam in 1182 and Palestine in 1187.

The crusaders, however, were able to take the strongly fortified city of Acre in 1191 and hold that position – along with similar fortresses in Palestine – for another century. But they would actually exercise little control beyond the walls of those fortresses.

Of course further efforts (additional crusades) were made to restore the lost crusader kingdoms. But the efforts came to little ... except to introduce European courts to the wealth and splendor of the Muslim courts, which now became something of cultural models to the primitive Europeans.

The crusading monks. Interestingly, the crusades also brought the creation of religious-military orders (such as the Knights Templar and the Knights Hospitaller) ... something like fighting monks, or at least warriors who had taken a solemn vow of a life of service to the cause. These military-priest orders would become wealthy and powerful in their own right ... so much so that they drew the ire and eventually persecution of a number of suspicious or envious European kings and dukes.

The *Knights Templar*, founded in 1118 in Jerusalem, was a holy order of knights (soon ordained even by Pope Honorius II in 1128), involved not only in fighting the Muslim "infidel" in the Holy Land (only about 10% of their order was actually engaged this way) but in collecting monies for various charities. They became so skilled in this latter venture, developing sophisticated banking techniques and placing themselves strategically all across Christendom (Europe plus the crusader holdings in the Middle East) that the Knights Templar order became vastly rich.

This then began to stir the envy and fear of Europe's various dukes and princes, who became increasingly resentful of the Templars. Finally in 1307, using the secrecy by which they operated as his excuse, French King Philip IV (deeply in debt to the Templars) had the leaders of this order arrested, tortured (seeking to get "proper" confessions out of them), and burned at the stake. Then five years later he pressured Pope Clement V to officially disband the order.

Surviving the realm of European politics better than the Templars was the *Order of the Knights Hospitaller*, formed actually a bit earlier in Jerusalem – even before the first of the crusades – from the foundations of a Benedictine hospital located in Jerusalem, by monks who had committed themselves to taking care of the sick and poor who came to Jerusalem as pilgrims. Then with the conquest of Jerusalem in 1099 by the crusaders, the monks were joined by various knights in forming a new order (also chartered by the pope), the Knights Hospitaller, dedicated to defending and caring for the Christian community in the Holy Land.

The order was ultimately forced to move to the island of Rhodes when Muslims first retook the Holy Lands in the late 1100s.

But the order continued to survive as the ruling authority in Rhodes and then later at Malta, then eventually in Sicily as a vassal state under Spanish authority. The Hospitallers would not draw the resentment of Europe's monarchs, and would continue to serve Europe charitably. However, the split in the Church that occurred during the Protestant Reformation of the 1500s would also divide the order – portions of which still survive down to today.

The urban Republic of Venice gets in on the act. Included (from the 1120s onward) in this great crusading venture were also soldiers and sailors from the rising city-state (or Republic) of Venice, strategically located at the top of the northeastern coast of Italy. This just happened to be the best jumping off point for central Europeans to reach the Holy Lands by water rather than the long and hazardous overland journey through the unfriendly Balkans and the wary Byzantine lands.   It also happened to be well-protected by the fact that Venice was actually a maze of offshore islands, virtually impossible to reach by a land army ... and well protected by a massive navy.

The ongoing crusading effort. Times of truce between Christians and Muslims would occur ... followed by the resumption of fighting, frequently as a result of a call of a pope to yet another crusade (4th, 5th, 6th) ... on into the mid and late 1200s.

Even the Byzantines got caught on the wrong end of the crusades, especially the 4th (1202-1204) which seems to have been waged only against the fellow-Christian Byzantine Greeks under the orders of the Venetian authorities for whom the sacking of Constantinople was the price exacted on the crusaders in order to have Venice's ships then take them on to the Holy Lands (they never made it there ... but did cripple Byzantine power greatly!

✳ ✳ ✳

MEDIEVAL EUROPE IN 1200

If you were to look at a map of the world at around 1200, you would see an amazing patchwork of colors indicating a huge variety of empires, kingdoms, duchies, caliphates, sultanates, emirates, khanates, etc. by which the world was then divided. In some instances, these colors would show ethnic or tribal territories. But in most cases, they would indicate the territories held by great landowners.   Emperors and Kings, popes and bishops, dukes and barons, sultans and amirs, khans and warlords, gave identity to the land over which they presided – and also over the people and animals and housing and barns and roads found within these lands. These great landowners added (or lost) land through wars with neighboring rulers, through marriages in which land was exchanged as huge dowries, or through inheritances via family bloodlines. Their rules or laws were the law of the land, their measures, their currencies, their taxes were the standards of their particular territory. They consulted whom they wanted to consult, they fought with whom they wanted to fight, they negotiated treaties and exchanged diplomats with whom they wished to do so. They defined life (subject to long established custom, of course) within their own borderlands.

The ability to give precise physical definition of the realms of these landowners on maps would seem to give their communities a more physically "real" character. But in fact, this was not exactly the case.

As for medieval Western Europe, in theory it was a single political entity roughly termed "Christendom" and in theory presided over by a dual rulership of Holy Roman Emperor (military ruler) and Christian Pope (religious ruler). Certainly, there was such a society as Christendom, and indeed it was symbolically held together by at least the religious rule of the Pope – though that hold was very loose outside of central Italy. The Emperor also had effective rule – though only in a small part of Christendom: in parts of Italy (particularly the South of Italy) and parts of Germany.

Actually what held Christendom together was more importantly the idea of what Christians were *not*: namely Muslims, their ancient political and cultural arch rivals still located across the Pyrenees in Spain and in occupation of many of the Christian holy sites in the Middle East (the Christian crusades to "liberate" these holy sites East were still underway at this time).

Neither the Pope nor the Emperor possessed the means to rule directly this sprawling Christendom.   Postal, commercial and military communications were greatly hampered by the dangerous conditions of the roads. The Emperor for instance had to trust the loyalties of his "vassals," individuals theoretically appointed by the Emperor to fill regional governorships as princes and kings, acting supposedly under the authority of the Emperor and for his benefit. But as these individuals operated at some distance from the Imperial palace it was impossible for the Emperor to oversee their work directly. Worse, as princes and kings were adamant about passing on their political positions to their children it was even more difficult for the Emperor to hold the right of lordship over their appointed subjects, their vassals. These more local rulers were developing a very well-developed sense of political independence.

For the Pope the situation was much less difficult, for Christian priests were celibate (not married and thus supposedly childless) and thus not able as easily to develop entrenched interests of their own. However, it was not uncommon for certain important families to expect the popes to name family members to particular bishoprics.

The looseness of this feudal pattern was repeated at lower rungs on the political ladder as well. These appointed kings in turn could not effectively rule the whole of their large kingdoms. They too had to turn to trusted vassals (dukes, barons, counts, etc.) to rule on their behalf. Here too, certain families expected to pass the right of such regional appointments on to their children and thus developed a keen sense of their own political independence. As these local lords could add to their own political holdings through war and marriage, in many cases these dukes and barons not infrequently ended up holding more power than the kings to which they supposedly were vassals.

For instance, around the year 1200 the Plantagenet family, through conquest and marriage, held the strategic duchy of Normandy and the kingdom of England, as well as the very rich duchy of Aquitaine (which briefly was associated with France before it was transferred to England through marriage). In short, the Plantagenets as mere French vassals or dukes effectively held several times the land and wealth of their French lord and king. However, this relationship held true only when the Plantagenets were in France serving as dukes; when in England they were kings by their own right. It would thus be very hard to say exactly how it was that the French king held rule over Normandy when their Norman vassal's power greatly exceeded their own! Our maps show Normandy as part of the French kingdom at that time. But was it really? That this was part of France was only an idea – a very weak idea at that.

As far as the little people – the peasant farmers – were concerned, none of this was their business. The lords over them came and went, none of that however from any of their doing. The peasant might wake up one day to hear that title over the region had been transferred in marriage or exchanged through treaty to another family. Though they had a new lord over the land, life went on much as before. Hopefully the new ruler, whether a son born to his father's title or a new ruler through transfer, would rule well so that the land would prosper. But these were matters beyond their control. These affairs belonged to the lords – and to God, who supposedly established these lords as their rulers.

✳ ✳ ✳

A SLOW SHIFT IN THE POLITICAL-CULTURAL DYNAMIC

The impact of the crusades on Europe itself

A shocking cultural awakening. In the 1100s Europe broke out of its dark isolation as its new energy took European crusaders East to "liberate" the Holy Lands from the West's long-standing rivals, the Muslims.
But upon arrival at the Holy Lands, the Christian knights were shocked in discovering how truly backward their own Christian or Western feudal culture was in comparison to the lavish culture (architecture, furnishings, clothing, food, music ... and scholarship) of the Muslim Middle East. But such a jolt of cultural awakening was truly the beginning of great things.

To be sure, the crusaders were victorious in their "freeing" the Holy Lands from "infidel" control by enemy Muslims – at least initially ... but only briefly.   This was not destined to last.

Islam soon got its act together, and by the late 1100s had begun the process of reclaiming the lands recently lost to these invading European crusaders. Eventually (late 1200s) all the Norman kingdoms in the Holy Lands were overrun by a strong Turkish Muslim revival ... and the crusades came to a close.

The rise of East-West commerce. But the Turkish overlords saw great economic benefit in keeping open trade relations with Western Europe, which was now stirring in its lust for the silks, spices, trinkets and even gold of the East, which the crusades had introduced to the folks back home. Likewise, the Europeans had goods that interested the Arabs and Turks, such as lumber, metals, fish, grains, and fine woolen cloth. So the Muslim East indicated that it was willing to continue relations with the Christian West ... as long as it involved trade and not crusading.

Cultural exchange. Thus it was that the East-West relationship of two centuries awakened an important symbiotic relationship between the two worlds ... intellectual as well as economic. Christian Westerners came in rather large numbers to experience the world of Islam – but not just to Palestine in the East but also to Spain in the South. Indeed, in particular the Spanish South is where most normally the Muslims opened up to these Christian pilgrims a new world, not only in the realm of material culture ... but also in the realm of scientific knowledge.

The impact of Europe's urbanization. These newly emerging European commercial cities that grew up under the stimulus of the East-West world of trade (Venice, Genoa, Siena, Florence, Marseille, London, Antwerp, Bremen, etc.) constituted a distinct entity apart from the rural feudal societies of the European interior. They were quite independent economic entities largely living off the wealth of overseas trade. Of course, they traded with the European interior – much as they traded with their customers in the Arab East. But they were dependent on nothing more than the income they were able to generate in their workshops, banks and shipyards. They were a literate (needing to communicate trade terms and keep commercial records) and industrious lot. Thus these cities grew quite wealthy ... and also politically quite powerful.

Whereas wealth in land (as in the European feudal system) is easily kept within a single-family domain – ownership easily being passed on from father to son over many generations – wealth in commercial and industrial capital is not so easily preserved within dynastic circles. It is easily lost in the hands of lazy or foolish offspring – just as easily as it is acquired by the ambitious and the industrious of society ... who can spring up from most any corner of society. Thus there was a much more dynamic quality to the way social and political power worked in these cities.

Also ... these city-states tended to be more responsive to its citizenry – unlike the grand feudal estates which kept their vast number of peasants effectively excluded from the political life of their own societies. Something like democracy or republicanism was being stirred in these European city-states. For instance, Venice even called itself a "Republic" (as would also other Italian city-states) ... where the urban citizens – at least those most active in the upper circles of the banking and manufacturing industries – actively participated in the economic and political decision-making of their cities.

The Italian city-states

It was some of the port cities of Italy that first derived the greatest benefit from this East-West trade. These city-states got the start of their development in the servicing of the crusaders – who by necessity required the strategic offerings of these cities: water transportation. Crusaders on their way to the Holy Lands basically needed to complete the trip by sea (overland routes generally required them to pass through the very hostile territory of the Turks). In good weather, the Mediterranean was indeed something of a superhighway (as the Greeks had discovered centuries earlier).

Two Italian port cities, Venice and Genoa, served the crusaders very well in this matter. Consequently, both of these cities developed naval fleets for the purpose not only of transporting crusaders to their military destinations, but also transporting the rich treasure in plunder that these crusaders brought from the Middle East on their return. Both cities grew enormously rich from this service.

The Republic of Venice. It is hard to say when the Republic of Venice was actually founded. The city, located in a lagoon – which made it very easy to defend – evidenced a strong political independence from even as early as the 600s. And its strategic location gave it natural advantages in the world of trade, beginning early-on simply with the salt industry.

As it grew in power, thanks to the business of shipping crusaders to the Middle East, it also developed ever-stronger political foundations. Thus in the year 1172, the city established a Great Council, run by individuals drawn from the city's leading aristocratic and commercial families. This council was authorized to oversee the city's affairs – and to elect its *doge* (from the older Latin *dux* or "leader"), individuals who served as doges for life. The Council and Venice's Doge not only supervised closely the commercial-financial development of the Venetian Empire – which by this point extended along the shores of the Adriatic as well as in various parts of the Eastern Mediterranean – but also the city's development itself of its art and architecture, and just in general its own strategic urban development.

By the 1300s Venice had become a massive maritime empire in the Mediterranean with thousands of ships moving among Venetian-controlled ports extending from Eastern Italy all the way to Syria and Palestine.

It must also be remembered that one of its citizens, Marco Polo, became very famous in his efforts in the later part of the 1200s to extend Venice's commercial ties all the way to China. Consequently, in his publication in 1300 of *The Travels of Marco Polo*, he opened the eyes of the Christian West to the vast wealth and geographic extent of Central and Eastern Asia.

The Republic of Genoa. At the same time, the crusaders in the 1100s and 1200s, coming by way of France, found the port city of Genoa – located on the other or Western side of northern Italy – to be their best maritime link to the Holy Lands.

Here too, the Genoese Republic worked along lines very similar to Venice's, a number of aristocratic-commercial families dominating the city's affairs as municipal consuls – and an elective doge overseeing the entire political process.

And like Venice, Genoa developed a very powerful navy to support the huge commercial empire that the city developed in those days, an empire which reached all the way into the Black Sea just South of the Russian world and north of the Turkish world.

And here too, it must be remembered that it was a Genoese, Christopher Columbus, who had the audacity in the late 1400s to seek sponsorship here and there (ultimately securing Spanish support) in his own quest for a supposed alternate route – westward across the Atlantic Ocean – to the fabled wealth of the East.

The Republic of Florence.   At around the same time, the Italian city of Florence developed its own Republican government.   The Republic was founded in 1115 when the Florentines rose up in rebellion against the Canossa dynasty, feudal rulers (margraves) of the Tuscany region, and established their own independent commune, ruled by the Signoria of Florence, a council made up of regularly-elected representatives of the various industrial-commercial guilds in the city.   There was some back and forth on their independence, with the city brought back under the rule of the margraves when Holy Roman Emperor Henry VI invaded Italy in 1185.   But when Henry died twelve years later, Florence regained its independence.

But unlike Venice and Genoa, the Republic of Florence was built not on maritime commerce as much as on international banking, in which it excelled, making its florin (introduced in the mid-1200s) something of an international monetary standard.

But family rivalries within Florence constantly shook Florentine politics, with the Guelphs (supported by the Florentine commoners) and the Ghibellines (supported by the noble families of Florence) actually going to war against each other.*   In 1303, that dispute resulted in a great fire which destroyed a great part of Florence ... and its economy.   But it bounced back fairly quickly.

Then, just as the Florentine economy hit amazing heights in its prosperity, tragedies in the mid-1300s burst the Florentine bubble, due in part to the default on the Florentine loan to English King Edward III (but Europe itself was also suffering from a huge economic recession) and because of the impact of the Black Death (the Bubonic plague) at around

---

*The ongoing and very bitter Guelph-Ghibelline contest originally arose around the issue of selecting church leaders – especially the pope – (the investiture controversy), a political contest which would run all the way into the 1500s, in the process drawing in other city-states across Northern Italy, and even various German and French rulers.

the same time.

Nonetheless, despite the varying fortunes of Florence, the city did serve as a home base to some of Europe's best intellects of the day: Dante, Petrarch and Boccaccio, whose writings in the Tuscan vernacular (instead of High-Church Latin) not only popularized the world of Italian literature, it created an Italian national language built on these Tuscan foundations. More about these writers in the pages that follow.

Other Italian city-states. Besides the big-three of Venice, Genoa and Florence, there were other Italian cities that had thrown off the older feudal system in order to secure their urban independence, and who too were able to do so because of the wealth they were able to acquire in the rising world of East-West trade – and with that wealth develop the military strength sufficient to protect that independence.

Unsurprisingly, like Venice, Genoa, and Florence, they too were proud players in the larger European political game, often fighting among themselves for political prominence. Thus Siena became a major contender in Tuscany with the Florentines for local dominance (actually ahead of Florence in this matter, until the collapse of the Bonsignori banking family in 1298). But Milan, Pisa, Ferrara, Mantua, Verona, Lucca, Arezzo and others also played the game, some of them, Pisa and Milan quite well.

European cities of the North

But the Italians were not the only ones to get in on the East-West act. Soon joining the Italians in this rich trade were the port cities along the Atlantic (Portuguese Lisbon, Belgian/Flemish Ghent, Bruges, Ypres, etc.) ... or having access to the Atlantic via the Thames River (London), or from the North and Baltic Seas (the German Hansa cities of Lübeck, Hamburg, Cologne, Bremen, Danzig, etc.). These became not only shipping and banking centers but also important manufacturing centers.

Flanders, and its capital, Ghent. Of particular note was the excellent wool sheared by English sheep farmers ... which was then spun into fine cloth by Flemish textile guilds – in high demand in the Muslim East. This would come to produce in Flanders an economic miracle just as grand as the one developing in Italy at the same time. For instance, in the 1200s, Ghent was the second largest city on the European continent north of the Alps, some 65,000 people within its walls busily manufacturing that famous Flemish wool cloth.

Paris. However, most important of all the cities of the north was Paris, the political base for the Capetian Dynasty, a dynasty which progressed from counts to dukes and eventually to French kings. Paris would possess both a very impressive royal residence and a magnificent cathedral built on the island (Isle de la Cité) – positioned at a strategic crossing point of the Seine River – and a famous university just opposite the Cité in the Latin Quarter. By the early 1300s, Paris had a population of around 200,000.

London. Also of increasing significance was London. In the latter part of the 1100s, the Norman kings built a strong political-religious base there: the Tower of London to intimidate the local population, Westminster Abbey as part of the king's role as "Defender of the Faith," and then Westminster Palace itself as a key royal residence. But the City of London itself would develop as an increasingly important trading center for the wool that was shipped from England to the European continent, and as a banking center that managed this vital trade. Thus London grew in population from some 18,000 in the year 1100 to nearly 100,000 by the year 1300.

The Hanseatic League. Lübeck, located at the western end of the Baltic Sea in Northern Germany, and possessing vital trade relations with various cities eastward from there reaching all the way to Novgorod in Russia, was the originator and leader of an ever-growing alliance of German cities. This alliance, the Hanseatic League, originally formed in the mid-1200s, became deeply involved in the rapidly-expanding trade in wool, eventually fine cloth (even silk), metal products such as armor, finished wood items, but also timber, fur, salted fish, iron ore – sought eagerly by merchants in London and Flanders.

Among those joining the Hanseatic League were the cities of Hamburg, Cologne, and Bremen, possessing strategic river-access to the North Sea, becoming major cities themselves in the process. Joining them, by the 1300s, were nearly 200 cities of various sizes – spread across Northern Europe, from today's Netherlands in the West to today's Lithuania in the East.

These Hansa cities were politically "free" in the sense that no local counts or dukes ruled over them. Only the Holy Roman Emperor stood above them in authority, although it was an authority which was mostly symbolic in nature. In fact, the Hanseatic League was a political force by its own rights, even at one point (1360s) conducting successfully a war against the Danish King, forcing him to recognize their trading rights throughout Scandinavia. That event marked the height of Hansa power.

The European monarchs get in on the act

However, city-states were not the only political forces arising under the stimulus of Europe's economic change. Princely rule was also organizing itself into stronger political units. The previous Viking invaders themselves added strong blood to the ruling lines of Europe – especially the adventuresome Normans who settled at coastal France.

And skilled princes or kings of Northern Europe found that in working with these rising cities (granting the cities certain political rights and protections ... in exchange for taxes paid into the kings' treasuries) their own power increased greatly. They could afford their own armies made up of paid mercenaries, who were more reliable than the volunteer armies led by noblemen supposedly serving under the kings as vassals.

As royal or kingly power increased, kings forced these subordinate noblemen into more complete submission to their royal authority. As kings learned to develop political power of their own, independent of the old feudal relationship which bound lord and vassal, something like a "state" belonging to the kings began to develop. The kings developed their own magistrates to inspect their territories, collect taxes and hear court cases over local disputes. The "king's law" and bureaucracy began to spread and deepen in the life of European society.

Particularly prominent in this development were such princely rulers as the German Hohenstaufens, Conrad III and his nephew Frederick I Barbarossa; the Norman-English Plantagenets, King Henry II and his son Richard I "the Lionheart"; and the French Capetians Louis VII and Philip II Augustus, all of these followed up by another Hohenstaufen, Frederick II, the highly ambitious Holy Roman Emperor. These individuals gained enough of a hold over larger territories that they were able to offer some degree of peace and prosperity to the land in Germany, in France and in England, when they weren't off crusading – or simply contesting each other for territorial holdings in Europe.

Conrad III of Germany (ruled 1116-1152). Conrad was an early leader of the Hohenstaufen family of Swabia (today's southwestern Germany) first appointed as Duke of Franconia by his uncle, the Holy Roman Emperor Henry V, for his support in Henry's Italian campaign, when the Tuscan Margrave was overthrown by the Florentines.

Actually, it was Conrad's vital support of other royal and imperial candidates that stood behind his enormous increase in power. It was all part of the political game played by such candidates, everything from the duchies to the kingships, to emperorships, even the Christian papacy itself. And in recognition of such service, Conrad, received the title of King of Italy (1128-1135) and, after some political setbacks, King of Germany – which he self-styled as "King of the Romans" (1138-1152).

The titles meant little at the time, unless they could be backed up by real power. In this matter Conrad seemed quite talented – although his earlier experience as King of Italy had not proven greatly effective. He kept himself busy putting various relatives in positions of power across central Europe.

In 1146 he was moved by the preaching of the monk Bernard of Clairvaux to "take up the cross" (become a crusader), joining French King Louis VII and Conrad's nephew Frederick Barbarossa in the effort. This "second crusade" turned out to be disastrous, with Conrad and a small remnant of his army able to escape the wrath of the Turkish victors and then Conrad turning very ill in late 1147. In early 1148, they regrouped and headed on to Acre and Jerusalem, but crushing failure met them again at Damascus. Thus Conrad returned to Germany, where he continued his activities, on a more diplomatic basis, until his death in 1152.

Louis VII of France (r. 1137-1180). Although he was well-educated early in anticipation of a future role as church clergy, when his older brother died, this put Louis in line for the French kingship. He would remain a devout Christian (considered rather "monkish" in nature), and, in the early years of his reign, close to his (and his father's) religious advisor, the Abbot Suger. Louis was early on (1137) married to Eleanor of Aquitaine, with the expectation this this would add enormously to the holdings of the Capetian family. Following his coronation as French king that same year, he found himself involved in the typical feudal contests for land and titles across France, most notably with the Plantagenet Henry II.

In 1147, Louis – accompanied by his wife Eleanor – joined the Second Crusade and headed overland through Germany and Hungary, joining Conrad III at that point. Battling the Turks along the way, they finally arrived at the Holy Lands in 1148, laying siege to Damascus – which ended disastrously. Despite Eleanor's wanting him to stay and continue the effort with her uncle Raymond of Poitiers, at this point he decided to give up the effort and head them home. In all, the Second Crusade proved ruinous, to both the French royal treasury and to his marriage with Eleanor. After the annulment of the marriage with Eleanor, he married Constance of Castile, who birthed only two girls before dying during a third childbirth. He immediately married a third time, finally securing a male heir, Philip, in the process.

Although politics always challenged his rule (he seemed to be constantly caught up in competition with English King Henry II), his heart was heavily in the world of religion and education. Thus he not only undertook the building of the Notre Dame Cathedral of Paris (construction beginning in 1163) but also the founding of a college in 1150 as an annex to the Cathedral – which would combine with the Sainte-Geneviève Abbey and the School of Saint-Victor to become the future University of Paris (by the edict of his son Philip Augustus in 1200) – to which hundreds would then flock for study.

In later years Louis found himself very sick, had his 14-year-old son Philip crowned French king at the Cathedral of Reims in 1180, and then died the following year.

Frederick I Barbarossa of Germany (r. 1152-1190). It was Frederick, eventually nicknamed "Barbarossa" (Italian for Red Beard) – rather than his son (also Frederick) – that Conrad, on his deathbed, designated as his successor as King of Germany (soon confirmed by the German electors). But Frederick also received the title of King of Italy (1152-1190) and soon thereafter – and most importantly – was elected as Holy Roman Emperor (1155-1190).

Frederick commanded enormous power, in that his very person combined the two most important families in Central Europe at the time, his father's Hohenstaufen side, known in Italian also as the Ghibellines (from the name of the family castle), and his mother's Welf side, known also as the Guelfs. This would enable Frederick to make his titles something vastly more than just symbolic designations. He was able to turn both his royal titles and his imperial title into powerful offices. He took his responsibilities in Italy seriously, in 1155 returning the city of Rome back into the hands of the papacy, after a time of Republican governance – gaining the enormous support of the Church in the process (including the title as Holy Roman Emperor). He then busied himself in bringing order back to the massively divided Germany (1600 principalities, from very large to very tiny), and was called on repeatedly to bring Italy back under papal-feudal order (taking sides in the papal contests going on at the time) ... not always met well by the increasingly independent-minded Italians.

Then he took up the call of crusaders in the Holy Lands to come and liberate them from Saladin's Muslim rule (which Frederick had himself earlier acknowledged in 1177). Thus in 1189 the "Third Crusade" got underway ... Frederick joined by English King Richard I ("The Lionheart") and French King Philip II Augustus.

But once again, things did not go well for the crusaders, and even worse for Frederick, when in June of 1190 he drowned in a river in what is today Southern Turkey – well before his goal of reaching the Holy Lands and liberating them.

Henry II of England (r. 1154-1189). Although Henry started out in 1150 merely as a Norman duke serving under French King Louis VII, he was very ambitious, and succeeded in making his Plantagenet family not only England's new royal family (known also as the Angevins), but ended up extending Plantagenet power across much of France, and even into parts of Ireland and Scotland. And it was he that made England a truly independent power.

As a grandson of English King Henry I, he inherited in 1150 through his mother, Matilda, the title of Duke of Normandy. And in 1151 – through his father, Geoffrey – the title of Count of Anjou (thus Angevin), a huge county just to the south of Normandy. And by way of marriage in 1152 to the just-divorced or papally "annulled" Eleanor (previously the wife of Louis VII), he received her holdings of Aquitaine in Southern France.

The following year, former English King Stephen of Blois came out of his "retirement" to support his own son William, clearly contesting Henry for the position of King of England. But Henry carried the day, and Stephen had to align himself with Henry's supporters, opening the way for Henry to be crowned King of England (1154). Henry would eventually extend informal control over Brittany, and Eastern Ireland and Southern Scotland.

Naturally Henry would face many bitter contests in holding his vast dominion ... which greatly exceeded in size that of his supposed sovereign or lord (when in France) Louis VII, who anyway was very bitter over Henry's marriage to Eleanor. By the mid-1160s, Henry and Louis would find themselves at war on multiple fronts. And so things went for Henry.

But Henry was no fool, and worked hard to bring all the warring to an end, and build his rule more securely on the solid basis of royal law, in essence founding England's Common Law.

But politics within Henry's own family and the circle immediately around him became less stable with time. Eleanor, a strong-willed woman, birthed eight children, and eventually became caught up in family rivalries that inevitably developed.

And when it became apparent that his candidate for the vital position as Archbishop of Canterbury, Thomas Becket, was blocking Henry's effort to bring the Church of England under his own authority, not only would the two former allies part company (Becket even had England put under papal "interdict" or condemnation), but Henry unintentionally had Becket murdered (not simply arrested). The shame Henry experienced over this matter would weaken him considerably.

Ultimately it was family rivalries within his own family and among his barons that would do him in, over the matter of the inheritance of all of his titles, but now most importantly the title of King of England. Then, in the midst of a huge revolt by his own children, his eldest son Henry died of a fever, leaving the royal inheritance in the hands of Richard (or possibly his son John – Henry's own preferred candidate). Then the new French King Philip Augustus joined forces with Richard to attack Henry's position in France, although papal intervention not only brought a truce but also a stepping back of Richard and Philip Augustus – in order for them to take up the call to crusade in the Holy Lands. But Richard and Philip took one last shot at Henry before their departure, as Henry himself was dying of a bleeding ulcer. Then when it was announced that Henry's son John had joined forces with his brother Richard, this finished off Henry, who soon died (1189).

Richard I "The Lionheart" (r. 1189-1199). Richard figures more importantly in legend than in actual political history. He was undoubtedly a fierce warrior, thus his name "the Lionheart." He inherited all the titles and land held by his father Henry, including importantly the position as King of England. But he actually spent very little time in England as its king, possibly only as much as six months. Naturally French-speaking, he found himself mostly in the very wealthy and quite fashionable Aquitaine ... when he wasn't off crusading.

When news came in 1187 that Jerusalem had fallen to Saladin, both Richard and his French ally Philip agreed to go on a Third Crusade. After collecting a huge amount of taxes in order to build a royal treasury needed to conduct this crusade, he headed off in 1190, coming to Sicily, establishing there by military means the Kingship of Sicily for Tancred. He and Philip then headed onward, went through a destructive storm at sea and ended up at Cyprus, where they battled and defeated the local ruler – who had taken advantage of the crusaders' plight in grabbing their monies and imprisoning them for ransom. Ultimately, Richard turned the Island over to the Knights Templar to rule. Thus Richard's reputation as a warrior developed quickly.

They arrived at Acre (1191), with both Richard and Philip becoming sick, even as the crusaders attacked the Muslim forces inside of Acre. They did succeed in driving Saladin from the fortress. But Philip, at that point, had enough of the venture and returned to France, leaving Richard to carry on the effort by himself. But a split in the crusader ranks as they approached Jerusalem, plus rumors that Philip and Richard's brother John were plotting against Richard back in Europe, forced Richard to come to terms with Saladin (1192), and Richard headed home.

But he had troubles at sea on his return, and had to take the land route across Central Europe to get home. But when he came to the territory of Leopold of Austria, who was angry with Richard on a number of counts, he was seized and imprisoned. Threatened by Pope Celestine III for having seized a crusader while on his mission (a grand crime) the pope excommunicated Leopold (cut him off from the privilege of Christian worship – considered at the time as absolutely necessary for eternal salvation). With Philip's encouragement, Leopold then (1193) simply transferred Richard into the hands of the Holy Roman Emperor, Henry VI. But with the Emperor being so powerful, the pope dared not excommunicate him. Then Henry demanded an enormous ransom for Richard's release. Under his mother Eleanor's direction, heavy taxes were again levied on the people of the Plantagenet domains, and Richard (despite John's opposition, also encouraged by Philip) was finally released (1194). On his return Richard forgave John, but found himself at war with Philip in his effort to regain his French holdings. Again, raising taxes, he built castles where he could to strengthen his position, and attacked the towns and castles of the opposition. But he died of an infectious wound in the process in 1199.

His brother John (infamous in the legend of Robin Hood) would then take over his holdings ... and fall into dispute not only with Philip (now an adversary) but also with his English barons, who forced a deeply humiliated John (loss of a key battle in 1214) to agree to terms (the *Magna Carta* of 1215) granting greater political independence to those same barons.

Philip II Augustus of France (r. 1180-1223).   When Philip II was crowned in 1180, approximately the Western half of today's France was held by the Angevin dynasty – under the rule of English King Henry II. The young Philip was determined to change this political relationship, not just in bringing the Angevin dukes back under Capetian royal authority, but ultimately in pushing them entirely out of France, extending Capetian rule tremendously in the process. Indeed, by the time of his death in 1220, the Angevins held only a small portion of French territory in southwestern France. At this point nearly all of France was held by Philip as the Capetian inheritance.

Philip performed this amazing political feat both in increasing massively the size of his royal army (adding to it a sizeable navy) and by playing on the feudal rivalries going on not only around the larger North-European realm but also within the Angevin family itself, for instance in allying himself with Richard and John in their rebellion against their father Henry – and then later in allying with John in his dispute with his brother Richard. He took on independent feudal lords, forcing them under tighter royal control, again both militarily and diplomatically.

We've seen that he joined Richard in the ill-fated Third Crusade, and then turned against Richard at every opportunity thereafter, step by step reducing Richard's Angevin holdings. But it was not until John took the English throne in 1199 that the largest part of the Angevin family territorial turnover to Philip occurred, most securely so as a result of the Battle of Bovines in 1214 – when John and some of his feudal allies failed horribly in their effort to retake territory lost to Philip.

Frederick II (r. 1220-1250). Another grand figure of those days was the Hohenstaufen, Frederick – King of Sicily (as of 1198 when only 3 years old!), King of Germany (as of 1212), King of Italy and Holy Roman Emperor (as of 1220), and King of Jerusalem (by marriage as of 1225).

Although the title Holy Roman Emperor, the most important of his political claims, was largely based on German holdings, Frederick spent little time there, preferring to base himself in Sicily, or be on crusade. Italian politics also commanded much of his attention as he fought to keep the rebellious republic-minded Italian cities under imperial control. Complicating matters further was the political battle going on between Frederick (supported by the Ghibellines) and the Roman Popes (supported by the Guelphs).

Frederick had disappointed Christian Europe when he failed to show up for the Fifth Crusade (1217-1221) and then finally did pursue the matter with the Sixth Crusade (1227-1229) but did not get very far in the venture before turning back, claiming sickness – causing him to be excommunicated by Pope Gregory IX for not respecting his crusading pledge. The next year he did finally make the venture, but to the anger of the papacy because being excommunicated, he did not have papal authorization for this venture. Nonetheless he arrived in Jerusalem, conducted diplomatic exchanges with the Muslim Ayyubid sultan, Al-Kamil, securing crusader holdings in Jerusalem, Bethlehem and Nazareth, and Frederick's official coronation as King of Jerusalem (1230). In exchange, he promised numerous rights to the Muslim population. This made local crusader noblemen, Templars, and Hospitallers very unhappy. But it also made the papacy furious, because this had been transacted outside of papal authorization. But it did succeed in securing the Holy Lands once again as Christian territory, although in 1244 Muslims were once again able to retake the area.

Relations between Frederick and Pope Gregory turned heated, as the order of excommunication was lifted, then re-imposed when Frederick took an ever-stronger hand in Italy's political conflicts. Then, as he marched his army on Rome to confront the pope in 1241, Gregory died, and Frederick backed off.

He was then forced to turn his attention elsewhere when Mongol invaders reached the borders of his imperial territory. But the Mongols, after burning and pillaging Poland and Hungary, found the going now extremely difficult, and simply retreated to Russia (1242).

Relations with a new pope, Innocent IV (1243-1254), merely worsened as Innocent supported the Guelph cities attempting to throw off Frederick's rule. The pope also worked with German princes to undercut Frederick's position as Holy Roman Emperor. In the end, Frederick was able to send Innocent fleeing to France, and to hang onto or even retake some of his domain. But it all served to exhaust him. Then, as he knew himself to be dying, he was able to assign various lands to family members and allies, and promised to return the lands he had seized from the Church.

Frederick died in 1250. And with the death of his son Conrad four years later, the Hohenstaufen dynasty came to an end.

Louis IX of France ("Saint Louis") (r. 1226-1270). Louis IX was the grandson of Philip II, and considered a model king in his very "goodness" – both political and personal. In fact, the Catholic Church, only 27 years after his death, proclaimed him as a "saint," the only French king to be honored this way.

He came to the French throne at age 12, and had his mother, Blanche of Castile, rule as regent, overseeing and in 1229 bringing to political success the lengthy "crusade" against the Albigensian heresy that had been sweeping Southern France.

Finally taking full rule soon thereafter, Louis found himself facing the usual feudal problems with various French nobles, plus English efforts to regain lost Angevin territory in France. But he took on those challenges in a way that was considered at the time exceptionally fair or "just." He was also well-known for his work with the poor within his kingdom, personally rather than just politically involved with them in the process.

But his sense of Christian "goodness" extended to the realm of dealing with heretics, a problem still shaking France – even after the successful completion of the Albigensian Crusade against the Cathars in Southern France (1209-1243). He was quick in responding to the call of Pope Gregory IX for action against the Jewish heresy, Louis in 1242 ordering the seizing and burning of some 12,000 copies of the Jewish Talmud and other Jewish writings. And he continued to oversee the confiscation of Cathar properties in Southern France – all the way to his departure on the Seventh Crusade in 1250. He expanded the role of the French Inquisition, requiring the mutilation of the tongue and lips of anyone found guilty of blasphemy. But this kind of rigor was exactly what was expected of a "good" Christian king.

He also exemplified the role of the crusader king, involved in not just one, but two crusades to the Holy Land. In his involvement in the Seventh Crusade, he first found himself rather quickly defeated in Egypt in 1250 by Ayyubid troops, and released only upon payment of an enormous ransom demand. He did however remain in the Holy Land, helping to strengthen the lines of defense of the crusaders in Jerusalem, Acre and other points in the area. Finally, in 1254, Louis and his army returned to France. Then he was back at the venture again in 1270 in response to the calling of the Eighth Crusade. But he got no further than Carthage (Tunisia) when he caught dysentery there and died of the disease.

Edward I of England (r. 1272-1307). Edward was the son of one of England's longest ruling kings, Henry II (1216-1272) ... which had been a highly troubled time for England ... Henry not being a strong king and not doing well in his efforts to reconquer lost Plantagenet lands in France – or in keeping radical barons under his control. His son Edward however proved able to bring these barons back under his father's rule ... and then headed off on the 9th crusade to the Holy Lands in 1270. Two years later, on his return to England, Edward learned of his father's death and his own assumption of royal rule.

Edward not only spent time reforming England's feudal laws and administration but he also engaged himself in conquering Wales (1283) and then taking control of a leaderless Scotland (1290) – in turn sparking a revolt and then on-going war (with Scotland's ally France joining the action), as a result. His wars however produced a huge tax burden for his English subjects to deal with, he performed the very cruel act of ordering the expulsion of England's Jews (1290), and his hanging and quartering of the rebel leader William Wallace (1305) simply succeeded in turning Wallace into a Scottish hero. And when he died in 1307, a very corrupt son, Edward II, was to take his place as English king.

✳ ✳ ✳

CULTURAL-INTELLECTUAL-SPIRITUAL STIRRINGS

In so many different ways, the West was on a major rebound during those vital years of the 1100s and 1200s. While European commerce and trade began to revive, so did the realm of scholarship, artistry and spirituality. Monasteries reformed as centers of learning, cathedrals began to be built and cathedral schools began to draw professors and students to form the nucleus of European universities.

The huge intellectual debt owed to the world of Islam

The new contacts (even the crusades) with the Muslim East had the unintended effect of assisting the Christian world in a major way in this new development of Western scholarship, artistry, and spirituality. In fact, even before the beginning of the crusades, there had begun a procession of Christian scholars to nearby Muslim Spain, to study Islamic medicine, mathematics, and general science.

Classical scholarship. Thankfully the Muslims had rescued from earlier Christian purging of pre-Christian Greek literature a huge realm of ancient scholarship, scholarship which otherwise would have been lost forever. Some of the works of Plato and Aristotle had been preserved in the Christian West. But the works of other Greek scholars had been purposely suppressed, because of their "pagan" origins. Muslims however, in coming across this same literature, had no such trouble with the material. They were in fact careful to protect this legacy ... even translating much of it into Arabic. But now with Muslim translations (and Greek originals) of the vast field of pre-Christian Greek scholarship quite available, Christian scholars could turn to the business of creating their own Latin translations of these formerly forbidden and thus forgotten ancient works, opening their world of Christian scholarship to new horizons.

Mathematics. Contact with the world of Islam would have a tremendous impact on Christian culture and its offerings in other areas as well. For instance, it was from the Muslim development of *al-jabr* (the "completion") – which came to be known in the Christian West as algebra – that Western scholarship was able to do its own advancement in the realm of mathematics.

Cathedrals. Moreover, the new cathedrals that came under construction in the 1100s and 1200s were able to reach ever-higher in structure – and yet be built with walls of stained glass rather than heavy stone – because of the discovery of the Muslims' pointed arch. This arch is what allowed such light, airy and high-reaching ceilings, and huge, and awesomely beautiful, colored glass windows to serve as the side walls.

This produced what is oddly enough termed "Gothic" architecture ... a term assigned to that particular architecture style by Italian critics of the Renaissance period that followed (1400s-1500s) ... who considered such architecture crude (thus Germanic or "Gothic") – even ugly! – in comparison to the classic looks of the older Romanesque style.

Spiritual "heresies"...
deviations from the official Roman-Christian "Order"

But the new spirit arising in the Christian West would find itself going in all sorts of new directions, ones which would upset deeply the keepers of the older Christian social order.   For instance, this strong revival of the European intellectual spirit was also accompanied by religious or evangelical "awakenings" among the common people – often which had as its object the reform of an obviously corrupt institutional church. This in turn brought Papal condemnation, for mere disobedience and the embarrassment it caused Rome, as much as for doctrinal errors.

The Albigensians (or Cathars). One of the principal heretical movements, brought back from the East during the crusades, was the Cathars (from *Catharos*, a Greek word meaning "Pure One") – also known as Albigensians from Albi, a town in southern France where the Cathars were numerous (also, northern Italy and Germany). The Cathars were dualists: believing that historical events were the product of the struggle of two forces, even gods – one good, one evil. Evil had dominion over the visible world; but through good works of extreme asceticism (including the avoidance of all sexual intercourse and the dissolution of marriages), the souls of individuals were restored to the Good God. Membership into the elect required such good works.

According to the Cathars, being elect assured one of eternal salvation; but those who died without being saved were merely reborn into life (the living hell) and given another chance to try to achieve eternal salvation. There was no eternal hell to which the damned went.

Furthermore, according to the Cathars, Christ did not truly have a human body – for that would have placed him under Satan's dominion; neither did Christ experience true bodily death or bodily resurrection.

These particular elements of doctrine were held mostly by the more "sophisticated" of the Cathar community. The common people who followed the Cathar teachings did so mostly for the moral or ethical elements of the faith – not the doctrinal elements, of which they remained largely ignorant.

In strong contrast to the times, women were admitted to the caste of "chosen" and could perform priestly rites – since sex was seen as a distinction only of the devil anyway, though usually only the men became evangelists and teachers out in the open world.

The Cathars were exemplary people in their personal lives of piety and charity (in obvious contrast to the average run of Christian priests of the times) and well-loved in their communities. In the south of France they may have even become a majority of the population – though most of these Cathar followers would have continued to see themselves as "good Christians" and would have continued their observance of regular Christian worship.

The Waldensians.   Another heresy of the times was the Waldensians, named after their founder Peter Waldo (or Valdes), a wealthy merchant of Lyons who, around 1175 gave up his wealth and took up the way of an itinerant preacher of the gospel. He promoted the shocking idea that only scripture should be the ground of faith, and that any Christian belief or practice that had no scriptural warrant should be rejected.

Though he gathered many local supporters, he unsurprisingly also drew the opposition of the local bishop for preaching (which was restricted to clergy). Tragically, an appeal to Rome in 1179 resulted in a refusal to support or even permit his work. For a time, the Waldensians observed the restriction – but then returned to evangelical preaching – resulting in their excommunication in 1184 (along with the Cathars – with whom they had nothing in common).

However, excommunication and suppression seemed only to draw more support – principally in northern Italy and southern France as well as along the French and German Rhine. They also had adherents in northern Spain, in Bohemia and in Austria.

Theologically, the Waldensians remained completely orthodox – on all points to which Scripture gave warrant. They even held out hope of being reunited with the church. But eventually, the more rigorous branch of the Waldensians in northern Italy began to select their own ministers to dispense the sacraments – putting a strain within the movement which wanted to avoid offending the church as much as possible.

The crusade against the heresies. Distressed at the popularity of these grass-roots spiritual movements, and the seeming danger they posed to the all-important authority of the Roman Church, in 1215 dealing with these heresies became a critical part of the business of the powerful Fourth Lateran Council, presided over by Innocent III. Not only were the Cathars declared to be heretics but so were the Waldensians, authorizing their brutal suppression (actually already underway at that point).

In France, a crusade against the Cathars had already been announced in 1209 by Innocent III, and northern barons took this opportunity to invade the south of France in the quest of new lands. As a result, over the next 20 years southern France's cities and countryside were laid waste, and her culture shattered. In 1243 the last bastion of Catharism in southern France was destroyed.

At the same time, the Waldensian movement was either destroyed or driven underground. Only in the removed heights of southern Switzerland did the movement hold out in any strength – until it was integrated into the Protestant Reformation 300 years later.

The new teaching orders (early 1200s)

Dominic de Guzman (1172-1221) and the Dominicans. In the early 1200s, a Spanish Augustinian canon, Dominic de Guzman, urged the local monks in Southern France to fight Waldensianism and Catharism by emulating the apostolic poverty of the heretics – thereby winning back the support of the people. As the Albigensian crusade swirled around him, Dominic actually began to organize a new but very orthodox teaching movement, ultimately receiving papal recognition in 1217 as the Order of Preaching Brothers – though the term "Dominicans" became the popular designation of this new order.

This evangelical and service organization spread rapidly throughout all Europe, reaching by 1230 from England and Spain to Denmark, Poland, Greece and the Holy Land.

In short order also, the Dominicans were given chief responsibility in administering the Inquisition (which was in direct violation of Dominic's original understanding of their mission).

But they also sought and obtained professorships in the new universities, becoming highly influential within the life of the institutional church.

Francis (Giovanni Bernardone) (1181-1226) and the Franciscans. Francis was a man who in so many ways gave humankind a most visible characterization of the very nature of Jesus Christ ... deeply caring for others, especially the ones most likely to be rejected by society: the poor, the outcasts (notably lepers), the most common of commoners. But by the same spirit, he could bring the very wealthiest, most socially noble, to join him in the same work with the poor and outcast.

He could identify with both worlds, high and low, because he was born into considerable wealth as a son of a very prosperous Italian cloth merchant. Yet as a young soldier he fell into the lowest condition in life as a year-long prisoner in a horrible prison ... where finally the payment of a huge ransom brought him out of captivity ... but as a very sick person.

But he early on found himself receiving words from God ... most mysteriously at first – and then by ever-deeper spiritual discipline (hours in prayer) as he developed.

In 1206 or 1207, he received a totally life-changing call from God to "rebuild my church" – which he did (morally and spiritually), at first with some of his father's money. This got him in deep trouble with his father (who expected his son simply to take up the family business) and local authorities. And, to the shock of all, when brought before a town gathering presided over by the local bishop, and forced to make a choice of which road he was to take in life, he determined to shed himself of all earthly connections (including even the clothes he was wearing at the time!) in order to be able to pursue this religious calling

He at first supposed this call to "rebuild" was in reference to an abandoned and decaying chapel in the region, and proceeded to rebuild it himself, stone by stone. This attracted onlookers, whom he engaged in discussions about God, Christ, salvation, etc. Soon a crowd joined him in his work.

Then he began to see his call in larger terms: to devote himself to serving the hungry souls around him, especially those among the poor and socially marginal (something he had been doing for years, although originally only as a side line). He had no plan, no long-range goal except to live and serve as Christ had done, rebuilding Christian communities and aiding the poor, the sick and the outcast. Soon joining him in his work was a whole community of fellow workers ... future Christian evangelists.

Thankfully, he succeeded where the Waldensians failed – ultimately gaining papal authorization for his work in 1210, though he had come close to being declared one of the heretics bothering the institutional church in those days. However, he was willing (though slow to actually do so) to put himself and his group under papal supervision. Thus in 1210, his movement was recognized as the Friars Minor (lesser brothers) by Pope Innocent III.

But the Franciscans became fully organized under the subsequent pope Honorius III (1216-1227) as a newly-recognized monastic society ... through the considerable help of cardinal Ugolino. Francis himself retreated more and more from the responsibilities of leadership, having little heart in seeing his movement institutionalized. When he died in 1226, he died as a very smple monk within his own monastic order!

But two years later, with Ugolino as the new pope Gregory IX (1227-1241), Francis was declared officially to be a Christian saint ... an unprecedented speed by which this process occurred – so great had been the impact of Francis on his times (and even since then!).

And his Franciscan Order, inspired by his charismatic legacy, spread rapidly throughout Europe – in parallel with the Dominicans. However, not surprisingly, the Dominican and Franciscan scholars actually vied with each other for intellectual leadership of Europe ... with the Franciscans a bit more mystical (Platonic-Augustinian) and the Dominicans a bit more naturalist (Aristotelian).

The Augustinian Friars. Actually, no single individual founded this new order of monks … a monastic order that grew up in the mid-1200s with the coming together of a number of monastic communities in the Tuscan region of Italy … small communities of laymen seeking simply a life of quiet devotion. To avoid being condemned by the "anti-heretical" mood of the papacy – suspicious of any religious grouping that did not have papal authorization – they adopted for themselves the name "Augustinian" in order to legitimize themselves as an orthodox community … claiming that they were simply following up on Augustine's Rule dating from the 400s. This ploy worked … and in 1243 Pope Innocent IV accorded them this legitimacy. Then in 1255 Pope Alexander IV formally authorized them as the Order of Hermits of Saint Augustine.

From this point on, the Augustinian Order spread quickly around Europe – not on the basis of some well-organized effort but instead rather spontaneously here and there … because the order clearly met the spiritual hunger growing with the times.

✳ ✳ ✳

SCHOLASTICISM, AND THE RESTORATION OF "HUMAN REASON"

As ancient works of Aristotle were reintroduced to the West from the Muslim East, scholars began to gather at the new "universities" which were growing up out of the cathedral schools. Here language, logic and science came under rigorous study.

A new and very strong interest in Aristotle was brought to the West through the works of the Muslims, Avicenna (early 1000s) and Averroes (mid 1100s).

This intellectual import owed nothing to Christianity but relied purely on secular reason. In consequence, Christian learning among scholars moved away from Platonic-Augustinian theory and into "natural" theory.

Albertus Magnus (c. 1200-1280). Magnus was a Dominican teacher in Cologne (briefly also in Paris). He stressed the importance of the study of secular, even pagan, empirical science (Aristotle) – along with Christian theology. For Albertus, there is only one Truth. Thus theology should not fear philosophy/science.

Thomas Aquinas (1224-1274). The most famous of the Dominican scholars was Thomas Aquinas, who taught in Paris and in Italy. He was deeply influenced by Aristotle's empiricism (taught by Albertus Magnus). He attempted to couple it with the Platonic foundations of Christian philosophy of his times.

Ultimately his great lifetime work, the *Summa Theologica*, is a massive effort to sum up all correct or "Catholic" theology ... forming the massive theological foundations on which Catholic Christianity stands ... even to today.

Aristotelianism.   Being instinctively Aristotelian rather than Platonic (or Augustinian), Aquinas felt that knowledge came principally through the rational ordering of what our senses revealed to us about the natural order. The world around us was the reality that we truly had to deal with in the here and now. And this world was not in itself evil, not something to be dismissed, as did the Platonist-Augustinian mindset still strong in his times.

True, following up on Albertus' views, he constantly affirmed the primacy of "higher" revelation knowledge which alone gives us understanding of the divine mysteries of faith. But for Aquinas, such revelation knowledge meant only the logical revelation of Scripture – as interpreted traditionally by the Church Fathers.

Aquinas opposed Platonic-Augustinian mysticism with its emphasis upon truth derived from Spirit-inspired insight. To Aquinas, mystically derived wisdom seemed too dubious a source of knowledge. Mysticism was, to his way of thinking, terribly liable to abuse by milk maids and overly imaginative cowherds.

Thus Aquinas downplayed the role in knowledge of the Holy Spirit and replaced it with the power of the Church and its wide range of sacraments in dispensing God's grace.

Further he explained works (of love) as the means by which faith is formed and the individual is justified before God and thus saved – although these works are possible only through the enabling power of God's Church-dispensed grace (through the sacraments).

The Human Intellect. To Aquinas, things physical and spiritual – body and soul – are not independent phenomena but of one substance (in distinction to the dualism of the Platonist Augustinians), though he acknowledged that the soul alone survives death, where it rests while it waits to be reunited with the body at the Last Day.

Aquinas took the view that the human mind was essentially a blank slate at birth. Gradually in its own development, the senses begin to organize physical perceptions in the mind, slowly bringing us to the awareness of reality (physical reality) as fact or data. At the same time, the active intellect (nous) focuses on this data and organizes it into useful information – or ideas or truths.

The source of this organizational power of the mind comes as a gift of

God, who has placed an element of His own divine light within us – so that we might recognize forms or ideas.

God. God's essence is in the way all existence is summed up in Him – not just in certain Ideas or Forms (as an architect's blueprint does not sum up the architect himself). Further, God is existence – not just a part of it. God is the very force giving rise to all life or existence within creation (working according to specific Ideas or Forms to be sure – but transcending the function of being merely a prototype of all things).

God draws all things from potentiality to actuality. It is God Himself who draws us ever forward in our thoughts, helping us to realize our humanity, in order to approach fulfillment of His Divine Plan. Indeed, it is God's design that man's purpose in life is to come to know fully all things – because the sum of all things gives testimony to the essence of God.

However, God does not impart knowledge by impressing every human thought with His thought (Platonism), but by fully endowed man at birth with his own potential, through his own human reason, to come to the knowledge of all things.

By expanding his own mind, man is making an intellectual journey toward God, is being conformed to God, is participating in God – a matter of great pleasure for God. And by "expanding his own mind," Aquinas meant rational inquiry, empirical investigation of reality, the pursuit of science. Thus to Aquinas the pursuit of empirical knowledge was the way of mystical union with God.

"like straw." However, ironically enough, in late 1273 he abruptly ceased his lifetime of writing ... alarming his Dominican brothers. When asked what was the matter, he merely replied, "I can write no more. All that I have written seems like straw." But he offered no further explanation of his decision to stop writing ... or his "straw" comment about his previous work. But with that, his life-work ended. He would then die a few months later (March 1274).

The unexplained comment has consequently been largely ignored by those who continue to hold his scholasticism in virtually worshipful regard!

The ongoing development of scholasticism

The spirit of wide-ranging and intense study of the world around us continued to move forward – guided by ever-tighter rules of logical inquiry built on Aristotelianism, giving both discipline to the endeavor, and a certain rigidity to it at the same time.

Siger of Brabant (c. 1240-1284). Siger was what might be termed a "secular Averroist" – one who believes in the autonomy of human reason. Siger felt that we lived in a "double truth" universe where theology and natural science were quite capable of being contradictory in their "truths." He undermined Aquinas' idea of the interdependence of science and theology. In turn, Siger focused on the study of physical science for its own sake – ordered by its own rules of logic – quite unrelated to theology. The spirit of secularism was clearly on the rise!

Anti-Scholastic skepticism

However not all great European minds were willing to go down this same path of holding human reason itself to be of divine nature.

Duns Scotus (1265-1308). One of the early voices to attempt to back down a bit from all this Scholasticism was Duns Scotus, an anti-Thomist (or anti-Aquinas) Franciscan. He felt that the study of creation neither was the pathway to an understanding of God nor an affirmation of the basic harmony of life. Each thing in the universe had a distinctness about its own existence. This was the foundation of reality: the world is made up of a multitude of separate things which have their existence quite independently of the existence of their defining "forms." It is this separateness between particular things and common forms that calls forth human thought – forcing the human mind to make the connection between form and particulars. This exertion of the human mind, however, is what gives dignity to human life and is reflective of God's own determining influence on nature.

God, in all his sovereignty, is not limited to the rules of human reason in the way he operates. God is not under any constraint to work within the logic of "forms" or "universals" – but can create anything as he particularly sees fit. Plato's (and Aristotle's) "universals" are not compelling as the starting point of knowledge.

Further, there is no way that we can use science or the study of the physical world to reflect back to the nature of God. The physical world we see around us is the product of the free choice of God – who is able to make this world any way he wants to. His choices reveal no necessary qualities about God.

With this last idea, Scotus began undermining the confidence of medieval scholars who felt that human reason was going to be able to bring all reality – including divine reality – under human scrutiny (and ultimately control). To Scotus, the exercise of human reason was good – even necessary, even dignifying of the individual. But it was not going to usher in some great age of human management of life through human reason.

William of Ockham (1285-1349). In a way, Ockham was even more hard-hitting than Scotus in his critique of the optimistic rationalism of the scholasticism of his times. This English Franciscan living in Paris was an ardent nominalist, claiming that what was truly "real," that is, open to human understanding through direct observation and reason, were the individual or particular things belonging to the physical world. However, the mind naturally reached beyond this reality to create broad mental categories or universals (names for things, thus "nominalism") of closely-related particulars. Thus the mind created for its own logical use the category of "dog" – a broad class of all animals that we recognize individually as dogs. In this the human mind was abstracting from the particular to the universals (Plato's "forms").

But these abstractions or universals had no reality in themselves. "Universals" were only mental constructs, nothing more – useful, of course, in helping us come to some kind of appreciation of reality, though by no means 100% reliable as a tool for establishing the truth of things. Ockham was thus a skeptic with respect to the claims made on behalf of "human reason" by the scholastics of his day (anticipating David Hume by centuries).

From this observation resulted "Ockham's Razor": the idea that we must be very careful in our use of human reason not to become too complex in our rational handling of particulars – lest we leave reality behind in the process. The simplest explanation of things is not only the more testable of things, it is normally the most accurate explanation of things!

With respect to religion, Ockham (echoing Scotus) pointed out that we cannot move in our reasoning from our observations about the particular aspects of creation to produce general conclusions about the Creator. God is not constrained to work according to the rules of human logic. Logic, in fact, can tell us nothing about the nature of God or of ultimate things in creation. God can be known only by faith – a quite different enterprise than using logic. Only faith, not human logic, can touch God's absolute sovereignty and freedom.

Ockham, in an effort to rescue faith from Scholastic rationalism, acted to sever the relationship between religion and secular science, a unity which Aquinas had worked carefully to develop. To Ockham, reason was a useful tool for observing the natural world. But it was useless in probing the realm of God. Only Divine revelation, received through human faith, would bring us knowledge of that higher realm.

Ockham's nominalism had the effect of freeing secular science from theology. Science no longer had to serve as the handmaiden of theology – or be justified by its theological value. But at the same time, neither did theology require anything from science in order to validate itself.

The decline of scholasticism

Thus in the 14th century (1300s) the *via moderna* (modern way) was born – rising to challenge the *via antiqua* (old way) of Aquinas. Thirteenth century scholasticism, built on the rationalism of Plato and Aristotle, came under challenge. So did the worldview of the Christian Middle Ages – and all of its certainties.

The contradicting positions of Aquinas, Scotus and Ockham not only undermined the unity of scholastic thought – they produced ongoing schools of thought which deepened the divide.

Further, scholarly thinking lost its freshness as scholars seemed more focused on carrying on these old debates to the point of total tedium. As the freshness died, so did the vitality of the scholastic enterprise at the universities.

Finally, the Black Death of the mid-1300s and the too-obvious politicization of the church (at about the same time) put the finishing touches on the collapse of the rational certainties of medieval scholasticism.

✳ ✳ ✳

MYSTICISM

Yet at the same time, while scholars argued over the nature of human reason and the location of absolute Truth, the hearts of the common people (and some not so common!) still continued to seek, perhaps even more devotedly, a deeper, more vital personal relationship with God.

Religious mystics, such as Meister Eckhart, Jan van Ruysbroek, Walter Hilton, Julian of Norwich, and Catherine of Siena, plumbed the depths of the soul and its relationship to God – and left records of those journeys for others to consider. Thus Christian mysticism flourished richly right alongside a growing secular-humanism during these times.

These "mystics" were looking for the great Truths of life not through systems of reason or intellect, but instead simply by seeking a personal piety by way of a direct spiritual contact with God. This piety tended to distance itself from religious formalism (the outward observance of religious rites and ceremonies) and to focus instead on the process of spiritual conversion (inner reform of the heart). Others pushed even further in their quest for "unity" with God, seeking true "mystical" experience

Hildegarde of Bingen (1098-1179). An early leader in this movement was Hildegard of Bingen, an amazingly prolific writer, artist, musician, poet, doctor and herbalist who was also the abbess of a dual male/female monastery. Much of her reflective work survives to this day. The Rhineland mystics were strongly influenced by her works two centuries later.

Joachim of Fiore (1132-1202). Another early leader of the rising mysticist movement, Joachim of Fiore understood the mystical mood developing here and there in Christian Europe as a key sign of the times. In fact, he allegorized human history into three periods: that of the Father (patriarchal times of the Old Testament), the Son (the priestly or clerical times of the New Testament church), and the Holy Spirit (a new age of individualistic spiritualism about to burst forth fully into human history). It seems that he was expecting some kind of "Great Awakening" (not the first nor by far the last of such "divine interventions" to shake the Christian West!).

The Church and the mystical Impulse. The "experiential" impulse within Christianity, despite domestic crusades and despite the orthodox teaching of the Dominican monks and the regular clergy, was always hard to contain by hierarchical authorities. The masses always stood ready to be swept up by any new wave of spiritual revival – a constant source of threat to the political position of the church ... for such spiritualism was always privatistic and by-passed the official church with its energy.

The church hierarchy watched these developments rather nervously, fearing that they might produce among the faithful a tendency to seek one's own way to God apart from the administration of the graces and sacraments of the church.

Also, new mystical orders grew up almost spontaneously around Europe – much to the chagrin of the church. Combined with the rapid spread of the teaching orders (principally Franciscans and Dominicans), the priestly church hierarchy was losing its grip on the scheme of things. The "church" was coming more and more to be understood as being within the hearts and minds of the faithful.

The German or Rhineland Mystics (1300 to 1350). By the early 1300s A group of German mystics was having a huge impact on the times. In fact, it would be this group who would actually lay the foundations for what would become the "Reformation" of the Church. In preaching (using the German vernacular) to the Beguines and Dominican nuns under their care, these particular mystics touched their feminine piety with their Dominican theology, with its stress on the care of souls and the importance of spiritual self-sacrifice ... rather than physical or outward renunciation which at the time was understood to be the path of true piety. In short, they stressed the importance of a Christian life of service to others in need, rather than service to one's own sense of self-righteousness (much like the Spiritual

Franciscans)!

Johannes "Meister" Eckhart (1260-1328). Then too, a more "creative" (and widely appealing) approach to Christian mysticism was offered by Johannes Eckhart, a prominent German Dominican studying, teaching and preaching in Paris, Strasbourg and Cologne. Taking the route that, centuries later, the Quakers would go down, Eckhart viewed the human soul as containing a "divine spark," and thus being truly of the same nature of God's own spirit or soul. To Eckhart, the human soul was not just a mere reflection of God's soul, created in his image. The spark of the human soul contained in its very "ground" the same elements as God's soul – having existed at a point before creation in complete unity with the soul of God.

Eckhart urged the faithful to retreat from the world to search for this divine spark in the ground of their own souls, to discover there the nascent Word of God, and to become mystically reunited, not just with God but with "Godness" itself: to become one with Divinity once again.

In his later life, as he came under suspicion of heresy as a neo-Platonist or even pantheist, Eckhart admitted to having been guilty of "exaggeration" and in the last years of his life backed into a more orthodox Thomist position. Nonetheless, shortly after his death (1329) parts of his writings were condemned by Pope John XXII.

Johannes Tauler (1300-1361).   Tauler, a Dominican and disciple of Eckhart's in Strasbourg and Basel, preached and taught a more orthodox view, that God gifts his people with a spiritual grounding crafted in his own divine image. This is conferred as a matter of divine grace; it is not (as per Eckhart) self-discovered as a matter of natural property of the human being. To Tauler, the return to "oneness" with God is a matter of having our human wills united with God's – not a matter of absorbing our human nature into God's divine nature.

Tauler's example and sermons (the only surviving part of his writings) had a great influence on the Rhineland school of mystics, and after them on Luther, because of his stress on suffering and self-denial (experienced poignantly during the Black Death) and on the reliance on grace as the center pieces of Christian faith.

✳ ✳ ✳

EARLY HUMANIST STIRRINGS

The natural inquisitiveness that peace and prosperity brought was met as much by a new exploration of the immediate world of the believer as it was by the new exploration of human reason, or even the glories of Creation and its Creator. Musicians and poets touched the hearts of Europe with a new love for the world which God had placed them in. Dante, Petrarch, Boccaccio, and Chaucer, for instance, wrote poetry and prose that also focused on human life as it was actually lived by real people around them – objects of interest (though not yet quite objects of reverence) in a world that had heretofore been focused more on the life beyond this earthly existence.

Giotto di Bondone (1267-1337). So also, the Florentine artist Giotto, though commissioned to paint religious art, designed his people to look real, very human, and quite alive – depicted as involved with others in the course of actual events – and not just formalized human icons who possessed only symbolic existence. His murals on the walls of the Arena Chapel in Padua are famous for his realism in depicting in various scenes the lives of Mary and Jesus ... as well as his very life-like 27 murals in the San Francisco basilica in Pisa, depicting the life of St. Francis.[*]

Dante Alighieri (1265-1321). Dante would have a huge impact on his times, daring to write magnificently in what he termed the "Italian" language – based principally on the Tuscan dialect of his birthplace, Florence – rather than on the classical Latin used rather universally. This was a major step in bringing the world of learning to the broader reaches of the common citizenry of Italy. But his work also connected the realm of religion and theology with the rising world of the ordinary passions of the people, especially the matter of romantic love.

He himself was betrothed by way of contract at age twelve and ultimately completed the contract in marriage with Gemma Donati of the powerful Donati family of Florence. But at an equally early age he developed a love-at-first-sight condition with a female named Beatrice, whom he would in his later writings elevate to nearly divine status – even though his contacts with her had always been, and always remained, minimal. Rather, she became a symbol representing the power of "courtly love" which was rising at the time.

Dante was ambitious politically, becoming early on involved with the Guelph party (pro-Pope) – which was politically dominant in Florence in his early days of politics – in opposition to the Ghibellines (pro-Emperor). He even served in a Guelph-Ghibelline battle in 1289 – thankfully coming out on the winning side. This would begin his political career.

But the times politically were very unstable, and the Guelph party itself soon divided into two hostile groups, the Guelph Whites (and Dante)

---

[*]Giotto also happened to be an excellent architect, designing the beautiful bell tower of the Florentine Cathedral.

– tending to distance itself from papal rule in the quest for more political freedom – and the Guelph Blacks – eager for a tighter rule in Florence of the papal party. At first the Whites dominated, and expelled the Blacks. But Pope Boniface VIII intervened and turned the political tables in Florence against the Whites. Dante was then sent by the Whites to negotiate with the Pope, but instead was arrested upon his arrival in Rome. Meanwhile the Blacks took over Florence, and deep revenge was taken against the Whites (including Dante) who were expelled from Florence and their property seized. Thus in 1302 Dante found himself in exile. He would never be allowed to return to Florence.

It was in exile that he did nearly all of his writing, *La Vita Nuova* (1294), a collection of poems and prose about courtly love, being the only work completed prior to that exile. His world of exile was not easy either. With the publication of his *De Monarchia* (1313 – actually written in Latin as a serious political study) his call for a secular monarch similar to the Emperor to bring peace to Italy (rather than solely the officers of the Church) distanced him further from the Church (the work was finally banned by the Church in 1515).

But it was his *Divine Comedy*,* written representing three stages of human progress, with Dante himself being the main character, and Virgil, Beatrice, and St. Bernard serving as guides in the three-staged journey: *Inferno* (Hell or the challenges of our earthly life); *Purgatorio* (Purgatory or the phase of the afterlife in which our sins are purged); and *Paradiso* (Paradise or our eternal reward as companionship with God in heaven). Stories of various individuals in his life were presented allegorically to portray this journey, all presented in a very beautiful poetic structure.

Francesco Petrarch (1304-1374).   Petrarch was born and raised in Arezzo in Tuscany to a family deeply involved in the business of law. Although Petrarch himself was trained in the law, he viewed the profession as one in which a person made a "merchandise" of his mind. Nonetheless he would be very active in the world of politics, moving to Avignon and doing much of his work there when Pope Clement V moved there to escape dangerous Roman politics, beginning the long-running Avignon Papacy.

Petrarch's political involvement also sent him on ambassadorial missions around Europe, which he used as an opportunity to collect historical material, notably ancient Greek and Roman writings, which served to deepen the foundations of his own writings. He continued the tradition of writing in Latin, but focusing not on theological matters (as was the habit of the time) but on historical scholarship. Clearly he understood that

---

*"Comedy" at that time meant more a process in life that, with God's help, brings a person to the happy state of a well-ordered life.

something important was happening: Europe was moving out of some kind of Dark Age into a new world of Light, modeled closely on classical antiquity. It was thus that his writings would have a huge impact on his times – and those that followed in the 1400s "Renaissance" – in bringing forward not traditional Christian but instead pre-Christian (Greek and Roman) culture as the social ideal that his world should be imitating.

Giovanni Boccaccio (1313-1375). Boccaccio was another Italian writer, deeply influenced by Dante's literary legacy – but also in close touch with Petrarch as friends. Boccaccio also forms a bridge between the High Middle Ages and the Renaissance. His chief work, *The Decameron* (completed in 1353 soon after the era of the Black Death), is a collection of 100 short stories told by ten literary characters passing the time (some ten days) while escaping the Black Death tearing through Florence. Much of the narrative simply describes the daily lives of these individuals and the political-religious controversies swirling around them at the time, as well as their own personal affairs – whether business, love or whatever. This was pure "Humanism" in literary form.

Geoffrey Chaucer (c. 1343-1400). Chaucer came from a well-positioned family in English society, serving as a high-ranking public official, involving apparently much diplomatic travel abroad. Possibly a trip to Italy had a huge impact on his story-telling career.

Certainly Chaucer was something of an English Boccaccio, also in his famous *Canterbury Tales** presenting, in the common English of the day, 24 stories told by various individuals (a knight, friar, physician, lawyer, clerk, miller, cook etc.) on a pilgrimage together from London to Thomas Becket's shrine in Canterbury, stories told simply to pass the time, but also done so in contest to see who could tell the best story!

Here too, the motif was quite Humanist rather than theological. And thus Chaucer helped step English society into the rising world of the Renaissance.

✳ ✳ ✳

THE CLOSE OF THE MIDDLE AGES (THE 1300s)

Marco Polo's amazing discovery of another world to the East

---

*These were composed over a period running from 1387 to his death in 1400, not fully complete, as he had hoped to write many more such tales told by these same pilgrims.

Around the year 1300, Westerners were very surprised to learn from an account, *The Travels of Marco Polo*, of a world in the Far East largely unknown to Westerners ... in particular, the very advanced civilization of China. Marco Polo's tradesmen father and uncle had first made the journey east from their home in Venice in the 1260s, meeting Chinese emperor Kublai Khan in the process. When then in 1271 they returned to China at the emperor's request (and Pope Gregory X's support), they had Marco with them – the young man impressing the emperor so much that he had him remain in China to serve as an imperial emissary. Marco thus was sent on many diplomatic missions in and around the Chinese Empire. Consequently, over the next 17 years he became quite familiar with China and its ways. Then he and his father and uncle had the additional opportunity to explore the neighboring societies of Vietnam, Burma, Indonesia, India, Sri Lanka and Persia ... before returning to Venice (in 1295) after 24 years away from their home.

Upon their arrival back in Venice, Marco found himself involved in a very vicious trade war going on at the time with Genoa ... and got captured and imprisoned in the process. But this did give him the opportunity to spend that time dictating the account of his travels to his cellmate. He was finally released in 1299 and returned to a very palatial home – thanks to the wealth he and his family had acquired in Eastern gems.

Very importantly, his depiction of a highly civilized China – and the Far East in general – awakened a Western society already highly stirred by a rising curiosity about the surrounding world ... and all of its fantastic material offerings. This would merely add to the dynamic that was taking Europe out of its humbler Christian ways ... and ever-deeper into the world of material wealth and power

The Avignon Papacy ... or "Babylonian Captivity" of the popes in France (1309-1377)

We have seen how clearly the papal office of the Bishop of Rome had long been the center of social-cultural politics – even military politics. During the crusades, European kings had served essentially as military commanders for Christian armies understood to be operating under the authority of the Pope. Only the crusading Holy Roman Emperor Frederick II acted independently of the Pope (for which he was excommunicated not once but twice!).

With the close of the crusades in the late 1200s this dynamic changed. Ambitious kings and princes (and even powerful Italian families) began to operate increasingly independently in their own territories – in disregard of the presumed unity of Christendom represented by the Church and its papal leadership. Popes found themselves in opposition to many of these new authorities – a situation which politicized heavily the papal office. Excommunications were imposed – and then lifted – against kings and ministers of state when the interests of the papacy and these rising authorities either clashed or conformed.

A number of diplomatic crises plus local circumstances in Rome upset greatly the political standing of the Roman papacy: infighting between two powerful Roman families (the Orsini and Colonna) over control of the papacy, the increasing influence of French clergy in the Papal Curia, the effort of French King Philip IV to have Pope Boniface arrested and brought to France for "heresy" in 1303 (but Boniface died soon after this assault) and finally the election of a French pope (Clement V) in 1305. This resulted in the decision of the Curia that year to move the papal office to France – eventually in 1309 to the city of Avignon in southern France. Here supposedly the pope would be under the French king's "protection." This begins the period of the papacy often termed the "Babylonian Captivity"!

Pope Clement was clearly a tool of French king Philip IV and agreed to the destruction of the Knights Templars, a very wealthy crusading order whose land and financial assets in France Philip IV coveted deeply. Clement also became deeply engaged in battles with the growing commercial empire of Venice, and led a brutal crusade at the beginning of the 1300s against some of the "Dulcinian heretics" whose Franciscan-inspired spirituality was deemed offensive to the church.

Then popes after Clement integrated the papacy more and more with the interests of the French monarchy. Thus as the 1300s rolled along, the popes gave more the appearance of being mere participants or even pawns in the political struggles of Europe than they did of being grand leaders of Europe's huge religious community.

The Scots secure independence from England

Edward II of England (r. 1307-1327) proved inept (and corrupt) ... losing the Battle of Bannockburn (1314) to Scottish leader Robert the Bruce – and thus securing Scotland's independence from England, with Robert now serving as Scottish king ... confirmed in 1324 by Pope John XXII's decree and further secured with a new Scottish alliance with France in 1327.

By this time the English were so tired of Edward that they (aided by Edward's wife Isabella ... who was also French King Philip IV's daughter) forced him to abdicate that same year in favor of his son Edward III. He was subsequently murdered ... probably under the orders of Isabella.

The First Phase (1337-1360) of the "Hundred Years' War"

The "Hundred Years' War" – actually a series of three wars, interspersed with times of truce – was basically an ongoing battle between the Plantagenet and Valois families over the question of the right to govern France. It is often identified as a battle between the English and the French, which is what it eventually became as Plantagenet troops and support took on an increasingly English nationalist character, with the Valois increasingly appearing to be the more "French" of the two contenders.

The Plantagenet family held the peculiar position of being both vassals or barons under the kings of France, yet – since the Norman victory over the Saxons in England in 1066 – at the same time kings by their own right in England. The two families were also connected by lineage or mutual descent from the Capetian royal family ruling France – starting up a bitter contest between the two families when the last king of the Capetian line ruling France died without any direct heirs. At first the Plantagenets – led by English King Edward III – attempted to assert his right to the French throne … he being the nearest male in line to that throne through his mother Isabella, the only sister of the just deceased French King Charles IV. But ultimately he acknowledged the Valois claim to the French throne by way of his cousin, Philip VI. But in 1337, Edward decided to press his own claim to the French throne when Philip moved to support the Scottish in their long-standing war with the English. Thus began the first phase of a contest that would span five generations of these two families.

Edward III (1327-1377) offered England another long period of rule … though he was deeply challenged during much of that time by that "Hundred Years' War. Initially, during the "First Phase" (1337-1360) of the war, it appeared that Edward would succeed in his bid for the French throne – as the fortunes of war favored his forces greatly in battle after battle. His son, Prince Edward "The Black Prince," was given command of his Plantagenet or "English" forces … and defeated the Valois or "French" forces soundly at Crécy (1346) and Poitiers (1356). And the younger Edward's path to securing his position as Prince of Aquitaine and Gascony in the South of France involved him in many other successful (and highly destructive) battles with the Valois forces.

But the intervention of the Great Plague (or "Black Death") hit England – as all of Europe – very hard … killing much of the English momentum. But the war then resumed as England recovered … resulting ultimately in the capture by Prince Edward in 1356 of French King John II … who, however, was merely held for ransom. But it was a most humiliating defeat for the French.

Then in 1360 a strange hail storm killed over 1,000 of the English troops as they were undertaking the siege of Chartres … on their way to then seizing Paris. The storm so devastated the English army (the largest loss of life in the war so far) that King Edward was forced to accept terms of peace with France. This would bring this first phase of the Hundred Years' War to a close.

The Black Death (1348-1350)

In the mid-1300s the Black Death struck Europe – wiping out 25 million people. It originated in Central Asia and made its way along the silk route to Constantinople in early 1347. From there it was brought to Sicily and Italy, spreading over Italy early the following year, and from there quickly into France and southern England by the summer of 1348. In Florence alone, it killed three-fourths of the city's inhabitants. In England, in a 3-year period it wiped out half of the population of 4 million people. After this a wave of other epidemics swept a much-weakened Europe.[*]

Overall, the Black Death left Christian Europe shattered, economically, socially, culturally, not to mention spiritually. Where was God in all of this? Was he actually not the powerful God they had been led to have full faith in? Or was he an angry God, angry at the moral-political dissolution that had hit the Christian community, especially at the level of its "Christian" leaders? What exactly was one to make of this disastrous event?

The Church did not rebound well from the Black Death, having been able to give neither explanation for nor relief from this mysterious devastation. A lot of faith in the Christian cosmos was deeply undercut by this tragedy. Worse, not able to account for the cause of the tragedy, the Europeans' frustration and wrath turned on defenseless targets such as Jews, Gypsies, lepers and foreigners, Europeans blaming them for having brought the disease. Whole communities of European Jews were completely wiped out in the reaction.

Nonetheless Europe rebounded fairly quickly, though with a greatly depleted population.

Urban optimism. Indeed a secular spirit rising among the people – particularly those living in the rapidly growing cities – was too strong to be long-intimidated by the calamities of the Black Death and the Babylonian Captivity ... or the diminishing of sacred tradition caused by the Papal Schism. As things actually turned out, many urban laborers benefited financially from the labor shortage caused by the Black Death.

———————————————————

[*]Waves of attack by the plague would hit Europe again and again over the years ... though not with the severity of the 1350 Black Death ... though very devastating and frustrating nonetheless. It would not be until the 1600s that Europe would reach the populations size it had before the Black Death.

Indeed urban life tended to bounce back quickly in spirit ... and keep moving forward, lured onward by a sense of better things lying ahead.

But rural serfdom (virtual slavery). However, it must also be noted that in the feudal countryside this same labor shortage caused many feudal lords in fact to tighten up on the ability of their peasants to shift around in the quest for better conditions elsewhere.

In England, efforts by landowners (including the church) to hold scarce labor captive through a tightening of the laws permitting the peasants to move on to new economic opportunities – instead gradually turning the English free peasants into serfs – eventually produced a massive uprising in East Central England known as the Peasants' Revolt (1381). Although it was brutally suppressed, it left among the commoners a legacy of discontent with the wealth of the landowners ... and the church.

In Central and Eastern Europe, the lords of the land now tended to lock their vassals in place as rightless serfs ... whose social-political status was now hardly different from that of a slave.

The rising threat of the Ottoman Turks in the East

Osman I (1281-1326) founds the Ottoman Empire. In 1281 a local Oghuz Turk took up his father's position as bey (governor) of a small beylic (Turkish state) in northwestern Anatolia (in modern-day Turkey), very near the border of a weakening Byzantine Empire. Choosing to take his aggressions out on the failing Byzantine Empire rather than on his Turkish neighbors (the more usual direction of Turkish military politics) he drew a large number of other Turks to his cause – notably Ghazi warriors (volunteer militia) abandoning what was by then a collapsing Seljuk empire – Osman building up a very strong military in in the process. Thus he proceeded to expand the boundaries of his own beylik, but also through diplomacy and strategic marriages as well as by the engines of war. By 1299 he was ready to accept the title "Sultan of the Ghazis." Thus the Ottoman Sultanate, the forerunner of the Ottoman Empire, was born (and soon named after him).

Orhan and Murad I. Osman's son Orhan (1326-1362) and Orhan's son Murad I (1362-1389) continued the Ottoman expansion, Orhan taking Bursa with his Ghazi troops, making it his new capital, very close to the Byzantine capital at Constantinople. At this point the Byzantine power in Anatolia was almost completely eradicated.

In taking power in 1362, Murad immediately conquered the city of Adrianople, to the north of Constantinople, beginning the encirclement of the Byzantine capital ... and the permanent move of the Ottoman Sultanate onto the European continent. Murad turned this Balkan city into his new capital in 1363 and renamed the city "Edirne." He then began his expansion into neighboring Bulgarian and Serbian lands, aided greatly by the internal divisions and infighting going on within those two Christian societies, and by the pressures on the Bulgarians coming from the Hungarians to the north and the Greeks rising up in rebellion against the Serbs to the southwest. In 1387 his troops were able to seize from the Italian Venetian Empire the strategic city of Thessaloniki sitting at the vital juncture of the land of the Bulgarians, Serbs and Greeks.

Finally in 1389 at the battle of Kosovo, Murad's new army, now including Janissary troops,* was able to crush the Serbian army (though the Ottoman forces themselves were greatly devastated by the battle), weakening the Serbs so much that they soon accepted vassalage within the growing Ottoman domain ... though Murad himself lost his life in the battle.

Bayezid I (1389-1403). Murad's son Bayezid gathered a massive army – interestingly made up of a large number of Serbian and Byzantine soldiers – to consolidate his hold on the remaining independent Turkish beyliks to the south of the Anatolian peninsula. Meanwhile (1389-1395) his troops were active to the north in Bulgaria and Wallachia (today's southern Romania), although the Wallachians were able to hold him in check. And in 1395 he laid siege to the Byzantine capital of Constantinople, but was unable to breach its thick walls or cut off its supplies by sea – although a Christian relief force – another "crusade," led by the King of Hungary – was defeated at Nicopolis (1396).

Tamerlane - A step backward for the Ottomans. The Ottoman assault on Constantinople continued until 1402, when the Ottoman troops were called back to Anatolia to hold off the ever-expanding central-Asian realm of Timur (or "Tamerlane"), who had allied with the local Turkish beys that had proven resentful of Bayezid's domination of Anatolia. At the Battle of Ankara (1402) Bayezid was captured, and died the following year in captivity.

For a brief period (ten years) it looked as if the Ottoman threat to Europe had been dismissed. But that was not to be. In the next century (and after) the Ottoman Turks would play a major role in European affairs.

The Papal schism closes out the Middle Ages (1377-1418)

---

*The Janissaries constituted something of a new personal guard, in effect slave soldiers who had been taken from Christian homes at an early age and trained as Muslim warriors totally dedicated in life and death to the Ottoman sultan. They proved to be very fierce warriors, even in taking on the Christian world they had originally been born to.

When in 1377 Pope Gregory returned the papal court to Rome, he soon died ... and the College of Cardinals elected a new pope, whom they quickly grew to dislike, and thus elected another pope. But the first pope refused to step down ... and now there were two popes.

European princes and kings soon lined themselves behind one or another candidate, making the papal schism even more catastrophic to the status of the Church. Eventually there would be even other candidates (and their political supporters) to step forward to claim the papal position ... before a compromise was finally achieved at the Council of Constance (1414-1418).

But Christianity, as the spiritual underpinning of the old Christian community, by that time had lost ground badly.

CHAPTER EIGHT

THE RENAISSANCE AND REFORMATION

✳ ✳ ✳

THE RENAISSANCE: AN OVERVIEW

A time of transition. Though there was no specific event to mark the end of the middle ages and the onset of the modern era, the 1400s seem to be the all-important transition time.

This period of transition into modernity, known today as the "Renaissance," ("Rebirth") was based heavily in Italy, especially in the cities of Venice, Florence, Siena, Mantua, Pisa, Milan, Urbino, Rome and Naples – but was also found in significant portions of Northern (mostly coastal) Europe … through the natural links that commerce produced – and by scholars who studied in Italy and took its learning north. Thus in addition to a number of vibrant Italian cities, the Renaissance also extended to Bordeaux and Paris (France), London and Bristol (England), Bruges and Antwerp (Flanders) and the coastal German cities (such as Lübeck and Hamburg) of the Hanseatic League … among a number of other European cities.

On the face of it, it appears that the Renaissance was essentially an economic affair – resulting from a rapid growth of commercial wealth that aided greatly in producing an intellectual revival in the form of a strong interest in pre-Christian Greco-Roman philosophy, and in a dazzling flowering of the fine arts (painting, sculpture, architecture) – dedicated more to the glorification of man and his talents ("Humanism") than to God and his traditional role in the Christian world.

The rising power of the European city. All of this wealth in trade flowing to the rising European cities would change deeply the way Christians or "Westerners" formed social bonds in order to advance and defend life. In general, the merchant cities of Europe went at the matter of acquiring new powers differently than did the princes, the latter tending to see politics as a rather personal matter, something impacting their own status as grand landowners, as overseers of the masses of peasants working those lands for them, and personally as the primary benefactors of the wealth this system provided.

The rising cities went at life with a different attitude directing them. Like the richest of all of them, the Republic of Venice, urban politics tended to be corporate, drawing into the position of leadership a wider circle of local interests than the single-individual-dominated kingdoms and principalities. Most cities were run or managed by a corporate council ... led by individuals elected to office on a regularly recurring basis by committees or guilds of tradesmen and manufacturers.

Urbanites were also a different breed of Europeans. Their business world required the ability to read, write and perform complicated mathematical processes – at a time when the rural feudal princes of the vast European countryside were often illiterate, reading and writing not being a very important factor in their rule. Europe's urban world was also larger than the traditional world of rural feudal Europe. Travel and business connections abroad – not to mention the ability to read and write – gave them a much bigger view of the world ... and how that world worked.

Europe's urbanites were an independent-minded lot, adventurers and risk-takers, and always a potential challenge to the medieval ways of rural feudal Europe. But they were tolerated, even encouraged, by local princes in whose territory these cities found themselves located. They were, after all, a source of mobile or moneyed wealth ... increasingly more important to local princes and their ambitions than the feudal vassals who were supposed to offer full support at the princes' command ... but who proved most unreliable in times of real need.

So the princes "chartered" the cities ... contracting with them to receive tax monies in exchange for the prince's support of their rather independent ways, ones that the cities required in order to do business successfully. Once a prince or king granted a city its charter, it had full rights to operate as it saw fit. Needless to say, cities guarded jealously those chartered rights. But also kings tended to respect carefully those rights ... because they depended so much on their cities' financial support.

Nonetheless this shift in the local political scene still had its dangers. The independence of these towns – in keeping with their actual power in this early stage of development – did not provide the air of legitimacy that they needed to feel secure in their liberties within the newly rising order. At any time these urban charters might be revoked by the local prince or bishop by any whim or fancy (or suspicion). There really was no "right" of their own that the towns could hold up to these lords in order to demand equitable treatment, at least not until the Protestant Reformation in the 1500s gave them the sense that they had the right to accept or reject political authority in accordance with what their own consciences dictated. There was no power on earth, only God alone, who had the right to judge them in matters of conscience, even political conscience.

Technological development. But in any case, the rapid growth of the trade in European goods called forth industrial growth – and industrial growth called forth new technologies. The number of inventions from newly emerging European inventive minds was phenomenal. But a few stand out – not only because they added so much to industrial development but because they also came to have such a profound impact on the European mindset or spirit.

The clock, with its carefully interworked systems of gears and wheels, seemed to serve as a symbol of the new sense of order which underpinned the whole universe – an order which existed by its own right.

Likewise, the compass gave the traveler, especially the new bold class of seafarers, a sense that life had key foundation points – which man of his own could fathom and use for himself.

Widespread printing of the Bible. But there is no question that the one technological development that most revolutionized the times was the invention of the printing press. In around 1450 Johannes Gutenberg introduced the new printing process (moveable type) which revolutionized the production of written material – using this new process to produce his amazingly high-quality *Gutenberg Bible* (in the Latin or Vulgate).

The printing process would soon revolutionize the printing and distribution of the Bible in the various European languages actually spoken at the time. Thus a wide number of local-language translations of the Vulgate Bible soon began to appear in widely available printed form: German (1466), Italian (1471), Dutch (1477) Spanish (1478 – but subsequently suppressed), French (1487), and Czech (1488).

William Tyndale's English translation, the first printed English translation, did not come out until much later,[*] around 1525 – after much resistance from the Church and from English King Henry VIII. Tyndale was eventually executed for this "crime" (1536). Oddly enough, only four years after Tyndale's execution, Henry VIII authorized his English-language *Great Bible* to be published, a translation based largely on Tyndale's work!

A shifting sense of history. The 1400s mark both a definite continuity with the long development of Western Christian culture, and yet at the same time a strong departure from many of the ways the Christian community had understood the cosmos around it. The Christian mind had long (a

---

[*]Copies of Wycliff's English Bible (completed around 1384) in manuscript form also were circulated widely – although not in printed form until the early-to-mid 1500s.

thousand years) seen the sweep of history in a profoundly dualistic fashion: there were the times before Christ and the times since then. Everything before Christ's appearance in history (Before Christ or "BC") had meaning for them only as preparation for this grand event. Everything since that event (*Anno Domini* – the Year of the Lord, or "AD") was measured in terms of how it gave fulfillment to God's plan of salvation for human life.

Christians traditionally had been certainly mindful of the importance of Rome. It seemed to them to be no mere coincidence that Rome reached its greatness (presumably in the reign of Augustus) at about the time Christ was born. To the Christian mind, this was God's way of preparing the civilized world physically to receive the gospel. They were aware of many of the unique features of Roman thought – but either they dismissed that thought as a carryover from darker days – or as metaphor, pointing to and confirming the gospel message. Thus they read Virgil, Ovid, Cicero, Livy with a profoundly Christian interpretation of the meaning of their works. So also did they understand Plato and Aristotle.

But by the 1400s, without dismissing their Christian loyalties or pieties, the Renaissance mind was looking back on the days of Greece and Rome through a new set of eyes. There had been growing, since the early 1300s (perhaps even earlier) a fascination with Roman ways in themselves, without having to go through some kind of Christian interpretation. This was timed with the reaction against scholasticism as an arid, intellectually arrogant ambition of human reason to bring all things under systematic theological mastery. This was timed with a desire to explore more deeply the "humane" features of human life: the simple passions, the loyalties, the love that connected human life with God and Christ – and with the rest of the human community. Things came to be of interest in themselves to the enquiring European mind as it moved through the 1300s and entered the 1400s. They came to be of interest not because they conformed to some great intellectual system but because they gave life to human existence. Thus did they now approach Virgil, Ovid, Cicero, Livy … not to further undergird a well-rehearsed medieval worldview, but to listen to them speak out of their own times, as fellow humans trying to find in life the same deeper qualities of human existence.

Having discovered this wealth of ancient human testimony and being deeply touched by the profundity of its spirit – pagan though it might be (and certainly was!) – they began to detach themselves all the more from the "darker" Christian mood of the centuries that stood between themselves and that "golden age" 1000 years earlier. They saw ancient history now not as part of a single Christian continuum, but as a time in which the once greatness of Roman civilization was lost and was now, a thousand years later, being rediscovered.

The development of the Renaissance mind. We need to make note at this point that those who had such a "Renaissance mind" actually composed only a small minority of the people of those days. By and large the mass of the Europeans living in those times probably retained the older medieval world view. When we are talking about the "Renaissance mind" we are describing a small group of wealthy and powerful businessmen, an equally small number of intellectuals, both secular and religious, and a small, curious group of adventurers.

However, though small in number, they were very powerful in terms of shaping the events of their day. In any case, it is to them that we look when we describe the Renaissance mind.

Though these individuals remained Christian to the core, they began to take a dimmer view of the way that their faith had been mediated by the Church during a thousand-year "dark ages." They instead sought to validate their Christian faith on the basis of personal loyalties and personal virtues. These people were doers – who used their minds in service to the needs of the family and local community – the "patria" as they understood it. They were not contemplatives; monastic life was not for them a Christian ideal. They were not knights living to honor the code of chivalry; that was much too abstract a notion for them. They were practical, "earthy" in their interests, and sought to use their considerable worldly talents for the common good. This was their understanding of their Christian responsibilities, their accountability before God.

The Roman Church under challenge. The church was thus finding itself hard-pressed to maintain its traditional place of authority within the European cultural sphere. It tried to resist its loss of status – but found that circumstances were making it increasingly difficult to hold its own.

For instance, the translation of the Bible from Latin into the languages of the people gave them the power to discern for themselves the word of God. Through the rapid growth of literacy that accompanied the growth in Bible and other book publication, this development became quite extensive. Thus the church became very alarmed by the publication of the Bible – more alarmed than it was over the publication of pagan Roman and Greek literature – protesting that this wide dissemination of the Bible would cause the emergence of wrong interpretations and subsequently the spread of new heresies. The church well understood that it was thus rapidly losing its monopoly on learning and authoritative knowledge.

Also, with the rise of the Humanist spirit, especially in Italy, religion was becoming seen more and more as a matter of internal religious disposition of the individual, and less and less as a matter of the sacraments, teachings and traditions dispensed by the church.

Yet interestingly, many of the church leaders themselves chose to join in with the rising humanist spirit of the times. Certainly there were those clergy who objected. But by and large, the view of the church – notably of its popes, who during the 1400s could be very worldly fellows – was that this intellectual revolution was something to be pursued. Thus the church was a active sponsor in this matter.

Indeed, the worldliness of the church was becoming a well-recognized feature. The Roman hierarchy was viewed widely as being venal and corrupt – as secular politics rather than spirituality preoccupied the popes of the 1400s. The dreams and schemes of the Roman church became more grandiose, overstepping even the wealth of Italy, and beginning to drain the wealth of the church north of the Alps. And the personal conduct within the highest offices of the church, including the papacy itself, was at times scandalous.

Discontent against the Roman church thus began to spread in the North of Europe by the end of the 1400s. Led especially by a number of northern Humanists, many Europeans began to demand reform of the church, not only in its ethical behavior but also in its very lines and features as an institution. Reform-minded individuals were beginning to demand that the church should drop its medieval trappings and purify itself along the lines of the early church described in Scripture.

✳ ✳ ✳

RENAISSANCE PHILOSOPHY, LITERATURE AND THE ARTS

Philosophy and literature

In their "worldliness," Renaissance scholars and writers were an incredibly curious lot. We have already noted in the pre-Renaissance writers Dante, Boccaccio, and Chaucer a new spirit, one which would take full form in the following century, that of the full "Renaissance" or "rebirth" of the pre-Christian or classical mindset. Thus Renaissance philosophers/writers studied carefully all the classic works they could get their hands on. They already knew Latin; they now took on Greek and even Hebrew. They wanted to go back to the "sources" themselves of the intellectual foundations of their world. They took in the works of the early church fathers – more authoritative for them because they were closer to the original events of Christ. But they also became quite as familiar with the wide range of "pagan" works of Greece and Rome. The idea was that if it came out of that older age, it was truer, purer, certainly a vast improvement over the political corruption and violence of their own days. Their writings were thus deeply suggestive of what a better world should look like. And by taking up this challenge, some of them became literary scholars of the first order.

Lorenzo Valla (1407-1457). Valla studied the linguistic structure of the ancients – and was able to demonstrate that the "Donation of Constantine," by which the popes claimed vast temporal powers received from the Emperor Constantine (early 300s), was actually a much later document employing a much later Latin more characteristic of the Middle Ages – when it was probably written!

Thomas Malory (c. 1415-1471). Although little is known about this English writer himself, his *Le Morte d'Arthur* (*The Death of Arthur*, published in 1485) was – by bringing back to notice the chivalry of the legendary heroes Arthur, Lancelot, Merlin, Guinevere, and the Knights of the Round Table – possibly demonstrating, through the narrative, the dangerous results of moral failure, in an attempt to restore just such legendary chivalry to an English world shattered by the devastating War of the Roses ... going on since 1455.

Desiderius Erasmus (1466-1536). Erasmus was a Dutch Catholic priest more interested in promoting a rising Humanism than in defending his own church, which was coming under increasing criticism for its "unchristian" behavior. He and his close friend Thomas More both were alarmed at the moral corruption infecting the Church, and the kinds of moral pretensions of church officials (even the popes). Erasmus's views were cleverly presented in his work *The Praise of Folly* (1511) as humorous satire. He also tried to find middle ground between the Catholic Church and the early Protestant Reformers, pleasing neither side in the increasingly bitter debate.

In his later years he would offer a written rebuttal to Luther's strongly anti-Catholic writings, particularly over the matter of free will. Luther did not believe in such free will, because he saw the human heart as fully captive to original sin. Erasmus depicted God as leaving a large realm of moral choice to the personal will of any individual, making each person quite responsible for the good or bad in the outcome.

Niccolò Machiavelli (1469-1527). The rather cynical political writer of the Renaissance, Machiavelli,* was involved personally as an official for the Republic of Florence, working in the world of Italian diplomatic and military affairs during the 14 years that the Medici were out of power (1498-1512). In his classic work, *The Prince*, written most probably in 1513 (but not

---

*Actually he also wrote poetry and several plays that were quite popular in his time!

published until 1532, five years after he died), he merely described that political world quite bluntly – and analyzed its operations quite accurately. He was particularly direct in describing the acquiring and then wielding of power by any successful political leader ... based on what he knew personally about the deceitful and brutal – even murderous – behavior of the political leaders of the day.

Machiavelli would be condemned by later Humanists for his less-than-utopian views on human motivations and behavior. But he was merely an analyst, hoping that a certain amount of very tough political realism, which he had come to understand quite clearly, could be employed by a strong-handed Prince to bring about a united Italy. His ultimate purpose was to advise such a leader (or perhaps he was also simply informing the commoners of his Republic on such political methods, ones certainly already well-known by any would-be leader of the day) in how to hold off non-Italian European princes (notably the French and Spanish kings) ... who viewed the disunited Italian peninsula as a place where they might pick up more territory in their personal rise to power.

Baldassare Castiglione (1478-1529). Castiglione, as an experienced and amazingly honorable diplomat caught up in the world of Italian political intrigue, wrote *The Book of the Courtier* (1528), in an effort to bring that world of corrupt and greedy political diplomacy under some degree of moral restraint and operational civility. His work became very well-read in Italian court circles – wearied by all of the political intrigue disrupting Italian life – although in the end, it seemed to have had hardly any actual impact on the rough nature of Italian politics of the day.

Thomas More (1478-1535). More was a high-level English lawyer, writer and politician, serving as English King Henry VIII's Lord High Chancellor (1529-1532). As a loyal Catholic, he was deeply opposed to the Protestant Reformation, especially after the very bloody Peasants' Revolt – which he blamed Luther for. At the same time, he was strongly supportive of his own version of the rising humanism of the day. He went on to describe what a well-designed human society should look like in his famous 1516 fictional work *Utopia* (Greek, actually meaning "no place"), a Republic located on a mythical island – functioning by human design almost like some kind of perfect monastery!

But he got himself in trouble with the king when he opposed Henry's efforts to have the pope "annul" his 24-year marriage to Catherine of Aragon (the marriage had failed to bring Henry an all-important male heir) – in order to take on a new marriage with Anne Boleyn (not an uncommon event in those days), and then in Henry's taking the Church of England out from under papal authority when the pope refused to do so – placing the Church under Henry's own authority as its Supreme Head. More's refusal to take an oath recognizing Henry in that role ultimately brought about More's execution as a "traitor" in 1535.

François Rabelais (? – c. 1553). Rabelais started out as a Franciscan monk, who left the monastery to take up medical studies and then become a doctor. But he also had a strong interest in scholarly academics, and then ultimately simply writing for pleasure. And that sense of pleasure led him to write over the period c. 1532 to 1548 a *Gargantua and Pantagruel* series of four (possibly five) humorous books – which the church disapproved of highly, because they were not only rather vulgar in language but also rather insulting about the behavior of church officials – although they received royal endorsement from both kings Francis I and Henry II of France.   And they proved to be very popular with the French commoner.

Michel de Montaigne (1533-1592). Montaigne was a French politician who enjoyed accompanying his work with written commentaries on society and its ways, and life in general, those writings summed up most beautifully in his collective work *Essais* (1580). There was a frank realism about his work – touching on a huge number of issues in life – which subsequently shaped deeply not only French but also other Western authors, all the way up to the present.

William Shakespeare (1564-1616).   Shakespeare, about whom we know very little personally, was an absolutely outstanding English playwright who formed a bridge between the world of the Renaissance and the rising "modern" world. His portrayal of the human condition under all sorts of varying circumstances is absolutely unparalleled, for all times and circumstances. He was well-recognized in his own time, but would achieve even greater fame over time, as the brilliance of his works became more clearly understood by subsequent generations. He could be historical. He could be comical. He could be tragic. He always reached deep inside the human psyche, especially in the tragedies written in the latter part of his career. Consequently, he left a dramatic legacy behind him, one that no one else has come close to duplicating.

Italian Renaissance art

This Renaissance spirit of "earthy reality" was well reflected also in the development of the arts. Art reached beyond traditional religious themes to reflect this interest in the individual – and the passions of the living person.

Classic art would play a huge role in redefining the shape that Renaissance art took on. The field of architecture also was deeply and widely developed ... not only to build new churches, but also trade halls and private homes – these too influenced greatly by classical styling.

Filippo Brunelleschi (1377-1446) was a Florentine architect who designed and supervised the construction of the massive dome of Florence's Santa Maria del Fiore Cathedral ... as well as some of the decorative bronze sculpture adorning the cathedral. He was also called on to do the design and oversee the construction of several other churches and chapels in Italy. He also developed the concept of linear perspective – which gives depth to pictorial art.

Donatello Bardi (1386-1466) was a Florentine sculptor, encouraged by Brunelleschi and supported financially by Cosimo de' Medici, whose classical works – most notably his statue David (not to be confused with Michelangelo's David) – would influence other early Italian sculptors and artists, in the move away from medieval church styles to the classical (Greek and Roman) style, which was on its way to dominating the Renaissance world.

Leon Battista Alberti (1404-1472) was a very early full example of the "Renaissance Man." A quite athletic and high-ranking priest of a noble family, he developed outstanding skills in a wide variety of literary, philosophical, artistic, mathematical and scientific fields. He was particularly well-known in his time as both an outstanding mathematician and architect (designing the churches of San Sebastiano and Sant' Andrea in Mantua). But his fame today reaches most notably in his works of art.

Sandro Botticelli (c. 1445-1510) was an excellent Florentine artist of both religious subjects (his *Madonna and Child with John the Baptist* – c. 1475), and classical mythological subjects (such as his famous *Birth of Venus* and *Primavera* paintings – c. 1485). He also did several of the wall frescoes in the Vatican's Sistine Chapel.

Leonardo da Vinci (1452-1519). Without a doubt the greatest artistic genius of the Renaissance was Leonardo da Vinci, not only an outstanding Florentine artist and architect, but an equally talented scientist and engineer. He was exceptionally talented in so many fields that he represented the very highest form of the "Renaissance Man," an outstanding Humanist! Leonardo not only produced the famous *Mona Lisa* painting (1503-1506 and possibly continuing after that) and the equally famous *Last Supper* mural (1492-1498) – along with many other excellent works of art – his notebook and sketches include some of the most advanced ideas in math and engineering. These include items ranging from solar power, to optics, to geology, to fighting machines, and insightful portrayals of man's anatomy. So famous in his own time was Leonardo that French king Francis I had him brought to France, where Leonardo lived out his last days in company with the king.

Michelangelo Buonarroti (1475-1564). On a par with da Vinci, at least in the realm of art and architecture, was Michelangelo, a Florentine artist of exceptional abilities. In the realm of sculpture, he produced most notably his *Pietà* (1498-1499) and *David* (1504). In the realm of murals, he produced most notably the famous ceiling frescoes of the Vatican's Sistine Chapel, a task which occupied him fully in the period 1508-1512. In his later years, he was commissioned by Pope Paul III to be the chief architect for the St. Peter's Basilica in Rome (1546-1564), at that point still in its early stages of construction. It was Michelangelo who designed the most notable church dome of the Renaissance.

Raphael Sanzio da Urbino (1483-1520) was another Renaissance artist and architect of great note, even at the early age of eleven, taking up his father's court painting business in Urbino when his father died. His early works brought him such attention that in 1508 Pope Julius II had him come to Rome to undertake the production of murals for the pope's library, later known as the "Raphael Rooms"! Among those murals was his famous *School of Athens* (1509-1511) ... Raphael – strongly influenced in style by Michelangelo's work on the Sistine Chapel at that same time – actually using individuals of his day (Michelangelo and da Vinci, for instance) to represent these ancient figures! From this point on, Raphael would be kept busy (until his early death at age 37) by subsequent popes working on various projects in the reworking of the Vatican buildings.

These three artists – da Vinci, Michelangelo, and Raphael – would influence deeply the character of Italian art (and elsewhere) for the next several generations.

Some artists of the Northern Renaissance

Albrecht Dürer (1471-1528) was a German artist from Nuremberg – patronized by Emperor Maximilian I – who produced elegant church altarpieces and personal portraits. He brought traditional Gothic woodcuts into modern usage, introduced landscape art with his watercolors, and wrote treatises about mathematically precise perspective and ideal proportions to be employed in artwork.

Hans Holbein the Younger (1497-1543) was a Swiss-based German famous for his masterful portraits of European nobility – most notably the person and court of Henry VIII of England.

Pieter Bruegel (1525?-1569). But of another style was the Flemish (Dutch) artist Bruegel. He took humanism to a new level, painting scenes of local village life, in all kinds of seasons – involving all kinds of local activities. Well-known today are such works of his as *The Hunters in the Snow* (1565) and *The Peasant Wedding* (1567), all depicting simply local life.

RENAISSANCE POLITICS

This new spirit of Renaissance humanism also captured the hearts and souls of a number of princes or secular military rulers who developed quite large views of themselves, individuals who were coming alive to the possibility of undergirding and extending their personal political rule through very worldly means, including crude violence if necessary. These new rising leaders varied from feudal kings and even barons and dukes of Northern Europe, to the powerful Medici family (extremely rich banking family of Florence), to the professional soldiers or condottieri such the Sforza family ruling Milan ... who all sought greater independence from the restraints of the Church and the Holy Roman Empire in the pursuit of their more local ambitions.

European Christendom was clearly fracturing morally and politically, and these princes each wanted their own portions of that dividing Europe. And they were willing to do most anything to acquire those portions.

The Hundred Years' War resumes (1369-1453)

The Second Phase (1369-1389). In 1369 the Hundred Years' War would resume – and continue for another twenty years. French King Charles V broke the previous peace when Edward, the Black Prince" refused to answer to Charles about complaints coming from the people of Aquitaine concerning Edward's heavy taxes levied on them in response to the huge cost of Edward's involvement in a Spanish royalty conflict going on next door. Charles thus claimed full sovereignty over Aquitaine. This meant war.

This time things did not go so well for the Plantagenets, either on land or at sea. Bit by bit the English lost most of the holdings in France they had acquired during the First Phase of the war. Then in 1376 the Black Prince Edward died, followed the next year by the death of his father King Edward

III. Coming to the throne (under a regency council) was then the 10-year-old Richard II, the Black Prince's son.

Finally in 1389, Richard II – who had recently weathered the Peasant's Revolt in England in 1381 and was simply tired of all the political strife around him – was able to acquire a series of peace treaties with France that left him in control of Aquitaine … though his actual legal relationship with the French monarchy remained unresolved.

The beginning of Third Phase. In the early 1400s Henry V of England turned the Plantagenet-Valois conflict strongly in favor of the English Plantagenets. The Valois army was crushed at the Battle of Agincourt (October 1415) and soon Henry drew various French barons to his side. At this point he stood on a number of legitimate grounds ready to inherit the French throne. But Henry died (1422) before he was able to take the French throne, leaving the Plantagenets in the hands of his nine-month-old son … and a number of adult regents who attempted to keep the Plantagenet interest in France alive.

Nonetheless, at this point the Plantagenets or "English" were still the more victorious. And indeed it was only a 17-year-old girl that reversed the course of the ongoing war, and finally secured French rule for the Valois dynasty.

<h3 align="center">France</h3>

Joan of Arc (c. 1412-1431) and Charles VII (r. 1422-1461). Joan of Arc was a girl of only 13 when she first heard the voices that would call her to save France from disintegration. For four years she quietly listened to these voices – until they became most insistent that she act immediately. By the beginning of 1429 not only was France widely overrun by the English, but Charles, the Dauphin of France (heir to the French throne), was rapidly losing authority within even the small portion of France (a small area along the Loire River) that remained his.

Her reception by French authorities was about what she expected – total rejection. But she knew the voices were serious, so she persisted. With the help of some "signs" from the same voices, she was finally able to convince Charles of the legitimacy of her call. Finally, in April of 1429, given command of a French army, she quickly routed the English army besieging Orléans, chased the English out of the Loire valley and by July had delivered Reims from the English so that Charles could be crowned king (Charles VII) in this traditional coronation site.

But now events began to move against her. She continued to try to rout the English from France – even though Charles himself seemed to have little appetite for such doings. When, yielding to public pressure to liberate Paris, in September she moved against the English in Paris. She was wounded and the effort failed. Meanwhile Charles made a truce with his enemies (and England's ally) the Burgundians. But the next spring (1430) she took up arms again – only to be captured by the Burgundians in an effort to rally the French at Compiègne against an English-Burgundian assault on that town. She was sold by her captor to the English, after Charles showed no interest in purchasing her release (jealousy?).

She was then turned over to a French ecclesiastical court (with strong pro-English sentiments) in Rouen to be tried as a witch. After a lengthy trial she was found guilty of sorcery and heresy and sentenced to death. On May 30, 1431 (age 19) she was burned at the stake as a witch.*

Charles then went on to get the powerful Burgundians to reverse course and become allies of his (1435), develop a professional army of his own (not dependent on feudal support of unreliable barons) – equipped with cannons – and then defeated the English at the Battle of Castillon in 1453. From this point on, the English held no more territory in France except at the port of Calais just opposite England on the French coast.

The Hundred Years' War was finally over.

The ongoing Valois. The French kings who followed Charles, Louis XI (r. 1461-1483) and Charles VIII (r. 1483-1498), found themselves deeply involved in the rather typical feuds over dynastic inheritances, and wars over extended territorial claims – principally in Italy – wars which would absorb both French and Italian politics for a half-century. When Charles VIII had no male heir, the crown then passed to a junior branch of the Valois: the House of Orléans – the head of which was Louis XII, King of France (r. 1498-1515), (briefly) King of Naples, and Duke of Milan.   Then when Louis had no male heir of his own, the crown passed to his cousin (and son-in-law) Francis.

Francis I (r. 1515-1547). Francis, in his long reign, would exemplify the Renaissance Man in French office, a major patron of the arts and letters – even as he continued French involvement in the affairs of Italy. At the same time, he found himself facing a new challenge in the rising Habsburg family, led by Charles of Habsburg, who started out as Dutch Lord (to the North), then by inheritance becaming King of Spain (to the South), and finally by election Holy Roman Emperor (to the East). Finding himself thus surrounded by this rising Habsburg power, Francis attempted an alliance with English

---

*Almost immediately it was recognized that rather than being a witch she had been in fact a true agent of God. Over the centuries her popularity grew until in 1920 she was canonized as a saint by Pope Benedict XV.

King Henry VIII. But not getting anywhere in the effort, he instead formed an alliance with the rising Ottoman Turkish Empire in Southeastern Europe ... principally with its Muslim sultan, Suleiman (the Magnificent)! Quite a bold thing for a Christian sovereign to do!

But truly, he was a king as interested in Renaissance culture as he was in the dynastic squabbles of the Renaissance sovereigns. Thus he is still well known for his love of cultural refinements: art and architecture,* fancy social occasions, etc. ... but also a certain decadence that accompanied his fancy lifestyle. Nonetheless, Louis assembled a huge library of books (requiring a copy of every book published in France!) and historical manuscripts (which he apparently took the time to actually read), then brought in scholars to study and discuss these works.

In the realm of architecture, he built (by da Vinci's own design) the fabulous Château de Chambord. He also rebuilt the Louvre Palace in Paris and the Château de Fontainebleau – converting them from medieval structures to Renaissance beauties.

He also founded the port city of Le Havre – sending out ships to America and the Far East, in competition with the Spanish and Portuguese, despite the monopoly that the papacy had established for these two powers through various papal bulls. Thus in 1524, under Francis's sponsorship, Giovanni da Verrazzano reached today's New York City, then headed north, to claim Newfoundland for Francis. In 1534 Francis sent Jacques Cartier to explore Quebec, then in 1541 Jean-François Roberval – to begin the French settlement of Canada, and the region's conversion to Catholicism.

However, the realm of European politics proved highly problematic for Francis. In 1525 he and his army suffered a massive defeat in Italy at the hands of Charles of Habsburg's Spanish troops. Francis was then taken to Madrid as a prisoner and released only the following year after he agreed to humiliating terms (including his abdication, the surrender of all French holdings in Italy, and the delivery of his two oldest sons as hostages to Charles's court) ... which, once free, he largely refused to honor. However only after paying two million gold crowns to Charles did he get his sons back (four years later). Then his war with Charles was resumed in 1536 – in alliance with the Turks – and continued all the way to Francis's death in 1547.

England

The War of the Roses (1455-1487). The humiliating English loss in

---

*Francis was a great importer of Italian Renaissance art ... including even the person of da Vinci, who served Francis during the first three years of the king's reign (1516-1519) ... which was also the last three years of the aging artist's life.

the Hundred Year' War resulted in a split within the Plantagenet dynasty between two factions: the House of Lancaster – identified by its *red* rose on in heraldic shield – and the House of York – thus identified by its *white* rose, a horrible dispute which came to be known as the "War of the Roses."

But the dynastic rivalry was anything but an internal English civil war, with the Lancastrians supported by the kingdoms of Scotland and France, and the Yorkers supported by the Burgundians – with the duchy of Brittany switching sides.

Henry VII (r. 1485-1509). In the end, the only thing that the 32-year war achieved was the destruction of the Plantagenet family – both sides – thus opening the door for the House of Tudor, led by Henry Tudor, which in a victory at the Battle of Bosworth Field (1485), gained the crown for him and his Tudor family. As actually a "Lancastrian," Henry married Elizabeth of York the following year, bringing the royal families together ... and moving England forward in a fresh period of peace – and thus prosperity – which Henry used (often corruptly) to work to his personal advantage.

Once king, he proved to be a cautious but very focused ruler in the matters of the royal finances, putting them, through careful tax measures, back on a firm footing. He rebuilt English power in his support of the independence of Brittany against an expansionist France. He also helped build English industry and trade in the way he challenged and then allied with competitors in that field, the Flemish and their cousins the Dutch.

Henry VIII (r. 1509-1547). Henry's son (also a Henry) had the ongoing task of trying to keep the English barons under royal control ... and coming up with a male heir to receive the Tudor legacy. He had married the aunt of Spain's King (and also Holy Roman Emperor) Charles ... a strategic move for the Tudors. But Catherine of Aragon had succeeded in delivering only a girl, Mary, in their 24 years of marriage.

Like his father, Henry was not a man of chivalrous scruples ... something more like Machiavelli's Prince – which was becoming more the norm in political high places. He needed a son and would do whatever was necessary to secure one. He finally divorced Catherine ... not only straining the relationship between Henry and Charles but also between Henry and the Pope – who refused to annul Henry's marriage to Catherine.

Thus Henry broke from Rome and declared himself (instead of the Pope) the head of the Church in England. Then to augment his treasury he not only ended all payments to Rome, he proceeded to seize the treasuries of wealthy English monasteries, selling their lands to various English supporters (including members of the rising merchant class) seeking entry into – or advancement within – the ranks of the aristocracy. Not only did this make the Tudor monarchy rich and powerful, those who received such lands (including Henry himself) were a guarantee that the Roman Church would be hotly resisted in England in any attempt to retake its lost position there. While all of this did not put England into the Protestant camp (Henry was highly opposed to Luther's reforms, though later he took some steps in the Protestant direction) it certainly helped open the way for Protestantism to find a foothold there.

In any case, further marriages (six in total!) proved no more successful in delivering Henry a strong male child to continue the Tudor line. His sickly son Edward* died at age sixteen after only six years of official – though hardly effective – rule.

Henry could be ruthless to those who fell out of favor, Cardinal Thomas Wolsey, his Lord Chancellor (Prime Minister) dying on his way to London to be tried (and most certainly executed) for "treason" after failing to secure the annulment with Catherine. Likewise, his replacement, Thomas Cromwell was executed for treason soon after arranging a brief and "unconsummated" marriage with an unattractive German princess.   At least his Archbishop of Canterbury, Thomas Cranmer, would die of such charges not by Henry, but by his daughter Mary. Politics in England was a very dangerous game.

But politics abroad was just as dangerous, as Henry found himself constantly involved in wars and shifting alliances with Francis of France, Holy Roman Emperor and Spanish King Charles, or with the Scottish King James. In the end, all that this activity accomplished was merely the emptying of Henry's royal treasury.

Castile

At the heart of what would become the future "Spain" was the ever-expanding kingdom of Castile. From its starting point in north-central Spain it included (by inheritance of Ferdinand III in 1230) the equally large neighboring kingdom of Leon, making it by far the largest political entity in Spain. Thereafter, and up until 1479, only the Christian kingdoms of Portugal (to the West) and Aragon (to the East) and a fast-declining Muslim Grenada) (to the South) remained outside the huge Castile domain.

As was typical of the times, Castile, and its ruling House of Trastámara, found itself constantly absorbed in dynastic infighting over rights to the throne, as well as over baronial positions outside the royal family itself.

Henry IV of Castile (1454-1474). Henry was something of a combination of both the Castile and Aragon legacies, his father John II of Castile and his

---

*Edward was born of Henry's third marriage – with Jane Seymour... who died soon after giving birth to Edward in 1537.

mother Maria of Aragon, although such a marriage did not yet unite those two kingdoms into one. Besides, personally he was a very weak ruler, letting his barons, notably the Duke of Trujillo, direct his political affairs. Family feuds also shook his rule when he had his childless marriage with Blanche of Navarre annulled and married his first cousin Joan of Portugal (their mothers were sisters). But Joan had an affair with a bishop, and this second marriage produced only a female heir – herself of dubious origins.

Thus it was that Henry formally recognized his half-sister Isabella, as heir to the throne of Castile.

Aragon

We commonly identify Aragon as a huge region in Western Spain, regained by Christian forces from the Muslims as they were pushed back southward in the Spanish Reconquista. But actually, Aragon was early-on the seat of a much larger empire reaching across the Mediterranean all the way to Greece. It was also, in typical feudal fashion, constantly involved in a contest with other Spanish families for dominion in Spain, and with the French for control of Southern France – and ultimately also Southern Italy. This Mediterranean dynasty and its empire reached the heights of its power in the 1200s and just prior to the end of the 1300s, when it lost its territory in Greece. But in 1442, it was able to take the huge kingdom of Naples in Southern Italy from French Angevin control and bring it into Aragon's Mediterranean empire.

Alfonso V of Aragon (r. 1416-1458). Bringing the Southern Italian Kingdom of Naples into Alfonso's Aragon Empire was a very complicated diplomatic, as well as military matter (employing some of the latest military technology), as feudal lords, Italian urban republics and ultimately the papacy became directly involved in the process. But ultimate success in the matter made Alfonso one of the leading political figures of his day. He too proved to be a patron of the arts (he himself being an avid reader of classical literature), and once his reign was secure did much to better the economic foundations of his empire.

But his marriage with his cousin Maria (their fathers were brothers) proved childless, and thus his brother John (who had been governing the Spanish holdings anyway) received title to his Spanish realm, and his illegitimate son Ferdinand title to his Kingdom of Naples.

Ferdinand I of Naples (r. 1458-1494). Ferdinand would go on to be a dominating figure in Italian – and European – politics, involving not only the French, the papacy, the powerful Venetian Empire, and other Italian city-states but also the rising power in the Eastern Mediterranean of the Ottoman Turks.

And he would turn his kingdom away from its political dependence on feudal barons, and instead on the rule of law defended by a growing royal estate – something that would become the trend of the times as Europe moved away gradually from feudalism into royal absolutism.

But, like his father, he was also a major patron of the arts, something considered extremely important in the thinking of Renaissance Europe.

John II of Aragon (r. 1458-1479). Alfonso's brother John would come to hold several titles: King of Aragon, King of Navarre, and King of Sicily. But in his case too, family conflicts over titles and jurisdictions would trouble his rule, resulting even in civil war (the Navarrese Civil War and the Catalan revolt), as well as an ongoing fight with the French monarchy.

Overall, his greatest success as king was in having his son Ferdinand betrothed to the heir to the Castilian throne, Isabella, at a very early age ... although this would be deeply challenged by other fortune-seeking families.

Finally: Spain!

Ferdinand II of Aragon (1479-1516) and Isabella I of Castile (r. 1474-1504). At the end of the 1400s things came together for Spain in a dazzling way. With the marriage of second-cousins Ferdinand and Isabella, popularly termed "The Catholic Monarchs"* – thus producing the union of Castile and Aragon – Spain's rise in importance began in earnest.

Ferdinand inherited all the Aragon titles (Aragon, Sardinia, Sicily, Naples and Navarre) and, by way of marriage, King of Castile and Leon. He would of course have to fight to make good his claim to Naples and Navarre. Catalonia would also challenge his claim. And there would be battles within the family for this or that claim as well. But he proved to be a tough warrior.

Isabella, after many efforts were made to marry her off to this or that individual and, after securing (questionably) a papal bull allowing these cousins to marry, she and Ferdinand snuck away to get married in 1469. Then upon receiving the throne at her half-brother Henry's death in 1474, she had to face all sorts of challenges to her right to the throne, including even a war with the Portuguese – which dragged on for years, on the land and on the sea. And the Portuguese seemed to be able to hold onto the claim that the Atlantic belonged solely to the Portuguese to exploit.

----

*Pope Alexander VI (himself a Spaniard) gave recognition to these two monarchs as vital "defenders of the faith" by giving them the title, the Most Catholic Monarchs. It was a title that they and their descendants were particularly proud of.

But the Genoese naval explorer Columbus was able to secure support from Isabella for a venture he claimed would give Spain access to the Far East, by heading West across the Atlantic. His subsequent discovery of America in 1492 would then give Spain a countering claim to Portugal's Atlantic monopoly, leading to an agreement, the Treaty of Tordesillas (1494), between the two powers as to which part of the Atlantic venture belonged to which of the two powers – and had it endorsed in 1505 by Pope Julius II. In this treaty it was agreed that all land to the east of a line of longitude – thus constituting something of an eastern hemisphere – would be Portugal's to exploit. All lands in the western hemisphere would be Spain's to exploit.[*]

The year 1492 was also a very big year for the Spanish in another way: it marked the military defeat of the Muslim Kingdom of Grenada, and the completion of Spanish expansion across the Iberian Peninsula (Portugal, of course excepted). But it also marked the announcement (the Alhambra Decree) that the Muslims (Moros) – along with the Jewish population in Spain – would subsequently be expelled from Spain, unless they agreed to convert to Christianity.

IIndeed, previously, in 1478, Ferdinand and Isabella had established the Spanish Inquisition, to hunt down those who could not be considered "authentic" Christians within the Spanish realm. And after the decision to force the conversion of Jews and Muslims, the Inquisition found itself focusing in particular on those who had converted from Judaism or Islam to Christianity – and whose "conversion" therefore was highly suspect.[†]

"Mad" Joanna of Castile and Philip "The Handsome" of Habsburg. Ferdinand and Isabella's sole surviving heir unexpectedly ended up being their daughter Joanna – who had married Philip of Habsburg. She was reputed to be insane, supposedly driven mad by the death of so many family members around her – and because of her husband's constant infidelities. She was thus institutionalized – placed in isolation at a convent ... and held there until she finally died at age 75.

Charles of Habsburg (1500-1558). This allowed her sixteen-year-old son Charles – who actually had grown up in his father's Habsburg land of Dutch-speaking Flanders – to take the throne directly as Charles I, King of Spain ... and three years later the vast Habsburg holdings in the Netherlands, Burgundy and Germany as Charles V, Holy Roman Emperor –

---

[*]The line, running approximately 46 degrees west by today's measure, basically assigned all of the Americas to Spain, except for the coastline extending east into the Atlantic – which comprises most of today's Brazilian coastline.

[†]The Spanish Inquisition would continue its work all the way up until it was finally abolished in 1834.

and Archduke of Austria. Charles also received title to the Spanish lands in Southern Italy ... and the popes also named him King in Germany (Pope Leo X) and King in Italy (Pope Clement VII). This undoubtedly made him the most powerful monarch in Europe.

Added to this was the constant flow of gold from his vast Spanish holdings in America, making Charles also (at least potentially) the wealthiest man in Europe. But his wars were very, very costly.

Charles also was a major player in the Catholic Counter-Reformation against the Protestants, in particular in his effort to silence the German "nuisance" Luther. As imperial "Defender of the Faith," he supported strongly the three popes who presided over the Council of Trent (1545-1563), called to tighten the definitions of Catholic theology and practice. He supported also the creation of the Jesuits, a special order of soldier-priest-monks called to teach and enforce papal doctrine ... and in the process to retake from the Protestants as much territory of Old Christendom as possible in order to place it back under papal control.

All of this kept him busy traveling from state to state within the Holy Roman Empire and his Spanish territories (he never established a capital city of his own). He assisted Venice in its defense against the Turks, but was not able to hold off the Turks in their assault on Budapest in Hungary.

And as far as the Spanish holdings in America went, he managed land assignments there along traditional feudal lines, but also sent priests to his American colonies – to bring the "Indians" or natives living there into the Catholic Church, and to protect them as "his subjects" against massive exploitation by the local Spanish lords. Thus to the mix of a rising Spanish feudal system in America, in which Spanish noblemen ruled the surrounding land and its inhabitants from their feudal manors or "haciendas," Charles added the political oversight of his colonies through the church's hierarchy of priests and bishops. These were called on to help keep the American social order under the control of the political authority back in Spain.

At the same time, he moved Spain into the position as major commercial competitor with the Portuguese in the African slave trade with the Caribbean Islands. Slaves were not of the same political-legal order as the peasants (Hispanic or Indian), and thus did not receive the same royal protection.

Then, most oddly, in 1556 Charles simply stepped down from his positions, turning the rule of Spain over to his son Philip and the Holy Roman Empire over to his brother Ferdinand. Now the Habsburgs had two parallel dynasties – generally fairly cooperative with each other. Then Charles retired to a monastery, and died the following year (1558).

Italy

At the time of the Renaissance, Italy was not a nation, but instead a territory with varying political systems, under constant dispute for control among various dynasties, French, Spanish, German as well as Italian. Southern Italy, with its political center at Naples, was under what had to be considered "Spanish" or Aragonese dynastic rule, challenged by French political interests. Northern Italy, with Milan as the leading city, was under local rule, except when the French were attempting to bring the region under French rule. Then there was the huge territory in Central and Eastern Italy identified as the "Papal States" and under direct papal rule, the papacy changing hands constantly as various families vied for this very important position. Then there were the "republics" or city states of Northwestern Italy, Florence, Siena, Pisa, Mantua, Ferrara, Verona (and, at times, Milan) belonging to this category. Then, as we have seen, there were the huge maritime domains of Genoa and Venice located at the upper edges, East and West, of the Italian peninsula.

Thus it is very hard to "summarize" Italian politics during this period, except to say that dynastic conflicts and the ongoing battle between the Guelf and Ghibelline coalitions were constant and quite violent.

Siena. It was Siena, not Florence, that first took the lead in the development of the very progressive and enormously prosperous region of Tuscany (the name derived from the ancient Etruscans based there). The town of Siena was the location of a university dating back to 1240, the city prospered enormously from the salt mining and wool trade, and from the banking business supporting this wealth in trade. And it was governed by its own Republic (founded in 1125), until 1555, when it lost a major war against Spain – and its long-standing Tuscan rival, Florence.

The Medici of Florence.   But it was the Medici family of Florence that would come to dominance – not only in Tuscany, but throughout much of Italy, and eventually even Europe itself.

The family started its rise to prominence in Florence's wool guild as textile merchants, eventually branching into the banking business as well. And it would be the latter occupation, as bankers, that would bring the Medici family to enormous wealth, and power.

Giovanni di Bicci de' Medici (1360-1429). The rise of the Medici to power began under Giovanni, who founded the family bank in 1397, in competition with the Albizzi family of Florence – who had previously taken command of the Tuscan banking realm when the Bonsignori family of Siena went bankrupt a century earlier in 1298. Giovanni was able to extend the Medici banking position by placing banking branches in Venice, Geneva – and most importantly, in Rome (and briefly in Naples) – managing the Church's finances. This of course would bring the Medici into fierce competition with other banking families for the position as financial foundation of the Church.

Cosimo di Giovanni de' Medici (1389-1464). The battle between the Medici and Albizzi was especially a bitter one, the Albizzi – in alliance with another powerful Florentine family, the Strozzi – succeeding in having Giovanni's son, Cosimo, exiled by Florence's Signoria (city council) in 1433. But when Cosimo relocated to Venice, most of Florence's banking dynamics went with him, forcing Florence a year later to lift the exile order and return Cosimo to Florence. From then on Florentine politics found itself under the firm direction of Cosimo, and much of the fast-rising art-world under his enormous financial patronage.

Cosimo was also to send a *condottiero* (a commander of an army-for-hire), Francesco Sforza, to Milan to secure matters after the death of the head of the Visconti family governing that city. Francesco had married the Visconti daughter Bianca years earlier, Bianca being also the sole heir to the Visconti family. They would henceforth rule Milan together. And thus Milan and Florence would also form an important political bond.

Lorenzo di Piero de' Medici (1449-1492). The Medici dynamic would reach its height under Cosimo's grandson, Lorenzo, also known as "Lorenzo the Magnificent." Lorenzo was a huge patron of the arts – supporting Verrocchio, da Vinci, Botticelli, Michelangelo and many others.

Lorenzo's diplomacy also played a huge role in bringing peace to Italy, most notably through the Treaty of Lodi (1454), ending the war between Milan and Venice. On the basis of this treaty the Italic League was founded. The Kingdom of Naples and the Papal states soon joined the League – as did many other Italian city-states. This therefore brought to Italy a relatively long period of peace, one absolutely vital to the development of Renaissance Italy!

Of course his political and financial success made Lorenzo many very jealous enemies, and an attempt was made on his life in 1478 (the Pazzi conspiracy), which wounded him and killed his brother Giullano. Lorenzo survived, but now found himself in bitter conflict with Pope Sixtus IV, who had authorized the assassination attempt (Rovere family versus Medici family?). When the Medici fought back, Sixtus seized what Medici financial assets he could grab, put Florence under an interdict (the Florentines had rallied to Lorenzo's support), allied with the duke of Naples, and had an army sent to conquer Florence. The war dragged on, until Lorenzo went to Naples and put himself at the mercy of the king (Ferdinand I) and negotiated a peace finally.

Then things settled back down, so that Italy could continue forward in peace. And this it did so, until shortly after Lorenzo's death in 1492.

The Papacy

As already suggested, the Church chose to join the political action which was disrupting Europe at the time. Certainly there were those who objected to the Church taking up such a worldly manner. But by and large, the view of the Church – notably of its popes, who during the 1400s could be very worldly fellows – was that intellectual revolution and political intrigue were things to be pursued. Indeed, the papacy was as much an object of dynastic competition as the kingdoms and republics were proving to be. Families such as the Roveres, the Borgias, the Medici, constantly vied for the all-important papal appointment by the College of Cardinals. Thus the church was as active a player in the Renaissance political game as were the European kingdoms, duchies and republics.

Sixtus IV (pope 1471-1484). For instance, Pope Sixtus IV (Francesco della Rovere) was both a grand patron of the arts and letters, constructing the Vatican's Sistine Chapel and developing the Vatican Archives, as well as bringing various artists to Rome to develop Rome's own artistic age. But, as we have seen, he was an organizer of the Pazzi conspiracy, designed to destroy the Medici family.   He also annulled the decrees of the Council of Constance, which had tried to bring the Church under the control of an ecumenical council rather than under the singular rule of the pope. And he authorized the Spanish Inquisition in 1478, in an effort to eliminate those of the Jewish community who had chosen to convert to Christianity rather than face expulsion, and whose true Christian loyalties were thus highly suspect. In all likelihood, this round of the Inquisition was in part an effort of the Spanish to demonstrate clearly that their former tolerance of Muslims and Jews (which had earned the Spanish Christians the reputation in the rest of Christendom as being less than "pure" Christians) had come to an end.

Innocent VIII (pope 1484-1492). Sixtus was followed by Innocent VIII (Giovanni Battista Cybo). As the son of the viceroy of Naples (the next most important person behind King Ferdinand I), Cybo worked his way up the clerical ranks until, with Rovere's help – and despite King Ferdinand of Naples' opposition (Ferdinand wanted Rodrigo Borgia as pope) – he became pope.

Alexander VI (pope 1492-1503). Then the Borgia family found itself back in power when Rodrigo Borgia was elected to the papacy as Alexander VI. Part of the prominent Borgia family of Aragon, Rodrigo became a cardinal after his uncle was elected as Pope Callixtus III (1455-1458), and he served the next four popes in various offices – until his election as pope in 1492. Alexander was a strong supporter of the Church and its political powers, but also a strong supporter of the Borgia family and its powers as well. And personally, he let no lust stand in his way!

His illegitimate son, Cesare, became a prominent *condottiero*, after having served briefly as a Catholic cardinal upon his father's election as pope. But he resigned to serve French King Louis XII in the latter's military ventures in both Northern and Southern Italy, aided immensely in taking on his own political realm in the process through his father's influence. But after his father Rodrigo's death in 1503 – and the election of a political rival Giuliano Della Rovere as Pope Julius II (nephew of Pope Sixtus IV) – Cesare's fortunes would change, despite his very strong military talents. Cesare would eventually become the model for Machiavelli's *Prince*, a strong, ruthless leader – who Machiavelli hoped would unite Italy. Eventually, Cesare was betrayed and murdered (1507) in one of the political games shaking Italy at the time.

Cesare's sister Lucrezia was considered quite the beauty, married three times, had affairs with others, and was mother of ten children, and was also very much a part of the program of political intrigue in the Borgia family's quest for power and status.

And so things went in Renaissance Italy!

Julius II (1503-1513). Not only did Pope Julius challenge rather successfully the Borgia family but, through much clever political intrigue, he was able to extend considerably the power of the papacy ... in a supposed effort to bring some degree of peace and stability to Italy. He brought Swiss Guards to serve as his military arm, conducted treaties of military alliance with various European princes, hired the artist Michelangelo to do the famous paintings in the Sistine Chapel, and ordered the selling of indulgences (payments to the Church designed to speed the sinner through Purgatory, and onward to Heaven after death) in order to finance the building of the massive Saint Peter's Basilica. Again, his role as pope was very much more a matter of personal politics than moral or spiritual leadership.

Leo X (1513-1521). Giovanni di Lorenzo de' Medici, in becoming Pope Leo X, finally brought the Medici family to full center-stage in terms of church politics. He was a massive spender of church funds – using such funds extensively to bring his nephew to power in Urbino as its duke – and having to sell "indulgences"* to the faithful in order to cover the massive costs involved in continuing building of the new St. Peter's Basilica.

He would also be the pope who would answer Luther's call (his 95 Theses) for church reform, with the papal bull of 1520 condemning Luther and his challenge, helping to break the ranks of Christian Europe into two fiercely opposing theological parties of Catholics and Protestants.

The Italian Wars (1494-1559)

In 1494, Charles VIII of France saw an opportunity, and invaded Italy on the basis of a dynastic claim to Milan. This would set off a series of "Italian Wars," involving claims and counter-claims to Italian territory of the French Valois and the Spanish and Austrian Habsburgs – in alliance with one or another of the Italian city-states, and with the popes deeply involved in the process. The whole thing turned very ugly, and very lasting in that ugliness.

The Turks on the rise in the East

Mehmed I (r. 1413-1420).   The Ottomans' humiliating defeat by Tamerlane's forces was followed by a decade of civil war (the "Interregnum"), as Bayezid's sons battled among themselves for the position of Ottoman Sultan. Finally in 1413, one of the sons, Mehmed I, emerged victorious and was able to reunite the Ottoman Sultanate. Three of the brothers were killed, though another brother Mustafa and nephew continued to challenge him during his reign.

Under Mehmed's direction, Albania in the West and the Armenian Kingdom of Cilicia in the East were added to the Ottoman holdings.

Murad II (r. 1444-1446 and 1451-1481). To secure his own power, Murad had to defeat his uncle Mustafa, released from captivity by the Byzantine Emperor Manuel II in order to block Murad. In defeating Mustafa, Murad received significant help from the Genoese navy! An angry Murad then turned on Constantinople, and backed off only when paid a huge tribute by the Byzantines. At the same time, he took on and crushed numerous beyliks in Anatolia that had been set up by Tamerlane.

The Byzantine Emperor then turned over to Venice some Byzantine lands, in the effort to get Venice (a former Ottoman ally) to block further

---

*An indulgence was a way of paying for one's sins, usually an act of confession, prayer or good works. But by the time of Leo, they were monetary contributions made by the people to the papacy specifically for the work on St. Peter's Basilica, contributions that would – according to the Pope's Grand Commissioner (chief indulgence salesman), Johann Tetzel – help speed their soul through purgatory on the road to heaven.

Ottoman expansion. In response Murad looked to some of his Christian allies in the Balkans to help him in what had become a Balkan War, which eventually simply came to a halt (1444). Murad then retired, and turned his government over to his young son, Mehmed.

Sensing an opportunity in this, Pope Eugenius IV soon called for another crusade, designed to drive the Turkish "infidel" out of Europe. This in turn brought Murad back out of retirement, to direct Ottoman operations alongside his son Mehmed. Meanwhile, Venice and Serbia had seemed unable to decide on which side to support, weakening greatly the "Christian" effort.

Also, having trouble with Turkish noblemen within his own domain, Murad built to greater importance the *devşirme* – the system by which Christian subjects were forced to turn over (often as many as 20 percent) of their male children, to serve as what would become highly privileged Janissaries within the Ottoman ranks. With full reliance on Janissary military support, Murad was able to bring his Turkish noblemen under full control, and have at arms a military force of enormous strength.

In 1448 Murad's troops defeated the Albanians at the second battle of Kosovo, bringing the Balkan powers (Thrace, Macedonia, Bulgaria, Greece, Serbia and now Albania) under Ottoman mastery. Only the city of Constantinople, the last position held by the dying Byzantine Empire, still found itself unconquered by the Ottomans. But that was about to change.

Mehmed II "the Conqueror" (1451-1481). Soon after his father died (1451) Mehmed prepared to take on Constantinople, building Rumeli Fortress near Constantinople to oversee operations. When he was ready, in only a matter of weeks (April-May 1453), Constantinople was finally conquered.

Mehmed proved to be a very wise ruler. He chose to be merciful to the inhabitants, because, recognizing both its strategic and symbolic importance, Mehmed intended to make Constantinople his new multi-ethnic (Muslim, Christian, Jewish) Ottoman capital. He also set up the *millet* system allowing each religious group making up his empire to continue to live according to their respective religious laws, customs, languages under their own respective leaders, operating however in full support of the presiding authority of the Ottoman Sultan. The generosity of these terms in fact guaranteed that support (even from Christians). But it caused grumbling among the old Turkish nobility, leading Mehmed to move even more decidedly in the effort to replace traditional feudal support of the unreliable Turkish noblemen with the devşirme as the basis of his rule.

Selim I (r. 1512-1520). Over the run of the next series of sultans, Turkish expansion slowed up, the Sultans having constantly to deal with rebellious Turkish noblemen (and family members) within the Ottoman Empire. Finally, under Selim I, the Ottoman empire was able to get back in the business of Ottoman expansion, extending Ottoman rule into Egypt and northern Iraq ... and making the Turkish navy a major force in the Eastern Mediterranean.

Suleiman the Magnificent (r. 1520-1566). Suleiman was a contemporary of Charles of Habsburg and French King Francis ... and adversary – or ally – of the two in the rough and tumble European diplomacy of those times.

Suleiman's troops expanded Ottoman power north against the Serbs and Hungarians, and reached as far north as Vienna, the seat of Charles's eastern empire. This assault against Charles's position in East Europe rather naturally made Suleiman a military ally of Francis. They joined forces in Hungary in support of the Turks, and along the Mediterranean coast in the area between Southeastern France and Northeastern Italy in support of France.

And although Suleiman ultimately failed to capture Vienna, his two assaults there gave Luther and the Schmalkaldic League the opportunity to build up their forces in Germany, ready to face the full wrath of Charles, the "Defender of the Faith." And Francis, though anti-Protestant, even allied with the German Schmalkaldic League against Charles. So things went in those days.

✳ ✳ ✳

RENAISSANCE EXPLORATION

This was also the "Age of Exploration" – a term we use in reference to the beginning of the exploration of the seas and continents around Europe by a wide variety of Italian, Portuguese, and Spanish explorers – professional adventurers really.

Some of the Major Figures in the Process

Prince Henry of Portugal. In 1419 Prince Henry of Portugal established at Sagres a school with a library and observatory to study the earth in support of his love of overseas exploration. He gathered at Sagres scholars from all around Europe to improve his maps – and general knowledge of the earth's geography (such as was available to early 15th century Europe). At the same time, Henry was sending out numbers of sailors to explore the African coast in search of a southern route around Africa to the East.

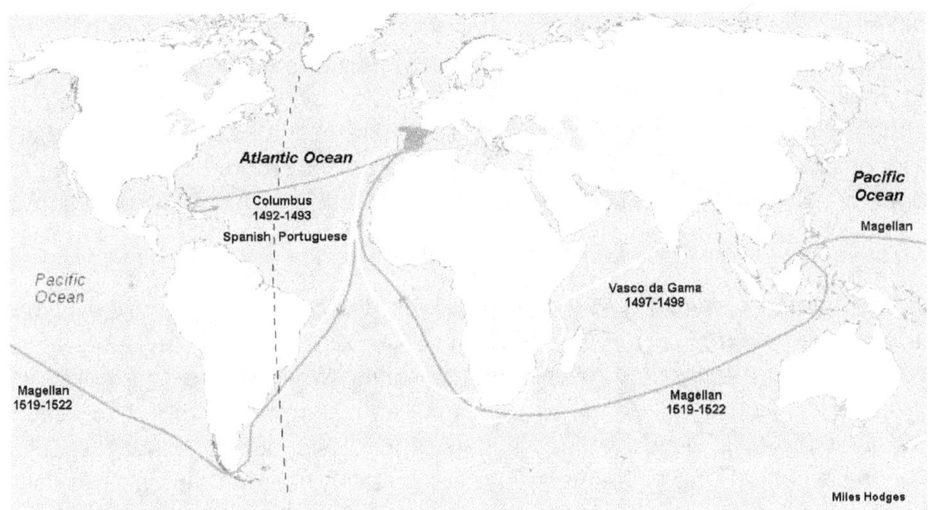

Bartolomeu Dias (c. 1450-1500). Dias was a Portuguese explorer who in 1488 was the first to sail around the southern tip of Africa at the Cape of Good Hope and point the way east to the Indies via the Indian Ocean.

He was later lost at sea off the Cape of Good Hope in 1500 during a new naval and commercial mission to India headed by Pedro Alvares Cabral.

Christopher Columbus (1451-1506). Columbus made four journeys to America. The first trip (1492-1493) he returned after creating a settlement, La Navidad, on the huge island he called Española. After leaving half his crew there, he was able (through storm and political problems with the Portuguese) to return to present the King and Queen with a chest of gold items and some Indian "interpreters."

The second trip (1493-1496) was undertaken with a huge fleet (17 ships and 1200 men), but failed to find any gold, struggled with some of the Indians, and faced a huge rebellion of his men. He left his brothers in charge and returned to Spain, with no gold.

The third trip (1498-1500) was undertaken mostly to block an effort by John of Portugal to match the Spanish effort. But Columbus found only chaos upon his arrival at Española. News of the chaos reached back to Spain, and Francisco de Bobadilla was sent to Española to clear up the mess. He and Columbus fought, and Bobadilla sent Columbus back to Spain in chains.

Columbus, after much pleading, was then authorized to undertake a small, fourth trip (1502-1504). But he was refused entry at Española when he arrived there. So he moved, via Cuba and Jamaica, on to the mainland (Honduras, Nicaragua and Panama). In Panama he discovered his gold, but also naval disaster and personal sickness. He managed to get back to Jamaica, but waited for a year for support allowing him to make his return to Spain. He was not received officially on his return (the Queen was dying) and only belatedly managed to receive his share of the gold profits. He died a very sick man at age 54 (1506), largely forgotten, though his two books, *Book of Privileges* (1502) and *Book of Prophecies* (1505) would leave some kind of legacy.

John Cabot (c. 1450-1498). Cabot was an Italian explorer who came into service to English King Henry VII. Like Columbus, he had long been convinced that Asia could be reached by sailing West. News of Columbus' discovery encouraged Henry to take up Cabot's proposal to try to reach the East by sailing West. Thus in 1497 Cabot set out to reach the East for the English king. He instead encountered North America (possibly Newfoundland or Labrador), though on his return to England he affirmed that it was northeastern Asia he had encountered. In any case he brought news of the wealth of fish and good land for settlement in the land he had encountered.

The following year, this time with five ships and 200 men, Cabot set out again on the same journey West. But the details of what then occurred are hazy. In any case his expedition failed to return to England. As a consequence, little of lasting value resulted from his efforts.

Vasco da Gama (1469-1524). Da Gama was a Portuguese explorer who first reached India in 1498 by sailing around the southern tip of Africa at the Cape of Good Hope, continuing up the eastern shores of Africa, and crossing the Indian ocean from (modern-day) Kenya to Calicut in India.

He sailed for India a second time in 1502 at the head of a fleet of 20 ships that was charged with punishing the Zamorin (Muslim ruler) of Calicut for having massacred the Portuguese left behind in India by Cabral. Treaties were concluded with neighboring Hindu enemies of the Zamorin and an effort of an Arab fleet to drive away da Gama was defeated. In early 1503 da Gama returned with his fleet to Portugal.

In 1524 he was sent by King John III to be the Portuguese viceroy in India. He established an administrative center at Goa and immediately began the process of strengthening the Portuguese commercial position in India. But he became sick and died before the year was out.

Pedro Álvares Cabral (1467-1520). Cabral was a Portuguese explorer commissioned by Manuel I to follow up on da Gama's exploration of India in 1498 and consolidate the Portuguese position in India.

In March of 1500 Cabral left for India with 13 ships, but headed westward into the Atlantic to sail around the becalmed waters of Guinea – and discovered the shores of Brazil in the process. He then headed east for the Cape of Good Hope (where he lost 4 of his ships and the fellow explorer Bartolomeu Dias).

In September he arrived at Calicut and signed a commercial treaty with the Zamorin, permitting him to establish a fortified trading post at Calicut. But disputes arose with the Muslim merchants and in December the trading post was attacked and most of the inhabitants massacred before Cabral could get a rescue party ashore from the boats offshore. Cabral took revenge by bombarding the city and capturing 10 Muslim ships – before sailing on to Cochin where he received a friendlier reception. Here he traded for precious spices.

In early 1501 he set sail for Portugal – but disasters along the way permitted him to complete the voyage with only four of the ships he had originally started the expedition with.

Despite his warm reception by the Portuguese King Manuel, it was da Gama and not Cabral who then received the commission to follow up Cabral's commercial venture, with da Gama's even grander expedition in 1502. Cabral retired from royal service and lived out his life quietly on his rural estates until his death in 1520.

Juan Ponce de Leon (c. 1460-1521) was a Spanish nobleman-soldier who was appointed governor of the eastern portion of the island of Hispañola. Stories of gold to be found on the adjoining island (Puerto Rico) led him to explore and settle the first Spanish settlement on that island (near present-day San Juan) in 1508-1509. He was appointed briefly as governor of that island – until political intrigue led to his removal from that position.

But he was not to be pushed aside and he was soon off exploring to the north in pursuit of a story about a fountain that could restore a person's youth. This brought him in early 1513 to the Bahamas and to Florida (which he first supposed was also an island – until he started sailing south along its coast and discovered its true extent). He returned to Spain in 1514 and had himself confirmed by the King as Governor of Bimini and Florida. He returned to Florida in 1521 with 200 men, with the intent of establishing a Spanish colony there. But upon his arrival he was hit by a Seminole arrow and died soon thereafter in Cuba

Ferdinand Magellan (1480-1521). Magellan was born in Sabrosa of Portuguese nobility – though in his late thirties he renounced his Portuguese citizenship and came into service to the Spanish King Charles I. It was to Charles that he announced his idea of avoiding the well-entrenched Portuguese positions along the route to the East Indies – by sailing west from Spain across the Atlantic and continuing in that direction (by-passing the Americas) until he arrived at the Indies from the East! He received Charles' support and on September 20, 1519, he set sail from Sanlúcar de Barrameda with five ships.

He crossed the Atlantic and in November arrived at modern-day Argentina, exploring the Rio de la Plata and coming ashore for the winter at Patagonia.

Late the next spring he then continued southward around the storm-tossed and rocky straits off the southern tip of South America (the "Straits of Magellan") – taking 38 days to make that dangerous passage – and then headed westward across the Pacific. He arrived at the Marianas. He then continued on to the Philippines – arriving there in March of 1521.

Ever the nobleman, he got himself involved in a political alliance with the ruler of Cebu island – and joining his Spanish forces with his ally's he launched an attack on the Mactan islanders – and was killed in the process.

His fleet, or what was left of it, arrived at the Moluccas on November 6, 1521. The sole ship to survive the entire voyage, the *Victoria*, commanded by Juan Sebastión del Cano, finally arrived at Seville on September 6, 1522.

Hernán Cortés (1485-1547). Cortés was of a lower rank of nobility, and sought adventure to improve his social status – coming to the New World in 1504 for that exact purpose. He and the governor of Cuba, Velázquez, fell into disagreement, and Cortes, hearing rumors of great wealth to be had in the of mainland Mexico, decided to undertake in early 1519 an expedition to seek his fortune there. Velázquez attempted to block his move, but Cortés was able to hold him off, and secure assistance from the local Mexicans (and find a wife and interpreter, La Malinche. He also scuttled all his ships, to make it clear that there would be no retreat from this venture. Then he marched on Tenochtitlan with 600 of his soldiers and many anti-Aztecan local warriors, massacred a mass gathering of Mexican aristocrats in order to strike fear in the Aztec emperor Moctezuma – and finally in November met Montezuma at his capital. Cortés was received lavishly and accorded various political honors. At first their relations were friendly.

The following year, 1520, Cortés had to go East in order to take on an army that Velázquez had sent to crush Cortés. However, Cortés not only defeated this army but added it to his own forces, and returned to Tenochtitlan. The situation in Tenochtitlan at this point was chaotic, and Montezuma was killed (by whom exactly?) – and Cortés and his men fled an angry Indian population. But gathering new forces, Cortés marched again on Tenochtitlan, and was able to defeat the Aztec forces there. He then took control of the realm, which he claimed for Spain – and renamed Tenochtitlan as "Mexico City."

King Charles appointed Cortés as governor of "New Spain," but sent "advisors," to keep things there under tight royal control. Yet, as the situation required that the king's new Indian subjects become properly "Christian," Cortés proved to be very supportive of the effort by Franciscan and Dominican monks to see this conversion achieved throughout the land.

Cortés would also lead a military expedition south into Honduras, to prevent a Velázquez agent from taking control there, and possibly threatening Cortés's position in New Spain. This effort put him in trouble back in Spain, which he returned to in order to defend himself. He succeeded grandly, and was returned to New Spain – where, after bringing some end to the political intrigue going on there, he lived out the rest of his days rather grandly (very wealthy from his silver mines).

Francisco Pizarro (1478-1541).   Pizarro was of illegitimate and poor background – though cousin of Cortés, and endowed with the same ambition as his cousin. However, he would make his fortune his own way, joining Balboa in crossing Panama ... and then eventually settling there, assigned finally the office of mayor of what would become Panama City.

But the rumors of "El Dorado" coming from the South interested him more, and led him to form up a three-man partnership with fellow-soldier Almagro and priest Luque, and they put together plans for an expedition South in the quest of this Land of Gold. Two ventures (1524 and 1526) from Panama along the Pacific coast brought them no further South than Colombia, and lots of trouble from the local Indians – although the discovery of some gold, silver and jewels on the second voyage confirmed rumors sufficiently for Pizarro to overcome Panamanian opposition and head to Spain to plead his cause (a third expedition) before King Charles. Receiving royal support, he returned to Panama to set out on that third expedition (joined by another explorer, de Soto) at the end of 1530.

Meanwhile, Incan society was facing chaos from a major plague (probably smallpox which had made its way south from the Spanish settlements) and from a bitter battle between brothers, Huáscar and Atahualpa, for the title of Incan emperor. Arriving at the moment that Atahualpa proved successful in the fight, and hearing of these developments, Pizarro sent word to Atahualpa, inviting him to meet with him in celebration of his victory. Tragically this is what Atahualpa did, unconcerned about the dangers posed by these intruders into his realm, with 8,000 Incan warriors meeting 168 Spanish troops for the occasion. But Pizarro was determined to capture Atahualpa, realizing already the terror that his guns caused among the Inca. Ultimately Pizarro succeeded in his plans, seized Atahualpa and held him for ransom, which turned out to be a room filled with gold – and two side rooms filled with silver.* Then after the ransom was delivered, Pizarro sentenced Atahualpa to death for the murder of his brother Huáscar. With Atahualpa's death, the Incan Empire found itself in chaos, making it easy for the Spanish (with added troops) to eventually bring the empire under Spanish-Catholic rule.

Then Pizarro and his partner Almagro fell into dispute over the city of Cuzco and whether their respective Peruvian domains – Pizarro's New Castile and Almagro's New Toledo that they now governed – included that vital city. Eventually (1538) Almagro was defeated in battle and executed, and Almagro's son stripped of his inheritance. But two years later, supporters of the younger Almagro assaulted Pizarro's palace, killing Pizarro. But the following year Almagro himself was killed in battle.

Massive fortune is not really the solution to life's problems. And thus ended up the grand quest of these fortune hunters for the gold of El Dorado! But in the end all this gold and silver (the Spanish silver at Potosi, Bolivia, would produce an additional $36 billion for Spain) would end up hurting the Spanish monarchy as well, setting off a massive price inflation across Europe – ultimately forcing the Spanish monarchy itself to have to declare bankruptcy three times before the century (the 1500s) ended.

The shift in political-economic focus
from the Mediterranean to the Atlantic

Of critical importance to what was developing as something of a grand Western revival, all this political and commercial activity initiated by Spain and Portugal – but soon also France, the Netherlands and England – naval superpowers ranging far and wide from their bases in the North Atlantic, would shift tremendously the dynamic away from the Mediterranean ... and into their own Atlantic-centered world. Italy, once prospering greatly from the East-West trade running between Europe and the Arab Middle East, would now find itself slipping in importance in this new dynamic.

This would have not only economic implications but also strong political ones as well ... as all Italian political units – which at this point also included the Roman papacy – would find themselves to be of much less significance in the changing scheme of things.

---

*Estimates are that the value of the ransom equaled over 1.5 billion in today's dollars, and the amount then seized from the Incan treasury to be another $1.5 billion. This would be the beginning of Spain's massive rise to power on the basis of the wealth the Spanish monarchy was able to extract from its American holdings.

✳ ✳ ✳

THE PROTESTANT REFORMATION
(The early to mid-1500s)

Growing conditions for religious reform

A sense of growing decadence in the Church. The deep corruption of the church – from popes down to parish priests – was a source of major frustration to the faithful – who had a profound sense of God's judgment over His people, the Christian community. Judgment would fall on this New Israel as surely as it did the Old Israel.

A growth of independent personal judgment. Combined with this sense of frustration with the church was a growing independent-mindedness on the part of the new humanist intelligentsia. The Church no longer held a monopoly over the thinking of such scholars and teachers. The new printing presses had put in their hands a wider range of reading that had ever been available previously. Some of it was pagan, most of it was Christian. But in any case, it opened up a world that was not automatically sifted through the scrutiny of the religious hierarchy.

Oddly, one of the most unsettling elements of this new literature were the Hebrew and Greek manuscripts of the Old and New Testaments that became widely available. The new Biblical scholarship that this engendered not only pointed out (minor) flaws in the Latin Vulgate – but gave the new scholars a sense of personal judgment superior to that of the official church.

The age of the individual conscience was being born! The Church could no longer expect automatically to command the thinking of its Christian subjects. Within the context of this independent and very critical mood – at least on the part of a new breed of humanist scholars – "business-as-usual" on the part of the Church was bound to create a massive reaction.

A major shift in the traditional political order of medieval Christendom. For centuries, the whole of the medieval Christian order had been a single piece – understood to be ordained and supported by the will of God. It was the widely understood principle that all the social orders, from kings and popes down to the vast multitudes of peasants, all had their respective "place" in that medieval political, economic, social, cultural, religious, spiritual order – such places determined by God's natural ordering of all people. A person was placed into that order by the logic of his or her birth – and that by the will of God. It was God that determined who would be born a king, who would be born a peasant. This all being by

God's righteous decree, there was little further thought that could be given to a rearranging of this larger medieval social or political order.

True, kings and bishops, who both belonged to the upper aristocratic orders, had been battling among themselves since the 1100s for dominance over this larger medieval social order. But such disputes did not involve the masses of European peasant farmers. They simply awaited the outcome of such struggles to see how marriages, political alliances, wars would move them from the domain of one lord (priestly or princely) to another. They themselves had no say in such matters. Their job was to till the soil and pay the lord their feudal dues. They always prayed that God would set over them a fair or just lord. But they themselves had no voice in the matter of who ruled over the land that they themselves worked so hard to cultivate.

The rising urban power base of the Renaissance. However, the rise during the 1300s and 1400s of European commercial wealth – in competition with the traditional wealth of rural landholdings – was bound to upset this arrangement. Bankers, merchants, industrialists – who congregated along key trade centers – did not fit easily into this older social order. Though certainly their guilds and unions attempted to formalize their wealth, in fact their wealth was dynamic and always subject to a rapid shift in fortunes. The success of their labors was related to the wisdom of investment decisions that they made. To prosper, they needed a free hand – and a mind open to new and ever-changing opportunities.

During the 1400s this group sat uneasily under the traditional rule of the medieval Church and Crown. Medieval feudal dues in the form of agricultural and military service owed the lord were cumbersome and at times counterproductive to the larger success of this new urban entrepreneurial class. It was inevitable that these towns would become centers of resistance against the medieval land-based social system.

Early efforts at reform

Actually, religious reformist urges reached all the way back to the 1200s and 1300s over a growing concern about the moral corruption rising within the Church ... and a similar desire to return the Church to its earlier, pre-Constantine ways – where the believer stood directly before God in faith and not just through the priestly ministrations of an institutional Church.

John Wycliff (1320-1384) and the Lollards. In 1370s England John Wycliff got himself in trouble teaching just such ideas. He also attacked a multitude of practices and features of the church – especially the way it accumulated for itself enormous wealth, at a time when so many of the faithful lived in deep poverty. And he succeeded in offending the Church hierarchy by having Scripture translated into English so that individual believers might come to Godly knowledge on their own. He consequently was dismissed from Oxford University in 1381 for his actions. But his ideas would live on after him, picked up by the later reformers of the 1500s.

Wycliffe's followers, contemptuously called "Lollards," from a Dutch word of derision meaning "mumblers" (originally directed at the Beguines), preached church reform in England. At first they were protected by some of the English nobility, basically as an excuse to bring some of the Church's vast wealth to their own hands. But then a Peasants' Revolt broke out in 1381 – mostly due to the huge social stress caused by the Black Death and the ongoing Hundred Years' War. In this, the rebels justified their actions employing Lollard themes. Consequently, the nobility turned against Lollard leadership, despite the fact that the Lollard leaders themselves were no supporters of the rebellion.

Wycliffe's Lollard movement was thus suppressed. But so was the intellectual ferment of Oxford university where his teachings had been widely accepted.

The Conciliar Movement. Also, the political turmoil of the Papal Schism pointed to the obvious need at the turn into the 1400s to get the Church to drop its political programs and get back to its major spiritual duties. Thus various Church councils were called (the Conciliar Movement) to unify and reform the Church – and at the same time bring independent voices of reform under submission.

But church politics was not going to be easily put aside ... if at all. For a time it appeared that the various church councils held in the early 1400s might take precedence over the authority of the Pope. But ultimately the Conciliar Movement died on the basis of its own politics.

The Council of Pisa (1409). This key council, in order to end the embarrassment of having two contending popes claiming to be the sole head of the Catholic church, deposed the two contenders, Gregory XII and Benedict XIII. This reform was undertaken even by the cardinals of both popes – who then elected a new pope, Alexander V. But when the two popes refused to step down, there were then three contending popes!

Jan Hus (1374-1415). Caught in this firestorm was the Bohemian or Czech reformer Jan Hus. Wycliff's teachings had reached Bohemia after his death and were eventually picked up by John Hus, who took up Wycliff's cause at the University of Prague in the early 1400s. Hus translated Wycliff's works into Czech and presented Hus's reform ideals to the Czech people.

The Czech reform led by Hus was geographically closer to the Imperial powerbase of the Habsburg Holy Roman Emperor (based in nearby Austria), and thus less able to be conducted quietly. Thus in 1414 Hus was called (under the Emperor's promise of safe conduct) to the Council of Constance to explain himself. But treacherously, he was arrested for "heresy" by the Council, and burned at the stake in 1415.

This was clearly intended to be an object lesson to those who had similar ideas of shaking up the Mother Church with their unwanted ideas of ecclesiastical reform. But instead, this display of Church "discipline" merely sparked deep anger over Hus's treatment ... which in turn led to widespread revolt in Bohemia. At first, attempts to put down what had become a popular national revolt failed. Finally, a compromise of sorts was reached with the Hussites.

The Council of Basel (1431-1449). It was a council held at Basel that made the first steps of progress toward reconciliation with the Hussites. Then it went further in defying a papal order to move to Bologna, claiming superior authority to that of the pope (Eugenius IV: 1431-1447).

But the Council's subsequent efforts at reform of the ecclesiastical hierarchy caused it to overstep its true power – and Eugenius used this to his own advantage. Also, the pressing problems of the Turks and the need for closer relations with the Eastern church provided the occasion for the pope to split the council's power – bringing a portion of the council to Ferrara while the remainder carried on in Basel. Then its decision in 1439 to elect a pope in opposition to Eugenius undermined most of the council's residual authority.

In the meanwhile, the papacy in Rome emerged as an ever-stricter defender of its ecclesiastical authority.

Girolamo Savonarola (1452-1498). Florence briefly (the 1490s) came under the direction of a religious reformer, the Dominican monk Savonarola, a very popular figure among the poorer classes of Florence and a thorn in the side of the Florentine aristocracy and the Roman church.

His prophecies about a new age arising out of corruptions of the former age seemed validated when the French king invaded Italy and the Medici fled Florence, allowing Savonarola to establish something of a puritanical Republic in Florence in taking on a grand effort to clean up the morals of Florentine society.

But the Pope and his agents challenged Savonarola to a public test by fire – which he failed miserably. He thus confessed (under torture) to fraud, he lost his popular support at home, and in 1498 was arrested, hanged and his body burned in Florence's public square.

Again, this was supposed to provide an object lesson for those inclined to challenge the religious-political status quo of old Christendom.

A "Protestant" revolt breaks out in Germany

Martin Luther (1483-1546).   But another monk (Augustinian Friar), Martin Luther, was not so intimidated and threw a new challenge of church reform in the face of the Pope ... and his close associate, the "Defender of the Faith" Charles V of Habsburg – the powerful Holy Roman Emperor (and also king of the dominant political power of the day: Spain). Such a challenge was quite daring ... if not even suicidal.

Behind Luther's defiant spirit was a long personal pilgrimage he had been on, one based on a deep desire to unburden himself of a profound sense of guilt and personal condemnation before God's judgment. For Luther, a personal breakthrough occurred as the message sank into the head of this Augustinian professor concerning Paul's teaching (Galatians and Romans) about divine Grace and forgiveness received through the simple faith of the believer – and not through the demands of any religious law or requirements of a religious system. So "liberated" was he that he felt that his discovery had to be brought to the world.

Luther was a teacher of the Bible to his fellow Augustinian monks. His complete familiarity with Scripture made him aware of and angry about the huge disparities between the way the early Church and the contemporary Church functioned ... plus a much anticipated visit to Rome turned into a very disillusioning experience for Luther when he came face to face with the political intrigue and corruption going on in the holy city.

Clearly the Church needed to clean up its act. Even Emperor Charles knew that. The popes had become famous for their corruption, epitomized at the beginning of the 1500s by the notorious Borgia family ... Father Rodrigo (Pope Alexander VI), his murderous condottiero son Cesare, and his beauty-queen daughter Lucrezia – among other illegitimate offspring ... not that a celibate pope was supposed to have children, much less mistresses!

However, what finally sparked Luther's bold challenge to the Church was the sale of indulgences ... to finance the building of the pope's elaborate cathedral in Rome. This led Luther finally to post in late October of 1517 his 95 theses on the door of the Wittenberg castle church. It was time for the church hierarchy to answer for its actions and behavior. It was time for the church hierarchy to clean up its act!

This action of Luther's seemed to be the signal for a number of German (and Scandinavian) princes to rise up in revolt against the political status quo of old Christendom defended largely by the Pope and the Holy Roman Emperor. In Luther they saw their chance legitimately (i.e., on the basis of Christian morality) to break away from the monopoly of power held by both Pope and Emperor ... and develop their own "Christian" sovereignty.* Thus one of them, Frederick III, Elector of Saxony, took Luther under his protection just as the pope declared Luther a heretic and consequently to be denied all personal support and even to be eligible to be killed legally by anyone who encountered him.

Emperor Charles V tries to suppress Luther. The newly elected Holy Roman Emperor, Charles V of Habsburg now took up the issue ... on the side of the Roman church. Luther, now excommunicated but still under the protection of Frederick and widely popular in Germany, was called by the Emperor to an Imperial Council (Diet) at Worms in 1521 to give account of his views. Here Luther stood firm in his views against the Roman church. And under an Imperial guarantee of his freedom, Luther was able to get away from the Council before the guarantee was retracted.

From then on for the rest of his life, Luther remained in seclusion in Frederick's Wartburg Castle, translating the Bible into German ... and publishing numerous works denouncing in vivid language the leadership and practices of the Roman church. These writings spread rapidly (thanks in part to the new printing press) throughout Europe – until talk of Luther and his challenges to the Church (and thus Christendom) was under discussion everywhere.

In the meanwhile, the Emperor found himself preoccupied by an on-going war with France over control of various cities and principalities in Italy. Then the Turkish threat to the Emperor's Austrian holdings rose again. Thus the Emperor was seriously distracted in his effort to quiet Luther. Luther was relatively safe.

The Peasants' War of 1524-1525. But when German commoners took his challenges as an invitation to rise up against the burden of all of Christendom's traditional authority, civil as well as religious, Luther came out passionately against the revolt.

Indeed, Luther was no revolutionary ... only a reformer. For Luther his call for religious reform was related to the matter of a sinner's personal justification before God. Luther showed little interest in making broader changes within Christianity beyond the throwing off of Roman spiritual authority – with its traditions of works-righteousness. Substantial changes in worship, for instance, were of lesser interest to Luther. Also the episcopal

---

*Also there was huge resentment in Germany for the heavy taxes imposed on the Germans in support of the Roman Curia ... and especially for the massive and very expensive cathedral being built in Rome with the goal of restoring the majesty of the papacy.

or hierarchical form of church government (rule "from above" by bishops) was not itself questioned by Luther – although he did strongly support the idea that the bishops were answerable to the local princes ... not to Rome.

Thus it proved to be the case that he stood strongly on the side of the princes against the German rebels (Müntzer and the "Zwickau prophets") who took up the political cause of the German commoners against their rulers. In the course of this peasant rebellion, Luther came down harshly against the peasant rebels, denouncing them in the same strong language that he used to denounce the hierarchy of the Roman Church.*

The peasants and their leaders were put down cruelly by the local princes and their mercenary troops (6,000 peasants lost their lives alone in the one-day battle of Frankenhausen).

The result of the Peasant War was to move real power over to the various German princes. Thus in Germany, the rule of the church was not a matter either of local congregational power – nor of the power of popes and bishops. Rather, it was the ruling prince in each of the many principalities that made up Germany who now determined each in his own territory its particular Christian character. Some remained loyal to Rome (the southern German princes). Some followed the Lutheran line (the northern German princes) with their new Schmalkaldic League, a powerful political alliance which was dedicated, among other things, to backing Luther in every way possible. But in any case, it was the local princes who made that determination. The dependence of church on state was thus set as the characteristic feature of German Christianity.

Thus in the end, although he was willing to break from the feudal Church, Luther was not willing to break from the feudal civil government in Northern Germany. Consequently, Luther's reforms would go only part-way in bringing Germany out of its medieval background ... and leave it still with a feudal social system, one that would last all the way up into the early 20th century. Furthermore, because Luther's religious movement was constructed deeply on these social foundations of a rather permanently medieval (*rural*) north-central Europe, "Lutheranism" would have almost no impact on any of Europe's rapidly developing industrial (*urban*) areas.

Thomas Müntzer (c. 1490-1525). Müntzer was the active leader of the unsuccessful Peasants' Revolt in Thuringia (1524-1525) that so upset Luther. Müntzer took a mystical view about the humble classes being the true

---

*In his *Wider die Mordischen und Reubischen Rotten der Bawren* [Against the Robbing Murderous Hordes of Peasants] (1525) he advises the German princes to take necessary action against the peasants: "Let everyone who can, smite, slay and stab, secretly and publicly, . . . a poisonous, devilish rebel, like one must kill a rabid dog."

repository of God's Spirit and the proper instrument of God's transformative work on earth. His theological writings and personal leadership were of major importance in motivating the peasants' revolt against the German ruling classes. At the Battle of Frankenhausen in May of 1525 his peasant forces were defeated – and Müntzer was taken prisoner and executed.

The Swiss Reform Movement

Ulrich Zwingli (1484-1531).   As a young man, Zwingli received a humanistic university education in Vienna and Basel. As a parish priest he continued his studies in Greek and Hebrew and of the humanist Erasmus and the classics. In 1518 he was brought to Zurich, Switzerland, as its pastor, where he gained a reputation as a brilliant preacher and scholar.

It was here that his inquiring mind also began to draw him toward Luther's reform movement. In 1522 Zwingli began to make his own moves to establish Scripture as the sole religious authority for the Christian. He opposed the Lenten Fast, citing the lack of Scriptural warrant for the practice – a position which was supported by the Zurich civil government. The bishop of Constance tried to suppress this innovation, but lost out to the Zurich government, which moved to take control of ecclesiastical matters within its jurisdiction. Zwingli supported this shift in authority, claiming that the civil government, under the Lordship of Christ and guided in its work by the dictates of Scripture, was the sole legitimate voice or conscience of the believing community.

He also moved to reform various features of worship, whenever there was no specific Scriptural warrant for such things, though he did so through a practice of gradualism. By 1525, however, he had eliminated statues and relics from the Zurich church, eliminated the Latin mass (substituting a memorial celebration of the Lord's Supper in its place) and placed at the heart of worship the sermon (a rather extensive exposition of Scripture) – the key feature of the Swiss Reformation.

But the conservative rural cantons of Switzerland remained firmly opposed to the Zwinglian reforms ... that is, strongly Roman Catholic. Relations grew bitter and hostilities resulted – with Zwingli himself being wounded and then put to death in a losing battle with the rural cantons in 1531.

The more gentle-natured Heinrich Bullinger then took over the Zurich reform movement.

The split within the Protestant ranks. Meanwhile, the reform movement was beginning to move in different and opposing theological directions. To Zwingli and the Swiss reformers (identified as the Reformed party) there were strong interests in restructuring the organization and practices of the church around its original constitutional base: Scripture. There was a stripping away of every feature of Christianity that could not be supported by Scriptural warrant. This was in keeping with Zwingli's humanist background – and his focus on the Greek and Hebrew origins of the church, and the sense that everything that was a departure from this classical age was a perversion of an original purity undergirding the church.

This would not probably have kept Luther and Zwingli from working closely together – except that one portion of Zwingli's reforms were violently opposed by Luther: Zwingli's treatment of the celebration of the Lord's supper. Zwingli (for whom the sermon, not the celebration of the eucharist, was the central point of Christian worship) interpreted Christ's words concerning his presence in the wine and bread as purely symbolic. To Luther, this was a shocking diminution of the power of the "real presence" of Christ in the elements of the eucharist. The gap was, in both their minds, unbridgeable by the mid-1520s. Others of both parties tried to effect a compromise. But Luther, even after Zwingli's death, would not hear of compromise. Thus Lutheranism and the Reformed faith split permanently.

But Zwingli's legacy lived on, taken up importantly by Johannes Oecolampadius in Basel. But it spread as well to Bern and Constance, and ultimately Geneva. And this Reform Movement also made its way down the Rhine River to Strasbourg – where under the leadership of Martin Bucer – who tried to unite the Lutheran and Zwinglian Reform Movements (but Luther was not supportive of the effort) – the Reform Movement took on the more thoroughgoing Swiss character (as distinct from the more conservative Lutheran variety).

John Calvin (1509-1564). But it would be John Calvin in Geneva that would bring the Swiss Reform Movement to full power.

Calvin was a Frenchman, schooled in the new humanist tradition, and prepared at the universities of Orléans and Bourges to be a lawyer. He fell in with a circle of French humanists who read with great interest the writings of Luther. Then, somewhere in the period 1532-1534, Calvin experienced a "sudden conversion" (the details of which unfortunately he never discussed publicly.) From this point on his well-organized mind was given over to theology rather than the law. At the same time his theological associations became very dangerous to an increasingly suspicious French king, Francis I.

In 1536, Calvin felt compelled to write – with all respect to his king – a reply to Francis I's suspicions about the "protestants": *The Institutes of the Christian Religion.** It was Calvin's hope that Francis, through this long

---

*This work underwent numerous editions, increasing in coverage with each new issue, from a single volume of six chapters in 1536, ultimately by 1559 to four volumes of 80 chapters, indicative of his own development as a scholar-teacher.

essay, would come to understand that the Protestants posed no threat to his rule – but only sought to revitalize the original Christian ideal on which the whole Christian realm ought to be properly based. Though it was the most compelling theological treatise explaining the Protestant position – it did not have its intended effect of swaying the views of Francis. Instead, it identified Calvin as a voice of religious dissent ... not tolerated in France. Calvin was thus forced to flee France. He intended to relocate to Strasbourg, where the reform movement was well underway.

His path there took him to Geneva (Switzerland) ... where the Protestant reformer William Farel prevailed upon Calvin not to head on to Strasbourg but to stay in the city and help him strengthen the Swiss Reformed Movement which was growing rapidly there. Calvin agreed. But for Calvin, this proved to be a stormy decision. Geneva was an unruly city, and Calvin's natural bent toward orderliness and discipline quickly made him many enemies in the city. In the spring of 1538 Calvin and Farel were banished from Geneva. Calvin headed on to Strasbourg, where, by that time, the "Reformed" movement was well established.

But in 1541, the old group of Calvin's supporters in Geneva urgently requested his return to the city. Calvin somewhat reluctantly decided to go back to Geneva – but on his terms. Upon his return, Calvin organized (accepting many compromises with the city Council) the religious life of the city around his new *Ordinances* – the foundation of Reformed polity. Geneva in turn became identified under Calvin's leadership as the model Christian city, the "New Jerusalem" of Protestantism.

Calvin's reforms help develop a strong European "Middle Class." Calvin was an urban European, steeped in the bourgeois mindset of the rising European urban "middle class." Calvin's interest in reform of the crumbling medieval moral-legal order involved importantly a vision of the new urban order as central to a purified Christianity. Thus his interest in reform did not limit itself merely to matters of religious doctrine – as was the case for Luther. Calvin truly was interested in a comprehensive reordering of every aspect of post-medieval life: political, economic, and social as well as theological.

Importantly, he gave a theological rationale for the independent-mindedness of the urban commercial class – arming them with Scriptural justification for going their own way within God's creation. Indeed, he encouraged them to establish purified political-economic-social orders as a way of purging Christendom of its corruption and of bringing glory to God in Jesus Christ. He made their soul-searching independent-mindedness a matter of the greatest importance in their standing before God. They not only had the right to be accountable to God alone as sovereign over them –

they had the Christian duty to see that this was the case. The supposition was that any earthly lord who positioned himself between them and God was going to be problematic in their "purified" relationship with God and their covenantal life in the purified Christian commonwealth.

Certainly the followers of Calvin attempted to convince the rich and powerful kings of Europe that their movement had no treasonous instincts – and that they planned to be good citizens in the realms where they lived. The kings were not convinced. And rightly so. Everything about Calvinism pointed to the idea of these people being accountable to no earthly ruler but to God alone. Switzerland, which was the birthplace of Calvin's Reformed Movement, was well recognized for its independent-mindedness and refusal to acknowledge the rule of any princely lord over the land. No ... Calvin's Reformed Movement, or "Calvinism" was destined to bring a clash with traditional princely and priestly rulers who claimed to rule by "divine rights." That was exactly what the Calvinists claimed for their own "self-rule": the common people's own self-rule *by divine right* – even by divine imperative. There was no way these two mind-sets were going to work cooperatively.

The extensive spread of Calvinism to urban Europe. It was not long before word spread widely of what was happening in Geneva under Calvin's reforms. Thus it was that during the second half of the 1500s, individuals from all corners of Europe came to Geneva to be a part of this new Reformed Movement. There they learned of ways to rebuild their communities as "covenant" communities ... covenanted with God to live solely by Scriptural standards. And there in Geneva they busied themselves also in translating and publishing exactly those scriptural standards (the Bible) in the various languages spoken across the European continent.

And thus it was that "Calvinism" came to be well-planted in the towns and cities of England (the Puritans), Scotland and Northern Ireland (the Presbyterians), Netherlands (the Dutch Reformed), France (the Huguenots), Western Germany, Bohemia and Hungary (the German, Czech and Hungarian Reformed Movement) – and even parts of Poland and Spain, where it later got eradicated by the Catholic Counter-Reformation overseen by the Catholic popes and Habsburg emperors.

The Michael Servetus affair (1553). Theologically, the times were very intense ... as we have just seen in Luther's reaction to the peasant revolt in Germany. But the intensity of the times does not offer much of an excuse as to Calvin's behavior in the face of a bitter theological attack on him (just words!) offered by a highly self-important Spanish intellectual (and accomplished medical doctor), who took delight in accusing Calvin of the evil of Trinitarianism, which – according to Servetus' book *Errors of the*

Trinity (1531) – was nothing more than a grand deception of the devil ... and those who held to it, servants of the devil.

Furthermore, Servetus presented himself (in his book *The Restitution of Christianity*) as the Michael of Scripture (from *Revelation* and *Daniel*) who was called to fight the antichrist, in order to usher in the End Times.

Calvin got involved with Servetus back in 1546, when Servetus sent Calvin a copy of *The Restitution of Christianity* ... resulting in a correspondence between the two men which started out calmly enough, but which quickly grew increasingly bitter as accusations and counter-accusations intensified. Calvin thus stopped the correspondence ... totally embittered by Servetus. But Servetus went on, announcing abroad that not only was Calvin the imposter Simon Magus, but both Calvin and the Pope were antichrists, needing to be dismissed in order to restore Christianity to its original character.

Servetus eventually got himself condemned by French authorities for his supposed Unitarianism ... escaped imprisonment, and decided to head to Italy for refuge. But strangely, he stopped by Geneva (1553) and decided to attend a worship service conducted by Calvin – when he was spotted and arrested. Servetus was duly tried and convicted of heresy ... and sentenced to be burned at the stake. Calvin tried to soften the sentence somewhat by calling for a beheading ... but could not get the Council to back down. Calvin and his friend Farel also visited Servetus in prison to get Servetus to recant his Unitarian beliefs. But Servetus would not recant. And thus the sentence was carried out.

To this day it is debated as to whether Calvin could not have exerted more pressure – for instance, to have Servetus banished rather than executed. But Calvin at the time was having his own political difficulties with the town council over matters of town governance, and seemingly needed to appear to be no less strong than the council in the (typical) handling of heretics.

In any case, it is another example of how frequently Christian theological precision gets way ahead of the Gospel of Jesus Christ. And it certainly was not the first time, nor certainly also the last. In fact, in those days a lot of this sort of thing would be going on ... doing the West's Christian foundations a huge disservice ... not to mention a huge disservice to Jesus Christ.

Scotland during the Reformation

We must at this point mention one of these "Calvinists": John Knox, the great Protestant reformer of Scotland. Knox not only helped direct Scotland to Calvinist Protestantism in the mid-1500s, but also left a powerful political legacy within the Calvinist or Reformed branch of Protestantism, a political legacy we call "Presbyterianism." Knox's Presbyterianism not only determined the organization of the Church of Scotland but also laid the foundations for the growth of representative democracy in the American middle colonies in the 1600s and 1700s.

As with many Protestant reformers, Knox began as a Catholic priest, highly discontent with the moral and spiritual corruption that had overtaken the Mother Church. He was attracted to the Lutheran teachings of the early Scottish reformer, George Wishart; was appalled when in 1546 the Catholic cardinal had Wishart burned at the stake as a heretic; and then joined the group of rebels who moved to overthrow the hand of the Catholic church over Scotland. This put him in opposition to the pro-French party that ruled Scotland – and when French troops in 1547 crushed this Protestant rebellion in Scotland, Knox was led off to captivity as a French galley slave. His release was finally secured by the pro-Protestant English King Edward VI, leading Knox to come to England to be a Protestant pastor and then chaplain to the King.

But when Edward died in 1553 and Catholic Mary Tudor ("Bloody Mary") came to the throne, Knox left England and made his way eventually to Geneva where he joined a community of English expatriates living and studying under the direction of Calvin. Knox took a great liking to both Calvin and his teachings and subsequently became a major voice in the English/Scottish Reform Movement not only in Geneva, but through letters, to a growing Protestant movement back in Scotland.

He returned briefly to Scotland in 1555, then back to Geneva to become pastor of the English church there ... and then finally in 1559 he returned definitively to Scotland to take over the spiritual leadership of the Protestant rebellion against the French-Catholic regent of Scotland, Mary of Guise.

Seeing that things were not going well in Scotland for the Protestant party, Queen Elizabeth of England came to their aid against the French in Scotland. But when Mary of Guise died suddenly in 1560, the French Catholic cause in Scotland was dead. Scotland was now won for Protestantism.

At this point Knox and his supporters began to reshape the Scottish church – not only theologically along the lines of Calvin's Reformed faith born in Geneva, but also politically in a way that was Knox's special contribution to the Protestant cause. Knox took the idea of representative government characteristic of Calvin's Reformed churches (communities led by elected elders or "presbyters"), and applied it locally, regionally and nationally in total reversal of the top-down or hierarchical fashion of Catholic or "Episcopalian" government. Thus local councils ("Presbyteries"), regional councils ("Synods" ... from the term "Senate") and national councils ("General Assemblies") that presided over the faithful were made up of representatives not of the political rulers over the church but of the people themselves. Thus was born "Presbyterian" or representative church government – the source of inspiration for the new Democratic or Republican forms of government that led eventually to the Constitution of 1789 underpinning the new American Republic.

Despite success in the Protestant takeover of the Church of Scotland, the continuing existence of a Catholic monarchy in Scotland under Mary of Guise's daughter, Mary Queen of Scots, made life still highly problematic for Protestant Scotland – and for John Knox personally ... as the two locked wills in on-going battle. But eventually Mary's political blunders forced her to flee to England, where Elizabeth put her under house arrest ... and eventually had her put to death.

In any case Knox, worn out and sickly, died from his labors in 1572. But his work in Scotland was carried forth faithfully by others, notably Andrew Melville.

The Catholic "Counter-Reformation"

The papal party finally realized the seriousness of the challenge to its moral authority – and in 1546 called a Council at Trent to answer the Protestant charges of ecclesiastical corruption and theological deviation. Rigid discipline was re-imposed over the priests who remained loyal to Rome. Luther's teaching on divine grace and justification alone by faith was condemned. A campaign was readied to wipe out any "heretics" not ready to return to Roman discipline. The war was thus on.

The Roman church, championed by the most powerful ruling family in Europe (the Spanish Habsburgs) – well-financed from their plunder of South and Central America – fought back cruelly, trying to stamp out the fires of the Protestant revolt. They succeeded in many places, and might have been fully successful had not the Muslim Turks attacked Vienna – the Eastern center of Habsburg power – during the height of this struggle. With the Habsburgs thus distracted, Protestantism dug in.

Pope Paul III and the Council of Trent. Pope Paul, under some considerable pressure from King Charles, called the Council of Mantua (1537) to begin dealing with some of the issues of the Reformation. But that Council got disrupted by a new round of warfare between Francis of France and Charles. In 1542 Paul again called a Council, this time located at Trent (Austria) – though it did not begin deliberations until the end of 1545.

At the same time, Paul established the Supreme Tribunal of the Inquisition – a remake of the old Papal Inquisition, which in the previous century had largely been suspended in its operations. The revival of the Inquisition in Spain under the Spanish monk Thomas de Torquemada – who for 18 years used its techniques of torture in a very "successful" manner against Muslims, Jews and Christian heretics – no doubt persuaded Paul of its constructive use in stamping out heresy. But political realities kept Paul's wonderful scheme limited to Italy – where it did a masterful job of discouraging Protestantism among the Italians (as the Spanish Inquisition did in Spain).

Paul's Council of Trent continued its meetings after his death in 1549, though he had by then clearly laid out the lines it would take. The Council of Trent met until 1552 (though it had to move to Bologna from 1547 to 1551 to escape an epidemic).   After 1552 it did not meet again until 1562 and completed its work the following year.

At the Council (as in his life) Paul took a very reactive position in the matter of the need for reforming the church. To him it was a straightforward matter of organizing the powers of the church to stamp out the Protestant heresy.

But Charles was deeply desirous of reform in the church in order to steal the ideological advantage the Protestants enjoyed over a number of issues dividing the church. Charles wanted the church to tighten up its moral laxness and make significant compromises in matters of doctrine pressed by the Protestants – in order to restore unity within Christendom.

But Paul held the line against anything that looked like a concession to the Protestants. Thus the Council of Trent, under his leadership, moved to anathematize (condemn) the Protestant position and to reaffirm the church's position that Tradition stood as a coequal with Scripture in determining church issues and doctrines.

The Latin *Vulgate* was pronounced the only authoritative version of the Bible. No translations into the languages of the day would be allowed. Further, no copies of even the Latin Vulgate were to be printed or distributed without authorization from church authorities.

Also, the Council reaffirmed the doctrine that *faith and works jointly* formed the path to salvation – and *not faith alone*, which was a central Protestant position on the subject of salvation.

Latin was to continue to be the language of the mass, the cup was to continue to be withheld from the laity during the sacrament of Holy communion, celibacy was to continue to be the order for the clergy – and a number of other doctrinal matters would remain unchanged. There were no doctrinal concessions to be made to the Protestants.

However the Council did move to tighten moral discipline in the church – a major Catholic embarrassment in the dispute with the Protestants. Clerical appointments were to be scrutinized more closely for moral-spiritual justification. Education of the clergy was to be stressed. And the preaching skills of the clergy were to be improved.

Overall, the tightening up of Catholic doctrine made the church look much less confused in the face of Protestant challenges. And the new moral regimen removed the matters that were the most obvious source of popular discontent against the church among the people (most doctrinal issues escaped popular understanding anyway).

Indeed, Pope Paul and the Council of Trent gave the Catholic Church a new crusading spirit against the Protestant "heresy."

The Jesuits (Society of Jesus). In 1540, Pope Paul III authorized Ignatius of Loyola and six companions to form a new priestly order, the Society of Jesus. Unsurprisingly, given Loyola's own background as a nobleman-soldier, the new order took on the character of a military unit, tightly disciplined to undertake very challenging work, as ordered by the Superior General (Ignatius initially) ... himself under the personal command of the pope. They were to serve the papacy as frontline missionaries, "soldiers of God," taking Catholicism to all parts of the world – from Canada to Paraguay, to Ethiopia, to Japan, and everything in between! In Christian Europe itself, they would serve principally as teachers of classical theology, rhetoric, mathematics, even music! – most notably to the youth of Europe's ruling class. And as evangelists, they dedicated themselves to countering the evangelism being undertaken by the Protestants.

Success! Thus it was that through tough political and cultural actions, the Counter-Reformation was able, step by step, to cripple Protestantism in Southern Germany, Bohemia, and Poland-Lithuania – and bring these areas back into Catholicism.

CHAPTER NINE

THE DEVELOPMENT OF THE DYNASTIC STATE

✳ ✳ ✳

THE SECOND HALF OF THE 1500s

By the mid-1500s the breakdown of the unity of Christianity and the weakening of the hold of the medieval church on the political hearts of Europe were affording a number of rising princes and kings a new opportunity: the immediate accumulation of vast amounts of wealth through the confiscation of church lands. Many of these new rulers got involved in the Reformation seemingly only for the opportunity it gave them to grab land and wealth from the church, even to make themselves the head of the church in their own lands. At the same time, political sovereigns as "kings" were taking full control over their royal domains in bringing their barons under tighter royal grip.

And also at the same time, Christian Europe was dividing itself not only along Protestant and Catholic lines, it was doing so also along Secular versus Christian lines themselves. Thus it was that the political unity of "Christian Europe" was fracturing, deeply.

Spain and the Holy Roman Empire

Philip II. Philip, unlike his Flemish father, was thoroughly Spanish: rich, powerful and arrogant ... in keeping with the dominant place Spain occupied in European affairs. During his reign, Philip's rule extended even to England (at least briefly during his four-year marriage to Mary ... also known as Bloody Mary for her persecution of English Protestants), to the Netherlands, to America, even to East Asia (the Philippines ... named after him).

Problems with the Dutch. But he was not without major problems during his reign. The Dutch, many of whom had become strongly Protestant

(Calvinist), were wealthy and independent-minded enough that they were able to hold off successive attempts of Philip to force them back under Catholicism (actually the Spanish did reclaim the Southern half of the Netherlands i.e., Belgium). This badly drained Philip's treasury and led to a number of financial crises during his reign.

Defeat of his mighty Armada by the English (July 1588). Philip's fleet, bringing to Spain the gold from America, was constantly raided by English pirates under authorization of Elizabeth, Queen of England (who had also allied with the Dutch rebels). Philip was so infuriated by all this (plus Elizabeth's murder of her Catholic rival, Mary, Queen of Scots in 1587) that in 1588 he sent a huge naval force (the Mighty Armada) against the English, with the intention of destroying English independence ... and bringing the country back under full Catholic rule.

God apparently had other plans. Instead his fleet was caught by foul winds and weather which the English exploited and sent the fleet, or the portion that survived, in miserable retreat (few made it back to Spain). Protestant Europe took great notice of the side which God seemed to have favored.

Nonetheless, Philip rebuilt his fleet and the war with England continued ... until both Elizabeth and Philip were dead (beginning of the 1600s). It was a standoff ... but one which spoke well of English power ... and rather poorly of Spanish greatness. It in fact marked the beginning of the decline of Spanish power.

France and its own religious civil war

Catherine de Medici (or Medicis). Francis died in 1547 and his son Henry, married to the strong-willed Catherine de Medici, ruled France during the next dozen years. He, like his father, was a great patron of the arts ... but unlike his father seemed more interested in peace than in war. He did attempt to hold back by force the growth of Protestantism in France, but the Calvinist Huguenots grew rapidly in number in France during his reign, Calvin's Reformed Movement reaching even into significant portions of the French nobility.

But Henry died early in a jousting accident. His sons were very young and his wife, Catherine, thus took over as Regent of France. In one role or another she would subsequently retain control over French politics, even as her sons reached majority and one by one briefly took the French throne.

The St. Bartholomew's Day Massacre (1572). Catherine was a devout Catholic and eventually took upon herself the challenge of curbing or even eliminating the Huguenot threat to Catholic France. The pinnacle of her success (and her ruthlessness) was when all nobility was invited to Paris to celebrate the wedding of her daughter Margaret and the distant (and Protestant) cousin Henry IV of Navarre (of the Bourbon line). It was a well-laid trap. A few days after the wedding, on St. Bartholomew's day, Catholics caught the Huguenots off guard and proceeded to the slaughter of most of the Huguenot nobility ... and then thousands of other Huguenots throughout the land (the groom Henry IV managed to escape). It effectively achieved what Catherine had purposed: it crippled greatly (though did not eliminate totally) the huge Protestant position in the country (though later she would attempt a compromise with them).

Henry IV of Navarre. But the one thing Catherine wanted the most was not to be achieved ... the passing on of the throne to another Valois offspring. Instead, in 1589, when both Catherine and her last son died, the crown passed to Henry IV of Navarre. The Bourbon distant cousins were now the rulers of France.

But after four years as king, Henry – finding the capital city Paris still holding out against him because of his Protestantism – decided that it was politically prudent to abandon his Protestantism and remake himself as a Catholic. However, he did not completely abandon the Protestants, issuing in 1598 the *Edict of Nantes*, granting religious toleration to the Protestants and finally bringing the wars of religion in France to an end.

Henry conducted very successful diplomacy with the powers around him (including even an alliance with the Ottoman Turks), put the royal treasury in good order (thus lightening the financial burden of the monarchy on the French), conducted numerous public works benefitting all levels of French society, and in general took the rather unusual path of truly caring about the welfare of his subjects, commoners as well as nobles. France prospered greatly during his reign. He would thus be remembered as "The Good King." But a fanatic Catholic assassinated him in the streets of Paris in 1610, bringing this period to an end.

Dutch independence

The industrious Dutch. The northern or Dutch-speaking part of the immense Habsburg Empire had benefited greatly from the Spanish plunder of America ... not because the Dutch were involved directly in the plunder itself. That was the contribution that the Spanish conquistadores (conquerors) made to the wealth of the Empire. But the money did not seem to stay in Spain ... but rather seemed inevitably to make its way north to the lands of the Dutch – principally to Flanders and the commercial cities of Antwerp (at that time the largest commercial city in Europe), Bruges, Ghent and other Flemish towns. Whereas the Spanish quickly spent their wealth in acquiring the trappings of aristocratic status (lands, fine houses, furnishings, clothing, servants, etc.) the Dutch put the money to work, investing in the manufacture and trade in those very goods desired by their Spanish associates. In other words, the Spanish spent their wealth, the Dutch invested theirs.

The Calvinist work ethic. Whereas Spanish culture was caught in the embrace of medieval aristocratic norms ... especially in its avoidance of manual labor (such labor being the clear indicator of inferior social status) the Dutch were heavily Protestant Calvinist. Calvin had taught that labor in the vineyard of God was the surest way to show honor to God. According to Calvin, labor exalted the human spirit ... rather than degraded it. As a consequence, the Dutch developed what we would call a very strong work ethic.

And it truly paid off for them. Indeed, the economic success of the Dutch cities was dazzling to behold. Thus, little by little, such wealth led to an increase in Dutch industrial and maritime power ... drawing them on their own terms into the political games of the European monarchs.

The Spanish reaction. But this urban Calvinist (Protestant) work ethic also brought suspicion and ultimately reaction from the feudal Spanish (Catholic) portion of the Empire. The intensely Spanish Catholic King Philip II resented the Protestant ways of his father Charles V's homeland ... and was even more determined than his father Charles to force religious conformity within his realm. He thus went after Calvinism in the Netherlands with an unrelenting zeal. He replaced local municipal rule with royal agents answering to him through his half-sister Margaret of Parma, he reorganized a Catholic hierarchy to supervise the religious life of the region, and he set up a Dutch Inquisition to chase down heretics.

However, so oppressive was Philip's hand in the Netherlands that local Dutch nobility quickly came to be the rallying points of resistance by the frustrated Dutch. They refused to cooperate in enforcing Philip's orders.

The Duke of Alba. Ultimately Philip sent Fernando Álvarez de Toledo – the Spanish Duke of Alba (or Alva) – and 10,000 troops to crush what had by 1567 become outright rebellion. However, the North's leading nobleman, the Prince of Orange, escaped Alba ... then sent a petition to Philip reminding him of the chartered rights of the Dutch cities that were being violated (not that Philip would be moved by such an appeal) – and then organized a military response to Alba.

It was bad timing for Philip ...because he had other major problems (such as France and the Turks) facing him at the time. Peace was made, then broken, then made again. But Spain was in trouble – nearly bankrupt from fighting crises on multiple fronts.

Meanwhile, Alba met with some success in the southern Dutch provinces (today's Belgium) by seizing and executing the noblemen leading the resistance there ... along with thousands of other individuals. This greatly weakened the South's ability to resist the Spanish hold over the land. Ultimately, Alba undertook the cruel strategy of surrounding and starving the Dutch cities one by one – killing thousands of the citizens of those cities in the process ... as for instance in Antwerp where possibly as many as 10,000 died during the 1576 "Spanish Fury" massacre. But thus did he finally succeed in breaking the independent spirit of the southern portion of the Dutch lands.[*]

But a kindlier Spanish governor however replaced him, letting Flemish Protestants leave the Catholic South. Thousands took the opportunity, emptying the Flemish cities of their industrious Protestant citizenry, who moved to the Dutch North in droves ... to the lands the Spanish seemed unable to conquer.[†] Catholics at the same time were allowed to leave the North in something of an exchange, though the flow of Catholics south proved to be a mere trickle in comparison to the floods of Protestants moving north.

The new Dutch Republic. By 1579 the Northern Dutch provinces were effectively independent ... but without a proper leader. A king (or queen) was needed ... but Elizabeth of England refused, and the Duke of Anjou did not work out for the Dutch. Thus in 1583 the Dutch Estates-General declared their Dutch union a Republic.

But Philip had no intentions of giving up his Dutch holdings, and sent a new Spanish army north ... seizing the remaining Southern Provinces and their main cities. Antwerp again fell to the Spanish ... and over half of the city's population fled to the North – as did most of the Flemish population of Bruges, Ghent and nearly all of Niewpoort and Dunkirk. As a consequence, Flanders nearly died economically ... and Antwerp ended its status as the commercial center of northern Europe. That honor now moved north to Amsterdam, turning it from a small village into what Antwerp had formerly been: the most active commercial center in Europe. But other northern

---

[*]Also, unwanted Calvinist fanaticism coming from the North did not help matters in the Southern Netherlands where Catholic sympathies were still strong.

[†]The fact that much of the urban coastal North had been built on land reclaimed from the sea by means of dikes and water pumps ... allowed the North to easily reflood those same lands ... making the movement of Spanish troops there almost impossible.

Dutch cities benefited as well.

The Northern Dutch secure their independence. At this point English Queen Elizabeth stepped in to give assistance to the Northern Dutch. Also the Dutch Republic came under the capable leadership of the younger Prince of Orange (his father having been assassinated a few years earlier). Finally, with the Protestant Henry IV taking the kingship in France and Philip's determination to punish the English for their piracy (and Protestantism), Philip at this point gave up on his program of forcing the Dutch back under his personal control. He had bigger problems.

Elizabethan England (second half of the 1500s)

Bloody Mary (r. 1553-1558). When Henry died in 1547 his young son Edward came in line to receive the kingship of England. But he was a mere youth and England was placed under the rule of a number of adult advisors who tried to guide the monarchy through the treacherous path created by the split in Christendom. But the sickly Edward died before he reached his majority, and his half-sister Mary came to the throne.

As a feudal bargaining chip, Mary earlier had been proposed in marriage to a number of European monarchs. But when her father Henry divorced her mother not only did she lose her value, she had good cause to fear for her life. She – and soon her half-sister Elizabeth – would both become outcasts as their father moved on in his marriages. Mary took refuge in her deep Catholic faith, which she saw as her sole protection. Finally in 1553 she found her faith rewarded when she became English queen. She married Philip II of Spain and with him attempted to restore the Catholic faith – on her part in England. The Pope however was of no particular help to her, demanding the return of the Church's lands confiscated by her father. This she was unable to do.

But she did make a move to kill off the most influential of her Protestant opponents at home, such as Cranmer, Ridley and Latimer (and several hundred others) – earning her the title "Bloody Mary." She also attempted to undermine the industrial and commercial wealth of the new nobility by placing various restrictions on their operations. She cowed the Protestants – but at the same time heightened their sense of outrage against Catholicism. Then, never a very healthy person, Mary died of a disease after only a quite short rule of five years.

Elizabeth (r. 1558-1603). Elizabeth now faced the same perilous dynamic ... though she played her hand very differently than Mary. At 25 she was attractive and a natural object of marriage in the dynastic system of Europe. But Elizabeth was not about to become a pawn in a male-dominated game (though that would change as the 1500s rolled along and a number of European women came to be major players by their own rights in the political game). She had no desire to surrender England as dowry in marriage, enhancing some European king's landholdings. And thus she would remain all the way to her death the "Virgin Queen."

As far as her personal loyalties in the Protestant-Catholic debate splitting Europe, she gave little indication as to where she stood. She once had been under the protection of the Protestant Catherine Parr, the last of Henry's wives ... and many supposed her to be a Protestant in her accession to the throne. But outwardly she appeared neutral ... at least initially. Thus she tried to mediate between her Catholic and Protestant subjects. But efforts from abroad to pressure her to return England back to Papal supervision tended to hurt badly the position of the English Catholics. Also, she found herself increasingly having to look to the industrial/merchant class of England for support ... a class that was becoming increasingly Protestant.

Furthermore, she found herself being dragged into the Protestant-Catholic battle going on to the north of England in Scotland. Another young Mary, very pro-Catholic, was waiting to receive the crown as Queen of Scots, with her own mother Mary of Guise meanwhile serving as regent ... the Guises being the group heading up the Catholic anti-Huguenot party in France. Opposed to the two Marys were a large number of Scottish noblemen, led by the tough Calvinist John Knox.

For Elizabeth, Scotland constituted a major problem with its strong French influence there. Although Knox seemed to have Scotland well in hand after Mary of Guise died suddenly in 1560, the younger Mary – who was now Queen of Scots – remained a thorn in Elizabeth's side. She was Elizabeth's cousin ... with strong claims of her own to the throne of England. However, Mary's poor political skills proved to be her undoing in Scotland, and in 1567 she was forced to flee Scotland to England – where Elizabeth immediately put her under house arrest. Now she intrigued all the more against Elizabeth. Finally having enough of her cousin's interference, Elizabeth had her put to death in 1587 ... part of the reason for Philip II to send his Armada to crush English arrogance (as he saw things).

The Puritans. Although clearly England was heading in a Protestant direction, the speed of this movement was not fast enough for some of the reformers. This latter group eventually received the title of contempt as "puritans" by other reformers. Both reforming groups were Calvinist, so Protestant theology was not the issue, at least not initially. Mostly the arguments originally occurred over style and ritual: for instance, the wearing of fancy vestments (surplices or lace gowns) by the clergy – which the Puritans opposed fervently.   Questions arose over free prayers (which the Puritans supported) versus recitations from the *Book of Common Prayer* (supported by the more traditionalist reformers). Puritans wanted the elimination of everything from Christian practice that did not have a direct warrant in Scripture. Clearly liturgical prayers and fancy vestments did not have such Scriptural warrant. Then too Puritans insisted on the importance of the preaching/teaching ministry at a time when the vast number of churches performed on Sundays only liturgies drawn from the prayer book. Elizabeth herself saw no need for the preaching ministry. But for the Puritans this was a major matter.

Tempers heated up when the bishops pushed the use of the prayer book as a matter of great principle (and threatened persecution) ... which then led the Puritans to the question of "why bishops at all?" Geneva under Calvin, Scotland under Knox and the Huguenots in France had eliminated this religious hierarchy. Calvinist congregations were largely self-supporting and united their churches not through a top-down episcopal hierarchy but through bottom-up gatherings of representatives of the churches at the Presbytery (region) and Synod (larger or national) level – a system termed Presbyterianism.

Overall ... at the time of Elizabeth's death in 1603 ... little had been resolved concerning the challenges raised by the Puritans.

Meanwhile ... Italy

Much to the distress of Machiavelli, the Italians found themselves unable to answer the challenges to Italian independence posed by the intrusions of the rising monarchs to the west (Spain) and north (France) of Italy (and occasionally the other Habsburg power, the Holy Roman or Austrian Empire). Italy became the playing ground for the military matches between these non-Italian powers ... aided and abetted by Italian city-states who foolishly hoped that an alliance with one or the other of these greater powers would increase their own hand in Italy. It did quite the opposite, making the Italian city-states political dependents, either of Spain or of France.

Italy itself thus appeared to be totally unable to do anything to fend off these intruders. Consequently, the southern half of the Italian peninsula below Rome fell into the hands of the Spanish. And the French moved with increasing boldness to take lands directly (Nice) and to dominate or control directly much of Northern Italy.

From 1494 to 1559 foreign wars fought in Italy became a regular and highly destructive feature of Italian life. The once powerful city-states of Italy at this point simply ceased to be able to control further their own destiny. Most shocking of all, in 1527 Spanish and German troops sacked

Rome at will during one of Charles and Francis's feuds – making the Pope look even more helpless in the larger scheme of things.

Finally, the drift of the vital East-West trade out of the Mediterranean and instead onto the high seas of the Atlantic, Indian, and Pacific Oceans drew away from Italy its earning powers, transferring them to the European city-states and monarchies bordering the Atlantic. From its grandeur as the leading European cultural/economic center during the 1400s Renaissance, Italy in the 1500s fell into a grim decline that it could not slow up, much less halt. By the year 1600 Italy was only a dim reflection of its former glory.

The Polish-Lithuanian Commonwealth

Since medieval times Poland and Lithuania had been closely connected through the person of the King of Poland, who was also the Duke of Lithuania. In 1569 this East-European union became formalized as the Polish-Lithuanian Commonwealth, making it at that time one of the largest and most populous of the European states. The ethnic makeup of the Commonwealth was diverse ... as was its religious makeup. Catholics and Protestants lived side by side in a relative degree of tolerance unusual for the times, especially unusual with the Wars of Religion raging around the borders of the Commonwealth.

The Commonwealth was based on a constitutional monarchy where the king's power was greatly limited by the power of the rather independent nobles ... a power exercised through their ruling council, the Sejm.

But with foreign (Swedish) sovereigns occupying the Polish-Lithuanian throne after 1572, huge troubles descended on the Commonwealth ... as the Catholic branch of the House of Vasa (governing Poland-Lithuania) found itself constantly at war with the Protestant Lutheran branch of the House of Vasa (governing Sweden). Sadly, the Polish Vasa kings tended to be more interested in their personal standing within Vasa family disputes than with the issues facing their Polish-Lithuanian subjects. Thus with a distracted monarchy and a powerful set of subordinate noblemen angling for power, the Commonwealth found itself increasingly divided and politically weakened.

Further to the East: Russia under Ivan IV ("The Terrible")

Ivan's predecessors. Ivan was the grandson of the Grand Prince of Moscow, Ivan III – whose 43-year reign saw Moscow expand its territory against the Republic of Novgorod ... and then throw off the yoke of the Golden Horde and go on to establish a highly autocratic Russian state (against much opposition from the Russian noblemen or boyars – and also from some of his brothers.)

The strong-handed Ivan III passed his reign on to his son Vasilli III, who continued the expansion of Moscow against other Russian city-states (most importantly Smolensk), against Lithuania (which dominated Eastern Europe from the Baltic to the Black Sea – including Kyiv) and Lithuania's ally Poland (immediately to the West and then South of Lithuania) ... and against the Khanate of Crimea. So that when Vasili passed his reign on to his own son Ivan, Ivan IV already had a legacy of heavy-handed Russian expansion through the ever-strengthening Grand Prince of Moscow's personal government.

Ivan IV (1533-1584). But in fact Ivan could be even more brutal than his predecessors ... though at the same time he was a patron of the arts, science, literature and commerce, was personally devout, quite intelligent, and an excellent diplomat – and in general very popular with the Russian commoners. But he suffered from bouts of paranoia which turned into insane rage ... at one point in a fit of rage accidently killing the son he was grooming to succeed him.

Despite his struggle with insanity, he actually succeeded in a number of ways in building up his Russian economic and political power base. He worked hard to build economic relations across the Baltic and North Sea with England, leading to the creation in 1555 of the Muscovy Company in England – the forerunner of the English trading corporation that would be at the heart of an eventual English rise to power. He took protective interest in Eastern or Byzantine Christianity in the Middle East. And he moved boldly eastward conquering the Khanates of Kazan (1552) and Astrakhan (1556), securing the Volga region for Russia.

His reign was constantly troubled by the strong neighbors to the west, the close allies, Lithuania and Poland – and also Sweden. Wars on that front were constant ... producing little by way of rewards for Ivan.

And like his father and grandfather, he had on-going problems with the nobility or boyars – who resented his absolutist hold over Moscow.

In 1565 He created a personal bodyguard of some 1000 soldiers (eventually 6,000), the *Oprichniki* by which he targeted opposing boyars for execution. ... and by which Ivan sacked and burned the fabulous Novgorod (1570) when, during a great plague which ripped through the city, he grew suspicious that the Novgorod noblemen were about to turn to Lithuania for help. He turned the Oprichniki loose on the Novgorod population, slaughtering countless numbers (2,000-3,000?) ... leaving the once noble city unable to ever rise to greatness again.

Likewise, his problems with the Crimean Tatars were ongoing. Relations finally came to a head in 1572 over the slave raids conducted by the Tatars deep into Russian lands. A huge Tatar army heading north was met by a Russian army half the size. But the capable *streltsy* (soldiers carrying firearms) routed the Tatar army so thoroughly that it broke both Tatar and Ottoman Turkish ambitions to advance into central Russia. However, in that same battle, the Oprichniki failed so miserably against the Tatars that Ivan ordered the Oprichniki unit dissolved.

Finally, in the latter years of Ivan's rule, Russians pushed eastwards toward the Ural Mountains, then crossed those mountains and continued moving eastward into Siberia. Ivan authorized the Stroganov family to settle to the east of the Ural Mountains. Employing a small force of Cossacks, they brought the tribes under Russian domination – and under Tsarist, not Stroganov, authority. With the help of Ivan's streltsy sent to work with the Cossacks, Ivan thus towards the end of his life (1584) came into the position of being the Tsar of Siberia.

✳ ✳ ✳

THE FIRST HALF OF THE 1600s

An overview

The Wars of Religion. It is usual to caption the first half of the 1600s as the time of an almost endless series of "Wars of Religion." Indeed, religion played a part ... though it was not really religion that caused these wars. Religion only justified these wars. What this tumultuous period was all about was the realignment of political power caused by the collapse of Christendom. The old moral order overseen by the Pope and Holy Roman Emperor had definitely disappeared ... and there was a scramble of rising political figures bent on securing for themselves a stronger position in the emerging status quo. This really was therefore a war of rising states, both monarchical (kings) and commercial (city-states). With the collapse of old Christendom, there were no rules in the struggle ... and so it became an all-out war of player against player. Therefore, the period properly ought to be termed "The Era of the Political Wars of the Post-Christendom States"!

The Thirty Years' War (1618-1648). It is also termed the period of the "Thirty-Years' War." Actually, wars among the rising European states had been going on rather constantly over the previous century, though they tended to reach a particularly devastating proportion in the 30-year period of 1618 to 1648. And the exhaustion experienced by all the players in this 30-year struggle finally brought something of a more enduring truce (though by no means end) to the inter-state conflicts. Indeed, it seemed to mark the beginning of a new era in European politics (and European history).

The Treaty of Westphalia (1648) and the dawn of a new era. The peace treaty of 1648 would end up not being just another one of the many truces that had provided only a temporary pause in the fights. Westphalia marked a deep resolve among the contenders to accept things as they had come to be politically by 1648 ... and to turn to something other than religion on which to guide their political ideals and justify their ambitions. Thus it was that non-religious or secular science would begin to take the place of Christian theology as the new worldview undergirding the new thoughts and dreams of political philosophers and political activists appearing at the end of this period of war.

Indeed, at this point Christianity itself would enter into a time of deep contempt by the more "enlightened" Europeans ... who were certain that they were on the path of discovery of something much higher, more noble than the worn-out moral-spiritual standards of Christianity.

Spanish power begins to slip. The wars had been costly to all of the dynastic and urban contenders, but to Spain most of all. In all the years of Spain's great wealth in American plunder, Spain had never put that wealth to work, but had merely consumed it as it rolled in across the Atlantic ... squandering that wealth in a grand display of status-enhancing material splendor – and in a constant round of wars with other European powers. The latter had proven costly to Spain, especially the ones waged against both the rebellious Dutch and the piratical English.

The drying up of the American plunder in gold. Everything about the Spanish economy depended on the continuous flow of American wealth. But the plunder would run out as the Spanish stripped the Indian societies of their stock in gold. Confiscated silver would soon be substituted ... and then slavery of the Indian population to force them to continue to dig the precious metal from the ground – in order to feed the material appetite of Spain. But this substitute of silver would not permit Spain to continue to live at the material level it had grown accustomed to when it was living on plundered gold. The silver mines would not suffice to pay the mercenary armies fighting the king's wars, the navy needed to protect this flow of wealth from the Americas, and the thousands of government officials and noble families dependent on this flow. Thus Spain would decline ... inevitably.

The beginning of the Spanish decline

Mediocre kings and royal advisors. Besides the all-important factor of the gold flow to Spain slowing up as key to a relentless decline that set in upon Spain in the 1600s, was that this this process was greatly accelerated by the line of mediocre Habsburg kings (and their advisers) who followed Charles and Philip in the 1600s: Philip III (King of Spain, 1598 to 1621) and his son Philip IV (King of Spain, 1621 to 1665). They were not bad kings ... just not the caliber of leaders needed by a great society to hold on to that greatness ... a problem common to all great societies in decline. Both kings depended on their chief ministers, the Duke of Lerma under Philip III and the Count-Duke Olivares under Philip IV. Further, Philip IV was burdened financially by the costliness of the wars on land and sea that were a central piece in the 30 Years' War. The English and French had allied against Habsburg Spanish power – a challenge that Philip knew he had to answer. Under Olivares's advisement, Philip attempted to reform Spanish government to make it more efficient so that he could cover the costs of war (the flow of American gold and silver having slowed up) ... but in the process only alienated the traditional Castilian aristocracy that had been the bedrock of royal power. Then he began to lose further control of the political situation when in 1640 first the Catalans, supported by the French, revolted – soon followed by the Portuguese (who sixty years earlier had been brought into the Spanish Habsburg realm) who did likewise. Compromise (and removing Olivares) would eventually bring some of the crisis under control – though from 1640 on, Portugal would remain independent under the new Braganza dynasty.

The Battle of Rocroi. But the biggest blow came in 1643 when Philip's army was sent south from the Spanish Netherlands (Belgium) to attack France in order to divert the French from their support of the Catalan revolt. But the tactic turned out to be a disaster for the Spanish. It was the first major defeat of the Spanish army since Spain's rise to power in the 1500s – and clearly signaled a huge slippage of Spain as the leading power of continental Europe. France would soon be occupying that prestigious position.

The rise of France

King Louis XIII and Cardinal Richelieu. The first half of 1600s-France belongs largely to Louis XIII (reigned 1610 to 1643) ... and his capable (and shrewd) advisor, Cardinal Richelieu. Louis was only nine years old when his father Henry IV was assassinated – thus the monarchy came immediately under a regency ... that of his manipulating mother, Marie de Medici and her corrupt Italian entourage.[*] At age 16 Louis took full control,

---

[*]She had a reputation as a schemer. It was believed by many at the time (and by some still today) that she was somehow involved in Henry IV's death.

soon sending his mother into exile ... and executing her Italian friends. She was eventually restored to privilege ... but continued to intrigue against her son and her son's trusted advisor, Armand Jean du Plessis, the Cardinal-Duke of Richelieu.

Against the French nobility. Louis had other problems at home (besides his mother and his rebellious younger brother Gaston!): the independent-minded French nobility and the Protestant Huguenots. Richelieu convinced Louis to order the destruction of all the castles of the nobility, sparing only those of clear strategic worth to the monarchy. This not only deprived the nobility of their prestige, but also of their real power. It was the beginning of the French monarchy as an absolutist institution (all power to the king ... and to him alone!). Thus he was widely hated by the French nobility. But Richelieu was not one to be contended with.

Against the Protestant Huguenots. Richelieu also stood at the center of the decision to bring to an end the power and influence of the French Protestant Huguenots. Early efforts at seizing their various strongholds located around France (mostly in the South) met with mixed results. Finally in 1628 the major Huguenot fortress of La Rochelle was overrun by Louis's army ... led personally by Richelieu. The defeated Huguenots however were still permitted to practice their religion as per Henry IV's Edict of Nantes (which had promised certain religious freedoms to the Huguenots). But in losing La Rochelle, the Huguenots no longer had any muscle of their own to protect themselves against any further attacks on their religious freedoms in France.

In the New World (New France). Since the early 1500s, France had been involved in exploring the lands to the north of the Spanish Habsburg holdings in Central and South America.   Francis I had sent (1520s) first the Florentine navigator Giovanni da Verrazzano to explore these coastal regions (the first European to discover what is today New York) ... then Cartier (1530s) to explore even further north along the St. Lawrence River – which they hoped was a river route which would cross the Americas and permit them to continue to sail West to Asia – laying claim to New France in the process. But French settlements there at first failed to take hold. Later (1564) Huguenots escaping troubles in France settled in the area of what is today northern Florida (Jacksonville) – though the Spanish quickly reacted and sacked the French settlement there. Not until the early 1600s would the French under Samuel de Champlain try again to establish settlements in the New World ... at Quebec (1608), on commanding heights above the St. Lawrence River, and here and there along the islands lying to the

South of the entrance to the River ... what would eventually become French Acadia. French settlers were encouraged to befriend the Indians ... whom the French considered as fully French in accepting Catholicism and learning the French language. French fur hunters and traders took Indian wives and soon informally extended French influence deep into Canada.

But until Richelieu took a strong interest in the American project, French settlement itself remained thin ... particularly in comparison to New England, just to the south of New France (where by 1630 thousands of English were beginning to settle). Huguenots were not permitted to settle in New France ... and thus just as New England was devoutly Protestant, New France by careful design was devoutly Catholic. Extending feudal rights to French lords or seigneurs willing to organize and oversee communities of settlers, New France finally began to grow (only in the second half of the 1600s however ... and slowly at that).

Against Spain. A continuous problem, inherited from Louis's predecessors, was Habsburg Spain. Despite efforts to forge a friendship with Spain through marriage (Louis was married to Anne of Austria, daughter of Philip III of Spain), and despite both kingdoms being staunchly Catholic, the Spanish and French kings (Louis and Philip IV) were natural contenders for dominance in continental Europe ... especially as Spanish holdings surrounded French holdings on virtually every front: Spain itself, Belgium, Luxembourg, Western Germany, and Northern Italy. Thus it was that the Catholic Cardinal Richelieu advised Louis to ally with the Protestant Netherlands in the on-going Spanish-Dutch war which raged during the Thirty-Years' War. But similarly, Catholic Spain sent aid to the rebellious French Huguenots to keep Louis occupied at home in France while the Spanish strengthened their position in Northern Italy!

Louis did not live long enough to see the massive French victory over the Spanish at Rocroi in 1643 (he died in Paris of tuberculosis just days before the battle). But he left to his 4-year-old son Louis XIV a monarchy well on the way to being the major player in the European dynastic game.

The onset of the Dutch "Golden Age"

Cruel adversity toughens the Dutch spirit. The Dutch North or Netherlands, though tiny in size on the European map, had turned itself into a powerful commercial center ... complete with its own vast commercial empire, soon reaching around the world. Cruel adversity had steeled the wills of the Dutch and, along with their work ethic, had transformed them into the most industrial-minded people of Europe. They were very creative in their industriousness, setting up in Amsterdam the first multinational bank, doing business with interested investors across all sorts of political boundaries. Also, at Amsterdam the first stock exchange was established, where investors (or "adventurers") could put their money in a new enterprise ... with the hope of making a huge profit when the enterprise met its industrial or commercial goal. Of course there were risks of failure. But the strong-willed Dutch were willing to take those risks.

Dutch commercial expansion. While they made much of their money in manufacture, the greatest portion came through commerce or trade. The Dutch were superior tradesmen, purchasing the goods of distant lands and returning those goods by sea to Europe ... making huge profits in the process. They thus developed a vast merchant fleet (the Dutch possessed more merchant ships than all other European powers combined) protected by a very able navy. They quickly outpaced the Portuguese in terms of their commercial reach. Indeed, the Dutch East Indies Company soon became the largest commercial enterprise connecting Europe with Asia.

The Dutch-Portuguese War (1598-1663). This process of Dutch expansion – largely at the cost of the Portuguese – did not happen overnight, but took decades to achieve. The contest between these two commercial empires was global, from the Americas in the West to the Indies in the East ... though the East Indies portion of the war would prove to be the more important engagement of the Dutch. Success in overrunning most of the Portuguese positions there turned out to be very profitable for the Dutch ... as the demand for the spices nutmeg, mace and cloves found in the Spice Islands was running very high at the time.

Dutch South Africa. Although the Dutch did not succeed in displacing the Portuguese in coastal southern Africa, when it came to the vital position at Africa's southern-most tip at the Cape of Good Hope, the Dutch were most focused. From that strategic point they could then proceed directly east to the Spice Islands of the East Indies. But they secured the area not only militarily, but also demographically ... establishing a large Dutch settlement at what would come to be known as Cape Town.

Local resistance from the native African population was rather light. The San (Bushmen or Hottentots) were a very primitive hunting society, thinly spread across the region. The more dangerous Bantu African tribesmen had not yet reached the area in their own expansion southward along the East African coast. In fact, both groups, Dutch White and Bantu Black were very surprised to run into each other a century later (the later 1700s) when the two groups, the Dutch spreading northeastward and the Bantu (Xhosa tribesmen) spreading southwestward, met at the Fish River (about halfway across today's South Africa).

In short, the Dutch were doing in South Africa what the English were doing at that same time in North America: extending their population deeply into overseas lands. And – just as the English of America were beginning to identify themselves primarily as "Americans" – so too the Dutch of South Africa were calling themselves "Afrikaners"! And like the English-American frontiersmen who were largely self-sufficient Protestant farmers, so too were the Afrikaners – identifying themselves as such also with the name "Boer" (Dutch simply for "farmer) – and quite proud of that identity ... as these Boer families spread themselves ever-deeper into the South African interior.

Dutch America. Also, like the Spanish, Portuguese and French (and soon the English) the Dutch, through their West Indies Company, got deeply involved in opening up commerce and settlement across the Atlantic in the Americas. They established a "New Netherlands" in the middle reaches of North America, ranging from what is today Connecticut in the north to Delaware in the South – with New Amsterdam (today's New York City) as its capital. They particularly focused on the "North River" (Hudson River) ... hoping it was the waterway that led across the American continent to the Pacific. Eventually finding this hope groundless, they nonetheless placed Dutch forts and numerous Dutch settlers along the fertile shoreline of this mighty river, and opened up trade in furs with the Indians. Here too, the Dutch population began to grow.

Dutch independence. Meanwhile, the Habsburg Spanish were refusing to give up in their effort to retake their ancestral northern Dutch or Habsburg lands ... as they had so successfully retaken the southern Dutch lands (Flemish lands actually). But besides the fact that the entrepreneurial Dutch were quite capable at self-defense, both the English and the French tended to ally with the Dutch against powerful Habsburg Spain. Finally, in 1648 the Spanish had had enough of the effort and in the Treaty of Westphalia acknowledged the independence of the Dutch Republic.

The highly sophisticated Dutch culture. But the Dutch were not just about business. Art and architecture flourished, with Dutch artists being some of Europe's finest (Rembrandt van Rijn and Jan Vermeer, for instance ... among many others). Education and science took a huge lead in the Netherlands, with the establishment of a number of outstanding universities ... and excellent scholarship. The practical Dutch were fascinated by the physical world around them and studied it closely, Christiaan Huygens and Antonie van Leeuwenhoek being among the leading scientists of their times. But the Dutch could also lead in the world of scholarly philosophy, Baruch Spinoza – a Dutch Jew of Amsterdam – being an example. So free (relatively speaking anyway) was the academic atmosphere for study and writing that other Europeans relocated there ... such as the famous French philosopher Descartes (from 1628 to just before his death in 1650).

Some of the other major players of the day

Gustavus Adolphus's Sweden. Under the kingship (1611 to 1632) of this exceptionally talented military commander,* Gustavus Adolphus, Sweden in short order grew in status from being merely a regional power to being one of the major powers of early 1600s Europe. Pressing the Protestant cause in the Thirty Years' War or Wars of Religion, he took on most notably the very Catholic Eastern Habsburg Empire (the Holy Roman or Austrian Empire) ... and his Catholic cousin, Sigismund, King of Poland and Grand Duke of Lithuania. Much of the Thirty Years' War centered on this competition between Sweden and the two huge Eastern European states of Austria and Poland-Lithuania. Spain, Prussia and France also weighed in big in the War. But Gustav Adolphus's Sweden seemed to be at the heart of things.

Interestingly, when Gustav Adolphus was killed in battle in 1632, his five-year old daughter (his only surviving child) Christina took over the Swedish throne (actually in 1644) ... focusing as much on learning and culture as her father had on warfare. Meanwhile the business of state, as well as the excellent Swedish military, was handed over to Christina's Chancellor Axel Oxenstierna. He effectively governed Sweden until his death in 1654. He not only maintained the strong military tradition of Sweden, but worked hard at developing a modern bureaucracy by which to govern the holdings of the Swedish Vasa dynasty.

Unfortunately at this point (1654), when Christina abdicated, Sweden fell into the hands of a less able king, Charles X Gustav, who continued to involve Sweden in a constant round of battles in North-central Europe (Germany and Poland) which ravaged the cities and countryside of the region. However, he lived only a half-dozen years before passing on the throne to his son Charles XI, who was largely a man of peace during the next four decades.

The Polish-Lithuanian Commonwealth.   In the mid-1600s the Commonwealth was assaulted from all directions, but principally from the

---

*Many – such as the Prussian Clausewitz, the Frenchman Napoleon and even the American Patton – considered Gustavus Adolphus a military genius, and studied carefully his use of heavy artillery, smaller but very mobile infantry units, and speed rather than mass in the employment of his troops.

East by the Russians who overran the eastern half of the Commonwealth and from the north by the Swedes who overran almost all of the western half of the Commonwealth (the "Swedish Deluge") ... the latter invaders creating such mayhem that nearly a third of the Commonwealth's population died from military action, hunger or disease. Worst hit were the cities, hundreds of which were totally destroyed by the invading Swedes (Warsaw lost about 90% of its population). This began the rapid decline of the once-great Poland-Lithuania, until both societies disappeared completely in the late 1700s, absorbed by their neighbors Russia, Austria and Prussia.

Germany. We mention Germany at this point only to make the point that Germany really did not exist as a political player in the 1600s. Instead Germany was a collection of a vast number of kingdoms, duchies, cities ... in theory all under the authority of the Holy Roman Emperor ... that is, the Habsburg Emperor of Austria. The reality was however that the Habsburg Austrian Emperor governed effectively less than a third of Germany (in the East and South of the German region). The rest of Germany was made up of small mini-states under one or another local ruler. This made for such weakness that an unprotected Germany typically served as the useful battleground for the various contending parties during the Wars of Religion of the first half of the 1600s.

Germany was devastated by these ongoing wars ... losing over a third of its population (in some areas far worse than that figure) ... through the battles, the devastation of the land (again, in great part by the Swedes) and the resultant hunger, and the diseases which accompanied all of that. Unfortunately for Germany, it would remain a victim-territory until well into the 1800s ... when finally (1870) the Prussians (led by the skillful Chancellor Bismarck) would succeed in uniting most of Germany as the Second German Empire.

Stuart England

James I Stuart and the Divine Rights Theory. During the reign of Queen Elizabeth (1558-1603) there had been a moderately tolerant working relationship between the Queen and the Protestant (Calvinist) reformers. The burghers of London and other English cities were for her an invaluable source of financial and other support for her rule – which was continually on the defensive against the likes of the "Catholic" defender Philip II of Spain.

Lacking an heir of her own, it became apparent that Tudor rule would eventually pass into the hands of the Stuarts of Scotland. Although Elizabeth's cousin Mary Stuart had been an ardent Catholic, her son James (king of Scotland as James VI) had been raised in Protestant (Calvinist) circles. Thus, in 1603 when Elizabeth died and indeed James came to the English throne as James I, it might have appeared that the going would henceforth be better for the Protestants in England.

In many ways James played to the Protestant reformers. He sponsored a new English translation of the Bible (the venerable King James version!), which pleased the reformers greatly (though the Puritans seemed to continue to rely mostly on their beloved English-language Geneva Bibles). He also was himself strongly opposed to the re-opening of England to Catholicism – though mostly for political reasons than for reasons of religious conscience.

But he also was a very strong "royalist," fully supportive of the "divine rights theory" of monarchy by which the claim was put forth that kings were responsible to God alone – and not to any human agency (such as Parliament). Unfortunately, he would soon discover that Parliament had a mind of its own and expected the king to share rule with Parliament. Little by little, tensions began to mount as the King and Parliament came into conflict.

Part of his difficulty would be over the matter of religion. James had during his earlier days as King of Scotland tired of the "upstart" behavior of the Scottish Calvinists. He was now prepared to rule directly over the Christian community in England – through an episcopal system of archbishops and bishops that linked all the Church of England to his personal rule as Head of the Church of England. Thus he was much opposed to the Calvinist idea of Presbyterian government by "elders" or leaders chosen from among the commoner or burgher class at the local level. During his rule (both in England and Scotland), he actively opposed the growth of such independent or "separatist" communities and congregations – that is, local communities and churches that tried to work independently of the episcopal system.

Overall, this was not a position all that different from Elizabeth's – except that he lacked her political insights and thus found himself in trouble on a number of fronts at the same time.

The development of Puritan power. Cambridge University was at this time a hot-bed of Calvinist religious thinking. Sons of prosperous English burghers came to this venerable institution to explore a world of widening economic, intellectual and spiritual opportunities. Here at Cambridge young men began to fashion a purist or "Puritan" vision of a newly emerging society, one operating directly under the sovereignty of God ... making the place of the sovereign king a bit problematic. They supported what was sort of a theory of "divine rights" of burghers – in opposition to the "divine rights" theory of the monarchy. These independent-minded scions of the burgher class came to see themselves not as essentially subjects of the English crown, but as subjects of God. According to their Calvinist or

Puritan mindset, individuals were to be led in living out their lives guided or governed only by their own scripturally-disciplined minds and their own prayerfully-cultivated Christian consciences. Nothing was to stand between themselves and their beloved God. Not even an English king.

Separatists and Puritans. It was not long however before there was a growing division taking place within the English Calvinist or Puritan ranks ... between those who sought simply to "purify" the mother Church of England of its non-Scriptural theology and behavior .... and those who came to be termed as "Separatists " – who had simply given up on the project of trying to reform the Church of England. The Separatists had come to the conclusion that the King was so adamantly opposed to serious reform that there was no point in continuing to try to reform the Church of England. Separatists were Puritans who simply were ready finally to "separate" from the mother Church.

The other Puritans were not pleased with Separatism, considering the Separatists as being something like traitors to the reform cause. Puritans were not ready to give up the fight to reform the mother church ... not yet anyway.

Charles I (1625 – 1649). When James died in 1625, his son Charles I came to power. Generally, policies continued much as they had under James – except that the debate over royal power was now widening and deepening in intensity. On the continent the doctrine of royal absolutism (all power rightly belongs to the king) was being aggressively put forward in the French (Louis XIII) and Spanish (Philip IV) courts. Inevitably the issue came to England.

Charles immediately upon his accession to power brought an even more aggressively royalist and aristocratic (or "cavalier") mood into English politics. Charles favored the old landed families (many of whom had Catholic sympathies) over the new independent-minded burgher (urban middle class) families in his appointments to the royal court. In particular, he allowed himself to come under the dominating influence of Buckingham, one of his father's advisors. Buckingham was very much a royal absolutist – one who was inclined to make no compromises with the burgher interests of Parliament.

Charles also stirred considerable political resentment by immediately putting aside all the laws that had blocked Catholicism from English politics. Likewise, his diplomacy of befriending Catholic kings on the continent (even marrying his son to a Catholic Spanish princess) was interpreted as the precursor of even reestablishing Catholicism in England. This was not something that the Puritan majority in the House of Commons would take lying down. The stage for violent confrontation was thus being set even from the outset of Charles' rule.

Charles tried for eleven years to rule without Parliament – which meant also ruling without the financial support of this powerful group of English merchants. This forced him to take very contrived and largely unsuccessful measures to raise his own monies in order to maintain his royal courts and armies. Charles simultaneously tried to engage in foreign ventures he hoped would rally the English to his side. But tensions only mounted with the gentry who would not play into his programs.

Rapidly deteriorating political conditions. Charles eventually turned more and more to William Laud, archbishop of Canterbury, for ideological support. The appointment of Laud, a self-professed Arminian,[*] as Archbishop of Canterbury angered the Calvinist Puritans enormously – who saw this as a move against their own position (which it was!). Further, Laud's efforts to put the entire Christian community in England under episcopal rule and in total conformity to the Prayer Book only drove the wedge deeper between the royal court and the Puritans in Parliament.

When a rebellion in Ireland flared up, the issue of who should control the army came to the fore. Pym, leader of the more reformist members of Parliament, narrowly succeeded in a vote to place the army under Parliamentary authority. But Charles refused to yield. With this, England found itself in a state of deep political division between King and Parliament. It now had two armies: the King's and Parliament's. Things were heading towards a show-down.

But it was his Scottish subjects who would actually start the open rebellion against Charles ... when he attempted to unite the heavily Calvinist Church of Scotland with his Church of England. Specifically, when Laud tried to impose the Prayer Book on the Scottish church, an explosion in Scotland occurred. In 1639 Charles sent his ill-paid royal army into Scotland to force acceptance of this decree ... only to find himself met strongly by Scottish forces. A truce was agreed on, which Charles soon broke in a second attack on Scotland the following year.

Parliament takes the initiative. Again, things went poorly for Charles in Scotland ... and desperate for funding for his army, he called Parliament

---

*The Dutch Reformer Jakob Arminius (1560-1609) questioned the strict Calvinist (Pauline) understanding that salvation was by grace extended by God alone ... not by human good intentions or good works. His supporters, the Remonstrants, insisted that salvation was at least in part a matter of the free choosing of the individual. A Dutch synod held at Dort in 1618-1619 – attended by Calvinists from other parts of Europe – opposed strongly the Remonstrants and their "Arminianism."

back into session in late 1640. But when Parliament put forth its own demands for the undoing of Laud's episcopalian reforms in exchange for its cooperation – the King dissolved Parliament (the Short Parliament) immediately. But the king's situation only deteriorated and soon he had to call Parliament (the "Long Parliament") back into session. This Parliament would not be dissolved until 20 years later. It was about to become the effective ruler of England.

Parliament now took action ... to remove (and subsequently execute) Laud, to greatly restrict the King's ability to raise revenues, and to make it impossible for the King to dissolve Parliament without its own consent.

Charles at first complied ... hoping to avoid what was clearly becoming a drift toward war in England itself.

But the King fought back, especially when he saw division setting in among the ranks of Parliament as to how to proceed, whether moderately or radically. In early 1642, Charles moved to have five of Parliament's leaders arrested ... but warned ahead, the five had already fled when Charles showed up with an armed guard. This event proved to be politically disastrous for Charles, now driving the Parliamentary moderates into the arms of the radicals.

Fearing what might happen next, Charles immediately headed north. But then in mid-1642, he decided to return to London. Some of the country was coming out in support of him (basically the conservative countryside) and he was hoping to force his way back into supremacy. But urban England (and the navy) supported Parliament. And thus the two sides gathered armed forces in direct opposition to each other. The English Civil War was now underway, initially taking the form of local battles here and there around England.

The Civil War (1642 – 1649). At first the war seemed to go in favor of Charles and his "Cavaliers." But by 1643 the fortunes of war seemed to be turning in favor of the Parliamentary troops and their army of "Roundheads" (identified by their short haircuts ... in distinction to the long curls of the Cavaliers, which was the fashion at the time in the royal courts of Europe). Charles's army, though superior in size, proved timid ... and gave the Parliamentary army an opportunity to organize itself. Also, the Scottish army in 1643 came into the struggle on the side of the English Parliamentary forces.

Finally, in 1644 the very capable Oliver Cromwell began to make his way forward as a military leader. He mixed Puritan spiritual discipline with incredible military discipline to produce a "New Model Army" – which proved itself to be a powerful fighting instrument on behalf of Parliament. In 1645, the entire Parliamentary Army, reorganized along Cromwell's lines, met and crushed the royalist forces at Naseby and Langport. The King escaped to Scotland, surrendering himself to Scottish authorities, only to have them in the following year (1646) – after receiving a huge payment from the English – turn him over to the English Parliamentary authorities. With Charles in prison the Civil War (at least its first phase) simply came to a close.

Disagreement within the Protestant ranks of Parliament. At this point a split occurred within the ranks of the Parliamentary coalition. Most of the Protestant members of Parliament were "Presbyterian" in persuasion and were willing to free the King in exchange for the establishment of the Presbyterian form of church government throughout England. But many of the English Protestants, numerous in the Parliamentary army, were "independents" or "congregationalists" and wanted local congregations to have the right to organize themselves as they saw fit.*

This division led Charles to undertake from prison secret negotiations with the very Presbyterian Scots, promising the Scots to institute Presbyterianism in England in exchange for support by the Scottish army. Thus the character of the Civil War now shifted into something of a nationalist struggle – an English Parliamentary Army under Cromwell and a Scottish Presbyterian Army supporting Charles.

But again, in this second phase of the civil war (1648-1649), things did not go well for Charles ... or the Scottish Presbyterian army. Also Charles had been counting on his former supporters in England to retake arms. But most refused (having previously promised under oath not to do so). Those that did were quickly seized ... and beheaded (for breaking their oath).

The Rump Parliament. This led to the question of what to do about the King. The matter was quickly decided by the army itself when it marched on Parliament ("Pride's Purge") and arrested the MPs (Members of Parliament) who had been willing to work out a compromise with the King ... and blocked the entrance of most of the rest. The small number of MPs remaining (only

---

*As previously explained, Presbyterians supported the idea of a system of church unions, all the churches at the local or regional level constituting a Presbytery, a number of Presbyteries joined together to constitute at a higher level a Synod (Senate), and the Synods united into a General Assembly. Positions of membership and leadership in these bodies were entirely elective on a regular (even annual) basis by church members ... to ensure a democratic character of the whole. This was quite unlike the traditional episcopal system of church appointments from the Pope (or king!) on the top of the ecclesiastical order, on down to the archbishops, and then to the bishops. However, the independents or "Congregationalists" wanted to have no higher union above the local churches, each of which was supposed to be entirely self-running. The difference between the Presbyterian and Congregationalists was thus political, not religious, because both groups were strong Calvinists theologically.

75 of the original 470 members of the Long Parliament)* were ordered to set up a High Court of Justice to try the King on charges of high treason.

The King is beheaded (1649). Fearing that the King and the Presbyterians might work together to create a new pro-royalist Presbyterian Parliamentary army, there was only one verdict likely to be forthcoming from just such a court. Thus in January of 1649 the court found Charles guilty as charged ... and at the end of the month the King was beheaded.

The nation was shocked – but subdued by this show of power. In any case, this effectively removed the rallying cause for opponents of Cromwell and his army of Independents.

Charles II is proclaimed King ... but flees to France. Nonetheless, his eighteen-year-old son (also "Charles") was immediately proclaimed by the Royalists as King of England, Scotland and Ireland. Royalists in all three countries attempted to take power in the name of the new king. But all this did was to return all three lands to violent civil war.

Reacting to the announcement of Charles II's assumption of royal rights in Scotland, the Rump Parliament now moved to abolish the monarchy and the House of Lords, declaring England under a newly-drafted Constitution to be a "Commonwealth" directed by a Council of State. Actually ... it was Cromwell and his army which were in effective control of England at this point.

✳ ✳ ✳

ENGLISH AMERICA

Spain had not appeared as interested in North America in its efforts to bring the Western Hemisphere under Spanish control and therefore that area seemed to offer the best possibilities for others to get in on the act. By the beginning of the 1600s it seems that the time was right for others to do exactly that – particularly after the Spanish army and navy had experienced a string of disastrous setbacks trying to keep both their Dutch subjects from breaking away from Habsburg authority and the English privateers (actually merely pirates officially authorized by English Queen Elizabeth) from harassing the Spanish fleets bringing gold from America. Thus (as we have already seen) the French sent traders to Canada to take advantage of its great wealth in animal furs – and sent priests to Canada to bring Indian

---

*Actually, the Rump Parliament would see the gradual return of almost half of the original Members of Parliament ... most of whom considered the other half still to be fully Members of Parliament – and hoped to see some kind of compromise able to bring about their return.

souls to Christ. Also the commercially-minded Dutch set up a merchant corporation to bring back the wealth of the central shores of North America – and to find passage through America to Asia, hopefully up the Hudson River where they positioned some Dutch settlements.

The Virginia Company

A strictly commercial venture. Likewise, the English formed a similar merchant corporation, the Virginia Company, to do the same for the area along the shores of the Chesapeake Bay. In 1607 a small fleet set out to site a colony named Jamestown along the James River – both named after the English King, James I. The motif of the venture was the same as it had been for the Spanish: for the adventurers to find Indian gold and thus secure their positions as rising noblemen ... or at least as something like "gentlemen."

However, gentlemen did not perform manual labor – which presented a problem for the Virginia Company, as most of the participants in this venture were attempting to establish for themselves ratings as "gentlemen." John Smith succeeded in making himself unpopular by commanding his fellow merchant adventurers to take up necessary labor if they hoped to eat. Some had brought along indentured workers to do the work for them. But most of the adventurers attempted to avoid the responsibility of manual labor. As a consequence, the new plantation at Jamestown suffered tremendously from the lack of food. This, plus not taking the time to properly site the new colony (they put it alongside a mosquito-laden swamp) caused the adventurers to sicken and then die in droves. More workers were brought in, but the venture had enormous difficulty trying to function as a successful settled community.

Tobacco to the rescue. No gold of any significance was to be found in Virginia. But an entrepreneurial individual, John Rolf, picked up some tobacco seed when at first stranded in Bermuda and then was able to bring his discovery along with him to Virginia ... and start up what became a very thriving tobacco industry. Others caught on, and soon tobacco farming and shipping back to England became the economic mainstay of Virginia.

A Virginia aristocracy develops on the European model. However, the colony began slowly to settle in ... and develop a degree of social order. In 1619 a governing Assembly (the House of Burgesses) representing all male landowners in Virginia gathered in Jamestown as the first elected government in English America. However, it was understood that the representatives themselves to the House of Burgesses were naturally to be drawn from the class of local Virginia aristocrats or gentlemen owners of the major Virginia plantations. Virginians held the social or cultural understanding that it was the proper thing to do in deferring to one's social betters – just as one did back in England.

Then in 1622 a major Indian attack which resulted in the death of some 300-400 colonists – and rumors of the deputy governor's mismanagement of the colony – caused King James to end the Virginia Company's charter in 1624, converting it into a royal colony directly under the King himself (but governed by a royal Governor appointed by the King.) The House of Burgesses continued to meet, though its power was reduced somewhat. But the real power of the royal colony was now located in the Governor's Council consisting of the Governor and a small group of advisors drawn from the wealthiest Virginia plantations (the Virginia aristocracy).

Servitude and slavery.   Despite the emphasis placed on the event of 1619 when some 20 Angolan Africans were brought to Virginia as slaves, slavery was hardly a novel institution in the New World. It had been going on, particularly in the nearby Caribbean Islands, for a century. And it simply fit right into the idea that there were two classes of people at the time, property-owners, and those who worked that property. Indenture and slavery had much in common, in that those who fit the category as either indentured worker or slave had no particular rights of his or her own under that category. Even indentured workers were considered the "property" of the person ("master") possessing their indenture ... an indenture that could be bought and sold to other wealthy owners if need be. But there were some key differences. A person usually chose to accept indenture in order to receive funding to cover the cost of the trip to America ... and with the understanding that at the end of the tenure of the indenture (usually seven years) that individual would receive not only the training developed during the indenture but also land rights and tools to allow himself (or herself) then to set himself up independently in the New World. Slavery had no such options ... but involved a lifetime of service ... and a similar servitude passed on to any offspring of such slaves.

Actually at first, slavery in Virginia was not a tightly defined institution ... some Africans actually being classed as indentured workers – presuming that upon attaining personal freedom, they would be able to take on indentured workers of their own. But with time (the later 1600s and certainly by the beginning of the 1700s) slavery became a fully-legalized part of the Virginia social scene ... and identified most closely with those of African origin.

Virginia's God. Despite this rather "un-Christian" picture of the very rich lording it over the poor, both black and white – Virginia was not Godless. Attendance at church (the Church of England directed by the King and the bishops he appointed) was required of everyone. But there were few pastors that accompanied the early settlers to Virginia and, as in England, attendance at worship was viewed more as a duty than as a right or privilege. Ultimately Virginia was no more or less religious than most of "Christian" Europe of those days.

New England

Meanwhile to the north of the Virginia colony in an area that would come to be known as "New England" an English settlement of a very different character was taking shape. Whereas the Virginia colony was from the very outset an experiment in personal social improvement through the acquiring of wealth and thus status in a largely feudal cultural setting, New England was a definite religious experiment based on the strong religious feelings stirred by the Protestant Reformation (of the Calvinist variety) in England. New England was an experiment in building a "Reformed" society, from the ground up, according to strict Biblical principles. It was an experiment in building a "New Jerusalem," a "city on a hill," able to shed Christian light to the rest of the world.

The Separatist "Pilgrims." The first to make the move to New England in this matter would be a group of Separatists ... who would gain for themselves the title of Pilgrims, for their world was indeed a world of pilgrimage – religious pilgrimage. Under the threat of imprisonment for their religious "treason," a small community of Separatists escaped to the Netherlands to live among fellow Calvinists like themselves. But it was a bad time to be looking for help in the Netherlands, as the Dutch were fully occupied at trying to keep themselves from being destroyed by the Spanish troops that had invaded their country. Thus economic hard times – plus watching their children abandon their English heritage as they began to take up Dutch culture – decided a number of these English Separatists to make yet another move: to America.

After political and economic complications with English investors and with royal authority, plus missteps in getting themselves across the Atlantic so late in the season (November 1620), and having suffered the loss of half of their members that first winter in America (50 of the 100 Pilgrims), these Pilgrims were able to set up a new community on the shores just opposite Cape Cod in Massachusetts. Here with the help of friendly Indians they were able to found the colony of "Plymouth" ... and begin to live out the religious experiment they had long been seeking.

The Puritans join them.   With so much persecution back in England after Charles took the throne as English King in 1625 ... the Puritans who had looked down on the Separatists as traitors to the Reformed cause now themselves realized that "separation" was the only option available to them ... short of civil war. Thus in 1630 and for the next twelve years after that, some 20,000 Puritans left England and sailed to America to found and develop there the Massachusetts Bay Colony, just to the north of the Plymouth Colony. John Winthrop, the spiritual mentor to this venturesome group of Puritans, was quick to link up with the Plymouth Pilgrims ... and to learn from them some of the secrets of survival in this strange new world.

These were not economic refugees or social climbing adventurers. These American Puritans came from stable Middle Class English stock which (unlike the Virginians) had developed the Calvinist attitude toward hard work as not only the way to please God but also the way to build for themselves and their families fairly prosperous lives.* They were literate (the ability to read the Bible was an absolute requirement) ... indeed, well-educated in the three "R's" (*R*eading, w*R*iting and a*R*ithmetic), and well led by university-educated (usually Cambridge) clergy, with usually just such a pastor chosen for each of the many New England villages.† The Massachusetts Bay Company which sponsored this mass movement of Puritans carefully laid out each new village with a certain size of population and a specific allotment of farmland, complete with a meeting house at the center of each village – serving as a church on Sundays, a school for children during the daytime on weekdays, and a hall for town meetings as needed in the evenings.

A deep sense of the equality of all (reflective of their understanding that all are esteemed as equals in the eyes of God) stood at the heart of the social agenda of New England. They worked together as equals, studied together, and defended themselves together ... such as the "minute men" who were trained to assemble from their fields or homes in a moment's notice if the village were threatened – usually by an Indian attack.

Being able to work as a community, there would be no "dying time" such as the Virginia Colony experienced repeatedly. Thus the New England colony prospered well beyond the level of the Virginia colony ... and grew accordingly.

This is not to say that New England did not have its problems. People

---

*This was the origin of the famous "Yankee work ethic" for which Americans would become world famous.

†Thus it was that Harvard College was founded (1636) in Boston shortly after their arrival to America, primarily to educate just such pastors. The heavily Episcopalian Virginia would not do the same (College of William and Mary) until almost the end of that same century (1693).

brought their personal issues with them to New England, such as the pastor Roger Williams ... for whom the Puritan settlements were never religiously "pure" enough and who finally was invited in 1636 to take his purity elsewhere ... though in establishing his own colony of Providence (Rhode Island) he quickly ran into many of the same problems himself and soon restored a close friendship with Massachusetts' leader John Winthrop. And there was Anne Hutchinson ... who believed herself to be more "spiritual" than the colony's pastors – except for the pastor John Cotton, whose favor she cultivated with breathtaking flattery. Eventually, in 1638, she was forced to leave the colony ... before her "prophetic pronouncements" shattered the social foundations on which the struggling new community was built.[*]

✳ ✳ ✳

A MAJOR INTELLECTUAL SHIFT

Religious fatigue. It is impossible to overstress the importance of two factors that played heavily in the lives of Westerners by the year 1650. One of these was a growing sense of relativism about revealed or divine truth. Watching Protestants and Catholics slaughter each other in the name of revealed truth did nothing beneficial for the cause of either "revealed truth" in the long run. Instead it tended to scatter the seeds of religious skepticism around the land. People were tired of the fiercely combative religious claims on people's sense of truth.

Consequently, the simple straightforwardness of truth built merely on human observation and reason seemed to be a much more useful – not to mention safer – approach to truth. The European was thus very receptive to a worldview which grew up from the foundations of "natural philosophy" – one that proceeded not from tradition, or scripture, or divine revelation, but one which seemed to stand simply on observed "fact." This was truth enough. This could even be, as in the example of the theory of the heavens, a greater truth. The European was thus beginning to be very open to what such natural philosophy (the forerunner of modern science) might now be having to say about life ... anywhere, everywhere – even in the heavens above.

---

[*]Anne Hutchinson would become a major hero of the American feminist movement for the way she stood up to the male authorities of the colony, attempting merely to "exercise the right of free speech." The fact that she created a circle of individuals, male and female, who were deliberately attacking the legitimacy of the colony's leadership with their claims that all the pastors but Cotton were serving the Anti-Christ or Devil is a most critical social matter conveniently overlooked in the extolling of Hutchinson's "bravery."

The development of the secular-scientific mindset. The second factor playing a very big role in the development of Western culture in those days was the growing interest in the immediate world around us – the physical, secular world. Somehow there was a growing sense that it was not a mere transient place – merely a staging area for eternal life. Rather – it had value, great value, in and of itself.

True, this kind of thinking had its roots as far back as the 1300s, with its love of physical beauty found in the human form and the natural world around us; and it developed rapidly in the 1400s during the Renaissance in Italy and Northern Europe with the rise of the spirit of entrepreneurship and the accumulation of personal fortunes.

But what is particularly notable about this intellectual movement of the 1500s and 1600s was how our interest in the world around us came to have a value in and of itself – apart from how it might help us in our relationship with God. Not that this implied a diminished regard for God. It's just that a new mindset was growing up – that could consider the study of anything apart from some implicit religious significance.

The "dethronement" of the earth

Despite the concern about the cruelty of the religious debate between Protestantism and Catholicism, none of these new free-thinkers had any desire to disestablish the larger matter of the Christian faith and its general worldview. But ultimately, what they would discover in their free-wheeling inquiry into their newly expanding universe would throw the whole moral-intellectual-spiritual paradigm of the West into further confusion.

The earliest upheaval came in a new view about the heavens and the earth. But this story goes back well before 1600. Let's therefore go back a bit and see how things evolved.

Since time immemorial it had been assumed that the earth was the fixed center of the universe – and that the "heavenlies" (sun, moon and stars) circled the earth – in accordance with divine law.

True – there were "fluctuations" in the heavenly movements of these supposedly divine and thus "perfect" celestial bodies. But these fluctuations ("imperfections") had been accounted for in numerous sub-theories that seemed to preserve intact the original doctrine. But these sub-theories were so complicated that it made for an almost incomprehensible vision of the precise movements of the heavens.

Nicolas Copernicus (1473-1543). In the mid-1500s Copernicus had come up with an alternative theory: the sun, not the earth, is the center of the universe (he apparently was not aware that almost 2000 years before him, Aristarchus had also come up with such a theory).

His purpose – so his publisher states – was not to challenge the obvious truth of the earth's centrality to the universe – but rather to make "astrological" calculations (for the purpose of fortune-telling) less complicated. His heliocentric (sun-centered) theory was simply to be viewed as a hypothetical system designed to simplify astrology. He did not intend to posit this theory as a new theory of Truth or Reality. It was simply a device of convenience. This anyway is what his publisher wrote in the preface, possibly to protect Copernicus. Whether Copernicus himself thought that his theories were or were not matters of mere convenience is much less certain.

Indeed, though his theory seemed to work, it still had many flaws – and needed a lot of further working out before it might be significantly better than Ptolemy's theory. As long as the motion of the planets around the sun was seen to be perfectly circular – rather than as was later discovered to be elliptical – Copernicus himself would need theories and formulas and sub-theories and sub-formulas to make his astrological calculations useful.

In his own days there seemed to be nothing particularly revolutionary about his theories. They were interesting ... perhaps even useful. But actually, he had put out in front of the European mind the suggestion that the sun, not the earth, might be a better starting point in computing the movements of the heavens. His ideas were not forgotten.

Tycho Brahe (1546-1601).   At the turn of that century (late 1500s/ early 1600s) Tycho Brahe made an enormous contribution to the growing field of inquiry about the universe and the place of our world in it. He was astrologer and mathematician for the Holy Roman Emperor. In pursuit of astrology, he carefully collected observations about the movement of the heavens. Though these were not intended at the time to serve the interest of science, they would prove very useful for later advances in the rising science of astronomy, studying the planets and stars in order to acquire knowledge of their movements in and of themselves – quite apart from their "fortune-telling" qualities.

Galileo Galilei (1564-1642).   But still the matter was not given much weight at the time – until in the early 1600s when it came into the hands of the Italian astronomer Galileo Galilei. Galileo announced loudly and long that from his direct observations of the stars, it was clear to him that the heliocentric theory was not just a conjecture but was in fact the Truth. Beyond a shadow of doubt, the sun – not the earth – was the center of things.

His impact did not stop there. Galileo had been armed with a newfangled instrument we know as a telescope (even claiming its invention – though it seems he fudged a bit on this truth). With this telescope he was able to make many unprecedented observations of the heavens beyond even the all-important fact of the earth's loss of central position in the scheme of things. He observed the pock-marked surface of the moon and the solar flares of the sun – discounting the ancient Greek religious doctrine that these heavenly bodies were the epitome of perfection (actual Platonic Ideals or Forms).

He also observed the moons of Jupiter in their regular orbit as together they all moved about the sun – giving rise to an explanation of how our moon could be similarly held in orbit around the earth as it makes its way around the sun.

Also, his telescope revealed considerable mass on the part of some of the heavenly bodies (the planets) which had appeared to the naked eye only as points of light in the sky, demonstrating their existence as substantial material entities: neighbors of the earth. But oddly, even under the powerful scrutiny of the telescope, other lights in the heavens (the stars) still remained as only points of light – giving indication that their distance from our earth must be vastly greater than had been previously imagined!

At first his announcement was met with much interest from the Italian Catholic hierarchy ... which initially seemed to be quite supportive of his studies. But Galileo was a bit of a theatrical publicity-hound who found that his celebrity status could be greatly enhanced by clobbering the church with the metaphysical implications of his discoveries. In case people had not understood the metaphysical implications of his findings, he was glad to make them clear. Thus he was loud in his announcement that both tradition and Scripture – hitherto considered the bedrock of all truth – seemed to be very wrong on their placement of the earth at the center of the universal scheme of things. Indeed, he seemed to be eager to demonstrate every point he could find where his studies challenged traditional authority.

But this was not a good time to insult the Church and its truths. Europe was in the midst of the violent Protestant-Catholic religious wars, and the Protestants were delighting in another excuse to verbally attack the Catholic Church. As they picked up on Galileo's threat to the traditional Christian worldview, they attacked the Pope fiercely for his tolerance of this vile theory. To the Protestants this was another example of how far the leadership of the Church was willing to stray from the Truth.

As Protestant criticisms grew sharper, the Pope became increasingly frustrated by the way Galileo's grandstanding was stirring up even more controversy within a disintegrating Christendom. Galileo really didn't need to press this point so much. Also the Church was getting tired of

Galileo's criticisms of its traditional authority. A show-down between Galileo and the Church thus became inevitable – given Galileo's personality and the Church's highly defensive position.   Eventually the Pope threatened excommunication if Galileo persisted. For Galileo, grandstanding was one thing, excommunication was quite another. So Galileo yielded. But he also succeeded in letting it be known that, whatever the Church might force him to say or do, the fact remained that the sun, not the earth, was the center of things.

However, because he built his sun-centered theory on the notion of *circular* paths of the planets around the sun (the paths are in fact elliptical, not circular) his calculations were flawed – a fact that many were quick to jump on as proof of the basic falseness of his theory.

Nonetheless, in this struggle between Galileo and the Medieval Christian worldview, Galileo struck a hard blow on behalf of Secularism's view that Christianity was hopelessly lost in ignorance, and was willing to enforce that ignorance in order to preserve itself. Galileo was a major contributor to the idea that there was another truth, another reality than the one put forth by Christianity.

Johannes Kepler (1571-1630). But very soon after Galileo's grand splash upon the European stage, his work (also the early 1600s) was backed up by further studies by Johannes Kepler. Kepler succeeded Brahe as astrologer and mathematician for the Emperor. As such, he had studied the heavens in search for a more rationally "beautiful" explanation of the movement of the heavens.

However, Kepler came at this work from a quite different angle than Galileo. To Kepler, his work was an almost mystical (Pythagorean) enterprise. Unlike Galileo, who sought (in the vein of the modern mindset) to exalt himself as the heroic intellectual explorer, Kepler sought to glorify God with his work. To him science was there to validate God – not man.

Kepler employed Brahe's data to refine Copernicus' heliocentric theory. In an amazing departure from long-held conventional thinking, he put the circular theory of the movements of the planets aside. In its place he substituted the amazing theory that the planets move in elliptical orbits around the sun, in precise and mathematically simple relations to the sun. In doing so, he cleared away all the unresolved details of Galileo's (or Copernicus's) heliocentric theory.

The simplicity and accuracy of Kepler's theory was now too compelling to be put aside by any religious authority: He was clearly giving accurate description to a physical reality – and not just a "useful" theory for making astrological calculations. The Christian world was going to have to come to terms with Kepler's science. It was no longer going to suffice simply to point to the authority of Scripture on the subject. Science was moving into a position of authority all its own. It was now going to be up to Christianity to figure out how to handle this newly emerging intellectual authority.

The development of "natural philosophy" (modern science)

Francis Bacon (1561-1626). In this regard, Bacon is often considered the first expounder of this new "scientific" method of arriving at Truth – giving the method a legitimacy as an alternative to religious truth.

Bacon's approach was empirical – collecting bodies of actual observations or data and then bringing them under the careful study of a community of scholars. He led scholarship away not only from the Platonist schools but also the Aristotelian schools that had long been prevalent in Europe. He, like Aristotle, felt that Truth was found in direct observation of things and their behavior. But he was opposed to the quickness by which the human mind likes to jump "deductively" to develop grand generalities (both Aristotelians and Platonists). Instead he proposed to work "inductively" from the hard facts and let them carefully suggest their own theoretical order – at the same time attacking such theories with doubts and constant testing, to see at what point they might not hold. In this he was laying the foundations of empiricism – which would take a strong hold over the English scholarly mind.

Bacon was a major bridge between the traditional religious worldview and the newly-arising secularist worldview. He acknowledged the importance of both, proposing that science and theology were two separate enterprises because of two different systems of proof required by each: direct observation and divine revelation. Furthermore, to Bacon, theology still remained the primary enterprise of the two

René Descartes (1596-1650). Taking this idea of Truth being found not from some ancient or higher religious source – but instead from the principles of life active all around us – was the French philosopher, René Descartes. His own understanding of this new approach to Truth would have a huge impact on Western philosophy.

In some ways Descartes was still a medieval rationalist – who believed (in keeping with Plato) that all things in the world around us are merely "extensions" of some variety of mathematical or geometric abstractions. The underlying truth about our world "out there" was discoverable really only through careful mathematical meditations on that world – which could be done at home or in one's closet.

But in any case, what he came up with in his musings was the idea that the world "out there" was essentially a mechanical device that worked according to fixed rules of motion. Events occurred as the result of impacts among the various material bodies that are in constant motion within this "machine."   The machine itself is devoid of soul or vitality of its own. It simply responds to the "laws" of motion in a mathematical way.

Impressed by those recent discoveries of Galileo and Kepler concerning the mathematical formulations that described simply and elegantly the movements of the heavens (permitting the world to set aside the horribly cumbersome formulations of the Ptolemaic tradition) Descartes jumped easily to the belief that all of life was undergirded by such pure or clear mathematical formulations.   Just as pure reason had discovered those celestial formulas, pure reason would surely also unlock the formulations for life here on earth.

Believing this to be so, Descartes set about to begin just that task – to start to lay out the fundamental or foundational truths on which a mathematical edifice of formulas describing earthly life could subsequently be built, his *Discourse on Method* (1637).

This Method was to go to the most fundamental of propositions that could be demonstrated through logic to be absolutely true – which for him had to be the reality of his own consciousness, the mind that posed the question in the first place. It was also a natural starting point for him, given his underlying faith in the human mind's ability to embrace the mathematical undergirding of the universe.

The cogito.   Thus his theories all began from the starting point of the "natural philosopher" (scientist) himself: the famous *cogito ergo sum* – "I think, therefore I am." This was the only "certainty" in the world of ideas, thoughts, or "truths" that lay beyond all doubt.

From that point he moves forward logically in a rather Platonic manner. Even though he cannot say with any certainty that things outside him exist – he can be certain that he is having thoughts about them! Furthermore, these thoughts can easily embrace the idea of the existence of things in their perfect form – as for instance a perfect circle. His thoughts also embrace the idea of the existence of a perfect God. Where do such ideas come from? He concludes that there has to be something beyond himself, "out there," something that sets such thoughts into motion. And that reality out there cannot be less perfect than what his own thoughts can formulate – for how could he conceive of something as being more perfect than it actually is? It could not come from his own mind – for his own mind is itself imperfect, given to doubt. No ... the Perfect then must exist beyond himself, giving rise to his present thoughts about such Perfection.

From this he jumps (and it is a jump indeed) that the very Perfection of God is such that God could not deceive him. Therefore, the thoughts he was having about a Perfect God had to be true. [Ingenious, but not very compelling logic!] Further, being God by nature, God would not allow deceptive thoughts to come among us – that God would allow only real or true thoughts to come to Descartes' mind [Descartes does not allow for the existence of a Deceiver – other than his own flawed doubts].

Probing the Question of Physical Existence or "Physics." Now he moves in his thoughts (outlined in particular in his 1649 book *Passions of the Soul*) to probe more deeply the matter of his own existence – both body and soul. His body he treats as a physical extension beyond his conscious mind or soul. But the two, body and soul (or mind) are closely linked so that they affect each other directly – supposedly through the pineal gland, located at the base of the brain!

Nonetheless, it is only the body, as an actual extension, that is guided by the mathematical laws of physics. The soul, not being an extension of any kind, does not exist on the basis of these same laws. It is of a different order of being.

Qualities such as color, sound, smell, temperature, flavor, etc. are also not extensions themselves but are "secondary" qualities – as opposed to the primary qualities such as mass and velocity or movement. Only these primary qualities point to real existence. Only these primary qualities respond to the laws of physics – mathematical laws describing the physical machinery called reality.

Descartes was very unclear in his thinking about how then these secondary qualities actually existed.

Descartes' Contribution to Western Thought. It was Descartes' thinking on this matter of the surrounding physical world – its substance, its physical "extension," as the only true base of existence – that got the Englishman Newton to thinking ... ultimately to refute Descartes' notions of mass and motion. The fellow Englishman Locke also would reflect on Descartes' theories – and adopt some of his thinking about the differences between primary and secondary qualities of being.

Of course, physics has developed in such a way that many of Descartes' ideas have been put aside. But overall, he was very persuasive in his effort to apply rational theories to the existence of physical matter here on earth. He was very influential in getting natural philosophers/scientists to begin to probe the nature of material-being here on earth – as a matter now open to human enquiry.

The purpose was no longer to apply human inquiry to physical life in order to discover the magical formula for turning base elements into gold – but to explore physical reality simply for knowledge of such reality in and of itself.

But some unanswered questions. However, that left the question of the human soul and will – and the divine soul and will. Where do we fit in? Are we merely elements of this mechanical/material world? Is God merely an element of the mechanical/material world?

To Descartes the answer was clearly a "no" to both questions. But in affirming our own vitality – and God's – Descartes was forced to separate the human soul (and God's) from that soul-less mechanical/material creation "out there." Fine. But how then were we connected to that world – except as removed observers? Where was our ancient sense of unity with all creation? Where in fact did that leave us in relation to God – and to each other?

Those questions were never adequately answered. The human soul now seemed to be left cut adrift by what was considered to be a very compelling philosophical statement – one which swept powerfully through the philosophical circles of Europe in those days.

Hugo Grotius (1583-1645). Another person who made a great contribution to the development of this new mindset was the Dutchman, Hugo de Groot (Grotius). In his 1625 work, *De jure belli ac pacis* (*On the Law of War and Peace*), dedicated to the Bourbon King Louis XIII of France, he appealed to the European conscience to seek a new spirit of openness or tolerance about matters of Truth, a broad-mindedness about inquiry concerning Truth.

To further buttress this appeal he set out to try to systematically collect a listing of rules and legal norms that might in the future become the underpinning of a new cooperative international order. He scanned history for laws that had found use in guiding nations toward peace – and laid them out as a new system of international law. By basing these laws on proven behavior, he hoped to be establishing a natural (i.e., scientific) basis for founding peaceful international behavior. He is thus considered the "Father" of modern international law.

Thomas Hobbes (1588-1679). The religious fatigue exhausting the Christian West in those days also had the effect of developing a political viewpoint that was both cynical and utilitarian (much in the vein of Machiavelli). Thomas Hobbes, in his book *Leviathan* (1651), called for an all-powerful sovereign who would serve the interests of the larger political community (i.e., England) by holding it tightly together under his sovereign authority – in order to curb the kind of human wantonness experienced in the Wars of Religion. For Hobbes, such powerful rule was not to be founded on the ancient rule of the "divine rights" of monarchs – but on the basis of the needs, even rights, of the community to be served by such an all-powerful ruler. In justifying this utilitarian approach to state-building, he used "natural" theory or logic rather than scripture or tradition, putting forth the first efforts to establish a modern "political science."

However, his arguments were not greeted warmly by the English monarchy, which found "divine rights" – rather than society-serving utilitarian rights as the foundation of its power – much more to its liking!

✳ ✳ ✳

EUROPE DURING THE ASCENDANCY OF THE BOURBONS

France under the "Sun King" Louis XIV (r. 1654-1715)

As the 1500s was clearly the age of Habsburg Spanish domination (under Charles and his son Philip) in Europe, by the end of the 1600s it was clear that Bourbon France under Louis XIV was the dominant power in Europe. Not only did Louis's armies manage to hold off European grand alliances formed against his growing power, but his court with all its particular French refinements became the model that virtually every other European monarch attempted to emulate in one fashion or another.

Louis got off to a very tough start (only 16 when crowned in 1654). He was only four in 1643 when his father Louis XIII died, leaving France in the hands of a regency under Queen Anne (r. 1643-1651), who was aided greatly by another politically skilled clergyman, Cardinal Mazarin (First Minister, 1642-1661). WIth the king so young there was always political intrigue going on by various noblemen attempting to take advantage of the situation. Twice Louis and his mother had to flee Paris and once both of them were even put under something like house arrest in their Paris palace (the Louvre). Cardinal Mazarin had his hands full trying to keep Louis and his mother from falling victim to all the political intrigue that swirled around the two of them.

The Fronde and royal absolutism. A big part of the problem arose from the 1648 Treaty of Westphalia to which Mazarin had been a major contributor. The Treaty contained an agreement among European powers assigning rather absolute religious (and thus political) powers to the ruling royal families of the various states involved in the treaty, empowering the sovereign rulers alone to determine which religion – Catholicism or Protestantism – would be practiced in their lands.

The noblemen of France realized that in assigning such an important power to the sovereign kings (and other heads of state) this took away traditional feudal rights of the lesser nobility. Thus there was a general revolt (the Fronde) of the French noblemen (including even close relatives of the young king) against French royal authority, authority promoted and protected by Mazarin. In theory the revolt was aimed at Mazarin, not the king. But with the formal crowning of the young king in 1654, that excuse no longer could be justified, as Louis stood strongly with the terms of the Treaty. Thus the revolt lost its justification and soon died away. From 1654 until he died in 1661, Mazarin held off further attacks on the king's powers ... adding to those powers here and there as he went along. Then with Mazarin's death, Louis was ready to take control of the affairs of state entirely on his own. He would make all the decisions, large and small. He made it clear that noblemen and other court officials existed only to carry out his orders. And thus Louis XIV began his rule of royal absolutism.

Life at the Palace of Versailles. Louis moved his court out of a dangerous Paris to the nearby suburb of Versailles – and then required the entire French nobility to move there with him to his new, enormous palace ... so that he could keep a close eye on them. He lavished his "guests" with endless banquets, balls, musical recitals, plays, etc. – to gloss over the reality that they were in fact something like prisoners there. But since there was little they could do to escape their situation, they made the most of it. In fact the proceedings at the Versailles Palace were so elaborate (and the logic behind it so very clear) that other sovereigns began to copy closely the political and cultural style of Versailles. And thus it was that French culture (and politics) came to be the standard for the ruling classes in virtually all of Europe.

The endless round of dynastic wars over European land rights. While other sovereigns honored Louis by mimicking him culturally, they fought him fiercely politically or militarily. It was always about land: who won it, who lost it. Land could change hands among Europe's sovereigns peacefully, such as in marriage where the exchange of lands accompanied the exchange of wedding vows. But most land holdings changed hands simply through fights over it ... territorial titles changing back and forth from one sovereign to another as the fortunes of war shifted back and forth. Louis and the other kings were constantly involved in wars, great and small, in an attempt to expand their territorial holdings. It was a confusing and draining process that occupied Louis until his death in 1715.

The revoking of the Edict of Nantes (1685) and the flight of Huguenots out of France. The ongoing existence of communities of Protestants in his

Catholic France was a major irritant to Louis. And thus he set out to bring religious uniformity (as per the Treaty of Westphalia) to France. He began the process almost immediately after assuming full royal powers in 1661. He harassed the Protestant Huguenots in every way possible, banning worship, destroying churches, closing schools, and placing his rough-edged troops in Protestant homes in order to break their spirit. And hundreds of thousands of Huguenots did break, finding it prudent to convert to Catholicism.[*]

Finally in 1685, he made a full move against Protestantism, issuing the Edict of Fontainebleau – declaring any further toleration to have come to an end. Although it was also very illegal to leave his realm without royal permission, perhaps as many as 200,000 Huguenots fled France for Protestant lands in Europe and elsewhere … taking with them the valuable entrepreneurial and professional skills that naturally arose from their Calvinist mindset. Other sovereigns (notably the Protestant variety) were shocked by Louis's behavior. But they did little to counter it. They were in fact quite glad to receive these talented refugees. Nonetheless, even as cruel as it was, expelling the Protestants finally brought religious harmony to France.

Louis's legacy. Louis came to the throne with the royal treasury virtually empty, then under the direction of his economic advisor Colbert had it restored … then Louis bled it dry again over the years with his countless wars. He refashioned French politics so tightly around his personal will that if future kings were not made of the same grit as he was, they would have big troubles maintaining control. And that is exactly what happened.

On the positive side, he made French language, learning and culture the European standard for many future generations. He also advanced the boundaries of France all the way up to the Rhine River in Germany and incorporated Flanders into the French kingdom, along with a number of other smaller acquisitions. And he sponsored further French exploration in America through Jesuit missionaries and explorers such as La Salle. Louis was able to lay claim to vast amounts of American territory from Canada in the north to the Gulf of Mexico in the South, from the Appalachian Mountains in the East, across the Mississippi River to its far sources in the West. The vast area below French Canada was in fact named after him, Louisiana.

---

[*]A group of Huguenots were able to hid themselves in the isolated mountains of Auvergne in Southern France, and maintain their Protestant faith in doing so. They were also the community, centuries later, that was able to help over 3,000 Jews hide in their town (Chambon) and thus avoid the Nazi deportation of French Jews (some 80,000 were deported) during World War Two, these brave Huguenots – brave because the penalty for helping Jews escape deportation was death – having themselves learned how to avoid detection by the French authorities all those years!

Meanwhile, an English Civil War drags on

The Puritan Commonwealth (1649-1653). With the beheading of Charles I in 1649, the Rump Parliament declared England, Scotland and Ireland to be no longer royal territories but instead parts of a new Republic ... or in Anglo-Saxon terms, a "Commonwealth" (like a Republic, a government belonging to the "commoners" of the land). The House of Lords was abolished as part of Parliament and a Council of State took over the executive responsibilities of the new government. But actually, relations between the members of the Rump Parliament running the new government and the army (at the time engaged heavily in putting down royalist resistance) was not an easy one. It was, after all, the army that had put the Rump Parliament into power in the first place ... and the army – especially under Cromwell – seemed to take a great interest in directing English (and Scottish and Irish) politics according to its own interests.

Also, political interests varied widely within the Rump Parliament ... some MPs wanting a government of a most definite republican nature and others still believing monarchy to be the most appropriate form of government for England. But in moral and spiritual terms the Rump Parliament was more united in wanting to see the country reformed under Puritan ideals ... especially in the matter of closing down theaters (considered the source of lewdness) and the requirement of strict Sunday church attendance (although a variety of religious denominations were nonetheless permitted). Neither of these moral "cleansings" of English society however were designed to win the hearts of most Englishmen – who enjoyed a rather looser moral life!

Domestic reforms. Actually, true political reforms proved to be few once the king had been eliminated. It was mostly lesser gentry that stood behind the Commonwealth ... and they were not interested in serious economic reform, especially of the variety demanded by the "Levelers" who wanted full equality for all, economically and politically. Mostly the changes that could be felt throughout England under the Commonwealth were in the form of the rigid moral order which descended on England. Worse for the new Commonwealth, heavy taxes had to be imposed on the citizenry to pay for the wars which went on constantly during this brief time period.

The Irish Rebellion. Most importantly, Cromwell faced challenges to the Commonwealth in both very Catholic Ireland and very Presbyterian Scotland. He set about the task of reducing the resistance of Ireland, brutally vengeful against Drogheda and Wexford (as revenge for the massacre of Protestant settlers who had earlier come from Scotland to Northern Ireland) ... though for the most part of the rest of his conquest of Ireland (and in the context of the times of the Religious Wars) he was fairly merciful to the towns that did not offer opposition. Nonetheless when he was called back to England to take on the Scottish problem the next year (1650), his subordinate officers continued the campaign in Ireland – on a much less merciful level* – earning Cromwell the eternal hatred of the Irish.

The Scottish Rebellion. Meanwhile in Scotland things underwent confusion as at first the Royalists tried to raise the Catholic Highland clans against the Lowland Covenanters (Presbyterians) ... but failed miserably in the effort. Then the Royalists joined the Covenanters under the renewed Royalist promise of instituting Presbyterianism generally within the royal realm.

At this point Cromwell left Ireland to deal with the Scots. Here too he was as determined a foe ... though conducting his campaigns so that the ravages of war there were greatly reduced. Scottish resistance was thus less intense ... and he soon succeeded in crippling the Royalist threat there.

But Charles II in the meantime (1651) had moved his army south from Scotland to England. Thus Cromwell went in pursuit of Charles, leaving George Monck to clean up the last of the Scottish resistance... which collapsed fully in 1652.

In September of 1651 Charles's Royalist forces and Cromwell's Puritan forces met in battle at Worcester ... where Charles's forces were completely routed – forcing Charles to flee to France.

Cromwell's Protectorate (1653-1659). In 1653 Cromwell simply dismissed the Rump Parliament and took direct control of English politics ... supported by a small "Barebones Parliament" (composed of representatives elected by local congregations) which he expected would come up with specific reforms – but possessed very little political expertise and subsequently was dismissed by Cromwell after only a few months of service.

It was at this point that a Cromwellian Constitution was put into force, making Cromwell "Lord Protector" for life (thus something like a king), and restoring the role of Parliament and the executive Council of State. But the real power in England remained Cromwell's loyal army ... and the military governors he appointed to preside over Scotland and Ireland.

At this point peace returned to the land (though anguish in Ireland continued ... and the Scots were always on the edge of rebellion ... which

---

*Tens of thousands of Irish were subsequently shipped off to Bermuda and the Caribbean islands to live in servitude there; and possibly as much as nearly half of the Irish population ultimately died of exposure, hunger and disease because of the intentional ravaging of the Irish countryside by Cromwell's generals (designed to break the will of the Irish) in the years after Cromwell's departure for England.

Charles II from his exile in France was watching closely). One of the big events of the time was in fact a commercial war with the Dutch ... fellow Protestants, but fellow competitors in the important world of international commerce.

Richard Cromwell ... and the demise of the Commonwealth (1659). In September of 1658 Cromwell suddenly became quite sick and died (urinary infection most likely) ... and – in royalist fashion – his office as Lord Protector was directly taken up by his son Richard. But Richard enjoyed no power base of his own (as his father had with the army) and thus he had no leverage by which to control the many political factions that constantly vied for power in Parliament. Richard was soon (May of 1659) driven from power by one of the faction leaders.

Monck takes command. With the political situation deteriorating rapidly, General George Monck left his position as Scottish Governor and marched with his army on London (January-February 1660) and placed the original Long Parliament back in power. And Monck and the MPs then took up the work of negotiating with the exiled Charles II concerning the restoration of the English monarchy, by this time desired by most of the English. Terms of pardon and compensation were agreed on and in May a newly reconvened Parliament invited Charles to retake the throne of England.

The Stuart "Restoration (1660)." By the end of May Charles was back in England, the following April (1661) he was formally crowned King (though in effect he had been governing the country since his return the previous year), and in May the Cavalier Parliament that would rule England for the next 17 years was fully in power. The Puritan experiment was over ... as well as England's only attempt at Republican government. Indeed, England – like the war-weary European continent after the long period of the Thirty Years' War – was ready to enter a new era of peace.

The Dutch and the English

These two societies at this point are discussed together because during the latter part of the 1600s their destinies seemed so intertwined ... in peace and in war. Both being rising sea-powers, their disputes were largely commercial. Both being a mix of Protestant and Catholic, the dynastic disputes that focused on the matter of religion required them to be very flexible in their handling of these disputes. In general, they moved cautiously through the thicket of religious-dynastic feuds. But when they did not, the results were calamitous.

The "Restoration" of the Stuart monarchy in England (and Scotland) under Charles II. The grand experiment in Puritan republicanism died a quiet death, with few seeming to mourn its passing. However, Charles's situation as "restored" king was still precarious. He had the support of the aristocratic "High-Church" or Episcopalian Cavaliers in Parliament ... but had to work with the Presbyterians who occupied an equally strong position in Parliament.

Political intrigue swirled around him all his days ... in part brought on by his wanton ways. He kept a seemingly endless string of mistresses – who bore him numerous illegitimate children (who would become nobles of the realm nonetheless) – in contrast to his Portuguese wife, by whom he gained valuable Portuguese territory ... but no living offspring.

Advisors rose and fell at the rate that they succeeded or failed in public policy, which was frequent – given all of the dynastic wars going on that invited Charles's participation. All this confusion merely encouraged the court intrigue which Charles seemed unable to control. He dissolved Parliament again and again to try to gain increased support for his rule, but to no particular avail. Parliament remained divided between Tories and Whigs* over a piece of legislation making it illegal for a Catholic (such as Charles's brother James) to inherit the throne of England (thus Catholic "Exclusion"). Finally during the last years of his life he attempted to rule without Parliamentary support (a difficult matter since it was from Parliament that he received his financial "supply" in the form of approved taxes).

William III of Orange and the Dutch Republic. William was the son of another William II, the Dutch Prince of Orange, and Mary, the eldest daughter of King Charles I of England. Charles II had taken refuge in the Netherlands with his cousin William II during the years of Cromwell's Commonwealth, and William supported him strongly in his exile. But William II died in 1650 after only a few years of service as Stadtholder (something like "President") of the Dutch Republic ... one week before the birth of his son William III.

During William III's youth, the Dutch and the English engaged in commercial conflicts as they both attempted to extend their commercial privileges to various places around the globe.† They also found themselves

---

*These were terms of contempt that one party assigned to the other: Tories, the name for Irish Catholic bandits, assigned to those who were opposed to the anti-Catholic Exclusion Bills, and Whigs, the name first for Scottish horse thieves and then later for Scottish Presbyterian rebels, assigned to those favoring Exclusion!

†The First Anglo-Dutch War (1652-1654) occurred during the time of the Puritan Commonwealth. The Dutch lost over a thousand of their merchant ships and thus sued for peace. But Dutch power was by no means broken. The Second Anglo-Dutch War broke out in 1665 during the early years of Charles II's reign. It was a more balanced conflict, with the English gaining New Netherland (New York), but losing a major naval battle, bringing the war to an end in 1667.

involved in the competing dynastic alliances formed across Europe.

William found his rise to the position of his father as Dutch stadtholder blocked by a number of political opponents in the Holland province, and William appealed to his English uncle Charles II for assistance in advancing his cause. But he did not know that his uncle had secretly agreed to an alliance with France ... directed at the Dutch Republic. Charles actually believed that defeating the Dutch in war was the proper way to force the Dutch to accept William. William would have none of it when he figured out what was going on.

In any case, the Franco-Dutch and Third Anglo-Dutch War broke out in March of 1672. The Dutch were at first devastated by this French-English combination. William was finally appointed stadtholder of key Dutch provinces in July, and refused to surrender to the English, even when the offer of dynastic rule over the Netherlands was offered in compensation. The Dutch flooded their low-lying fields ... and with that the French overland invasion came to a halt. The English then quickly lost interest in continuing the conflict. Thus the war ended in 1674. But it had been very hard economically on the Dutch society.

Then William moved to marry his young English cousin Mary, daughter of James of York, Charles II's brother (1677).* He did so in the hope of improving relations with the English ... and strengthening his own claim on the English throne as Charles I's grandson.

The Glorious Revolution (1688-1689)

This question of who would inherit the throne of the childless Charles II at his death troubled England greatly. Next in line was his brother, James, Duke of York, an avowed Catholic. The effort to pass an Exclusion Bill had been aimed at him ... in order to prevent him from inheriting the throne. Nonetheless when in 1685 Charles died, his Catholic brother James became King of England as James II (and Scotland as James VII). It was also the year that Louis XIV revoked the Edict of Nantes, driving hundreds of thousands of Huguenots from France.

Much of Protestant Europe was up in arms about this revoking of the Edict of Nantes – reactively forming something of a Grand Alliance under William of Orange's strongly Protestant leadership. When in the spring of 1688 James II concluded a naval agreement with Louis XIV, suspicions mounted quickly in England that this was the prelude to a formal pro-Catholic/anti-Protestant English-French military alliance.

Then when James's Italian-Catholic wife, Mary of Modena, delivered

---

*Although her father James was a Catholic, Mary and her sister Anne had been carefully brought up under their grandfather Charles I's orders as Protestants.

a baby boy in June of that year, it appeared that England was in line eventually to inherit a Catholic successor to James. A group of English Protestants agreed with William that it was time to act. Soon a coalition was formed against James II and his close ally Louis XIV, which included, at least indirectly, the strongly anti-French Holy Roman (Austrian) Emperor and the Pope! Louis took the first action – which then erupted into full scale war.

Now it was the turn of William to act. He quickly gathered a huge Dutch naval invasion force – to which James responded rather feebly. With William's landing in England, noblemen began declaring themselves as "Whigs" for William. James began to lose courage quickly, fearing even the loyalty of his own "Tory" army. Defeat in small skirmishes and growing anti-royalist or Whig rioting in England's cities decided him to flee to France in mid-December. But he was caught before he could complete his escape and was returned to London. However, William did not want the responsibility of taking personal action against his father-in-law James. Clearly, the best strategy was to allow James to again "escape" to France. And so at the end of December James slipped off to France to become an exile living there as the guest of Louis XIV.

William and Mary.   Parliament quickly (February 1689) empowered William and his wife Mary II to rule as joint sovereigns – under the authority of Parliament. It also passed a Bill of Rights (December 1689) clarifying the rights and powers of Englishmen and their government (civil rights and powers elaborated further in John Locke's very important *Two Treatises of Government*, published in 1689). England still had a monarchy (which it does even to this day) but it was in fact under Parliament's unquestioned sovereignty. Thus to the Protestant point of view, this was indeed a "Glorious Revolution."

Only five years later (1694) Mary died childless ... and William continued as both King of England and stadtholder of the Netherlands until his death in 1702. During that period, the followers of the exiled James (the "Jacobites"), encouraged by the active support of Louis XIV, refused to accept William's title ... and undertook rebellions in Scotland and Ireland – and an assassination attempt – all of which failed. But it certainly troubled constantly the first ten years of William's reign. Along with this was an ongoing war with France that occupied much of William's time, keeping him abroad in Europe on military campaigns. But he succeeded importantly in blocking much of the limitless ambition of Louis XIV which had the rest of Europe constantly up in arms.

The refinement of the mechanistic/materialistic vision of life

Meanwhile, the work of studying the physical structure and behavior of the surrounding physical world continued to move ahead – especially in England which led the way in the new "empirical" or scientific study of our world.

It was the age of mechanical clocks, precision telescopes and sextants, mechanical war-machines, and other such useful instruments. It was the age which reduced the movement of the heavenlies to a precise mathematical formulation. It was the age which began to look at life as a precise "natural" composite of various material elements – physical and chemical. It was an age which was thrilled by the idea of unlocking all the mysteries of "natural" life by bringing such life (seen more and more in mechanical/materialist terms) under precise intellectual formulation. It was an age of heady "natural philosophy" and "natural philosophers" (the name given to the scientists of the 17th century).

This was particularly the case in England which led the way in the new "empirical" or scientific study of our world – such study eventually termed "positivism. " In 1660 the Royal Society was founded, bringing this new breed of "natural-philosophers" (as they saw themselves) together to encourage each other in their work.

Isaac Newton.   In the latter part of the 1600s one of these English naturalists, Isaac Newton, picked up on Descartes' theories of motion and completed the mechanistic vision of the universe that Descartes had laid out. In Newton's *Principia* (1687) he so thoroughly pulled the mechanistic/ materialistic vision together that it became the single most important foundation piece for the modern worldview.

Following the ancient thinking of Democritus and the atomists, he "demonstrated" that all things within the universe were made up of minute bits of matter. There was something absolute or eternal about the existence of these particles: once created by God, they remained in permanent being. They did, however, combine and recombine into different elements, which in turn combined into different physical forms of matter. But Newton asserted that while the larger forms of life changed, the atoms themselves did not. They were unchangeable, possibly even eternal in their being.

These tiny particles were held together in their shape and movement to take the forms we see before us through the force of natural attraction or gravity (the gravitational attraction of two bodies is equal to the product of their mass divided by the square of the distance between them).

This theory appeared to explain quite fully *everything* from the movement of the planets through the skies, to the movements of the tides, to the velocity of falling objects – and more.

Just as importantly – the completeness of the theory left no possibility of seeing creation as a "living" thing. Creation was without life of its own;

it was instead mere "matter" responding mechanically to a set of fixed mathematical laws.

Newton depicted God in such a way that God actually lost "personality" and the realm of sovereign action. God was left a role in nature largely as "First Mover" or original architect of this mechanistic universe, with no further significant intervention in life. God became identified with the eternity or infinity of the universe.

Deism was being born.

Gottfried Wilhelm Leibniz. Leibniz was a German mathematician and rationalist philosopher – who, simultaneously with Newton, invented the differential and integral calculus. He was a widely talented and traveled individual – and kept up friendships and correspondences with a wide range of scientists, philosophers and political figures of the day.

Leibniz was born and educated in Leipzig, eventually studying law at the University of Leipzig. From 1667 to 1672, he worked for the Elector of Mainz as a lawyer and diplomat.

He traveled widely coming into close contact with a number of political and scientific luminaries of his day. In 1672 he traveled to Paris where he came into contact with Huygens and Malebranche. His travels also took him to England (1673, 1676) and to Amsterdam (1673), where he spent time with Spinoza. During these days he began his work on calculus.

In 1676 he went to work as a librarian to the Duke of Brunswick, and took up work on a number of mechanical devices that utilized his mathematical and technical talents. But he also turned his attention to philosophy, completing works on metaphysics and systematic philosophy during the 1680s and 1690s.

John Locke. Very shortly after Newton's *Principia* was published, Britain's well-known political essayist, John Locke, demonstrated his talents in the broader scientific world with his publication *Essay on Human Understanding* (1690)!

Locke's psychology. Locke brought the human mind into this mechanical world by positing a theory of knowledge in which the mind at birth is simply a blank receptacle, possessing no "innate" ideas. Over the years the mind has data added to it from the outside world. This comes in the form of "sensations" that strike this blank mind through the sensory devices of sight, hearing, feeling, taste, and smell. These data in turn are developed into full ideas by the mechanism of the mind, which sifts this imported information in the search for the agreement or disagreement of two thoughts or ideas. From this mental process develops a well-articulated vision of the world around us – and its causes and effects.

As far as "moral" ideas were concerned, Locke felt that prudence and long-term self-interest would serve the rational mind as the determiner of human action.

This theory of human knowledge stood in strong distinction to the traditional understanding that the mind possessed fully – even at birth – a vast store of innate understanding that was vitally a part of its soul quality. The old theory accounted for "learning" by seeing the task not one of inserting information from the outside (as per Locke – and almost every Western educator since), but instead one of drawing out (thus the ancient word "education" which means "draw out") the wealth of innate understanding already present in the human soul. One didn't make discoveries about things "out there." A person made discoveries about things already located deep down inside oneself.

Though Locke's theory could offer no hard evidence that what he hypothesized was indeed true – the time was ripe for such a theory. "Science" was rapidly stripping life of the sense of "soul" or "sacredness" to it. The wars of religion had also helped immeasurably. So Locke's theory "made sense." That was all that was needed to leave a lasting impression on the rapidly shifting world-view of the West.

Locke's social science.   Furthermore ... Locke employed his scientific methodology not only in the explanation of workings of human thought and action, he employed the same methodology in the explanation of what might be termed "social dynamics." Locke was pleased to discover that societies too worked according to a number of basic principles ... which careful study revealed quite clearly to be behind all social action. And these principles, once understood, could be used scientifically to improve dramatically the mechanics of social behavior. In other words, society itself could be – in fact, should be – reformed through the rising principles of science ... obviously a process that should be directed by those with the knowledge of just those principles (such as Locke himself)!

Thus "social reform" by enlightened individuals came to be understood as making much more sense than waiting patiently for God to intervene to put troubled societies back on the road to health and progress.

Locke's "Grand Model" for the Carolina colony. So it was that Locke was called on by his personal patron (and Britain's Chancellor of the Exchequer – the second most important political position in the King's cabinet) Baron Anthony Ashley to put together a structural plan for the new Carolina colony in America. This new colony offered the perfect opportunity to construct a society that actually worked according to the laws of social science.

Thus it was that in 1670 Locke came up with what was termed "The

Grand Model." This plan included not only The Fundamental Constitutions of Carolina but also the physical designs for the actual settlement of the colony. Thus were detailed some 120 principles designed to make the colony indeed a "Grand Model."

Basically, it followed English principles of social structuring in terms of class, property allotments, and the political rights accorded each level of society ... ranging from Black slaves and property-less Whites – all the way up to the largest landowners (who were naturally the eight Lords Proprietors themselves).

The problem was that Locke knew very little about the actual lay of the land in the new colony, the social traits of those who would actually be taking up residence in that colony, and the matter of the Indians and their own sense of property rights. Needless to say, the Model proved to be beautiful on paper ... but of limited use in actually moving the Carolina settlement forward. Consequently, although the Grand Model would remain in place, it would have to be amended or updated numerous times.[*]

Social design for England. But Locke would be given yet another opportunity to put forward his views on the shaping of a more enlightened society ... when England's Glorious Revolution broke forth in 1688. In 1689 Locke published (anonymously at the time) his *Two Treatises of Government*, the first treatise critiquing the social science of Sir Robert Filmer, the second treatise being Locke's own "Essay Concerning the True Original, Extent, and End of Civil Government."

Of course events in England were taking their own political course at the time. But Locke's work would be used frequently to justify "scientifically" some of the developments of the day. And it would serve as something of a Bible for future "social reformers" – such as Thomas Jefferson in his drafting of America's Declaration of Independence.

Benedictus (Baruch) de Spinoza (1632-1677). Spinoza was born of Jewish parents who had escaped the Inquisition in Portugal by coming to

---

[*]Tragically, there would be more than just this Ashley-Locke disappointment arising from the effort to find the right utopian formula in the face of life's ever-developing challenges. In fact, failure rather than success – and often very brutal failure at that – would be the normal outcome of such ventures ... over and over again. But there would always be the strong temptation to try again anyway – especially on the part of those who made such armchair social design their main work in life, social philosophers, social critics, journalists, progressive politicians, government technocrats, etc. Despite the miserable historical record of failure of such social ventures, that record would be completely disregarded, so certain were such intellectuals that their newest formula would finally be the one that would bring grand social success (also making them therefore the social geniuses of their day).

Amsterdam where Baruch (Latin: Benedictus) was born. Spinoza was a very unorthodox thinker – and his ideas eventually got him expelled from the Jewish community (1656). Because he saw God as present in everything – as the source and essence of all substance – he was viewed variously as a pantheist, a materialist, an atheist.

He was a moral relativist, who did not believe in some set of transcending religious or civil laws that we ought to conform ourselves to, but who instead believed in following out our own natural personal imperatives – ones that no one else had a right to pass judgment on.

This was not a philosophy designed to make the religiously conservative community around him very happy. But it certainly spoke to those souls who were tiring rapidly of the mean-spiritedness of the religiously orthodox – a growing number of youthful minds who hoped to rise to truths which were vastly higher than the traditional variety that had brought Europeans to war against each other mercilessly.

Giambattista Vico (1668-1744).   Vico was an Italian jurist/social-philosopher who receive little notice in his own lifetime – but was someone who would have a tremendous impact on later intellectuals, especially the German "Romanticists" of the 1800s such as Herder and Goethe ... and even (in part at least) Karl Marx. But that influence lives on even today!

Vico might be properly termed an "anti-positivist" in the way he differed so strongly with the way Descartes had captured the thoughts and imaginations of the scientific world of the 1700s (even also down to today). In many ways Vico agreed with Descartes about how natural philosophy was truly valid in the realm of the study of the natural world – the Cartesian or "positivist" approach to the study of the world of material things around us. But Vico also affirmed most strongly that it was absurd to apply this same mechanical approach to the study of the very creative world of human social dynamics. Social truth does not exist apart from human experience, but is created by that very experience.

In his 1725 multi-volume work *Scienza Nuova* (*New Science*) he demonstrated that scientific "Truth" in the realm of the highly complex and infinitely varied workings of human society does not exist apart from what human hands themselves have put into place (the social order). In other words, social truth is to be found only in the realm of human experience. The social truths that man seeks come to him only to the extent that he is able to learn from and understand such experience. They do not exist abstractly in the form of strict human behavioral laws or mathematical social rules.

As much as it was for Aristotle, the truths therefore that interested Vico were to be found in the record of human history: the realm of actual human experience. Thus the types of truths sought by the scholars studying social order (in order to improve their social orders) Vico was certain would be found only in the careful study of history.

But such study also demonstrated that societies are subject to the cycle of rises and falls, cycles that had little to do with mechanical rules of social order. However, Vico was no cynic about the lessons of history. He believed that history clearly demonstrated that, in the longer run of human history, definite human progress had taken place ... and would continue to move forward – even to a time in which human equality could be achieved socially.

The furthering of the mechanization/materialization of the soul

Natural Religion or Deism. Despite the rapid secularization of Western culture, most philosophers were not willing to give up on the all-important idea of God – not yet. It was too soon to make an abrupt departure from the traditional worldview in which a providential God was all-important to the Western sense of order, predictability, security, hope.

Indeed, Newton thought of himself as being religiously quite devout. His theory of the universe – so he thought – was intended as a powerful tribute to the Grand Architect who designed such a wonderfully complex yet beautiful creation.

However, the observation was unavoidable that, having created such a masterful work, the Grand Architect was really no longer necessary to the functioning of creation. Indeed, the view was inescapable that, from the time of creation eons ago, creation had been completely self-running according to God's own laws of nature. It did not need further "intervention" from God. Truly, since that time, God had been entirely redundant to the workings of the universe.

Reforming Christianity along more secular lines. In fact, from this standpoint one would have to say that there was no need to hear further from God – for God to be involved in the course of the world's affairs. Accordingly, there was also no need to pray to him – even to acknowledge him really – though few were yet willing to jump to this next step in their line of logic.

Thus the feeling was growing among the "enlightened" philosophers that those that continued to insist on the life of piety were self-deluded – and possibly dangerous. Still fresh were the memories of the great slaughter undertaken in the name of Protestant and Catholic piety.

So the Enlightenment was not a matter of just leaving religion alone – and going on without it. This matter of religion too had to be addressed.

Now the intention of the Enlightenment philosophers was not to destroy Christianity, but to take its "best" features, particularly the high moral-ethical character of Jesus, and focus on that instead. The rest, the miracle stories and the divine "revelations," all that could be/should be carefully removed from Christianity.

Thus the West saw the publication of a mass of works at the end of the 1600s in the order of John Ray's *The Wisdom of God Manifested in the Works of Creation* (1691); Locke's *The Reasonableness of Christianity* (1695); and John Toland's *Christianity Not Mysterious* (1696).

But by the 1720s and 1730s, the Deist voice had now become one of intense criticism of traditional Christianity. Take for instance the work of Matthew Tindal, *Christianity as Old as the Creation* (1730) – which became something of the official Deist "Bible" in his time. Here Tindal laid out the argument that all that was valuable in Christianity was that which universal reason alone would hold true. All else (i.e., revelation) was superstition – the most evil form of subjugation of the human mind.

Or consider the work of Thomas Woolston, an English Deist. In his *Discourse on the Miracles of Our Savior*, he debunked the miracle stories of Jesus and the resurrection accounts in Scripture – on the basis of rationalist arguments.

These were not just voices "outside" the church. In fact they were essentially voices "inside" the church, clamoring for its "enlightenment." Even the English Archbishop Tillotson joined in the chorus of those calling for a "natural religion," a Christianity brought up-to-date with enlightenment thinking.

Also, problems within a maturing English America

Social stress in Virginia. A major problem was developing in Virginia as the prime real estate along the shores of the various rivers (James, York, Rappahannock, Potomac Rivers) of the rich Tidewater region of coastal Virginia was largely claimed by the earliest of settlers. Within a couple of generations manor homes overseeing thousands of river-front acres began to be built ... and the "first families" began to take their place at the head of Virginia society. A Virginia aristocracy was beginning to take shape.

At that point, newcomers (after working off their time of indenture) were forced to head to the mountainous interior to find land for themselves. Besides the fact that the soil was rocky and the distance to the ports that would ship their products back to England great (whereas the wealthy plantations could load their products on ocean-going ships right at the plantations docks along the river), the "poor whites" of the interior were always faced with the problem of very bloody Indian attacks. The lives of these later Virginians were very hard ... their earnings marginal at best.

Bacon's Rebellion (1676). In 1676 the frustration felt by those later arrivals exploded in a major uprising by Virginia's Western frontier farmers and also by some of the English indentured workers in the East ... led by a young aristocrat Nathaniel Bacon (and thus termed "Bacon's Rebellion"). A number of grievances motivated this rebellion. Their world stood in such stark contrast to the privileges of Governor Berkeley and the handful of wealthy Virginians with which he surrounded himself. The rebels were particularly furious about what they felt was the indifference to their problems characteristic of the Jamestown government ... and especially the lack of protection against the Indians by that government.

Bacon's Rebellion was put down by Governor Berkeley only with much difficulty – and only after the rebels, worked up to intense anger, succeeded in marching on the Virginia capital Jamestown and burning it to the ground. Then in the midst of events Bacon became sick and died. Leaderless, the rebellion quickly collapsed.

The growth of slavery. The net result of the revolt was a deepening of the social gap between the Virginia aristocracy and the Virginia frontiersman. But also, the aristocrats were so unnerved by the anger of the rebels at this point that the Virginia wealthy lost interest in white indenture – and moved to use fully slave labor in its stead.

Slavery as an institution had been recognized as a permissible institution only in 1654. But as slavery extended its place in the Virginia economy, the laws regulating and controlling slavery advanced in accompaniment. By 1705 the Virginia Slave codes defined the institution fairly much as it would be practiced in Virginia for the next 160 years.

Human "Enlightenment" ... and witchcraft in New England. Meanwhile a serious problem would gradually develop in New England because of the very success of the colonies there. The strong dedication arising from royal persecution that had so greatly focused the early work of the New England colonists would soon fade away. As it became clear that the King was far away, preoccupied with major problems of his own brewing back in England (problems which the New Englanders carefully stayed out of), the sense of religious-social urgency which had originally inspired the heroic activity of the New England colonies gradually got lost. The generations which followed became complacent about the life that had been passed on to them by the founding generation. Ritual and routine replaced spirit and bravery. Human (or "secular') logic – termed at the times as human "Enlightenment" – seemed to offer better answers to life's ongoing issues ... much better than merely "waiting on the Lord" (who to the original settlers had always been the moral and spiritual guarantor of their success).

And right along with a rising trust in purely human logic grew the illogic of a growing acceptance of witchcraft and sorcery as a supplemental understanding of life's dynamics ... a measure of the distance New Englanders were beginning to put between themselves and the disciplines of Biblical spirituality. The political-moral authorities of the Massachusetts colony attempted to keep some degree of control over this development.

But in the late 1600s this new mood got away from them. Unexplained diseases, sudden Indian attacks, and quarrels over property-rights among the English settlers themselves deeply rattled the peace.

Finally, in February of 1692 in Salem Village, Massachusetts, an accusation of witchcraft aimed at one individual quickly led to an explosive claim of such practices aimed at others (tragically, the fear of witches was common across all the Western world in the 1600s). Some 200 individuals were accused of the crime, 30 found guilty in trial, and ultimately 19 hanged ... before the colony's authorities could get sentences overturned and things finally brought to a halt (April 1693). The impact of this event would forever bring deep shame to the Puritans and their legacy ... though the event itself actually had little to do with Puritanism.

What was happening to America's covenant with God ... to make the American settlement a "Light to the Nations," a "City on a Hill"? As the 1600s came to a close in America, it looked as if America had indeed fallen into the ways of Ancient Israel ... wandering from God when life had finally become so successful that the idea of God and his sovereignty again got lost in the process. What then would the future hold for America ... and for the Western or Christian world in general – which was going through a similar cooling of its Christian spirit?

✳ ✳ ✳

EUROPE DURING THE FIRST HALF OF THE 1700s

The War of the Spanish Succession (1701-1714). As Spanish King Charles II approached death, the question of successor began to trouble greatly Europe's various monarchs.   He himself was childless and the Spanish Habsburg line had no heir to receive the throne ... though there were other claimants to the throne because of marriage ties of ancestors. Charles, after much hesitation named Philip, Duke of Anjou as his heir. But he was a grandson of Louis XIV and though not the first in line to inherit the French throne, that stood as a possibility. In other words, a single individual of the French Bourbon family might end up ruling over a combined French-Spanish state ... a thought so frightening to other European powers that an anti-Bourbon Grand Alliance of England, the Netherlands (both under

William III) and Austria was formed to block this development.

But no one at this point was very ready for war, just having gone through a period of mutual warfare that exhausted most all European powers economically as well as physically. But there was too much at stake for cool diplomacy to work out a compromise ... and the Grand Alliance declared war on France (and its ally Bavaria).

The war did not go well for Louis and his French armies in the surrounding areas of the Spanish Netherlands (Belgium) and in French-held Italy. But neither did it go well in Spain for the Alliance. Opposition began to grow at home to bring the conflict to an end. Finally by the terms of two treaties (1713 and 1714) the war did come to an end, with the Bourbon Philip on the Spanish throne as Philip V ... but with the pledge that the Bourbon kings of Spain would remain independent or separate from the Bourbons of France. With Louis XIV dying in 1715, there was little likelihood that the French would be willing or able to break this pledge. And thus the balance of power among the European monarchs was preserved.

Europe at this point would get something of a break from the intense dynastic rivalry that had been going on since the rise of the powerful monarchies in the 1500s ... but not because the rivalries ceased. They in fact continued ... but with much less drive behind them, because the major European powers came under the rule of less driving personalities and because sponsoring commercial ventures rather than just accumulating European land became the object of the game that occupied the European monarchs. And this took much of the rivalry away from Europe ... and pointed it towards other parts of the globe.

France during the early years of Louis XV (1715-1743). Louis XIV was succeeded by his five-year-old great-grandson, Louis XV,[*] with France thus being placed under the Regency of his great-uncle Philippe (Duke of Orléans). Philippe reversed the diplomatic course of Louis XIV by forming a French alliance with Great Britain (England, Scotland and Ireland were now united as a single kingdom), the Netherlands and Austria – aimed primarily at Spain. But Spain was an easy mark at this point, and this alliance thus fairly easily brought peace to Europe. An economic catastrophe was the only blemish in Philippe's eight-year Regency.[†]

---

[*]Louis XIV had ruled so long (72 years) that he outlived a whole line of successors.

[†]The catastrophe resulted from a speculative investment bubble that developed as the French followed the lead of the Scottish economist John Law, who urged the greatly expanded use of paper money over gold to stimulate the economy. This in turn led to wild investment in the Mississippi Company developing land in American Louisiana. As all speculative bubbles ultimately do, it burst in 1720, ruining financially all sorts of investors.

When Louis finally reached his majority (1723) and Philippe died a few months later, Louis turned to his old tutor, the Catholic Priest Fleury, who in 1726 became both Catholic Cardinal and Louis's first minister. Fleury restored the royal finances that had been exhausted by Louis XIV and guided France diplomatically in such a way that the kingdom was largely at peace during his 17-year premiership, which ended only with the aged Fleury's death in 1743. At this point Louis took full personal control of the running of his kingdom.

The War of the Austrian Succession (1740-1748).   When the Habsburg Holy Roman Emperor Charles VI died in 1740,[*] Europe got drawn into a dispute over who should inherit the throne. When his daughter, Maria Theresa, took the throne, fighting broke out. The ruling families of Britain, France, Spain, the Dutch Republic, Bavaria, Prussia, Denmark, Saxony-Poland, Russia – all got involved in one side or another. The rising German power Prussia, under Frederick II (the Great), made the first move by invading Silesia – thereby doubling Prussia's size. At this point the race was on to see what other parts of the Habsburg holdings one or another European king could swallow before the Habsburgs could get their act together during this time of contested succession.

Military madness.   Indeed, French King Louis XV jumped at the chance to move against Habsburg Austria and take portions of Bohemia; Maria Theresa's Austrian and Hungarian troops countered with an advance against French ally Charles of Bavaria, who was claiming the position of Holy Roman Emperor. The Saxons joined the action as allies of the French and the Prussians. The King of Naples, Charles (soon to be also Spanish King as Charles III), attacked Milan in the North of Italy, drawing an Austrian counter-move. Then English King George II's British army got into the act in order to "balance" the odds, gathering a coalition of smaller German states to support Maria Theresa, thus again pitting the English against the French. Russia tried to get into the action ... but troubles at home weakened the Russian participation. Then Louis XV tried to distract the English by supporting the exiled rebel, "Bonny" Prince Charles Stuart, who had never given up his right as a Stuart to inherit the Scottish – and also English – throne. So the chaos thus spread to Scotland. With the English thus distracted, the French, and their Spanish allies, attempted an invasion of England by sea ... which ultimately went badly for the French and Spanish. Failing there, the French then invaded and occupied the Austrian

------

[*]At this point the lands held by the Habsburg Emperor included Austria, Hungary, Bohemia (the land of the modern-day Czechs), Croatia, Parma (Italy) and smaller scattered holdings in East-Central Europe.

Netherlands (or Belgium – being held since 1714 by the Austrians rather than the Spanish) ... with the Dutch further north being forced to respond.

Action in the Americas. Meanwhile there was also much military action overseas in North America.   The French and their Indian allies conducted many raids against English settlements, which led the colonists of Massachusetts to organize a strong countering move against the strategic French fortress of Louisbourg on Cape Breton Island. They captured the fort (1745) ... and continued to hold it against a French effort to retake it. But at the end of the war in 1748 English King George II returned it to the French in exchange for the Indian port of Madras ... much to the great annoyance of the American colonists who had sacrificed greatly for their victory.

But after all, European wars were not understood to be fought on behalf of any subject people like the colonial Americans – but instead for the personal gain of the ruling families of Europe. Nationalism, focused on the interests of the common people, was not yet (except among the Dutch and the colonial Americans) a driving force in European politics. But it soon would be.

Action in India. India was also brought in as a key piece in the European dynastic competition. The French made the first move (1746) by seizing the port city of Madras, a lightly defended commercial outpost of the British East India Company. When the regional prince or Nawab, an Indian ally of England, attempted to retake Madras, his army was crushed by the French. The British then countered by attacking the commercial settlement of the French Compagnie des Indes at Pondicherry. But it was well fortified and the British soon abandoned the effort. However, at the end of the conflict the British had Madras returned to them in exchange for the return of Louisbourg to the French.

The overall results of the war. In the end, all that this long War of the Austrian Succession produced was the entrance of Prussia into the ranks of Europe's major powers (Prussia got to keep Silesia), the confirmation of Maria Theresa as Austrian Archduchess and Empress of the Holy Roman Empire, France's withdrawal from the Netherlands, France's promise to end support of the Scottish rebellion, and the restoration of French and English overseas territories lost during the war. To the embarrassment of the major players themselves – except Frederick of Prussia, who emerged a hero among his people – little else was achieved by all this military effort ... except the depleting of the treasury of a number of royal families of Europe and the disgruntlement of the civilian populations burdened with the responsibility of replenishing the empty royal treasuries. This would become a source of major trouble in the years ahead.

England (actually now "Great Britain") during these years

Anne. In 1702 William died suddenly from complications of a riding accident. Rule passed directly to his wife's sister, Anne, in accordance with the Act of Settlement of 1701 passed by Parliament to ensure that no Catholic ever became the future ruler of England.

Anne's rule of the next dozen years continued pretty much along the same lines that it had under William at home – with the War of the Spanish Succession being a major focus abroad.

George I (1714-1727). When Queen Anne died in 1714, some fifty eligible heirs to the English throne were passed over because they were Catholic, and the throne was instead given to the German prince-elector of Hanover, who was crowned as George I. The elderly and publicly shy George was hugely German rather than English in spirit and in culture, spoke little English, distrusted the Tories with their pro-Stuart sympathies, and leaned heavily on Whig support in Parliament for his rule. Indeed, by the later years of his thirteen-year rule, effective government of England was in the hands of the leader of the Whig Party in Parliament, Robert Walpole ... making him in essence the first of a long line of "prime ministers" overseeing the governance of Great Britain.

A major event during George's rule was the South Sea Bubble, a wild speculative scheme engineered by the South Sea Company offering stock in support of its goal of taking over most of the huge national debt. With some fraudulent behavior involved, almost immediately stock prices rose so quickly that there was a rush to buy up the company stock. The government then attempted to put a halt on the wild speculation – which had the effect of panicking investors. Thus the value of the stock quickly fell away to one tenth of its peak value. Fortunes were lost and investors ruined – including members of the ranks of the nobility. George himself had not been directly involved (though he personally lost some money himself in the Bubble). In fact, he had been away in Hanover during the wild months of the summer and fall of 1720. Nonetheless George and his cabinet ministers received much of the wrath of the people who lost their fortunes. Eventually the politically rising Walpole was able to restore the kingdom to some degree of financial stability and move the blame away from George ... where it really did not belong anyway.

George II (1727-1760). When George I was away on another trip to Hanover he suddenly died – and his son George (also Germanic rather than English in culture) inherited his father's princely and royal titles in both Hanover and Great Britain. George wanted to replace the politically dominant Walpole, but his wife dissuaded him from doing so because it would have made Parliament impossible to deal with. Indeed, Walpole and Parliament merely strengthened their control over British politics in the years ahead. Anyway, George preferred life in Hanover where he was more of an absolutist ruler ... than England where Parliament dominated.

During the War of the Austrian Succession George spent summers in Hanover conducting the summer military campaigns. Back in England Walpole retired and George's ministry was led by a number of individuals, most importantly by Lord Carteret, a leader of the group wanting to get involved in the War. Despite the military victory at Dettingen (Germany) of a large anti-French coalition which included Britain (led in battle personally by George), the war was unpopular with the English – who felt strongly that George had Hanover's German interests at heart more than Britain's.

Before the war was over George had one other major issue to attend to: the Scottish rebellion under "Bonnie" Prince Charlie (receiving limited aid from France). After initial Scottish successes, the rebellion started losing steam – with France then withdrawing its support. At the Battle of Culloden (1746) George's troops crushed the Scottish forces. Charles was able to escape to France. But many of the Scots were executed. The Jacobites or Stuarts would never again pose a threat to the Hanoverian dynasty ruling Great Britain – England, Scotland and Ireland - as well as Hanoverian Germany.

Rising Prussia

Frederick I and Frederick William I. Actually, Prussia started out as two distinct principalities, Brandenburg-Prussia, united in the person of the leading member of the Hohenzollern family (of the Franconian branch). In 1701, the Duke Frederick of Prussia took for himself the title of "Frederick I, King in Prussia." His son, Frederick William, who took Frederick's place at his death in 1713, turned out to be an ambitious reformer of Prussian life, disciplining the Prussian bureaucracy, strengthening considerably the Prussian military, conducting successful diplomacy in order to keep Prussia out of any expensive wars, and leaving a surplus in the state treasury at his death in 1740.

Frederick II the Great. For the next 46 years (1740-1786), Prussia was under the rule of the extremely capable Frederick II, a patron of the arts and philosophy ... but most importantly the military. He built up a standing army (including a very mobile cavalry) of 80,000 well-trained men, able to move quickly and decisively in action in accordance with Frederick's own exceptionally skillful tactical and strategic direction. Thus the War of the Austrian Succession confirmed Prussia as not only a new "great power," but the only one to gain any real or lasting benefits from the war.

Russia joins the game

Russia since Ivan IV. Ivan had left an infirm son, Feodor, to rule after him, who in turn in 1598 had died childless, ending the Rurikid dynasty that had ruled Moscow since the 800s. During Feodor's reign his brother-in-law and chief minister, Boris Godunov, had actually governed Russia ... and at Feodor's death the Zemsky Sobor (national counsel) voted him as Tsar. Godunov worked hard to open up Russia to Western ways ... but was only very partially successful. When he died in 1605, he left the Russian throne to his son, Feodor II – who was immediately murdered by another claimant to the throne, throwing Russia into the "Time of Trouble."

One individual after another rose and fell as Tsar ... and Russia collapsed socially into devastating disorder. The 1601-1603 famine, accompanied by the plague and the roaming of the countryside by cutthroat brigands, killed approximately one-third of the Russian population. Also the Polish-Lithuanian Commonwealth took advantage of this time of chaos to dominate Russia.

The rise of the Romanovs. Finally in 1613, the Zemsky Sobor turned to the 16-year-old Michael Romanov (whose grandfather, Nikita Romanov, had been a key counselor to Ivan IV), pleading with Michael to become Tsar ... and bring the chaos to an end.

Actually, it was Michael's father, Feodor Romanov, who did the governing of Russia during the first 20 years of Michael's reign. Feodor had been a powerful military boyar (nobleman) who had been forced by a jealous Godunov to take up monastic life ... and who now years later had become the head of the Russian Orthodox Church as Patriarch Filaret! Having the leader of the Orthodox Church as co-ruler with the secular Tsar was actually quite in keeping with Byzantine tradition!

During this period (1613-1633) of father-son governance, Russian political power began to be drawn more closely into the hands of the Tsar ... and economic control over the Russian populace tightened considerably, the aristocracy finally brought under taxation ... and the peasants locked to the land they were born to so that they could not escape to the steppes (where they had been able to avoid taxation).

In 1645 when Michael died, his place as Tsar was taken by his son Alexis (or Alexei) I. His 31 years of rule were marked by a continuing and hugely financially draining war with Poland (1654-1667) and Sweden (1656-1658); a horrible split (or *Raskol*) in the Russian Orthodox Church between the "Old Believers" and the ritual reformers following the heavy-handed lead of Patriarch Nikon; and a Cossack rebellion (drawing the poor in revolt against the oppressive tax system of Russia) in Southern Russia during the period 1667-1671 which had to be put down brutally by the Tsar's streltsy.

When in 1676 Alexis died, his oldest surviving son Feodor III took over at age 15. He was of a liberal nature ... but also sickly and weak. He was a reformer ... but mostly interested in matters of church rather than state reform. In any case he ruled only 6 years before he died.

Peter I Romanov – "The Great" (ruled 1682-1721). The Boyar Duma (council of noblemen) then turned to Feodor's half-brother Peter to take the throne. But he was opposed by followers of another of Alexis's sons, Ivan – whose candidacy was promoted brutally by Ivan's older sister Sophia. She and her streltsy supporters murdered some of Peter's family and friends and then forced the Duma to accept a dual Tsardom of her brother Ivan and her step-brother Peter. Tough as she was, over the next seven years she herself effectively governed. Finally (1689) Peter faced down Sophia ... and had her sent off to a convent, thus ending her political interference. Ivan (as Ivan V) continued formally to rule with Peter. But Ivan was another sickly Romanov... and probably even mentally so. In any case Peter now moved to take charge of Russia personally.[*]

Peter had a tremendous impact on Russia in two important ways. First of all was his modernization of the Russian military and the creation of a Russian navy. To better inform himself of modern Western naval matters – and to try to create a political alliance for Russia that he could use against the Turks – Peter traveled (1697-1698) to Western Europe to study Western ways and to meet with various political leaders. He even worked "incognito" (how exactly could a 6'8" Russian work "incognito"?!!!) for four months at a Dutch shipyard, studying modern shipbuilding. And though he did not achieve his grand alliance, he picked up all sorts of key points about diplomacy. He was an outstanding learner.

With his navy he seized the Turkish Ottoman territory of Azov (adjoining the Black Sea) in 1696 and built his first naval base there (1698). He then turned his attention north to the Baltic Sea. With an alliance of Denmark-Norway, Saxony, and the Polish-Lithuanian Commonwealth, he faced Sweden, dominators of the Baltic Sea. His first effort at fighting Sweden (1700) proved to be largely a failure and he backed off ... but used the time while Sweden continued to fight his allies to reorganize the Russian military. He also began to build his new capital facing out on the Baltic Sea

---

[*]Ivan would die in 1696, making Peter sole ruler at that point.

– St. Petersburg!

Having finally defeated Poland, Sweden now turned its attention to Russia (1708) ... launching an invasion which now went poorly for Sweden. The next year the two armies met further south in Ukraine, which ended disastrously for the Swedes. Unfortunately for Peter, pumped with his sense of military success, he decided to go it alone against the Ottoman Turks (1710-1711). The results were disastrous for Peter ... and he had to return the territory he had earlier seized along the Black Sea (including valuable Azov). But he was soon ready to resume action in the North and challenged the Swedes on sea and on land, taking Livonia (Estonia and Latvia) and Karelia (southern Finland), the vital territory he would need protecting his new capital at St. Petersburg.

But besides the impact he made on Russian military organization and strategy, he also had a huge impact on Russian culture ... having studied culture as closely in his trips to Western Europe as he had studied the art of Dutch shipbuilding. He was particularly interested in West European architecture, and modeled his new capital city after the cities of Western Europe. He even placed a heavy tax on the wearing of the traditional beard and robe, in order to push his noblemen to look more "modern." He did what he could as a follower of the Western "Enlightenment" to curb the powers of the clergy ... leaving the position of Patriarch unfilled after 1700, replacing the Patriarchy with a Holy Synod. He personally also saw to the naming of bishops. And he restricted entry into monasteries until a man reached at least 50. Thus the traditional power of the Byzantine Church in Russia was weakened deeply.

When Peter died in 1725 his position was taken up by his wife Catherine ... though she reigned only two years before she died in 1727. She was followed by their son, Peter II whose also short rule ended in early 1730.

Anna (1730-1740). His place was taken by his cousin Anna, who proved to be as autocratic as any of the most autocratic of her predecessors. In her ten years of rule (1730-1740) she had over 20,000 Russians arrested and subjected to her program of cruel punishment for a variety of political crimes. She favored Germans over Russians as counselors – much to the irritation of her Russian subjects. And she drained the state treasury fighting the Turks in a (successful) effort to regain Azov. Yet despite the expense, this action demonstrated to the world (and the Turks) that the Russians were now a serious power in Eastern Europe.

Elizabeth (1741-1762). The infant Ivan VI was designated future Tsar by his grand-aunt Anna prior to her death ... but was immediately arrested and imprisoned (along with the rest of his family) by the supporters of Elizabeth, daughter of Peter the Great's second wife – of questionable legitimacy in the eyes of many Russians. She would rule Russia for the next 20 years.

But she was unlike Anna, executing not a single person during her reign, but instead devoting herself to developing the fine arts and education in Russia. She established or constructed the University of Moscow, the Imperial Academy of Arts, the Peterhof, the Winter Palace and the Smolny Cathedral in St. Petersburg ... very expensive Baroque monuments to her rule. But perhaps most importantly, she laid the groundwork for her eventual successor, Catherine "the Great."

Catherine II "The Great" (1762-1796). Although Catherine belongs mostly to the last quarter of the 1700s, this is an appropriate time to bring her under discussion. She was (like so much of European royalty) not a native of the land she would eventually govern ... but was instead a German (originally Sophie von Anhalt-Serbst-Dornburg). She was married to Peter III (also actually a German in culture) – who ruled Russia as Tsar only six months (1762) before he was deposed in a plot organized by Catherine (Ekaterina, her Russian Orthodox name).

In her 34-year rule as Russian Empress she worked hard – with only small success – at bringing Russia up to the standards of the European Enlightenment going on in the West. However ... with the outbreak of the French Revolution in 1789, she would turn in opposition against these same principles.

She was very successful in extending Russia's frontiers deeper to the South around the Black Sea, westward into Poland – which she helped to carve up among Prussia, Austria and Russia in a series of divisions or partitions which completely eliminated Poland In 1795 – and eastward even into Alaska on the North American continent. It was her rule that finally brought Russia fully into the ranks of Europe's great powers.

✱ ✱ ✱

THE TURNING POINT: THE SEVEN YEARS' WAR
(ACTUALLY 1754-1763)

Once again, the dynasties of Europe fell into bitter conflict, a conflict that raged not only across Europe, but also North America, Central America, West Africa, India and the Philippines. It involved a number of regional rivalries – between France and Great Britain, Prussia and Sweden, and also Prussia and Austria – though the greatest action was between France and Great Britain. Alliances were formed, quite different from the ones of the War of the Austrian Succession – now involving former enemies as allies.

France now allied with its traditional enemy Austria, joined by Spain, Sweden and Saxony. England allied with Prussia and a number of smaller German states (including naturally Hanover) – and eventually Portugal. Russia also got involved, at first as an ally of Austria, then switching sides in 1762 to become a Prussian ally.

In the Americas. The war started as a dispute over the control of Canada, with France – and its Indian allies – fighting the British and the English-American colonists – and their Indian allies.[*] The Indians resented the rapid expansion of the English colonists into the North American interior and conducted bloody raids on the settlers in an attempt to block this expansion. The French, with interests around the perimeter of these English colonies (Canada to the north, the Mississippi River Valley to the West and the Gulf of Mexico and Florida coast to the South) were just as interested as the Indians in seeing this English expansion in America halted – even reversed.

It was the rush of the English and French to place their own forts in the upper reaches of the Ohio River valley (the river beginning in Western Pennsylvania and flowing west until it joined the Mississippi River) that started the conflict in 1754. The action did not go well for the English (including a young George Washington) and the next year the English swung the action north to New France (Canada) – though here too the French largely held their own over the next couple of years.[†] The British immediately reacted by beginning the expulsion (1755-1763) of some 11,000 of the French Catholic population (the Acadians or "Cajuns") living in British Nova Scotia ... because of their (rightly) suspected disloyalty to the British crown.

Then when the conflict spread to Europe itself, the French pulled troops out of Canada ... and the military situation reversed itself in America. In 1758 the English captured a number of key French forts and the strategic town of Quebec. And in 1760 the British were able to surround and capture Montreal, sealing the fate of Canada, which was now fully in British hands.

In the Caribbean the British navy fought the French navy for the key sugar-producing islands of Guadeloupe and Martinique (considered even more valuable to the British than the English colonies in North America!). Then when Spain got involved, the English quickly took Cuba.

In Europe. War in Europe itself finally broke out in 1757 when France and their allies attacked Prussia (allied only with England and George II's German lands). That did not go well for the French, so they attempted instead to

---

[*]Thus the conflict and ensuing war was known in the English colonies as the "French and Indian War" (1754-1763).

[†]The only British success that year (1755) was their recapture of Louisbourg.

take the war to England. But the expanded French navy proved no match for the British navy (the Battle of Quiberon Bay – 1759) and the French invasion of England had to be called off. When "neutral" Spain* finally got militarily involved in order to help the French by invading Portugal, Spain – like France – found itself in major trouble.

In Asia. Much like the alliances with the Indians in America, the French and English had established conflicting alliance systems with the Asian Indian princes, who had their own local conflicts to deal with. But here too things did not go well for the French, who one by one lost their Indian forts and trading centers to the British. Then with the French rather completely knocked out in India, Britain turned its attention to the Spanish Philippines, taking the capital Manila ... humiliating the Spanish along with the French. In 1763 an exhausted France and Spain finally called for peace.

"Peace." The war had been costly to everyone involved, but particularly to the Spanish, who now fell even lower in political status, and the French, whose royal treasury was on the verge of bankruptcy and whose King Louis XV had also lost major political status even among his own people. On the face of it Great Britain had come out a big winner. But the cost involved in victory would prove to be very problematic ... especially in America where the colonists saw little advantage for themselves in comparison to the burdens they themselves had assumed in helping achieve this English victory.

---

*Spain was not so neutral when it bankrolled the French royal treasury just as its borrowing power had become exhausted by the war. The immense French royal debt at that point appeared to have expanded well beyond the control of the French themselves.

CHAPTER TEN

ENLIGHTENMENT ... AND REVOLUTION

* * *

A DEEP COSMOLOGICAL SPLIT DEVELOPS WITHIN THE WEST

Christianity under fire

This all occurred at a time when the Western Christian world was beginning to see itself faced with an issue bigger than even the persistent animosity between Protestantism and Catholicism.

What was at issue was the question: is Christianity truly an "inspired" religion – its great Truths "revealed" by God through the prophets, and through Jesus, and subsequently through the saints of the Church? Is Christianity a religion designed to bring people to live in humble submission to the historical or continuing and fully active outworking of God's will? Is Christianity a "way" for those seeking to live on eternally (thus also in the "hereafter") in the company of God?

Or is Christianity essentially a moral-ethical program – useful for the orderly behavior of the citizens of this world? Is Jesus to be understood most importantly as the Good Teacher who offers outstanding moral-ethical instruction – and a lofty moral example himself – for the benefit of those choosing to live this life in dignity and with compassion?

By the early 1700s the Christian split was obvious – and profound. On one side of the divide were the "spirituals" or "pietists." On the other side were the "rationalists" or "ethicists." Both claimed to be defending the correct Christian approach to Truth and Order. But their positions were almost mutually exclusive. There was absolutely no common ground that could pull these two "Christian" groups together.

America's "Great Awakening" religiously ... and politically

Then, in the late 1730s and early 1740s – just as it appeared that the Christian foundations of early English-America were also about to die out because of a lack of spiritual interest or even cultural support – something mysterious infected the American heart. The "Great Awakening" suddenly broke out upon the American scene ... to restore the warmth of American affection for God and Jesus – and the belief once again in God's total sovereignty in America.

Actually the event first broke out in England, as a result of the evangelical ministry of the brothers John (the preacher) and Charles (the musician) Wesley ... and their "Methodist" supporters.* On a (rather unsuccessful) missionary trip (1736) to the newly established American colony of Georgia, John came into the company of some Moravians – who modeled for him a strongly-grounded Christian faith ... one that would impact Wesley deeply. It inspired John to go about churches in Britain and Ireland – then even the streets and open fields – to call his fellow Englishmen to repentance and spiritual salvation. Thus his "Methodism" spread itself across his English world.

Joining him in this effort was fellow Oxford student George Whitefield ... who also had an interest in taking the message to America. He would spend the rest of his life moving back and forth from England to America – preaching wherever he could.

But the Americans put forward a number of outstanding evangelists of their own ... who had a huge impact in restoring the Christian faith in their world – for instance, Theodore Freylinghuysen, William and Gilbert Tennent, Jonathan Edwards, David Brainerd, Samuel Davies ... and others.

But without a doubt the greatest impact on America came from Whitefield, who repeatedly moved north and south through the colonies, drawing hundreds of thousands to hear his preaching, calling on Americans to repent of their indifference to God and to return to live under his sovereign rule as free and equal followers of Christ.[†]

The net result of this grand revival was three-fold. It revived the Americans' sense of personal responsibility to serve a higher cause as a covenant people, pledged to live socially to the high standards of the Christian faith. It worked to build in the colonists a collective *national* spirit as "Americans" – producing an identity well beyond that of being just "Virginians," or "New Yorkers," etc. And it restored among these Americans the understanding that in crossing the great Atlantic Ocean they had cut their ties with an English political system that held millions in servitude to absolutist monarchs ... and that in America, their sole responsibility was to

---

*The term "Methodist" was originally a term of derision used by fellow Oxford University students who mocked the Wesleys and fellow members of their Holy Club for their efforts to develop a more disciplined Christian faith during their studies at Oxford.

†Estimates are that he preached over 18,000 sermons to as many as perhaps ten million people in Britain and America ... until his death in 1770 at age 50.

God and neighbor alone. They would defend that notion with their lives if need be. And just such a need there would be ... quite soon.

"Enlightened Despotism"!

Back in the second half of the 1600s (and into the early 1700s), French King Louis XIV had justified his heavy-handed rule along philosophical lines not unlike that which Hobbes had earlier called for: the need of the people to come under an "enlightened" Leviathan, an absolute or "despotic" father-figure who would rule the people with an iron fist for their own best interests.

Louis was careful to pay close attention to all the discussions of enlightenment thinking, sponsoring scientific research (especially when it could be beneficial to his military ambitions) and giving the appearance of being an earnest contributor to the new thinking coming out of the emerging scientific age. This was what the ideal of "enlightened despotism" was supposed to be all about.

But it came at a great social price to France, leaving that country after his death in 1715 in a state of economic and intellectual dependency on the massive French monarchical system, which it was unlikely that any personality less than Louis XIV's could sustain. Indeed, the French state began to slide into economic disarray shortly after him, leading to the entire collapse of the French state in the late 1780s.

The Jesuits

By the time of Louis XIV, the most militant defenders of the "True Faith" (Roman Catholicism, or more particularly the authority of the Pope) – the Jesuits – had lost much of their original spiritual character ... and had become a quite thoroughly political organization. They not only linked themselves with Catholic kings who promised support of the Catholic cause, but they became closely involved in the political intrigue not only aimed against Protestants but also directed to the rise and fall of particular monarchs. They were politically astute – and dangerous to work with.

Louis XIV used them to help drive the Huguenots out of France – though he was also cautious with them because of his "Gallican" policy of bringing the church in France directly under his own political supervision ... thus in political contest with the Roman Pope – whom the Jesuits were pledged to serve at all costs. But those costs would come to them ... when European monarchs finally moved to shut down the Jesuit order.

Charles Louis de Montesquieu (1689-1755)

Montesquieu, was a well-traveled French nobleman – including time spent in England (1729-1731), where he became impressed with the social progress underway there since the "Glorious Revolution" of the late 1600s ... and the growth of Parliamentary power under the Hanoverian kings. He was to have a tremendous impact on rising political thought – especially in America where his writings, most notably *The Spirit of the Law* (1748) would eventually guide the Constitutional Framer and future U.S. President Madison greatly in his understanding of what constitutional law is all about: what it is to achieve, and how it is to do that.

The law as simply a man-made social instrument. To Montesquieu, the "law" is simply the set of rules that a society goes by in order to keep itself together and moving forward, in accordance with some kind of basic social principle. In his study abroad – and historically (for instance his 1734 work, *Considerations on the Causes of the Greatness of the Romans and their Decline*) – he understood that social laws are definitely merely man-made. And such legal creativity varies widely from culture to culture ... and from geographic location and climate to geographic location and climate. And these laws sometimes have been effective social instruments. And sometimes they have been sadly ineffective in serving societies, notably when they faced serious challenges.

He most definitely was not a believer that there existed some set of universal social laws – universal laws such as existed in the material world of physics and chemistry – universal social laws that other philosophers (the "Positivists") hungered to discover. To Montesquieu, law was a highly varying product of human invention – and that alone. This could be very good; this could be very bad.

The system of checks and balances. He was not a person who favored one particular social type over another.   But he definitely understood that whatever social principle a society worked by (whether democratic republic, aristocracy, or monarchy) it had to guard carefully against allowing governing power to fall into the hands of those who used their positions of power solely for selfish purposes – a development he termed "despotism."

And since human nature tends over time to like to gather into its own hands as much power as possible, the best way to guard against this despotic tendency was to set up a system of laws that separated the powers of government ... particularly through the separation of legislative, executive, and judicial authority. In doing so, they would check and balance each other in authority ... so that despotic power could not develop.

How history has validated Montesquieu.   It was this insight of

Montesquieu's that had a huge impact in the shaping of the 1787 American Constitution – with its "checks and balances system." However the French – and in particular the despot Robespierre – chose to ignore Montesquieu's wisdom ... and turned their French Revolution into a horribly murderous affair (1789-1795) – pretty much along the lines that Montesquieu predicted would happen if power fell into a single set of hands.

Jean-Jacques Rousseau undercuts the idea of royal sovereignty

A key individual coming onto the European political stage a generation later was the French-cultured Swiss, Jean-Jacques Rousseau (1712-1778), whose writings, especially *The Social Contract* (1762), became quite popular in France. Rousseau raised the question of political sovereignty, where it was lodged and how it functioned to best serve the people.

Rousseau claimed that originally man lived in some kind of simple natural state of harmony, without laws or government. But life had evolved over time into a more complex form – civilization – requiring as it developed greater mutual dependence among men for the orderly working of society, and thus also a more complex system of moral instruction or law to guide society. Man accordingly had to give up his total personal sovereignty to come under the protection and nurture of this more complex society. But he was giving it up not to some ruling individual but to the larger idea of the society as a whole, the general will – in particular its laws, which were the clearest expression of a people's general will.

The laws, not any particular individuals, were the locus of sovereignty in the truly good society. Unfortunately, ignorance of this good had clouded people's political understanding, causing them to slip into all forms of political tyranny – absolute rule over society by particular individuals such as kings and dukes, which was the general pattern of Rousseau's day.

Rousseau's hope was to open men's eyes to the understanding of what was truly right and good about society, that such knowledge would free men to usher in a good or utopian society that was truly the right of everyone to enjoy, not just the privileged few. All the superfluous fluff of decadent civilization – in particular French civilization as it was viewed in his own time – would be simply swept away by the opening of the eyes of the people to the Truth.

With the *Ancien Régime* – the *Old Order* comprised of the officers of the king and church that dominated all European society in the 1700s – thus swept away, society would be free to create or contract a social system as simple and basic as possible, a social system directed by a set of basic laws that restored to man his fundamental liberties, allowing him to live as close to the original state of nature as possible.

The French were strongly impacted by Rousseau's theories – as have been many revolutionary-minded secular philosophers since Rousseau (as well as modern hippies trying to go back to nature in simple communal living). Rousseau's vision of primitive society even found its way into the polite social gatherings or salons of Europe's ruling classes and their intellectual tutors. Thus it was that the future queen Marie Antoinette used to love to play in the Versailles palace gardens with fellow maidens at the French court at being a peasant girl herding her sheep. It was all so quaint, so romantic.

The French monarchy was sick, very sick. Reform was needed. But by Rousseau's logic, that reform was going to have to be extensive for the good society to result. The Ancien Régime was going to have to be set aside in its entirety in order to make way for the new. Thus with Rousseau's encouragement, the French political mood was becoming increasingly revolutionary as the political debate in the late 1700s intensified in France.

British Pragmatism takes a different path

British empiricism. Across the channel in the British Isles, the British were of a more practical mindset in their love of hands-on experimentation than their continental cousins, who loved to sit at their desks or gather at polite salons to indulge themselves in the world of pure thought. During the Enlightenment, the British were too busy inventing new material technologies – and developing the industries to put those technologies to practical use – to be wasting time speculating about hypothetical realities. They were all, by nature, Empiricists.

David Hume promotes empiricism. In the mid-1700s the Scottish philosopher David Hume (1711-1776) had his own answer to the Rationalism that infected so much of European society. As a philosophical empiricist, the widely read and respected Hume found sufficient Truth for life in simply observing actual behavior, and the results it produced. Results were to Hume real Truth. Long-abiding custom – in other words, social rules that actually worked over the long run – were for Hume the foundations on which to build human life.

Likewise, Hume was most unimpressed by the great intellectual "spins" that philosophers wove around hypothetical behavior in building their great systems of thought. For Hume, reality was in the doing, not in the hypothesizing about life.

Widely studied, Hume became well-known in his time for his skepticism about speculations about God, or great systems of religious Truth, or the validity of "objective" ethical systems, even the claims of science to have established an explanation of all life in terms of cause and effect. All this was to Hume mere intellectual humbuggery.

Hume's impact lived long after him. In fact it was Hume that awakened the great German philosopher Kant from his "intellectual slumber" (as Kant himself put it) and caused Kant to undertake the task of responding to the challenge that Hume had issued to those who would claim to understand human nature, even life itself.

Adam Smith explains capitalism. In the meantime, the British were very busy inventing new material technologies, and developing the industries to put those technologies to practical use.

Building on this attitude was the fellow Scot, Adam Smith (1723-1790), who in his *Wealth of Nations* (1776) wrote a compelling explanation of how simply letting the competitive marketplace bring forward the material blessings of life – and the pricing involved for such wealth – would also naturally bring forth human progress. He was much opposed to the idea of forcing on society the designs of utopian social planners, who would soon enough make a mess of things with their well-reasoned schemes.

In fact, Smith was strongly opposed to any kind of "intervention" into this market mechanism by the government or any other outside societal institution. To Smith (and all capitalist philosophers since then) this independence of commercial action was the key doctrine of Capitalist philosophy.

But at the same time, Smith was highly opposed to market insiders getting together to conspire to set prices through a withholding of goods or services to create an artificial scarcity. He was thus opposed to cartels, monopolies, and unions, of any variety. He also considered the danger of rapid population growth distorting the labor market and driving prices down to subsistence levels. But he felt that economic growth of the whole industrial sector would constantly increase the demand for labor and thus prevent such cruelties from occurring.

Kant attempts a compromise
between British Empiricism and French Rationalism

Immanuel Kant (1724-1804) was something of a father to German philosophy, setting out, just prior to the French Revolution, to locate some kind of intellectual bridge between the powerful philosophies of French Rationalism and British Empiricism.

Kant agreed with Hume's empiricism, namely that essential to human knowledge is our sense experience – the experience of the seeing, feeling, hearing, etc. of real material objects around us. But he also agreed with the continental Rationalists (most notably Leibniz, whose writings also were a major influence on Kant) that knowledge is also a matter of the exercise of human reason, in particular the use of innate human ideas ("categories") which we are born with and which help us to organize this empirical information. Thus Kant saw himself as closing the intellectual gap between the British Empiricists and the Continental Rationalists.

Kant also saw himself as answering Hume's skepticism about ever knowing with any degree of certainty the Truth of transcendent ideas, such as moral laws or ethical principles (not to mention the idea of Heaven itself). In Kant's *Metaphysics of Morals* (1785) and *Critique of Practical Reason* (1788), he proposed a new moral/ethical "categorical imperative, " one that did not require the existence of God for its validity. It involved an ingenious piece of moral logic: we ought to act in such a way that our act could become accepted as a universal principle of behavior. If it were not able to attain such a universal validity – because, for instance, of an internal contradiction in logic – then that action, by "practical reason," was obviously not to be pursued.

Taking this logic of "practical reason" a step further, he turned to the issue of the existence of God. He agreed with Hume that no rational argument could be given for God's existence – that is, "pure reason" could not build a case for God's existence. But "practical reason" could. Pursuing a traditional line of reason that went back at least as far as Ockham in the early 1300s, Kant claimed that human reason cannot establish the "fact" of God. But in observing the moral instincts of people we can see – through the eyes of faith – that there is some kind of source beyond the mere human will itself that directs life. That higher moral grounding is by definition God. Thus God exists. (This kind of theological reasoning did not, however, impress the Prussian government – which censured his work).

Finally, so impressed was Kant that we humans could live in accordance with such higher moral imperatives that in his *Perpetual Peace* (1795) he laid out a vision for a new world order. Here (despite the Reign of Terror going on viciously in France at the time) he contributes greatly to the utopian idealism that will absorb the thoughts and aspirations of intellectuals for generations to come.

Jean-Baptiste de Lamarck places the idea of "natural progress" on a scientific basis

Change was in the air. A sense that something new, something revolutionary, was about to break forth seemed to be the understanding of the times (the latter part of the 1700s). "Progress" was the new by-word.

Clearly history had always been pointing toward some great new development in life on this planet ... politically, intellectually, morally, even spiritually.

Reinforcing this idea was the way the new "science" itself pointed to such "progress" as the inevitable move of all history. Things had long been moving forward in a state of constant progress ... progress that now seemed about to reach its highest achievement.

A big step in the early development of the theory of evolution by "natural" development was made by the French botanist, Jean-Baptiste de Lamarck (1744-1829). He was concerned about the overwhelming body of empirical "facts" that were being collected by scientific observers – pointing to a need for systematization (in the manner of Linnaeus) and for the construction of theories that would make all this material speak to our sense of understanding in a useful way. Thus he began publishing a number of works of a wide scientific scope, all designed to explain the process of the earth's natural, physical life: *Research on the Causes of Principal Physical Facts* (1794); *System of Invertebrate Animals, or General Table of Classes* (1801); *Hydrogeology* (1802).

Most importantly, in his 1809 *Zoological Philosophy* (which he presented to the French dictator Napoleon) he demonstrated that through chemical influences acting on organisms to create new traits and by the environmental forces shaping these traits through necessary adaptation, organisms had progressed over time. This included humans, in which human learning did not start out with a blank sheet (as per Locke's theory) but was built in part not only on the development of natural biological adaptation but also on the received aspects of learning derived by a person's ancestry. Thus learning could be understood as potentially progressive, evolving from one generation to the next, if carefully engineered with that understanding.

But he then went much further ... in theorizing that life, in all its varied form, had evolved historically over the very long run of the earth's history. He conceived this evolution as a step-by-step development of plant and animal life by which ever more evolved forms replaced more primitive forms – as if life had scaled a ladder from lower to higher forms, culminating after eons of earth time in the emergence of human life.

He identified the driving force behind this evolution as being that of a dynamic process by which life urges itself forward toward perfection and changes along the way of this process as organs and characteristics are either taken on or dropped on the basis of their usefulness (or lack thereof) to the species in this quest. Giraffes thus developed longer necks and legs because this proved useful to them in reaching the higher vegetation on a tree.

There were, of course, many flaws in such bold, far-reaching theorizing. For instance, how such alterations in species form are preserved and passed on to a new generation was not really answered by Lamarck. Ultimately, a lot of his theorizing was overturned later with the development of genetic science. But at the time, the apparent reasonableness of his utilitarian theories gave great impetus to the notion of a "natural" development of life – one that needed no divine intervention to explain its workings.

✳ ✳ ✳

THE AMERICAN "REVOLUTION" (1770s-1780s)

The monarchical principle in trouble. When Prussia's popular King Frederick II (the Great) blocked an Austrian attempt to retake Silesia with his own surprise attack on Austria's ally, Saxony – and then treated high-handedly the Polish-Saxon royal family (directly connected to Louis XV of France) in their defeat – European nobility (and even French commoners) were outraged. This was not how royalty were to be treated.

But in fact, royal absolutism was beginning to slip. Questions were now being raised on the European continent about the divine rights of kings. As humanist rationalism blossomed among Europe's intellectuals and aristocrats, the very idea of *God-given authority* certainly found itself losing its compelling qualities. If divine rights lost its grip on the minds and hearts of Europeans, what then, morally speaking, justified all this royal absolutism?

Indeed, the Enlightenment had unleashed all sorts of philosophical conversations about reforming European governments in order to make them more rational, more "enlightened." The debacle of the French role in the Seven Years' War, plus the shocking state of the French king's finances, plus rumors about the king's mistress, Madame de Pompadour, and her role in the rapid turnover of the King's advisors, all became topics of conversation by intellectuals and noblemen (female as well as male) who gathered in the "salons" of fashionable French homes to discuss the decaying state of French society. But the conversations could also be heard in the streets of Paris by commoners, who raised many of the same questions.

The American colonies move to full independence

George III's royalist absolutism. During the course of the recent Seven Years' War, George II died (1760) and his place was taken by his 22-year-old grandson George III. However, this George was not a German ... but was fully English (he never even visited his estates in Hanover). He was very well-educated or "enlightened" in his youth ... and was tightly disciplined by his mother, who took the responsibility of making sure that her son would someday be every bit the absolutist king (that the first two Georges were not!) that the Bourbon family of France modeled for the rest of Europe's royalty.

For the American colonies, who under the first two Georges (1714-1760) had been left largely alone to conduct their own political and economic affairs, George III's efforts to live up to his mother's expectations of him as an absolutist king – over America as well as over his holdings in Europe – would come as a huge political shock ... which soon enough would fuel the fires of full rebellion.

Taxation without representation. Because of the Seven Years' War, George III's debt had nearly doubled in size and he needed new taxes to replenish his royal treasury. His thinking was that the colonies had benefited from his military action in America and therefore they should pay up ... without considering that they had carried much of the burden of the action themselves without compensation. Worse, he simply imposed new taxes without first consulting the colonial tax payers themselves – in direct violation of an ancient right of all Englishmen to be consulted first. The Whigs in the English Parliament were sympathetic to the colonials when they began to object loudly; the Tories however supported the King's rather autocratic move. And at this point George was relying principally on his Tory supporters.

Growing conflict with "Yankee" independent-mindedness. Also, the King began to take the attitude that the colonials – especially those of New England – were far too independent-minded and needed in principle to be shown who now was in charge (unlike his immediate predecessors). Thus the King sent soldiers to unruly Boston to protect the tax collectors ... to which the citizens of Boston reacted by dumping tea into the Boston harbor (1773).* (Also other American towns were boycotting the British tea.)

George countered (1774) by shutting down the port of Boston and forcing their citizens to house the often unruly soldiers ... to break their spirit. Then he moved to make good on his promise to France to outlaw the further expansion of colonial settlements westward so that the Catholic French could place their own settlements there. Also there were the rumors that he was going to bring the independent congregations of Protestant New England and the Middle Colonies under episcopal authority (rule by bishops ... a system which Virginia and the Carolinas were already under) ... and thus under his direct control as head of the English Church.

––––––––––––––––

*Actually, the reaction was not only about taxes but also about the fact that the King was subsidizing the earnings of the struggling British East India Company ... forcing the colonies to buy their tea, when in fact Dutch tea was much cheaper.

War. Finally, war started (1775) when he sent his troops by night to seize the gunpowder stored in Concord ... producing actual shooting on both sides (which the British received the worst of). When colonial troops then gathered in the heights above Boston, the English counterattacked ... and finally after much loss of life (twice the numbers on the British side) the colonials withdrew. But the colonial troops returned that winter – but this time with cannon – in the heights around British-held Boston. The British then wisely vacated Boston ... never to return. But a British-American war was now clearly underway in any case.

That next summer (1776) the colonials made formal (their *Declaration of Independence*) what was clearly evident in their behavior: they considered themselves a fully independent and thus self-governing people – under the authority of their own elective Continental Congress. It was a daring move. The Dutch had performed this same feat ... but it had taken them some 80 years (1568-1648) of agonizing war to carry off their own independence from Habsburg Spain. Furthermore, the American colonials were considered in comparison to the sophisticated Dutch to be a rather boorish people. The English expected the crushing of this rebellion to be short work. Other Europeans stood by wondering.

The French join the action. But the wondering ceased when in 1777 the colonials destroyed a British army of 6,000 men at Saratoga. France now joined the war on the American side ... the recently crowned French King Louis XVI more than happy to make whatever trouble he could for British King George III.

The Impact on French thinking. Thus the new conflict began to take shape the way dynastic conflicts typically did ... except that Louis had no idea of what he was getting involved with. The idea of a subject people rising in rebellion against their king was not a principle he should have been supporting ... no matter how much trouble it brought France's traditional enemy England. But Louis simply could not think past the idea that all politics was simply a matter of relations among the members of the feudal ruling classes. It had always been this way. Thus all that Louis saw in this dynamic was his ability to take political advantage of the troubles encountered by a fellow monarch.

However, his soldiers who served in America would become quite infected with the idea that the people had political rights of their own ... and that it was okay for them to break free from their sovereign king when they possessed the moral right to do so. Considering that the Enlightenment conversations in the French salons were already bringing up such questions as the right and wrong of politics, the American rebellion was likely to prove toxic to French politics. And indeed it did.

American victory. With key French help in the huge British defeat at Yorktown (1781), the colonials finally broke the last of the English will to continue the conflict ... and the English sued for peace. The Americans had done it ... secured their independence from royal rule in basically six (but very hard) years!

The uniting of the 13 new states as a federation. In coming together to fight George III's aggressions, the inhabitants of the English colonies in America had certainly thought of themselves quite seriously as "Americans." Otherwise they still typically saw themselves as Georgians, Virginians, New Yorkers, etc.

Thus when the English armies were finally sent back to England at war's end, they proceeded to look to the development of their former colonies as newly independent states, Massachusetts, Pennsylvania, New Jersey, Virginia, South Carolina, etc. Despite a continuance of the Confederation that had held them together during the recent war, the lack of a continuing common cause had demonstrated the weaknesses built into this union. Thus they were beginning to compete diplomatically and economically with each other in their ongoing relations with the Old World of Europe. They were even erecting trade barriers against each other's products in the hope of encouraging the development of the industry and commerce of their particular state.

Those who had given so much of themselves during the war now grew alarmed at where this new narrow view of patriotism was taking them. Not only was this hurting the Americans financially, but their disunity could give opportunity to one of the major European powers (Spain, France or even England) to come and force them back into colonial status.* Particularly now choosing to work independently of each other, any one of these small states would be an easy pickoff by the more powerful European monarchs.

Thus delegates from twelve states (Rhode Island refused to participate) gathered in Philadelphia in the summer of 1787 to put together some kind of a stronger constitutional union that would face them outward in common defense ... and inward with an agreement to do away with these trade barriers they had been erecting.

But many were suspicious of a central power (they had just fought off the power of the English King and Parliament) and would come to support

---

*Treaties in those days were indications only of a pause in a conflict ... not its resolution. Treaties were made and unmade in rapid succession. Thus the Treaty of Paris recognizing American independence by the British could be broken at any time the British noticed a weakness among any of the American states.

the idea of a union only under the promise of a number of guarantees that this federal union would not compromise the powers of the states ... and the people themselves. Thus a promise was made to add a Bill of Rights to the Constitution as soon as it was ratified and a new government formed under its provisions.

The Constitution itself provided for a system of power distribution that would use the natural human tendency of those in power to want to accumulate even more power ... to have that tendency offset by other parts of the governing system acting in the same way. As already noted, this system was well recognized at the time – thanks to the writings of the French political philosopher Montesquieu, who had studied carefully the mechanics of the British government – and was termed the "checks-and-balances system." Law-making powers were assigned to a Congress of two Houses, a Senate representing the States and a House of Representatives representing the citizen voters. But the legislative powers of Congress were carefully limited to only those outlined in the Constitution itself. A President was designated as the chief executive officer (and head of the military and the diplomatic corps) whose job was to oversee the implementation of the laws made by Congress. And a federal judiciary was designated to try cases coming under constitutional law. All other powers, most particularly the laws that guided the daily affairs of the American people were (by the Bill of Rights) reserved to the States ... and to the people themselves. Thus the Constitution provided for a limited government to protect the unity of the individual states ... and little more than that, lest it should want to take upon itself ever-wider powers. It was understood that sovereignty remained with the people and the states.

Whether or not this system would continue to work as originally intended would ultimately depend on the people themselves. The historical record for popular vigilance in this regard was not good. Thus when America's well-recognized wise one, Benjamin Franklin, was asked at the end of the meetings that had been held in secret as to what kind of government they had come up with, his answer was: "a Republic ... if you can keep it."*

✳ ✳ ✳

---

*__Note: of critical importance.__ Keeping those powers separate and not having them come – by human instinct itself – into the hands of a smaller and more powerful group of authorities has been very difficult, even in America, where the national authority has slowly stripped state and local authorities of much their power, where federal judicial authority (most notably the Supreme Court) has taken on greater legislative powers than Congress, and where the president employs executive power solely in accordance with his own personal tastes ... and through extensive bureaucratic control of the nation's life – control that Congress seems unable (or unwilling) to check.

THE FRENCH REVOLUTION (1789-1799) ... AND NAPOLEON

Supporting the war in America of course had only worsened the situation for the French royal treasury (once again!). Taxes would have to be raised. And because both the Church and the nobility were exempted from taxation, this would all fall on the French tax-paying commoners (the moneyed middle class), who were already heavily burdened with taxes. Discussions about revising the tax system led nowhere. Eventually the discussion moved to the idea of taxing the nobility ... gaining opposition from that quarter... but merely highlighting all the more the privileges of the nobility versus the burdens of the commoners. At this point (May 1789) Louis XVI was forced to turn to the Estates-General (a French National Assembly representing all three estates of: church, nobility and commoners). Because of the practice of royal absolutism, this august body had not been convened by a French king since 1614. With this call to assemble, French politics exploded.

It was apparent from the beginning that the Third Estate (commoners) was going to dominate the proceedings ... and had a number of economic and political reforms they were demanding to be put in place or they would not be willing to cooperate with the King. Seeing the calling of the Estates-General as a mistake, Louis then tried to shut down the assembly (June), only to have the members of the Third Estate move to a nearby tennis court, and there swear an oath to not leave until a new constitution was granted by the king.* Indecisive behavior by the King, the arrival of troops to Paris, and all sorts of rumors circulating around the streets of Paris, set off rioting and looting culminating in the storming of the Bastille castle (July) and the complete breakdown of royal authority when the King's troops began to side with the Paris mob of *sans culottes* (workers who wore trousers rather than knee-length silk breeches or *culottes*).

At this point the Third Estate was now meeting as the "National Constituent Assembly," working on a new Constitution for France, which included the ending of all the privileges of the Church and the nobility. Frenchmen of all classes now stood equally before the law, stated clearly in the new *Declaration of the Rights of Man* (August). In one stroke, French feudalism had come to an end.

Some noblemen were willing to go along with the new France. But many (émigrés) showed their opposition by fleeing to other countries ... and appealing to the rest of European nobility to form a counter-revolution in order to restore the nobility's ancient feudal rights in France. This merely put all the nobility (and upper-level Church authority) in the eyes of the new

---

*Certainly influencing French thinking along these lines was the coming into full effect of the new American Constitution, when just a couple of months earlier (April) Washington was sworn in as the new American President.

French "citizen" under suspicion of treason.

Then when the King himself attempted to escape France (June 1791) and was caught at the border, he was returned to Paris now also under similar suspicion.

The target of reform was not only the old royal-feudal structure of France but also the Church organization that had long supplied it its legitimacy. Church property was turned over to the Assembly, which then sold the land in order to raise needed revenues. Clergy now became civil employees paid by the State, required to swear loyalty to the State rather than the Pope. Most clergy refused and were treated as traitors.

The Constitution was finally approved in September of 1791, providing for a constitutional monarchy: a single legislative body (basically the National Assembly), a monarch with limited veto powers, and an independent judiciary. But it was short-lived ... as the King used his remaining powers to protect priests who had refused the oath of loyalty to France rather than the Pope. He was also accused of showing little interest in organizing a national army to protect France from the larger reaction against the Revolution by the surrounding powers. Thus when French action against the Austrians and then the Prussians proved dispirited and unsuccessful, the blame fell on the King.

The insurrection. The Assembly now seemed to be given over to increasingly radical voices calling for the King's abdication. At the same time, however, anti-Revolutionary sentiment seemed to be spreading in the conservative (and still quite pro-Catholic) countryside ... especially the Vendée ... adding to the nervousness of Paris. Finally in August of 1792, a bloody Paris insurrection exploded and the indecisive King lost the last of his powers ... and was arrested and imprisoned. At this point the Assembly (heavily represented by lawyers) also lost its powers, as Paris came under the control of local committees made up of a variety of radicals, some of even a working-class background.

The Convention. Elections were then called (with all adult male Frenchmen voting) to send representatives to a new constitutional Convention. When it met in September it decreed the end to the monarchy, the beginning of the French (First) Republic, and a new non-Christian calendar beginning at year 1 (1792).

The King is guillotined. The Girondins, led by the more pragmatic Georges Danton, were less radical than the Jacobins. The Girondins were less interested in bringing the King to trial than in keeping the Paris Commune from totally dominating all aspects of the French Revolution. The Jacobins, led by the Idealist Maximilien Robespierre – and which interestingly included in their ranks a number of noblemen, including even the King's cousin Louis Philippe – reflecting Paris radicalism, were in favor of the King's death. A vote in early 1793 on the matter split the Convention, with the Jacobins (and some Girondins) gaining a small majority. Thus the King was executed at the guillotine like a mere commoner three days later.

It was shocking. A king had been executed by his own people. But this merely marked the beginning of the Republic's struggle to find some semblance of political structure. With the King out of the way, Girondins and Jacobins turned on each other. Robespierre's Jacobins accused Danton's Girondins of conspiracy to betray the Revolution ... with every attempt to answer the accusations making the Girondins look all the more guilty. The Paris mob now was at the door, demanding the expulsion of the traitors (the Girondins). Twenty-nine Girondin leaders were arrested and carried off. The Girondin party was devastated (summer 1793).

The Republican Constitution (1793). The way was clear now for the finishing of the new Constitution. The preamble was even more utopian than the earlier *Declaration of Human Rights*. Not only was freedom of speech and press and equality of all before the law guaranteed, the Declaration proclaimed that all French had the right to education, to work, to receive public assistance, even to rise in rebellion if the government failed to deliver on these rights.

Even though the Constitution provided for a Legislative Assembly, since the days of the Convention the real work had been performed through a series of committees, the most important of which was the Committee of General Security (which searched for enemies of the Revolution to bring to "justice"). With the creation of the Republic, that function was then taken over by the Committee of Public Safety.

The "Reign of Terror" (1793-1794). In October, trials of the enemies of the Revolution began in earnest. The Queen was guillotined, then much of the Girondin leadership as well. As arrests began to become more widely sweeping through French society, the Committee of Public Safety, now headed by Robespierre, became more absolute in its control. Indeed, by the end of 1793 Robespierre was the virtual dictator of Republican France.

Not only did the Paris guillotine work overtime to kill thousands of enemies of the Revolution, the French army found itself busy in the French countryside putting down anti-Revolutionary rebellions. Worst was in the Vendée where the army conducted something akin to genocide in bringing the people of that province into submission. Estimates of those who died in the Vendée range from a quarter to over a half of the population of 800,000.

By the next summer (1794) the Revolutionary Tribunal was at its most active in trying and executing the Republic's enemies at home. The Jacobins were persuaded that only terror could shake the people's feudal Catholic mindset and free them to rise fully to the rule of human "Reason."

Indeed, the Cult of Reason was intentionally set forth as the new state-sponsored atheistic worldview (or religion), designed to replace France's long-standing Catholic foundations. As such, "Reason" was required of all those true to French Republicanism. Thus it was that in November of 1793, at the height of the Reign of Terror, churches across France were forcibly transformed into Temples of Reason, including most importantly Paris's Notre Dame Cathedral – where a huge procession followed a newly appointed "Goddess of Reason" and her white-clad girls into the cathedral and placed her on the altar to be worshiped. This worship of "Human Reason" in turn merely stirred more deeply the radical instincts of those most dedicated to the "social cleansing" taking place in Paris and across much of France.

But the public mood itself was now beginning to turn against all this social terror, a terror that Robespierre praised as the hallmark of true Republican Revolution. When in July (1794) 16 nuns went singing to the Paris guillotine for the crime of choosing to remain nuns, things took a turn for Robespierre. Political jealousy within the Committee of Public Safety also motivated his arrest (end of July) ... and execution the next day.

With the downfall of Robespierre (and other Jacobin leaders) the Committee of Public Safety lost influence ... and eventually the use of the word "terror" itself became a crime. The Thermidorian Reaction had set it.

The Directory (1795-1799).   Surviving Girondins now took charge, wrote a new constitution and put it before the people, who approved it overwhelmingly. The new constitution provided for a bi-cameral legislature and a five-man executive committee, termed the Directory. Unfortunately for France this executive scheme proved largely unworkable (in part also because of the poor level of political talent among the directors). The Directory tried to step back from the excesses of the Revolution ... and was able to do so only because politically the country was exhausted. But these were shaky foundations. Besides, the French government still had not solved the problem of an empty state treasury ... and the economy in general was in very bad shape. And corruption was a problem the new government seemed unable to overcome.

The French army.   The major difference between the French army and those of its enemies was that the French army, by the end of 1792, was made up of masses of conscripted or drafted commoners ... literally hundreds of thousands of new "citizens" called on to defend their Republic ... whereas the armies of their adversaries tended to be paid soldiers, forming smaller armies limited in size by the size of the treasury of their royal employers. Also the French developed the use of different services in tactical support of each other, particularly the use of artillery in support of the infantry (and of course cavalry for the same purpose). Particularly skillful in this regard was a young artillery officer, Napoleon Bonaparte ... who would soon distinguish himself as an excellent tactician.

Advance against other European powers. The French found some degree of sympathy for the Republican cause in other parts of Europe ... in particular among the Dutch, who in 1795 set up (with the help of the French army) a new Batavian Republic – something of a sister republic of France's. Also, Prussia turned the west bank of the Rhine over to France ... in order to concentrate on its war with Poland. Spain was pacified (1795). Then Napoleon advanced into northern Italy, defeating both Italian and Austrian efforts to block his advance (1796-1797). From Italy he headed north to attack Austria, which soon called for a peace that recognized the various expansions of the French borders (1797). Napoleon was a fast-rising name in France.

Napoleon Bonaparte

Rise to prominence. Napoleon had first distinguished himself by firing his cannons on a royalist uprising in Paris (1795) attempting to overthrow the new Directory. This earned him (age 26) his appointment by the Directory as General of the Army of Italy... which he honored with his subsequent victories in Italy (against principally the Austrians and the northern Italian states they dominated). As a national hero he was able to cultivate political supporters within the Directory in Paris ... making the Directory increasingly dependent on him personally.

The Egyptian campaign. Finding that the French navy was not ready for a direct assault on Britain, Napoleon decided to take the war to the Middle East in order to seize for France Britain's vital trade route to India. At first (1798) he scored an easy victory against the Mamluks' Egyptian Army. But Lord Nelson's British fleet soon showed up, destroyed Napoleon's French fleet, and ended any idea of France controlling the vital trade route to India. But Napoleon pushed on from Egypt to Syria anyway (early 1799) ... into a world of hunger, disease (the plague) and brutality – devastating his troops as well as the local population.

Consul (or dictator) 1799. Hearing of mounting political confusion (and growing unpopularity of the Directory) back in France – and finding no further opportunities for glory in the Middle East – Napoleon decided to return to Paris. Upon his arrival (oddly enough, to a hero's welcome) he shut down the Council of Five Hundred and the Directorate, and named himself Consul of France ... confirmed in a new French constitution which in turn received in a national plebiscite almost total approval (a rather suspicious tally of 3 million in favor, only 1500 opposed).

Emperor (1804). There were numerous attempts to unseat, even at one point to assassinate, Napoleon ... and he used one such incident to move (with another highly approving plebiscite) to make himself "Emperor of France" ... with the rights of succession to the title on the part of any of his personal heirs. And so with the Pope in attendance, Napoleon had himself crowned French Emperor in December of 1804. He thus re-established in France the ancient principle of monarchy, with himself as an imperial monarch. The First French Empire was thus born.

Reforms. In so many ways Napoleon brought France into modern culture. Besides modern military strategies, he introduced a new legal code – one which would outlive him as a model followed not only in France but widely in Europe (particularly in those countries where Bonapartist rule once held sway) and even in many other parts of the world. It replaced the complex mix of feudal customs with precise written rules applied equally to all citizens regardless of social rank. He reorganized the administration of France, ending its confusing maze of feudal districts, instead dividing France into 80 *départements* of more or less equal size, governed by prefects which he himself appointed, thus tightening Paris's control over the rest of France ... and giving it a truly national or French identity in replacement of the regional loyalties characteristic of traditional France. He freed up the sale or exchange of property ... and opened the trades or professions to anyone trained for the work – and not just to those born to specific guild families.

He extended to Catholic France, brutalized by the Revolution, his Concordat of 1801 – restoring the Church and its priesthood to its place of religious privilege ... though he did not return to the Church properties seized during the Revolution. On the other hand, he shut down the Catholic Inquisition and ended the restrictions against Protestants and Jews. He liberalized France's divorce laws. He also pushed for the development of more secular public secondary schools (lycées). And he started France thinking in metric terms (though full conversion to the metric system would not take place until the mid-1800s).

Wars and more wars. However, it is in the conduct of his many wars that

Napoleon is largely remembered. He was hugely successful ... most of the time. In 1800 he pulled success out of a near disaster at Marengo (Italy) and won overwhelmingly at Hohenlinden (Germany) against the Austrians.

In 1805, with the birth of a new round of war by a new coalition (the "Third") of Britain, Sweden, Russia, and Austria, things got off to a poor start for Napoleon when his own French-Spanish naval coalition was defeated by the English at Cape Finisterre (Spain), ending his hopes for an invasion of England by his Grande Armée. He then turned his army east towards the Austrians, crushing them at Ulm. But in the meantime, his combined French-Spanish navies were again defeated – decisively – at Trafalgar (Spain) by the English under Lord Nelson. But the French were able to capture Austria's capital Vienna ... and then move on to destroy a combined Austrian-Russian army at Austerlitz before the end of the year. The resulting peace saw Napoleon remaking the face of central Europe, putting to an end the Holy Roman Empire and combining the hundreds of small but semi-independent German states into a Confederation of the Rhine.* Napoleon was at the height of his glory at this point.

In 1806 he marched against the ("Fourth") coalition of Prussia and Russia, crushing Prussia at Jena and Auerstedt. He then turned to face Russia, fighting to a stand-off at Eylau ... and then to an overwhelming defeat of Russia at Friedland. The Prussians lost half of their territory in Germany when Napoleon created the Kingdom of Westphalia and placed his brother Jerôme over it as king. With the Russian Tsar, Napoleon was kinder in his victory, hoping to create a friendship that could serve French interests in East Europe.

He now focused his thoughts on Britain, attempting to tighten his "Continental System" of a blocking of all commercial relations with Britain on the European Continent ... in an effort to cripple the British economy and thus force Britain to finally fall under his rule. But his effort to discipline Portugal (which had not been honoring the boycott) drew him into the Iberian Peninsula of Spain and Portugal ... where Spanish sensitivities to French intervention in the region's political affairs drew him into a draining round of local fights with Spanish guerrilla bands. His appointing his brother Joseph as King of Spain (1808), in the hope of getting on top of the situation there, only made matters worse. He was forced to position a huge portion of his army in Spain to hold things together there ... while he faced continuing threats to France elsewhere. Indeed, the British under Wellington would take advantage of Napoleon's troubles elsewhere by sending their own troops to Spain and gradually help end French control there.

At this point (1809), Austria (part of the "Fifth" Coalition) re-entered

---

*He had also promoted himself earlier that year from the position as President of the Italian Republic (since 1802), to now being King of Italy.

the fight against France, actually defeating the French in a battle at Aspern ... but then being devastated by the French in a second engagement at Wagram. Politically this resulted in a huge loss for Austria. But at least peace would reign in Europe for the next few years.

But the Russian Tsar was being pressured by his nobles to join with Britain in an offensive against the French ... in the hope of retaking Poland. Napoleon heard of these plans and instead decided to take the initiative. Thus in 1812 he headed a French army of nearly half a million troops into Russia. A big mistake! The Russians fell back instead of offering direct resistance to the invaders (except at bloody Borodino) destroying their own crops and animals to keep the French from securing food for their troops. Napoleon made it all the way to Moscow, just as the harsh Russian winter set in ... finding nothing in this abandoned and burned-out city to mark this as a victory. The Russians simply would not surrender. After five weeks of pointless occupation, and with political problems brewing back in Paris, Napoleon decided to withdraw. The retreat was so ruinous that less than one-tenth of his army made it back alive to France.

Encouraged by Napoleon's failure in Russia, a Sixth Coalition was formed against him in 1813. Once again, Napoleon – with a rebuilt army – humiliated the Coalition at Dresden. But the numbers were against him, and a few months later at Leipzig, Napoleon's army was crushed. Humiliating terms were put before Napoleon, which he delayed too long in accepting. Napoleon attempted to hold off with a number of smaller engagements ... but he was running out of soldiers. Finally the French Sénat took action in deposing him. Napoleon now had no choice but to accept exile to the Island of Elba (off the Italian coast) which he was allowed to continue to rule as "emperor."

The victorious allies then reinstated in France the Bourbon monarchy under Louis XVIII. Their hope was to put this whole 25-year nightmare of the French Revolution and the Napoleonic Empire behind them and move back to business as usual. That was not to be.

The Battle of Waterloo (1815). In early 1815 news reached the allied delegates to the Congress of Vienna that Napoleon had escaped from Elba and was gathering a new French army in order to restore his French Empire. Britain, Russia, Austria and Prussia were determined to put to an end forever Napoleon's efforts to undo their work. By the summer, Napoleon was ready to act against this new coalition, moving into (today's) Belgium where outside the village of Waterloo he met the combined army of Britain (under Wellington) and Prussia (under Blücher) ... and went down in defeat. This time he was exiled to a small island (St. Helena) in the middle of the

Atlantic Ocean where he would remain until his death six years later.

The American and French Revolutions compared

The American Revolution. Actually, the American Revolution was no revolution at all – socially and culturally speaking. It was revolutionary (unprecedented) only in the sense of a people rising up against their feudal king and succeeding in the short span of a half-dozen years in securing their full independence as a people. But America before the war and America after the war was pretty much the same. 150 years of colonial self-rule (according to the precise laws and regulations of their own particular colonial charters) since the early 1600s had taught the Americans how to take care of themselves – from building their own communities of homes, barns, workshops, schools and churches, to defending themselves from their local enemies, the Indians – and occasionally the Spanish and the French. The American "Revolution" occurred simply because an English king decided to take away the personal liberties to which these Americans were well accustomed. Their "Revolution" merely confirmed those liberties ... not create them as if they were new.

Even the Constitution they drew up in 1787 was a rather limited political document, more a treaty among thirteen independent states (each of which was already self-governing under its own state constitution) providing for cooperation so as to keep them from splitting into little contending states, vulnerable to the continuing imperial designs of the great powers of Europe. The Constitution did not provide for a "government" such as we think of today when we think of an institution which governs over people. Government in that sense remained a strictly state and local affair (except occasionally in times of war) ... up until the mid-1960s when President Johnson and his "Liberal"* brain trust decided to lay the foundations for a "Great Society" that would govern, from Washington, DC, on virtually every matter affecting American life. But that took nearly two centuries to come

---

*There is considerable confusion over the term "Liberal" in today's America. Originally the term meant liberal in the sense of being free ... in reference to being liberated from the autocratic governments of Europe which attempted to control all social life from above by higher authority. Liberal meant full grass-roots self-government of the people themselves. In America today it means almost the opposite ... where a Liberal is actually what Europeans would term a Socialist, meaning someone who believes that society would work better (or more "progressively") under the extensive guidance and control of high-level government experts – an idea which American "Liberals" have supported since the mid-1960s. Supposedly, with such higher governmental authorities (bureaucrats mostly) managing larger society and its needs, this then leaves the Liberal "free" to focus on his or her own personal matters.

into existence after the American "Revolution."

The French Revolution ... and its wider impact on Europe. But what happened in France in follow-up to America's Revolution was indeed truly "revolutionary" in every social-cultural respect. The French Revolution killed the feudal system that had governed Europe for a thousand years. And the follow-up Napoleonic Empire put in its place a new system by which the masses of common people, not the select lords and ladies, formed the foundation of French social power. The French armed their people ... and in the process of fighting their own wars gave real strength to the notion of the "people" – or (as this new concept would develop through the 1800s) the "nation."

It was not just France that the Coalition powers of Britain, Austria, Prussia, Russia, Spain and Sweden were fighting. It was their Revolution they were trying to undo. They were quick to support the French Bourbon monarchy that the French Revolution had nearly decapitated.

In many ways Napoleon was one of them ... another monarch. But he was a monarch who stood for the ideals of the European Enlightenment. They were opposed to those ideals more than the person of Napoleon ... though it was hard to differentiate the two, Napoleon had so completely embraced Enlightenment ideals.

For this reason, at first many of the European upper-middle class (university educated) intellectuals were very supportive of the French Revolution ... even at first of Napoleon. But in bringing the idea of the sovereign "people" forward, the French Revolution also raised the question of how to define those people. Though most of the European aristocracy already spoke French among themselves, the commoners around them spoke a multitude of languages ... which carried the songs, the poetry, the stories, the dreams of the common people. And thus local language became an important factor in defining "the people."

In this way "nationalism" was born ... aided greatly by the cultural arrogance of the occupying French governors and their troops. Thus the idea of "German" and "Italian" began to take form, to be joined by the already rising sense of being English (but also Irish), Spanish, Portuguese, Russian, Swedish, Polish, etc.

Thus feudal Europe was entering a truly revolutionary social phase ... one which would bring forth the pride of the European nation ... but also the tragedy of the *national* bloodying of World War One (1914-1918) ... and the consequent undermining of European dominance throughout the world.

CHAPTER ELEVEN

THE "MODERNIZING" OF THE WEST

✳ ✳ ✳

THE BUDDING SPIRIT OF NATIONALISM IN EUROPE

The role of Romanticism in growing the sense of nationhood.   The French Revolution had initially challenged Europeans to investigate further this idea of building human progress on the basis of the ability of man (any man or woman / all people, potentially) to reason clearly, if properly brought up to do so.   But when given the chance to put this utopian dream into practice, the French ultimately had failed miserably – very, very miserably.

A reaction against such worship of Human Reason naturally set in, not just among the skeptical British Empiricists but among a number of continental scholars, especially the German Romanticists.   This latter reaction developed on the European continent, especially when it became obvious that under Napoleon what stood behind French power was not Reason, but some kind of special Spirit that rose naturally out of the soul of an energized people themselves (French peasants becoming national warriors).

This quest for such Spirit (German *Geist*) would mark much of European philosophy during the 1800s, especially that coming out of Germany, whose philosophers seemed to dominate the field of intellectual inquiry on the European continent that century, the way the French had done so the century before.

The German Romanticists Herder and Goethe. Two young Germans, Johann Gottfried Herder and Johann Wolfgang von Goethe helped found together the *Sturm und Drang* (Storm and Drive) Movement of the 1770s, celebrating the spirit of struggle as the necessary element in achieving what the Rationalists had felt would be achieved simply through pure reason.

The clergyman Herder studied under Kant at Königsberg, but moved away from Kantian rationalism into a mystical world presided over by God. As a young pastor he met Goethe, inspiring the latter with his insights into Biblical literature. He recognized that the Hebrew literature of the Old Testament was more of the nature of poetry and folk narrative than technical science (which was how Rationalistic Western society was coming to think and operate at that point), and that it was necessary to understand the Hebrew writings as such – not as mechanistic science but as deeply inspired narrative or parable – in order to comprehend their great truths.

The two men became good friends whose speculations together about human knowledge birthed the Sturm und Drang Movement of the 1770s, elevating human emotions above human intellect. Eventually their thinking would settle down a bit and evolve towards Classicism, or love of the styles of classical or ancient Greco-Roman antiquity, in an attempt to balance human emotion and human intellect.

Herder was a strong German nationalist, at a time when Germans were attempting to construct the idea of a German nation (Germany at the time was divided into hundreds of independent states, large and small). Yet he was cautious about letting the highly emotional tribal spirit of nationalism get too far away from practical reason.

Then with the outbreak of the French Revolution in 1789 Herder would support the Revolution, producing a split between himself and many of his friends, including Goethe. Finally, his dedication to refuting Kant's theories would place him pretty much in isolation within the German academic community.

Goethe was an individual of wide tastes and talents, being a poet, dramatist and scientist all in one. He was early influenced by Herder, who inspired in him a deep appreciation of German folk culture and consequently a spirit of German nationalism.

But Goethe was also a profound individualist, intrigued by the power and depth of personal experience and emotion. In his first play, *Götz von Berlichingen* (1773), Goethe explored the depths of individual human sentiments – helping to lay the foundation for the Sturm und Drang Movement, which, among other things, advocated personal freedom in the face of oppressive, medieval attitudes in Germany concerning the role of the individual in society. This Sturm und Drang Movement would later blossom into German Romanticism.

In the 1780s Goethe went to Rome to study classical art, architecture, and literature and for a while came under the more formalistic style of the neo-classicist movement. But on his return to Germany he found little appreciation for his new views. He then turned to science for a while. But his longer-standing romantic inclinations reasserted themselves, and his independent, individualist style returned to the fore. This culminated in his all-time great work, *Faust* (actually written and rewritten in two parts over a long period of time reaching perhaps from 1772 to 1829), which was an epic tale of the search of the individual for that which is of a lasting or transcending value in the face of freedom's great opportunities – and uncertainties.

His *Faust* would become the best-read work of German literature (roughly equivalent to the place which the works of Shakespeare have long enjoyed in English literature), inspiring young Germans for generations to quest for the German ideal, the romantic spirit or soul that made Germany unique among the nations.

Herder's and Goethe's ideas would leave their mark on German nationalist thinking by putting into place a powerful intellectual legacy for others to pursue, with the idea of exploring the spirit of man as well as his intellect. However both of them eventually moved on to the philosophy of Classicism, which idealized the cultural and political achievements of the ancient Greeks and Romans, who became for them models that Europeans should attempt to emulate (as it was also for Americans at the time, who took up the Roman idea of the Republic as the political structure they were trying to set up in 1787).

Georg Wilhelm Friedrich Hegel: historical progress through struggle. Just as Goethe was to become Germany's grand poet of the century in Germany, Georg Wilhelm Friedrich Hegel would become Germany's grand philosopher of the century. Hegel built on the Sturm und Drang idea of the blessings of struggle, seeing in the tension between opposing forces (usually in the form of newer, radical ideas and practices challenging older, established ideas and practices) the possibilities of birthing a new standard, one operating at a higher social level than previously. This idea eventually became his famous *dialectic*, the struggle of two opposing things eventually birthing a third, superior thing – a dialectical dynamic supposedly found in all aspects of material as well as biological and social or cultural development on this planet.

But he added to this purely mechanical formula the idea that the process itself was not random, but instead guided by a superior *Weltgeist* / World Spirit or World Mind (or just simply God) that was directly involved in the entire process as part of a quest for the completion of history, with the full union – in a state of perfect love – of all things together. Even God (especially in the form of the living Jesus) was part of this process, seeking his own completion in union with man – or man in union with him, when all would be one in a perfect state of love and peace.

From this point on, virtually all the 1800s sense of progress (not just in Germany but in much of the whole of Western Civilization) was shaped by the idea not just of philosophers sitting in their salons directing others rationally toward a utopian world, but by the direct involvement of those who would bring history forward, through noble struggle, struggle directed by some great Spirit. Without such struggle, violent though it might be, progress was impossible.

Hegelianism also touched on group pride, as nations or classes came to see themselves as being under the special anointing of the World Spirit to take the lead to direct history into the next era. This fed powerfully into German nationalism, with its sense of special German historical destiny.

But this also fed powerfully into the working-class movement also arising at that time, a movement which came to view the industrial workers of the world as the true moral underpinning of the world to come.

Schleiermacher and Protestant Liberalism. Interestingly, just as it was a German Hegel and soon to be a German Marx that would leave a huge impact on 19th century Western philosophy and political theory, it would be a German, Friedrich Schleiermacher, who would initiate something of a German lead in the 19th century world of Western theology. Thus he would come to be known as the "Father of Modern Liberal Theology."

Basically, he reacted to the supposedly rational world of the Enlightenment – and its clear failure in the French Revolution – as much of the surrounding intellectual world did also at the time (the early 1800s). But he was also as reactive to the strict Biblical literalism of the Reformed Church he was schooled under. As a pastor and professor (Halle, then Berlin), he followed the rising Romanticism trend sweeping Europe's intellectual circles at the time, in emphasizing the idea that faith was a *feeling* derived from a direct spiritual connection to God – rather than a set of strictly traditional or even well-reasoned religious principles.

Then he added, Christianity as faith was and always had been *contextual*, socially and culturally. He found the truth in Scripture not in the way the Bible met modern standards of fact-based science, but in the deep faith that led the Gospel writers to put into writing the ways events in Christ's days touched their hearts so profoundly. In his own extensive study of Scripture, he affirmed that Scripture was never to be taken as "fact," but instead as spiritual testimony – and should always be understood as such.

✳ ✳ ✳

SOCIAL UPHEAVAL DURING THE FIRST HALF OF THE 1800s

From the defeat of Napoleon in 1815 to the outbreak of World War One almost exactly a century later (1914) Europe experienced its first long period of relative peace in 300 years – since the onset of the Protestant Reformation in the early 1500s marking the beginning of the break-up of old Christendom. "Relative peace" is the correct term because there would be European wars during the 1800s. But they would be brief and limited in scope compared to the previous European dynastic wars.

To a great extent this was so because the Europeans focused their energies more on overseas opportunities for their own imperial expansion. Also the Napoleonic wars had put such a scare in the hearts of the European monarchs and aristocrats that they realized the absolute importance of not letting their rivalries get out of control. Thus was birthed the "Concert of Europe" – regular gatherings of European heads of state to work out their differences – a diplomatic system that guided European continental politics fairly well during the rest of the 1800s.

It was the foolish disregarding of this system in the early 20th century that would finally push Europe into two tragic rounds of a devastating rivalry (World Wars One and Two) ... which would result ultimately in Europe's fall from its position as the political center of the world.

The restoration of Europe's monarchies

The Congress of Vienna (1814-1815). The Congress of Vienna first assembled with Napoleon's initial defeat in 1814 ... for the purpose of putting Europe back together again in a form as close as possible to the way it looked before the French Revolution. Kings, emperors, and diplomatic delegates came from all over Europe (even Turkey) to participate in this grand event. The major concerns were what to do with a post-Napoleon France ... and how to reorganize and distribute among the victorious European powers – in particular Great Britain, Prussia, Austria and Russia – the various lands (most notably the Netherlands, Italy, Poland, western Germany, Norway and Finland) previously shaped by Napoleon's dominating influence. A balance of power among those four major powers was their goal. This balance was the best guarantee that their own squabbles would not get out of hand again. They had no intention of allowing the lower social orders or classes to get involved ever again in any future political conflicts arising among Europe's royalty. Thus they signed a Quadruple Alliance (1815) promising to meet regularly (the Concert of Europe) over a period of at least twenty years to consult on any matter affecting their relationship.[*]

France. But treaties *among* Europe's kings and emperors would not take care of issues brewing *within* each of the countries. France in particular would have a very difficult time with lingering domestic social forces unleashed by the Revolution.

---

[*]France would join the alliance in 1818.

The Bourbon dynasty was restored to the French throne, with Louis XVIII, brother of Louis XVI, now King of France.* The 60-year old, gout-inflicted Louis XVIII had come to the throne after watching the butchering of the French royalty and much of the French aristocracy during the Revolution – and watching the success of Napoleon at the head of a popular ("the people's") French army. He was wise enough to draw some important conclusions for his own tenure in office: the days of royal rule, conducted without concern for the people, were over. Consequently, Louis issued a very Liberal Charter of 1814, guaranteeing a bi-cameral legislature to govern with him ... and freedom of the press and religion. He retained most of the governmental reforms put in place by Napoleon. He also promised the rising middle class or bourgeoisie that he would abolish a number of key taxes. But he would not – could not – keep such a promise. His treasury was empty. Nonetheless, his reign proved to be a time of greatly appreciated peace.

Austria. Not only was the post-Napoleonic gathering held in the Austrian capital, Vienna, but much of its work in redrawing the post-Napoleonic map of Europe was engineered by the Austrian Foreign Minister, Klemens von Metternich. It might even be said that the European diplomatic era following the defeat of Napoleon was something of the "Age of Metternich" (1815-1848).

Napoleon's politics had finished off the ancient position and title of Holy Roman Emperor, but Austria's ruler, Francis I, kept for himself the title of Emperor of Austria. Austria was however just about as complex a political entity as the Holy Roman Empire had been. The Austrian Empire was German at its core, but spread widely so as to incorporate many other ethnic or national groupings, including Hungarians, Poles, Italians and Czechs. With the Napoleon-inspired rise among the various ethnic groups of Europe of a distinctly popular or "nationalist" spirit, directing Austrian politics on a stable course was going to be extremely difficult for Austria's Habsburg Emperor and his Foreign Minister (and, after 1821, Chancellor) Metternich.

Great Britain. Since 1810, when the British King George III had fallen rather permanently into a state of insanity, Britain had been led by George's son George as Prince Regent, and by a number of capable cabinet ministers, including notably Jenkinson (Lord Liverpool), Castlereagh, Wellington, and Canning. When George finally died in 1820 his son took the throne as George IV ... and British politics took a decidedly more reactionary

---

*Ten-year-old Louis XVII, son of Louis XVI, died in a Republican prison in 1795.

turn (1820-1830). The main issues impacting his short reign were the Catholic Question – George IV being strongly opposed to any loosening of the restrictions against Catholics in office – and his scandalous efforts to divorce his wife. On both matters he failed to get his way, diminishing his stature considerably. Towards the end of his reign he became reclusive, being massively overweight and nearly totally blind. When he died in 1830, there was no sadness or regret among his people.

The Netherlands. Napoleon had replaced the Batavian Republic, established during the French Revolution, with the Kingdom of Holland – placing his brother Louis Bonaparte as its king. With Napoleon's downfall, William Frederick of Orange, son of the last stadtholder, declared himself King of the Netherlands. Then during the Congress of Vienna, the Catholic southern provinces – that had been exchanged back and forth among Spain, France, and Austria – were combined with the northern provinces to create a new United Netherlands ... with William Frederick as its King William I.

The logic behind the major powers creating this stronger entity was to put some kind of barrier state or neutral territory separating Great Britain, France and Germany from each other.

Prussia. Prussia continued after the war to be ruled (1797-1840) by Frederick William III. He was not a particularly outstanding king, relying on his ministers to bring Prussia her diplomatic and military successes.[*] His one burning desire personally seemed to be to impose a rigid Protestant regime over his lands, forcing the unity of the Lutherans and Calvinists as a single Prussian Protestant Church (1817) ... over which he personally presided.

The *Deutscher Bund* (Germanic Confederation). The 39 German states of the old Holy Roman Empire (including Prussia) were loosely united (1815) as a Germanic Bund or union. The Bund had its own legislature (the Diet) ... but was under the presidency of Austria ... and thus, to the extent it had any real power at all (which indeed was slight), was shaped by the conservative or reactionary policies of Metternich.

Russia. Russia continued under the rule (1801-1825) of Alexander I ... a strange personal mix of mystic ... plus sometimes liberal (the earlier part of his reign), sometimes reactionary (the latter part of his reign), in personality.

---

[*]The one diplomatic success most urgently sought by the Prussians in Vienna was the acquisition of Saxony. But Austria and Great Britain, seeing danger in such a growth of Prussia, blocked this move. Ultimately the Prussians had to give up the quest.

When he came to the Russian throne in 1801, he announced himself as a liberal reformer – though he was slow to act on these reforms, and did not get far before he proved himself to be a rather traditional autocrat. In fact by the end of his reign he had become quite a reactionary. It was rumored that he had come under Metternich's powerful influence – although Napoleon's earlier betrayal as an ally with his attack on Russia, plus popular uprisings Alexander did not understand or sympathize with (such as the Greek anti-Ottoman revolt), and growing discontent among young Russian officers, unhappy over the backwardness of Russia, played their own part in Alexander's retreat from liberalism.

He was the one who dreamed up the idea of a "Holy Alliance" to which he invited all the participants at the Congress of Vienna to join ... largely as a defensive alliance against the kind of political culture unleashed by the French Revolution and Napoleon. Ultimately only Austria and Prussia humored him by joining his Alliance. France and England had no interest in getting entangled in Alexander's religious crusade – though they did participate in the Quadruple / Quintuple Alliances, with something of a parallel political agenda.

Huge troubles in the land of the Ottoman Turks

From the high point of their assault (but ultimate defeat) at Vienna in 1683, the Turkish Ottoman Empire had been on a steady path of decline – militarily, politically, socially and morally. The quality of the Ottoman sultans had deteriorated steadily, personal weakness and even insanity increasingly affecting the character of the sultanate.

The Imperial Harem of *Valide Sultans* (mothers of the sultans) gained dominance over the process of selecting sultans (usually minors when sultans first took their thrones) and then the *Haseki Sultans* or wives of the sultans took over the positions of dominance after that. Consequently, the objective of Ottoman rule ceased to be the welfare of the Ottoman Empire, but instead became the advancement of the fortunes of one or another of the harem families (run by women slaves) in competition with each other.

Also the Janissary military corps had become highly privileged, wealthy, corrupt ... and largely useless as a military institution. Sultans had been made and unmade (murdered usually) by various Janissary groups ... weakening even further the Ottoman Empire.[*]

––––––––––––––––––––

[*]The Janissaries had once (the 1400s and 1500s) been an elite fighting force made up of slaves taken from their Christian homes as boys and raised in both Islam and in a spirit of total devotion to the sultan. They had no other stake in life and thus fought fiercely for the sultan. But eventually (the late 1500s) the Janissaries were allowed to marry, own property and have children of their own, becoming something of an Ottoman aristocracy. They now had political interests

Sensing the need for deep reform, in 1826 Sultan Mahmud II (ruled 1808-1839) made the decision to disband the Janissaries ... facing a bloody revolt from the Janissaries in the effort. But he did succeed – killing and executing 6,000 of them in the process – and began the process of rebuilding Ottoman power based on a more modern army (but a very slow process at this point).

Then there was the matter of the pashas, Ottoman noblemen who were given increasing responsibility in the governance of the provinces and the Ottoman military. As the sultan's effective governance over the empire weakened, his responsibilities were gradually taken up by a number of the pashas, thus constituting themselves and the regions of their governance as increasingly semi-autonomous realms within the empire.

Quite notable in this regard was Muhammad Ali Pasha, governor of Egypt. This Albanian-born Muslim reformer – who in 1811 slaughtered off several thousand of the Mamluks who had long governed Egypt – worked hard to bring up to European standards the army and bureaucracy of Egypt (Napoleon's activities in Egypt having been the keen motivation for doing so). He also helped develop an industrial economy able to support such an army. Soon, with the introduction of cotton farming into Egypt, the country began to develop independent economic and political power.

In the process, Muhammad Ali established his own dynastic rule in Egypt (which would last until 1952) ... creating the question of just exactly how much was Egypt still a part of the Ottoman Empire. The British by and large worked with his successors (now entitled "Khedives") as if they were in fact fully sovereign heads of state, able to conduct political policy in Egypt without consulting with the Ottoman sultan.

The *Tanzimat*. Meanwhile, Sultan Mahmud II was keenly aware of the deficiencies of the Ottoman government, and authorized a vast number of reforms of Ottoman government and society in an attempt to modernize or reorganize (*tanzimat*) the empire.[*] French government provided the model for most of the reforms.

Yet whereas the hope of the sultans was to integrate more closely all the various Ottoman sub-communities with the sultan's rule, the reforms had something of the opposite effect, opening up to these sub-communities the idea that they had their own sovereign rights to develop as distinct peoples.

---

of their own to pursue ... and they soon became centers of corruption rather than military discipline. The Janissaries grew so powerful that they were able to make and depose sultans at will, weakening greatly the sultanate.

[*]And also did his sons, Abdül Mecid I (ruled 1839-1861) and Abdül Aziz (ruled 1861-1876), who tried to keep their father's reforms moving ahead.

Thus a greatly weakened Turkey was beset by revolts of subject peoples from within the Empire ... and assaults from without by surrounding powers (principally Russia and Austria), attacks which steadily chipped away at the outer borders of the Ottoman Empire.

Greece. Then in 1821 it was the turn of the Wallachians (Romanians) to attempt a similar revolt. But it was put down by the Turks.

But the Wallachian uprising had inspired the Greeks of the Peloponnesian Peninsula also to revolt at that same time. This revolt, however, soon spread to the Greeks of Macedonia and the Island of Crete.

Greek atrocities against Turks were answered by even greater atrocities against the Greeks by the Turks (the Greek Patriarch hanged outside his residence in Constantinople ... and 27,000 Greeks executed on the island of Chios). This then prompted European involvement.[*]

Sultan Mahmud then enlisted Muhammad Ali to send his army to Greece to crush the rebellion. Muhammad Ali largely succeeded in this task (1825) ... prompting Britain, France and Russia to intervene. In 1827 the three powers finally sent their navies to break the Turkish-Egyptian hold on Greece. This gave the small and struggling Greek Republic some relief.

But Mahmud would not back down ... until the Russian army took the key town of Adrianople just north of the Ottoman capital at Istanbul ... and a French expeditionary force was sent at the same time to the Peloponnese (Southern Greece).

Bit by bit, protocols were signed by the Turks recognizing various aspects of Greek independence ... until full independence was formally acknowledged in the Treaty of Constantinople in 1832. The treaty also established a monarchy for Greece, with Otto of Bavaria (actually a minor at the time, and thus putting Greece under a regency until 1837) becoming Greece's first king, replacing a short-lived Greek Republic.

His rule would face some difficulties in that Otto was a strong German in his tendency to demand strict adherence to government rulings – putting him in conflict with some of the more active former revolutionary fighters – and was a strong Catholic in a very Greek Orthodox world. But he did get Greece's independence secured for its people ... although the Greeks could not get past the idea of continuing the revolution until all Greek lands were out from under Turkish rule, and the country had its capital back in Constantinople (Turkish Istanbul). Troubles developed between the King and his very popular former admiral Konstantinos Kanaris, with the blowup resulting finally in Otto being forced to leave Greece in 1862.

Upon the urging of the major Western powers, the Greeks accepted

---

[*]It also inspired the British Romantic poet Lord Byron to go to Greece to fight for its independence ... and die there of a fever in 1824!

Danish prince George, who converted to Greek Orthodoxy and worked carefully to win the support of the Greek people. He would reign as a very popular king ... until his assassination by a crazed Socialist in 1913.

Serbia. Revolt against the Turks had actually started earlier in Orthodox Christian Serbia when in 1804 a peasant uprising, assisted by Christian Orthodox Russia, was able to hold off efforts of the Turks to force Serbia militarily back into the Ottoman fold. But in 1812, Russia was being pressed deeply by Napoleon's army – thus pulled out of the game, leaving the Serbs to face the Turks alone. For several years Serbia was made to submit ... then in 1815 revolted again, this time successful in holding off the Turks.

  Finally in 1830 the Turks were forced to recognize Serbia officially as an autonomous state, with the Serbian rebel leader Miloš Obrenović as the new Serbian prince. ... ruling under a new constitution as of 1835.

A growing spirit of rebellion

Germany. University students around Germany found themselves hopeful that a united Germany might be established at the Congress of Vienna ... but were disappointed at how Germany was ultimately split into three parts: a strong Austria, a strong Prussia, and a weak Bund or German Confederation. A number of student organizations (the *Burschenschaften*) – calling for the creation of just such a unified German fatherland – spread rapidly ... much to the distress of Metternich. He called a congress of German princes to stand together against this growing movement. They jointly issued the Carlsbad Decrees, agreeing to curb the freedoms of the press and of the universities ... even outlaw the use of the Burschenschaften's colors: red, black and gold (the colors of Germany's flag today!). But all this achieved was the driving of the student movement underground ... which then became increasingly revolutionary.

Spain. A similar problem developed quickly in Spain after the war. Ferdinand VII had been removed from power by Napoleon in 1808 but returned to his throne by Napoleon in 1813. At this point Ferdinand turned into a bitter reactionary ... and what is considered today Spain's worst king in its long history. He quickly alienated the Spanish people by rejecting the liberal constitution of 1812 ... and then re-instituted the Inquisition, shut down all newspapers except the official journal, and imprisoned or executed every liberal voice in the country. And he seemed unable to work with any other Spanish political figure, changing – and even arresting – his ministers at frequent intervals.

  Spanish revolt actually started up first in the Spanish colonies in

America during the Napoleonic Era. Initially these revolts were anti-French ... though liberal in political character. But with the restoration of Ferdinand as Spanish king, the spirit of rebellious liberalism began to turn against Ferdinand ... and take on the character of independence movements aimed at securing the colonies' freedom from Spanish authority. Then the spirit of revolt extended to Spain itself in early 1820 among Ferdinand's troops that he had assembled in Cadiz with the intention of sending to America to suppress the colonial rebellions going on there. Ferdinand lost the contest with his troops and was thus forced to accept the liberal constitution of 1812.

But another meeting of the Concert of Europe was called by Metternich, where it was finally decided to authorize the French to invade Spain (1823) and restore the absolute rule of Ferdinand. In this France succeeded, ending for a while all open talk of liberal reform of Spain.

The continuing independence movement in the Americas

Haiti. The French Revolution and its strong political ideals infected deeply the inhabitants of the French sugar-producing colony (known at the time as Saint-Dominique) ... inhabitants made up mostly of slaves brought generations earlier from Africa to work those extremely profitable sugar plantations.

Unfulfilled promises of freedom sent back and forth between revolutionary France and Haiti finally inspired a group of mostly Black freedmen in 1791 to take up their own cause of liberation (ending slavery altogether) ... beginning a revolt that would brew through the next ten years – led by the militarily talented Toussaint Louverture. Indeed, slavery was pronounced at an end in 1794, confirmed by the subsequent Directorate, and then also by Napoleon. But the actual status of the colony itself remained uncertain ... especially as Louverture switched back and forth in his loyalties to France (partly shaped by political intrigues going on within Haiti itself).

Napoleon moved in 1801 to resolve the matter by sending a huge force to Haiti to bring the colony back under full French control ... and by having Louverture and his colleagues arrested and deported to France in the process. But the Haitians fought on, led by Louverture's lieutenant Jean-Jacques Dessalines ... the Haitian effort aided greatly by a huge outbreak of yellow-fever, which decimated the French army. When in 1803 the French were defeated in a battle at the end of the year, it was clear that French rule in Haiti had come to an end.

Indeed, Haiti now came under the firm rule of Dessalines, who butchered the remaining French White and most of the freed-Black population in Haiti (a total of 3,000 to 5,000 executed), and then became Haiti's new emperor. But he himself was assassinated in 1806! Thus it was that Haiti set off down its own quite peculiar path ... one often very brutal in nature.

Mexico. When Napoleon invaded Spain in 1808, deposed the Spanish king Charles IV and placed his own brother Joseph over Spain as its new king, the Spanish colonies in America found themselves in a state of political confusion. At first it appeared that the huge viceroyalty of New Spain (as the Spanish colony was termed at the time) was going to come under the independent governance of a group or *junta* of local leaders ... except that this was blocked by those (usually those originally born in Spain) with continuing Spanish loyalties.

But then a call to revolt issued in 1810 by a local priest, Father Miguel Hidalgo y Costilla, was taken up enthusiastically by locals ... and a contest between the pro-Spain and pro-independence supporters broke out ... brutally – both sides executing captured opponents, including Father Hidalgo, who was executed in 1811. A Declaration of Independence was issued formally in 1813 ... but the civil strife within New Spain continued nonetheless.

In 1820, when Spanish Liberals were able to take control in Spain, the question of the status of the Catholic Church and the matter of a republic or a monarchy to govern Spain and its overseas holdings merely intensified the struggle in New Spain. Finally in 1821, a compromise was agreed on in New Spain (now giving itself a local name as "Mexico") between the leaders of the two parties – declaring Mexico independent and all citizens now of equal status politically ... but Catholicism still the sole religious underpinning of the country and monarchy as the ongoing form of government. The monarchy was, however, very soon replaced by a republic of sorts.

So Mexico was independent. But what it was beyond that was never very clear. The military stepped in frequently to resolve personal contests at the top of the political hierarchy – making for very unstable governance ... a problem that seemed never to go away!

Central America. At the same time the Spanish lands to the south of Mexico, set themselves up separately from Mexico as the Federal Republic of Central America (1823). But the different regions making up the federation fell into civil war in 1838 – liberals versus traditionalists, eventually joined by just "separatists" in the fight. But by 1841, everyone was exhausted ... and the federation was ended – with Guatemala, Honduras, Nicaragua, El Salvador, and Costa Rica acknowledged as fully independent countries.

Simón Bolívar and his Republic of Colombia (Gran Colombia). Much the same dynamic was going on further south, in Spanish territories located in the northern part of the South American continent. Again ... the French Revolution and Napoleon's role in upsetting deeply Spanish government both home and abroad played majorly in the developments in this region. But here a single individual, Simón Bolívar, played the key role of being the central figure in these events.

In 1810 Bolívar took up fighting in support of a Venezuelan republic that had declared its independence from Napoleonic Spain. At one point (1815) he was forced to flee to Haiti, but returned with Haitian support and was eventually (1821) able to set up a new Venezuela republic ... actually entitled the Republic of Colombia – with Bolívar quite naturally serving as its president. But he did not stop at that, but kept up his conquests by liberating other lands in the region – Ecuador (1822), Peru (1824) and Bolivia (1825). These were then merged into what was termed "Gran Colombia."

However political differences developed between Bolívar (a strong centralist) and former supporters who wanted greater autonomy in the regions ... ultimately even independence on the part of Venezuela, Colombia, Ecuador, etc., that made up Gran Colombia. In the dispute, he lost control of those regions, was nearly assassinated (1828), and – tired of the whole mess – finally resigned (1830) ... and soon died.

But here too what followed was simply government by various military-supported autocrats (*caudillos*) ... who, however, would never attain the respect and authority that Bolívar had possessed. But it was all the government that these new states were to know ... for the longest time (even up to today).

Brazil. As a colony, Brazil played a role quite different from that of the Spanish colonies when in 1807, to escape Napoleon's aggressions, the Portuguese Prince Regent João (or John) VI moved himself and his court to Brazil's Rio de Janeiro ... making Brazil the center of Portuguese operations. And in doing so, João went on to develop Brazil's political institutions to a rather high degree of sophistication. And then, to the great irritation of the Portuguese back home in Portugal, when the Napoleonic threat was over in 1815, there seemed to be little interest in the royal court in leaving the vast lands of Brazil to retake residence in the much smaller Portugal. The idea of making Brazil and Portugal co-equals in the Portuguese political system did not please the domestic Portuguese either.

But the Liberal Revolution in Portugal (1820) brought to power those able to force João to return to Portugal to resume rule there (1821). Nonetheless, he left his son Pedro to continue as Regent in Brazil. Then also, when the Portuguese revolutionaries tried to return Brazil to the status of being a mere Portuguese colony ... the Brazilians resisted strongly – led by Pedro. The following year (1822) the Brazilians then made their country a fully independent "Empire" ... with Pedro as their emperor. But Portuguese military efforts to counter this move did not work well ... and the Portuguese court finally (1826) recognized Brazil as being fully independent.

Of course independent Brazil faced some of the same contentious issues as the newly independent Hispanic states around them: liberalism versus traditionalism. Keeping Brazil from falling into civil war exhausted Pedro, who died in 1831 ... leaving Brazil in the hands of a Regency while his son remained in his infancy. Unsurprisingly, the political turmoil merely continued during this period. Finally in 1841, Pedro II was crowned ... way before his adult years.

But overall, Brazil prospered and remained fairly stable politically during the 58-year reign of Pedro II ... until in 1889 the Brazilian military conducted a coup, establishing a Brazilian republic.

The Monroe Doctrine (1823). Meanwhile (going back to the 1820s), during all this turmoil brought on by the French Revolution and Napoleon's Empire, there was no way that either Spain or Portugal were ever going to allow the independence of their colonies ... and thus they both fought back fiercely against the independence movements going on there.

But all of this confusion had allowed the very entrepreneurial British to quietly slip into the American dynamic ... to develop strong commercial ties of their own with these colonies. Thus Britain had no intention of ever letting their American clients be drawn back into the mercantilist privileges[*] of Spain and Portugal.

But, most cleverly, the British let the American President Monroe state the case for both Britain and America in this matter: *America* would not let any European power restore its colonial empires on its side of the Atlantic. That might have appeared as an incredibly stupid pronouncement coming from a very recently established and untried republic. However ... it was well understood by all that the might of the British navy was what stood behind this "Monroe Doctrine" (1823), giving it its muscle.

The European Revolutions of 1830

At this point the sole agenda of the Congress of Europe – now including only Austria, Russia and Prussia as its mainstay – was the defense of the autocracy of these three powers. But that was going to come under increasing challenge from liberal quarters.

____

[*]Mercantilism: where colonies were permitted to trade only with the imperial mother country ... and no one else.

France. Unsurprisingly, there had existed in France a very anti-revolutionary, anti-Napoleonic mood amidst the returned nobility ... and even in some parts of the French countryside. Louis had tried to walk a line of moderation between those French with fond memories of the Empire and those French with a burning hatred for everything and everyone Napoleonic. But he was old and sick ... and up against his younger brother, who was a leader of the anti-Napoleonic reaction. Worse, Louis had no heirs himself and it looked as if the throne would pass to his younger brother upon his death.

Indeed, only ten years on the throne, Louis died in 1824 ... and his brother Charles X became France's king. Unfortunately, Charles was too thick-headed to understand what his older brother had understood ... and proceeded to try to move the Bourbon monarchy back to the status it possessed prior to the Revolution. The only people this would please was the small group of ultra-royalists among the returning émigrés. Consequently, Charles's actions greatly alienated much of the rest of French political society – a large section of France comprising the middle and upper middle class ... and the citizens of Paris of all social orders.

Finally bringing things to an explosive head, Charles foolishly responded to the growing opposition to his rule by publishing the "July Ordinances" of 1830, which dissolved a newly elected Chamber of Deputies (which had returned an even larger number of liberals opposed to Charles), and called for new elections ... allowing only a very small number of voters to participate. A number of Paris journalists protested his move ... and were soon joined by a Paris mob filling the streets. Soldiers sent out by Charles to suppress the mob were attacked savagely by the protesters ... with many soldiers soon joining them.

Fearing that all of this was heading toward a restoration of Republican France, French political leaders Charles Maurice de Talleyrand-Périgord[*]

---

[*]Although this period is known as "the Age of Metternich," Talleyrand was himself a most outstanding individual in the field of European politics during this same period. He began his political life as a Catholic priest, representing the Church in the court of Louis XVI. He represented the First Estate (Church) in the Estates-General of 1789. Then, becoming anti-clerical, he joined the Jacobins! He was sent to England in 1792 to represent the new French Republic ... and remained there when France began moving toward the Reign of Terror. He was forced out of England in 1794 and went to America, staying there for two years. The new Directorate permitted him to return to France ... and then appointed him as its Foreign Minister! But he soon became a supporter of Napoleon, aiding Napoleon in taking control of France from the Directorate. And thus he became Napoleon's Foreign Minister! But his relationship with Napoleon cooled when he found himself disagreeing with some of the Emperor's diplomatic decisions, and he resigned his position in 1807. Then in 1814, Talleyrand played a key part in the restoration of the Bourbon monarchy ... and was appointed as France's chief negotiator at the Congress of Vienna.   However, for the next fifteen years he stepped out of the limelight of French politics. But he re-entered the spotlight in

and Adolphe Thiers put before the Chamber of Deputies the name of Louis Philippe, Duke of Orleans, as a new king to replace Charles X (who was forced to step down) ... entitling him as "king of the French by the will of the people" (rather than the old Bourbon formula: "king of France by the will of God"). Thus the Orleanist wing of the old Bourbon monarchy took power in France ... with Louis Philippe I posing himself as the "bourgeois king" (mostly an act!).

The uprising (which had never extended outside of Paris) quickly settled down. Overall the French were enjoying a period of rising prosperity brought on by the fifteen years of peace and were now relatively content with the shape of things politically in France.

Belgium. The people of the southern provinces of the new Kingdom of the Netherlands had, in earlier generations, been brought back forcibly to Catholicism. This alone made them quite different from their heavily Protestant northern neighbors. Also, the upper and middle classes of this region spoke French rather than Dutch ... and were greatly upset when their new king, William I, demanded that all government work be done in Dutch (exempting only the French-speaking Walloon districts bordering France).

William's high-handed ways so upset these "Belgians" that in August (partially inspired by events in nearby Paris) protesters took to the streets of Brussels as a result of an opera which stirred Belgian feeling to a point of high indignation. Soon a street mob developed, and began looting and pillaging the city through the night. A group of alarmed citizens formed a Council of Regency and proposed a separation of Belgium and Holland, with the king's brother as viceroy of Belgium. William reacted to this challenge by sending an army to Brussels ... which ran into such stiff resistance that it was forced to withdraw. William was now willing to agree to the Council's proposal. But it was too late. A Provisional Government had been formed in Brussels.

At this point the other powers of the Concert of Europe weighed in on the matter ... Prussia and Russia ready to invade, but France's Louis Philippe threatened to counter their move. At a meeting in London the Big Five powers called for an armistice ... then moved to recognize Leopold of Saxe-Coburg as the king of Belgium. The Dutch nonetheless sent an army to Belgium ... only to be countered by a French army and a British-French blockade of the Dutch coast. William now had lost the contest. But it would not be until 1839 that he would finally recognize the independence

---

arranging for Louis-Philippe to take the French throne in 1830.

Today his name mostly evokes the image of a cynical, self-serving politician willing to pull almost any deal that would advance his career. But actually, it was the gain of France that seemed to inspire most of his craftiness ... behind and above all else that he did.

of Belgium.

Poland. Not every such event in Europe ended up so successfully. Poland had once been a powerful society (1500s and 1600s) but decline had set in during the 1700s and the Poles found their society carved up in three different stages of partition (1772, 1793 and 1795), being completely absorbed or "disappeared" by the surrounding major powers, Russia, Prussia and Austria with the last partition. But Polish patriots fought alongside Napoleon in his wars against those same three powers ... and Napoleon rewarded Polish support in 1807 by setting up a Duchy of Warsaw. But at the Congress of Vienna in 1815 the duchy was re-designated as a kingdom ... with the Russian Tsar as its king!

At first Alexander respected the more liberal character of the Polish society and state, even allowing the Poles to continue to keep their own flag, currency, military uniforms, and particular political organization. But as Alexander turned more conservative – even reactionary – he began placing tighter restrictions on Polish society. When his brother Nicholas I took the Russian throne in 1825, he at first attempted to relax the restrictions ... until an attempt on his life in 1829 turned him also towards repression of the people under his rule.

Towards the end of the following year (1830) the spirit of rebellion spread to Warsaw, then to the whole of Poland. At first the Poles were able to hold off an invading Russian army. But the Poles' own lack of a unified command structure undercut their effort, and in 1831 Warsaw fell to the Russians, ending the revolt. At this point Nicholas declared the Polish monarchy expired, with Poland now simply absorbed into the Russian state. However, although this stopped Polish independence activity, it did not end the Polish dream of national independence. In fact, it served in the coming years to make the dream even stronger in the hearts of Polish nationalists.

Political reform in Great Britain. Whereas the House of Lords was made up of high Church officials and the British aristocracy, the House of Commons supposedly was a more "democratic" part of the British Parliament. Since even the Middle Ages, two members were elected from each of the counties and towns (boroughs) making up the kingdom. But over the centuries economic fortunes had changed and many of the towns had disappeared, yet still sent two representatives to Parliament ... whereas major industrial centers that had grown up in the past century (Manchester, Birmingham, etc.) had no representation whatsoever. Furthermore a few landowners of the empty boroughs ("rotten boroughs") controlled a number of seats; other seats were bought and sold like clothing goods. The whole system therefore actually ended up representing only a tiny portion of the entire

British population.

    With the democratic spirit spreading across the European continent in 1830, the mood soon reached the British shores as well. In 1830 the unloved George IV died and his place was taken by his more liberal-minded brother, William IV ... who called for an election, which brought to power a reformist Whig majority led by Earl Grey. After much action back and forth, a reform bill was finally passed into law in 1832. It wiped out the rotten boroughs, gave new representation to the industrial cities and made voting standards uniform across the kingdom. It increased the suffrage, bringing the comfortable middle class into the voting public ... though it still set voting qualifications high enough that it excluded the multitudes of industrial and farm workers making up the bulk of the British population. Nonetheless, this marked a significant step forward toward full democracy in Britain.

The expansion of "Democratic America"

The Jacksonian "Democratic Revolution" (the 1830s). The vote of the common people (at least for members of America's House of Representatives) was not a new thing for the Americans. But with the development of Andrew Jackson's Democratic Party (shaped and directed in its activities by Jackson's assistant, Martin Van Buren), America was understood to be led no longer by aristocrats (particularly the Virginians – Washington, Jefferson, Madison and Monroe) or the Bostonians (the Adams, father and son) ... but by "one of the people" – Andrew Jackson. Actually, Jackson was himself of aristocratic background ... but played to the idea that he was just an ordinary American. And indeed ... the common people, muddy boots and all, invaded his presidential reception in 1829 (smashing dishes and furniture in the process) to get close to their war hero and now president, Andrew Jackson.

    And so a new understanding filled the political atmosphere of America ... certifying the fact that politics belonged to the people themselves ... and not just a group of select aristocrats. Politics could thus get very vulgar at times ... part of its being so "democratic"! But America was very proud of itself in taking the lead in this matter of "democratizing" their society's politics.

The "Second Great Awakening." Behind this peculiar self-development of "Democratic America" was a renewing of the popular spirit ... one that had guided America through the dark days of its war of independence from British King George III. But this was a spirit then that had, like most things when a crisis is over, settled back into a more mundane nature – a humanistic spirit that sees itself guided by reason and logic rather than unpredictable passion ... and unpredictable sources, such as God himself.

The French found this American spirit most interesting, because it was so different from what was the norm back in Europe. This curiosity brought Alexis de Tocqueville and his associate Gustave de Beaumont to America in 1831 to study America more closely. Then in 1835 and 1840 Tocqueville published his two-volume findings, *Democracy in America*, noting not only the basically egalitarian spirit of the American people (easily challenging those who would take on airs of superiority), something he understood derived from America's basically Puritan origins. He also noted the restless and purpose-driven heart of the American individual – who however (from his point of view) tended to move on to new challenges before completing the old ones! He also was most alarmed at how the slavery issue was crushing the American soul, predicting (correctly) that failure to soon resolve this issue would most likely lead to civil war in America.

But the American world of cool reason and logic supposedly characteristic of the comfortable Americans soon came under attack. A huge economic depression that hit America in the period 1837-1841 undercut deeply the idea that life basically worked along quite rational lines. Such an event seemed at the time to be unprecedented. Thus, even in the East, talk grew that America was facing God's great Day of Judgment, the long-awaited return of Christ to Earth – to judge all humankind. Americans needed to get their act together spiritually.

Also ... apparently masses of Americans, especially those that had crossed the Appalachian Mountain Barrier and were heading ever-deeper into Indian territory, were not seeing things in America's supposedly humanistic fashion. Here on the Western frontier, hunger, disease, and angry Indians awaited these bold souls willing to step into such an unpredictable world. But comforting them was their strong Christian faith that they were answering a call that God himself had put on them ... a covenantal call to advance their Christian realm into the darker world of the American interior. And they understood this challenge as one calling them to deal with this world in front of them but also the world within themselves. They needed to cleanse themselves of their own sins so that they could find greater success in taking on this larger life – and ultimately get themselves right with God.

To cultivate and direct this strong American spirit was a range of individuals, most of them simple men who took up the call to pastor (preach, teach, baptize, pray) the wide-ranging collection of frontiersmen and their families. But a large number also were just as active in the more settled East. There were also a number of "prophets" who stepped forward to offer "updated" versions of the Christian gospel, also collecting a huge following in the process.

By far the most active were the Methodist circuit riders, who braved weather, hunger, and Indians to reach the scattered settlements of the frontiersmen with their preaching and counsel. These were ordinary men with extraordinary commitment, fueled by a religious fire that actually started back in England at the turn of the century and had been brought to America under the guidance of America's Methodist Bishop Francis Asbury, a man himself who in a period of 1784-1816, preached some 16,000 sermons over a course of as much as 275,000 miles on horseback, and who grew the American Methodist community from 1,200 to 214,000 – with eventually 700 preachers to guide this huge flock. He was followed by an even greater number of circuit riders, some 3,500 of them, and nearly 6,000 Methodist pastors, who by 1840 had this community up to 750,000 members in size, the largest denominational community in America.

Even the Black community got in on the act, with the African Methodist Episcopal (AME) and AME Zion communities developing among free Blacks in Philadelphia and New York City. These two groups would play a huge role after the Civil War (1861-1865) in shaping the religious lives of the multitudes of newly freed slaves.

And the folks back East were also invited to the world of camp meetings, largely designed by the Presbyterian pastor Albert Finney, who turned these meetings into well organized "revivals," ones that would become something of a model for other revivalists – in his days and even since then. So active was his revivalist ministry that it seemed that there was no more work to be done in up-state New York. It had become, what Finney himself termed, "a burned-out district"!

Then there was the most unusual development with the up-state New Yorker William Miller, who was able to bring a huge number of followers to purify themselves in preparation for the "Advent" or Second Coming of Christ ... which he predicted would bring the "Rapture" in April (then October) of 1844. But disappointment did not discourage his followers – who reformed themselves under the guidance of the female prophet Ellen White as the "Seventh-Day Adventists," a group that would grow internationally as well as nationally.

Also arising from the same "burned-out district" of New York was an even stranger quasi-Christian movement: The Latter-Day Saints, or "Mormons." Its founder Joseph Smith claimed angelic direction (1827) in getting his new religious movement started up, complete with its own Bible (*The Book of Mormon*) and its own way of preparing for the second coming of Christ. But so radically different was his "Mormonism" that his movement not only grew monumentally in size, it succeeded in stirring up equally monumental opposition from Christian neighbors. Thus he had to move his huge community several times, before he himself was killed in another such confrontation (1844). Ultimately a member of his staff, Brigham Young, took the bulk of the Mormon community (there would be other communities elsewhere as well) all the way to Utah, and there set up his "Zion" headquarters for what would become a huge international religious community.

There was, however, a calmer version of America's Second Great Awakening, arising amidst the more traditional American denominations ... principally the Congregationalists, Presbyterians, and Dutch Reformed, although many Methodists (and Baptists) would soon join this development. Two areas of action grew huge within these Christian communities: the founding of colleges to further the world of Christian knowledge and the creation of missionary societies to spread the word – even abroad. Thus it was that jointly these communities created the American Bible Society (to put a Bible in every American home), the Sunday-School Union (to develop Biblical literacy among America's children and youth), the American Tract Society (offering an easy explanation of Christianity's basic themes and doctrines), etc., etc. Equally amazing was the number of Christian seminaries and colleges that were established during this period, some 500 of them by the mid-1800s.

Literacy and knowledge were never intended to be the privilege of just the upper ranks of society - as was the case back in Europe. This was a privilege available to any American seeking such a goal in life. America's democratic sense of the basic equality of all its people depended on such opportunities being available to one and all. You would have to work for it. Equality would not just be handed to you on a silver platter. But it was there, freely available to any and all who sought it. And Americans were definitely just such seekers!

And that was America spiritually in the 1830s and 1840s!

The Mexican-American War (1846-1848). Indeed, it was the urge of the American people themselves rather than the designs of any government that had long been the foundation of America's birth, growth and ultimately substantial national power. And this democratic instinct driving America was not likely to weaken ... as long as there was land to the West for Americans to settle.

Texas would play a particularly key role in this matter at this point (1830s) ... as thousands of Americans poured into what the neighboring Mexicans viewed as a northern province of theirs (but sparsely inhabited by Mexicans themselves at the time). Ultimately this American "intrusion" brought war between the two groups ... with the Texas-Americans soundly defeating the army of Mexican caudillo Santa Anna in 1836. Mexico was thus forced to acknowledge Texan independence.

But then the matter arose as to whether Texas would stand as an independent nation or as an add-on to the United States, with the Texans soon resolving the matter in favor of the latter. But this presented a huge problem for the U.S. government... fully understanding the outrage that Mexico would feel if Texas were to join the Union.

After being avoided as an issue by American presidents for the next ten years, President Tyler and the U.S. Congress moved finally (1846) to accept Texas's request for admission to the Union ... bringing Mexico to immediately issue a formal declaration of war against the U.S. But to the surprise of everyone (including most Europeans) the Mexicans were quickly and decisively beaten in various battles ... not only in Texas but in all of Mexico's northern territory – reaching even to California. In fact, by September of 1847, American troops found themselves fully in command of Mexico.

Thankfully both Congress and President Polk were wise finally to award Mexico a $15 million payment for the territory taken from Mexico, softening the blow greatly ... and gaining formal Mexican acceptance of the transfer of lands. This piece of diplomacy would soon prove to have been very, very important ... for in short order, defending the American claim to these Western territories in the face of a Mexican counter-move would have made a huge crisis hitting America at the time (the American Civil War, 1861-1865) all the more disastrous for the American Union.

The Revolutions of 1848

France. Louis Philippe had cultivated his reputation as "citizen king" ... yet at the same time he was as absolutist in his heart as any other European monarch of his day. His prime minister, François Guizot, skillfully kept a working majority in the French parliament in support of the king's increasingly restrictive policies, which clearly favored the prosperous industrial upper middle class ... at the expense of the French working class.

But the French working class – which had been the backbone of the 1830 Revolution, but which had been denied any political fruits from its sacrifices – was not unaware of its political rights – and importance – in the French scheme of things. French intellectuals attracted to the lofty ideas of "socialism" had been clear about the key role that the working class was destined to play in the industrial society taking shape in France. Being hounded by the French police, secret societies began to be formed by such socialists ... and also by republicans hoping to see France returned to the status of a republic. All this (plus numerous attempts at assassination of the king) made Louis Philippe and Guizot all the more resistant to any call for political reform.

By mid-late 1847 even members of the middle class began to gather at special banquets to discuss the need for immediate reform. Then in February 1848, a massive banquet was scheduled to take place in Paris ... though Guizot convinced involved members of the legislature to call off the event. But it was too late – for things began to move forward anyway: the streets of Paris were filling with people demanding Guizot's dismissal. The National Guard was called out to disperse the rowdy crowds ... but refused to go against the crowds, with some guardsmen even joining them. The panicked king then dismissed Guizot ... but crowds gathered at Guizot's home, protected by army regulars. Shots were fired and some 50 individuals were shot ... then carried through the streets on carts that night. The next day a huge mob gathered at the king's Tuileries Palace ... causing Louis-Philippe to flee the country in disguise.

A new Republic was declared by a provisional government ... and, following the lead of the socialist Louis Blanc, the new government proposed – as a matter of the "right to work" – the creation of workshops for the unemployed. At this, thousands of unemployed workers gathered in Paris for jobs ... greatly exceeding the government's real ability to set up workshops. Instead, the government agreed to pay the unemployed a small financial compensation ... which (because of this generosity) by early summer had swelled the ranks of the unemployed to over a hundred thousand! This not only threatened the treasury of the new Republic, but left industries unable to hire workers, who were content to live off the small dole rather than the earnings of their labor.

The effort to bring some control over the program by setting tighter qualifications for the dole now produced its own political problems in the Paris streets. The Republic's military was called in to disperse angry crowds, the soldiers fired on them (and they fired back), with over ten thousand people killed or wounded in the encounter. Martial law was extended over the country ... while the Republican politicians quickly prepared the new Republican constitution – which provided for universal adult male suffrage.

Finally in December of 1848, elections were held ... and Louis Napoleon, nephew of the Emperor, was elected by a huge majority of the French voters. A new era had begun in French life.

The failed effort at Rome. In Italy, revolutionary radicals were demanding the creation of a new Roman Republic - replacing the Papal States. In the chaos, Pope Pius IX's Minister of Justice Peligrino Rossi was assassinated (November 1848). Also, the Pope's protective French troops had just been called back to France to deal with the chaos there ... leaving the Pope's own small army unable to hold back a much larger Italian army intent on taking Rome. At this point Pius escaped to Naples ... and the revolutionaries announced the formation of their Roman Republic (also November 1848). The hope was clearly that this Roman Republic would be the springboard for an even larger Italian Republic.

The Republicans authorized the pope to return to Rome to continue his religious duties ... even though his political role as Head of the Papal States was to be ended. But the pope was not interested in the compromise. Indeed, in retaliation, Pius threatened excommunication of those Catholics supporting the Republic ... even of those who simply voted in the Republic's new elections (there was a 50% turnout however).

But newly elected French President, Louis Napoleon decided to come to the aid of the Pope and sent a huge French army (along with some Spanish troops) into Italy (April 1849). After a month's siege at Rome, the Republicans agreed to a truce ... which reestablished the pope's political powers - although Pius would not return to Rome until the French troops agreed to full support of the papacy.

These troops would indeed continue in that role ... until 1870 when another round of revolutionary events in Europe led to the creation of the Kingdom of Italy – by many of the same individuals who had directed the effort to establish the Roman Republic in 1848-1849.

The Austrian Empire. Meanwhile, events in France had spread quickly eastward to Vienna, inspiring equally dramatic events there. In March (1848) university students and craftsmen joined forces to march on the emperor's palace calling for Metternich's resignation. When members of the court aristocracy joined in the demand, Metternich realized that he had lost his political grounding ... and escaped to England. When the Emperor agreed to institute a number of liberal reforms, the revolt seemed to have achieved its objectives.

At the same time the French events had also stirred up a similar spirit of revolt in Prague ... where demands for liberal reform of the imperial government took on strongly Czech nationalist tones. Now hard pressed by this spreading spirit of revolt, the Emperor agreed to the demand to make Czech co-equal with German.

Hungary was next. Protesters gathered in Budapest demanding a constitution and parliament of their own ... which the Emperor agreed to institute. But then when other minorities living within the Hungarian realm (Serbs, Croatians, Romanians) asked for similar rights, it was the Hungarians who refused ... causing war to break out between Hungary and the minorities.

In Austrian-controlled northern Italy similar events unfolded. With the fall of Metternich in March, an Italian mob in Milan forced the Austrian garrison to evacuate the city. Venice then joined the revolt, then all of

Lombardy and the Tuscany province ... with Charles Albert, king of Sardinia-Piedmont, sending troops to aid his fellow Italians. By that summer, Austria had vacated all of Northern Italy.

The Habsburg empire seemed to be crumbling everywhere. So distressed was Emperor Ferdinand over all this that he abdicated in December, elevating his 18-year-old nephew, Franz Joseph, to the Austrian emperorship.*

Prussia. Prussian king Frederick William IV (who had come to power in 1840) had made it clear that he ruled by the will of God alone. But with the retreat and fall of royal absolutism all around Europe, the king found himself facing the same demands in Berlin for liberal reforms of his government. With seemingly no other options, he yielded ... promising such reforms ... meanwhile waiting for the tide to turn. Which it soon did.

The Frankfurt Assembly (1848-1849). A major hope of the German Liberals, calling for a constitution and written guarantees of citizens' rights, focused on the German Confederation, which gave its authority over to a constitutional assembly voted on by a large German electorate. This Assembly gathered at Frankfurt to begin the writing of a new constitution for a united Germany. Although it was somewhat slow going, the serious hitch in the program did not appear until the Assembly was ready to finalize its works in early 1849. Only one question remained: who would reign over Germany as a constitutional monarch: a Hohenzollern (Prussia) or a Habsburg (Austria)? The Habsburgs were not willing to separate their non-German territories from a new Germanic empire ... and thus they would not take the position at the head of the new German state. By the time in April when the Assembly turned to Prussian king Frederick William IV to take over the new constitutional Germany, William had recovered much of his lost political strength and made it very clear that he would not head any kind of a state that gave authority to its ruler through the popular will. He would answer to God and God alone.

 The Reaction. Now without any prospect of a king to lead their new state, the whole constitutional project began to fall apart. Although many German states had signed onto the project, four major German states (in addition to Prussia) announced that they would not accept this arrangement. With that the Frankfurt Assembly dissolved.

But that was not the end of the matter. Frederick William not only shut down the Prussian Parliament, but after having subdued protests in

---

*This would be the beginning of the 68-year reign of Franz Joseph, which would last until his death in 1916.

his own land, sent Prussian troops to crush the rebellions in some of the other German states. Thousands of liberal reformers were forced to flee Germany; those who failed to do so were imprisoned.

And much the same event occurred in Habsburg Austria. Austrian troops even bombarded their own capital into submission, and then turned on the Hungarian reformers. When the Hungarians fought back fiercely, Tsar Nicholas sent Russian troops to help the Austrians to crush the new Hungarian Republic and force Hungary back into the Habsburg Empire as an Austrian province.

Likewise, the Austrians were able to retake (brutally) the territory they had just lost in Italy ... leading the aged king of Piedmont, Charles Albert to turn his throne over to his son, Victor Emmanuel II, hoping that this would soften peace terms with Austria.

Nonetheless, despite this huge victory of monarchical absolutism, Victor Emmanuel kept his father's liberal constitution of Piedmont in place ... thus preserving for him the leading position in the hearts and minds of Italian liberals, who continued to dream of an independent Italy.

✱ ✱ ✱

THE URGE TO RATIONALIZE AND CONTROL SOCIAL DYNAMICS

Jeremy Bentham's Utilitarianism

Going back a bit in our narrative, it is important to mention the legacy that Bentham (1748-1832) had on the development of British social thinking at the end of the 1700s and beginning of the 1800s.

Bentham is considered to be the founder of British Utilitarianism ... a philosophy built simply on the idea that "the greatest happiness of the greatest number is the true measure of right and wrong." In short, he was a strong advocate in favor of "human rights."

He was highly opposed to slavery, believed in equal rights for women, was a strong advocate of the separation of church and state, was opposed to physical punishment, and believed strongly that there should be no restrictions on speech. He even supported the idea of animal rights. But he spent his greatest energies on the matter of prison reform. In short, he was a very "modern" philosopher and jurist!

But he did not believe that all of these came simply by lifting traditional Christian moral standards ... as if these "human rights" would come into place on their own in a rather natural manner (as did Marx and other philosophers that came after him). To him, human rights would come only through proper moral and political reform of society ... enlightened social reform – principally by enlightened public authority. In short, under British utilitarianism, the primary role of government was to oversee the process of human progress.

Auguste Comte (1798-1857)

The Frenchman Auguste Comte reacted to the sometimes wild speculation of French rationalists, who during the previous century had built their philosophical theories on "reasonable" propositions – rather than on the observation of actual phenomena. In short, he introduced British empiricism to French or continental philosophy, terming his approach "positivism."

He was particularly interested in seeing social philosophy built on very careful observation of actual social behavior rather than mere rationalist speculation ... such as Rousseau's social theories a half-century earlier, which had helped push France towards the tragedy of its recent Revolution. Thus Comte laid the groundwork for the field of modern sociology with its demand for "factual" foundations for all assertions of truth.

In his major six-volume work, *Course of Positive Philosophy* (published in the period 1830-1842), he stated that human knowledge began in its primitive stage as theology, or laying all events at the feet of divine forces or God (related to the Divine rights claims of monarchical authority). The next stage, the rationalist or philosophical stage, was then characterized by broad abstract principles as the foundation of truth or knowledge (he had in mind the rhetoric of Revolutionary France). But the rising stage that the world found itself entering at this point (a pragmatic, bureaucratic post-Revolutionary France) would now be built on the works of scientific scholars who would direct society through their knowledge of actual fact-based science.

Most interestingly, none of Comte's Positivism or Progressivism itself was itself based on the empirical methods he called for in his study – but was instead a continuation of the French rationalist approach to knowledge!

Nonetheless his ideas would catch the imagination of 19th century Europe and help move it toward the notion that all truth is built on fact and fact alone.

John Stuart Mill (1806-1873)

Mill was an amazing child prodigy, reading classic Greek literature (from Aesop to Plato) by age 8, then a full array of Latin and Greek works by age 10 ... plus history, math, physics and astronomy. In all of this, he was carefully "home schooled" – pruned and protected in his infancy and youth by his father, James Mill – in order that the son would be "associated" only with the sharpest minds (his father's and that of the family friend Jeremy

Bentham) ... and not with lower social orders of his own age ... a key part of the educational philosophy of the British "Positivist" movement. His father's goal was to grow his son into "a bright light of Utilitarian philosophy that might light the world." In part the father succeeded, though at a deeply heavy emotional and spiritual cost to the son.

Utilitarianism, Positivism, or Liberalism – all amounted to pretty much the same thing: holding the common view that a person is born with no a priori thoughts or abilities ... but as a thinking creature is simply the result of careful development by guiding hands – hopefully ones that care deeply for the happiness of those in their care. It was all very personal. Liberals (both Americans and British, from Jefferson to the Mills) viewed with great distrust the intervention of public authorities in this process. In short, "the best government is the one that governs the least!" This would be a central tenet of Mill's Utilitarian or Liberal philosophy.

The understanding was that simply a person becomes what the surrounding world brings to that person ... nothing more, nothing less. Therefore that surrounding world – physical as well as social – must be carefully shaped, engineered, protected. But this must be carried out on a personal or individual basis ... not on a public or Socialistic basis. Personal freedom was essential to proper development.

Thus it was that Mill would later reject deeply the ideas of his former mentor, Bentham. Mill would disagree strongly with Bentham that social progress would come best through the process of well-constructed government action ... Mill holding to the later developing idea that social progress would fare better under personal or private development than under official governmental action ... which to subsequent British Liberals was central to their idea of the critical importance of personal freedom

However ... Mill was closely connected with the British administration of India – being a high-ranking official from 1823 (at age 17!) all the way to the end of the East India Company in 1858. In this matter, he would, take a broader view of the responsibilities that fell to "more enlightened" social hands in face of a "barbarian" society. Something akin to social action or "benevolent despotism" would be required under such circumstances ... but must be carefully conducted so as to benefit and not just merely subdue such a barbarian society.

And as far as an issue under much discussion at the time, Mill felt that religion was the highly laudable ability of human thought to rise above the merely physical or natural condition of life to contemplate and be moved by ideals of excellence. But whether there was a supreme Deity or consciousness to which human thought draws itself – or which energizes the forces of life as Creator and Sustainer – was a most uncertain proposition for Mill.

In any case, the very simplicity and the very attractiveness of Utilitarian or Positivist "Liberalism" would catch on widely in the fast-changing political setting of 19th century Britain. And Mill, with his many publications, would be one to give great clarity and appeal to this idea ... also helping to make the British Liberal Party a growing force in British politics.

Darwinism

When in 1859 Charles Darwin published his book, *On the Origin of Species* – the culmination of years of research and earlier publications – he shook the moral foundations of Western civilization. This occurred not because Darwin invented a new worldview out of thin air. The ideas of progress through social struggle were by this time rather widely accepted. The British Whig party, in fact, was built on this idea: that Britain should be run by those proven strongest in life's competition and that no tears should be wept for the poor swept aside by life's struggles, because that would only hinder human progress.

No, it was not the newness of Darwin's ideas that made his works so spectacular, but it was because he gave such precise explanation – and justification – to these Whiggish ideas. His great contribution to this debate of worldviews was that he built his Darwinist theory of life on a vast field of scientific evidence, something that had by that time become the absolute requirement for any claim to Truth.

Also, he was building his ideas on a well-established base of earlier works on this matter of evolution.

Thomas Robert Malthus, and early versions of "survival of the fittest." Since the publication in 1798 of the book *An Essay on the Principle of Population* by the English clergyman Thomas Malthus, there was considerable discussion in England about the problems created by a rapidly expanding human population on the earth, the issues of hunger, disease and war that this would produce. Consequently, by the time of Darwin's 1859 publication, a number of leading political and intellectual figures in England had already taken the social position that the best thing to do about the rising number of English poor was – by a process of natural de-selection – simply to let them maintain a natural balance with their world by the thinning of their ranks through hunger and disease. It was thus wise not to encourage their expansion through unnecessary charity.*

––––––––––––––––

*It was this very un-Christian attitude that inspired Charles Dickens to write in 1843 his famous *A Christmas Carol* (the greedy and socially insensitive businessman Ebenezer Scrooge having to deal painfully with his own conscience) ... along with other works written from the same moral point of view.

Charles Lyell (1797-1875). In the early 1800s, at the same time that biology was moving toward the development of a theory of natural evolution, similar work was moving ahead in the area of geology. The most notable figure behind this work was Charles Lyell.

Lyell had developed an early curiosity about different earth formations in England into a full-blown quest to give an explanation for the layers of the soil that he observed within the country's cliffs and mountains. On a trip to Italy in 1828-1829 where he studied Mt. Etna, he came up with the idea that all these geological features (mountains, valleys, islands, deserts, etc.) did not occur abruptly – but were the process of gradual shifts (volcanos) and decay (erosion) in the earth's surface ... taking place naturally over a very long stretch of time, a process continuing even into the present.

Further study in Spain the next year led him during the period 1831-1833 to publish his 3-volume work, *Principles of Geology*. Loaded with supportive data for his theory, the book was to make a tremendous impact on his time.

Overall, Lyell presented a view of the earth as being both very old (older than the calculus of those who reckoned the earth's age on the basis of adding up the Genesis chronologies) – possibly even millions of years old – and very much still in the process of becoming. To him the earth was even to be looked upon as a living organism.

An earlier Darwin. We have already introduced Lamarck as a major part of this dynamic. But it is also interesting to note that Lamarck was himself influenced by Darwin's grandfather, Erasmus Darwin (1731-1802), who in 1796 described in his publication *Zoonomia* how species had developed slowly over the generations by their abilities to pass on from generation to generation not only their basic traits, but also useful alterations in those traits. Thus Erasmus's grandson Charles Darwin came from a family already securely located in the evolutionist camp!

Darwin himself. Then what Darwin achieved in his 1859 book *On the Origin of Species* was to show through actual scientific analysis how living creatures on this planet could have evolved slowly over an enormous expanse of time from a small number of simpler forms into a vast array of much more complex species. All of this could have been achieved entirely through a natural or mechanical process by which the very competitive nature of life rewarded the stronger offspring of any species the better chance for survival, and the privilege of birthing a new generation that retained that superiority. Eventually this struggle for life – and its continuation from generation to generation – would, over time, bring into existence a distinctly new, more complex species, one better adapted to the complexities of life.

Thus every living creature we saw around us was naturally evolved from a less complex ancestor by a process termed "natural selection." In short, morally speaking, life was at its core simply a matter of the survival of the fittest.

It was Darwin's Cambridge University teacher, John Henslow, who arranged for Darwin in 1831 to sail on the British naval ship *Beagle* to the South Pacific islands just off the coast of South America ... and who urged him to take with him a copy of Lyell's *Principles of Geology*. Lyell's vision of even the earth itself as a living, developing organism touched Darwin's thoughts deeply. With this sense of a dynamic earth in mind he thus came up with an unprecedented (and correct) explanation of how coral atolls were formed out on the high sea.

Nature cooperated in the process. While he was in Chile an earthquake took place in which he actually observed the land rise in front of him. Thus the concept of a dynamic earth was not merely a theoretical one for him. He also observed strata of sea shells in the mountains at a height of 12,000 feet, lifted over time from an earlier position as a sea bed.

What he was doing was giving further support to Lyell's view of the earth's natural life – support so extensive that the world of learned scholars felt themselves forced to look upon the earth in this way from this time on.

Upon his return to England in 1836 he was greeted easily as an accomplished colleague by the scientific community. But he was just getting started. His thoughts returned to the questions of why life took the shape it did – which increasingly left God out of the picture.

Darwin was not really a radical by nature, and for years kept his thinking to himself. But he was thinking thoughts that he knew would not be well greeted by many in his times, including his devoutly Christian friend, Henslow.

Actually it was in 1842 that Darwin first drafted a brief version of his theory and then two years later a full draft version – but was unwilling to bring it before the public because of the furor he knew it would stir. He would show it only to close friends such as Lyell and Thomas Henry ("T.H.") Huxley. Finally in 1858 he was inspired to act when he received a paper from Alfred Wallace, a botanist working in the Malayan islands, a paper which pointed to the same hypothesis he had been developing. His friends urged him to bring out his own thoughts on the subject in a joint paper worked up with Wallace – presented that summer. With this he was ready to bring out his full work, *On the Origin of Species by Means of Natural Selection, or The Preservation of Favoured Races in the Struggle for Life*. In November of 1859 he presented his first edition – which was bought up immediately and quickly went to further editions (6 such editions over the next 13 years). The English scientific community was highly approving; the clergy were adamantly hostile, as he expected.

His friend Huxley only added fuel to the fire by extending the logic of his friend's theories into the realm of social action, cultivating a theory known as "Social Darwinism." It was Huxley who came up with the idea that brutal competition in society or "survival of the fittest," was a necessary part of the advance of mankind.

Darwin was himself not a proponent of this view – but soon became identified with it.

Other books by Darwin followed over the next years – the most important of which was *The Descent of Man and Selection in Relation to Sex* (1871). Here he came out directly with what had only been implied in his *Origin*, namely that even man himself was the by-product of the evolutionary process, not only physically but also morally and spiritually. This of course challenged the notion that man was a very distinct part of the Creation process – but instead was merely another, albeit a highly evolved, by-product of the on-going mechanism of evolution. In 1872 he went a step further in his *The Expression of the Emotions in Man and Animals*, stating the the emotions we attribute uniquely to man are in fact shared in some less evolved ways with other members of the animal kingdom.

Herbert Spencer. Darwinism was further buttressed by the writings of other social philosophers of the day. Besides Darwin's pupil Huxley there was Huxley's friend Herbert Spencer, who had been moving in the direction of Darwin's thinking even before Darwin published his first work in 1859. Spencer had been working on both social theory (his 1851 *Social Statistics*) and personal development theory (his 1855 *Principles of Psychology*), his work heavily influenced not only by Malthus but also by the theories of Lamarck. Then when Darwin's work was published in 1859 Spencer came out in full force in his support of evolution as the basic doctrine of life, in every aspect of life on earth.

Soon Spencer would even outdistance Darwin as the most recognized philosopher of the late 1800s. But the very names Darwin and Darwinism would still serve as the most powerful symbols able to raise strong debate, pro and con, not only well into the 20th century but still even today.

Friedrich Nietzsche. The German philosopher and writer Friedrich Nietzsche was not exactly a Darwinist, but certainly was – or would soon become – a voice of his times ... a period deeply steeped in the Darwinist mindset. In his multi-volume series *Also Sprach Zarathustra* (*Thus Spoke Zarathustra*), he gave the German culture the ideal of the *Übermensch* – except that he was referring to the highly achieved individual – not some racial group, such as the Nazis would eventually use the term in reference to the German people as a whole, seeing themselves as a superior breed. Nietzsche was referring to the highly self-cultivated individual who (reflective of Nietzsche's own personal struggles) had come to put aside all other values (wealth, sex, even happiness) in order to focus completely in meeting fully the high calling that fate had placed on that person. Such a person strove to rise above the mere animal call to life – to rise above (*über*) mere common existence as a person (*Mensch*).

In fact, with respect to the ideal of the racial Übermensch, he was actually much opposed, getting himself in trouble with the German authorities for his strong anti-nationalism. He even at one point renounced his Prussian citizenship. No, Nietzsche was extolling the powerful individual that he claimed should be directing human life on this planet, not the group-think of the rising nationalist spirit that he saw developing around him – one which would eventually lead Europe into the disastrous national or tribal conflict known in its time as the Great War and to us today as World War One (as well as its continuation as World War Two a generation later).

He also was distinctly an atheist – informing the world that "God is dead." He (like Marx) saw the Judeo-Christian religion as offering humanity only enslavement to earthly commonness by teaching people to aim not for greatness in this life – but instead to aim for some supposed afterlife that Judeo-Christianity claimed awaited the humble and faithful at death. Nietzsche was very emphatic in stating that there was no evidence whatsoever that such a Heavenly life actually existed.

The assault on Christian morality

As an Anglican clergyman, Malthus himself had, back in the late 1700s, wrestled with the problem of why God would allow suffering to occur within his creation. Malthus finally concluded that God wanted man to rise to the challenge of life, to succeed in the face of life's difficulties through the discipline of hard work. Those who fell short of the challenge were simply some kind of disappointment to the great Creator. Those who failed merely reaped that which they had sown.[*] This in essence was the British version of Sturm und Drang!

Malthus's explanation of course was a terrible reading of what the founder of the Christian faith himself had taught the world. Jesus put the challenge not in terms of natural selection, but quite the opposite. According to Jesus, the challenge of life was to find ways to help the poor in the face of the huge challenge of survival in a competitive world of economics and politics. This ability to do charity, when the opposite would be so much

---

[*]It is truly amazing the extent to which man can go in rationalizing about God and God's intentions.

more tempting, was for Jesus the measure of greatness of anyone in God's kingdom.

At some point people were going to have to choose between the two, Jesus or the Darwinists. The original Puritans had chosen Jesus, and built an experimental society of mutual service among social equals based precisely on the spiritual ethics of Jesus Christ. The Virginians, not exactly Darwinists but of the same mindset, chose instead personal success at the cost of others (the slaves). Thus by the mid-1800s this was not a new issue. It is simply that Darwinism finally gave aggressive selfishness the moral justification that an increasingly aggressively selfish society seemed to require.

But Darwin himself, very sensitive to the importance of human charity and mutual concern in human society, was quite aware of this ethical matter, and actually troubled by how many were choosing to read cruel ethical justification into his theories.

Marxism

At the same time that German (and other) social philosophers were seeing in the fast-changing dynamic of their days the fulfillment of history through the rise through struggle of the tribal nation (France, Germany, Italy, etc.), German expatriate philosopher (in exile in London) Karl Marx headed down an entirely different road in his explanation as to where history was headed. He saw history fulfilled not in the struggle among nations but instead in the struggle among economic classes, principally between the owners of wealth and the subject classes (proletariat)[*] that produced that wealth for the owners through their labors. Marx was so insistent on this matter that he actually despised nationalism and all the discussion going on about nationalist struggles, seeing that as a distraction leading people away from the real struggle that lay before them, the industrial class struggle that was about to unfold – and lead the world into its final stage in history.

The Hegelian dialectic applied to Marx's economic theory. In 1848 Marx published his famous 30-page *Communist Manifesto* in the hope of capitalizing on the spirit of political rebellion that was rocking continental Europe at that time.

His *Manifesto* outlined history as a series of quite Hegelian dialectical struggles over time between those who legally owned the land, tools, machinery (what Marx summed up as social property or the "means of production") that produced the wealth that the people of society lived off

---

[*]A term drawn from Roman times in reference to the members of the Roman working class who held little or no property and thus few or no political rights.

of, and the proletariat who, though they owned none of those means of production, labored physically in using those means of production to bring forward the wealth that society lived off of. Typically in history, in the distribution of the wealth that a society jointly created for its survival and prosperity, nearly all of that wealth went to the class of property owners, with very little making its way to the hands of the proletarian workers.

This would bring tremendous tension to society, which eventually would turn into physical conflict because of this social injustice. Again, in Hegelian (and eventually Darwinian) dialectical fashion, such conflict or class struggle would then move history forward to a new, and better social system, shaped by the way the opposing classes synthesized their social positions into a new social structure.

Continuing his analysis in a further work, *Das Kapital*,* he carefully described the situation around him in Europe where the feudal system, once dominated by landed aristocrats, had been challenged by a new social class of industrial and financial capitalists, thus creating the age of capitalism. But he also saw how capitalism in turn had created its own opposing social force in the form of the industrial workers (the industrial proletariat) whose labors supported the capitalist system. And he predicted that conditions were quickly rising that would cause the industrial proletariat in its turn to rise up against the capitalist class, and – through the necessary historical conflict or revolution – open the way to a new social system.

Time was on the side of the worker, because capitalism by its very nature is highly competitive even among the capitalists themselves – each capitalist trying to eliminate his competitors in order to gain greater control over the market. This way they could increase their profits, even establish total or monopolistic control over the whole process. But of course as they drove each other out of business, they were inadvertently thinning out their capitalist social ranks, making their numbers smaller at the same time that the ranks of the proletarian were growing. Thus simply the calculus of the few against the many meant that the days of capitalism were numbered. At that point (which supposedly was now upon them) all the proletariat had to do was rise up and seize control of the means of production, thus destroying the power of the capitalist class ... and the public government (the "state") that had been protecting the capitalists. Thus in rising up against their capitalist oppressors, they had "nothing to lose but their chains."

A property-less, state-less, utopia. But, according to Marx, the resultant

---

*Marx was a prolific writer ... who found getting his work published difficult because of the opposition it always faced from the authorities. Of his multi-volume *Das Kapital*, the first volume would be published in 1867. Additional volumes would be published by his friend Friedrich Engels after Marx's death in 1883: volume two in 1885 and volume three in 1894.

social system would be different, it would be utopia itself. There would be no further class of dominators or exploiters of the proletariat, because the new society would be made up solely of industrial workers. There would be no other class of people in the new society but this one single industrial class. Everyone would now live as social equals – as comrades, rather than as a two-class system of gentlemen lording it over a servant class. Being equals, all would live communally, as in all land, tools and machines being owned jointly by all – and by nobody in particular.

Consequently, there would be no need for the political enforcing agency of the state or government. It would simply wither away, because the sole purpose of the state was to protect the interests of the privileged class of property owners, whether feudal, capitalist or whatever. In the communist society there would be no personal property, thus no state. Something like a Rousseauian bliss would then hold this happy world together.

Communism as the last stage of history. Also, the new society would end the long historical dialectic of a ruling class and a proletariat class finding themselves once again in conflict. With no division under communism between a propertied class and a proletarian class, there would be no cause for social conflict, no tension, no stress, only blissful peace. Thus this last historical revolution would bring history to a completion, the kind of millennialist completion that everyone was expecting because of the unprecedented progress they had been observing coming forth at mind-boggling speed. All history was supposedly about to fulfill itself, and Marx was showing how that was to be accomplished.

All very scientific. This was all pretty powerful stuff. And it appealed to the interests not only of European industrial workers, but also to intellectual Progressivists – not only in Europe but also in America. Marx's theories seemed to be irrefutable because they were built on hard fact. Unlike the philosophical speculations of social philosophers before him, but quite like Darwin, Marx had thrown a lot of historical data into his analysis, supposedly hard economic data, thus qualifying his theory as "scientific socialism," making him – and those who followed his lead – "scientific socialists."

Marx's militant atheism. As all materialists or mechanists, Marx had no need of the concept of God, or some divine hand driving forward the economic process he had outlined. It all worked – similar to Darwin's theories – entirely mechanically. Marx personally was an atheist. In fact he was quite opposed to the Christian religion, or any religion that saw history shaped and judged by a Supreme Being. As for Christianity, he saw the religion simply as a cruel psychological tool used by Europe's ruling classes (most lately the capitalists) that savagely exploited their own servants or workers, by excusing their horrible treatment of the workers under the promise that if the oppressed workers all cooperated with the system and behaved themselves (not rebel against their oppressors) they would be rewarded in the next life with heaven. To Marx, such religious theory was only a form of spiritual opium given to the masses to keep them docile.

The spread of Marxism among Europe's intellectuals. Meanwhile, as Europe headed into the Twentieth Century, clearly a growing number of social and political philosophers were convinced that, through some kind of Darwinian process, Western civilization (and, via the West, also world civilization as well) was moving into a bright future in which utopian existence for all – even (and especially) the unwashed masses – seemed to loom into view. Society just needed some adjustments here and there – led of course by these political philosophers or social scientists – in order to bring this process to completion. "Historical progress" and "democracy" – however conceived specifically (and the variation was indeed huge) – were the bywords, the slogans, the shibboleths, of those who supposed that they possessed special intellectual insights into where the world was headed.

Within that group of Western social reformers was a large group of Marxist ideologues and political activists – forming the Social Democratic Party in a number of European countries – whose expectations were that Marx's Communist revolution would soon break out across Europe. This supposedly would occur naturally first in a society experiencing the most advanced state of capitalism, probably Great Britain or Germany. After all, Marx's scientific socialism would not work except under the historical circumstances he had so carefully described. Every stage of historical development had to be completed before history would be ready to move on to the next step or phase in its development. The dialectical method demanded that kind of historical precision.

INDEX

A

B